£37·50

Language in the British Isles

Language
in the British Isles

Edited by PETER TRUDGILL

Professor of Linguistic Science
University of Reading

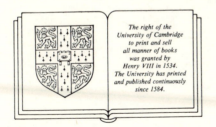

The right of the
University of Cambridge
to print and sell
all manner of books
was granted by
Henry VIII in 1534.
The University has printed
and published continuously
since 1584.

CAMBRIDGE UNIVERSITY PRESS

CAMBRIDGE

LONDON   NEW YORK   NEW ROCHELLE

MELBOURNE   SYDNEY

Published by the Press Syndicate of the University of Cambridge
The Pitt Building, Trumpington Street, Cambridge CB2 1RP
32 East 57th Street, New York, NY 10022, USA
296 Beaconsfield Parade, Middle Park, Melbourne 3206, Australia

First published 1984

Printed in Great Britain at the University Press, Cambridge

Library of Congress catalogue card number: 83-7616

British Library Cataloguing in Publication Data
Language in the British Isles
1. Great Britain–Languages
I. Trudgill, Peter
409′.41   P551.G1

ISBN 0 521 24057 3 hard covers
ISBN 0 521 28409 0 paperback

AO

Contents

The contributors

A. J. Aitken
Dictionary of the Older Scottish
  Tongue
Edinburgh University

G. M. Awbery
Department of Dialects
Welsh Folk Museum, Cardiff

Michael Barnes
Department of Scandinavian
  Studies
University College London

Michael V. Barry
Department of English
The Queen's University of Belfast

Wynford Bellin
Department of Psychology
Reading University

A. Bliss
Department of English
University College, Dublin

Jenny Cheshire
Department of Applied Linguistics
Birkbeck College, London
  University

R. D. Clement
Linguistic Survey of Scotland
  (Gaelic)
Edinburgh University

Ellen Douglas-Cowie
Department of English
The Queen's University of Belfast

John Edwards
Department of Psychology
St Francis Xavier University, Nova
  Scotia

V. K. Edwards
Department of Applied Linguistics
Birkbeck College,
  London University

A. C. Gimson
Department of Phonetics and
  Linguistics
University College London

Ian Hancock
Departments of English and
  Linguistics
University of Texas, Austin

John Harris
Department of Linguistics
Sheffield University

Kenneth MacKinnon
School of Business and Social
  Sciences
Hatfield Polytechnic

Marilyn Martin-Jones
Department of Linguistics and
  Modern English Language
Lancaster University

J. Milroy
Department of Linguistics
Sheffield University

L. Milroy
Department of Speech
  Newcastle upon Tyne University

Cathair Ó Dochartaigh
Institiúid Teangeolaíochta
  Éireann, Dublin

Euan Reid
Institute of Education
London University

Cynthia Shuken
Linguistic Survey of Scotland
Edinburgh University

N. Spence
Department of French
Bedford College, London University

David Sutcliffe
Bulmershe College of Higher
  Education, Reading

Alan R. Thomas
Department of Linguistics
University College of North Wales,
  Bangor

R. L. Thomson
School of English
Leeds University

Peter Trudgill
Department of Linguistic Science
Reading University

Martyn Wakelin
Department of English
Royal Holloway College, London
  University

J. C. Wells
Department of Phonetics and
  Linguistics
University College London

Preface

It is sad but true that many British and Irish linguists are relatively uninformed about the languages spoken in the British Isles and about the current sociolinguistic situation here – the linguistic situation in, say, India may actually be more familiar to some of them. (In this book, 'the British Isles' is taken to include the Channel Islands, the Isle of Man, Orkney and Shetland as well as mainland Britain and Ireland.) It is a matter for some regret that British and Irish linguists have carried out comparatively little research into many of the languages spoken here (much of the important work on Gaelic, for example, has been carried out by Scandinavians), and that students in our schools, colleges and universities often have little acquaintance with the rich linguistic heritage of these islands.

This book is both an attempt to rectify this situation and a reflection of the fact that interest in British languages on the part of local scholars and others is beginning to increase – an interest which, it is hoped, this book will further stimulate. It is also hoped that much of the information contained in this work will percolate into spheres outside those inhabited by academic linguists. Many educationists, journalists, broadcasters, lawyers, social scientists and politicians have begun to realize, and many more will surely do so, that they need more information about languages and language situations to aid them in decision-making and policy-forming of various sorts. This is particularly clear in the field of education, where adequate information on languages and dialects, particularly those spoken by immigrants, is often very seriously lacking. Part IV of this book is intended to confront this problem.

Parts, I, II and III, on the other hand, are more purely linguistic in emphasis. Part I is devoted to English, the *lingua franca* in these islands, and the language spoken, either as a first or second language, by the vast majority of the inhabitants of the United Kingdom and the Republic of Ireland. Part II is devoted to the Celtic languages, the earliest languages in the British Isles for which we have any records, while Part III deals with the other languages. The number of chapters devoted to each language is a reflection, not of any kind of linguistic or cultural importance, but of our knowledge to date; and a final hope for this volume is that it will act as a spur to further research.

Peter Trudgill

Acknowledgements

Chapter authors wish to acknowledge the helpful advice of colleagues and friends in the preparation of this volume.

The author of chapter 2 thanks Colin Biggs, Alice Davison, Jean Hannah and Jim Milroy.

The author of chapters 5 and 12 thanks Diane Wakelin for much valued collaboration.

The author of chapter 7 thanks Brendan Adams, Jim Milroy and John Wells for helpful comments on the initial draft, and Michael V. Barry for making available material from the Tape-Recorded Survey of Hiberno-English Dialects, on which the treatment of South Ulster English in chapter 7 is based.

The author of chapter 13 thanks John Harris, Jim Milroy, Michael McTear and John Wells for their help and advice.

The author of chapter 24 wishes to thank his colleagues Thomas Acton, John Holm, Donald Kendrick, Ruth Lehmann, Bruce Rodgers, James Sledd and Keith Whinnom for their useful comments on, and criticisms of, an earlier draft of this chapter.

The author of chapters 25 and 26 thank their colleagues and fellow members of the Linguistic Minorities Project, without whom their chapters could not have been written: Xavier Couillard, Anna Morawska, Michael Morawski, Verity Saifullah Khan and Greg Smith. The author of chapter 26 also wishes to thank David Barton, Elizabeth Rowlands and Roy Truman for helpful comments on the first draft of her chapter.

The author of chapter 27 thanks David Newell and the Broadcasting Research Department of the BBC for permission to use survey data and for advice; Dr J. Roger of the Applied Statistics Department, Reading University, for advice on multivariate statistics; Dan Lynn James of Dyfed LEA, Eluned Ellis Jones of Gwynedd LEA and Gerson Davies of Clwyd LEA, for reports and for permission to use figures; Dr D. Collett of the Applied Statistics Department, Reading University, for advice on loglinear models, help with GLIM and for looking over the discussion of tables 27.5 and 27.6 and the breakdowns by age and sex in the censuses; the Publications Department, Office of Population, Censuses and Surveys, for sending Census County

Monitors for the 1981 Census as they appeared; Mrs Yvonne Robinson and Mr Ted Miller of the Psychology Department, Reading University, for assistance with maps and graphs.

The author of chapter 28 thanks John Harris, Seán de Fréine, Brian Ó Cuív and Máirtín Ó Murchú for their comments on an earlier draft of his chapter.

Abbreviations

In addition to ME (Middle English), OE (Old English), RP (Received Pronunciation) and SE (Standard English), which appear in the text, the following abbreviations occur when preceding linguistic examples:

A	Angloromani	NAE	North American English
AN	Anglo Norse	NHE	Northern Hiberno-
BBE	British Black English		English
BJC	British Jamaican Creole	OF	Old French
BV	Belfast Vernacular	OI	Old Irish
Corn	Cornish	ON	Old Norse
Cr	Creole	ONF	Old Norman French
Du	Dutch	O Sc	Older Scots
EModE	Early Modern English	OW	Old Welsh
ESSE	Educated Scottish Standard English	OWN	Old West Norse
		Pres Eng	Present English
Fr	French	R	Romnimos
G	Guernsey-French	S	Sark-French
Gk	Greek	Sc	Scots
Gmc	Germanic	ScE	Scottish English
HE	Hiberno-English	SEE	Scottish Standard English
IE	Indo-European	SHE	Southern Hiberno-
It	Italian		English
J	Jersey-French	SUE	South Ulster English
JC	Jamaican Creole	SW	Dialects of east Cornwall, Devon and, usually west Somerset, sometimes areas further to the east (chapter 12)
LF	Lingua Franca		
LG	Low German		
MDu	Middle Dutch		
MLG	Middle and Low German		
Mod E	Modern English	US	Ulster Scots
MUE	Mid Ulster English	V Lat	Vulgar Latin
MW	Middle Welsh		

Part I

English

Introduction

English is by a very long way the dominant language in the British Isles. The vast majority of the population of the islands are native speakers of English, and those who are not native speakers generally use English as a second language. This, of course, has not always been the case: English was preceded in the British Isles by languages of Celtic origin. The process of the replacement of Celtic by English began in the fifth century A.D., and continues to the present day. The Celtic languages are the topic of Part II of this book; and the subject of the retreat of the Celtic languages, and their survival, is dealt with there and in Part IV. The geographical expansion of English within the British Isles, being simply the other side of the coin of the contraction of Celtic, is also covered in Part II, with the spread of English in Wales, Ireland and the Scottish Highlands being further covered in chapters 27, 28 and 29 respectively. (For the spread of English in Lowland Scotland, see also chapter 30.)

In Part I, we look at the history of the English language in the British Isles, taking a perhaps rather more social focus than is usual but concentrating nevertheless on linguistic characteristics; and on the linguistic characteristics of those modern varieties of English in the British Isles for which we have information. The sociolinguistic position of varieties of English, and their interaction with other languages, are dealt with in Part IV (with the exception that the sociolinguistic characteristics of Highland, Cornish and Welsh English are covered briefly in the present section). The extent of our coverage of particular varieties of English in this book has been determined by the state of our knowledge as well as by linguistic and sociolinguistic considerations. It is notable, for example, that relatively little seems to be known about variation in English syntax in the British Isles. And many of the advances made in the study of urban varieties, the subject of chapter 13, *Urban dialects in the British Isles*, have been theoretical and methodological rather than descriptive. We have not yet been provided with detailed descriptions of many of the urban dialects spoken by the majority of the population.

In his book *Accents of English*, Wells (1982: 2ff) makes a sensible and useful distinction between 'General English' and 'traditional-dialect'.

2

Traditional-dialect is 'restricted to a small area of the geographical territory where English is spoken as first language' and is recessive even there. It is found in areas of England 'well removed from London, particularly the north and the rural west'; and in eastern, central and southern Scotland and in the north of Ireland, where it is known as 'Scots'. Scots is discussed in this section of the book in chapter 6, *Scottish accents and dialects*, and in chapter 7, *English in the north of Ireland*. Traditional-dialect in England is the subject matter of chapter 5, *Rural dialects in England*.

With the possible exception of traditional-dialect varieties in the American Appalachians and the Canadian Maritimes, and with the additional exception of English-based Creoles (see chapters 14 and 33) and creole-influenced varieties, all other varieties of native-speaker English come, according to Wells, under the heading of 'General English'. One variety of General English is 'Standard English', which differs from nonstandard varieties (as indeed they differ amongst themselves) in syntax, morphology and vocabulary. Relatively little is known about the grammatical characteristics of nonstandard varieties of English in England, but what is known is discussed in chapter 2, *Standard English in England*, and in chapter 13. Standard English itself comes, of course, in a number of different forms in different parts of the English-speaking world. Chapter 6 includes discussion of the Scottish variety of Standard General English, while chapter 2 is devoted to a discussion of the form of Standard English employed in England. (My own preferred label for varieties of English from England is 'English English', by analogy with 'American English', 'Australian English' etc., but other writers use the term 'Anglo-English'. Note that, whatever label is used, we have been careful in this book to distinguish between the terms' 'English English' and 'British English'. The latter is often used in the literature, particularly, it seems, by Americans and writers on English as a foreign language, where it is really the former that is intended.)

Differences within General English of pronunciation alone are described by Wells as constituting differences of accent. Chapters 3 and 4 in this section deal with accents of General English in England, with chapter 4, *English accents in England*, treating local accents (as does chapter 13 also) and chapter 3 discussing the non-localizable English English accent known to linguists as 'Received Pronunciation' or 'RP'. As Wells points out, RP 'is characteristic of the upper class and (to an extent) of the upper-middle class. An Old Etonian sounds much the same whether he grew up in Cornwall or Northumberland.'

Chapters 8–12, *English in the south of Ireland*, *Highland and Island English*, *Manx English*, *Welsh English* and *Cornish English*, deal with varieties of English spoken in areas where Celtic languages survive or where they were spoken until comparatively recently, and where the substratum influence of these languages is therefore still in evidence (for attitudes to Irish English see chapter 28). Chapter 14, *British Black English and West Indian Creoles*, on the other hand, discusses substratum influence of a different type. It looks at the linguistic interaction, set in motion by migration from the Caribbean, between General English and African-influenced, English-derived West Indian Creoles.

1

The history of English in the British Isles

J. MILROY

Introduction

Typological change

During the past nine centuries, English has undergone more dramatic changes than any other major European language in the same period. Old English was moderately highly inflected for case, number, gender, tense, mood and other grammatical categories. Present English, however, has a vastly simplified inflectional morphology with total loss of inflections in, for example, adjectives and the definite article, and very considerable inflectional losses in every other word-class. There have also been many phonological changes, and the lexicon has been altered from mainly Germanic to a mixed Germanic–Romance type. In syntax, a mixed SVO–SOV word-order has become mainly SVO, and there have been great changes in the tense–aspect system of the verb. These changes, taken together, amount to a typological change from mainly synthetic to mainly analytic, and at the lexical level to considerable modification of the Germanic character of English.

As a result, OE (Anglo-Saxon), unlike, for example, medieval Icelandic, is not immediately accessible to the modern native reader. This will be apparent from OE quotations on pages 23–4.

Geographical spread

The geographical spread of English has been no less remarkable. Around 400 A.D. it was a series of obscure Germanic dialects spoken along the northern European coast between Jutland and what is now north-eastern France. By around 800 it had been established in south, east and central Britain as far north as Edinburgh, while dialects of Celtic (Cymric) were still in use in the west from Cornwall to Cumbria and Strathclyde. In contrast, English is now the most important language in the world with the second highest number of native speakers (approaching 400 million) and many millions of users as a second language. This dramatic increase (from about 2 million speakers in 1600) is a result of the rise of Britain as a colonial, commercial and industrial power, and (more recently) the importance and prestige of the USA.

Variation and change

The aim of this chapter is to attempt to account for the very considerable changes that have taken place, not merely to chronicle those changes. For this reason, and for reasons of space, the changes discussed are selected as being those of major importance. In the discussion attention is given to the fact that no language is monolithic, but exists in many varieties at all times; and also that change may be associated with social (including political) factors. The history of a language is not a set of easily verifiable facts, but depends on the interpretations put on accidentally surviving texts by generations of scholars. The present account differs from many standard histories of English in that it is relatively sensitive to social and stylistic variation: therefore, it is assumed, for example, that certain types of change at given times may have been more advanced in colloquial speech than in the more 'formal' written texts that happen to survive. Similarly, it is assumed that changes have taken place at differential rates in different varieties, so that at any given time some varieties may have been more advanced than others.

Origins

English is descended from the Germanic group of the Indo-European family of languages. Within this group it belongs to the West Germanic branch, and its nearest relative is Frisian (still spoken by a few thousand people on the coasts and islands of northern Germany and Holland), with which OE shared some common developments, (for example, raising of Gmc /a/ to /æ/: 'Anglo-Frisian brightening'). It is also closely related to Dutch and Low German, but less closely to High German (which exhibits divergent phonological developments).

Chronology

Scholars have traditionally distinguished three periods in the history of English. The OE period lasts from the Anglo-Saxon settlements in Britain (traditionally dated 449 A.D.) until just after the Norman Conquest, i.e. 1100–1150. The linguistic break between OE and ME (Middle English) appears to be sharp and obvious, even in the earliest extensive ME text (the Peterborough extension to the *Anglo-Saxon Chronicle*, *c.* 1154). There is no such clear linguistic break between ME and Modern English texts. The conventional date for the transition (*c.* 1500) is dictated by cultural factors such as the beginning of the Renaissance in England and the introduction of printing by Caxton. Even the 'Great Vowel Shift' (see below), which can be held to differentiate Modern English from ME, is not a safe guide: it may well have been in progress in some areas before 1400 (Kökeritz, 1953; Lass, 1976) and is still retarded in some dialects at the present day.

In what follows, I shall focus on accounting for the typological and lexical changes that have taken place between OE and Modern English. ME is regarded as a transitional stage in which the characteristics of OE were rapidly altered and in which the foundations of Modern English were laid.

Old English as a Germanic language

Phonology

OE, like other Germanic languages, usually has its main stress on the root syllable of words. This results from a very early change known as Germanic accent shift, and it has some consequences for the general phonology. A series of Indo-European vowel-shift rules, known collectively as 'ablaut', are preserved more systematically in Germanic than in other Indo-European languages, particularly in the 'strong verb' system. Thus OE:

Infinitive	Pret. sing.	Pret. pl.	Past part.	
drīfan	drāf	drifon	ȝedrifen	'drive'
singan	sang	sungon	ȝesungen	'sing'

The vowel variations are ascribed to variable pitch-accent and stress-accent in Indo-European. The preterite plural/past participle forms had stress on the suffix in Indo-European with a 'zero' vowel in the root syllable. Ablaut variation affected other parts of the lexicon besides the verb and is responsible for some residual alternations in Present English, such as *ride* (v.), *road* (n.).

In the consonant system, OE shares with other Germanic languages the reflexes of the 'First Consonant Shift' (Grimm's Law), which stipulates that certain series of Germanic obstruents correspond to related series in Indo-European. For example, the Indo-European voiceless stop series: /p, t, k, k^w/ (as in Latin *piscis, tres, cornu, quando*) correspond to Gmc /f, θ, x, x^w/ (as in Pres Eng *fish, three, horn, when*). When this fricative series occurred in syllables that did not bear the main stress in Indo-European, they were additionally subject to voicing in Germanic (Verner's Law). OE preserves many of the reflexes of Verner's Law, for example in the accent-shifted preterite plural/past participle of strong verbs such as *weorþan* 'become' (pret. sing. *wearþ*, pret. pl. *wurdon*). Verner's Law alternations have been largely levelled out in the course of time but are preserved in, for example, Pres Eng *was/were*; *seethe/sodden* (OE *seoþan* 'boil').

Of the various vowel changes that took effect within the OE period, the most important is 'i-umlaut' or front mutation. This was pre-literary in date and had, amongst other things, the effect of creating new vowel alternations within noun and verb paradigms: thus, OE *mūs* 'mouse', *mȳs* 'mice'; *fōt* 'foot', *fēt* 'feet'. i-umlaut operated when, in Germanic, [i] or [j] followed in the succeeding syllable: under these conditions a low or back vowel in the root syllable was raised and/or fronted. The process can be thought of as vowel harmony or anticipatory assimilation in height and/or frontness. All other extant Germanic languages (except Gothic) have i-umlaut, but they appear to have implemented it independently.

OE is also affected by common West Germanic changes, for example consonant gemination before original [j] (cf OE *sittan*, but ON *sitja* 'sit') and rhotacism, whereby [z] → [r]: thus, OE *wǣron* < Gmc **wǣzun* 'were'.

Various specifically OE changes, such as breaking and back mutation, have few consequences at the present day; however there was a general tendency towards palatalization of [k, sk, g] (under various conditions) which gives the following contrasts: Pres Eng *choose, cheese, edge, fish* (OE *cēosan, ciese, ecg, fisc*); cf. Gothic *kiusan*, German *Käse, Ecke*, Danish *fisk*.

Morphology

Although less highly inflected than Latin, OE was still quite a highly inflected language with, for example, three genders, four cases (with residues of a fifth – instrumental), highly inflected articles and pronouns, and many different conjugations of verbs and declensions of nouns.

The Germanic features not shared with other Indo-European languages affect chiefly the adjectives and verbs. OE distinguishes between the 'strong' (definite) and 'weak' (indefinite) declensions of adjectives, the weak declension being used when some 'definite' element precedes the adjective (e.g. the definite article or demonstrative) and the strong declension otherwise. The distinction was finally lost in late ME.

Verbs are divided into two inflectional types, also known traditionally as 'strong' and 'weak'. Strong verbs are inflected for tense by undergoing a change of the root vowel (see above), whereas weak verbs form their preterite and past participle by adding a suffix containing a dental consonant. Whereas the strong verb vowel alternations are descended from Indo-European, the dental preterite weak verbs are peculiar to Germanic. They are of more recent origin and can often be shown to be derivatives of strong verbs, or of other parts of speech. The relation between the following pair, for instance, is causative, and the weak verb is derived from the preterite of the strong:

	Infinitive	Pret. sing.	Pret. pl.	Past part.	
Strong:	licgan	læʒ	læʒon	ʒeleʒen	'lie'
Weak:	lecgan	læʒde	læʒdon	ʒelæʒd	'lay'
					(i.e. 'cause to lie')

The strong and weak verbs remain in Present English, with some tendency for strong verbs to transfer to the weak system, but with certain transfers in the opposite direction. Thus:

	OE	Pres. Eng
help	strong	weak
weep	strong	weak
wear	weak	strong

Some original weak verbs like *hide, feed* owe their 'strong' appearance to early shortening (see page 19).

Syntax

Many of the syntactic differences between OE and Present English can be attributed to the typological difference between a highly inflected and weakly inflected language. Thus, OE clearly had many more surface rules of agreement, concord and government than Present English has. The history of syntax is discussed on pages 21–4.

Lexicon

The OE vocabulary is predominantly Germanic. A few items, e.g. *sceap* 'sheep', are confined to West Germanic and not found in North Germanic. Some everyday words, however, were borrowed into West Germanic (before the Anglo-Saxon migration to Britain) from Latin (or from Greek though Latin) and are therefore common to West Germanic languages. These include OE *ciese* 'cheese'; *strǣt* 'street'; *cyrice* 'church'; *biscop* 'bishop'; *cealc* 'chalk'; *mīl* 'mile'.

Borrowing from Latin and Greek in the OE period is often ecclesiastical in type and includes *candel* 'candle'; *mynster* 'monastery'; *reogol* 'rule' (for much more detail see Serjeantson, 1935).

The influence of the indigenous Celtic vocabulary is minimal and includes *brat* 'apron' and *brocc* 'badger'. Scandinavian influence on spoken language was very far-reaching in many areas in late OE, but does not become evident in surviving texts until after the breakdown of the West Saxon scribal and literary tradition (i.e. after the Norman Conquest).

The Germanic character of the OE lexicon is most obvious when we consider its methods of word-formation. Abstract, technical and intellectual terms were derived by compounding and affixation from the basic wordstock. Examples are: *þrīnes* 'trinity' (lit. 'three-ness'); *rīmcræft* 'arithmetic' (lit. 'rime-craft': skill in numbers); *þrōwung(e)* 'suffering', 'passion'; *ārfæstnesse* 'piety' (lit. 'fastness', i.e. firmness, in reverence).

The later English preference for borrowing abstract terms from French, Latin, Greek (and Arabic) came about not because the OE language was incapable of expressing the ideas in its own terms, but because of the socio-political consequences of the Norman Conquest. Much of the OE abstract vocabulary was gradually displaced in the ME period.

Dialectal variation in OE

The three Germanic tribes that settled in Britain, the Angles, Saxons and Jutes, appear to have spoken slightly divergent dialects from the beginning, and their patterns of settlement and influence are evident in the four main literary dialects. The Angles settled in the Midlands and east between the Thames and the Forth. The two Anglian dialects were Northumbrian (spoken north of the Humber) and Mercian (from the Humber to the Thames). The Jutes settled in Kent and along the south coast to the Isle of Wight: the OE dialect of that area is Kentish. Amongst the Saxons, the West Saxon dialect proved dominant and was used in the rest of the OE-speaking area to the south and west of the Thames.

The approximate boundaries of these areas continue to be discernible throughout ME and in some rural dialect characteristics today. After the Viking invasions and wars of the eighth and ninth centuries, the Anglian-speaking areas were virtually annexed and came under Danish rule (the Danelaw). Thus, West Saxon (the language of King Ælfred) became the standard OE literary language, while the Anglian dialects seemingly underwent rapid changes as a result of contact with Danish. It is of some importance to note this, as the Modern English standard language that began to form after the Norman Conquest was based not on West Saxon but chiefly on the south-east Midland (Mercian) dialect of London.

The rise of Modern English

Variability in early ME

The ME period can be viewed as transitional between OE and Modern English. The first substantial ME text (the Peterborough extension to the *Anglo-Saxon Chronicle*, composed *c*. 1154) shows considerable changes. As the West Saxon scribal tradition has been disrupted, the orthography is variable, already considerably influenced by French conventions. There is French influence on vocabulary, a certain amount of levelling of OE inflections and a loss of grammatical gender. Subsequently, texts dating from *c*. 1200–1300 show very considerable variation in orthography and dialect, with varying degrees of lexical influence from French and Scandinavian and varying simplification of inflections. The degree of conservatism in texts from *c*. 1200–1300 is related to their geographical origin. South-west and south-west Midland texts (*Ancrene Wisse*, Caligula text of Laȝamon's *Brut*) are conservative in that they maintain, amongst other things, relatively full inflection and grammatical gender. Southern and south-eastern texts are grammatically conservative: the more innovatory texts tend to be from the east Midlands, with north-east Midland texts the most 'advanced' (e.g. *Havelok*).

The 'conservative' appearance of west Midland texts as against the 'advanced' and variable character of east Midland ones is plainly a consequence of the Norman Conquest (but see also page 11 on Danish influence). It is known that whereas Saxon bishops and other leading men were rapidly replaced by Normans in many areas, the west Midlands remained less directly influenced, and texts in 'classical' OE continued to emanate from that area. In language, as in other matters, the effects of the Conquest were felt most rapidly in the south-east and east Midlands.

It has usually been argued that the sharp break between OE and ME is more apparent than real. First, many orthographic changes may be purely scribal, not reflecting phonological changes. For example, the substitution of *a* for OE *æ* does not necessarily indicate lowering and/or retraction of OE /æ/ (ME *sat*, OE *sæt*). Second, the conservative West Saxon scribal tradition may well have concealed the presence of changes already beginning in spoken OE by the tenth century or so.

Despite this necessary caution, it is clear that these medieval changes (if compared with changes taking place in a comparable period between, say, 1600 and the present) were by any standard rapid. Fourteenth-century English is quite evidently more similar to Present English than to OE: it is typologically well advanced towards the analytic stage, even in the relatively formal literary texts that are preserved.

Language contact in early English

Although some changes may proceed 'naturally' without external factors being responsible, rapid and large-scale change affecting all levels of the language is normally a consequence of language contact. Early medieval England was twice subjected to massive political and social changes involving speakers of foreign languages: the Scandinavian invasions and settlements of the ninth to eleventh centuries, and the Norman Conquest followed by Norman rule.

Certain general principles that operate in language contact situations are now well known to sociolinguists and creolists. These include: (1) gross morphological simplification; (2) some loss of segmental phonological distinctions; (3) relexification (i.e. replacement of much of the lexicon of one language – the subordinate one – with the lexicon of the other) and (4) a preference for a fixed SVO word-order. ME shows clear signs that at least three of these (1, 3 and 4) had operated: loss of a number of consonantal distinctions seems also to have taken place if the orthography of some thirteenth-century texts is to be trusted (Milroy, 1983).

The influence of Norse and Anglo-Norman was not confined to the vocabulary – as traditional accounts often imply. Scandinavian place names in the Midlands and east of England (in some areas in the order of 90%) show that Danish settlement was extensive in the Danelaw (east of a line from London to Chester) in the tenth and eleventh centuries. The place-name evidence suggests that in some areas (e.g. north Yorkshire), a form of Danish must have been generally used for some time. However, as it is most unlikely that OE and ON were fully mutually comprehensible, contact forms (Anglo-Danish pidgin) must have been used to some extent in trade and commerce. As the bilingual situation receded, the varieties that remained must have been effectively Anglo-Norse creoles with a tendency in the post-creole situation to restore some of the grammatical distinctions lost in pidginization.

Contact with Norman French was of a somewhat different kind. The

Norman settlers were quite few in number, but they immediately seized positions of national political power. Contact with Normandy was maintained until 1204, and until that time Anglo-Norman was quite widely spoken. By the thirteenth century, however, Anglo-Norman as a first language was receding sharply and its use became largely confined to ceremonial and administrative purposes. But again it is clear that in daily life between 1066 and the early thirteenth century, pidgin-type contact forms or interlanguages must often have been used, continuing and spreading the tendencies to structural simplification that were already present in Anglo-Norse areas.

The effect of these contacts was not, in general, direct borrowing from the grammatical apparatus of Scandinavian and French. The structural simplifications did not chiefly result from any particular characteristics of Old Norse and Norman French, but from the contact situation itself, in which speakers in daily use abandoned distinctions that might be considered redundant or inessential to everyday communication. The ME texts that survive are not, of course, composed in a creole language, but the simplifications they display are best accounted for by the hypothesis that the language had at some point been subjected to creolization. Everyday spoken English in some areas may well have been further advanced in inflectional loss and other post-creole characteristics, and it is from these spoken varieties that Present English is chiefly descended.

The rise of Standard English

After the thirteenth century, English in Britain was never again subjected to the cataclysmic effects of invasion followed by bilingualism and language contact. The language has, however, been subjected to other important influences, chiefly that of Central French from about 1250 to 1500 and the classical languages (Latin and Greek) from 1500 onwards. These effects have come about through literary rather than everyday spoken channels and are largely lexical (see pages 27–8). Their importance has been to increase the vocabulary available for formal and technical uses of the language and hence to contribute to the functional elaboration that is necessary in a national standard language.

Although West Saxon had developed a standard literary form, English after the Conquest was cut off from any immediate possibility of developing into a national 'standard'. There were many reasons for this, including great variability in written forms, but the chief reason was that Latin and Norman French, rather than English, were used for official and administrative purposes, and so English could not acquire the status associated with official languages. A second reason for the low status of English was that Latin was the language of theology, philosophy and science, and this continued to be the case until about 1700.

In one sense the history of English since 1200 is one of rising 'respectability' and the gradual acquisition of more and more of the functions appropriate to a standard language. From the Middle Ages onward, there is a literature of complaint about the low status and inadequacies of English. Robert of Gloucester (fourteenth century) complains that a man must know French if he is to be well thought of. In the fifteenth century Caxton is faced with the problem of devising a normalized language for use in printed books. He is perplexed by the variability of English and complains that the language is like the moon ... 'which is neuer stedfaste/but euer Wauerynge/wexynge one season/and waneth and dyscreaseth another season'.

Sixteenth-century writers regard the language as lacking in eloquence and seek to 'improve' it by large scale lexical borrowing from Latin and Greek (Jones, 1953). Even in the seventeenth century writers can still think of English as ephemeral and unimportant: Waller's view is that to write English is to write on sand:

> poets who lasting marbles seek
> Must carve in Latin or in Greek.

It is not until the eighteenth century that the status of English is finally assured. Swift in 1712, while continuing the complaint tradition ('I do ... complain to your lordship ... that our language is extremely imperfect ...'), is confident enough of the importance of English to propose that the language should be fixed and standardized ('ascertained') by an Academy. However, the task of codifying and standardizing was in fact carried out by private persons: the lexicon and orthography are codified in Dr Johnson's *Dictionary* of 1755, and the grammar is codified in a spate of grammar books, the most influential of which was Bishop Lowth's *Introduction to English Grammar* (1762).

The chief linguistic symptom of a standardized language is normalization, i.e. the suppression of optional variants at most levels of the grammar. In this sense, standardization has been fully achieved only in the written channel: English speech is still extremely variable, especially in phonology but also in aspects of syntax (despite the present prestige of Received Pronunciation (RP) and the influence of SE grammar books). It is also clear that standardization has come about as a result of commercial, political and social needs rather than for purely linguistic reasons or through the direct influence of literary men. Technological advance (particularly the invention of printing and the commercial need to disseminate printed books as widely as possible) has been instrumental in spreading the influence of the standard language. The decision to base the standard on a particular dialect (that of the south-east Midlands) is also a result of commercial and political factors – the general importance of that region rather than any supposed linguistic superiority in its dialect.

Generally speaking, the sixteenth and seventeenth centuries are the centuries of vocabulary expansion in response to the need for functional elaboration of the developing standard – in science, philosophy and literature. In these centuries also there was an interest in defining a 'correct' standard pronunciation (by 'orthoepists' such as Hart, Gil and others, as discussed by Dobson, 1968). The eighteenth century was the century of syntactic prescription: many grammatical prohibitions, such as avoidance of the double negative, originate from that century. Nineteenth-century scholarly interest shifts to historicity – the provision of a historical pedigree for English and other non-classical languages. This involves a strong interest in the dialects and in the Anglo-Saxon basis of English. Much of the flavour of this research is anti-classical and nationalistic. The hybridization of English by French and Latin is often regretted (for a discussion see Milroy, 1977: 70–98) and the historical continuity from Anglo-Saxon to the present is emphasized and (in my view) exaggerated.

Interpreting the evidence

Progressive standardization of written records from about 1500 has had the consequence that in Modern English from 1500 we have less direct access to variation and nonstandard forms. There is therefore a tendency for histories of English to concentrate from that period on the history of SE alone. It should be remembered, however, that the very diverse dialects of Present English in the British Isles do have their own histories, greater knowledge of which would increase our knowledge of the nature and processes of linguistic maintenance and change.

The standardization of spelling makes Early Modern English phonology more difficult to recover than other levels of the grammar. Our sources for reconstructing pronunciation are: (1) the testimony of sixteenth- and seventeenth-century writers on pronunciation – the orthoepists (Dobson, 1968); (2) casual and informal spellings in personal letters and diaries (Wyld, 1920); (3) the evidence of rhymes and puns; (4) 'the use of the present to explain the past' – reconstruction of past uses from forms preserved in Present English dialects. Advances in social dialectology in recent years suggest that the fourth type of source has more to offer than has been realized (Labov, 1975; Nunberg, 1980; Milroy and Harris 1980; Milroy, in press). Some account will be taken here of the dialectal diversity of Present English (see pages 16–18).

Phonological change since 1100

The Great Vowel Shift

If we compare a selected set of OE words with their Present English descendants, it is clear that there have been great phonological changes since OE times. Consider OE īs 'ice'; mȳs 'mice'; fēt 'feet'; hām 'home'; gōs 'goose'; hūs 'house'. In these instances, the spelling suggests that the consonants have not changed; however, the vowels certainly have, for example, the long high vowels [iː] and [uː] as in īs 'ice'; hūs 'house' have become diphthongs with the

Table 1.1. *Long vowel system of ME*

CV1	/iː/ as in /biːt-/	'bite'
CV2	/eː/ as in /meːt-/	'meet'
CV3	/ɛː/ as in /mɛːt/	'meat'
CV4	/aː/ as in /naːm-/	'name'
CV5	(see below)	
CV6	/ɔː/ as in /hɔːm-/	'home'
CV7	/oː/ as in /roːt-/	'root'
CV8	/uː/ as in /uːt/	'out'

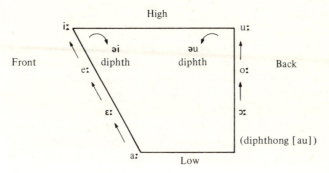

Figure 1.1. Model of the Great Vowel Shift

first element of the diphthong having been lowered in each case to a vowel as low as [a] in many dialects. Thus, we have [aɪ, ɑʊ] in *ice, house*. In general, consonants have not changed as much as vowels, and OE long vowels (as in the forms cited) have changed more than the OE short vowels.

The series of changes that brought about the present reflexes of the earlier long vowels is known collectively as 'The Great Vowel Shift'. This was a 'chain shift' in which low, low-mid and high-mid vowels were raised to respectively low-mid, high-mid and high positions, and the high vowels were diphthongized (possibly to avoid a clash with the mid-vowels that were rising into the high vowel space). There is dispute as to whether the Great Vowel Shift was a 'push-chain' or a 'drag-chain' or whether it had elements of both (see Lass, 1976).

The Great Vowel Shift is assumed to have operated on a ME long vowel system which was approximately as set out in table 1.1 (approximate Cardinal Vowel values are assumed). Note that ME /ɔː/ had already been raised from OE /aː/ (cf. OE *hām* 'home'). The chain shift pattern can be represented on a trapezoid model as in figure 1.1. Thus, by 1600 or so, ME /biːt-/ had become /bəit/, ME /meːt-/ had become /miːt/, and so on. At the vacant slot at CV5, it

Table 1.2. *Long vowel system of London English c. 1550*

ME			*c.* 1550		
CV1	biːt-	diphth. 1	beit/bəit	'bite'
CV2	meːt-	CV1	miːt	'meet'
CV3	mɛːt-	CV2	meːt	'meat'
CV4	naːm-	CV3	nɛːm	'name'
CV5	hauk-	CV6	hɑːk/hɔːk	'hawk'
CV6	hɔːm-	CV7	hoːm	'home'
CV7	noːt-	CV8	ruːt	'root'
CV8	uːt	diphth. 2	əut	'out'

is presumed that there was no ME monophthong. However, there was a diphthong /au/, as in the ME forms of *law, hawk, autumn*, which was monophthongized by the sixteenth century and had come to occupy the CV6 position /ɔː/, as ME /ɔː/ rose to /oː/ (as in *home, stone*, etc.).

The position by about 1550 in London English was probably as in table 1.2. Lexical items in the *meat* (ME /ɛː/) class were already showing a considerable tendency to merge either with the *meet* class or the *name* class. Thus, Shakespeare could rhyme *meat* items with *meet* items or with *name* items. By 1700 in London English, the three-way distinction between EModE *meet/ meat/mate* had been reduced – except residually – to a two-way distinction. Most *meat* items merged with EModE /iː/, but a few (*great, break, steak, yea*) fell in with the *mate, make, name* class, which had presumably risen to a vowel near /eː/. The stabilization of most *meat* items in the *meet* class took place after a considerable period of alternation between one vowel and the other.

Certain other ME diphthongs were also involved in the Great Vowel Shift pattern in London English. Thus, ME /ai/ as in *day, raise*, fell together with ME /aː/ by the sixteenth century, so that SE has the same vowel in, for example, *tail* and *tale*. Similarly ME /ou/ in *flow, know* fell together with ME /ɔː/ in *home, stone*. Some dialects, however, still maintain the ME diphthongs as distinct. Lowland Scots (variably) distinguishes *tail, soul* (diphthongs) from *tale, sole* (monophthongs). For a similar situation in East Anglia, see Trudgill (1974) and Trudgill and Foxcroft (1978).

It is clear that in subsequent London and SE, the sixteenth-century vowels have undergone phonetic changes. In particular there has been a tendency to diphthongize long vowels – especially obvious in EModE /eː/ and /oː/, which are now /eɪ/, /əʊ/ (as in *name, home*). The first elements of the Early Modern English diphthongs have been considerably lowered: thus /əi/, /əu/ are now (approximately) /aɪ/, /aʊ/. But the situation in present-day RP is extremely fluid and variable (see chapter 3), and this must always have been so.

Dialectal variations in the Great Vowel Shift

The pattern as described above applies mainly to RP and its Early Modern English London ancestor; other dialects have either implemented the same pattern at different rates or implemented a somewhat different pattern.

London urban speech, together with other southern and Midland dialects, has carried the Great Vowel Shift a stage further than in RP. For example, the first element of Pres Eng /ei/ (< EModE /e:/) has been lowered to [ai]: thus, since *mate* becomes almost identical to RP *mite*, the London diphthong in *mite* has undergone rounding to [ɔi] (see chapter 4). A clash between [ɔi] in such words as *pint* and the vowel in *point* is then avoided by raising of the *point* diphthong to [oi]. Dialects in many rural areas or in towns remote from London have, however, implemented the Great Vowel Shift more slowly than RP and may display a stage similar to Early Modern English. In some dialects, for example northern Hiberno-English (see chapter 7), the diphthongs arising from ME /iː/ and /uː/ have not lowered their first elements beyond the Early Modern English stage (i.e. /eɪ, əɪ; əʊ/). Some dialects maintain a vowel near low-mid in words of the *name, make* class, and some maintain a residual ME three-way distinction between words of the *meet/meat/mate* classes (Milroy and Harris, 1980). Hopkins (House and Storey, 1959: 219) reported in 1872 that in Devon dialect ME /iː/ had failed to diphthongize in the words *stile* and *high*, which were still pronounced *steel, hee*.

It appears, therefore, that the Great Vowel Shift was implemented first in south-east Midland dialects (perhaps in urban areas) and has spread to other dialects by geographical diffusion, perhaps reinforcing a general tendency for long vowels to rise in these dialects at slower rates and in slightly different patterns. The shift is most advanced in London and other south and south Midland areas.

In dialects derived from Old Northumbrian, the Great Vowel Shift took a different form. The main difference is in the 'original' back vowels, and its results can be seen in Lowland Scots. In these dialects OE *ā* as in *hām* 'home', was not raised to /ɔː/ in ME and /oː/ in Early Modern English, but was front-raised to /eː/; thus, Sc *hame, stane* for PresEng 'home, stone'. The mid-back vowel /oː/ (ME *fōt* 'foot') was probably not raised to a 'back' /uː/ but was fronted to /øː/ or /yː/ and then often unrounded. As these lower back vowels were fronted, there was less chain-shift pressure on original /uː/ (ME *ūt*); it remained undiphthongized (as in Sc *oot, hoose*) but with a tendency to be advanced to central or even front position.

The short vowels and typological change

While the ME long vowels have been massively changed in quality, the short vowels have changed much less. In RP, ME *ĭ, ĕ* and *ă* (accepting this last as a low front vowel: Lass, 1976) have changed relatively little, although they have probably been subject in the past to some fluctuation. ME *ŏ* has been lowered, and ME *ŭ* has been lowered and unrounded in southern varieties of English except after labials (cf. *sup/pull*, both from ME *ŭ*). Failure of the short vowels to change dramatically (while the long vowels were subject to raising and diphthongization) has resulted in a configuration of the vowel system that is very different from OE. In particular, these changes have made possible a large-scale loss of phonemic length. To explain this, we must first discuss the OE vowel system.

The OE (West Saxon) system is believed to have consisted of nine pairs of long and short vowels (six monophthongs and three diphthongs), each pair being distinguished mainly by length rather than quality. Thus OE *īs* 'ice' and *is* 'is' are thought to have differed only in length. In Present English the reflexes of such pairs are massively different in quality, as in *bite* (/aɪ/) vs. *bit* (/ɪ/).

The gradual implementation of the Great Vowel Shift seems to have resulted in situations in which phonemic length became to a greater or lesser extent redundant, as the pairs of vowels became different in quality. As a result we have in Present English two major types of vowel system, one which retains inherently long and inherently short vowels but with qualitative differences also, and another, in which most vowel phonemes can be either long or short according to the varying phonetic contexts in which they occur.

In the first type (e.g. RP), there is a clear qualitative difference between such pairs as *beet* (/i/) and *bit* (/ɪ/), but a length distinction is also present, although no longer necessary for distinguishing one vowel from the other (except in some northern English dialects). In the second type (Lowland Scots, Scots English, northern Hiberno-English – see chapters 6, 7, 30), length is mainly allophonic, so that the vowel in *beet*, *leaf* (ME long vowels) is as short as that in *bit* (ME short vowel), whereas the vowel in *breathe*, *sleeve* is long (before the voiced fricatives). So too, in northern Hiberno-English, the vowel in *bed* (ME short) is longer than that in *gate* (ME long), as for most vowels a following voiced consonant predicts a fully long vowel. In Anglo-English this reduction in the importance of vowel length has been gradual and variable, whereas in Scots a complete typological change from phonemic to allophonic length seems to have been implemented early (see, e.g., Lass, 1976).

Restructuring and alternations

The ME vowel system presumed as a basis for the Great Vowel Shift already showed phonetic and structural differences from the OE system. OE long and short /y/ had merged with /iː/ and /i/ respectively (there were some dialectal differences here), the OE diphthongs *io*, *eo*, *ie* (long and short) had merged with /eː/ and /iː/. New diphthongs /aɪ, au, ɔɪ/ arose in ME from various sources. ME /aː/ originated from OE *ă*, lengthened in open syllables, and then later participated as a long vowel in the Great Vowel Shift. OE /aː/ was raised and rounded to /ɔː/ in early ME in the south and Midlands and this /ɔː/ also subsequently participated in the Great Vowel Shift. This example shows that some tendency to raising of long vowels was already present around 1200: the Great Vowel Shift may therefore be regarded not as a particular change with a determinate beginning and end, but as a manifestation of a general tendency to raise long vowels, which was accelerated in late ME/Early Modern English, but which may have been in progress long before in some dialects and is still continuing today.

The results of the Great Vowel Shift are complicated by restructuring. In the history of English there have been a series of lengthenings of original short vowels and shortenings of original long vowels under specified conditions. Thus, for example, original long vowels that have been shortened have failed to participate in the Great Vowel Shift. Not only have lexical items with an original long vowel become short vowel items (and *vice versa*), but also derivationally and inflectionally related pairs in Present English may now be seen to alternate between the reflexes of the original 'long' and 'short' vowels.

Alternations generally arise from variation in syllable structure and syllabification. Thus, an alternation such as /iː/ vs. /ɛ/ in *steal/stealth* arises from ME open syllable lengthening. As ME /ɛ/ in *stelen* was in an open syllable, it was lengthened, whereas /ɛ/ in *stelþe* was not. Subsequently *stelen*, but not *stelþe* underwent the Great Vowel Shift. Alternations such as *keep/kept*, *five/fifty* arise from late OE shortening before consonant clusters (other than sonorant and homorganic voiced stop) and geminates. Pairs such as *south/southern, sheep/shepherd* arise from late OE/early ME shortening in trisyllabic words (see, e.g. Fisiak, 1968 for further details). Together with the reflexes of OE i-umlaut (as in *foot/feet, strong/strength*), these and other quantitative changes give rise to complex vowel-shift networks in related words in Present English.

The results of the Great Vowel Shift are also complicated by later shortenings that are apparently not associated with syllabification. Thus ME *flōd*, *blōd* should give [fluːd] etc., but these items (together with others – see Wyld,1920) underwent shortening early enough to participate in the southern English change of short /u/ to /ʌ/ (perhaps around 1600 or later). Other items from ME /oː/ (e.g. *good, foot*) underwent even later shortening in Early Modern English, and their vowel fell together with ME /u/ when it remained rounded (i.e. after labials as in *push, full*, etc.). Thus the RP /ʊ/ class today (*good, foot, full*, etc.) is largely composed of ME /oː/ items that underwent late shortening and ME /u/ items with initial labials.

Short vowel developments in Modern English

Major developments of the Early Modern English short vowels include:
(a) Lowering and unrounding of ME *ŭ* to /ʌ/, as in *cup, hut*; this was prevented after labials in southern varieties of English (as in *pull, full*) but seems to have extended even to labial environments in some Scots and northern Irish

varieties. In most northern English and many Midland dialects, EModE *ŭ* failed to lower and unround. In these, *look* and *luck* can often be homophonous (see chapters 4 and 5).

(b) Lengthening of ME *ă* and *ŏ* before /s, θ, f/ in southern England (see chapters 4 and 5). This is widespread (see Lass, 1976), and in some dialects (e.g. RP), backing has also taken place. Thus, the RP contrast between *pat* (/æ/) and *path*, *grass* (/ɑː/).

The history of short *ă* in Modern English is extremely complicated (for some discussion see Lass, 1976 and Milroy, in press). Here we may note that lengthening and backing in RP affects other environments in addition to the voiceless fricatives. Rounding of *ă* after /w/ is found in southern varieties of English; most other dialects retain /a/ in this environment.

Consonants

Changes in the consonant system have been less dramatic. Loss of OE consonant length (as in *sittan* vs. *witan*) probably started in the north-east Midlands and spread to most dialects by 1400. OE did not have a phonemic contrast between voiced and voiceless fricatives: the contrast begins to appear in intervocalic positions in the north-east Midlands around 1200 and is then reinforced in all positions by borrowing from French (e.g. *vertu* 'virtue'; OE had no initial voiced labial fricative). There have been numerous cluster simplifications: OE initial /hl, hr, hn/ were merged with /l, r, n/ in ME; initial /hw/ was merged with /w/ in some ME dialects, but still remains in some present-day dialects; medial and final /xt/, as in OE *riht*, remains in Lowland Scots, but the fricative was lost (with vowel lengthening) in some ME dialects and was probably generally lost in most London and east Midland areas by 1600. Final /b/ was lost after /m/ in ME (as in *lamb*, *dumb*, etc.), but parallel loss of /g/ after /ŋ/ (as in *sing*) has been variable: it was probably variable in London English in the Early Modern English period, and the stop remains today in west Midland dialects (see chapter 4). Loss of the alveolar stop /d/, after /n/, seems to have been widespread around 1700: its probable loss is indicated by hypercorrect spellings such as *gownd* 'gown' and the survival of the hypercorrection *sound* (ME *soun* < Fr *soun*) (see Wyld, 1920).

Consonant simplification has proceeded further in dialectal English than in the standard language. Syllable-initial /h/ is lost in many vernaculars; London English merges /ð, θ/ with /v, f/ in most positions; loss of final /t/ after other obstruents is very common, so common that in some dialects (Lowland Scots, northern Hiberno-English) the weak verbs *keep*, *sleep*, etc. have the past tenses *kep*, *slep*, etc. and are effectively re-analysed as strong verbs; loss of final /d/ after /l/ and /n/ is also widespread. In one important instance a consonantal loss has affected the standard language. Loss of pre-consonantal /r/ before /s/ had already taken place in some south-east Midland varieties by about 1500 and enabled forms like *cuss*, *hoss*, *passel* to be translated to the New World. General loss of post-vocalic /r/ was probably in progress in the sixteenth century (see, e.g. the spellings of Henry Machyn, *c*. 1550), but could hardly have been complete in 'polite' London English until around 1700.

Loss of post-vocalic /r/ in some dialects has resulted in a division into *rhotic* and *non-rhotic* dialects (Wells, 1970, 1982; and see chapter 4). At the surface phonemic level, rhotic dialects can be described as having fewer vowel contrasts than non-rhotic in that the vowels in the forms *here, fair, bore, moor* belong to the same phoneme as *heat, fate, boat, moot*. In RP and other non-rhotic dialects additional vowel phonemes /iə, ɛə, ɔə, ʊə/ in *here, fair, bore, moor* are postulated. Rhotic dialects include those of Scotland, Ireland and many Anglo-English dialects west of a line running from Hampshire to North Lancashire.

As it is clear that the vowel and consonant developments proceeded differentially in different forms of English, there is usually some difficulty in specifying precise chronology. This is particularly true of a complex change such as the Great Vowel Shift, which may well have been beginning in southeast Midland English in ME. In general, if we accept that changes first manifest themselves variably and then proceed quite slowly to completion (unless competing changes prevent this – Wang, 1969), then the beginnings of certain 'modern' English changes may well be located in some spoken varieties of ME (i.e. earlier than is usually admitted).

Syntactic and morphological change

Inflectional loss and simplification

At varying speeds in different dialects, OE inflectional morphology was greatly simplified in ME. Chaucer's English, being more conservative than some northerly dialects, still retained traces of OE adjectival inflection (now simplified to *-e* as in *shoures soote* 'sweet showers'), and rather more variation in noun plural inflections than those dialects that were rapidly generalizing the *-es* plural. London English (*c*. 1400) still maintained a distinction in the genitive case between feminine nouns (uninflected as in *his ladye grace* 'his lady's grace') and others (inflected in *-es*). There was still a distinction in conservative dialects between the singular and plural of the definite article/demonstrative (*the/tho*), but a new indefinite article derived from the numeral *ān* was becoming general. The 3rd person singular present of the verb was inflected in *-eth* in more southerly dialects and in *-s, -es* in northerly ones. Northern dialects showed a tendency to lose the *-en* inflection on strong verb past participles and hence a tendency to simplify the strong verb pattern. In Chaucer's English, the genitive of the neuter personal pronoun, *(h)it* was still *his*, and the Scandinavian forms of the 3rd person plural pronoun (general in the north from 1200 or before) had penetrated only to the nominative form (*they*). The oblique cases were still initial *h* forms descended from OE.

The chief mysteries of ME are the origin of the 3rd singular feminine *she*, and the present participle in *-ing*. The former, in various spellings (e.g. *scho*, sche) occurs in many east Midland texts as well as initial *h* forms (*heo* etc.) from OE. As for the participle, OE had *-ung* in the gerund (verbal noun), but *ende* and similar forms in the participle. Chaucer's English has the *-ing* participle, whereas the contemporary *Gawain* poet (north-west Midlands) has *-ande*.

Shakespeare's inflectional morphology is already virtually that of Present English. In the strong verb, it is actually simpler, as past participle forms are often identical to the preterite (e.g. *writ, rode, chose* for *written, ridden, chosen*). The 3rd singular present of the verb now varies between *-eth* and *(e)s* endings (and continues to do so in formal writing through the eighteenth century). The genitive of the neuter personal pronoun is still *his* in formal style, but a new colloquial genitive *it* (which later gave way to *its*) has appeared. Otherwise, ME morphological distinctions are largely lost in Early Modern English, e.g. the present plural ending of the verb (*-en*), the infinitive ending, and adjectival inflection; but there are sporadic residues, e.g. the *ge-* perfective prefix (by now *y-*, as in *yholpen* 'helped'). Some fossilized forms, of course, survive even to the present day: *whilom, seldom, random* are OE dative plurals, but that fact has been irrelevant to English synchronic morphology since before 1300.

While inflection losses and other morphological changes are often quite evident by the thirteenth century, syntactic changes are in general somewhat slower to manifest themselves.

General trends in syntax

As the history of English syntax is extremely complicated, only a few topics of general importance and current interest can be briefly treated here. There is a tendency to attribute changes in syntax to loss of inflections and the trend towards analytic rather than synthetic constructions. While there must certainly be some connection, it should be remembered that in some respects (e.g. the tense–aspect system) OE was not very highly inflected; yet tense–aspect usage today is very different from that of OE. Indeed, the rapid trend towards isolative or analytic structure itself requires explanation, unless it is held to be a diachronic universal. Morphological simplification and (possibly) the generalization of an SVO word-order (see below) seem themselves to be at least partly consequences of close contact with Scandinavian and French speakers – socio-political rather than internal linguistic factors may be paramount.

OE had a complex enough system of subordinate clauses (relative clauses were introduced by the indeclinable particle *þe*, or by forms of the demonstrative pronoun, – sometimes with *þe* attached; place and time clauses used the adverbials *þā* and *þær* – often as correlatives; adverbials of reason, cause, purpose, etc. often used prepositions followed by the demonstrative and, variably, *þe*: thus *for-þæm-þe*, 'because' (lit. 'for-that-which')). The OE relativizer system continues through the ME period, with modifications (e.g. *þæt*, which was originally the neuter singular demonstrative, appears as a relative with non-neuter and even plural antecedents as early as *The Peter-borough Chronicle, c.* 1154); however, by later ME, WH- relatives have made their appearance. In OE, these forms were confined to interrogative use. Their appearance as relatives (and the appearance of other WH- forms as adverbial subordinators) may be attributed to a tendency to interpret subordinate clauses as indirect questions and also to imitation of Latin and French models (for more detail on relative clauses see Romaine, 1982; Traugott, 1972).

Although WH- relatives were very well established by 1600, note that the specialization of *who/whom* to use with human antecedents and *which* to use with non-human antecedents post-dates 1600. Furthermore, WH- relatives are still today much rarer in spoken English than in written and formal English, and are confined in speech mainly to non-restrictive clauses. Otherwise, *that* and zero are preferred as in:

(1)   This is the man *that* I saw
     This is the man   I saw

In British English *This is the man whom I saw* is very formal.

Word-order

Although it has been said that OE word-order was relatively 'free', it did generally conform to rules not dissimilar to those of modern German. Main clauses normally had SVO order (except when they were second or subsequent in a set of co-ordinates). Embedded or subordinate clauses had SOV order. VS order occurred in interrogatives and in sentences introduced by certain adverbials and negative particles. Thus, the following sentence (with an embedded clause as object) has the same general order as Present English:

(2)   Ohthere sæde his hlaforde... þæt he ealra Norðmanna norðmest bude
     'Ohthere said to his lord ...that he of all Northmen   northmost lived'
       S   V ⌐—IO—⌐ ⌐————————————O———————————⌐

Within the embedded object clause, however, the order is SOV, and that order is also generally found in OE relative clauses and in subordinate clauses of time, place, result, condition, etc. The SOV order in a second or subsequent co-ordinate clause is demonstrated by:

(3)   He for on Bretanie ... and wið þa Brettas gefeaht
     'He went to Britain ... and against the Britons fought'

The SOV order in subordinate and co-ordinate clauses does not survive the ME period (except in poetry).

The VS order in negative statements is demonstrated in:

(4)   Ne con ic noht singan
     'I cannot sing' (*lit.* 'Not can I (not) at all sing')

The second clause in the following example demonstrates VS order after an adverbial:

(5) Ða ic ða ðis eall gemunde, ða gemunde ic ...
     'When I then this all remembered, then remembered I ...'

The inverted VS order after adverbials remains throughout ME and is quite usual in Early Modern English: in more formal literary styles, especially poetry, it remains (together with other 'inversions' such as optional SOV order in main clauses) until quite recently. In spoken Present English, the only traces of VS order in statements are with certain negative or quasi-negative adverbs, as in:

(6) *In vain* did I attempt ...
     Never have I seen such a thing
     Scarcely had he arrived ...

In these it is the auxiliary verb in Present English that is moved to the left.

In questions, an inverted order remains, also with the auxiliary verb moved to the left. Thus, for EModE *Go you?* and *When came you?*, Present English has *Do you go?* and *When did you come?* Otherwise, Present English has SVO order in statements, and this had become general by the fourteenth century.

From ME onward, with the loss of inflections and with a growing tendency to expect the subject in initial position, there is gradual loss of impersonal verb constructions. These were common in OE with certain 'private state' verbs (e.g. *think*, *like*). An OE sequence such as *þam cyninge licodon peras* is to be interpreted as IO (dat.)-V-S, i.e. 'to the king – were pleasing – pears'. By Early Modern English this construction leaves only an occasional residue, e.g. *methinks* 'it seems to me', and the original impersonals are normally re-interpreted as personal verbs in an SVO order.

Tense–aspect

The most interesting changes are those that have occurred in the tense–aspect–mood systems of the verb. The most general change since OE has been the development of a system overwhelmingly dependent on the use of auxiliary verbs. Already in OE the use of auxiliaries was fairly well developed, partly as a result of the loss of the Germanic inflected passive (Gothic in the fourth century had an inflected passive similar to that of Latin, but it had disappeared in OE, Old High German, etc.) and partly as the result of the failure of Germanic to distinguish more than two tense-forms (past and non-past). OE expressed the dynamic passive by the use of *weorþan*: *hē wearþ ofslæʒen* (he was slain) and the stative passive by *bēon/wesan*: *hē wæs ofslæʒen*. But the various aspects of the verb – stative, habitual, progressive, future – could normally be expressed by the simple present form. The perfective also was quite likely to be expressed by a simple form, as in *ic syngode* 'I sinned' (Luke 15: 21), to translate the Latin perfect *peccavi* 'I have sinned'.

Verb phrases using the auxiliaries *beon/wesan*: 'be', and *habban*: 'have' were quite common in OE, but not necessarily to express progressive and perfective aspects. Thus, in *Orosius* 12:35: *seo ea bið flowende ofer eal Aegypta land,* the phrase *bið flowende* seems to express a general condition rather than a progressive aspect. When constructions with *habban* + past participle occur, it is not always clear whether they are true perfect tenses, as in Present English; sometimes *habban* is a full verb denoting possession, as in *ic hæfde hine gebundenne* 'I had him in-a-state-of-being-bound'. Verbs of motion and verbs of becoming formed their perfects with *be* rather than *have* and continued to do so until Early Modern English. Shakespeare, for example, still preferred *be* to *have*, as in *The King himself is rode to view their battle (Henry V)*.

The history of the *do* auxiliary is complicated. By Shakespeare's time it has virtually become a dummy marker of tense, as in *he did go* ('simple' past meaning), replacing the earlier *gin* (from *begin*), favoured by Chaucer (in ME the *do* auxiliary is often causative in force). By about 1600, it has become more common in negative statements and questions than in affirmatives, anticipating Present English specialization to these uses. Note, however, that the *be* progressive (as in *I am going*) is not fully developed in Early Modern English literary use.

Modality

The development of the modern modal auxiliaries may be partly connected with the gradual disappearance of the subjunctive mood (as a result of inflectional levelling). In OE and ME many of them (e.g. *cunnan* 'to know') functioned as full verbs as well as auxiliaries (cf. Modern German), for example they could take direct objects. The specialization of *shall* and *will* as future auxiliaries is gradual: in ME *will* was strongly volitional in meaning, with *shall* preferred as a predictive; *shall*, however, could still carry strong connotations of obligation well into Early Modern English. In early varieties of English, *can* (as auxiliary) meant 'know how to' and *may* 'have the ability to'. Thus:

(7) I can ne I ne mai tellen . . .
  I do not know how (to count), nor have I the power to count. . .

By Shakespeare's time, forms like *should, might* function quite commonly (but not always) in subordinate clauses where earlier English would have used subjunctive inflections, with no auxiliary (on the verb system see Traugott, 1972; Lightfoot, 1980).

Chronology of syntactic changes

The precise dating of syntactic changes is difficult for several reasons. First, syntactic change diffuses extremely slowly. Second, literary texts tend to be conservative in usage. For example, although Shakespeare does not make extensive use of the modern *be* progressive, it is quite likely that the usage had become well established in speech in Early Modern English. Third, if a particular construction is used in some text, it is not always clear what semantic interpretation should be put on it. Therefore, we cannot always be sure that a particular usage represents habitual, stative, progressive, etc. Finally, we have to recognize that there is more variation in Present English than is usually admitted. Some dialects use only *will* (not *shall*) for prediction and may lack certain other modals, e.g. *shall, may*. Some dialects extend the use of the progressive construction to certain 'private state' verbs, as in *I'm not caring* for *I don't care*. Others avoid the standard perfect tense (see chapter 7), and use constructions similar to the OE 'possessive' + participle, as in *he has it bought* 'he possesses it in a bought condition'; in contrast, in SE the perfect construction seems occasionally to be preferred to the simple past, where the latter would be predicted (as in *He's won it last year*). Other dialects retain dummy *do* in statements, sometimes with 'habitual' force, as in Hiberno-English *He does be coming round now and again* (where no emphasis is intended).

Even in cases where we think we can date a given development precisely, e.g. the development of the passive progressive in the eighteenth century (*the house is being built* for *the house is a-building*), it may well be that the new construction had existed in colloquial use for some time before being noticed in written records.

Vocabulary change

Introductory

Present English vocabulary is rich in synonymy. Very often, two or more words exist with the same referent, distinguished not so much by difference in 'meaning' as by difference in potential stylistic usage. This richness is a result of borrowing from other languages. In pairs like *house/mansion*, *depth/profundity*, *child/infant*, *stink/scent*, the first item is native and the second French. In most (but not all) such cases, the native word is more humble and ordinary, or more appropriate to general usage, whereas the French word is more formal, technical or 'high-sounding'. The more formal and technical an English text is, the more likely it is to contain many words borrowed from French, Latin and Greek. It has been estimated that about 80 per cent of the items in a dictionary are likely to be from these sources.

Since the Norman Conquest, the English language seems to have been peculiarly willing to borrow massively from other languages, usually those considered to be carriers of a 'superior' culture. In this respect, English differs from modern German, which has preferred (like OE) to construct the words it needs from its own word-stock (sometimes on the model of Latin etc. as 'loan-translations'). Thus, German has *freiwillig* (cognate with 'free will') for English *voluntary* (from French) and *Hauptmann* (lit. 'head-man') for English *captain* (from Norman French). Since early ME times, English has progressively dropped the habit of creating new words from its own word-stock (e.g. *gospel* < OE *gōd spell*, < Gk ευαγγελιον 'good news') and has lost many of the words that were originally created in this way.

Influences on borrowing

It is difficult to specify a single reason why English (as against German) should have developed this mixed vocabulary. Several factors are involved: (1) the influence of translation from French and classical texts in the Middle Ages and Renaissance; (2) the need for precise technical terminology in science and philosophy as these branches of learning progressed in earlier centuries; (3) a general sense of inferiority about the English language – a belief that it lacked 'eloquence' and expressiveness.

But not all of the borrowing into English is due to these general cultural influences. There are two further kinds of influence: (1) the influence of language contact, i.e. adoption of Scandinavian and Norman French words through daily contact with settlers in England; (2) sporadic borrowings from other languages in the course of commerce and colonization from the late sixteenth century onwards. On this last type of source we shall have little to say: items like *yacht*, *schooner* are from Dutch, *bungalow* from Malay, and *tobacco* from an American Indian language (for further detail see Sheard, 1954). The influences through prolonged language contact and through cultural channels are more important.

Scandinavian loans in English (borrowed between *c.* 800 and *c.* 1050) do not normally appear in English texts until after the Conquest. They do not call attention to themselves as 'non-native' in the way that classical borrowings do. In fact, many of the Scandinavian loans are amongst the commonest words in the language. Apart from a few administrative terms surviving from Danish rule (*by-law* 'town-law', *husband* 'householder'), they include everyday verbs, adjectives and nouns such as *get*, *take*, *want*, *scrape*, *call*, *flat*, *ill*, *awkward*, *ugly*, *sky*, *skill*, *egg*, *leg*, *skirt*. Sometimes Scandinavian/OE doublets remain, e.g. *sky/heaven*, *skirt/shirt*, the last pair being cognates. Scandinavian words are particularly numerous in north Midland, northern and Scots dialects, e.g. *gate* (in the meaning 'way, road' as in street names such as *Briggate* in Leeds); *kirk*; *gar* 'do'; *kist* 'chest' etc. So pervasive was this early influence that even some 'grammatical words' are Scandinavian, e.g. the 3rd person plural pronoun: *they*, *their*, *them*. Thus, a very commonly occurring sequence – *they are* – is probably wholly Scandinavian: the OE form was *hie sindon* (for detail on Scandinavian see, e.g. Jespersen, 1942).

Many early French borrowings have also become very common words, e.g. *chair*, *table*, *just*, *faith*, *peace*, *war*, *catch*, particularly if they are Norman French (borrowed before *c.* 1250). Here again there was everyday contact, but also some cultural influence. Thus some literary and religious terms were borrowed from Norman French. However, Norman influence is clearest in those areas of life in which the conquerors were dominant: the legal, military and domestic fields, and in terms relating to social organization and administration. Basic vocabulary in these areas is largely Norman: *prison, burglar, attorney, war, captain, sergeant, soldier, table, boil, beef, duke, bailiff, rent, treasure.* Many OE words were displaced by French ones; some disappeared entirely (e.g. OE *friþ* 'peace'), whereas others remained with altered (and usually restricted) meanings (thus OE *bord* 'table' remains as *board*).

After about 1250, the Norman dialect lost status, and cultural borrowings in vast numbers now came largely through written channels from the Central French (françien) dialect. After about 1400, French influence began to decline, although we have continued to borrow French words occasionally ever since (e.g. *garage, c.* 1900). Often the same word was borrowed two or three times, first in its Norman French form, then in a later medieval French form and later again either in a Latinized French (or original Latin) form, or in a modern French form. For example, *kennel, cattle, catch, real* are Norman, whereas *channel, chattel, chase, royal* are the Central French variants; *jaunty* is Norman, *gentle* is Central French and *Gentile* a Latinized form; *chief* is early French and *chef* is modern French.

French influence was not confined to the borrowing of single items, but extended to the general rules of word-formation in English. Many of the prefixes and suffixes that we still use to form complex words are taken from French (or came through French influence ultimately from Latin or Greek). Thus, derivational systems exemplified by: *nation, national, nationality, nationalize, nationalization* were imported into English from French, and we can still attach French suffixes to native words, as in *like/able, word/age* (conversely there are French/English hybrids with English suffixes, e.g. *nation/hood*).

Although Latin had always had some influence on English (either directly or through Latinized forms in French), the main period of classical borrowing started with the Renaissance in England (i.e. from about 1500). Latin and Greek made the chief contributions to what we have called the 'functional elaboration' of English (see page 12); not only did they provide an immense battery of general abstract terms, they also contributed the entire vocabulary of technical terms that were needed in the developing sciences, e.g. *momentum, equilibrium, apparatus* (from Latin), *criterion, phenomenon* (from Greek). In sixteenth-century literary circles, there was some resistance to the borrowings that came in through written use, and they were labelled 'inkhorn terms'. Some of these, such as *immorigerous, obstupefact* were short-lived, but they were very numerous: even Johnson's *Dictionary* (1755) lists many such borrowings that did not survive his own century. Nevertheless, the influence of classical borrowing on the more elaborate styles of English is very considerable. It is worth remarking that mastery of the Latinate vocabulary of English is difficult and requires the support of a strong educational system.

Semantic shift

If we return to our comparison with German, which has not borrowed to the same extent as English but has relied for elaboration on its own word-stock, it is noticeable that ordinary German words commonly retain meanings that are close to the medieval ones. Thus, German *Tier, Stuhl, Himmel* have the same meanings as their OE cognates: *dēor, stōl, hēofon*, viz. 'animal, chair, sky'. The Present English cognates: *deer, stool, heaven* have been specialized in meaning as the French and Scandinavian borrowings have taken over their more generalized meanings. Similarly, many of the more learned classical borrowings have shifted in meaning as they have been pressed into everyday use. Sometimes an original literal meaning has become figurative only. The 'extravagant and erring spirit' of *Hamlet* did not spend lavishly or make mistakes – *extravagant* and *erring* both retained their Latin meanings, approximately 'wandering'. Sometimes there is shift to a meaning associated with the original in some quite rational way: thus, the Greek *hygiene* 'health' has come to mean 'cleanliness' presumably because cleanliness was believed to be necessary to good health. The Latin *sanus* 'clean' has undergone specialization: *sane* now means only 'mentally healthy'. It is not easy to point to convincing reasons WHY any given word should have undergone semantic shift in some particular direction: OE *deor* was a perfectly serviceable word for 'animal'; yet, it was displaced and specialized to refer to a particular species. However, semantic shift in English (even since 1600) has been so widespread that large-scale borrowing and resultant richness in synonymy must be in some measure responsible for it.

Conclusion

This chapter has addressed itself to the problem of accounting for the dramatic changes that have taken place in English since OE times. While every care has been taken to be sure that factual material (although selective) is accurate, the account given here differs from traditional treatments in at least two ways. First, more emphasis than is usual has been placed on social and political factors as possible underlying causes of linguistic change. Second, there has been avoidance of the *ad hoc* statements about possible causes of PARTICULAR changes that are scattered around in even the best handbooks. They are of the following kinds: (1) 'Scandinavian influenced English because the two languages were mutually comprehensible', and (2) 'Norman French influenced English because the Normans were culturally superior'. The first is unknowable and unlikely anyway, and the second depends on what is meant by cultural superiority. All that we know is that Scandinavian and Norman French influenced English as a result of conquest and settlement by speakers of these languages.

Although some suggestions have been made as to possible causes of change in general, it has to be admitted that we know less about 'causes' of change than we would like. Similarly, although non-specialists are very fond of arguing about whether the history of English has been one of 'progress' or 'degeneration', the linguist can only say that changes in some areas (mainly in vocabulary) may reflect cultural changes, and that if there is progress or decay then that is a cultural matter rather than a linguistic one. All languages and dialects are equally well adapted to the needs of their users at any given time. The fact that English is now an influential world language is not due to any superiority AS A LANGUAGE, but is a result of the activities of its speakers over the centuries.

REFERENCES

Chomsky, N. and Halle, M. 1968. *The sound pattern of English*. New York: Harper and Row.

Dobson, E. J. 1968. *English pronunciation: 1500–1700*. 2nd edn. Oxford: Clarendon Press.

Fisiak, J. 1968. *A short grammar of Middle English*. Warsaw: Polish Scientific Publishers; London: OUP.

House, H. and Storey, G. 1959. *The journals and papers of Gerard Manley Hopkins*. Oxford: OUP.

Jespersen, O. 1942. *Growth and structure of the English language*. Oxford: Basil Blackwell.

Jones, R. F. 1953. *The triumph of the English language*. Stanford: Stanford University Press.

Kökeritz, H. 1953. *Shakespeare's pronunciation*. New Haven: Yale University Press.

Labov, W. 1975. On the use of the present to explain the past. *Proceedings of the eleventh international congress of linguists*. Bologna, 1972. 825–51.

Lass, R. 1976. *English phonology and phonological theory*. Cambridge: CUP.

Lightfoot, D. 1980. *Principles of diachronic syntax*. Cambridge: CUP.

Milroy, J. 1977. *The language of Gerard Manley Hopkins*. London: André Deutsch.

―――― 1983. On the sociolinguistic history of /h/-dropping in English. In M. Davenport *et al.* (eds.) *Current topics in English historical linguistics*. Odense: Odense University Press. 37–53.

―――― In press. Present-day evidence for historical changes. In *Proceedings of the first international conference in English historical linguistics* Durham, 1979.

Milroy, J. and Harris, J. 1980. When is a merger not a merger? The MEAT/MATE problem in a present day English vernacular. *English World-Wide* 1, 2: 199–210.

Nunberg, G. 1980. A falsely reported merger in eighteenth-century English. In W. Labov (ed.). *Locating language in time and space*. New York: Academic Press.

Romaine, S. 1982. *Socio-historical linguistics*. Cambridge: CUP.

Serjeantson, M. S. 1935. *A history of foreign words in English*. London: Routledge and Kegan Paul.

Sheard, J. A. 1954. *The words we use*. London: André Deutsch.

Traugott, E. 1972. *A history of English syntax*. New York: Holt, Rinehart and Winston.

Trudgill, P. 1974. *The social differentiation of English in Norwich*. Cambridge: CUP.
Trudgill, P. and Foxcroft, T. 1978. On the sociolinguistics of vocalic mergers. In P. Trudgill (ed.) *Sociolinguistic patterns in British English*. London: Edward Arnold.
Wang, W. 1969. Competing changes as a cause of residue. *Language* 45: 9–25.
Wells, J.C. 1970. Local accents in England and Wales. *Journal of Linguistics* 6: 231–52.
——— 1982. *Accents of English*, 3 vols. Cambridge: CUP.
Wyld, H.C. 1920. *History of modern colloquial English*. London: Fisher Unwin.

2

Standard English in England

PETER TRUDGILL

Introduction

This chapter is concerned with the linguistic characteristics of present-day Standard English (its history and development have been outlined in chapter 1 and the role and changing position of SE in British society is discussed below in chapter 25). SE can be characterized by saying that it is that set of grammatical and lexical forms which is typically used in speech and writing by educated native speakers. It follows, therefore, that 'Standard English' is a term that does not involve phonetics or phonology, although, of course, accents do differ considerably in social status. Indeed, in Britain SE is spoken with a wide range of accents, although these normally include only Received Pronunciation (RP) and the 'milder' regional accents, the 'broader' regional accents most usually co-occurring with dialects that are nonstandard to varying degrees. It also follows that SE includes the use of colloquial and slang vocabulary as well as swear-words and taboo expressions. Thus, *Whoever did that was bloody stupid* must be considered SE, while *Whoever done that were very silly* is not SE.

Modern SE comes in two main, semi-autonomous varieties: North American English, as employed in the USA and Canada; and English-type English, as employed in England and, with differences that are minor except at the level of colloquial vocabulary, in Australia, New Zealand, and South Africa. (SE as used in Scotland, Ireland and Wales, insofar as it differs from Standard English English, is dealt with in chapters 6–9 and 11.) Other native and non-native varieties, such as those spoken in the Caribbean, Africa, India, Hong Kong etc. tend to look to either North American and/or English-type English as the norm. One should note, however, an increasing tendency towards autonomy on the part of, especially, Australian English.

Internal differentiation

Standard English English is described, lexically, in the great dictionaries such as the *Oxford English Dictionary*. Apart from obvious types of stylistic and register differentiation, SE lexical usage is fairly uniform, although age-group, sex and regional differences can certainly be found, especially at the level of colloquial vocabulary. Grammatically, Standard English English is described in grammars such as Quirk *et al.* (1972), and is even more uniform at this level than in the case of lexis. Age-group differences can, however, be noted (see below), as can a small amount of regional variation. Regional differences include those listed here:

Standard English English permits the following orderings of indirect object and direct object:

(1) She gave John a book   She gave a book to John
     She gave him a book   She gave a book to him
     She gave him it   She gave it to him
                                 She gave it to John

In many areas of the north of England, particularly the north-west, other constructions are also possible, even in educated usage. They are, in probable descending order of frequency:

(2) She gave it him
     She gave it John
     She gave a book John
     She gave a book him

Speakers of Standard English English in the south of England tend to use, in their speech, contracted negatives of the type:

(3) I haven't done it
     I won't do it

In the north of England, the alternative contraction is, in some areas, more common:

(4) I've not done it
     I'll not do it

Standard English English, as described in the grammar books, is generally said to employ *must* in positive epistemic usage:

(5) He must be at home – I can hear his radio

and *cannot/can't* in negative epistemic usage:

(6) He can't be at home – his light is off

In the north-west of England, many educated speakers employ instead *mustn't* in this latter usage:

(7) He mustn't be at home – his light is off
     (cf. American English *He must not be at home*)

Standard English English, as described in most grammar books, has the following forms, with *must* and *have to* expressing compulsion or obligation (see also Quirk *et al.*, 1972: 67–9):

Positive	*Negative modal*	*Negative main verb*
He must do it	He hasn't got to do it	He mustn't do it
He has (got) to do it	He doesn't have to do it	
He had (got) to do it	He hadn't got to do it	
	He didn't have to do it	
He will have to do it	He won't have to do it	

The forms with negated modals have the meaning 'He is not compelled to do it' etc.; while the negative main verb forms have the meaning 'He is compelled not to do it'. Note that no past tense or future form is possible in the case of the negative main verb usage. Instead, circumlocutions such as *He wasn't allowed to do it* have to be used. However, in many areas of northern England, educated speakers have an alternative form for *He mustn't do it*, namely *He hasn't to do it* meaning 'He is compelled not to do it'. This then permits the formation of past tense and future forms:

(8) He hadn't to do it
     He'll not have to do it

The second sentence of (8) is ambiguous, being possible also in the negative modal sense. This is also true of other possible northern forms such as

(9) He's not got to do it
     He hasn't got to do it
     He didn't have to do it
     He hadn't got to do it
     He'd not got to do it
     He won't have to do it
     He'll haven't to do it

(For other examples see Hughes and Trudgill, 1979: ch. 2.)

In the rest of this chapter we attempt, briefly, a negative characterization of Standard English English by comparing it to other varieties. In other words we try, for reasons of brevity, to illustrate the nature of Standard English English by saying what it is not rather than what it is. We then examine changes currently taking place within the variety.

Standard and nonstandard English English

Forms which occur widely in nonstandard dialects of English English, but which are not found in SE, include the following:

Multiple negation/negative concord

Nonstandard dialects permit forms such as:

(10)   He didn't want no supper
       I couldn't find none nowhere
       I don't like you no more
       None of them can't do it

SE equivalents are:

(11)   He didn't want any supper – He wanted no supper
       I couldn't find any anywhere
       I don't like you any more
       None of them can do it

There is some equivocation concerning the use of negative verb forms with *hardly*. Most authorities would not accept *I couldn't hardly see*, but forms such as these certainly occur higher up the social scale than other multiple negative forms.

Some nonstandard dialects permit negative concord with other forms such as *only*, *without* and *nor*:

(12)   I haven't only got one
       He stood there without no clothes on
       Don't you like it? Nor don't I

Past tense verb forms

Many nonstandard dialects have fewer irregular past tense verb forms than Standard English English. Differences include: (a) complete regularization:

   I draw   *I drawed*   *I have drawed*

(b) reduction of three verb forms to two, as *per* regular verbs, but without complete regularization:

   I see   *I seen*   *I have seen*
   I give   *I give*   *I have given*

This leads, in many nonstandard dialects, to a distinction between main verb *do* and auxiliary *do* that is not present in Standard English English:

   Main Verb: *do*   *done*   *done*
   Auxiliary: *do*   *did*   —

Thus:

(13)   You done it, did you?
        * You done it, done you?
       SEE: You did it, did you?

In other cases, irregular verb forms operate according to a different pattern from that found in Standard English English (cf. page 22):

I write   *I writ*   *I have writ*

It is also worthy of note that some nonstandard dialects employ the standard form of the past participle in the simple perfect, but not elsewhere:

(14)   I've gone   I could've went
       I've taken it   I might've took it

Ain't

Very many nonstandard dialects in England employ *ain't*, or some variant of *ain't* such as /ɪnt/, /ɛnt/, as the negative present tense form of *be* and of auxiliary *have*, for all persons:

(15)   I ain't doing that
       She ain't here
       I ain't got one
       We ain't done it

Present tense verb forms

Many nonstandard dialects differ from Standard English English, in which -*s* is a marker of the 3rd person singular, by having -*s* for all persons:

(16)   I wants it
       You likes him

Others lack -*s* even in the 3rd person singular:

(17)   He like her
       She want one

Relative pronouns

Many dialects differ from Standard English English by permitting *which* as a relative pronoun referring to humans as well as things; by using forms other than *who*, *which* and *that* as relatives; and by permitting the omission of subject as well as object relative pronouns:

(18)   He's the man which done it
       He's the man what done it
       He's the man as done it
       He's the man done it

Demonstratives

Many nonstandard dialects do not employ *those* as a plural demonstrative, using *them* or *they* instead:

(19)   They books over there
       Them boys on the bridge

Adverbs

Most nonstandard dialects lack the Standard English English distinction between adjectives and their adverbial counterparts in *-ly*:

(20)   He runs very quick
       She done it very clever

Many dialects other than Standard English English also permit unmarked plurality after numerals, as in *ten mile*, and double comparatives such as *more nicer*. Also typical of many nonstandard dialects is the regularization of the reflexive pronoun such that all forms are derived from possessive pronouns i.e. *hisself, theirselves* corresponding to *himself, themselves* in the standard variety. For further information on nonstandard dialects of English English, see chapters 5 and 13.

Standard English English and other standard varieties

Standard English English differs little from that used in Australia, New Zealand and South Africa, and differences are mainly lexical – see Baker (1966), Turner (1966), Ramson (1970), Lanham and Macdonald (1979), Trudgill and Hannah (1982). Grammatical differences are generally of a quantitative rather than qualitative nature, Standard English English being at some points more conservative, at other points less conservative than the other varieties (see below). South African English, however, does have a few forms which are probably the result of interference from other languages e.g. *This metal is capable to withstand great heat* (SEE ... *capable of withstanding ...*).

Differences between Standard English English and North American English (NAE), on the other hand, are very large as far as lexis is concerned, and numerous enough in the case of grammatical forms. It is worth pointing out, too, that many of the differences involve differences of frequency rather than the absolute absence of forms from one variety or the other. There are, too, spelling differences, and a few differences in punctuation.

No full study of differences between North American English and Standard English English lexis and usage is available, but information is available in the *Oxford American Dictionary*, as well as in Allwood (1964), Bähr (1974), Strevens (1972), Chambers (1975), Švejcer (1978) and Trudgill and Hannah (1982).

Grammatical differences – and we can do no more here than point to some of them – include the following:

The past tense forms of a number of irregular verbs TEND to differ between the two varieties:

	SEE	*NAE*
burn	burnt	burned
learn	learnt	learned
dream	dreamt /drɛmt/	dreamed
lean	leant /lɛnt/	leaned
dive	dived	dove
fit	fitted	fit

Habitual *would* is a good deal more frequent in North American English than in Standard English English:

(21) NAE: When I was little, I would go there every day
      SEE: When I was little, I used to go/went there every day

Corresponding to Standard English English:

(22) I wish I had seen one
      If I had seen one, I would have bought it

many spoken forms of North American English have:

(23) I wish I would have seen one
      If I would have seen one, I would have bought it

Standard English English usages such as:

(24) Ah! that will be the postman
      Would you be Mr Smith?

correspond most frequently in North American English to forms without *will/would*:

(25) Ah! that must be the mailman
      Are you Mr Smith?

Standard English English permits *do* substitution with auxiliaries, semi-auxiliaries and modals in a way which is unknown in North American English:

(26) You have finished it? Yes, I have (done)
      I haven't read it yet, but I will (do)
      I don't know if I'll go – I might (do)
      We left, although we shouldn't have (done)

This is less common with semi-auxiliaries:

(27) ?I haven't visited her yet, but I am going to (do)

and with progressive aspect:

(28) ?Will you be working next week? Yes, I will be (doing)

It is not possible with the passive voice.

In addition to being impossible in North American English, this construction is also not especially common in Australian, New Zealand, South African, Scottish or Irish English. It is, in other words, a feature which is particularly typical of English English.

The verb *to like*, in English, may take either an infinitival clause or a present participle clause as its object. Generally, Standard English English prefers the participle while North American English, on the other hand, more often has the infinitive:

(29) SEE: I like walking
     NAE: I like to walk

Similarly,

(30) NAE: I watched him do it
     SEE: I watched him doing it

The verbs *come* and *go*, when uninflected, are followed by *to* + infinitive, or *and* + another clause, while North American English often has simple uninflected verb:

(31) SEE: We'll come and see you soon
     NAE: We'll come see you soon
     NAE/SEE: We came to see you last week

Collective nouns such as *government, team* frequently take plural verb agreement and plural pronoun substitution in Standard English English, but most often take singular agreement in North American English. Singular agreement is probably also more common in Australian English than in Standard English English:

(32) SEE: Aston Villa are playing well. They are top of the division
     NAE: Aston Villa is playing well. It is top of the division

A number of nouns differ in count-noun/mass-noun membership between Standard English English and North American English:

(33) SEE: I want two lettuces
     NAE: I want two heads of lettuce
     SEE: John is good at sport
     NAE: John is good at sports

In written Standard English English, any use of the pronoun *one* is followed by further co-referential instances of *one*, while North American English normally has *he, she,* or *he or she*. (In speech, both varieties often have co-referential *you* or *they*):

(34) SEE: One must be honest with oneself
     NAE: One must be honest with himself

Those adverbs which can occur medially before the verb are generally placed after the first element of the verb in complex verb phrases in Standard English English but often occur before it in North American English:

(35)   NAE/SEE: He never does anything
       SEE: He'll never do it
       NAE: He never will do it
       SEE: He would never have done it
       NAE: He never would have done it

In constructions such as:

(36)   The table has books on it
       The bushes with flowers on them

where an object is described as having some other object *in*, *on* or *off* it, Standard English English permits the deletion of the pronoun (*it*, *them*):

(37)   The table has books on
       The bushes with flowers on

North American English does not permit this construction. Note, too, that even Standard English English tends not to have sentences such as:

(38)   *The table has a dog on

i.e. the object that is *in*, *on* etc. the other object must be relatively expected:

(39)   The soup has carrots in
       ? The soup has flies in

Standard English English permits the use of *immediately* and *directly* as subordinators. In North American English, this is not possible, and they must be used instead to modify some other subordinator, such as *after*.

(40)   SEE: Immediately we left, it started raining
       NAE: Immediately after we left, it started raining

For spelling differences between North American English and Standard English English, see, for example, Švejcer (1978).

Punctuation practices in the writing of Standard English English and North American English are more or less identical, but two differences can be noted: (a) Standard English English tends to have lower case after a colon, while North American English frequently has upper case:

(41)   SEE: There was only one conclusion to be drawn: the politicians had
              all been very foolish
       NAE: There was only one conclusion to be drawn: The politicians had
              all been very foolish

(b) If a sentence ends with a quotation, North American English places the inverted commas after the full stop. Standard English English often places the full stop last, unless the entire sentence is a quotation:

(42)   SEE: He said that the politicians had been 'extremely foolish'.
       NAE: He said that the politicians had been 'extremely foolish.'

For further details of differences within SE, see Trudgill and Hannah (1982).

Linguistic changes in progress in Standard English English

We noted above that there is a certain amount of regional differentiation within Standard English English. Other differences within Standard English English are due to linguistic changes currently taking place. Younger speakers, naturally enough, tend to favour more recent forms, but there is also some correlation with region, most innovations tending to be most common in the south-east. Some continuing linguistic changes appear to involve acceptance into Standard English English of forms already current in North American English. This is most apparent in the case of lexical and idiomatic innovations, but involves grammatical forms also. Other linguistic changes involve the acceptance into Standard English English of forms from nonstandard dialects, while yet others are probably simply changes internal to Standard English English itself. Changes currently under way include those described below.

Modals and auxiliaries

The verbs *ought to* and *used to* are changing their status from auxiliaries to full verbs. Earlier descriptions of Standard English English give the following negative and interrogative forms for these verbs:

(a) You ought not to do that
(b) Ought you to do that?
(c) Ought you not/Oughtn't you to do that?

(d) You used not to do that
(e) Used you to do that?
(f) Used you not/Use(d)n't you to do that?

Of these forms (f) has now more or less disappeared, and (e) is rare. Instead, especially in speech, as opposed to writing, we more normally find the use of *do*-support, as in *Didn't you use to do that?* and *Did you use to do that?* Form (d) is still common enough, but, especially in more informal usages, is increasingly being replaced by *You didn't use to do that*. The newer forms are already the only ones used in most nonstandard dialects and in North American English.

Of the *ought* forms, (a) is still common, and (b) and (c) reasonably common, but there seems to be a definite increase on the part of educated speakers in the use of the alternative forms, *You didn't ought to do that*, *Did you ought to do that?*, and *Didn't you ought to do that?* These forms are already usual in many varieties of nonstandard English. (North American English, on the other hand, seems to favour forms with *should* rather than *ought to*.)

Standard English English, as we saw above, has *must* in positive and *can't* or *mustn't* in negative epistemic usage:

(43)   He must be at home
       He can't be at home

More recently a form already current in North American English has begun to occcur in Standard English English, namely the use of *have to* or *have got to* in positive epistemic usage:

(44)   He has to be the greatest runner in the world
       That's got to be John – I recognise his voice

The rules governing the use of the present perfect in Standard English English seem to be altering somewhat, and there appears in particular to be an increase in the usage of forms such as:

(45)   I've seen him last year
       He's done it two days ago

The use of the auxiliary *shall*, already absent from Scottish English and unusual in North American English, is becoming increasingly rare in Standard English English also. Instead *will* or the reduced form *'ll* is used. *Shall* survives most strongly in 1st person interrogatives:

(46)   SEE: Shall I turn out the light?
       cf. Sc Eng: Will I turn out the light?
       NAE: Should I turn out the light?

One clear result of American influence on the Standard English English grammatical system can be seen in the case of the verbal forms *have* and *have got*. The older Standard English English usage, as described in the text books, was to form present tense questions and negatives of the type:

(47)   Have you (got) any money? I haven't (got) a penny

More recently, the North American forms have also become very common in Standard English English:

(48)   Do you have any money? I don't have a penny

For further details see Trudgill (1978), Hughes and Trudgill (1979), and Trudgill and Hannah (1982).

The sociolinguistic situation of Standard English English *vis-à-vis* other varieties is discussed in this book in chapter 25. It is not entirely possible, however, to divorce a discussion of the changing sociolinguistic situation from a discussion of changing linguistic characteristics. It seems probable, for example, that Standard English English is destined to become somewhat more heterogeneous and somewhat less monolithic in the next few decades. Just as Australian and other forms of SE are breaking away from Standard English English and achieving a certain amount of autonomy, so within England itself the boundaries between Standard English English and other varieties seem to be weakening. Forms that would formerly have been considered nonstandard regionalisms (see above, page 32) are probably now to be included within the realm of Standard English English, since they occur in the speech and writing of the highly educated. Similarly, the acceptance into Standard English English of forms from other external varieties, notably North American English, is perhaps more rapid than in the past, and less controversial. Controversy remains, however, and it is useful, in examining the prescriptive linguistic notions in which our society still abounds, to observe their relationships to the notion of 'Standard English'. Opposition can be observed, in the letters columns of newspapers and elsewhere, to: (a) the usage of clearly nonstandard forms such as *I done it*; (b) the usage of forms that were formerly nonstandard but have become, or are on the way to becoming, standard or marginally standard, such as the use of *than* as a preposition in, for example,

(49) He's better than me
      He's taller than what I am

(c) the usage of forms which are clearly standard, but colloquial, or informal, such as the use of slang and taboo vocabulary; (d) the usage of forms which are clearly standard, but are also innovations, such as *hopefully* as a sentence adverb, or *who* for *whom*; (e) the usage of innovations which are not yet standard but seem destined to become so, such as the use of *disinterested* for *uninterested*; (f) the usage of forms which are clearly standard but which have been singled out by prescriptive grammarians as being illogical or not conforming to the rules of Latin, such as *It's me* and 'split infinitives', as well as 'dangling participles'.

Hostility is clearly strongest in the case of (a), reflecting the status of forms such as these as nonstandard. In the other cases, opposition is more sporadic and less vehement, judgements about correctness shading off into notions about good and bad style. In all cases, however, we must notice that judgements about what is standard and what is not have changed and are changing, just as notions about what is BRITISH English (rather than North American English) have changed to keep up with the developing situation, and just as the linguistic forms themselves change. Standard English English, like any other language variety, is a somewhat fluid, dynamic and ill-defined entity.

REFERENCES

Allwood, M. 1964. *American and British: a handbook of American-British language differences.* Sweden: Habo Mullsjö.

Bähr, D. 1974. *Standard Englisch und seine geographischen Varianten.* Munich: Fink.

Baker, S. 1966. *The Australian language.* Sydney: Currawong.

Chambers, J. (ed.) 1975. *Canadian English.* Toronto: Methuen.

Hughes, A. and Trudgill, P. 1979. *English accents and dialects.* London: Edward Arnold.

Lanham, L. and Macdonald, C. 1979. *The standard in South African English.* Heidelberg: Groos.

Quirk, R. Greenbaum, S. Leech, G. and Svartvik, J. 1972. *A grammar of contemporary English.* London: Longmans.

Ramson, W. (ed.) 1970. *English transported: essays on Australasian English.* Canberra: A.N.U. Press.

Strevens, R. 1972. *British and American English.* London: Collier-MacMillan.

Švejcer, A. 1978. *Standard English in the United States and England.* The Hague: Mouton.

Trudgill P. 1978. Sociolinguistics and sociolinguistics. In P. Trudgill (ed.) *Sociolinguistic patterns in British English.* London: Edward Arnold.

Trudgill, P. and Hannah, J. 1982. *International English: a guide to varieties of Standard English.* London: Edward Arnold.

Turner, G. 1966. *The English language in Australia and New Zealand.* London: Longmans.

46
which refers to
persons wh...
school refers to

Recent origins and definitions

It is a remarkable fact that, for at least four centuries, the English have cultivated a concept of a form of pronunciation which has been considered more correct, desirable, acceptable or elegant than others. It has always been a matter of preoccupation for a small section of society, but this minority interest has grown in recent times, without a very precise specification of the standard or of the typical speaker having been given until this century. Henry Sweet (1908: 7–8) wrote that:

Standard English ... is now a class dialect more than a local dialect: it is the language of the educated all over Great Britain ... The best speakers of Standard English are those whose pronunciation, and language generally, least betray their locality ...

while Alexander J. Ellis (1869, vol. 2: 624) accepted that

there prevailed, and apparently still prevails, a belief that it is possible to erect a standard of pronunciation which should be followed throughout the countries where English is spoken as a native tongue, and that in fact that standard already exists, and is the norm unconsciously followed by persons who, by rank or education, have most right to establish the custom of speech.

Ellis was explicit on the correlation between social status and pronunciation, noting that the 'inferior' is generally 'anxious and willing to adopt the pronunciation of the superiorly educated, if he can but manage to learn it. How can he? Real communication between class and class is all but impossible.' Finally, he concludes (vol. 1: 23) that

In the present day we may ... recognise a *received* [my italics] pronunciation all over the country, not widely differing in any particular locality, and admitting a certain degree of variety. It may be considered as the educated pronunciation of the metropolis, of the court, the pulpit and the bar.

Later, Daniel Jones, having abandoned his earlier term for this standard, 'PSP', agreed with Wyld (1922: 2–3) in using in his *English Pronouncing Dictionary* (*EPD*) from 1926 the traditional label 'Received Pronunciation' (RP). He also retained in his definition of RP a specific social delimitation

45

the 'everyday speech in the families of Southern English
ose menfolk have been educated at the great public boarding-
s'. By Jones's time, it was widely agreed that, although the base of RP
was a southern type of pronunciation, this form of speech was generally
considered to be 'accentless' and to be used by the upper classes throughout
Britain. It was to this extent likely to be the most widely understood form of
speech, a matter of significance to the BBC's Advisory Committee on Spoken
English whose pamphlets *Broadcast English* (1928–1939) sought, mainly for
reasons of general intelligibility (Pamphlet I: 20), 'to secure some measure
of uniformity in the pronunciation of broadcast English, and to provide
announcers with some degree of protection against the criticism to which they
are, from the nature of their work, peculiarly liable'. The pronunciation
recommended was, broadly speaking, traditional RP.

The need for a revised definition of the standard

It is clear, however, that in modern British society several of the criteria used
hitherto to delimit RP are irrelevant. If we are to believe Sweet, Ellis, Jones
and other authorities of the last two centuries (see Johnston, 1764; Sheridan,
1780; Adams, 1794; Walker, 1825; Rippmann, 1914), any well-bred (preferably
upper-class) Londoner educated at a public school might be expected to
provide us with an example of RP. Moreover his social counterpart in other
regions of Britain could be assumed to use comparable speech forms. A
descriptive statement of RP could then be obtained by an analysis of the
speech of an appropriate sample of such a socially defined group, who would
themselves be aware of the exclusivity and prestige which their accent confers
upon them. This is clearly no longer the case. Certainly, since the Second
World War, a single and commonly agreed style of pronunciation cannot be
regarded as an unvarying characteristic of children at public schools; RP is
no longer a prerequisite for diplomats or for social success; and even the BBC
passed through a period of great permissiveness in its selection of newsreaders
for its internal services, though quite recently its standards have become more
rigorous and uniform.

It is clear, however, that there still exists a widely held notion, albeit ill-
defined, of a standard pronunciation (see chapter 32) and that this standard is
identified as having the features of RP. If social class and type of education
can no longer be used as defining factors in any description of the standard,
recourse must be had to other criteria.

A survey of the comments of grammarians and lexicographers on the
pronunciation of English over the last four centuries reveals, in the great
majority of cases, a single phonological system which has been evolving in
time. There is therefore a phonological tradition of a standard, of which we
can observe the latest stages of development during this century. This evolving
system with its varying phonetic characteristics is the most reliable basis for

Table 3.1. *Vowel and consonant phonemes of present-day RP*

Vowels*	iː ɑː ɔː uː ɜː
	ɪ e æ ʌ ɒ ʊ ə
	eɪ aɪ ɔɪ
	əʊ aʊ
	ɪə eə ʊə
Consonants	p b t d k g tʃ dʒ
	m n ŋ
	f v θ ð s z ʃ ʒ h
	l r j w

* The phonetic notation used is that employed in the *English Pronouncing Dictionary* (1977) and with two small variants, in my *Introduction to the Pronunciation of English* (3rd edn, 1980). This notation emphasizes the significance of the qualitative as well as quantitative oppositions in the RP vowel system. (See pp. 61–8 for details of lexical sets.)

our definition of present-day RP. The concept of RP is sterile if it is to be regarded as the unchanging property of a section of past society. What has remained constant is RP's regional base: its characteristic phonological features have always been those of the south-eastern region of England. Today's segmental system differs hardly at all from that described as the standard form by Sweet and Jones at the beginning of the century (see table 3.1). Most strikingly absent today are, among the vowels, the phoneme /ɔə/ in such a word as *pour*, and, among the consonants, the phoneme /ʍ/ as in *white*, which, although characterized as obsolescent by phoneticians of a hundred years ago, was nevertheless often recommended as appropriate in more formal styles.

As far as the prosodic features of accentuation and intonation are concerned, it is hardly possible to speak of evolving RP systems. If we rely on the evidence of Johnston, Sheridan and Walker, certain lexical items have undergone in southern English a change of stress-accent, e.g. such words (with an eighteenth-century stress pattern shown) as *admini'strator*, *adver'tise*, *bal'cony*, *de'monstrate*, *'frustrate*, *i'llustrate*, etc., and, if we extend our evidence to that available in an earlier century, a feature of recent RP has been the loss of a post-tonic secondary stress in such words as *territory*, *adversary*, *ceremony*, with a consequent weakening of the vowel to /ə/ and its frequent elision. However, there continues to occur in the present day a number of cases of stress-accent shift or uncertainty, such well-known examples as *controversy*, *dispute* (n.), *comparable*, *applicable*, *primarily*, *exquisite* being particularly striking. The reasons for the changes are various, so that it is not possible to discern a general pattern of evolution. Whether, therefore, a speaker pronounces *controversy* as _ ' _ _ _ or ' _ _ _ _ or *pejorative* as _ ' _ _ _ or

' _ _ _ _ cannot be taken as a factor in deciding whether he is to be categorized as RP or not. In the case of intonation, despite the accounts given by Walker nearly two hundred years ago, our knowledge of the patterns in use before this century and their functions is too sketchy to permit generalizations, especially as it is only in the last fifty years that the various facets of intonation have been analysed systematically with reference to data derived from ordinary discourse, though the functions of many of the patterns remain a matter of dispute.

It is one thing, however, to assert that present-day RP represents a stage in the evolution of a long-standing system; it is quite another to assess what may be regarded as the state of the system in the last quarter of the twentieth century. Since at any time we are in the presence of several co-existent systems representing the speech behaviour of more than a century, it is clearly necessary to limit the range of speakers examined. The most sensible solution restricts the informants to those of the middle age group 'general RP' speakers (Gimson, 1980: 92), avoiding the more conservative and obsolescent speech forms of older generations and the often eccentric and ephemeral innovations of the young. Given this source of data determined by age and the essential constancy of the traditional system, the investigator must seek evidence for any shared instability in the phonological system and for shifts in the phonetic realization of the system. A descriptive statement must give not only an inventory of the phonemic items within the system but also a phonetic specification of the realized forms of the phonemes. It is also necessary to note significant changes in the incidence of phonemes in specific words or groups of words. The description thus arrived at will constitute a definition of RP without reference to social class or education.

Present tendencies in RP

In an article written nearly twenty years ago (Gimson, 1964: 131–6), I made use of observations made by Daniel Jones in his works on English in order to speculate as to whether any of the phonetic tendencies which he had noted were capable of modifying the oppositional terms of the RP system. Although my speculations of that time were concerned mainly with vowels, which are particularly apt to exhibit evident change, often in the space of less than a century, there appears to be little evidence as yet that certain mergers of phonemic oppositions brought about by phonetic change, which I regarded as at least possible, have materialized. For instance, the final elements of the closing diphthongs /eɪ, oʊ, aɪ, aʊ, ɔɪ/ seemed for many RP speakers to be so weak as to be likely to disappear, leading to the oppositions *men* ~ *main* or *sell* ~ *sail*, *bide* ~ *bud*, *down* ~ *darn*, *tall* ~ *toil*, etc. being one principally of quantity. None of such mergers has taken place, though the potential remains for the future. But there is no doubt that the confusion between /əʊ/ (for /oʊ/) and /ɜː/ grows, especially before [ɫ]. On the other hand, the undoubted levelling (see chapter 4, on 'smoothing') of /aɪə, aʊə/ to either [aːə] or /ɑː/ (a development attested in RP for well over a century), though widespread and capable of producing homophones of the sort *shire, shower, Shah* or *tired, towered, tarred*, appears to be related to idiosyncratic variations of style.

As far as the centring diphthongs are concerned, the disappearance of /ɔə/ must now be regarded as accomplished, with /ʊə/ also very much in danger. Words previously pronounced almost invariably with /ʊə/ are now commonly heard with /ɔː/ among younger RP speakers, e.g. *poor, moor, tour, tourist* (the frequency of occurrence and functional load of /ʊə/ being extremely low). There is a tendency for /ʊə/ to remain, however, in rare or exotic words, e.g. in *gourd, Ruhr, bourse*, or where /ʊə/ is a variant of a disyllabic /uː/ + /ə/, e.g. in *jewel, truant, fewer*, etc. When /ʊə/ follows /j/, e.g. *cure, pure, furious*, etc., there was an identifiable variant /ɜː/ which I felt obliged to record in *EPD* (13th edn., 1967). Such a variant is regarded by the younger generations as both old-fashioned and affected, /ʊə/ or /ɔː/ being preferred. It is clear that the opposition between the front centring diphthongs /ɪə/ and /eə/ remains constant, the functional load in this case being high. The retention of this latter opposition and the decline of the back diphthongs /ɔə/ and /ʊə/ bring about an interesting imbalance in the system of centring diphthongs, which a century ago had exemplary symmetry.

In fact, some of the changes most evident today were not dealt with in my earlier article (Gimson, 1964), especially as regards the short vowels. The diphthongization of /ɪ, e, æ/, often mentioned by Daniel Jones, has not been productive phonologically and, like the use of /ɜː/ for /ʊə/ after /j/, is regarded as an obsolescent affectation; but the lengthening of /æ/ before /b, d, g, dʒ, m, n/, regarded by Jones and by Ward (1945: 202) as a recent development, is established. The lowering of /æ/ is also obviously more common amongst young speakers, possibly to avoid the comic effect made by the older RP form nearer to front half-open (i.e. only slightly more open than Cardinal [ɛ]) often with strong pharyngealization. The consequence of this lowering of /æ/ and the fronting of /ʌ/ (approaching Cardinal [a]) is a possible confusion of /æ/ and /ʌ/, e.g. in such pairs as *cat* ∼ *cut, match* ∼ *much*. It is difficult to believe that two vowels of such relatively high frequency of occurrence (/æ/ – 1.45%; /ʌ/ – 1.75%) should merge, though equal load has not always inhibited such mergers in the past, e.g. the vowels of *meet, meat*.

The case of /ʊ/ is of particular interest, as a result of the apparent change in its phonetic realization. The lip-rounding associated with this vowel is so weak among a large number of RP speakers that it could be regarded as a form of stressed /ə/. This loss of lip-rounding is apparent in the two diphthongs which have [ʊ] as a second element, resulting, in the case of /əʊ/, in the levelling in the direction of /ɜː/ already mentioned and also, in the case of /aʊ/, in a phonetic form [aɤ] or [aï] which so nearly approaches /aɪ/ that popular observers claim an identity between a pair such as *mice* and *mouse*!

/ɒ/ can now be said to be the regular vowel in such words as *off, cloth, loss*, etc., where previously /ɔ:/ had been an admissible variant. The evidence also suggests that the realization of /ɔ:/ with a higher tongue position and closer lip-rounding than was usual fifty years ago is becoming firmly established, a change no doubt brought about by the recent disappearance of back centring diphthong oppositions.

Again, as regards incidence of vowels, the use of /i:/ for /ɪ/ in final (open) positions, e.g. in *money*, *happy*, to which Jones had called attention as a tendency, is becoming more firmly established and, if a prediction can be risked, is likely to be a general feature early in the next century. Another tendency, the use of /su:-/ rather than /sju:-/ in such words as *suit*, *suitable*, *superior*, *superscript*, etc., which showed every sign of becoming general, does not attract unwavering support from the younger generations.

But perhaps the most interesting and wide-ranging change in RP concerns the incidence of /ɪ/ and /ə/ in weak syllables (I have summarized the chief changes in *EPD* (1977: xvi) and in *IPE* (1980: 104–5)). In many weak syllables where traditional RP had /ɪ/ (e.g. Sheridan and his contemporaries give /ɪ/ as the second syllable in such words as *blanket*, *bloodless*, *bucket*, *cabbage*, *captain*, *lettuce*, *pamphlet*, *toilet*, forms confirmed by nineteenth century observers) regional accents of English had overwhelmingly /ə/. It seems evident that the use of /ə/ in such syllables is now gaining ground amongst RP speakers of both middle and younger generations. Evidence for the progress of the change was sought by means of a small pilot investigation described below.

A pilot investigation of the incidence of /ɪ/ and /ə/ in present-day RP

In preparing the fourteenth edition of *EPD* (1977), I felt obliged to obtain new statistical evidence for the ordering of the variants and for the introduction of variants with /ə/ where they had not been given before. Some objective evidence for ordering had been sought in the thirteenth edition of *EPD* by means of a questionnaire sent to British phoneticians and others likely to be reliable judges, but there were surprising inconsistencies in the responses received. It clearly would have been more satisfactory if comparable speech samples had been examined and assessed by the same investigator, and this was the intention for the following edition. It proved possible to carry out only a pilot study with twenty informants. The speech of these informants was examined with particular reference to their choice of /ə/ or /ɪ/ in weak syllables. (Auditory discrimination between the phonetic areas of /ə/ and /ɪ/ is notoriously difficult. In the analysis, only those vowels readily identifiable as typically of the traditional RP /ɪ/ quality were classified as /ɪ/, all other qualities being classified as /ə/ even when the listener found it difficult to decide between /ɪ/ and /ə/.) In such an investigation, the first decision to be made concerned the selection of informants, class and educational standard having been rejected as prime criteria. The deciding factors adopted were (1) *age*: within the age range 20–45; (2) *phonological system*: a phoneme inventory corresponding to the traditional set of terms, a matching incidence of phonemes in words and a specification of their phonetic realization.

The factor of age was obviously a simple one to take into account, but for the criteria concerned with appropriateness of system and realization a test of acceptability had to be applied. Despite the fact that the reading of word-lists can produce unnatural results, there seemed no alternative, in the time available, to the use of this as a crude screening technique. Features required of the informants may be exemplified as follows:

(1) *System*: for instance, the oppositions /æ/ ~ /ɑː/, /ɒ/ ~ /ɔː/ should be maintained, e.g. in *cam* : *calm, knotty* : *naughty*; /ŋ/ should operate as a phoneme, e.g. *singer* /'sɪŋə/ without a voiced velar stop following the nasal; the oppositions /ɔː/ ~ /ɔə/ or /ʍ/ ~ /w/ would be optional.

(2) *Incidence*: for instance, /ʊ/ rather than /uː/ should occur in such words as *book, cook*, etc.; /ɑː/ in *pass, caster, demand*, but /æ/ in *ass, aster, expand*, etc.; /r/ should not occur post-vocalically except as a link. On the other hand, the use of /ɔː/ or /ɒ/ in *salt, fault*, etc. would be optional; similarly, /æ/ or /ɑː/ in *plastic, elastic, stance* or *trans-* or *-graph*, and /iː/ or /ɪ/ in unaccented word-final position.

(3) *Phonetic specification*: for instance, /iː/ and /uː/ should be realized as pure vowels or glides but not as wide as [əɪ, ʌɪ]; /ɑː/ with a mid-open articulation reaching neither Cardinal [a] nor Cardinal [ɑ]; /əʊ/ with a mid-central first element, variants such as [oʊ, ɔʊ, ʌʊ] being rejected; /aɪ/ with a mid to front first element, but not [ɑɪ, ɒɪ]; /aʊ/ with a mid to back first element, but not [æʊ, ɛʊ]; /t, d/ to be alveolar rather than dental; /r/ to be a postalveolar continuant rather than a trill [r] or uvular articulation.

It will be seen that there is a degree of tolerance especially in the vowel articulations (in *IPE*, 3rd edn: 308–12 I have given more detailed explanations of the possible phonetic tolerances within what I have labelled 'High Acceptability RP').

In order to achieve such requisite features in the informants' speech, subjects were asked to read 460 words arranged in five columns and 92 rows. As a check on the influence of context or of monotony, informants read the word-lists both in rows and in columns. Within the lists were placed certain crucial items which would help to determine the existence of the appropriate oppositions or incidences, e.g. *one, path, book, among, singer*, etc.

The majority of the items in the word-list, however, were designed to test the choice of /ɪ/ or /ə/ in such word-endings as *-less, -ness, -ible, -ity, -ical, -iple, -itive, -ace, -ice, -ate, -ite, -age, -ege, -ily, -est, -in (-en), -eign (-ain), -em, -ange (-enge), -inal, -imal, -es, -ed, -et*, and initial sequences such as *re-, de-, te-, be-, e-, se-, pre-, ne-, le-*, etc. To supplement this word-list, a fairy tale to be read by the informants was also concocted, especially to elicit further data on the termination *-et*. Finally, each subject was engaged in free conversation for two or three minutes, the informant and the investigator always being well-known to each other. Free speech of this kind can rarely produce sufficient data for useful generalization, but it does serve as a check on the more artificial reading procedures.

The results of the investigation made it clear that /ə/ had indeed made inroads in certain weak syllables where amongst more conservative RP speakers /ɪ/ is more typical. The shift is rarely 100 per cent. For example, in the case of /-ətɪ/ for /-ɪtɪ/ in the termination *-ity*, all informants used /ə/ in such words as *fidelity, security, suitability, visibility, authority*, etc., but there was a significant minority in favour of /ɪ/ in such words as *mobility, utility, charity, infinity, dignity*, etc., and even a slight majority for /ɪ/ in *enmity, unity*. But, in the 63 words containing this ending, pronounced by all subjects in the tests, the majority in favour of /-ətɪ/ was of the order of 90 per cent. Somewhat less marked, but nevertheless quite significant, shifts to /ə/ were to be found in the case of *-ible* (*terrible, horrible, possible, sensible*, etc., with /ə/, but /ɪ/ often kept in *eligible, crucible, negligible*, etc.); *-itive* (*positive, infinitive*, etc. with /ə/, but *fugitive* with /ɪ/); *-ate* (*immediate, fortunate, chocolate, legitimate*, etc. with /ə/, but /ɪ/ often kept in *private, climate*); *-ily* (*easily, family, angrily*, etc., but /ɪ/ often in *heavily, happily*); *-em* (*problem, item, emblem, system*, though /ɪ/ is preferred in *poem*). It is to be suspected that these changes towards /ə/ are of much longer standing than dictionaries would have us believe.

/ɪ/ remains completely dominant in other cases, e.g. *-age, -ege* (*vicarage, message, cabbage, village, college, privilege*, etc.; *-est* (*modest, tempest, honest, forest, biggest*, etc., though in the case of *interest* a majority used /-est/); *-ice* (*service, office, practice*, etc.); *-icle, -ical* (*article, medical, typical, musical, critical*, etc., though a minority used /ə/ in *bicycle, vehicle, physical*). What is more, there appeared to be no tendency for the morphemes *-ed, -es* to change from traditional /-ɪd, -ɪz/ to /-əd, -əz/, e.g. in *horses, raises, waited, dreaded* (though *-ed* in *hundred* generally was /-əd/). Similarly, /ɪ/ remains dominant in such initial syllables as *re-, de-, pre-, ne-, se-*, though more cases of /ə/ are to be found in *te-* (*terrific, tenacious*), *be-* (*between, believe, belong*), *pe-* (*petition, peninsular*), *fe-, phe-* (*ferocious, phenomenon*), *ve-* (*velocity, venereal*), *me-* (*mechanic, memorial*). Initial *e-* usually has /ɪ/ (*enough, edition*) but /e/ (rather than /ə/) also occurs, for example in *estate, explain, exist*.

In other weak syllables, the preference is less clear-cut, e.g. although *-et* is usually still realized as /-ɪt/, especially after a velar stop or an affricate (*sonnet, helmet, carpet, velvet, triplet, jacket, bucket, pocket, budget, hatchet*, etc.), /-ət/ is commonly heard in *violet, scarlet, claret, garret, toilet, bracelet, cabinet*, etc. Similarly, in the case of *-ace*, /-əs/ and /-ɪs/ are almost equally divided, e.g. in *preface, menace, necklace, surface, palace* – the last word losing the potential rhyme *Alice – palace*. Finally, there is a strong movement amongst the younger informants in the case of *-ess* endings to move towards /-əs/, though the overall dominance remains clearly with /-ɪs/, the ratio being of the order of 6 : 3 in favour of /-ɪs/. Although such words as *business, goodness, witness, highness, kindness, topless, painless, listless, laziness, wickedness, silliness*, etc., showed a marked preference for /-ɪs/, others such as *blindness, illness, dark-ness, seedless, foolishness* showed a strong minority for /-əs/ while *wireless, careless, toothless* had a majority with /-əs/. The results were complicated by the fact that a number of speakers used /-es/, for example commonly in *weakness, priceless, happiness, penniless.*

A pilot investigation of this limited extent reveals how badly we require a more ambitious survey of every aspect of RP, defined as strictly as possible, as well as a data-based assessment of the number of speakers who can be said to use this accent.

RP in the future

In conclusion, it can be said that, if a different set of criteria for defining RP, as has been suggested above, is adopted, together with a range of acceptable tolerances within the model, which will result in a somewhat diluted form of the traditional standard, the re-defined RP may be expected to fulfil a new and more extensive role in present-day British society. Its primary function will be that of the most widely understood and generally acceptable form of speech within Britain which can serve as an efficient and common means of oral communication, whether or not this speech style carries with it social prestige. But, in addition and more importantly for the future, this standard form of British speech can function as one of the principal models for users of English throughout the world (Gimson, 1980: ch. 12). It already has the advantage of being generally acceptable as a teaching norm because of its widespread intelligibility, because it has already been described in textbooks more ex-haustively than any other form and because recordings used in teaching abroad are usually made in this accent (quite apart from the prestigious aspects associated with it). It must share with a representative form of American speech the most likely candidature for a natural model to be imitated wherever English is taught. In many parts of the world it is the traditional model and is still recommended, e.g. Vassilyev (1980: 11):

RP is easily understood in all the English-speaking countries... RP has been recorded, investigated and described more comprehensively and thoroughly than any other type of English pronunciation. For all these reasons, RP is adopted as the teaching norm in the schools and higher educational institutions of the Soviet Union...

In this sense, if RP is retained as a label, 'received' must be taken to mean 'of widespread intelligibility and general acceptability'.

REFERENCES

Adams, J. 1794. *Euphonologia loquae anglicanae*. London.
BBC's Advisory Committee on Spoken English 1928–39. *Broadcast English*. London: BBC.

Ellis, A.J. 1869. *On early English pronunciation*. London: EETS.

Gimson, A.C. 1964. Phonetic change and the RP vowel system. In D. Abercrombie *et al*. (eds.) *In honour of Daniel Jones*. London: Longman.

────── 1980. *An introduction to the pronunciation of English* (*IPE*). 3rd edn. London: Edward Arnold.

Johnston, W. 1764. *A pronouncing and spelling dictionary*. London.

Jones, D. 1917. *An English pronouncing dictionary* (*EPD*). London: Dent. [Edited since 1964 by A.C. Gimson: 13th edn. 1967; 14th edn. 1977.]

Rippmann, W. 1914. *The sounds of spoken English*. London: Dent.

Sheridan, T. 1780. *A complete dictionary of the English language*. London.

Sweet, H. 1908. *The sounds of English*. Oxford: Clarendon Press.

Vassilyev, V.A. 1980. *English phonetics*. 2nd edn. Moscow: Vysšaja škola.

Walker, J. 1825. *A critical pronouncing dictionary*. London.

Ward, I. 1945. *The phonetics of English*. 4th edn. Cambridge: Heffer. [Later editions, Cambridge: CUP.]

Wyld, H. 1922. *A history of modern colloquial English*. Oxford: Blackwell.

English accents in England

J. C. WELLS

Introduction

'The English of most people', I wrote in 1970, 'is neither RP Standard English nor a rural dialect. The vast mass of urban working-class and lower-middle class speakers use a pronunciation nearer to RP ... than the archaic rural dialects recorded by the dialectologists. Yet their speech diverges in many ways from what is described as standard.' The aim of that article (Wells, 1970) was 'to sketch the principal phonetic variables among such local, mainly urban, forms of English'. The twelve years which have passed have seen important developments in our field. As well as Trudgill's well-known appli-cation of Labovian sociolinguistic techniques to the speech of Norwich (Trudgill 1972, 1973, 1974), we have had new descriptions (see also chapter 13) of the phonetics and phonology of London (Beaken, 1971; Bowyer, 1973; Hudson and Holloway, 1977), the West Midlands (Heath, 1980), the Potteries (Wilson, 1970), Liverpool (Knowles 1974, 1978), Greater Manchester (Shor-rocks, 1980) and West Yorkshire (Petyt, 1977), all with an emphasis on the variability to be found in the local accents in question and on the correlations observable between linguistic and social variables. In the north-east, the ambitious plans of the Tyneside Linguistic Survey (Pellowe *et al.*, 1972) have borne some fruit (Jones-Sargent, 1983) and the speech of two Northumberland villages has been excellently covered by Johnston (1979). Other new studies of English local accents, cast in more traditional moulds, include Weissmann (1970) on Bristol and Wakelin (1975) on Cornwall. There is also an excellent short introductory survey by Hughes and Trudgill (1979).

In the present chapter I aim not only to update Wells (1970) (while ex-cluding references to Welsh English, separately treated in chapter 11 of this volume), but also to recast the description of local accents in a conceptual framework corresponding to that developed in Wells (1982), where a more detailed treatment is presented (see particularly chapters 2.3, 3.1, 3.2, 3.4, 4.1–4 in that work).

Consideration of the indexically important questions of voice quality and intonation patterning lies outside the scope of this short chapter. Birmingham, Liverpool and Newcastle-upon-Tyne are all cities with characteristic intonation types; a good start at describing that of Liverpool has been made by Knowles (1974, 1978).

Consonants

Plosives

All accents have a six-term system of plosives, /p, t, k, b, d, g/. They differ to some extent in the phonetic realizations of these plosives.

The voiceless plosives, aspirated before a stressed vowel in the south, are unaspirated in parts of the north: thus /pɪn/ *pin*, southern [pʰɪn], some northern [p⁼ɪn]. This seems to be associated particularly with the Pennine valleys north of Manchester. Conversely, some southern speech, including Cockney, often has aspiration in other environments too, as in *upper, utter, soccer*.

In Liverpool and London /t/ and /d/ are often affricated, thus [tˢɛn] *ten*, [dᶻɒg] *dog*. In the broad Liverpool accent other initial plosives, too, may be affricated, thus [kˣɪŋg] *king*; medial and final Scouse (Liverpool) plosives are often phonetically fricatives, thus [ʃɔːʈ] *short* (where [ʈ] denotes an apico-alveolar slit fricative); ['dɔːʈə] *daughter*; [bax ~ baχ] *back*. London /t/ is frequently affricated not only initially but also elsewhere: ['letˢɐ] *letter*, [ʔɑːtˢ] *art* are elegant-Cockney variants of what might otherwise have bare [ʔ] for /t/.

Intervocalic /t/ is particularly subject to regional and social variation. The use of a tapped realization, usually voiced, is familiar as an Americanism, but is by no means uncommon in England. Pronunciations such as ['bɹɪɾɪʃ] *British*, ['mæɾə] *matter* are characteristic of casual style in at least some accents within RP; this 'voiced t' is, interestingly enough, what many Cockneys regard as the 'normal, "correct" variant' (Sivertsen, 1960: 119), as opposed to the 'posh' [tˢ] and the 'rough' [ʔ]. In Cockney it is particularly frequent across word boundaries, as in ['gɒɾɪʔ] *got it*. Apparently, though, [ɾ] is not used in slow speech or prepausally.

Northern speech exhibits a phenomenon presumably deriving from an earlier t-tapping rule, namely the use of what is perceived as /r/ in place of /t/ intervocalically across word boundaries, thus ['ʃʊɹʊp] *shut up*, ['gɛɹɒf] *get off*. Other examples of this t-to-r rule include [bəɹ i 'eɪnˀ 'gɒɹɪˀ] *but he ain't got it*, [wɒɹɪ 'sɛd] *what he said*. It is regarded as 'rough'.

In various syllable-final environments the voiceless plosives, and also the affricate /tʃ/, are increasingly reinforced by a preceding [ʔ]. Prepausal forms such as [stɒʔp] *stop*, [pɪʔk] *pick*, [nɒʔt] *not* can be found in both northern and southern speech, as can the deliberate-speech variants with the [ʔ] used to initiate an air-stream, [stɒp', pɪk', nɒt']. From this it is a small step to a glottal stop overlapping the oral stop so as to mask its release stage, and thence to a bare glottal stop. Not only in London Cockney, but also in many rural accents of the south and of East Anglia, and now increasingly in urban accents throughout England, glottalling of /t/ is widespread though overtly stigmatized. Forms such as ['bɪʔə] *bitter* are by no means geographically restricted to London. The glottalling of word-final /t/ before a following vowel, as *take i*[ʔ] *away*, *no*[ʔ] *interested*, can now be heard in the south-east almost throughout the social scale among younger people, and also in parts of the north (e.g. Leeds). (Before a consonant, as in *no*[ʔ] *bad*, it clearly extends into RP.)

Glottalling of /p/ and /k/ seems to be commonest after a nasal, thus [dʒʌmʔ] *jump*, [pɪŋʔ] *pink*. In this environment, of course, glottalling does not involve the loss of place-of-articulation information. In other environments it might, since [lɪʔ] would then represent any of *lip*, *lit*, *lick*. In fact Londoners seem to glottal /t/ much more readily than /p/ or /k/ in this environment. The same applies intervocalically, thus Cockney ['lʌɪʔə] *later*, but usually ['pʌɪʔb̥ə] *paper*, ['bʌɪʔg̊ə] *baker*.

Occasionally other consonants are glottalled in Cockney, notably /d/ and certain fricatives: ['breʔn̥ 'bʌʔə] *bread and butter*, [wʊʔn̥ʔ] *wouldn't*, ['dɪʔɹən] *different*, [ɒn i 'ʌʔə 'sʌɪʔ] *on the other side*.

Yorkshire speech is characterized by a special kind of assimilation involving a switch from voiced to voiceless obstruent before a following voiceless consonant, thus [sʊp'saɪd] *subside*, ['bratfəd ~ 'braʔfəd] *Bradford*. This makes *a white sheet* and *a wide sheet* homophonous.

Fricatives

It is probably correct to regard all accents as having the same 8-term fricative system, /f, v, θ, ð, s, z, ʃ, ʒ/. (The question of /h/ is discussed below.) But in Cockney and various other urban accents the dental fricatives tend to be replaced by (or realized identically with) other phonemes, namely /f/ for /θ/ and /v/ or /d/ for /ð/. th-fronting makes *thin* identical with *fin*, [fɪn], although speakers can apparently usually make the distinction if need be. The same applies to *lather* and *la(r)va*, often both ['lɑːvə]. A recent popular work on Cockney, Barltrop and Wolveridge (1980), is appropriately entitled *The muvver tongue*. The th-stopping option is used for initial /ð/, as in *this* [dɪs] (not usually *[vɪs]). But standard initial /ð/ is also subject to a wide variety of other possibilities in working-class running speech, as for example Cockney ['ɹæːnːiˈæːzɪz] *round the houses*. Hypercorrect [θ] is often to be heard in *feather* ['θeðə].

Nasals

From a taxonomic-phonemic point of view, most local accents agree with RP in having three nasal phonemes, /m, n, ŋ/. Adherents of a generativist model of phonology may well argue that there is no point in recognizing a phoneme /ŋ/, since all cases of [ŋ] may be regarded as deriving from an underlying /n/, thus /sɪng/ → [sɪŋ] (via assimilation and g-deletion rules). The argument for a two-term system of nasals, /m, n/, is rather stronger in certain accents of the midlands and north. Here words never end in bare [ŋ]: there is a phonetic plosive at the end of words such as *sing* [sɪŋg], *hang*, *wrong*. *Singer* rhymes perfectly with *finger*, and *kingly* with *singly*. This situation holds in the local accents of the area roughly bounded by Birmingham, Shrewsbury, Preston and Sheffield. (Elsewhere, the situation is as in RP, so that *sing, singer, kingly* have bare [ŋ], but *finger, singly* [ŋg].) It does not necessarily follow for all such accents that [ŋ] occurs only in the environment of a following velar, so as to make it beyond question an allophone of /n/. In Liverpool, for instance, *sing* and *wrong* have [ŋg], but *sings* is [sɪŋz] and *wronged* is [ɹɒŋd] (for an illuminating discussion, see Knowles, 1978: 85–6). In Cannock, Staffs., bare [ŋ] is reported in unstressed syllables only, thus *moving* ['muːvɪŋ]. But in Stoke-on-Trent it appears that *sings, wronged*, and *moving* may all contain [g] (-*ing* being [ɪŋg ~ ɪn]); so there is no phonemic /ŋ/.

As is well known, there is sociolinguistic variability in the pronunciation of the -*ing* ending in most of the English-speaking world, and certainly throughout England. However it appears that the point in the social class/ formality scale at which the crossover occurs between 'low' [ɪn ~ ən ~ n̩] and 'high' [ɪŋ] varies from place to place. In Cannock, according to Heath (1980), the alveolar variant is actually pretty rare, whereas in London it is very frequent.

Liquids

There are two liquids, /r, l/. When pre-consonantal or final, both are (or have been) susceptible to processes of vocalization, usually after triggering qualitative or quantitative changes in a preceding vowel.

The phonetic realization of the liquids themselves varies regionally. While /r/ is most frequently a postalveolar approximant, as in RP, it is also realized as a retroflex approximant (in the west country), as a uvular fricative, approximant, or tap (in Northumberland, though no longer in urban Tyneside), and as an alveolar tap (quite widely in the north, in an alternation with [ɹ] which usually involves determining factors which may depend on the phonetic environment, degree of formality, or both). In the case of /l/, the RP distribution of clear and dark allophones may not apply: in much of the north an intermediate 'neutral' [l] is found in all environments. In the far north /l/ is strikingly clear even when not pre-vocalic. The vocalized /l/ of London and the south-east, developed from dark [ɫ], is a back vocoid, often with lip-rounding, [ɤ ~ o]; thus *milk* [mɪok] (the usual Cockney form).

In rhotic accents (accents which preserve the historical distribution of /r/) /r/ occurs pre-consonantally and pre-pausally as well as pre-vocalically, e.g. *start* [stɑːɹt], *square* [skwɛəɹ]. In non-rhotic accents, including RP, /r/ (or at least /r/ realized phonetically as such) is restricted to pre-vocalic position, as *sorry* ['sɒɹɪ], *rip* [ɹɪp]; this includes the possibility of a following syllabic consonant or pre-vocalic word boundary, as in ['bæɹl̩] *barrel* (presumably = /'bærəl/), *square up*. Rhotic accents are found in two main areas, the west country (south and west of a line stretching from near Shrewsbury to around

Portsmouth) and a patch of Lancashire (north and east of the centre of Manchester). The prestige norm, however, exerts a steady pressure towards non-rhoticity. Thus the urban speech of, say, Bristol or Southampton is more accurately described as variably rhotic, the degree of rhoticity being reduced as one moves up the class and formality scales. The impact of r-dropping on the vowel system is discussed below.

Phonetic /r/ may occur in unhistorical environments for any of three reasons. One is the familiar analogical 'intrusive /r/' as found in RP (Gimson, 1980: 208–9), thus *put a comma in* [ˈkɒməɹ ∼ ˈkɒmə ∼ ˈkɒmər] etc. This is very general in England, at least in the environment of a preceding [ə], perhaps slightly less so after the PALM and THOUGHT vowels (*ask grandma in, law of averages*). In Cockney it can occur after MOUTH [æː ∼ aː] too (*how I did it* [ˈæːɹ ɑɪ...]). (See page 60 for my use of keywords, written in small capitals.) The second possible reason, sometimes difficult to distinguish from the first in practice, is, I think, a phonotactic constraint against final [ə] and in favour of [ɚ] (/ər/), which applies very widely in the traditionally rhotic areas to give forms such as *comma* [ˈkɒmɚ ∼ ˈkɑmɚ] not only before a following vowel (as applies with the first reason) but also before a consonant or pause. This often also affects words ending in unstressed RP /əʊ/, e.g. *window, yellow,* giving [ˈwɪndɚ] etc. over about half of the rhotic west (see map Ph205 in *The linguistic atlas of England, LAE*). The third possible reason, often difficult to distinguish from the second, is pre-consonantal/final /r/ by false analogy from RP and other non-rhotic models. Thus *khaki* is usually /ˈkɑːrki/ in rhotic accents of England, because of the equivalences in items such as *darkie, park*; so also *camouflage* with /-lɑːrdʒ/ because of *large, barge*.

Bristol is well known for its 'intrusive /l/' which occurs context-free in items which would otherwise end in [ə], thus [ˈɛːɹjəɫ] *area*, [ˈnɔːɹməɫ] *Norma* (which thereby become homophonous with *aerial, normal*).

Glides

The remaining consonants may conveniently be referred to as glides: they comprise the semivowels /j, w/ found in all accents and an /h/ whose status is variable.

Except where a diphthong /ɪu/ remains in the system, words such as *new, numerous* have either /njuː/, as in RP, or else plain /nuː/, as in Cockney and quite widely elsewhere in the midlands and south. After a preceding /t/ or /d/, as *tune, duke,* the yod-dropping innovation (/tuːn, duːk/) is in competition with a development we may call 'yod-coalescence' (/tʃuːn, dʒuːk/). The latter possibility is very much more widespread in England than the former (and appears to have displaced it quite recently in Cockney); it makes the first syllable of *Tuesday* homophonous with *chews,* and *dune* homophonous with *June.* Hypercorrections such as /djuːˈlaɪ/ *July* are frequent in lower-middle-class speech. RP, of course, resists yod-coalescence – at least in more formal styles of speech – even in unstressed environments such as in *postulate, educate*, where the American [-tʃ-, -dʒ-] sound faintly uneducated to ears attuned to the RP [-tj-, -dj-].

In East Anglia yod-dropping is not restricted, as elsewhere, to environments involving a preceding coronal consonant. Here we also find it after labials (*pure, beauty, music, few*), velars (*accuse*), and /h/ (*huge*). This leads to homophony (variable, because sensitive to social and stylistic considerations) in pairs such as *beauty, booty* ['bʉːti], *cure, cur* [kɜː].

h-dropping is perhaps the single most powerful sociolinguistic shibboleth in England. Nearly everywhere working-class accents are characterized by the absence (variable or categorical) of the [h] which RP speakers use. This makes *hedge* and *edge* homophones. Sometimes, though, by hypercorrection, [h] is introduced into items whose standard pronunciation has an initial vowel, thus [hiːstə] *Easter*. A strong correlation between [h] usage and social class has been repeatedly found by investigators; in London schools, for example, Hudson and Holloway (1977) found that middle-class girls dropped only 6 per cent of possible [h], while working-class boys dropped 81 per cent.

It is correspondingly complicated to establish the status of /h/ as a phoneme. It is oversimplifying merely to say that working-class accents lack /h/. A vowel bared by a dropped /h/ generally behaves like any other initial vowel, triggering the pre-vocalic forms of the articles and linking/intrusive /r/ (*an 'edge*, [ði ɛdʒ] *the hedge, your hedge*). But there is also some evidence that there are speakers who treat initial vowels in dropped-/h/ words differently from other initial vowels, so justifying the claim that they have underlying /h/ in such words, but with zero realization (Hurford, 1972).

The only parts of England to retain historical /h/ in working-class accents are recessive patches in rural Wessex and East Anglia, together with the extreme north of the country (Northumberland, Tyne and Wear, parts of Cumbria and Durham). In the cluster /hw/ retention of /h/ is even rarer, being found only in Northumberland. There are of course some speech-conscious speakers of RP or near-RP who have attempted (with varying success) to restore /hw/ in words spelt *wh-*.

Vowels

Many vowels and diphthongs exhibit a very considerable range of geographical and social variation. Thus the word *mouth*, for example, may be pronounced with vowel qualities as diverse as [eɪ], [ɛʊ], [æː], and [aɣ], as well as the more familiar [aʊ] and [ɑʊ] types. The same range of possibilities also characterizes words such as *out, house, loud, now* – in fact all the words which have RP /aʊ/. Since I wish neither to have to refer at every point to the English of seven hundred years ago ('Middle English /uː/ words') nor to make implausible claims about the non-RP native speaker's competence ('/aʊ/ is realized as [eɪ] in this accent'), I make use of a framework of keywords, each of which refers to a reference set of lexical items. This enables me to refer to *out*, *house, loud, now*, etc. as 'the MOUTH words' and to the vowel (monophthong or diphthong) used in them as 'the MOUTH vowel' (of that particular accent). Words so written in small capitals are therefore intended to stand for a whole such lexical set. The keywords have as far as possible been chosen in such a way as to minimize the possibilities of confusion when spoken aloud (in any accent): e.g. if *out* had been chosen it could easily have been confused with *art*, *eight*, or *oat* when said in this or that accent, while *mouth* benefits from the fact that there are no words such as might be spelt **marth*, **mayth*, **moath*.

Short vowels

The short vowels of southern accents are systemically the same as those of RP (see chapter 3), namely /ɪ, e, æ, ɒ, ʌ, ʊ/, in the lexical sets KIT, DRESS, TRAP, LOT, STRUT, and FOOT respectively. (The problem of [ə] and its distinctiveness *vis-à-vis* STRUT will be discussed below.) In northern accents, on the other hand, the short-vowel system comprises five rather than six members, namely /ɪ, ɛ, a, ɒ, ʊ/: the lexical sets STRUT and FOOT are combined in /ʊ/. This means that *cut* rhymes with *put*, *mush* with *push*, and *mull* with *full*, while *cud* and *could* (strong form) are homophonous. Historically speaking, this is not a merger but the failure of the phonemic split which applied elsewhere. The geographical area involved stretches northwards from a line running from the Severn estuary to the Wash, extending virtually to the Scottish border. The matter is, however, sociolinguistically sensitive; particularly in the midlands, the STRUT set is usually more or less successfully distinguished from the FOOT set in relatively formal or relatively higher-class local accents by the use of [ə] is STRUT words (i.e. by extending the phonotactic range of /ə/ by bringing it into stressed syllables). But hypercorrect forms (e.g. ['bətʃə ~ 'bʌtʃə]) are widespread and in some cases institutionalized, while remaining archetypal indicators of northernness to southerners and RP speakers. The resulting fuzziness of the systemic isogloss is discussed by Chambers and Trudgill (1980: ch. 8); see also Knowles (1978) and Lyne (1973). (See also page 72, map. 5.1.)

Some northerners also have [ə] in certain NURSE words, where however it does not appear to contrast with long [ɜ:]; thus *work* [wək ~ wɜ:k] (and in rhotic northern [wɚːk]).

Many southerners have two contrastive degrees of length in TRAP words, e.g. *pad* [pæd] vs. *bad* [bæːd] (as also for some RP speakers), *str*[æ]*nd* vs. *s*[æː]*nd*, *sh*[æ]*m* vs. *j*[æː]*m* (Fudge, 1977). There seems to be a lot of disagreement among individual speakers as to which words have the long vowel and which the short. Except in a few cases (such as adjectives in [-æːd]) Londoners tend to perceive lengthened [æː] as typical of country-dwellers.

In the south-west, on the other hand, short vowels all tend to be lengthened in certain environments, thus (under nuclear stress) [dɪːd] *did*, [tɒˑp] *top*, etc. Even distinctions of the type *gas* vs. *grass* may then be missing, so that with /r/ preserved in START words and often /l/ in words like *calm* there is actually no systemic opposition corresponding to RP /æ/ vs. /ɑː/ in parts of the west country. This may be tested by pairs such as *lagger* vs. *lager*, *matter* vs. *tomato*, *manna* vs. *banana*.

Realizationally, the quality of short vowels tends to correspond to the systemic symbols used for them above: i.e., DRESS is often opener in the north, [ɛ], than in London and the south, [e̞], while TRAP is fully open in the north, [a ~ a-], but nearer to half-open in the south, [æ ~ ɛ̞]. In old-fashioned speech in some parts of the south, LOT is unrounded, [ɑ] (otherwise [ɒ], at least weakly rounded). Unlike Americans, English people seem never to have *bother* and *father* as unconditional rhymes.

Northerners often have /ɒ/ rather than the expected /ʊ/ (acrolectal /ʌ/) in some or all of *one, once, nothing, among, tongue*.

Long vowels and diphthongs (1)

The long vowels and diphthongs may conveniently be divided into three part-systems, according as their final tendency is relatively front and close, back and close, or mid/open. We consider first those which tend generally towards a front/close quality. They are those of the lexical sets FLEECE, FACE, PRICE, and CHOICE, RP /iː, eɪ, aɪ, ɔɪ/ respectively.

Certain southern accents merge PRICE and CHOICE, using a diphthong of the [ɔɪ] type for both. (Comparison of maps Ph118 *lice* and Ph187 *voice* in *LAE* suggests their identity over about half of the south, including Essex, Hampshire, and Warwickshire, but excluding London.) This is one possible consequence of a sound change we may refer to as 'diphthong shift', characteristic of the local accents of London, Birmingham, and much of the south and midlands. In this development, similar in many ways to the Great Vowel Shift of half a millennium ago, FLEECE becomes [əi] (Cockney [bəi] *bee*; in some localities rather [ei], thus Cambridge [bei] *bee*); FACE becomes [ʌɪ] or [aɪ]; PRICE becomes [ɑɪ], [ɒɪ], or [ɔɪ]; and CHOICE (if not merged with PRICE) becomes [oi]. Thus the starting-points of the diphthongs are shifted counter-clockwise. The consequence is that Cockney *race* may sound like RP *rice*, *tie* like *toy*, and perhaps *mean* like *main*. The new [oi] quality for RP /ɔɪ/ can be heard from many southerners whose other diphthongs are not shifted (at least in relatively formal style): I hear it repeatedly from students in the term *voiced*.

There are local accents which preserve historical contrasts in the lexical set FACE which are lost in RP. In East Anglia there may be a distinction between [eː ~ eə] in *name, paper* (ME /aː/) and [æɪ] (etc.) in *nail, way* (ME /ɛi ~ æi/). In parts of the north of England [ɛɪ] is found in items such as *eight, straight, deign*, where there was once a velar fricative after the vowel, but [eː] in items such as *late, main, day*, where this was not the case. In both these types of accent we may recognize contrastive /eː/ and /ɛɪ/, both corresponding to the single RP /eɪ/. Such distinctions are, however, sharply recessive.

In an area of the south, to the west of London, MOUTH is realized as a diphthong of the [ɛɪ] or [eɪ] type (making *down* sound like RP *deign*). A report from High Wycombe, Bucks., suggests the possibility of variably merging

MOUTH and FACE as [ɛɪ], so that *out* is a potential homophone of *eight*. Usually, though, they are kept distinct, as [ɛɪʔ] vs. [ʌɪʔ] etc. (The only locality for which the [ɛɪ] type of pronunciation is reported in *LAE* is Tingewick, Bucks.: see maps Ph152, Ph154, for the first of which the editors see fit to comment 'sic' at [ɛ̈] in *clouds*. But laymen often comment on it.)

The realizations of FACE and PRICE in the north of England are rather different from those in the south. In the more conservative type of northern accent, FACE is a monophthong of the [eː] type (perhaps in opposition to an [ɛɪ], as discussed above); in the midlands and to an increasing extent in northern urban speech, a diphthong is used. In Tyneside there is an unusual opening-diphthong variant, [eə] or [ɪɐ]. The PRICE diphthong involves very little movement in some northern speech, being of the [aɛ] type; in any case, a Cardinal 4 starting-point is diagnostic of a northern rather than a southern accent. In some local dialects long monophthongs are used. Tyneside has an alternation between an [ɛɪ] and an [aɪ] type, apparently distributed in a way similar to that of Scottish accents (see chapter 6), i.e. [ɛɪ] everywhere except before voiced fricatives and # : [twɛis faɪv] *twice five*.

Some southern accents, together with RP (cf. chapter 3), exhibit a process which we may call 'smoothing'. This causes a diphthong to be realized monophthongally in the environment of a following vowel (as when in RP *showing* /ˈʃəʊɪŋ/ is pronounced [ˈʃəˈɪŋ]). This is a matter which has been very little investigated, but examples from Norwich include *seeing* [sɛːn], *saying* [sæːn], *going* [gɔːn], *knowing* [nɒːn] (Trudgill, 1974: 159; these also involve absorption of the /ə/ of *-ing* /-ən/); from Bristol, *playing* [ˈplɛːɪn], *going* [ˈgoːɪn] (cf. *play* [plɛɪ], *go* [gɔʊ]; Weissmann, 1970); and from London and many other localities *fire* [ˈfaːə ~ faː], *flowers* [ˈflaː(ə)z ~ ˈflɛː(ə)z].

Long vowels and diphthongs (2)

We consider next the long vowels and diphthongs which tend generally towards a back/close quality: i.e. those of the lexical sets MOUTH, GOAT, and GOOSE, RP /aʊ, əʊ, uː/, as well as certain possible new types, products of the vocalization of /l/.

As with FACE, so with GOAT there are local accents which preserve historical contrasts lost in RP. Thus in East Anglia many speakers distinguish *moan, sole, nose, toe*, with [ʊu], from *mown, soul, knows, tow*, with [ʌu]. Trudgill and Foxcroft (1978) show that while this distinction is retained in working-class Norfolk accents it is increasingly lost closer to London (Ipswich, Colchester) and among speakers further up the socioeconomic scale. Some Yorkshire speakers, too, have an /ɔʊ/ which is in contrast both with the /oː/ of most GOAT words and with the /aʊ/ of most MOUTH words, so that *know* /nɔʊ/ may be distinct from both *no* /noː/ and *now* /naʊ/ (Petyt, 1977).

The opposition between GOAT and GOOSE is clouded in Norfolk by the fact that some words fluctuate between the [ʊu] typical of GOAT and the [ɵʉ ~ ʉː] typical of GOOSE, so that pairs such as *soup* and *soap* may sometimes be homophonous. Some GOAT words, furthermore, have variants with the /ʊ/ of FOOT, thus *boat* [bʊt], *road* [ɹʊd].

The vowel system of certain conservative accents of the north and the easterly midlands retains the diphthong /ɪu/, with the possibility of minimal pairs such as *threw* /θrɪu/ vs. *through* /θruː/. (In the history of RP and other accents, a syllabicity shift converted earlier /ɪu/ into /juː/, with loss of the /j/ in certain consonant clusters.) While RP vacillates between /sjuːt/ and /suːt/ for *suit*, the form /sɪut/ persists, for example, in parts of Yorkshire.

The diphthong shift alluded to above in connection with front diphthongs also affects back diphthongs in London and much of the south, and also in Birmingham. The GOOSE vowel has become [əu ∼ əʉ] (at least in certain environments, such as in unchecked syllables), thus *boots*, Cockney [bəuʔs]; GOAT has acquired the wide-diphthong realization [ʌʊ ∼ ʌʉ], or sometimes [œʉ]; and MOUTH has shifted to [æʊ] or [ɛʊ ∼ eʊ] (with the further possibility of unrounding of the second element, discussed above; and in London with monophthonging to long [aː ∼ æː]). Hence London or Birmingham *soup* may sound like RP *soap*, *load* like RP *loud*, and London *brown* like something caricatured as 'brahn' but actually closer to RP *Brian* or some versions of *bran*.

In the north and far west, on the other hand, GOAT remains in some places as a monophthongal [oː] or a somewhat centralized mid [o̝ː], thus *don't know* ['doːnʔ 'noː]. This monophthong appears to be gradually losing ground to a diphthongal [ɔʊ ∼ əʊ]. In Tyneside there are local variants [ʊə] and [ɵː]. Northern MOUTH is usually [aʊ], but in Lancashire there is also an [əy] type; in the same area GOOSE, otherwise [uː], is realized as [ʏː].

The vocalization of pre-consonantal and final /l/ has given rise to new phonetic diphthongs in London and much of the south, as for example in [mɪok] *milk*, [sɛof] *self*, [væov] *valve*. Cockney exhibits various vowel neutralizations in the environment of a following [o] from [ɫ], e.g. *wheel* = *will* [wɪo], *fall* = *full* = *fool* [foː]. Since London GOAT and GOOSE otherwise have central starting-points, the retention of back allophones before tautosyllabic /l/ has led to new contrasts such as ['slʌʊli] *slowly* vs. ['gɒʊli] *goalie* (goal-keeper), ['trʊʉli] *truly* vs. ['fɔolɪʃ] *foolish*. Many London informants now intuit the [ɒʊ] of *goal*, *told*, *roller* as phonemically distinct from the [ʌʊ], middle-class [əʊ], of *go*, *toad*, *polar*.

In many other parts of the country GOAT has an [ɒʊ]-type variant before /l/ which may nevertheless be seen as allophonic.

Syllabic [ɫ], when vocalized, gives rise to a back monophthong of the [oː] type (rather closer than Cardinal 7), thus *table*, Cockney ['tˢʌɪboː]. It is not always distinct in London from the pre-consonantal realization of THOUGHT, or from this plus vocalized /l/, so that *apples* may end identically to *pause* and its Cockney homophone *Paul's*. Londoners do not make the RP distinction between [-fɫ] and [-fʊɫ], *painful* vs. *spoonful*.

Long vowels and diphthongs (3)

The remaining vowels and diphthongs are the mid/open long monophthongs and the centring diphthongs: those of the lexical sets PALM, THOUGHT, NURSE, and also NEAR, SQUARE, START, NORTH, FORCE, and CURE, insofar as their vowels have not been dealt with already. There are also the questions of incidence in the lexical sets BATH and CLOTH.

RP /ɑ:/ occurs in words of three lexical sets (distinguishable by their behaviour in other accents). One such is START, which in rhotic accents contain /r/; another is BATH, in which the TRAP vowel is used in northern accents; the third is PALM, where neither of the foregoing apply. The opposition between short /æ ~ a/ (TRAP) and its long counterpart (= RP /ɑ:/) is missing in certain western accents, so that *lager* is homophonous with *lagger* and *tomato–mulatto*, *bravado–shadow* are perfect rhymes. Pairs such as *palm* vs. *Pam*, *calm* vs. *cam*, *halve* vs. *have* may nevertheless remain distinct by virtue of the retention or restoration of /l/ in the items spelt with *l*. Rhoticity ensures the distinction between pairs such as *ham* vs. *harm*, *cat* vs. *cart*.

Otherwise all accents have a long /a: ~ ɑ:/ in contrast with short /æ ~ a/. Given this, we have the geographically and socially important question, which of the two vowels, long or short, is used in the fifty or so everyday words we designate as the BATH set (*staff, path, brass, shaft, grasp, fast, ask, plaster, dance, grant, branch, demand, sample, answer...*). In local accents of the north they have the short vowel, but in southern accents (as in RP) the long one. The isogloss (see page 72) runs approximately directly from south Wales to the Wash, slightly to the north of the other major north/south isogloss, that relating to the STRUT vowel. Bolton, in Greater Manchester, appears to constitute an enclave with the long vowel in BATH words, where the surrounding local accents have the short vowel (Shorrocks, 1980). Given that an accent has the contrast between long and short vowel, the matter of incidence can be readily tested by investigating whether pairs such as *staff–gaff, path–hath, brass–gas, grasp–asp, basket–gasket, plaster–aster, dance–romance, grant–pant, slander–gander, sample–ample* rhyme (as in the north) or not (as in the south and in RP). Expressions such as *gas-mask* (RP /ˈgæsmɑːsk/) are notoriously subject to hypercorrection by upwardly-mobile northerners (for an interesting subjective account of this see Knowles, 1978).

RP /ɔ:/, too, is found in words of several distinct lexical sets – distinct, that is, from the point of view of other accents. All accents of England seem to have a distinction between a long [ɔ:]-type THOUGHT vowel and the short LOT vowel, as shown by minimal pairs such as *caught* vs. *cot*, *gnawed* vs. *nod*, *naughty* vs. *knotty*. Just as there is a set BATH varying regionally and socially between TRAP and PALM, so there is a set CLOTH varying between LOT and THOUGHT. But in this case it is the north which agrees with current educated usage, with /klɒθ/, while the /klɔːθ/ form, now archaic in RP, is a southern provincialism, now obviously recessive. Examples of words in this set include *cough, froth, cross, soft,* and perhaps *Austin* and *gone.* (The historical parallelism between the BATH and CLOTH lengthenings with their virtually identical structural environments – principally that of a following voiceless fricative – are obvious, although the social and regional outcomes are rather different.)

Except in rhotic accents, NORTH words have the same /ɔː/, so that *gnaw* and *nor, stalk* and *stork,* are homophones, while *lawn* rhymes with *corn.* The historically distinct FORCE set, too, increasingly falls in with NORTH, making *hoarse* a homophone of *horse* and *sport* a rhyme of *short* (and hence, in non-rhotic accents, of *ought*). More conservative accents, though, may retain the distinction, with, for example, [doə] *door* (compare [lɔː] *law*). Informal evidence from Humberside suggests that this is now perceived as a dialectalism and stigmatized by schoolteachers.

A complication here is that in the north some THOUGHT words may be pronounced with the /ɔʊ/ discussed above on page 63, rather than with /ɔː/.

In London /ɔː/ has developed a noticeable allophonic range, with an opener, often centring-diphthong, variant in unchecked syllables but a closer, often closing-diphthong, variant in checked syllables: thus [fɔə] *four,* [lɔə] *law–lore,* but [foʊs] *force,* [loʊn] *lawn,* in the kind of broad Cockney which has the greatest phonetic distinction here. A morpheme boundary suffices to trigger the former variant, so that there are actually minimal pairs such as [bɔəd] *bore#d* vs. [boʊd] *board–bawd–baud,* [jɔən] *your#n* ('yours') vs. [joʊn] *yawn.* The absorption of vocalized /l/ into [oʊ] gives rise to further pairs such as [bɔə] *bore* vs. [boʊ] *ball,* [pɔəz] *paw#s–pour#s–pore#s* vs. [poʊz] *Paul's–pause.* So for some varieties at least of London speech it seems appropriate to recognize a phonemic split, with RP (etc.) /ɔː/ split into /ɔə/ and /oʊ/.

All accents have a long mid central monophthong, with or without r-colouring, in NURSE words (RP /ɜː/). It is contrastive with all other vowels except possibly /ər/ (in rhotic accents): this last can be tested by *foreword* vs. *forward,* (*ex*)*pert* vs. (*Ru*)*pert.*

Words of the lexical set SQUARE have a vowel of the [ɛə] or [ɛː] type (with or without r-colouring) in most parts of England. Speakers with rhotic accents do not, in my experience, react favourably to the suggestion that this might be regarded as a pre-/r/ allophone of the FACE vowel (as is clearly the case in Scottish English); so that for them, as certainly for most non-rhotic accents, we must recognize a phoneme /ɛə ~ ɛː/. The exceptions are those in some parts of the midlands and north (notably Liverpool), for whom SQUARE and NURSE are not distinct, with [ɜː] or [ɛ̈ː] in homophone pairs such as *spare–spur, fair–fur, staring–stirring.*

Some East Anglians give the impression of not distinguishing SQUARE from NEAR (e.g. *fair* = *fear* [feə]); but this may be a case of phonetic overlap rather than a phonemic merger (Trudgill, 1974: 123). Otherwise NEAR words have a centring diphthong of the [iə ~ ɪə] type. On the whole this seems to justify the recognition of a separate phoneme (RP /ɪə/), though its contrastiveness *vis-à-vis* the sequence /iː/ plus /ə/, or in rhotic accents *vis-à-vis* /iː/, is not always clear. In conservative accents, particularly in the north, historical /iː/ remains in the environment __rV, thus *serious* [siːr-] (compare RP etc. [sɪər-]).

Similarly, most accents have a diphthong of the [uə] or [ʊə] type in words of the lexical set CURE. In some cases this can be regarded as a realization of /uː/ plus /ə/ or /uː/ before /r/, but in other cases as a separate phoneme (RP /ʊə/). The trend towards /ɔː/ in place of earlier /ʊə/ is perhaps more advanced in local accents – urban ones at least – than in RP. Thus *sure* is increasingly a homophone of *shore* and *touring* a rhyme of *boring*. Where RP has /jʊə/, as *pure*, some local accents have /jɜː/. East Anglian yod-dropping then makes *pure* a potential homophone of *purr* /pɜː/.

The inventory of phonetic centring diphthongs may be increased by two types of continuing phonological process. One is the smoothing of diphthong plus [ə], giving [faə ~ faɑ] *fire*, [aə ~ aɑ ~ æə ~ ɛə] *hour* etc. Although this is a familiar feature of Cockney, it does not in general seem to be as fully developed in most local accents as in RP. The other is the 'breaking' of vowels before /l/ (as happened earlier before historical /r/), giving pronunciations such as [fiəl] *feel*, [seɪəl ~ sʌɪəl] *sail*. Some speakers have potential contrasts of the type *feel # ing* vs. *Ealing* with [iə] and [iː] respectively. Students often insist on transcriptions such as [fiːl] *feel* and claim that such words are disyllabic. Perhaps they are right: if so, the [l] could be regarded as deriving from [əl], the [ə] representing pre-l breaking. But I am not aware of any accent which operates breaking in the environment of a pre-vocalic /l/, e.g. *pilot*, RP /ˈpaɪlət/; (cf. breaking before pre-vocalic /r/ in *pirate*, RP /ˈpaɪərət/, though not in local-accent and near-RP /ˈpaɪrət/). Speakers in the West Midlands tend to have [-ʊuəl ~ -əuəl] in words like *tool*, *cool* (London [-ʊuɫ ~ -oʊ]).

Weak vowels

All accents have a phoneme /ə/ found in the weak syllable of *again*. In some accents, however, the opposition between /ə/ and the STRUT vowel is variable or absent. This may be tested by pairs such as *an ending* vs. *unending*, *hiccup* vs. *gallop*, *a large and tidy room* vs. *a large untidy room*. The opposition is particularly likely to be missing in western accents and in lower-middle-class northern accents (where [ə], rather than the stigmatized [ʊ], is used in STRUT).

Popular local accents often have [ə] at the end of words such as *yellow*, *window*, where the standard pronunciation has [əʊ]. This may trigger intrusive /r/: *tomat*[ər] *and cucumber production*. In some western accents (e.g. Southampton) both words of this type and words such as *comma*, *sofa*, *arena* are often pronounced with /ər/ [ɚ] in all environments, as mentioned above.

Most English people retain some sort of opposition between [ə] and [ɪ] in weak syllables, thus *zealot* vs. *sell it*, *callous* vs. *chalice*, *abbot* vs. *rabbit*, *Lennon* vs. *Lenin*, (non-rhotic) *dancers* vs. *dances*. But a clear drift towards [ə] is under way, with [ə] replacing a more old-fashioned [ɪ] in environment after environment. The last pair mentioned, for example, are homophonous ([-səz]) for some people (see the discussion in chapter 3).

Another drift away from [ɪ] concerns the final vowel in words such as *happy*, *valley*, *coffee*, where [i] seems likely to displace [ɪ] in RP. In local accents, [i] is on the whole found in the south of England and such peripheral parts of the north as Birmingham, Derby, Liverpool, Newcastle, and Scunthorpe, while [ɪ] (or even a rather opener quality) is found in the central north, e.g. Manchester, Leeds, Nottingham.

REFERENCES

Barltrop, R. and Wolveridge, J. 1980. *The muvver tongue*. London and West Nyack, NY: Journeyman Press.

Beaken, M.A. 1971. A study of phonological development in a primary school population of East London. Ph.D. thesis, University of London.

Bowyer, R. 1973. A study of social accents in a south London suburb. M. Phil. dissertation, University of Leeds.

Chambers, J.K. and Trudgill, P. 1980. *Dialectology*. Cambridge: CUP.

Fudge, E. 1977. Long and short [æ] in one southern British speaker's English. *Journal of the International Phonetic Association* 7, 2: 55–65.

Gimson, A.C. 1980. *An introduction to the pronunciation of English*. 3rd edn. London: Edward Arnold.

Heath, C.D. 1980. *The pronunciation of English in Cannock, Staffordshire*. Publications of the Philological Society no. 29. Oxford: Blackwell.

Hudson, R.A. and Holloway, A.F. 1977. Variation in London English. Mimeo, Dept. of Phonetics and Linguistics, University College London.

Hughes, A. and Trudgill, P. 1979. *English accents and dialects*. London: Edward Arnold.

Hurford, J.R. 1972. The diachronic reordering of phonological rules. *Journal of Linguistics* 8: 293–5.

Johnston, P.A. 1979. A synchronic and historical view of Border area bimoric vowel systems. Ph.D. thesis, University of Edinburgh.

Jones-Sargent, V. 1983. *Tyne bytes. A computerised sociolinguistic study of Tyneside*. Frankfurt-am-Main: Peter Lang.

Knowles, G.O. 1974. Scouse: the urban dialect of Liverpool. Ph.D. thesis, University of Leeds.

——— 1978. The nature of phonological variables in Scouse. In Trudgill (1978) pp. 80–90.

LAE = Orton, H., Sanderson, S. and Widdowson, J. 1978. *The linguistic atlas of England*. London: Croom Helm; Atlantic Highlands, NJ: Humanities Press.

Lyne, A.A. 1973. How broad was my 'u'. *Lore and Language* 9: 3–6.

Pellowe, J., Nixon, G., Strang, B., and McNeany, V. 1972. A dynamic modelling of linguistic variation: the urban (Tyneside) linguistic survey. *Lingua* 30: 1–30.

Petyt, K.M. 1977. 'Dialect' and 'accent' in the industrial West Riding. A study of the changing speech of an urban area. Ph.D. thesis, University of Reading.

Shorrocks, G. 1980. A grammar of the dialect of Farnworth and district (Greater Manchester County, formerly Lancashire). Ph.D. thesis, University of Sheffield.

Sivertsen, E. 1960. *Cockney phonology*. Oslo University Press.

Trudgill, P.J. 1972. Sex, covert prestige and linguistic change in the urban British English of Norwich. *Language in Society* 1: 179–95.

—— 1973. Phonological rules and sociolinguistic variation in Norwich English. In C.-J. Bailey and R.W. Shuy (eds.) *New ways of analyzing variation in English*. Washington DC: Georgetown University Press.

—— 1974. *The social differentiation of English in Norwich*. Cambridge: CUP.

—— (ed.) 1978. *Sociolinguistic patterns in British English*. London: Edward Arnold.

Trudgill, P.J. and Foxcroft, T. 1978. On the sociolinguistics of vocalic mergers: transfer and approximation in East Anglia. In Trudgill (1978) pp. 69–79.

Wakelin, M.F. 1975. *Language and history in Cornwall*. Leicester: Leicester University Press.

Weissmann, E. 1970. Phonematische Analyse des Stadtdialektes von Bristol. *Phonetica* 2: 151–81, 211–40.

Wells, J.C. 1970. Local accents in England and Wales. *Journal of Linguistics* 6: 231–52.

—— 1982. *Accents of English*. vol. 1: An introduction. vol. 2: The British Isles. vol. 3: Beyond the British Isles. Cambridge: CUP.

Wilson, D. 1970. The phonology and accidence of the dialect of the North Staffordshire Potteries. M.A. dissertation, University of Birmingham.

5

Rural dialects in England

MARTYN WAKELIN

Introduction

In this short chapter, I confine myself to citing examples of 'traditional vernacular', i.e., the sort of English characterized by old regional features and spoken mainly, but by no means exclusively, by older people in rural areas. The data presented here derive largely from the Leeds *Survey of English dialects* (*SED*, Orton *et al.*, 1962–71), and *The linguistic atlas of England* (*LAE*) based upon it (1979); also – for vocabulary – on the *SED*-based *A word-geography of England* (*WGE*, Orton and Wright, 1974). These largely replace Ellis (1889), Wright (1898–1905) and Wright (1905). Other *SED* derivatives are Kolb (1966) and Kolb *et al.* (1979). All of these should be consulted at the relevant points, and no further reference is made to them here. For widely distributed nonstandard grammatical features, see Hughes and Trudgill (1979: ch. 3). It may be objected that, since *SED* was conducted in the 1950s and early 1960s, using older informants, the material is in some ways obsolete or archaic. I have tried to indicate if and when this is the case. The continuing use of dialect by younger speakers, however, means that much of the material cited here is still relevant at the present day. In the phonology, I have attempted to define dialect areas, but this is not possible for the morphological and lexical data.

Phonology

It would be beyond the scope of this volume to provide a full conspectus of the vowels and consonants of the English dialects, so we shall confine ourselves to indicating the chief features of some main dialect areas which emerge on the BASIS of their phonology.

We may first distinguish two major phonological boundaries (see also chapter 4):

(i) A boundary from the Wash to the south of Northamptonshire, through north-west Berkshire, Oxfordshire, Gloucestershire and Monmouthshire, dividing northern /ɒ/ from southern and RP /ʌ/ in, e.g., *bucket, some, enough, hundred* (ME *u*; *ǭ*); see map 5.1.

70

(ii) A boundary from the Wash to the north of Northamptonshire, through the north of Herefordshire and Worcestershire, dividing northern short /a/ from southern /ɑː/ ([ɑː], [aː], [æː], etc., i.e. a long sound), RP /ɑː/, in, e.g., *chaff, laugh, pass, path* (ME *a* + /f, s, θ/); see map 5.1.

The areas so delimited, although not exactly co-extensive, are near enough to allow us to speak of 'northern' and 'southern' dialect areas. In each case the 'northern' sound is the earlier one; the 'southern' equivalents arose before and during the Early Modern English period and spread throughout the south, south-west and East Anglia. Within these main areas, we can distinguish several others, described below.

The area north of the Humber

This stretches southward from the Scottish border to a boundary running across England roughly from Humber mouth (but examples (iv), (v) and (vi, b) below also take in south Humberside and much of Lincolnshire) along the Ouse and Wharfe valleys, and out of north Lancashire via the Lune and Ribble valleys. The southern boundary marks the limit of a bundle of phonological isoglosses of the greatest importance (Rohrer, 1950) as well as that of many of the Scandinavian loan-words found in northern dialect (see pages 86ff, below). It also represents the boundary which in Anglo-Saxon times, probably running much further to the south, divided Northumbria from Mercia, and is therefore an ancient ethnic as well as linguistic boundary (Brook, 1965: 62). The traditional phonological features in question (see map 5.2) are:

(i) /uː/ in, e.g., *brown, cow, house* (ME *ū* undiphthongized). Note that the presence of an [ɔ] or [ə] on-glide or of hybrid forms /əʊ/ ([əʊ], [ʌʊ]) presumably indicates the influence of RP.

(ii) /ɪə/ ([ɪə], [ɪʊ], [jʊ], etc., and [ɪuː] (perhaps a hybrid from RP influence) in, e.g., *food, goose, moon*; also in, e.g., *cook, good; enough, gloves* (from an early fronted form of northern ME *ǭ*).

(iii) /ɪə/ ([ɪə], [ɪa], [ea], etc.) in, e.g., *bone, loaf, road* (RP /əʊ/; from the northern ME fronting of OE *ā*, ON *á* /aː/ to /eː/ instead of southern rounding to *ǭ* /ɔː/). Note that early attempts to conform more closely to RP have resulted in a distinctive and persistent /øː/ phoneme in Northumberland, north Durham and Tyne and Wear; /ɔː/ ([ɔː] or [oː]) pronunciations in the north represent a more recent attempt. The northern area is, however, also being invaded by the traditional north midland sound in these words (perhaps by influence from that in the class (iv) below), namely /ʊə/.

(iv) /ʊə/ in, e.g., *coal, coat, foal* (ME *ǭ* < *ǒ* lengthened). Note that /øː/ is found in the far north, with sporadic intrusions of /ɔː/ throughout.

(v) /iː/ or /ɪə/ in, e.g., *eat, speak* (ME *ę̄* < OE *ě* lengthened; for north midland and west midland /ɛɪ/ see below);

(vi, a) /ʊ/ in, e.g., *ground, pound* (ME *u* unlengthened before /nd/);

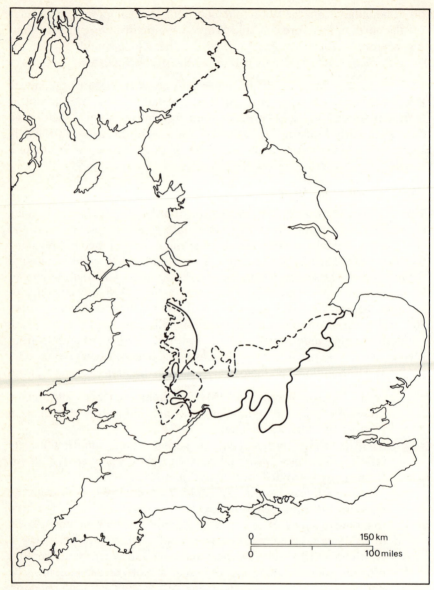

—————— General southern limit of /ʊ/ in *some*

– – – – – General southern limit of a short vowel in *chaff*

Map 5.1. *Some* and *chaff* (after *SED*, with permission of the Athlone Press)

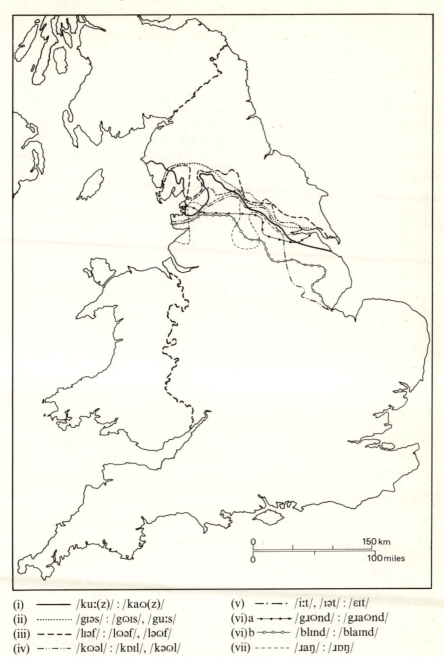

(i) ——— /kuː(z)/ : /kaʊ(z)/   (v) —·—· /iːt/, /ɪət/ : /ɛɪt/

(ii) ············ /gɪəs/ : /gɔɪs/, /guːs/   (vi)a +—+—+ /gɹʊnd/ : /gɹaʊnd/

(iii) – – – – /lɪəf/ : /lʊəf/, /ləʊf/   (vi)b ○—○—○ /blɪnd/ : /blaɪnd/

(iv) —··—··— /kʊəl/ : /kɒɪl/, /kəʊl/   (vii) – – – – – – /ɹaɪ/ : /ɹɒɪ/

Map 5 2. Northern/north midland isoglosses (after *SED*, with permission of the Athlone Press)

(vi, b) /ɪ/ in, e.g., *blind, climb* (ME *i* unlengthened before /nd/, /mb/);
(vii) /a/ in, e.g., *among, long, throng* ('busy', adj.), *wrong* (northern ME *a* lengthened to *ā* and then re-shortened).

Northumberland, north Durham, Tyne and Wear and environs

This small sub-area is characterized by the features set out below.

(i) Traditional retention of initial /h/ (also in Durham, Cumbria and parts of north Yorks). Note that this is also a feature of dialect in (a) Somerset, south Wiltshire and north Dorset; (b) East Anglia; (c) Essex, London, Surrey, Kent and north Sussex – where it may be due to RP influence (see also chapter 4).
(ii) Aspiration of /w/ in, e.g., *what, which, why*;
(iii) Realization of /r/ as [ʁ] in all positions, e.g., in *rabbits, tree, furrow, arm, ladder* (Pählsson 1972).

The north midlands/midlands

(i) In the old West Riding of Yorks /ɔɪ/ is the traditional development (long) of ME *ō̦* (/mɔɪn/ *moon*, /skɔɪl/ *school*; also /fɔɪt/ *foot*).
(ii) In *bone, loaf, road*, etc. (ME *ō̦*), the traditional north midland development is to /ʊə/ ([ʊə], [ʊa], etc.); (cf. page 71, example (iii), above).
(iii) In *coal, coat, foal*, etc. (ME *ō̦* < *ŏ* lengthened), south and west Yorkshire and part of south Lancashire traditionally have /ɒɪ/.
(iv) In the north midland and some west midland dialects the reflexes of ME *ē̦* < OE *ǣ, ēa* in, e.g., *deal, reach, team* are different from those of ME *ē̦* < OE *ě* lengthened in, e.g., *eat, speak*: the former giving /iː/, /ɪə/, the latter /ɛɪ/. The more northerly dialects, however, do not differentiate in this way, having /iː/ or /ɪə/ for both types. There is thus a contrast between northern /iː/, /ɪə/ and north midland /ɛɪ/ here (see page 71, example (v), above).

The west midlands

An area of the west midlands may be distinguished in respect of two features:

(i) /ɒ/ (RP /a/) before some nasals, e.g., in *man, hammer* (less regularly in *hand, land, stand*, etc.) within an arc extending from north Lancashire to south-west Gloucestershire;
(ii) /ŋɡ/ (RP /ŋ/) in *ring, singing, tongue*, etc. in a similar, but smaller, west midland area extending from central Lancashire to north Worcestershire and north Warwickshire. This is still retained by younger and educated speakers (see chapter 4).

The area west of Watling Street

(i) Rhotacism: pre-consonantal and final /r/ ([ɽ] or [ɹ]) occur throughout a large southern and western area in traditional dialect, extending from

Kent (though absent in the immediate environs of London) as far north as Cheshire (it is found again in Lancashire and its environs as well as more sporadically in the east in these positions); see map 5.3, and chapter 4. In a small area of south Somerset [ʈ] is aspirated in initial position (i.e. [hʈ]).

(ii) /w/ and /j/: in large areas of the south-west initial /w/ may be lost before /ɒ/, e.g. in *woman, wool*, but added initially or after a preceding consonant before long back vowels (more sporadically, it would seem) in, e.g., *old, whole, boiling, poison*, etc. Loss of /j/ in, e.g., *year, yeast, yes, yesterday*, etc. shows much the same geographical pattern as loss of /w/, except that there is also loss on the eastern side of the country (east Lincolnshire, Suffolk). Addition of /j/ is found (more sporadically again – Wiltshire, Berkshire, Gloucestershire, Oxfordshire, Hampshire provide examples) in, e.g., *earn, earth*.

(iii) Voicing of initial fricative consonants, as in /vɪŋgər/ *finger*, /zadl/ *saddle*, /ðʌm/ *thumb*, /ʒɪlɪn/ *shilling*, occurs as an archaic and recessive feature, mainly in Devon and the immediate neighbouring areas (plus Dorset, part of Wiltshire and south and west Hampshire; to a lesser extent in north Somerset, Gloucestershire, Avon and north Wiltshire, plus occasional outliers) and most regularly for initial /f/. In medieval times, on the basis of place-name evidence, it probably occurred as far north as Watling Street (Wakelin and Barry, 1968: 58). See maps 5.4 and 5.5, which both show relatively extensive distributions.

Front-rounded vowel sub-area in the south-west

In the south-west (west Somerset, Devon and east Cornwall) /uː/ and /ɒ/ (ME *ọ̄, u*) are realized as fronted types [ʏː], [ʏ] due to sixteenth–seventeenth century fronting processes. In this area, and only in this area, /aɒ/ (ME *ū*) is also realized as a fronted diphthong [œʏ]; see map 5.6. This is probably due to the same sixteenth–seventeenth century process (Wakelin, 1975: 125–54). Note that there is also a tendency towards fronting in parts of the north-west midlands and East Anglia, but it appears not as marked as in the south-west.

The 'Cornish' sub-area (west Cornwall and some of central Cornwall)

This area does not have the characteristics mentioned immediately above – /uː/ is [uː], /ɒ/ is [ɒ], /aɒ/ is [ɛɒ]. Neither does it have the voicing of initial fricatives, except where this has spread from the adjacent area. /a/ is [æ], which may be a relic of an old RP form. Inflections here also tend to be of a more 'standard' type, and there is a corpus of Cornish loan-words (see chapter 12).

Note that the whole area west of Watling Street is also characterized by the presence of archaic inflections and, in vocabulary, an absence of Norse loan-words (see below).

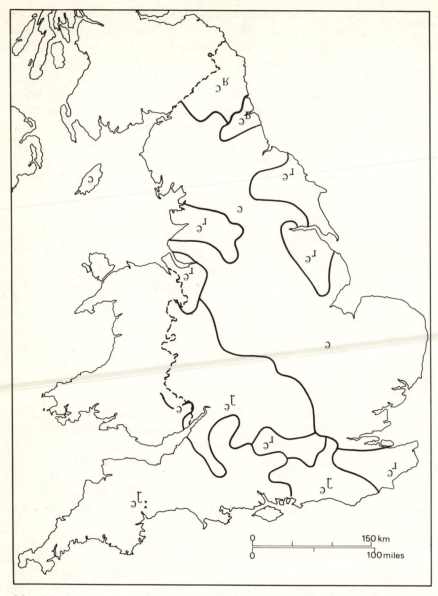

Map 5.3. General limit of final post-vocalic /r/ in *farmer* (after *LAE*, with permission of the Editors and of Messrs Croom Helm)

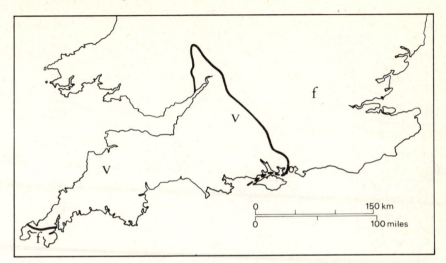

Map 5.4. General limits of /v/ in *finger* (after *LAE*, with permission of the Editors and of Messrs Croom Helm)

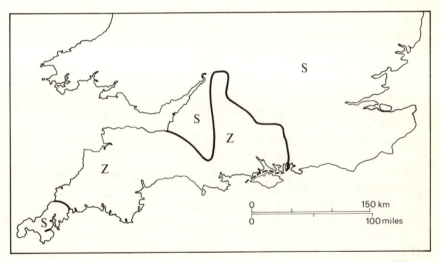

Map 5.5. General limits of /z/ in *-saddle* (after *LAE*, with permission of the Editors and of Messrs Croom Helm)

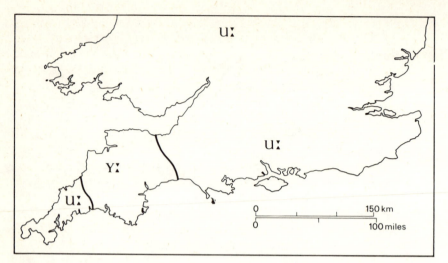

Map 5.6. General limits of south-western [Y:] in *moon* (after *LAE*, with permission
of the Editors and of Messrs Croom Helm)

London and the south-east

(i) In the whole south-east of England and East Anglia /a/ (ME *a*) is
regularly (i.e. in speakers of all ages) raised to [æ], sometimes becoming
/ɛ/ in Essex, Surrey, Kent and Sussex. (The close variety [æ] is also found
in Northumberland, in Somerset and some of the south-west midlands
and in west Cornwall – see above.)

(ii) /ʌ/ (ME *u*) is regularly realized as an unrounded, fronted vowel, approaching /a/ (see chapters 3 and 4).

(iii) In older forms of traditional dialect in the south as well as in popular
London speech and conservative RP (see chapter 3), /ɔ:/ (ME *o*) occurs
before /f, s, θ/, e.g., in *off, cross, cloth* (and also in some other words –
dog, gone, Tom); but this is now obsolescent and in RP has become so
within living memory.

(iv) In *cake* (ME *ā*), *hail* (ME *ai, ei*), *strange* (ME *ā* < OF *au*), etc., /ɛɪ/
regularly has a lowered front element ([aɪ], [æɪ]) in London and the
south-east.

(v) In *brown, cow, house* (ME *ū*), etc., the south-east regularly has /ɛω/ (cf.
popular London dialect, where a monophthong /a:/ obtains – see
chapter 4).

(vi) The glottal stop [ʔ] regularly replaces /t, k/, more rarely /p/, in medial
and final positions (e.g. [gɛʔ bɛʔə] *get better*, [av ə lɒʔ] *have a look*, [gəʔ ʌʔ]
get up) in south-eastern dialect.

(vii) /θ/ is regularly articulated as /f/ (/fɪŋk/, /klɔːf/) and /ð/ as /v/ (/vɛn/, /brʌvə/), in both popular London pronunciation and also that of the Home Counties. But in certain words – *that, the, there, these* and some others – initial /ð/ appears as /d/ (or a cross between /d/ and /ð/) in popular London dialect and the south-east; this may owe something to Dutch or Flemish influence (Samuels, 1971: 11ff).

(viii) /l/ is regularly realized as [ɫ] or with a back-vowel resonance [ö] in the south-east: [fɪöd] *field*, [bɪö] *Bill* (see also chapter 4).

(ix) In words which in OE contained *ȳ*, e.g., *hide, hive, lice, mice*, some very old forms of south-eastern dialect (Berkshire, Surrey, Kent, East Sussex, Essex, north Hertfordshire, Suffolk and south Norfolk) have /iː/, since here OE *ȳ* > ME *ẹ̄* > /iː/.

(x) Old East Anglian and south-eastern dialect is noted for its pronunciation of initial /v/ as /w/ in, e.g., *vinegar, viper*; a very old feature, which was preserved in Cockney up to the last century.

Grammar: general and widely distributed features

Nouns

The formation of double plurals (*mices, mens*, etc.) is a widely observable feature of most nonstandard speech: *SED* records, e.g., *bellowses, hawses* ('haws'), *mices*, etc., widely.

'Weak' plurals deriving either regularly from OE forms (e.g. *een* 'eyes' < OE *ēage, -an*) or having adopted a weak ending at a later stage (e.g. *shoon* 'shoes' < OE *scōh*, pl. *scōs*) also occur, though in diminishing numbers, in older forms of dialect (see further below).

Plurals are frequently unmarked after numerals, as in *ten foot, five pound*.

Pronouns

The personal pronoun *us* 'me' is widespread in nonstandard speech (*Give us it*, etc.); *thou* (subject), *thee* (object), *thy, thine* and *thyself* are often preserved in older dialect (to a lesser extent in the east midlands and south-east); also *ye*, usually reduced to *'ee* in the south, which may function as subject or object, singular or plural.

Except in the north (for reasons unknown), the possessive pronouns 'his', 'hers', 'ours', 'yours', 'theirs' may be *hisn, hern, ourn, yourn, theirn*, with final *-n* presumably on analogy with *mine* and *thine*; *hisself, theirselves* are in general use as distinct from SE *himself, themselves*.

The dialects retain a wider variety of relative pronouns inherited from an earlier period than does SE: *as, at* (reduced form of *that* or, in the north, < ON *at*), *that* and *what* (ubiquitous) are all in dialectal use, employed by people of all ages to refer to both things and people, as well as the simple omission of the pronoun in, e.g., *He's the man looks after the cows* (see chapter 2).

Adjectives

'Double' comparatives and superlatives are possible in dialect everywhere (*more kinder*, *more safer*, etc.), and the *-er*, *-est* endings are not restricted to monosyllabic adjectives: one may find, e.g., *usefuller* 'more useful'.

Verbs

Present singular. In the dialects an *-s* ending has spread generally, by analogy, to other persons of the verb than the SE 3rd singular form, giving *I sees, you goes, we sits down, they likes*, etc. (see also chapter 2).

Past tenses and past participles. Since the early ME period, 'strong' verbs, which formed their past tenses and past participles by a change of stem vowel (*ride, sing*), have tended to join the 'weak' class (see chapter 2) which is numerically stronger and which forms its past tenses and past participles by adding a *-d* suffix (*gather, kiss*). This analogical process is still widely observable in the dialects, and *knowed, growed, catched*, for example, are of widespread occurrence; we also find past tense and past part. *drinked* (also very occasionally past part. *drunked*), *speaked, weared, seed, stealed, gived*, past part. *doed* ('done'), as well as more exotic forms like past tenses *spoked* and *wored*, past part. *borned* and past tense and past part. *stoled*, which shows that dialects may simply add the usual *-d* to the past stem (*wored*) or to the 'strong' past part. (*borned*) to form a new past tense or past participle.

Some few verbs which usually became weak in ME (and are so in modern SE) have, however, retained their old strong forms in regional dialect, e.g. *crope* (past tense), *croppen* (past part.) 'crept' in south Lancashire and Merseyside.

Another familiar characteristic of ME reshuffling in the strong verbs was the 'levelling' of the vowel of the past tense plural under that of the singular, or the levelling of the vowel of the past tense singular under that of the plural or past participle. Thus the parts of OE *drincan* have emerged in SE via this process as *drink* (inf.), *drank* (past tense), *drunk* (past part.); but in the dialects the results of levelling may be different, thus *drunk* is general in non-SE speech as past tense, and conversely *drank* is frequent as past participle (except in the north and north midlands).

Grammar: regionally restricted features

Nouns

Archaic plural forms include:
 Kye 'cows' (regularly derived from OE pl. *cȳ*, SE *cows* being a later formation): all northern counties plus Cheshire and Staffordshire;
 Kine 'cows' (= *kye* + *-n* ending from OE *-n* pl. formation): west Cumbria and north Yorkshire;

Shoon 'shoes' (OE *scōh* + *-n* ending): all northern counties, plus Cheshire, Derbyshire, Staffordshire;

Een 'eyes' (regular development from OE *ēage*, pl. *ēagan*): all northern and some west midland counties;

Housen 'houses' (OE *hūs* + *-n* ending): once apparently general except in the north, now restricted to old dialect in Essex and East Anglia, Hereford and Worcestershire, Gloucestershire, Oxfordshire and Berkshire, plus occasional outliers;

Chicken 'chickens' (regularly formed from OE *cicen*, pl. *cicenu*; SE *chickens* is a double plural): south-western counties, sporadically in the western and south-eastern counties;

Childer 'children' (regularly derived from ME *childre* < late OE *cildru*; SE *children* is a double pl.): north midlands, also occasionally found in the south.

Pronouns

(1) Personal. I: in some very old south Somerset dialect there may still conceivably be left some traces of obsolete *utch* (ME *ich*), perhaps sometimes in the form *us* (Wakelin, 1977: 112), but this was regarded as rustic and provincial as early as ME times.

Him, it: in the south-west, old *'n* (OE *hine*) survives in the form /ŋ/ or /ən/, e.g. *I seed 'n* 'I saw him/it'. This was lost to SE because it was replaced by the OE dative form *him* in early times.

She: in addition to *she*, note the related *shoo* (ME *scheo*, with stress shifted to the second element of the diphthong, i.e. *scheó*, or a blend of *she* and *hoo*, below), found mainly in south Yorkshire and west Yorkshire; north-west-midland *hoo* (OE *hēo* 'she', later replaced by ME *scheo* [above], of doubtful origin); *her*, found in the central and southern-west midlands and south-western peninsula (except west Cornwall); see Duncan, 1972).

Them: an unemphatic form *mun*, whose origin and history are obscure, occurs in east Cornwall (Wakelin, 1975: 176).

The interchange of subjective and objective function, e.g. *her wear'th the trousers* (*SED*, VI.14.14), *brought he up* (*SED*, VIII.1.11), takes place in the south-west (and elsewhere) in certain apparently restricted circumstances, in general the object form being used for the subject when the pronoun is UNEMPHATIC, and the subject form being used as the EMPHATIC form of the object. Examples of the first are the use of *us* for 'we' in the south-west and west, *them* for 'they' in the south-west and much of the west midlands; examples of the second are the use of *I* for 'me', of *he* for 'him' and of *she* for 'her' in the south-west.

(2) Possessive. The obsolete (or obsolescent) use of the personal pronoun in a possessive sense has left a few relics: *us* 'our' in the old West Riding of Yorkshire, also in east Cheshire, north Derbyshire, north Staffordshire; *we*

thus used in south Staffordshire is now rare, and other personal pronouns used in like manner are apparently now completely obsolete.

Its was a sixteenth-century formation, replacing an earlier (*h*)*it*, and, before this, *his*. In older regional dialect *its* is still often avoided, either by using the old form *it* (north midlands and Humberside) or *his* (general), or a periphrastic construction (south-west), e.g. *cut the throat of him* (a pig) 'cut its throat'.

(3) Reflexive. The form of *-self*, *-selves* in the north and midlands may be *-sen*, *-seln* (sing.) and *-sen*, *-seln*, *-sens* (pl.) < ME *seluen*. The simple personal pronoun *me*, *thee*, etc., may be used as a reflexive form in the north and the west midlands, e.g. *wash me* 'wash myself'. And a reflexive form *yourself/you*, *thyself/thee*, etc., may be used in dialect in contexts where it is not so used in SE, e.g. *sit you down, sit yourself down, play them(selves)*.

(4) Demonstrative. Northern forms are *yon(d)*, *yonder* (OE *gēon*) 'that over there', *thir* 'these', *tho* (OE *þā*) 'those', *thon* 'that over there', *thon ones* 'those over there' (both perhaps < *yon* influenced by *th*- from *this*, *that*, etc.), likewise *thonder* 'yonder'.

Theseun, *thoseun* 'these, those' are still found in north-west Shropshire. The south-west uses the well-known *thick* (/ðɪk/), *thicky*, *thuck*, *thucker* forms for 'this', 'that' (< ME *þilke*), and *theseum* 'these' also emerges in Wiltshire. *They* 'those' (*in they days*, etc.) is also in frequent use (cf. ubiquitous nonstandard *in them days*).

Adjectives

The SE ending in *-en* (*wooden*, *golden*) is used more extensively in south-western dialect, and may apparently be added to any noun to form an adjective, e.g. *papern* 'paper', *boarden* 'made of boards', *boughten* (cakes) (Phillips, 1976: 119).

Verbs

Infinitives. In south-western verbs an archaic relic of the ME infinitive ending *-ien* may be found in their *-y* ending, e.g. *sheary* 'shear' (sheep); this is probably added indiscriminately to any verb now, whether or not it had an *-i-* in OE and ME times.

The uses of the verb *do* (in reduced or unstressed form) are extended in some south-western dialects to introduce a simple infinitive, as in *I d' know*, *they d' come*, etc. (see map 5.7).

Third person present singular. Very occasional traces of the old form in *-eth* (OE *-eþ*) may remain in east Cornwall and south Devon (e.g. *her'th returned*, and see above; it was replaced by *-es* from ME times onwards), and this is sometimes extended to the 1st person singular in, e.g., *I'th seen*. Sometimes, however, the 3rd person singular ending is brought into line with the rest of the SE verb paradigm, and thus 3rd person singular forms can still be found in the southern counties without any ending, e.g. *she wear*.

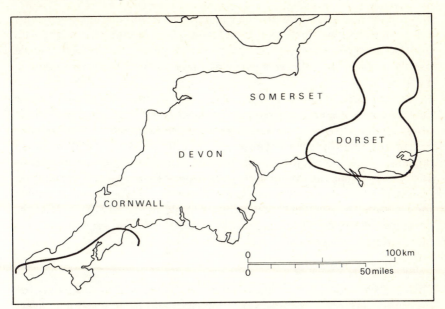

Map 5.7. General limits of periphrastic *do* (after *SED* VIII. 5.1, with permission of Mr S. F. Sanderson, Director of the Institute of Dialect and Folk Life Studies at Leeds University)

Present plural. An -(*e*)*n* ending sometimes replaces the OE -*aþ*, ME -*eth* ending in the present plural in a small area of the west midlands (mainly Derbyshire, Cheshire and Staffordshire), found already in ME times in this area: *we putten* 'we put', *han you* ...? 'have you ...?', *cutten* 'cut', *keepen* 'keep', etc. This ending is also sometimes extended to the 1st and 3rd persons singular, as in *I bin* 'I am', *I han* 'I have', *he han* 'he has', *doen he*? 'does he?'.

Present participle. An *a-* is prefixed (*a-boiling, a-riding,* etc.) in scattered places in the east midlands and west midlands as far north as Cheshire and as far west as Wiltshire and Gloucestershire, deriving from OE *on* + verbal noun (*on rīdunge,* ME *a-ridinge*).

Past participle. An *a-* is prefixed (*a-found, a-done,* etc.) mainly in the south-west, deriving from the OE prefix *ge-* (ME *y-, i-*).

Past tenses and past participles. Some verbs in dialect have, for historical reasons, obtained the vowel which historically belongs to another class, e.g., in the south-west *give* and *sit* are occasionally found with past tense and past part. *gov* and *sot*.

Archaic forms. Some verbs show interesting archaic forms in dialect. *Give* has past tense sing. *gav* in north Yorkshire; *get* has past part. *getten* and *gotten* in the north and north midlands. *Speak* has a wide variety of past tenses and past participles in addition to *speaked, spoked,* already mentioned: in the past tense *spake* is found (except in the east midlands and north); *spak* and *spok* occur in the north (*spok* also in the north midlands and the south-west); the past participle shows chiefly past tense forms – *spoke* occurs everywhere, with the short form *spok* in the north and north midlands (and south-west); the old past tense *spake* is found as past participle in rural Surrey, and *spak*, *spaken* in Yorkshire.

The verb 'to be'. This verb has a large variety of interesting forms, but we may note only one aspect here: looking at the form 'I am', we see England divided into two – *I be* in the west and *I am* in the east (and in west Cornwall: see chapter 12) – by a line roughly parallel with the ancient Watling Street boundary. *I bin* occurs in a small sub-area of the west (Shropshire and its environs), showing the *-n* ending characteristic of some west midland dialects (see above). *I are*, occurring sporadically along the *I be*/*I am* boundary and in the south-east, is an enigma but possibly a product of dialect mixing; *I is* in the north is probably derived from ON *ek es*. See map 5.8 for a summary of the distribution of these forms.

Syntax

Dialectal syntactical constructions often parallel those of SE, with only few exceptions, as far as is known. Note, however, south-western use of auxiliary *do* (page 82, above), and also south-western omission of *do* in negative commands as in *not go* 'do not go', *not wait* 'do not wait', etc. (Wakelin, 1977: 125). An apparently widespread dialectal preference (examples from Lincoln-shire, Kent and the south-west), although sparingly attested and clearly obsolescent, is for the use of the simple over the expanded form of the verb in the present tense: *the kettle boils* ('. . . is boiling'), *it rains* ('it's raining'), etc. (Wakelin 1977: 121–2). *SED* (IX.9.6) found a number of ways of expressing the notion 'whose' in the phrase 'whose uncle was drowned': *as*/*at*/*that his uncle was drowned*, *'s uncle what was drowned*, *that was his uncle drowned*, *what's uncle drowned self*, and (zero) *his uncle was drowned*. Finally, the definite and indefinite articles are sometimes distributed differently from SE: *the* is widespread before the name of an ailment (*SED* VI.5.8), and is also found before *church* (*SED* VIII.5.1) and *school* (*SED* VIII.6.1) (as in *go to the church*/*the school*) in the north. The indefinite article *a* is widespread before a numeral (*SED* VII.1.17, VII.2.8) as in *about a six*, *a one*, etc.

Vocabulary

This section will illustrate some regional lexical differences from SE by citing some among many possible examples of traditional dialect words with rela-tively clear geographical distributions. (There is regrettably no space here to illustrate traditional fishing vocabulary, for which see Elmer, 1973 and Wright, 1968.)

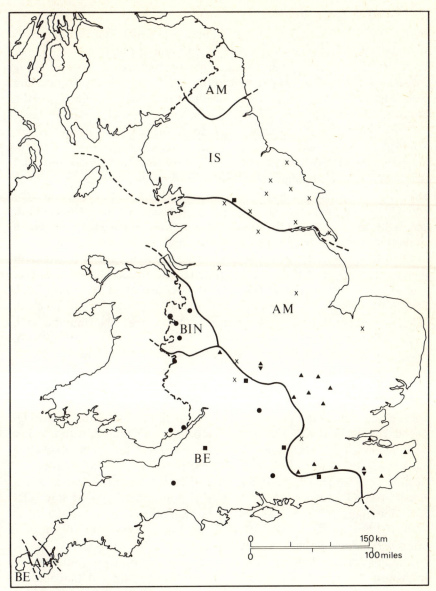

- • AM instead of usual local form
- ▪ AM as well as usual local form
- ▲ ARE instead of or as well as usual local form
- ▾ BE as well as usual local form
- × no response recorded

Map 5.8. *I am* (after *SED* IX. 7.7, with permission of Leicester University Press)

The region north of the Humber

Blushes 'blisters' (derived from OE *blyscan*, v.), now mainly restricted to Northumberland, Durham and south-east Cumbria; *cuddy* 'donkey' (? pet form of *Cuthbert*), far north and northernmost parts of North Yorkshire; *gay* (Fr *gai*), *gradely* (ON *greiðliga*), *right* (OE *rehte, rihte*), all adverbs meaning 'very', together constitute the regular northern intensifiers, *gay* mainly in the far north, *gradely* in Lancashire and *right* in Yorkshire and its non-northern environs; *ken* 'know' (OE *cennan*), now deeply eroded by its native and SE synonym *know* (OE *gecnāwan*); *poke* 'sack' (ONF *pogue, poke*), only in Northumberland, south-east Cumbria and north-west North Yorkshire, and even here clearly retreating; *ratten* 'rat' (OF *raton*) is found as far south as South Yorkshire, but is being eroded by *rat*; *side* 'clear' (the table; derived from OE *sīde*, n.) occupies most of the north except for the far north-east; *stanchions* 'door-jambs' (OF *estanchon*), only in a small area comprising south-east Northumberland, Tyne and Wear and east Durham and a strip of north North Yorkshire; *tomorn* 'tomorrow' (OE *tō-morgenne*, with retention of final nasal), widely distributed over the whole north except north Cumbria (*tomorrow*), Northumberland (*the morn*), Tyne and Wear (*morrow*); *wark* 'ache' (OE *wærcan*), cf. also *headwark* 'headache', *toothwark* 'toothache', all widely distributed; *whangs* 'boot-laces' (OE *þwang*), Northumberland, Cumbria, north-west North Yorkshire, north Lancashire, cf., further south, *thongs*, of the same derivation. *Shibbands*, literally 'shoe-bands,', is now present only in a relatively small area of north-east North Yorkshire.

The following are words adopted from the Scandinavian dialects (Wakelin, 1977: ch. 7). Some Scandinavian words which are well-distributed over the whole of the north, and penetrate into the north midlands, are: *clatch(ing)* 'brood' (of chickens; ON *klekja*), in competition in Cumbria with *laughter* (ON *lahtr*) and in Northumberland with *brood* (OE *brōd*), but extending south-east as far as north Norfolk; *clip* 'shear' (ON *klippa*), as far south-east as Norfolk; *ewer* 'udder' (ON *júðr*), but large areas of Yorkshire have *bag*, also a Norse word (ON *baggi*); *gallows* 'braces' (ON *gálgi*); *gilt* 'young sow' (ON *gyltr*), incorporates Norfolk and north-east Suffolk, and is also found in the south; *lad* 'boy' and *lass* 'girl' (both probably Norse); *teem* 'pour' (of tea, etc.; ON *tæma*); *thrang, throng* 'busy' (ON *þrǫngr*).

Scandinavian words found in a 'typical' distribution from south-east to north-west, but sometimes including south Humberside and Lincolnshire and/or excluding the far north or north-east, are: *addle* 'earn' (ON *ǫðla*); *beck* 'stream' (ON *bekkr*); *gimmer-lamb* 'ewe-lamb' (cf. ON *gymbr* + OE *lamb*); *ket* 'rubbish' (ON *kjǫt*); *laik* 'play' (ON *leika*); *lait* 'look for' (ON *leita*; but now very restricted); *lea* 'scythe' (ON *lé*); *loup* 'jump' (ON *hlǫupa*); *mun* 'must' (ON *munu*); *slape* 'slippery' (ON *sleipr*); *stee* 'ladder' (ON *stige*); *steg* 'gander' (ON *steggi*); *stithi* 'anvil' (ON *steði*) (see map 5.9).

Other Scandinavian words are found in different geographical patterns:

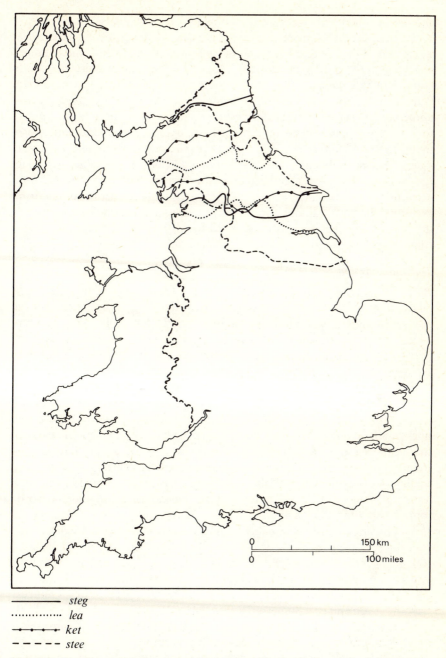

steg

lea

ket

stee

Map 5.9. Scandinavian loan-words (after *SED*, with permission of the Athlone Press)

drucken 'drunken' (ON *drukkinn*), mainly far northern areas, but extends to West Yorkshire and environs; *garth* 'paddock' (ON *garðr*) and *stackgarth* 'stackyard' (ON *stakkgarðr*), found in some areas of Yorkshire and counties to the north (cf. *garthman* 'cowman', found only in Lincolnshire and south Humberside); *gaumless* 'silly', etc. (ON *gaumr* + OE *-lēas*), Durham, north Pennine area, South and West Yorkshire; *gowk* 'fool' (ON *gaukr*), Northumberland, parts of Cumbria and west Durham; *grain* 'prong of (agricultural) fork' (ON *grein*), only in the west, but penetrates the west midlands and is also found again in Hampshire, Wiltshire, Berkshire and their western environs; *kale* 'charlock' (ON *kál*), parts of Cumbria and North Yorkshire; *lop* 'flea' (probably ON **hloppa*), restricted to the eastern half of the north, but extending into Lincolnshire; *nay* 'no' (ON *nei*), scattered areas of the north, excluding the far north, but also occurs in Leicestershire and Warwickshire – the pattern has been seriously disturbed by SE *no* (OE *nā*); *stower* 'ladder-rung' (ON *staurr*), parts of North Yorkshire only.

The midlands and East Anglia

Bing 'gangway' (in cow-house; ON *bingr*) is found only in the west midlands, an example of a Scandinavian word with a geographical distribution outside the norm; *pad* 'path' (through a field; Dutch or LG *pad*) demonstrates the midland debt to the Low Countries – now found in Lancashire, north-west North Yorkshire, west Cheshire and their environs and in south Humberside, Lincolnshire, Nottinghamshire, Leicestershire, north-east Northamptonshire and their environs, these two areas having been split by a large wedge of *path* (OE *pæþ*) driven through the centre; *snap* 'workman's snack' (apparently MDu or MLG *snappen*), found in parts of the central and north midlands and also in north-west Essex, with *bever* (AN *bever*) in parts of the south-east and the east midlands; *stale* 'handle' (of besom; OE *stalu*) is found in much of the west midlands and some of the central and south-east midlands, extending into Suffolk – *stick* (OE *sticca*) is also found in scattered areas; *tallet* 'hay-loft' (Welsh *taflod* < Latin *tabulat-*) is a west midland word, found there (and also in the south-west) in various forms – *tallent, tollet, tollent, tollart*, etc., which possibly found its way from Wales to England with travelling people such as cattle-drovers (Wakelin, 1970); *thongs* 'boot-laces' (OE *þwang*, cf. northern *whangs*, of the same origin, above), now found only in scattered areas of the west midlands and north-west midlands; *tump* 'ant-hill' (< ?) is found in the counties along the Welsh border, parts of west Gloucestershire, Avon and east Somerset; *wench* 'girl' (OE *wencel*) is found widely all over the west midlands, in competition with SE *girl* (< ?) and *lass* (Shropshire, south Staffordshire – see above); 'cow-house' is complex: *cow-house* and *cowshed* are the most widespread terms for 'cow-house', the first widely distributed, the second found mainly over the large central and southern portion of England. These two words together have pushed various other, more localized, words to the edge of the map, e.g., *byre* (OE *bȳre*) in the far north, *shippon* (OE *scypen*) in Lancashire, Cheshire and their environs and also in Devon and its environs (two residual areas remaining from a nationwide coverage), *stable* (OF *estable*) in south Humberside and north-east Lincolnshire, *mistall* (OE *mēox* 'dung' + *steall*) in West Yorkshire, *neat-house* (OE *nēat* 'cattle' + *hūs*) on the Norfolk-Suffolk boundary, *beast-house* (OF *beste* + OE *hūs*). See map 5.10 for a summary of the distribution of these forms.

Some East Anglian words are: *huh* 'askew' (OE *a-wōh* 'awry', etc.) in *on the huh*, *all on (the) one huh* from Norfolk and Essex – cf. *on the sosh* from Norfolk; *hulver* 'holly' (ME *hulfere* < ON *hulfr*), only in Norfolk; *mawr*, *mawther* 'girl' (apparently OE *mōdor*), Norfolk and Suffolk; *pit* 'pond' (OE *pytt*), found in Norfolk and east Lincolnshire, also in the west midlands and north-west, these areas having been separated by SE *pond* (OE **pund*); *push* 'boil', n., (cf. MDu, MLG *pust*), found all over East Anglia and adjacent regions to the west; *ranny* 'shrew-mouse' (apparently Latin *araneus*); *sall(y)* 'hare', Norfolk, Suffolk, Buckinghamshire and Essex (sometimes *Old Sall* or *Aunt Sally*). For substantial lists of Suffolk and Norfolk words see Claxton (1968) and Mardle (1973), respectively.

The south and south-west

Court 'farmyard' (OF *co(u)rt, curt*), parts of the south-west as far east as Wiltshire and Hampshire (also found in *courtyard* in Warwickshire and Oxfordshire), which it shares with *barton* (OE *beretūn*); *evil* 'muck-fork' (OE *gēafol*), found in Cornwall and most of Devon; *fitch* (early Du *fisse, visse, vitsche*) and *fitchew* (OF *ficheau*) 'polecat' share Devon and Cornwall, *fitch* in the south, *fitchew* in the north, *hasp* 'latch' (OE *hæpse*) is now found only in isolated areas of the south-west, where it is in competition with midland and SE *latch* (derived from OE *læccan*, v., – cf. northern and eastern *sneck* of obscure origin); *linhay* 'cart-shed' (cf. OE *hlinian* 'lean' + ?), in Devon and in small areas to the north-east and north-west, is in competition with *cart-house* (western areas from Dorset to Cumbria) and SE *cart-shed* (the south-east and Essex favour *cart-lodge*); *mow* 'stack', n. (OE *mūga*), north and south Devon, east and central Cornwall, is found beside *rick* (OE *hrēac*), which occurs throughout the central and some of the west midlands, and *stack* (ON *stakkr*), which is found in all other areas and SE; *pook* 'haycock' (< ?) is found in the counties south-west of Sussex. See further, Fischer (1976).

Many of the words cited in this section illustrate the antiquity of the English dialectal vocabulary (Wakelin, 1977: ch. 4; *WGE*), since they are of known OE origins, although such dialect words as *blush* (n.), *evil, hasp, ken, shippon* and *thongs* are now restricted to relatively small areas, while the SE equivalent, whether of OE or other origin, predominates in terms both of area and prestige.

During its history, English has borrowed copiously from other languages. Thousands of words were taken from Scandinavian sources, especially into

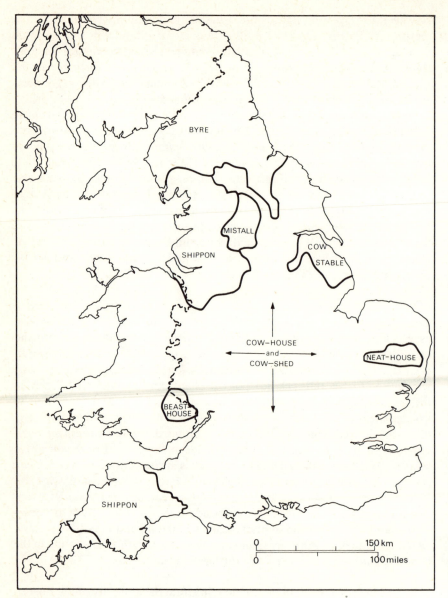

Map 5.10. Words for the cow-house (after *SED*, with permission of the Athlone Press)

the northern and eastern dialects, following upon the Viking raids (and, later, settlements) which began in the late eighth century, but many of them do not appear in the medieval records until several centuries later. Some of these, e.g. *both, ill, leg, same, they, them, their, window*, have become an indispensable part of the standard language, while others appear only in dialect, of which those listed in this section are representative examples.

Perhaps the most typical geographical distribution of Scandinavian words is a broad band across the north of England, whose northern and southern boundaries, however, fluctuate quite considerably from word to word. But some Scandinavian words extend far beyond their northern area, others are firmly restricted to parts of it, while yet others now display quite different patterns. Opposing tendencies of expansion and contraction have obviously been at work at different times.

French words also find a place in the dialectal stratum of English, deriving from the large number of such words which have come into the language from the Norman Conquest onwards. We could add many more to those cited above, and this applies too to the words cited of Low Dutch and Middle and Low German origins, stemming from the numerous contacts of the English with the Flemish and Dutch in various spheres of work and culture from the Middle Ages onwards.

There are, too, borrowings from other languages. In particular, there is a sizeable body of such words extant in west Cornwall deriving from the extinct Cornish language, which died out in the eighteenth century leaving few traces of its presence except for place names (see chapter 12). There are also a few other Celtic loans, of which *tallet* cited above is an example.

In this brief chapter I have necessarily given an overview and pointed to general features. There are a number of studies of specific regional dialects which have not been described in any detail here: for example, Campion (1976) on Lincolnshire dialects, Hedevind (1967) on Dentdale in the West Riding of Yorkshire, Kökeritz (1932) on Suffolk dialect, Orton (1933) on south Durham, Oxley (1940) on Lindsey, Parish and Hall (1957) on Sussex, Widén (1949) on Dorset and Wilson (1974) on Staffordshire. Geeson (1969) and Glauser (1974) discuss lexical aspects of Northumberland and Durham, and the Scottish-English linguistic border, respectively.

REFERENCES

Brook, G. L. 1965. *English dialects.* 2nd edn. London: André Deutsch.
Campion, G. E. 1976. *Lincolnshire dialects.* Boston: Richard Kay.
Claxton, A. O. D. 1968. *The Suffolk dialect of the twentieth century.* 3rd edn. Ipswich: Norman Adlard.
Duncan, P. 1972. Forms of the feminine pronoun in modern English dialects. In Wakelin (1972).

Ellis, A.J. 1889. *On early English pronunciation, part v: the existing phonology of English dialects.* London: EETS, ES 53.

Elmer, W. 1973. *The terminology of fishing.* Berne: Francke.

Fischer, A. 1976. *Dialects in the south-west of England: a lexical investigation.* Berne: Francke.

Geeson, C. 1969. *A Northumberland and Durham word book.* Newcastle: Harold Hill.

Glauser, B. 1974. *The Scottish-English linguistic border: lexical aspects.* Berne: Francke.

Hedevind, B. 1967. *The dialect of Dentdale in the West Riding of Yorkshire.* Uppsala: University of Uppsala.

Hughes, A. and Trudgill, P. 1979. *English accents and dialects: an introduction to social and regional variation in British English.* London: Edward Arnold.

Kökeritz, H. 1932. *The phonology of the Suffolk dialect, descriptive and historical.* Uppsala: University of Uppsala.

Kolb, E. 1966. *Phonological atlas of the northern region.* Berne: Francke.

Kolb, E., Glauser, B., Elmer, W. and Stamm, R. 1979. *Atlas of English sounds.* Berne: Francke.

Mardle, J. 1973. *Broad Norfolk.* Norwich: Wensum Books.

Orton, H. 1933. *The phonology of a south Durham dialect.* London: Kegan Paul, Trench Trubner and Co. Ltd.

Orton, H. *et al.* 1962–71. *Survey of English dialects, Introduction* and 4 vols. Leeds: E.J. Arnold.

Orton, H. and Wright, N. 1974. *A word geography of England.* London: Seminar Press.

Orton, H., Sanderson, S. and Widdowson, J. 1978. *The linguistic atlas of England.* London: Croom Helm.

Oxley, J.E. 1940. *The Lindsey dialect.* Department of English Language Texts and Monographs 8. Leeds: University of Leeds.

Pählsson, C. 1972. *The Northumbrian burr: a sociolinguistic study.* Lund: Gleerup.

Parish, W.D., revised Hall, H. 1957. *A dictionary of the Sussex dialect and collection of provincialisms in use in the county of Sussex.* Privately printed. Originally published Lewes: Farncombe and Co., 1875.

Phillips, K.C. 1976. *Westcountry words and ways.* Newton Abbot: David and Charles.

Rohrer, F. 1950. The border between the northern and north-midland dialects in Yorkshire. *Transactions of the Yorkshire Dialect Society* 8: 29–37.

Samuels, M.L. 1971. Kent and the Low Countries: some linguistic evidence. In A.J. Aitken, A. McIntosh and H. Pálsson (eds.) *Edinburgh Studies in English and Scots.* London: Longman.

Wakelin, M.F. 1970. Welsh influence in the west of England: dialectal *tallet. Folk Life* 8: 72–80.

————(ed.) 1972. *Patterns in the folk speech of the British Isles.* London: the Athlone Press.

———— 1975. *Language and history in Cornwall.* Leicester: Leicester University Press.

———— 1977. *English dialects: an introduction.* 2nd, rev. edn. London: the Athlone Press.

Wakelin, M.F. and Barry, M.V. 1968. The voicing of initial fricative consonants in present-day dialectal English. *Leeds Studies in English,* NS 2: 47–64.

Widén, B. 1949. *Studies on the Dorset dialect.* Lund: University of Lund.

Wilson, D. 1974. *Staffordshire dialect words: a historical survey.* Ashbourne: Moorland Publishing Company.

Wright, J. 1898–1905. *The English dialect dictionary*. 6 vols. Oxford: OUP.
——— 1905. *The English dialect grammar*. Oxford: OUP.
Wright, P. 1968. Fishing language around England and Wales. *Journal of the Lanca-shire Dialect Society* 17: 2–14.

6

Scottish accents and dialects

A. J. AITKEN

Scottish accents: vowel systems and realizations

The largely shared system of vowels and an indication of the widely differing selections of individual vowel phonemes by the two extreme contrasting varieties of Scottish speech are shown in table 6.1. These two varieties are: vernacular Scots, which archetypically selects according to historical Scots phonology and which is spoken by speakers of group 3 and, especially, group 4, (these groups are described in chapter 30, pages 521–2), and Standard English (SE) or rather, its Scottish variant, Scottish Standard English (SSE), or the 'educated' variety of this, Educated Scottish Standard English (ESSE), the Scottish variants of World Standard English. There exists also a very large body of Scottish speakers who variously compromise – in system, realizations, selections – between the fully vernacular variety of Scots presented in column 2 of the table and the Scottish Standard English of column 4. By way of comparison, there is given in column 5 the Anglo-English System (after Abercrombie, 1979: tables 5.1 and 5.2), here that of RP, of vowels in general and of 'vowel + r'.

A sketch of the underlying history of the Scottish system is given in Aitken (1977), where (also in Aitken, 1981a) the rationale for the choice of numbers for the various Scots vowel phonemes (see column 1 of the table) is suggested. How it was that Scottish Standard English speakers came to speak the SE DIALECT with the Scottish ACCENT presented here is explained briefly in Aitken (1979a: 99f).

Those accents which are in effect hybrids or compromises between the Scottish Standard English system of column 3 and the RP system of column 5 are identified at chapter 30, page 526, and described and discussed in Abercrombie (1979: 75–81) and Aitken (1979a: 110–14).

The Scottish Vowel-length Rule

As well as sharing the system of vowels of column 3 of Table 6.1 to the extent shown, all varieties of Scottish speech, from the fullest vernacular to Educated Scottish Standard English, operate in some measure the Scottish Vowel-length Rule (SVLR), of which a fairly detailed account is now available in

Table 6.1. *Systems and selections of Scottish vowels*

1. Vowel Number	2. Vernacular Scots	3. Scots vowel	4. Standard English (including Scottish Standard English)	5. Anglo-English
8a	ay 'always', gey 'very', May, pay, way			
10	quoit, avoid, join, point, oil, choice, poison	ɔi		
1*s*	bite, bide, price, wife, tide		bite, bide, price, wife, tide	aɪ / aɪə(ɹ)
1*l*	five, size, fry, aye 'yes', kye 'cows', fire	a·e	five, size, fry, eye, die, lie, tied, fire	
2	meet, need, queen, see, seven, devil, here	i	meet, need, queen, see, meat, steal, here	iː / ɪə(ɹ)
11	ee 'eye', dee 'die', dree 'endure', lee 'untruth'			
3	meat, breath, dead, head, steal, pear, mear 'mare, female horse'	(Merges with 2, 4, or 8, in vernacular dialects)		
4	ake, 'oak', ate 'oat', bate 'boat', sape 'soap', baith 'both', hame 'home', stane 'stone', hale 'whole', tae 'toe', gae 'go', twae 'two' (South-eastern dialects); late, pale, bathe, day, say, away, mare 'more', care	e	late, pale, bathe, day, say, away, May, pay, way, care, mare 'female horse', pear	eɪ
8	bait, braid, hail, pail, pair	eː (in many Central Scots dialects merged with 4)	bait, braid, hail, pail, pair	εə(ɹ)

Table 6.1. (*cont.*)

1. Vowel Number	2. Vernacular Scots	3. Scots vowel	4. Standard English (including Scottish Standard English)	5. Anglo-English
5	throat, coat, thole 'endure', rose, before	oː (merges with 18 in some, e.g. Central and South Scots, vernacular dialects)	throat, coat, rose, before, oak, oat, boat, soap, both, home, stone, whole, toe, go, shoulder, old, cold, mow, snow, grow, over, solder colt, roll, more, Forth	oʊ / ɔə(ɹ)
18	cot, God, on, loch, bocht /boxt/ 'bought', horse, Forth	o		
6	about, bouk 'bulk', poupit 'pulpit', loud, powder, shouder 'shoulder', room, mouth, house, louse, cow, now, fou 'full', pou 'pull', plow 'plough', oo /u/ 'wool', hour, sour	u	boot, fruit, moon, pool, rule, loose, poor, do, chew, blue, true, two, moor, sure	uː / ʊə(ɹ)
			put, good, hook, room, full, pull, wool, pulpit	ʊ
7	boot, fruit, good, muin 'moon', use (n.), use (v.), love, do, moor, poor, sure	ø (North Mainland: merged with 2, Central and South Scots: merged or merging with 4 (SVLR long), 15 (SVLR short).)		
9	Boyd, choice, noise, boy, joy	oi		

Table 6.1. (*cont.*)

1. Vowel Number	2. Vernacular Scots	3. Scots vowel	4. Standard English (including Scottish Standard English)	5. Anglo-English
9a		ɔe	Boyd, noise, boy, joy, quoit, avoid, join, point, oil, choice, poison	ɔɪ
12	faut 'fault', saut 'salt', fraud, mawn 'mown', auld 'old', cauld 'cold', hauch 'meadow', cause, law, snaw 'snow', aw 'all', faw 'fall', twaw 'two' (except in the south-east) far, daur 'dare', waur 'worse'	a: (in some Northern vernacular dialects merged with 17) ɔː		
12a		ɔ	bought, fault, salt, fraud, cause, law, all, fall, war	ɔː ɔə(ɹ)
18a			cot, God, on, loch, golf, knoll, horse	ɒ
13	nowt 'cattle', cowt /kʌut/ 'colt', gowf 'golf', sowder '/sʌudɪr/ 'solder', louse 'loose', chow 'chew', grow, know /knʌu/ 'knoll', four, owre 'over', row 'roll'	ʌu	about, loud, powder, mouth, house, louse, cow, now, plough, bough, hour, sour	aʊ aʊə(ɹ)
14	duty, feud, rule, heuk 'hook', neuk, beuch 'bough', teuch 'tough', news, dew, few, blue, true, plewis 'ploughs'	iu / ju	duty, feud, news, dew, few, use (n.), use (v.), cure	juː jʊə(ɹ)

Table 6.1. (*cont.*)

1. Vowel Number	2. Vernacular Scots	3. Scots vowel	4. Standard English (including Scottish Standard English)	5. Anglo-English
15	bit, put, lid, hiss, give, gird 'hoop', his, next, whether, yird 'earth', fir	ɪ†	bit, lid, hiss, give, his, fir	ɪ 3ː(ɹ)
16a		ɛ̈	seven, devil, next, whether, earth	ε
16	met, bed, leather, meh 'cry of sheep', serve, Perth, Ker	ε	met, bed, leather, breath, dead, head, leaven, revel, vex, serve, Perth, defer, Ker	
17	sat, lad, man, jazz, vase, warst, mar	a (see vowel 12 above)	sat, lad, man, jazz / vase, far, mar	æ / ɑː ɑː(ɹ)
18	See vowel 5 above	o		
18a		ɔ	See vowel 12 above	ɒ
19	butt, bud, bus, buff, buzz, word, fur	ʌ†	butt, bud, bus, buff, buzz, love, bulk, tough, word, worse, worst, fur	ʌ / 3ː(ɹ)

The continuance or non-continuance of horizontal ruled lines from either column 2 or column 4 across column 3 or column 5 signifies the presence or absence of phonemic distinction. Where a compartment is left vacant there is no selection of the phoneme in question, or the phoneme does not occur in the specified variety.
† not subject to SVLR

Aitken (1981a). [What Aitken modestly refers to as the SVLR is now very widely labelled by other writers on Scots – see, for example, chapter 7 of this volume – 'Aitken's Law'. – Ed.] SVLR potentially affects most Scots vowels except 15 and 19, and, in many dialects, 8 and 12. The vowels affected display a two-way variation between long duration in 'long' environments and short duration in 'short' environments, the regular long environments being: a following voiced fricative, /r/ or a morpheme boundary, all of these either final or followed by a consonant constituting a second morpheme. Thus we find, e.g., [lif] *leaf*, [bit] *beat*, [bid] *bead*, [fil] *feel*, [fild] *field* and [grid] *greed*, in the short environments, and, on the other hand, [liːv] *leave*, [diːr] *dear*, [ʌˈgriː] *agree*, etc., and [ʌˈgriːd] *agreed* (i.e. /ʌˈgri≠d/), in the long environments. Other curiosities thrown up by the Rule are [ˈfiːləin] *feline* beside [ˈfilɪŋ] *feeling* and [ˈlaˑedo] *lido* beside [ˈsəidl̩] *sidle*; but hiatus invariably realizes longs, as [ˈhiːetʌs] *hiatus*.

In some dialects the Rule has brought about phonemic splits. In a wide area of central Scotland vowel 7 no longer exists as a separate phoneme. Its lexical inventory has divided between vowel 4 [eː] in precisely the SVLR long environments, and vowel 15 [ɪ] in precisely the SVLR short environments. So in these dialects *moor* (originally vowel 7) and *mare* 'more' (vowel 4) are homophones, as also are *too* (vowel 7) and *tae* 'toe' (vowel 4), *ruize* 'praise' (vowel 7) and *raise* (vowel 8 or vowel 4), in the long environments, all with /e/ (i.e. [eː]); similarly for *boot* (vowel 7) and *bit* (vowel 15), *suit* and *sit*, *spoon* and *spin*, *fool* and *fill*, *school* and *skill* in the short environments, all with /ɪ/. In virtually all dialects, too, the long and short variants of vowel 1 can only be regarded as now displaying two distinct phonemes. One phoneme is realized as a slow diphthong, [aˑe] or the like, mostly in the long environments, 1*l* in table 6.1, as in *five*, *rise*, *fire*, *dry*, etc., *tied*, but also displays such irregularities as [saˑeθ] *scithe* and [kʌnˈsaˑes] *concise*. The other phoneme is realized as a fast diphthong, [əi] or the like, mostly in the short environments, 1*s* in table 6.1, as in *Fife, rice, bite, tide* etc. but also displays irregularities in [wəivz] *wives*, [ləivz] *lives* etc., and optionally [səiθ] *scithe* and [kʌnˈsəis] *concise*.

It will be seen that the vowel system of Scots and of Scottish Standard English possesses items, viz. the item comprising 1*s*, 10 and 8a, and vowel 16a, absent in other varieties of English; for further discussion of 16a see Abercrombie (1979: 74–5) and Aitken (1979a: 103, and 118 n. 13). Conversely, 18a is shared with other non-Scots varieties but NOT with the most conservative varieties of vernacular Scots, whose speakers adhere to 18, in some dialects merged with 5. For other ways in which Scots and Scottish Standard English differ from non-Scottish accents, in possessing fewer vowel phonemes at vowel 6 and vowel 17, but in maintaining pre-*r* vowel oppositions lost by non-rhotic accents of English, see Abercrombie (1979: 72–81) and Aitken (1979a: 100–101).

On the vernacular side of the system, in the North Mainland and North-eastern vernacular dialects (and in that of a small South-eastern pocket: see Mather, 1980: 34–5), vowel 7 has been disposed of, but quite differently from Central Scots as described above. In these northern dialects vowel 7 has long since (before the early sixteenth century) merged with vowel 2, in *beet* 'boot', *bleed* 'blood', *meen* 'moon', *eese* (nˈ) /is/ 'use', *eeze* (v.) /iz/ (i.e. [iːz]) 'use', *seer* /sir/)sure', *dee* 'do', *geed* or *gweed* 'good', *keet* or *kweet* 'ankle' /kit/ or /kwit/ (elsewhere *cuit* /køt/ or /kɪt/), *skeel* or *squeel* 'school'. So in these dialects *boot* and *beet* (the plant) are homophones, as [bit], as are *blood* and *bleed*, and *poor* (vowel 7), *pier* (vowel 2), *peer* (vowel 2), *pear* (vowel 3), as [piːr]. Some other mergers which have taken place in some vernacular dialects are shown in table

Table 6.2. *Variety of system in Scottish dialects*

	Vowel number	ESSE	Central Scots vernacular	Some Angus vernacular	Some North-eastern and Northern vernacular
meet	2	i	i	i	i
boot, soot	7	u (6)	ɪ	ø	
bit, sit	15	ɪ		ɪ	ɪ
gate	4	e	e	e	e
bait, wait	8			eː	
coat	5	o	o	oː	o
cot, lot	18 / 18a	ɔ		o	
caught, saut 'salt', salt	12		ɔ	aː	a
cat, sat	17	a	a	a	
about	6	ʌu (13)	u	u	u

6.2, which illustrates also the principal distinctions maintained by the more conservative dialects. More detailed displays of system variety over a larger part of the system, with more precisely specified realizations, can be seen in Catford (1957a: 113), Mather (1964: 41–4) and additional instances in Aitken (1981a; especially section 6).

Realizations

Pace the detailed exceptions which the *Linguistic Atlas of Scotland*, vol. 3 (*LAS* 3) will doubtless display when it appears, there are some realizational characteristics of vowels which do seem regionally and socially widespread in Scotland, taking in both the vernacular dialects and the more conservative or 'fully Scottish' forms of Educated Scottish Standard English. These are the characteristic Scottish close realization (near to Cardinal Vowel 1) of /i/ (vowel 2); and monophthongal (and near to Cardinal vowels 2 and 7, respectively) realizations of /e/ (vowel 4) and /o/ (vowel 5 or 18) (except when a sonorant consonant follows).

Most dialects in the central Scotland area have half-open peripheral realizations (near to Cardinal vowel 3) of /ɛ/ (vowel 16). In the north-east, however, a noticeably closer realization of this is found, [ẹ]. Conversely, the dialects of the south-east and south (the Border region) favour an opener diaphone of vowel 16, commonly symbolized as [æ]. Indeed, these dialects commonly have open realizations of all the low vowels, 16 (/ɛ/), 17 (/a/) and 12 (/aː/): vowel 16, with [æ], in *met, bed, penny, leather, heafer*; vowel 17, maintaining its distance with [ɑ] or [ɒ] in *cat, lad, man, lather, gaffer*; vowel 12 with [ɑː] or [ɒː] (or, often, merged with 17: see e.g. Wettstein, 1942 and Catford, 1957a) in *saut* 'salt', *maun* 'must', *hauf* 'half'. In some at least of the same dialects vowel 19 /ʌ/ is realized as [ä] or [ɐ]. Like many other (? especially East) Scots dialects, Border Scots realizes vowel 15 /ɪ/ as (more or less) [ɛ]. Thus is manifested the wide-mouthed or 'big-moo'ed' articulatory set of this dialect, of which some of its speakers are consciously aware (Mather, 1974: 50). It will be observed that vowel 16 in particular presents more and more open realizations as one moves south from Aberdeenshire.

Most Scottish dialects appear to favour realizations of vowel 15 /ɪ/ as half-open and/or centralized front vowels such as [ɛ], [ë], [ɜ], so that vernacular speakers with local accents differ audibly in this respect from their middle-class Educated Scottish Standard English-speaking neighbours with closer, RP-like [ɪ]. In Caithness and in central Scotland, including Glasgow and Edinburgh, vernacular speakers commonly realize vowel 6 fronter than else-where (or than local Educated Scottish Standard English speakers) as [ü] or [ÿ]. This may be selected not only for vernacular items such as *aboot* 'about' /ʌ'but/, *hoose* 'house' /hus/, but also for SE forms such as *boot, good, poor* /but/, etc. These realizations [hÿs], [bÿt], etc., are nevertheless realizations of vowel 6, not, as some have supposed, vowel 7, which in the Central Scots dialects, for instance, appears as [ɪ] or [eː]: [bɪt] *buit* 'boot', [peːr] *puir* 'poor'. These features are referred to again, as 'vulgarisms', on page 108, below.

Unstressed syllables and weak forms

Space is lacking to deal with phenomena affecting 'unstressed' syllables, such as 'vowel harmony' (Dieth, 1932: §§ 83–91; Hill, 1963: 452–5) and 'terminal stress' (Wettstein, 1942: § 60; Aitken, 1981a: 149), or with 'weak forms', for which I can only refer to dialect monographs, for example, those of Murray (1873: 134f), Grant and Dixon (1921: 63–5), Watson (1923: 31f), Dieth (1932: §§95–99), Zai (1942: §230–40), and, especially, Wettstein (1942: §72); see also J.Y. Mather's essays and, for Scottish Standard English only, Abercrombie (1979: 83).

Scottish accents: consonant systems and realizations

I merely recall here the following well-known Scottish features: / ʍ ~ w/ in *while* ~ *wile*; non-initial /x/ in *braw bricht moonlicht nicht* and in *Brechin, Buchan, technical, patriarch, Bach, loch* – as a prominent Scottish shibboleth this feature is not likely to disappear as it almost has in northern England (Wakelin, 1972: 101); and 'rhotacism'; and the well-known North-eastern /f/ for *wh-* as in *fa fuppit the fite fulpie?* ('who whipped the white dog(gy)?').

In most varieties of Scots speech initial voiceless plosives have little or no aspiration, whereas final voiceless plosives do: so [pitʰ] *peat*, [tikʰ] *teak*; this does not happen, however, in Caithness (see Mather, 1973: 58). Except in Caithness, Orkney, Shetland and Galloway, where clear or palatalized *l* and *n* appear to be the rule, other parts of Scotland favour dark realizations of *l*, which may be alveolar pre-vocalic, dental post-vocalic, so [ɫuɫu] *Lulu*, [ɫip] *leap*, [miɫ] *meal*. There is wide variation, both allophonic (and perhaps 'free') and also diaphonic, in realizations of *r*, including 'one tap', fricative and frictionless alveolars (and in some environments dentals), and, in a sizeable minority of speakers, not apparently local to any one area, uvular realizations also; the north mainland, and middle-class Edinburgh speakers, especially female, use a retroflex frictionless [ɻ] with or without lip-rounding (Mather, 1978: 8–9, 12–13); some middle-class speakers realize /r/ as a voiceless frictionless velar before alveolars, e.g. in *fort, ford, forth*. True, some rural speakers and others still retain in all environments the voiced alveolar trill popularly supposed to be characteristically Scottish.

Sporadic realization of the voiceless plosives /p/, /t/, /k/, when non-initial, with accompanying glottal closure or simply as the glottal stop [ʔ], formerly (*c.* 1900) believed to be a peculiarity of Glasgow speech (see, e.g., Aitken, 1982: 32, 34), is now widespread, at least as far north as Wick, and is perhaps absent in most regions only in speakers who are both elderly and conservative. This, especially when in the intervocalic position, is the most strongly and overtly stigmatized feature of 'gutter Scots': see further page 108, below and chapter, 30, page 529.

A number of other local consonant system and realization features are mentioned and illustrated in the various writings of J.Y. Mather listed among the References, also in Catford (1957b), Nicholson (1907: 61–3), Grant (1934), Dieth (1932), Wettstein (1942) and Zai (1942).

Suprasegmental features

Abercrombie (1979) has some remarks on intonation ('in Scotland almost certainly more varied than in England'), syllable division ('Scottish speakers make as many syllables open syllables as possible'), and rhythm; a description of one type of Scottish intonation is provided in McClure (1980). Apart from one investigation of voice quality in Edinburgh males (Esling, 1978), virtually nothing has been published on articulatory set and voice quality in any form of Scottish speech.

Selectional phonology

Column 2 of table 6.1 exemplifies some of the most characteristic of the vowel selections of vernacular Scots – those which differentiate vernacular Scots dialects generally (and in most instances northern dialects of England also: see below) from SE. To these characteristic vowel selections fall to be added large numbers of consonant selections similarly affecting all Scottish dialects and in most cases northern dialects of England as well, for example: Scots /ŋ/, SE /ŋg/ in *single, English, longer* (Scots *langer*); *rummle* (SE *rumble*), *chaumer* (SE *chamber*); *stoppit, jaggit, jaggt, ahint* (SE *behind*), *heelant* (SE *highland*); *fowrt* /fʌurt/ (SE *fourth*), *fift* (SE *fifth* but SSE *fift*); *lenth, strenth, fin* (SE *find*), *ahin* (SE *behind*), *blin* (SE *blind*), *han* (SE *hand*), *gran* (SE *grand*), *cannle* (SE *candle*), *thunner* (SE *thunder*); *birk* (SE *birch*), *kirk* (SE *church*), *caff* (SE *chaff*), *sic* (SE *such*); *brig* (SE *bridge*), *seg* (SE *sedge*); *doo* /du/ (SE *dove*), *hae* (SE *have*), *gie* (SE *give*), *deil* (also *deevil*) (SE *devil*), *ein* (SE *even*), *mou* /mu/ (SE *mouth*).

At a more local level, the interlacing and tangled bunches of isoglosses encompassing the several individual members of phonologically related word-sets within Scotland result similarly from earlier sound-changes, failures to sound-change and borrowings of cognates, especially from Old Scandinavian and Middle Flemish, events similar to those which produced the more widely distributed selectional northernisms just instanced. These more localized selectional differences include the dialectally divergent treatments of vowel 7 (see page 99, above), and of vowel 3 which, in all but the North Mainland dialects, had its lexical inventory variously re-distributed to vowels 2 and 4 in different regions (see Aitken, 1977: 8). Among the results of more 'combinative' sound-changes are the differing selections of the Scots vernacular equivalents of *two, who, where*, as *twaw, whaw* or *fa, whaur* or *far* with vowel 12, in all dialects except the South-eastern, and, in the south-east, *twae, whae, whare* with (regular) vowel 4 (see further Aitken, 1971: 187 and n. 31). (Other 'combinative' sound-changes are mentioned in Aitken, 1977: 10; Dieth, 1932: § 23, § 69.) For comprehensive lists of such features see Grant (1934: xvi–xli) and, on a more modest scale, Murison (1977: 32–6); see also the dialect monographs of Murray (1873), Wilson (1915, 1923, 1926), Watson (1923), Dieth (1932), Wettstein (1942) and Zai (1942), who detail those affecting their own regions.

Vocabulary

Like many of the selectional northernisms discussed above many 'Scots words' which Scots imagine to be peculiarly their own are still or until recently have been (see page 112, below and Glauser, 1974 *passim*) current in other nonstandard dialects of English, especially of course those of northern England. They include many well-known Scandinavianisms – *bairn, brae, gate* 'road', *kirk, lass, big* 'build', etc., and many items of other origins, for example, *cleugh* 'ravine', *haugh, heugh* 'steep slope', *canny, bonny, fozie* 'soft, spongy, flabby', *greet* 'weep', *loun* 'boy', *jag* 'prick', the idiom *let on* 'to admit to knowing', etc. Yet there is also a considerable, but, one guesses, rather smaller number which have always had their southern limit of distribution close to or within the Scottish border: Gaelicisms such as *airt* 'direction', *ingle* 'household fire', *oe* 'grandchild'; Gallicisms like *deval* 'stop', *douce* 'gentle', *vennel* 'lane in a town'; words from the Netherlands, Anglo-Saxonisms such as *beadle* 'sexton' and *but and ben*; and others. For a brief account of some of the principal etymological layers of both of these sorts of vocabulary see Murison (1977: 48–55).

As well as these more or less country-wide expressions, there exist also, as *LAS* 1 and 2, Glauser (1974), and several local dialect descriptions evidence, fairly numerous localized items of vocabulary. Some, but far from all, of these can be seen to result from the favouring by certain areas of particular etymological layers of influence, as a consequence of the special history of the locality. We therefore have Scandinavian items in Shetland, Orkney and Caithness (see chapters 22 and 30 of this volume; see also, especially, Nicholson, 1907; Jakobsen, 1928, 1932; Marwick, 1929; Murison, 1977: 36). There are Dutch items in Shetland (Murison, 1971: 175–6); Anglo-Irish in Galloway (Riach 1979, 1980); Gaelic in some northern (see Nicholson, 1907) and north-eastern areas and in Kintyre; Romani and Cant items in the Borders (Watson, 1923: 344; Mather, 1980: 41 and chapters 23–4).

Grammar

Until recently, 'grammars' of Scots have dealt almost exclusively in distinctive Scottish features of morphology and in lists of closed class items and of idioms. The fullest of these treatments are Murray (1873: 150–230) and Grant and Dixon (1921: 75–196), the latter including a section on word-formation; there are more selective sketches in Wilson (1915, 1923, 1926), Robertson and Graham (1952), Murison (1977: 38–47) and Graham (1977: 14–18).

Not a few of the features itemized in these accounts, like some of the selectional forms and vocabulary items in the same descriptions prescribed as 'good Scots' or, really, 'Ideal Scots' (see the discussion of 'Ideal Scots', page 522 and 'Good and Bad Scots', page 529), are now quite recessive and seldom heard outside conservative rural fastnesses and/or by group 4 speakers, though all are of course to be found in earlier and some modern vernacular literature. Some other grammatical features are discussed with the 'Covert Scotticisms' and 'Vulgarisms' described below. Some of the remainder which are still in fairly widespread and general use by groups 3 and 4 speakers, or as stylistic overt Scotticisms (see page 107, below) are the following: the irregular noun plurals *een* 'eyes', *shuin* 'shoes', *kye* 'cows' (and there are others more recessive); a three-term deictic system *this*, pl. *thir*, *that* pl. *thae*, *yon* (or *thon*), unchanged in the plural (Northern dialects also have unchanged plurals *this* and *that*); the numeral 'one' opposing its attributive (*ae*, *yae* (*man*)) to its absolute form ((*that*) *ane*, *yin*, *een*, *wan*). The forms of the negative differ from SE: clitic *-na*, *-nae* (*-ny*); isolate *no* (North-eastern *nae*). The syntax of verbs differs from SE:

Indicative: They say he's feart (/fɪrt/ 'scared')
    Thae laddies says he's feart
    Them that says he's feart
    They were feart
    Twaw weemen that wes there tellt me
Habitual: Every time I sees him I aye thinks that
Narrative: 'Heh! Wullie!' he shouts and belts aff efter him

The auxiliary *have* may ellipse after a modal or the infinitive-marker *to*, e.g., *I soud never gaen awaw.*

In Ideal Scots and some vernacular (group 3 and group 4) Scots, the forms of past tenses and past participles differ in numerous verbs from SE: lists are to be found in all of the 'grammars' mentioned above.

More localized items include the use in Shetland of gender-marked 3rd person personal pronouns (especially the masculine) for inanimates, as in *He* (the tub) *was half-filled with water, Pit her* (the kettle) *on da fire, He* (the weather) *was blaain half a gale.* The 2nd person singular personal pronoun *thou, thee* /ðu/ (Shetland /du/), /ði/ (Shetland /di/), formerly in general use as an intimate, or disparaging (and liturgical) pronoun of address, has been receding before the original plural forms *ye, you*, since the sixteenth century; it now survives in Shetland, Orkney and parts of North Mainland Scotland (including the Black Isle). The recession of the formerly general distinction between the present participle *-an* (/-an/ or /-ɪn/) and verbal noun *-in* (/-ɪn/ or /-in/), as in Grant's example, *He's aye gutteran aboot, He's fond o gutterin aboot* (both of these with vowel harmony in some dialects), has proceeded less far in the south: the distinction continues to be operated in Shetland, Orkney and North Mainland Scots and in Roxburghshire and East Dumfriesshire.

Covert Scotticisms

Most Scottish people are aware that the characteristic northern or exclusively Scottish locutions we have instanced above are either 'Scots' or 'slang' (see chapter 30, page 529). Yet it appears that there is also a substantial class of undoubtedly Scottish or, in some cases, northern English and Scottish expressions which seldom evokes either of these responses from native Scottish speakers. The extensiveness and actual membership of this class most probably varies from speaker to speaker and most probably in a way generally related to the usual social groupings. The following accounts for what appears to be in the main a common core of such expressions, used by a very wide social range of speakers, including middle-class Educated Scottish Standard English speakers. Expressions of this sort, which Scottish speakers use unselfconsciously, wholly or largely unaware that in so doing they are behaving peculiarly Scottishly or 'giving themselves away' as Scots, might be called 'unaware' or 'unmarked' Scotticisms: I have preferred 'covert Scotticism'.

Conversely, where a speaker is aware of an item's Scottishness, I have called it an 'overt Scotticism'.

Some, perhaps now a majority, of covert Scotticisms are optional alternatives to their 'English' equivalents: so the notion of the Scotticism *to mind* can alternatively be expressed by its standard equivalent *to remember*, *to sort* by *to mend*, the absolute pronoun *mines* equally be realized by *mine*, and *I'll better* (attend to it) by *I'd better*. These, therefore, take their appropriate places in columns 1 and 5 of table 30.1 on page 520. But there are others of this group which lack in speech available 'English' alternatives at all: the only modal of permission, for most Scots in informal speech (including many habitual Scottish Standard English speakers) is the verb *can*; *may* is not an option for them. Their only means of referring to a brook is by the noun *burn* or to the little finger as one's *pinkie*. As well as being covert Scotticisms, then, the latter are 'obligatory' Scotticisms. They are, however, obligatory only in un-bookish or informal speech. Indeed, in formal written English the category 'covert Scotticism' ceases to exist and virtually all its members are disallowed; in other words, as a rule Scots WRITE (and speak formally) standard literary English, with at most only a very occasional inadvertent 'covert Scotticism' and a few 'overt Scotticisms'.

Covert Scotticisms of selectional phonology are not very numerous. An apparent condition of entry to the set is that the phonological contrast with the corresponding non-Scottish SE form be slight and unobtrusive, i.e., that the differentiated segment should share most of its distinctive features with the non-Scottish SE segment it replaces. Instances are *lenth* /lɛnθ/ and *strenth* /strɛnθ/ (Anglo-English *length* /lɛŋθ/, /strɛŋθ/), *fift* etc. for *fifth*, trisyllabic *Wednesday*, and 'equal-stressed' pronunciations of *porpoise* and *tortoise* (for a more extensive list see Aitken, 1979a: 104–5). Some items – including the three last – are obligatory for all speakers, others for some speakers only. Among lexical Scotticisms, it is doubtful if alternative renderings for the following would readily occur to most Scots: *ashet* (large serving-plate), *bramble*, *haar* (sea-mist), *rone* (horizontal gutter on a house), *rowan* (mountain-ash), *to jag* (prick), *to swither* (hesitate) and, as we have seen, *burn* and *pinkie*; and numerous special constructions, applications and idioms, such as *I'm away to my bed*, *How's he keeping?* (= how is his health?), *to miss oneself* (to miss a treat), and other examples listed at Aitken (1979a: 106). A morphological covert Scotticism is the absolute pronoun *mines*. The other morphological Scotticisms mentioned or alluded to on page 104 mostly wear their Scottishness on their sleeve and so remain 'overt' and, largely, exclusively vernacular in their distribution. But there are many peculiarities of Scots syntax which differ rather strikingly from Anglo-English usage yet operate as covert, and mostly obligatory, Scotticisms.

In negative constructions Scots often reduces the operator rather than the negative, and prefers to do so with *will* and, especially, *be*: *He's no/not going*, *He'll no/not go*, *Is he no/not going?*, are preferred to *He isnae/isn't going*, *He willnae/won't go*; and **Isnae/isn't he going?* rarely, if ever, occur; similarly with *Will* (also *can*) *he no/not come?* rather than *Won't/can't he come?* (while **Willnae/cannae he come?* are scarcely possible, at least in Central Scots). *Shall, may* and *ought* hardly occur. As we noted above the permissive sense of *may* is expressed by *can* – *Can I come as well?*, the possibility sense by means of the adverb *maybe* – *He'll maybe come later*. Yet *should, might* and *must* do occur, though in a more limited range of uses than in other varieties of English: e.g., *You should go and see that play, You might let me have it, He must have forgotten to come*. Obligation is expressed by *have to* or *have got to*: *You'll have to find the money, You've got to do it. I'll better* may replace *I'd better* (*do it*). *Be to* (= be intended to) has a more complete paradigm than in other kinds of English: *He was to have been to do it*. Other Scotticisms of 'modal' and other verb usage, and of the forms of the relative pronouns, are instanced in Aitken (1979a: 105) and, more fully, in Millar and Brown (1979), Brown and Millar (1980), Miller (1980) and Miller and Brown (1982), from which reports the foregoing is largely drawn.

Overt Scotticisms

There exists a second type of Scotticism which resembles the covert Scotticism in not being restricted to the more vernacular and more working-class varieties of Scots speech and to vernacular literature: this we might dub the 'stylistic overt Scotticism'. Stylistic overt Scotticisms are used for special stylistic effect – as a deliberate deviation from normal style – by those whose regular or expected speech is Scottish Standard English (columns 3 to 5 in table 1 of chapter 30), that is by group 1 or group 2 Scottish Standard English speakers (the groups are described in chapter 30 also) and also by other Scots on formal occasions when an 'English' style is expected, for example, in a public speech or a piece of discursive writing. Frequently, though variably – by males perhaps more often than females, and especially, though not only, on occasions when it seems desirable to claim membership of the in-group of Scots, at a Burns Society meeting let us say – Scottish Standard English speakers will intentionally depart from their regular 'English' by selecting Scottish-marked expressions. This includes a large number of traditional vernacular Scots words and word-forms, e.g., *aye* [aˑe] for *yes*, *dinna* for *don't*, *hame* and *hoose* and *ben the hoose*; not, however, those stigmatized localisms which are regarded as 'vulgarisms'. In addition there exist for this purpose a substantial number of expressions which seem to occur most frequently, or only, under 'stylistic overt Scotticism' conditions. Paradoxically, that is, these are expressions of traditional Scottish origin, and overtly marked as of Scottish provenance, which are employed for special stylistic purposes only by Scots whose habitual speech otherwise disfavours vernacular Scottish elements, or by any Scot in an English-using register (such as public speaking); they are largely confined to use by 'English-speaking' not 'Scots-speaking' Scots. From the much larger list of instances in Aitken (1979a: 107–8) we may mention: *to keep a calm sough* ('not to get excited'), *it's back to the auld claes and parritch tomorrow* (or *the morn*), *darg* ('job of work'), *kenspeckle* ('conspicuous'), *thrang* ('busy'), and *stravaig* ('to wander aimlessly'). It is not too difficult to understand how this comes about. It is, after all, the 'educated' (and therefore Educated Scottish Standard English using) Scot who is also concerned for and informed about such esoteric subjects as the native literary tradition and the more or less archaic forms of Scots which are part of this.

The range of both obligatory covert and stylistic overt Scotticisms is not homogeneous throughout Scotland, but displays local variation with the local dialects. In particular, stylistic overt Scotticisms often display specifically local as well as simply Scottish allusion, such as the ritual use by middle-class Orkney or Shetland or Caithness speakers of local shibboleths such as *peerie* or *peedie* 'little' or Caithness *cown* /kʌun/ 'weep', or the middle-class north-easterner's ritual greeting in North-eastern 'Scots' to a friend from the same region: *Foo are ee, min?*, with its equally ritual response: *Jist chaavin*.

Vulgarisms

As is suggested in chapter 30, pages 529–30, virtually any identifiably verna-cular Scots feature, except as described in the two preceding sections, is liable to latent disapproval or open condemnation by some Scots under any circum-stances of spoken use, and by many, perhaps most, Scots under some quite common circumstances of interlocution (e.g., in a school classroom or on a grand social occasion). There exists also a more circumscribed set of specific features of Scots speech whose explicit condemnation even by enthusiasts for 'Good Scots' is an entrenched part of the linguistic mythology of Scotland (Aitken 1979a: 102–4, 108–10, 118, also Aitken, 1981b: 84–6 and Aitken, 1982). These are the features commonly specified as markers of 'Bad Scots' (see, e.g., Murison 1977: 56–7; also chapter 30 of this volume, page 529) and commonly (and correctly) localized to working-class speech of the larger cities, though they are by no means confined to these areas (see especially Aitken, 1982: 34). These explicitly stigmatized Scotticisms I label 'vulgarisms'.

A number of realization features already mentioned figure prominently among them: the glottal stop realization (the most notorious of all Scottish 'vulgarisms', and constantly condemned from 1895 till today), lowered and centralized realizations of vowel 15, fronted realizations of vowel 6; another such feature is the epenthetic vowel described by Dieth (1932: § 82), Wettstein (1942: § 59) and Aitken (1979a: 103–4, 118). Some selectional word-forms which are sometimes openly commented on and are clearly similarly dis-favoured are ['sʌmhɪn] or ['sʌmhm] *something*, ['nʌhɪn] or ['nʌhn̩] *nothing* and the realization of *thr-* as [ʂr-], [çɹ-] or [ɻ], as in [çɹiː] *three*, ['çɹʌʔm̩s] *threepence*, ['çɹoʔl̩] *throttle*. A number of lexical, idiomatic and grammatical 'vulgarisms' are cited in Aitken (1979a: 108–10 in a list which is, however, by no means exhaustive.

Morningside English

The markers by which the middle-class, so-called 'Morningside' or 'Kelvin-side', accent (see chapter 30, page 526), is identified appear to be the following: realizations (either sporadic or consistent) of vowel 1*l* and 1*s* (both) as a narrower diphthong of the [eɪ] variety; of vowel 17 as a half-open vowel of the [ɛ̣], [ɛ] or [ɛ̣] variety (these two are the well-known stereotypes); realizations of vowel 16 as a fully mid rather than half-open vowel, viz. [ẹ]; sometimes over-rounded or diphthongal realizations of /o/, vowel 5; lengthened realizations of vowels 2 (/i/) and 6 (/u/) in SVLR short environments, and r-less realizations of vowel + *r* sequences, [fa-ːm] or [fɑːm] for [farm] and the like. The latter two of these are adjustments and the first four hyper-adjustments from regular Scots towards RP-like realizations.

'Dying Scots'

Notwithstanding the claims made in chapter 30 anent the Scots' 'dialect loyalty', it is also true that many of the words and usages mentioned or alluded to on pages 102–5 above have restricted regional and/or social distributions, chiefly to vernacular (group 3 and group 4) speakers. Yet none of them is obsolete. Furthermore, the stock of Scotticisms is being continually enlarged by new creation, albeit many of the new creations begin life as (more or less) 'vulgarisms'. None of the following seems likely to be more than a hundred years old: *multy* 'multi-storey tenement', *scheme* 'local authority housing estate', *high-heid-yin* 'boss', *henner* 'gymnastic feat', (*the whole*) *jingbang* or *bangshoot* '(the whole) caboodle', *fantoosh* (adj.) 'fancy', *to miss oneself* 'to miss a treat', *to put* (another's) *gas at a peep* 'to deflate (him)', *to be up to high doh* 'to be over-excited' about something.

Even so, it hardly seems disputable that both the type and the token frequencies of the Scottish elements of form, vocabulary and grammar in Scottish usage is shrinking – fewer Scotticisms are being used less often by fewer people. One evidence of this is the fact that many words for common and permanent notions, such as *gowk* 'cuckoo', *graith* 'equipment' or *lift* 'sky', in most of their areas of survival, no longer display their former full semantic range, and that other such words or forms now survive only patchily across the dialect map – words such as *cuit* 'ankle', *nowt* 'cattle', *bate* 'boat', *lafe* 'loaf', *sape* 'soap', *leem* or *luim* 'tool, loom', *teel* or *tuil* 'tool', *shö* or *shae* 'shoe', *shoo* 'shove', *gnyauve* 'gnaw', etc.

'Good' or Ideal Scots may thus indeed be 'dying' (see Aitken, 1981b: 80–3), as is indeed to be expected from its socio-linguistic history and circumstances (see chapter 30 *passim*, especially pages 529–30). Clearly though, despite its generally low prestige, in the styles and registers to which it is appropriated, 'Scots', and more particularly 'Bad Scots', is far from dead, as much of the present chapter (along with Murison, 1976; Ross, 1972; Agutter and Cowan,

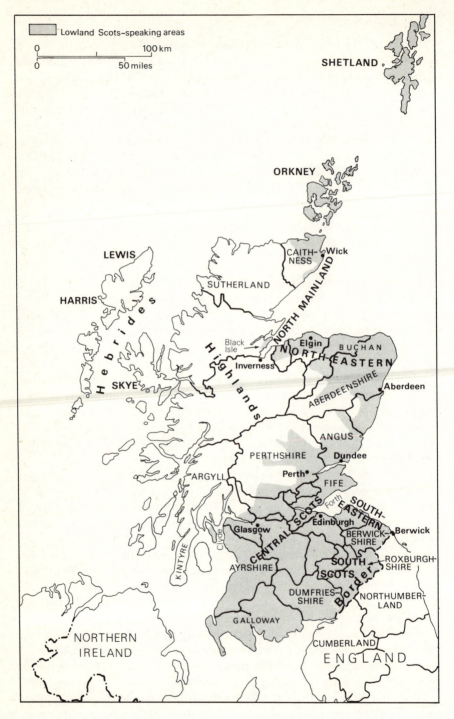

Lowland Scots-speaking areas

0   100 km
0   50 miles

SHETLAND

ORKNEY

LEWIS

HARRIS

Hebrides

SKYE

CAITH-NESS   Wick

SUTHERLAND

NORTH MAINLAND

Highlands

Black Isle

Inverness   Elgin   BUCHAN

NORTH-EASTERN

ABERDEENSHIRE   Aberdeen

ANGUS

PERTHSHIRE   Dundee

Perth   FIFE

ARGYLL

CENTRAL SCOTS   Forth   SOUTH-EASTERN

Glasgow   Edinburgh   Berwick

Clyde   BERWICK-SHIRE

KINTYRE   AYRSHIRE   SOUTH SCOTS   ROXBURGH-SHIRE

Border

DUMFRIES-SHIRE   NORTHUMBER-LAND

NORTHERN IRELAND

GALLOWAY

CUMBERLAND

E N G L A N D

1981; Wickens, 1980, 1981; and several other works listed in the References) illustrates.

The Highland Line and dialect districts (Map 6.1)

For a brief history of the several successive attempts to establish the Scots versus Gaelic or Scots versus Highland English linguistic frontier (the so-called linguistic Highland Line) see Speitel (1981). The pioneer linguistic investigation of the Highland Line was that of J. A. H. Murray (Murray, 1873: 231–7 and map). It was also Murray who, jointly with A. J. Ellis (Murray, 1873: 77–86; Ellis, 1889: 681–820), on the basis mainly of 'phonetic' (i.e. systemic, selectional and realizational) distinctions, established the division of the Lowland Scots-speaking area into four major areas, with a number of sub-divisions for three of these, an arrangement later refined by Grant (Grant, 1934: xxiv–xli, xlvii–xlviii); Grant's (and Murison's, 1977: 32–7) lists of distinguishing features (chiefly phonological), appropriated to his different divisions, have been mentioned above. In this essay I have employed my own, somewhat *ad hoc* but I hope transparent, set of labels for different broad regions, rather than follow one or other of the earlier labelling systems and the unrealistically precise delimitations of dialect division accompanying some of them (notably Ellis's).

The Border

As well as possessing a number of roughly distinct major regional dialects, Scotland is very certainly a dialect island within the English-speaking world and very probably far the most copious bunch of isoglosses in English is that running along the historical Border. Admittedly this is, as usual, a pretty tangled bunch, with a tendency to splaying, especially at the eastern end: see especially Glauser (1974: 283, fig. 88), and Speitel (1978). For a sketch of the earlier investigations of the linguistic Border, see Glauser (1974: 49–55).

It is true that there are many 'general northern' features whose southern limits lie far south of the Border – some front vowel or diphthong (i.e. some realization of vowel 4) representing Old English *ā* in *home*, *stone* etc., i.e. as *hame*, *hyem* or the like; vowel 6 undiphthongized e.g. in (north of England) /huːs/ *house*, and so on; many lexical features including some already mentioned; and some grammatical features such as the *yae* ~ *yin* distinction, and

Map 6.1. The Lowland Scots-speaking areas, showing the linguistic Highland Line and the dialect districts referred to in chapter 6
Note: The Highland Line is here adapted from that established by Speitel in Speitel (1981).
The term 'Northern' in the text embraces the dialect districts shown here as Orkney, Shetland, North Mainland and North-Eastern.

the word-orders *give me it, put the light on*. There are a number of other isoglosses which cut across the Border at an angle, including the *twaa ~ twae* opposition and others in phonology, and a large number of lexical features shown in Speitel (1978), Glauser (1974) and the linguistic atlases. Yet when all of these are discounted the number of (more and less) important Scotticisms which extend only to or just over the Border is remarkably high, including SVLR as a whole; Scots *nicht ~* English [nɛit] and other examples; innumerable realizational phenomena (a striking one is the realizations of vowel 19: universally unrounded in Scots as [ʌ], regularly rounded [ɷ] in northern England; another is the different treatment of the r-phoneme on either side of the Border); some selectional forms and innumerable lexical items attested, especially, in Speitel (1978).

According to Glauser (1974: 284), 'the dividing effect of the geographical Border can be expected to increase', as 'dialect words' – examples are *aye* 'always', *poke* 'bag', *redd* (v.) 'comb', *ingan* 'onion', *pooch* 'pocket', *steek* (v.) 'stitch', *soop* (v.) 'sweep', *gaed* (past tense) 'went', *kye* 'cows', *shuin* 'shoes', *een* 'eyes' and *nicht* 'night' (Glauser 1974; *passim* and 276) – recede to the Border in northern England, but are continued in daily use in Scotland, thanks, we assume, to the more persistent dialect-loyalty of the Scots.

REFERENCES

Abercrombie, D. 1979. The accents of Standard English in Scotland. In A.J. Aitken and T. McArthur (eds.) *Languages of Scotland*. Edinburgh: W. and R. Chambers. pp. 68–84.

Agutter, A.J.L. and Cowan, L.N. 1981. Changes in the vocabulary of Lowland Scots dialects. *Scottish Literary Journal* Supplement no. 14: 49–62.

Aitken, A.J. 1971. Variation and variety in written Middle Scots. In A.J. Aitken, A. McIntosh and H. Pálsson (eds.) *Edinburgh Studies in English and Scots*. London: Longman. pp. 177–209.

——— 1977. How to pronounce Older Scots. In A.J. Aitken, M.P. McDiarmid and D.S. Thomson (eds.) *Bards and makars: Scottish language and literature, medieval and renaissance*. Glasgow: University Press. pp. 1–21.

——— 1979a. Scottish speech: a historical view with special reference to the Standard English of Scotland. In A.J. Aitken and T. McArthur (eds.) *Languages of Scotland*. pp. 85–118.

——— 1979b. Studies in Scots and Scottish Standard English today. In A.J. Aitken and T. McArthur (eds.) *Languages of Scotland*. pp. 137–58.

——— 1981a. The Scottish vowel-length rule. In M. Benskin and M.L. Samuels (eds.) *So meny people longages and tonges: philological essays in Scots and mediaeval English presented to Angus McIntosh*. Edinburgh: Michael Benskin and M.L. Samuels. pp. 131–57.

——— 1981b. The good old Scots tongue: does Scots have an identity? In E. Haugen, J.D. McClure and D. Thomson (eds.) *Minority languages today*. Edinburgh: Edinburgh University Press. pp. 72–90.

—— 1982. Bad Scots: some superstitions about Scots speech. *Scottish Language* 1: 30–44.

Brown, E. K. Forthcoming. Relative clauses in a corpus of Scots speech. *English World-Wide.* Volume and issue no. unknown.

Brown, E. K. and Millar, M. 1980. Auxiliary verbs in Edinburgh speech. *Transactions of the Philological Society* 81–133.

Brown, E. K. and Miller, J. E. 1975. Modal verbs in Scottish English. *Work in Progress* 11: 146–84. Edinburgh University Linguistics Department.

Catford, J. C. 1957a. Vowel-systems of Scots dialects. *Transactions of the Philological Society* 107–17.

—— 1957b. Shetland dialect. *Shetland folk book* 3: 71–5.

Dieth, E. 1932. *A grammar of the Buchan dialect (Aberdeenshire).* vol. 1, *Phonology-accidence.* Cambridge: Heffer.

Ellis, A. J. 1889. *On early English pronunciation.* Part v, *Existing dialectal as compared with West Saxon pronunciation.* London: Philological Society.

Esling, J. H. 1978. Voice quality in Edinburgh: a sociolinguistic and phonetic study. Ph.D. thesis, University of Edinburgh.

Glauser, B. 1974. *The Scottish-English linguistic border: lexical aspects.* The Cooper monographs. Bern: Francke.

Graham, W. 1977. *The Scots word book.* Edinburgh: Ramsay Head Press.

Grant, W. 1934. Introduction. *The Scottish National Dictionary* vol. 1.

Grant, W. and Dixon, J. M. 1921. *Manual of modern Scots.* Cambridge: CUP.

Hill, T. 1963. Phonemic and prosodic analysis in linguistic geography. *Orbis: Bulletin international de Documentation linguistique* 12: 449–55.

Jakobsen, J. 1928, 1932. *An etymological dictionary of the Norn language in Shetland.* London: David Nutt.

LAS 1 1975. *The linguistic atlas of Scotland.* Scots section vol. 1 edited by J. Y. Mather and H. H. Speitel. London: Croom Helm.

LAS 2 1977. *The linguistic atlas of Scotland.* Scots section vol. 2 edited by J. Y. Mather and H. H. Speitel. London: Croom Helm.

LAS 3 Forthcoming. *The linguistic atlas of Scotland.* Scots section vol. 3. [the volume on phonology].

McArthur, T. 1979. The status of English in and furth of Scotland. In A. J. Aitken and T. McArthur (eds.) *Languages of Scotland.* Edinburgh: Chambers. pp. 50–67.

McClure, J. D. 1980. Western Scottish intonation: a preliminary study. In L. R. Waugh and C. H. van Schooneveld (eds.) *The melody of language.* Baltimore: University Park Press.

Marwick, H. 1929. *The Orkney Norn.* Oxford: OUP.

Mather, J. Y. 1964. Dialect research in Orkney and Shetland after Jakobsen. *Fróðskaparrit (Annal. societ. scient. Færoensis)* 13: 33–45.

—— 1973. The Scots we speak today. In A. J. Aitken (ed.) *Lowland Scots.* Association for Scottish Literary Studies, Occasional Papers no. 2. pp. 56–68.

—— 1974. Social variation in present-day Scots speech. In J. D. McClure (ed.) *The Scots language in education,* Association for Scottish Literary Studies, Occasional Papers no. 3. pp. 44–53.

—— 1978. The dialect of Caithness. *Scottish Literary Journal* supplement no. 6: 1–16.

—— 1980. The dialect of the eastern borders. *Scottish Literary Journal* supplement no. 12: 30–42.

Millar, M. and Brown, E.K. 1979. Tag questions in Edinburgh speech. *Linguistische Berichte* 60: 24–45.

Miller, J.E. 1980. Syntax and discourse in a corpus of spoken Scottish English; The expression of possibility and permission in Scottish English; GET in a corpus of Scottish English; The expression of necessity and obligation in Scottish English; Negatives in Scottish English; Reference to future time in a corpus of Scottish English. Working Papers, for subsequent publication. Department of Linguistics, University of Edinburgh.

Miller, J.E. and Brown, E.K. 1982. Aspects of Scottish English syntax. *English World-Wide* 3: 3–17.

Murison, D. 1971. The Dutch element in the vocabulary of Scots. In A.J. Aitken, A. McIntosh and H. Pálsson (eds.) *Edinburgh Studies in English and Scots*. London: Longman. pp. 159–76.

—— 1976. The speech of Moray. In D. Omand (ed.) *The Moray Book*. Edinburgh: Paul Harris. pp. 275–82.

—— 1977. *The guid Scots tongue*. Edinburgh: Blackwood.

Murray, J.A.H. 1873. *The dialect of the southern counties of Scotland*. London: Philological Society.

Nicholson, D.B. 1907. Dialect. In J. Horne (ed.) *The county of Caithness*. Wick: W. Rae. pp. 60–8.

Riach, W.A.D. 1979. A dialect study of comparative areas in Galloway. *Scottish Literary Journal* supplement no. 9: 1–16.

—— 1980. A dialect study of comparative areas in Galloway (2nd report). *Scottish Literary Journal* supplement no. 12: 43–60.

Robertson, T.A. and Graham, J.J. 1952. *Grammar and usage of the Shetland dialect*. Lerwick: The Shetland Times Ltd.

Ross, J. 1972. A selection of Caithness dialect words. In Donald Omand (ed.) *The Caithness book*. Inverness: Highland Printer Ltd. pp. 241–60.

Speitel, H.H. 1978. The word geography of the Borders. *Scottish Literary Journal* supplement no. 6: 17–38.

—— 1981. The geographical position of the Scots dialect in relation to the Highlands of Scotland. With maps by George Leslie. In Michael Benskin and M.L. Samuels (eds.) *So meny people longages and tonges* (see Aitken 1981a). pp. 107–29.

Wakelin, M.F. 1972. *English dialects: an introduction*. London: The Athlone Press.

Watson, G. 1923. *The Roxburghshire word-book*. Cambridge: CUP.

Wettstein, P. 1942. *The phonology of a Berwickshire dialect*. Zurich: Schüler S.A. Bienne.

Wickens, B. 1980. Caithness speech: studying the dialect with the help of school children. *Scottish Literary Journal* supplement no. 12: 61–76.

—— 1981. Caithness speech (Part 2). *Scottish Literary Journal* supplement no. 14: 25–36.

Wilson, J. 1915. *Lowland Scotch, as spoken in the Lower Strathearn District of Perthshire*. London: OUP.

—— 1923. *The dialect of Robert Burns*. London: OUP.

—— 1926. *The dialect of Central Scotland*. London: OUP.

Zai, R. 1942. *The phonology of the Morebattle dialect*. Lucerne: Raeber and Co.

7

English in the north of Ireland

JOHN HARRIS

Historical background and dialect boundaries

The term 'north of Ireland' is taken here to refer to an area roughly equivalent to the nine northernmost counties of Ireland which comprise the historical province of Ulster, i.e. Cavan, Donegal, Monaghan and the six counties of Northern Ireland: Antrim, Armagh, Derry, Down, Fermanagh and Tyrone. The English spoken in the north warrants separate consideration from that spoken in the rest of Ireland (see chapter 8), because it reflects historical conditions that are in many ways peculiar to the area. It was during the Plantation of Ulster in the seventeenth century that English was first introduced into the north of Ireland on a large scale, when Scottish and English settlers were given land that had been confiscated from the native Irish-speaking population by the British authorities. Scottish planters (predominantly from south-west Scotland) were concentrated in the north and east of Ulster but made their presence felt throughout the province, outnumbering by almost 6 : 1 the English colonists (mostly from the north-west Midlands and south-west of England), the majority of whom settled the Lagan Valley stretching south-westwards from Belfast Lough (see Braidwood, 1964). English is now spoken in most areas of Ulster, the domain of Irish as a first language being restricted for the most part to the Donegal *Gaeltacht* in the extreme west of the province (see chapters 18 and 28). These settlement patterns, although somewhat blurred by subsequent internal migration, are still reflected in the present-day linguistic geography of the north of Ireland. Irish, Scots and Anglo-English have all left their mark in varying proportions on the different types of English spoken in Ulster.

Dialectologists have concentrated on differences in vocabulary, vowel quality and the lexical distribution of phonemes when drawing linguistic boundaries within Hiberno-English (English as spoken in Ireland), e.g. between northern and southern Hiberno-English (Barry, 1980) and between Ulster Scots and other Hiberno-English dialects (Gregg, 1972). However, a more abstract typology of Hiberno-English dialects, based on vowel quantity differences, allows us to discern more clearly the competing influences of English and Scots source dialects. According to this typology, Hiberno-

115

English dialects can be categorized as 'more English' or 'more Scots'. A typically English dialect in this sense is one which preserves the original West Germanic system of phonemic vowel length, having one set of inherently short and one of inherently long stressed vowel phonemes (Lass, 1976: 54–6). Scottish dialects, on the other hand, are characterized by the disruption of this dichotomous pattern, resulting in the loss of phonemic length: vowel quantity is to a large extent conditioned by the phonetic environment (see chapter 6). The manner in which the English language was imported into Ireland (see chapter 28) has meant that the geography of the Scots–English linguistic divide in Britain has broadly speaking been reproduced in Ireland. The most northerly Hiberno-English dialects are clearly Lowland Scots in type, whereas southern Hiberno-English varieties have more in common with the dialects of England (see chapter 8). Between these two extremes lies a range of transitional dialects with phonological characteristics that exhibit in varying proportions a compromise between the Scots and English systems. According to the vowel length typology, we can recognize three broad categories of northern Hiberno-English (see Map 7.1):

(a) Ulster Scots (US) as spoken in parts of the north and north-east of Ulster (most of County Antrim, north-east Down, and parts of County Derry and County Donegal). The area in which this variety is spoken has been defined by Gregg (1972), who refers to the dialect as 'Scotch-Irish'.

(b) South Ulster English (SUE) as spoken in the extreme south of the province (south Armagh, south Monaghan, north Cavan, south Fermanagh and south Donegal); and

(c) Mid Ulster English (MUE), which is spoken in an area roughly sandwiched by Ulster Scots and South Ulster English (the Lagan Valley, stretching south-westwards from Belfast Lough, south Tyrone, north Monaghan, north Fermanagh and some coastal parts of central Donegal).

A transitional dialect, which displays features of both Ulster Scots and Mid Ulster English, is spoken in north Tyrone and parts of County Derry. In terms of number of speakers, Mid Ulster English is the dominant variety in Ulster. It is spoken in Belfast, the most economically important and populous city in the north, and is the dialect upon which the regional standard pronunciation is based. (See Milroy, 1982, for a discussion of the effects of standardization on northern Hiberno-English phonology.)

Ulster Scots, which is spoken in areas where Scottish settlement was at its densest, is recognizable as a dialect of Lowland Scots (see chapter 6) by, among other things, its typically Scots pattern of conditioned vowel length. Mid Ulster English, which is spoken in areas where Scottish influence was offset by the presence of English settlers, is a 'mixed' type in that it has a modified Scots-type vowel length pattern, in which English-type elements are discernible. South Ulster English, which is spoken in areas where the predominant non-Irish influence was English rather than Scottish, can be seen as

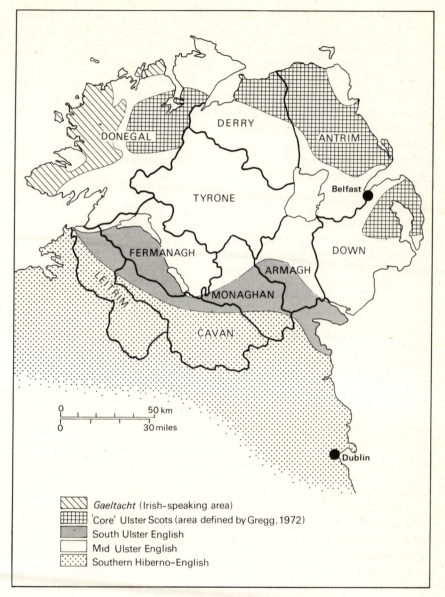

Map 7.1. Approximate boundaries of northern Hiberno-English dialects

a transitional dialect between southern Hiberno-English on the one hand and Ulster Scots and Mid Ulster English on the other, since it combines the English dichotomous pattern of phonemic vowel length found in southern Hiberno-English with some typically northern features of vowel quality. Because of the importance of vowel quantity differences in this typology of Hiberno-English dialects, attention will be focused here on the vowel phonology of northern Hiberno-English and in particular on how elements of both Ulster Scots and South Ulster English are combined in Mid Ulster English.

The influence of Irish (see chapter 8) can be seen to varying extents in most types of northern Hiberno-English. It is obviously most marked in the Donegal *Gaeltacht* where English is spoken as a second language, but it is also clearly discernible in dialects spoken in some peripheral areas of Ulster where Irish survived until recently. Many nonstandard features of Ulster Hiberno-English phonology have been ascribed to Irish interference (see, especially, Adams, 1966), but the evidence is somewhat ambiguous and the contribution of seventeenth-century Scots and English regional dialects is not to be underestimated. At the syntactic level, however, certain northern Hiberno-English constructions point more clearly to Irish origins.

Northern Hiberno-English phonology

Northern Hiberno-English dialects exhibit many phonological characteristics that are general throughout Ireland (see also chapter 8). These include: the retention of historical /r/ in all positions including pre-consonantally; the (often extreme) palatalization of /k, g, ŋ/ in the environment of front vowels; the realization of /l/ as clear in all positions; the merger of the Middle English (ME) ę̄ class (e.g. *meat*) with ME ā (e.g. *mate*) rather than with ME ẹ̄ (e.g. *meet*); the preservation of certain vowel oppositions before historical /r/ where they have been neutralized in RP, e.g. /ɛrn/ *earn* vs. /ʌrn/ *urn*, /fɔr/ *for* vs. /for/ *four*; and the failure of ME ă to back-round after /w/, e.g. /want/ *want*.

Besides the vowel length differences already mentioned, phonological characteristics that distinguish northern from southern Hiberno-English include: the realization of /u/ (in *boot*) as fronted [ʉ] in the north but as back [u] in the south; a higher than half-close, over-rounded articulation of /o/ (in *boat*) in the north versus lower than half-close in the south; the realization of /θ, ð/ as fricatives in the north but as stops in the south; and the absence in the north of the southern spirantization of final voiceless stops. Intonation in many northern Hiberno-English varieties is strikingly different from that of most other types of English including southern Hiberno-English. In Belfast English, for example, attitudinally unmarked statements typically have a rising nuclear tone rather than the more usual falling pattern (Jarman and Cruttenden, 1976).

Table 7.1. *Vowel system of Ulster Scots*

i		ʉ		əʉ
	ï			əi
e			o	ɑe
				ɔe
ε		ʌ	ɔ	
	ӕ			
			ɑ	

Ulster Scots vowels

It is necessary to distinguish within Ulster Scots between a conservative variety, spoken mostly in rural areas, and a standardized type (see Gregg, 1958, 1964; see also chapter 31, where Douglas-Cowie discusses bidialectalism in Ulster Scots-speaking areas). Although they share essentially the same phoneme system and allophonic realization rules, the two varieties differ quite widely in the lexical distribution of vowel phonemes. In this respect, conservative Ulster Scots and standardized Ulster Scots are equivalent to Lowland Scots and Scottish English respectively (see chapter 6). Conservative Ulster Scots is very similar to the Lowland Scots spoken in the south-west of Scotland: it preserves a typically Scots lexical distribution of phonemes, the present-day vowels being for the most part the outcome of a continuous development from Older Scots (OSc). In standardized Ulster Scots, lexical items have been re-allocated to the phoneme classes that are nearest to the equivalent standard classes. The system of stressed vowel phonemes in Ulster Scots is shown in table 7.1.

Some of the typically Scots features that are present in conservative Ulster Scots and usually abandoned in standardized Ulster Scots are: the undiphthongized reflex of OSc ū, eg [kʉː] *cow*; lowered and unrounded reflexes of OSc ŏ before labials, e.g. [tɑːp] *top*; the merger of reflexes of OSc ei with /i/, not with /əi/ or /ɑe/, e.g. [diː] *die*; the raising of OSc ă to /ε/ in certain environments, e.g. [fεːrm] *farm*; fronted and unrounded reflexes of OSc ō̜, e.g. [blïd] *blood*; the failure to raise OE ā beyond /ɔ/ in the environment of labio-velars, e.g. [twɔː] *two*, and the raising of the vowel elsewhere at the front rather than the back of the vowel area, e.g. [heːm] *home*; the retention of original /x/, e.g. [bɔːxt] *bought*; and the vocalization of final /l/, e.g. [wɔː] *wall*. The major correspondences between the conservative and standardized vocalic phoneme classes are illustrated in table 7.2. Standardized Ulster Scots lacks the /ӕ/ phoneme, transferring most items from this conservative Ulster Scots class into the /ï/ class (e.g. /θӕk/ → /θïk/ *thick*). Conservative /ï/ items are transferred into either the /ʉ/ or /ʌ/ class (e.g. /fït/ → /fʉt/ *foot*, /blïd/ → /blʌd/ *blood*), or, before /r/, into the /o/ class (e.g. /dïr/ → /dor/ *door*).

Table 7.2. *Lexical distribution of vowel phonemes in conservative and standardized Ulster Scots*

Standardized		Conservative	Standardized		Conservative
i	street	i	ɑ	hand	ɑ
	beat	e		grass	ɛ
ʉ	soot	ï	ɔ	pot	ɔ
	book	ʉ		top	ɑ
ï	thick	æ̈	ʌ	dumb	ʌ
	twist	ʌ		blood	ï
e	same	e	ae	my	ae
	hay	əi			
			əi	line	əi
o	foal	o		die	i
	home	e			
	floor	ï	əʉ	cow	ʉ
	snow	ɔ		howl	əʉ
	cold	əʉ			
			ɔe	noise	ɔe
ɛ	bed	ɛ			
	head	i			
	twelfth	ɑ			
	never	æ̈			

The most striking feature of Ulster Scots vowel phonology is the massive disruption of the original English pattern of phonemic vowel length. The stressed vowel phonemes of present-day Ulster Scots can be grouped into three categories according to their quantity characteristics: two groups exhibit phonemic length (i.e. they are inherently short or long), although not necessarily preserving the original Older Scots pattern; in a third group, length is no longer phonemic but phonetically conditioned. The first group preserves the original Older Scots phonemic length pattern: /æ̈/ < OSc ĭ and /ʌ/ < OSc ŭ remain short everywhere: /o/ < OSc ǭ, /ɔe/ < OSc oi and /e/ < OSc ā remain long everywhere. A second group shows phonemic length but not on the OSc pattern: /ɛ, ɑ, ɔ/ from OSc short ĕ, ă, ŏ are now long everywhere. In a final group, length is no longer phonemic but is now conditioned by the following environment: /ï/ < OSc ǭ is long before /r/ and short elsewhere; /əʉ/ is short before a voiceless consonant, or before a sonorant followed by a voiceless consonant, and long elsewhere; /i, ʉ/, and to a large extent /əi, ae/, conform to the Scots vowel length conditions often referred to as 'Aitken's Law' (Lass,

Table 7.3. *Realization of /i, ʉ/ in conservative Ulster Scots*

	/i/		/ʉ/	
Short__voiceless stop	[fit]	*feet*	[öt]	*out*
__voiced stop	[did]	*dead*	[föd]	*food*
__voiceless fricative	[tiθ]	*teeth*	[hös]	*house*
__nasal	[kin]	*keen*	[drön]	*drown*
__lateral	[fil]	*feel*	[töl]	*tool*
Long__voiced fricative	[sni:z]	*sneeze*	[bʉ:z]	*booze*
__/r/	[fi:r]	*fear*	[ʃö:r]	*sure*
__vowel	['fi:ət]	*Fiat*	[ʃʉ:ər]	*shower*
__ #	[di:]	*die*	[brʉ:]	*brew*
__ # consonant	[di:d]	*died*	[brʉ:d]	*brewed*

1974; Aitken, 1981, and chapter 6 of this volume). According to this 'law', vowels in Scots are long before /r, v, ð, z/, in hiatus, or before a morpheme boundary (#), and short elsewhere. In the case of /ï, ʉ/, allophonic variation in quantity is accompanied by quality differences. /ʉ/ is realized as close, central, slightly rounded [ʉ:] before /v, ð, z/, a morpheme boundary or another vowel (e.g. [brʉ:z] *bruise*); in other positions, it is a half-close, central vowel, long before /r/ (e.g. [ʃö:r] *sure*) and short elsewhere (e.g. [söt] *suit*). /ï/ in conservative Ulster Scots varies in quality according to area, ranging from slightly higher than half-close, central, unrounded [ï] (with a lower allophone [ë:] before /r/, e.g. [flë:r] *floor*) to [i(:)] or [e(:)], in which case it merges with /i/ or /e/ in some contexts.

The effect of the Aitken's Law length conditions on the realization of /i, ʉ/ in conservative Ulster Scots is illustrated in table 7.3. The distribution of the diphthongs [ɑe] and [əi] generally follows the conditions of Aitken's Law: [ɑe], in which both morae are long, occurs only in 'long' environments, and [əi], in which both morae are short, usually only occurs in 'short' environments, as illustrated in table 7.4. If this pattern of complementary distribution were rigid, [ɑe] and [əi] could be treated as allophones of one phoneme (as in Scottish English). However, in conservative Ulster Scots, the distribution only holds for reflexes of OSc ī. [əi] can occur word-finally as a conditioned reflex of OSc ai (which in other positions has developed into Ulster Scots /e/, e.g. [re:n] *rain*). The diphthongs [ɑe] and [əi] therefore contrast before #, e.g. [həi] *hay* vs. [tɑe] *tie*. The transfer of lexical items from their conservative Ulster Scots classes into standard classes is achieved in such a way as to leave the opposition between /əi/ and /ɑe/ intact, since they also contrast morpheme-finally in standardized Ulster Scots (see table 7.5). *Die*-items are transferred, not into the *my*-class (as in Scottish English), but into the /əi/ class left vacant by a transfer of *stay*-items into the /e/ class. The importance

Table 7.4. *Distribution of diphthongs* [əi] *and* [ae] *in conservative Ulster Scots*

Short—voiceless stop	[rəip]	ripe
—voiced stop	[gəid]	guide
—voiceless fricative	[məis]	mice
—nasal	[ləin]	line
—lateral	[wəil]	wild
Long—voiced fricative	[daev]	dive
—/r/	[taer]	tire
—vowel	['traeəl]	trial
—#	[tae]	tie
—# consonant	[taed]	tied

Table 7.5. *Reflexes of Older Scots word-final ei, ī, ai in conservative and standardized Ulster Scots*

Older Scots	conservative Ulster Scots	standardized Ulster Scots	
ei # ——————	i —————	əi	die
ī # ——————	ae —————	ae	my
ai # ——————	əi —————	e	stay

Table 7.6. *Aitken's Law minimal pairs in standardized Ulster Scots*

Aitken's Law 'long' environment —#				Aitken's Law 'short' environment —/d/, —/n/	
[tae]	tie	[taed]	tied	[təid]	tide
[mae]	my	[maen]	mine (poss.)	[məin]	mine (n.)
[niː]	knee	[niːd]	kneed	[nid]	need
[brʉː]	brew	[brʉːd]	brewed	[bröd]	brood

of # in the conditions governing length and quality in /əi, ae/ and length in /i, ʉ/ is illustrated by the standardized Ulster Scots minimal pairs in table 7.6. The similarities to Scottish English are clear.

At several points in the system, standardized Ulster Scots exhibits under-differentiation of vowel phonemes in relation to Received Pronunciation (RP). The RP opposition between /uː/ (as in *food*) and /ʊ/ (as in *good*) is

Table 7.7. *Vowel system of South Ulster English*

(a)	ı	ǫ	(b)	iː	ʉː		əi
	ɛ	ö		eː		oː	əʉ
	a	ɑ		aː		ɑː	ɑı

Table 7.8. *Lexical distribution of vowel phonemes in South Ulster English*

/ı/	bit	/iː/	feet	/əi/	my
/ɛ/	bet	/eː/	fate	/əʉ/	how
/a/	bat, Sam	/aː/	psalm, glass	/ɑı/	boy
/ɑ/	pot	/ɑː/	caught, loss		
/ö/	but	/oː/	boat		
/ǫ/	good	/ʉː/	boot		

represented by only one standardized Ulster Scots phoneme /ʉ/. Similarly, RP /ɒ/ (as in *cot*) and /ɔː/ (as in *caught*) correspond to the single phoneme /ɔ/ in standardized Ulster Scots. In Ulster Scots, the opposition between /ɛ/ and /a/ is neutralized in some velar environments, namely after /k/ or before /k, g, ŋ/. For example, *peck* and *pack* are both [pɛːk].

On the other hand, standardized Ulster Scots maintains certain vowel oppositions in environments where the corresponding RP contrasts are neutralized, particularly before historical /r/. For example, RP lacks a contrast equivalent to US /o/ː/ɔ/ before historical /r/ followed by a consonant, e.g. US [hoːrs] *hoarse* vs. [hɔːrs] *horse*. Similarly, in the same environment, Ulster Scots contrasts /ɛ/ and /ʌ/, where RP only has /ɜː/, e.g. US [ɛːrn] *earn* vs. [ʌrn] *urn*.

South Ulster English vowels

South Ulster English, as has been pointed out, is a transitional dialect, combining typically southern Hiberno-English vowel quantity with some northern Hiberno-English quality features. (I am grateful to Michael V. Barry of Queen's University, Belfast, for making available to me material from the Tape-Recorded Survey of Hiberno-English, on which this treatment of South Ulster English is based.) South Ulster English vowel phonology is markedly different from that of Ulster Scots, since it preserves for the most part the English dichotomous pattern of phonemic vowel length. Two sets of stressed vowel phonemes can be recognized, one containing inherently short vowels and the other inherently long vowels (including diphthongs) (sets (a) and (b) in table 7.7). Sample lexical items containing these vowels are listed in table 7.8.

Table 7.9. *Reflexes of ME ă, au, ŏ in South Ulster English*

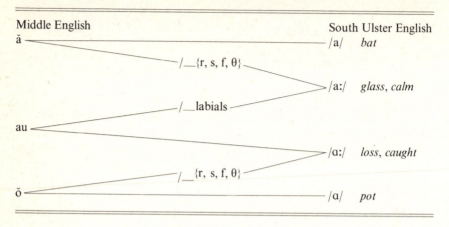

The lexical distribution of these phonemes is not identical to that of RP but resembles it more closely than does that of conservative Ulster Scots. Only some of the main divergences from RP lexical distribution need be noted here. The incidence of the South Ulster English phonemes /ö, ɷ/ is not the same as RP /ʌ, ɷ/: some RP /ɷ/ times fall into the /ö/ class in South Ulster English, e.g. *put, pull, bush*. The SUE /eː/ class includes a large number of items that originally contained ME ę̄ but now have /iː/ in RP, e.g. *leave, beat, decent*. When not shortened, the South Ulster English reflex of ME ǭ is /ʉː/ in all environments, including before historical /r/ where it has remained as /ɔː/ in RP, e.g. [flʉːr] *floor*, [bʉːrd] *board*. SUE /əʉ/ is the reflex not only of ME ū (as in [kəʉ] *cow*) but also, as in rural Ulster Scots, of ME ŏ followed by ld, with loss of the d, e.g. [əʉl] *old*, [kəʉl] *cold*.

The lexical distribution of the four South Ulster English phonemes /a, ɑ, aː, ɑː/, which correspond to RP /æ, ɒ, ɑː, ɔː/, can best be seen in terms of their development from ME ă, au, ŏ (see table 7.9). South Ulster English shares with southern Anglo-English dialects the Early Modern English lengthening of ME ă before /r, f, θ, s/ (but not before /n/ followed by a voiceless consonant, e.g. SUE [grant] vs. RP [grɑːnt] *grant*) and has preserved the lengthening of ME ŏ in the same environments, now abandoned in all but the most conservative types of RP, e.g. SUE [saːft] vs. RP [sɒft] *soft*.

The realization of South Ulster English vowel phonemes differs widely from that of Ulster Scots not only in terms of quantity but also in quality. Unlike US /ʌ/, South Ulster English slightly advanced from back /ö/ is rounded, being articulated as half-open [ɔ̈] or half-close [ö] depending on the dialect. In contrast to US back /ɑ/, SUE /a, aː/ are realized as central or front, with raised diaphones as high as [ɛ(ː)], e.g. [hɛːf] *half*. SUE /ɛ, ɑ/ are the main reflexes of ME ē and ŏ respectively, lowered from mid position and, in the case of /ɑ/, frequently unrounded, e.g. [bæt] *bet*, [pɑt] *pot*. Since /ɑ/, when unrounded, is often fronted, there is a good deal of 'crowding' in the lower vowel area; overlapping is common, resulting in occasional confusion over word-class assignment. This is particularly true of /a/ and /ɑ/ following a labio-velar approximant: since the Early Modern English rounding of ă after /w/ occurs only sporadically in South Ulster English (as in rural Ulster Scots), it is often difficult to determine whether a low, central vowel following a labio-velar is a realization of /a/ or of /ɑ/, e.g. [wa̱nt] *want*. In many South Ulster English dialects, the two vowels are clearly neutralized in this environment.

Realizations of some other South Ulster English vowel phonemes have a more 'northern' quality to them. /ʉː/ and the second element in /əʉ/ are usually more fronted than the typically back [uː] of southern Hiberno-English. /ɪ/ is normally pronounced lower than the corresponding southern vowel [i̞], although never as low as US /æ̈/. High allophones do occur before palatalized consonants, e.g. [k̟i̟k̟] *kick*. /oː/ is often realised as an over-rounded, back vowel slightly higher than Cardinal 7, as in Ulster Scots, but a 'southern' more open diaphone occurs in some varieties.

Belfast Vernacular vowels

Belfast Vernacular (BV) is taken here as representative of Mid Ulster English, partly because it is the most widely spoken variety and partly because it has been the subject of much recent research (see especially J. Milroy 1976, 1981; J. and L. Milroy, 1978). The vowel phonology of Mid Ulster English can be viewed as an accommodation of both Ulster Scots and South Ulster English systems. The lexical distribution of Belfast Vernacular phonemes is similar to that of South Ulster English, but at the allophonic level both Ulster Scots and South Ulster English can be seen to have exerted an influence. This compromise works itself out as a proliferation of vowel allophony in Belfast Vernacular, some phonemes displaying both typically Ulster Scots and South Ulster English allophones.

Ulster Scots influence is most clearly seen in the fact that Belfast Vernacular vowel phonology is characterized by large-scale loss of phonemic length. The system of Belfast Vernacular stressed vowels is displayed in table 7.10 as three sub-systems, grouped according to their quantity characteristics. The length of the vowels in set (a) is entirely conditioned by the following environment; the vowels in set (b) are invariably short, those in set (c) invariably long. Sample lexical items in which these vowels occur are given in table 7.11.

Several points of divergence from RP in the lexical distribution of these vowels need to be noted. The class of words containing BV /ɪ/ (whose realization varies along a continuum from [ɛ̈] to [ɪ]) includes a number of items that have /ɛ/ in RP, e.g. *yesterday*, *never*, *get*. Like Ulster Scots, Belfast Vernacular only has two phonemes that correspond to RP /uː, ɷ, ʌ/, namely /ʉ, ɔ̈/. The BV /ɔ̈/ class contains most of the core vocabulary items that have /ʌ/ in RP, e.g. *but*, *cut*; the /ʉ/ class contains items that have either /uː/ or /ɷ/

Table 7.10. *Vowel system of Belfast Vernacular*

(a)	i	ʉ		əi	(b)	ɪ	(c)	ɔː
	e		o	əʉ		ö		(aː)
	ɛ		ɔ					ɔe
	a							

Table 7.11. *Lexical distribution of vowel phonemes in Belfast Vernacular*

/i/	feet	/əi/	fight
/e/	fate	/əʉ/	shout
/ɛ/	bet	/ɪ/	bit
/a/	bat	/ö/	but
/ɔ/	pot	/ɔː/	bought
/o/	boat	/aː/	father
/ʉ/	boot	/ɔe/	boy

in RP, e.g. *food, good.* However, there is a third class of items that alternate between conservative /ö/ (from South Ulster English) and innovating /ʉ/ (from standardized Ulster Scots), where RP has /ʊ/, e.g. *pull, full, bush, took.* As with SUE /ʉː/, the BV /ʉ/ class contains a number of items, in which the phoneme is followed by /r/, that belong to the /ɔː/ class in RP, e.g. *floor, door, board.* This pronunciation is common in rural Mid Ulster English but is now recessive in Belfast, where it is being replaced by /o/, e.g. [dʉːr] → [doːr] *door.*

Another alternating class in Belfast Vernacular is made up of a number of items that originally contained ME ẹ̄ and now alternate between standard /i/ and a conservative pronunciation (predominantly South Ulster English in origin) near [e], e.g. *beat, decent, leave, Jesus.* This class is recessive in Belfast, where it only contains around thirty items, but it still maintains a vigorous existence in rural Lagan Valley speech. Recent research has revealed that, for some speakers, [e] realizations of this class are potentially contrasted with /e/, in which case another phoneme (/ẹ/) must be recognized (Milroy and Harris, 1980). The /e/:/ẹ/ contrast is marginal since, although /ẹ/ can be realized as slightly lower than /e/, realizations of the two phonemes often overlap.

Belfast Vernacular lacks the full /æ/:/ɑː/ contrast of RP or the SUE /a/:/aː/ contrast. BV /aː/ is of marginal status since it only occurs in a few words, e.g. *father, rather* (contrasting with /a/ in *gather*), although even in these words many speakers substitute /ɔː/. Because of the conditioned lengthening of /a/ discussed below, Belfast Vernacular collapses the SUE /a/:/aː/ distinction in all other instances, e.g. /sam/ *Sam, psalm.*

Within set (a) in table 7.10 we can recognize three groups of vowels, each with its own set of length conditions:

Table 7.12. *Length conditions on Belfast Vernacular vowels*

	/i/	/e/	/ɛ/
Long___#	see	day	—
___z	breeze	daze	Des
Short___n	keen	rain	pen
___d	seed	fade	dead
___s	geese	face	mess
___t	feet	fate	pet

(a) /i, ʉ/ are long before /r, v, ð, z/, #, or another vowel, and short elsewhere (Aitken's Law);

(b) /e, o, əʉ, əi/ are short before a voiceless consonant, or before a sonorant followed by a voiceless consonant, and long elsewhere;

(c) /ɛ, a, ɔ/ are short before a voiceless stop or affricate, before a sonorant followed by a voiceless consonant, or in any stressed syllable followed by an unstressed syllable in the same morpheme, and long elsewhere.

The length conditions on these three categories of vowels are illustrated in table 7.12 by /i, e, ɛ/.

For many Belfast Vernacular vowels, conditioned variation in length is accompanied by often extreme quality differences, and in this allophonic diversity it is possible to discern the competing influences of Ulster Scots and South Ulster English. The disruption of the English pattern of phonemic length, which has not affected South Ulster English to any great extent, clearly points to Ulster Scots influence. The conditions governing length in /ɛ, a, ɔ/ can be seen as an accommodation of the contrasting characteristics of the invariably long Ulster Scots vowels /ɛ, ɑ, ɔ/ and the short South Ulster English vowels /ɛ, a, ɑ/. BV /ɛ, a, ɔ/ retain South Ulster English shortness in the 'short' enviornments given in group (c) on this page, but elsewhere Ulster Scots influence makes itself felt by generalizing the South Ulster English lengthening of ME ă and ŏ before /r, f, θ, s/ to /ɛ/ and other environments. This compromise also manifests itself in the allophonic quality differences of these vowels. When short, BV /ɛ, ɔ/ have a typically South Ulster English low, and in the case of /ɔ/, unrounded and frequently fronted articulation, e.g. [bæt] *bet*, [pɑ̈t] *pot*. When long, the two vowels are, as in Ulster Scots, mid and, in the case of /ɔ/, rounded and slightly advanced from back, e.g. [bɛːd] *bed*, [pɔ̈ːd] *pod*.

/a/ exhibits the most extreme allophonic diversity of all Belfast Vernacular vowels, ranging from [ɛ(ː)] or [æ(ː)] before or after palatalized velars, through [æ] or [a] before /t/, [a] or [ɑ] before /p/, [ɑː] or [ɒː] before voiced obstruents and voiceless fricatives, to [ɒː] or even [ɔː] before nasals. Before /r/, /a/ remains central in some rural Mid Ulster English speech but is becoming increasingly backed and frequently rounded in more innovating Belfast Vernacular vari-

Table 7.13. *Realization of /a/ in conservative Belfast Vernacular*

[bɛːɡ̇]	*bag*	[hɔːᵊn]	*hand*
[bæk]	*back*	[bɒːᵊd]	*bad*
[flat]	*flat*	[pɒːᵊs]	*pass*
		[bɒːr]	*bar*

Table 7.14. *Realization of Belfast Vernacular /ɛ, a, ɔ/ in polysyllables*

− morpheme boundary		+ morpheme boundary	
['tænər]	*tenor*	['tɛːnər]	*tenner*
['banən]	*Bannon*	['bɑːnən]	*banning*
['rɑ̣bn̩]	*robin*	['rɔ̈ːbn̩]	*robbing*

eties. The short, mostly front allophones of /a/ are characteristic of South Ulster English, while the long, back allophones appear to have their origins in US. Long back /a/ as well as long /ɔ, ɛ/ tend to develop centring off-glides, e.g. [bɒːᵊd] *bad*, [bɛːᵊd] *bed*, [pɔ̈ːᵊd] *pod*. The pattern of fronting, backing and raising in /a/ is by no means rigid, since it is subject to sociolinguistic variation (Milroy, 1982). Nevertheless, the realizations in table 7.13 are typical of conservative Belfast Vernacular.

The proliferation of allophony in /ɛ, a, ɔ/ is responsible for several potential neutralizations which have been carried over into Belfast Vernacular from either Ulster Scots or South Ulster English. The Ulster Scots neutralization of the /ɛ/:/ɑ/ opposition under [ɛː] in velar environments reinforces typically South Ulster English front realizations of /a/. In Belfast Vernacular, the low allophone of /ɛ/ is apt to overlap with short front realizations of /a/ before /k/, e.g. [næk] *neck, knack*. Similarly, the Ulster Scots lowering and unrounding of OSc ö before labials and the South Ulster English overlapping of /a/ and /ɑ/ before voiceless stops combine in Belfast Vernacular to produce the neutralization of the /ɔ/:/a/ opposition before /p/, e.g. [tɑp] *tap, top*. The Ulster Scots merger of the *cot* and *caught* classes is partially adopted in Belfast Vernacular as the contextual neutralization of the /ɔ/:/ɔː/ contrast in all but the 'short' environments mentioned in group (c) on page 127, e.g. [kɑt] *cot* vs. [kɔ̈ᵊt] *caught*; but [dɔ̈ːᵊn] *Don, dawn*, [sɔ̈ːᵊs] *sauce*, [lɔ̈ːᵊs] *loss*. Back raised allophones of /a/ rarely overlap with /ɔː/, since the former are usually more peripheral than the centralized realizations of the latter.

The importance of the morpheme boundary environment in the conditions governing the length and quality of /ɛ, a, ɔ/ in polysyllables (see group (c) on page 127) is illustrated by the minimal pairs or near-minimal pairs in table 7.14. Short allophones of these vowels occur in stressed syllables followed by an

Table 7.15. *Realization of* /e/ *in Belfast Vernacular*

+ morpheme boundary				− morpheme boundary	
[dɛ:]	*day*	[dɛ:z]	*days*	[dɪəz]	*daze*
[frɛ:]	*fray*	[frɛ:d]	*frayed*	[əˈfrɪəd]	*afraid*

unstressed syllable, provided no morpheme boundary intervenes. If a morpheme boundary does intervene, length is conditioned by the following consonant as in monosyllables.

Scots influence on Belfast Vernacular is particularly obvious in the case of /i, ʉ/, in which length is determined by the Aitken's Law conditions that operate in Ulster Scots. Belfast Vernacular lacks the /əi/:/ɑe/ opposition of Ulster Scots, and although BV /əi/ has allophones that are reminiscent of the two Ulster Scots diphthongs, their distribution is not determined by Aitken's Law. In closed syllables, the first mora of BV /əi/ is similar to that in US and SUE /əi/ in that it is mid, although it is also usually fronted, e.g. [seid] *side*. Word-finally, however, the first mora is low as in US /ɑe/, although not backed, e.g. [tæːˑ] *tie*.

BV /e/ displays wide allophonic variation which seems to be Anglo-English in origin, since it occurs in some southern Hiberno-English varieties but not in Ulster Scots. When long, it is realized as [ɛː] morpheme-finally (e.g. [dɛː] *day*), as [ɜː] before /r/ (e.g. [fɜːr] *fair*), and as [ɪə] elsewhere (e.g. [dɪəz] *daze*); when short, it is realized as [ɪə] or [eə] (e.g. [fɪət] *fate*). The presence of the morpheme boundary in the conditions governing quality in /e/ produces minimal pairs not found in RP, as shown in table 7.15.

Before /r/, many Belfast Vernacular vowels undergo extreme quality alterations, resulting in a reduction in the maximal system of contrasts in this environment. The /e/:/ɛ/ opposition is neutralized under [ɜː] before /r/ in monosyllables but is maintained when an unstressed syllable follows in the same morpheme, e.g. [ˈdɜːre] *dairy* vs. [ˈdære] *Derry*. The three-way /e/:/ɛ/:/ʌ/ contrast before /r/ in polysyllables gives way, in conservative Lagan Valley speech, to a two-way /e ~ ɛ/:/ʌ/ contrast in monosyllables, e.g. [ɛːrn] *earn* vs. [ɔrn] *urn*, and to a complete collapse of the opposition under [ɜː] in innovating Belfast Vernacular, even when /r/ is word-final, e.g. [ɜːrn] *earn*, *urn*, [fɜːr] *fair, fur*. While /əi, əʉ/ are pronounced as triphthongs before /r/ in conservative Mid Ulster English (e.g. [ˈtəiər] *tire*), they are often monophthongized in Belfast Vernacular, with the result that the /əʉ/:/a/ opposition is often neutralized in this environment, e.g. [tæːr] *tire*, [taːr] *tower, tar*. The /ɔ/:/o/ opposition is maintained before /r/ in most Mid Ulster English varieties including conservative Belfast Vernacular (e.g. /fɔr/ *for* vs. /for/ *four*), but in progressive Belfast Vernacular it is often neutralized under /o/ in monosyllables.

Northern Hiberno-English consonants

Mid Ulster English consonant phonology also shows evidence of the mixing of South Ulster English and Ulster Scots features. Certain consonantal characteristics are common to most types of Hiberno-English, both northern and southern; for example, the retention of historical /r/ in all positions, the realization of /l/ as clear in all environments, and the preservation of the /ʍ/ (orthographic *wh*):/w/ contrast. Some of the consonantal characteristics of Belfast Vernacular appear to be South Ulster English in origin, for example, palatalization of /k, g, ŋ/ in front-vowel environments and tapping of intervocalic /t/; others of Ulster Scots origin, for example, glottalization of non-initial voiceless stops.

With southern Hiberno-English, northern Hiberno-English shares the retention of historical /r/ in all environments, although its realization varies throughout the country. Post-vocalically, /r/ in northern Hiberno-English is realized as the addition of a retroflex quality to the preceding vowel (e.g., in narrow transcription, [fɔɹ] *fur*). A dental tap occurs after dental consonants, e.g. [θɾiː] *three*. Initially, an alveolar approximant is usual, e.g. [ɹʌn] *run*.

The voiced/voiceless distinction between /w/ and /ʍ/ (e.g. *witch* vs. *which*) is maintained in much of northern Hiberno-English but has been lost in urban Mid Ulster English dialects. /l/ is realized as clear in all environments, including post-vocalically, although here an innovating velarized variant appears in some types of Belfast Vernacular.

Dental articulations of /t, d, n, l/ in all environments occur in some dialects where Irish influence is prominent as well as in some conservative South Ulster English and Mid Ulster English varieties. In other dialects, dental realizations only appear as allophones in some /r/ environments, alveolar articulations being usual elsewhere. In these dialects, sequences of /d/ or /t/ plus /r/ are realized as dental stop plus dental tap, e.g. [t̪ɾiː] *tree*. /d, t, n, l/ are also realized as dentals before /-ər/, provided no morpheme boundary intervenes, e.g. ['mat̪ər] *matter*, but ['fatər] *fatter*.

Palatalization of /k, g, ŋ/ in front-vowel environments is typical of both southern and northern Hiberno-English other than Ulster Scots. These consonants are also palatalized before originally front vowels that have now been backed, in which case a palatal glide often appears in northern Hiberno-English between the consonant and vowel, e.g. [kʲɑːn] *can*, [ba̱ːgʲ] (an innovating alternative to conservative [bɛːgʲ] *bag*).

Northern Hiberno-English lacks the typically southern spirantization of final voiceless stops. However, most northern varieties other than Ulster Scots share with southern Hiberno-English the lenition of medial /t/, which is realized as a voiceless tap, e.g. SUE ['pɪɾ̥] *pity*, or in some types of Mid Ulster English as a voiced tap merging with medial /d/, e.g. BV ['pëɾe] *pity*. The combination of the vowel length conditions and the tapping of /t/ in Belfast Vernacular produces minimal pairs that are also found in some types of North

American English, e.g. ['reɪɾər] *writer* vs. ['reːɪɾər] *rider*. In urban Lagan Valley speech, medial lenition also affects /ð/, which is often deleted in this position, e.g. ['brɔ̈ər] *brother*.

The velar fricative /x/ occurs frequently in rural Ulster Scots in words containing orthographic *gh* (e.g. [θɔːxt] *thought*), but it is general throughout Ulster in proper names and a few dialect words and pronunciations, e.g. /'dɔxərte/ *Doherty*, /lɔx/ *lough*. In dialects other than Ulster Scots, /x/ is usually lenited to [h] or zero, e.g. ['dahərte], ['daərte] *Doherty*, or occasionally merged with /k/, e.g. [lɑk] *lough*.

In Ulster Scots, but not in South Ulster English, voiceless stops and affricates are usually glottalized when medial or final, e.g. ['lʌˀke] *lucky*, [pəiˀp] *pipe*. Glottalized /t/ may lose its oral articulation, e.g. [pɔːˀ] *pot*. In Belfast Vernacular, this glottalization is only generally adopted before syllabic sonorants, e.g. [bɑˀtl] or [bɑʔl] *bottle*. However, in some types of Belfast Vernacular where Ulster Scots influence is strongest, voiceless stops are also glottalized in final position. The closing of the glottis is often accompanied by a raising of the larynx which produces compression of the air betwen the glottal and oral closures and results in an ejective release, e.g. [wik'] *week*.

Northern Hiberno-English morphology and syntax

Many features of northern Hiberno-English morphology and syntax are to be found in other nonstandard dialects throughout the English-speaking world (see chapters 1, 2, 5, 6, 8 and 11) or in records of earlier forms of the standard language (Milroy, 1981). These features include: the simplification of strong verb allomorphy, resulting in a reduction of Standard English (SE) three-form distinctions (e.g. *do/did/done*) to two (e.g. *do/done/done, see/seen/seen, go/went/went*) and SE two-form distinctions (e.g. *come/came/come*) to one (e.g. *come/come/come, run/run/run, beat/beat/beat*); contrasting singular and plural forms of 2nd person, personal pronouns (*you* vs. *youse*) and their use in imperatives (1); the deletion of subject relative pronouns (2); and the use of the *for-to*-complement to express purpose (3):

(1) Come you here!
(2) It was Bernie seen him
(3) He went up the street for to buy a paper

Two SE non-assertive forms can be used in positive sentences in some northern Hiberno-English: *yet* meaning 'still' (4) and *anymore* meaning 'from now on' or simply 'nowadays' (5):

(4) He's here yet
     (SE: He's still here)
(5) I'll be getting six or seven days' holiday anymore
     (SE: I'm getting six or seven days' holiday from now on)

Example (5) is from Milroy (1981). Labov notes a similar use of positive *anymore* in midwestern American English: *That's the way it is with airplanes anymore* (1972: 309). The morphological distinction between singular and plural in subject–verb concord is neutralized in many types of northern Hiberno-English: the singular marker -*s* appears on verbs with either a singular or a plural subject (unless the latter is a personal pronoun, in which case plural concord operates as in SE) (Policansky, 1982):

(6)   Them eggs is cracked, so they are

Some cases of nonstandard usage are apparently confined to northern Hiberno-English, for example: adverbial *but* meaning 'though' (7); *from* as a conjunction meaning 'since' or 'from when' (8); and the use of the conjunction *whenever* to mean simply 'when' without any implication of repeated action (9):

(7)   I never seen him, but
      SE: I didn't see him, though
(8)   She's living here from she was married
      SE: She has been living here since she was married
(9)   My husband died whenever I was living in the New Lodge Road

The northern Hiberno-English tense–aspect system exhibits many characteristics that are peculiar to Hiberno-English, some of which can be attributed to interference from Irish (see also chapter 8). The SE perfect tends to be avoided in conservative varieties of northern Hiberno-English; instead, a construction with the past participle positioned after the object may be used in transitive sentences (10), or, when reference is being made to the immediate past, a construction is employed which is formed with *be* followed by *after* and the present participle (11) (Harris, 1982).

(10) Aston Villa have the League won
      SE: Aston Villa have won the League
(11) She's after telling him the news
      SE: She's just told him the news

Otherwise, the simple past (12) or non-past (13), or the progressive (8) are used in contexts where the perfect would be appropriate in British SE:

(12) Did you see him yet?
      SE: Have you seen him yet?
      (But the Hiberno-English form is acceptable in North American
      Standard English.)
(13) He's a good while dead
      SE: He's been dead a good while

In some conservative varieties of Hiberno-English (both northern and southern), special habitual forms of the verb occur. These take one of three forms:

do plus the infinitive (14); *do* plus *be* plus the present participle (15); or a habitual *be*-form followed by the present participle (e.g. *I be going, he be's going* which contrast with the non-habitual forms *I am going, he is going*) (16). (Note that habitual *be* is by no means restricted to Hiberno-English. It is well known as a feature of Black American English, for which point see Traugott, 1972: 191.)

(14) There's a sawmill here and they do take a lot of timber for palings
(15) He does be coming round here a lot now
(16) They be planting trees every year at the Forestry

Conclusion

Speakers of British English often remark on the similarities between certain types of northern Hiberno-English and North American English. Indeed it is possible to identify particular linguistic features in northern Hiberno-English which also occur in many dialects of Canada and the United States but not in standard British English. At the phonological level these include: the retention of post-vocalic /r/; the tapping of intervocalic /t/; a low unrounded reflex of ME ŏ before voiceless stops (e.g. [gät] *got*, [bläk] *block*); and lengthened reflexes of ME ä and ŏ before voiced consonants and voiceless fricatives (so that, for instance, the vowels in *bad, ban, gas, god, Tom, loss* are long).

There appear to be at least three reasons for this reported similarity, all of which are rooted in the chronology of events that led to the spread of English beyond the shores of Britain. Firstly, the conditions of contact in the north of Ireland between the typologically distinct dialects of England and Scotland were similar to those that initially obtained in North America. Secondly, the arrival of a major British presence in Ireland during the sixteenth and seventeenth centuries roughly coincided with early large-scale British settlement of North America. Thirdly, the migration of large numbers of northern Irish Presbyterians (the so-called 'Scotch-Irish') to North America at the end of the eighteenth century had an important influence on the development of American English (not to mention the impact of more recent large-scale Irish immigration). It is natural in the light of these facts that the American and Irish varieties of English which both developed as a result of early British colonialism should share certain linguistic features that were characteristic of Early Modern English but have subsequently been lost from Standard British English.

REFERENCES

Adams, G. B. (ed.) 1964. *Ulster dialects: an introductory symposium*. Cultra: Ulster Folk Museum.
———— 1966. Phonemic systems in collision in Ulster English. In *Verhandlungen des 2. Internationalen Dialektologenkongresses: Marburg 1965*. Wiesbaden: Franz Steiner. pp. 1–6.

Aitken, A.J. 1981. The Scottish vowel-length rule. In M. Benskin and M.L. Samuels (eds.) *So mony people longages and tonges*. Edinburgh: Benskin and Samuels. pp. 131–57.

Barry, M.V. 1980. The southern boundaries of northern Hiberno-English. In R. Thelwall (ed.) *Linguistic studies in honour of Paul Christophersen. Occasional Papers in Linguistics and Language Learning* 7. Coleraine: New University of Ulster. pp. 105–152.

Braidwood, J. 1964. Ulster and Elizabethan English. In Adams (1964) pp. 1–109.

Gregg, R.J. 1958. Notes on the phonology of a Co. Antrim Scotch-Irish dialect. I. *Orbis* 7: 392–406.

———— 1964. Scotch-Irish urban speech in Ulster. In Adams (1964) pp. 163–92.

———— 1972. The Scotch-Irish dialect boundaries in Ulster. In M.F. Wakelin (ed.) *Patterns in the folk speech of the British Isles*. London: The Athlone Press. pp. 109–39.

Harris, J. 1982. The underlying non-identity of English dialects. *Belfast Working Papers in Language and Linguistics* 6: 1–36.

Jarman, E. and Cruttenden, A. 1976. Belfast intonation and the myth of the fall. *Journal of the International Phonetic Association* 6: 4–12.

Labov, W. 1972. *Sociolinguistic patterns*. Oxford: Blackwell.

Lass, R. 1974. Linguistic orthogenesis? Scots vowel quantity and the English length conspiracy. In J.M. Anderson and C. Jones (eds.) *Historical linguistics* II. Amsterdam: North-Holland. pp. 331–52.

———— 1976. *English phonology and phonological theory*. Cambridge: CUP.

Milroy, J. 1976. Length and height variations in the vowels of Belfast Vernacular. *Belfast Working Papers in Language and Linguistics* 1: 67–110.

———— 1981. *Regional accents of English: Belfast*. Belfast: Blackstaff.

———— 1982. Probing under the tip of the iceberg: phonological 'normalization' and the shape of the speech community. In S. Romaine (ed.) *Sociolinguistic variation in speech communities*. London: Edward Arnold. pp. 35–48.

Milroy, J. and Harris, J. 1980. When is a merger not a merger? *English World-Wide* 1: 199–210.

Milroy, J. and Milroy, L. 1978. Belfast: change and variation in an urban vernacular. In P. Trudgill (ed.) *Sociolinguistic patterns in British English*. London: Arnold. pp. 19–36.

Policansky, L. 1982. Grammatical variation in Belfast English. *Belfast Working Papers in Language and Linguistics* 6: 37–66.

Traugott, E.C. 1972. *A history of English syntax*. New York: Holt, Rinehart and Winston.

8

English in the south of Ireland

A. BLISS

Pronunciation

In general, the pronunciation of present-day southern Hiberno-English represents the accommodation of the sounds of mid-seventeenth-century English to the phonemic system of the Irish language: Irish speakers learning the variety of English used in Ireland interpreted and reproduced the sounds they heard in terms of their own phonemic system, and the resulting pronunciation has been handed down, more or less intact, to the present day. A good deal of information on pronunciation is given in Henry (1958), while some theoretical considerations are discussed in Bliss (1972a); for earlier forms of southern Hiberno-English see Bliss (1979).

Vowels and diphthongs

The variety of English on which southern Hiberno-English is based had six short vowel phonemes /i, e, a, ɔ, ʌ, u/, six long vowel phonemes /iː, eː, aː, ɔː, oː, uː/, and three diphthongal phonemes /əi, əu, ɔi/. Irish had (at most) five short vowel phonemes /i, e, a, o, u/, five long vowel phonemes /iː, eː, aː, oː, uː/, and a series of diphthongal phonemes, the precise number varying from dialect to dialect. There was, therefore, an insufficient number of vowel phonemes in Irish to match the vowel phonemes of English, so that the speaker of Irish would have difficulty in recognizing and reproducing the English sounds. However, the Irish vowel /a/ had two main allophones [a] and [ɑ], and the Irish vowel /aː/ had two main allophones [aː] and [ɑː]; by raising these allophones to phonemic status the requisite number of vowels was made up. The relationship between the vowel phonemes of seventeenth-century English and of present-day southern Hiberno-English is therefore that shown in table 8.1.

The English diphthongs /əi/ and /əu/ presented little difficulty, since all dialects of Irish had comparable diphthongs. Irish, however, had no diphthong which at all resembled the English diphthong /ɔi/; but this diphthong was very rare, and most of the words written with *oi* or *oy* were (or could be) pronounced with the diphthong /əi/; corresponding pronunciations are still common in southern Hiberno-English, e.g. /dʒəin/ *join*. The precise realization of the various vowel phonemes of southern Hiberno-English varies from

135

Table 8.1. *Vowels of southern Hiberno-English and seventeenth-century English*

17c. Eng:	ɪ	ɛ	a	ɔ	ʌ	ʊ
SHE:	ɪ	ɛ	a	ɑ	ɔ	ʊ
17c. Eng:	iː	eː	aː	ɔː	oː	uː
SHE:	iː	eː	aː	ɑː	oː	uː

Table 8.2. *Distribution of southern Hiberno-English vowels*

/ɪ/	bid
/ɛ/	bed
/a/	bad
/ɑ/	pot
/ɔ/	putt, nurse
/ʊ/	put
/iː/	bee, peer
/eː/	bay, pair
/aː/	path, calm, bard
/ɑː/	paw, talk, port
/oː/	boat, hoarse
/uː/	boot, tour
/əɪ/	buy
/əu/	bout
/ɔɪ/	boy

Table 8.3. *Consonant phonemes of Irish*

p	p′	t [t̪]	t′	k′	k	
b	b′	d [d̪]	d′	g′	g	
f [ɸ]	f′	s	s′ [ʃ]	x′ [ç]	x	h
v [β]	v′			ɣ′ [j]	ɣ	
m	m′	n	n′	ŋ′	ŋ	
		l	l′			
		r	r′			

district to district: this is what makes up the 'local accent' by which it is possible to identify what district a speaker comes from. Most realizations do not differ widely from the phonetic value of the symbols here used to identify the phonemes. The realization of the phoneme /ɔ/, however, (like the corresponding phoneme of Irish) is to a greater or lesser extent centralized, [ɔ̈]. The vowels of educated southern Hiberno-English are distributed over lexical sets in the way shown in table 8.2. For further information concerning phonetic details and social and regional variation, see Nally (1971) and Barry (1981).

Consonants

The consonant phonemes of seventeenth-century English did not differ much from those of present-day English. The consonant phonemes of Irish (see table 8.3) were, and are, very numerous, because every consonant phoneme except /h/ is duplicated, one form being palatal and the other non-palatal. The system varies slightly from dialect to dialect, that of the Munster dialect being the simplest; there is some reason to suppose that the English language was first accommodated to the Munster dialect, and from Munster carried into the other provinces virtually unchanged. In table 8.3 the palatal phonemes are distinguished by the accent ʹ; non-palatal phonemes are left unmarked. Generally the normal realization of each phoneme is close to the phonetic value of the symbol used; where this is not so the normal realization is given in square brackets.

Irish had 31 consonant phonemes (see chapter 18), English only 23 (excluding the affricates /tʃ/ and /dʒ/, which were treated as sequences /tʃ/ and /dʒ/.) Irish speakers could therefore take their choice when equating English sounds with their own. Generally the resemblance between Irish and English phonemes was obvious enough. In some cases the two members of a pair of phonemes were equated with two different English sounds: Irish /f, fʹ/ were equated with English /ʍ, f/, Irish /v, vʹ/ with English /w, v/; Irish /t, tʹ/ with English /θ, t/, Irish /d, dʹ/ with English /ð, d/; Irish /s, sʹ/ with English /s, ʃ/. In some cases only one member of a pair of phonemes came into play, the other being dropped: Irish /nʹ/ was equated with English /n/, Irish /lʹ/ with English /l/, Irish /r/ with English /r/, Irish /ɣʹ/ with English /j/. In some cases the two members of a pair of phonemes were equated with what in English were only allophonic variants: Irish /k, kʹ/ were equated with English /k/, Irish /g, gʹ/ with English /g/. Sometimes a neutral sound, not precisely resembling either of a pair of Irish phonemes, was introduced to reproduce an English sound; this is the case with English /p, b, m, ŋ/. The English phoneme /h/ offered no difficulty, of course. No sounds corresponding to English /z, ʒ/ existed in Irish, but since these are merely the voiced equivalents of /s, ʃ/ they were easily articulated. The inventory of southern Hiberno-English consonant phonemes is as follows:

/p, b, ṱ, ḓ, t, d, k, g,
ʍ, w, f, v, s, z, ʃ, ʒ, j,
l, r,ⸯ.
m, n, ŋ,
h/

Post-vocalic /r/, as in *nurse, car*, is preserved in southern Hiberno-English.

The equivalences between English and Irish consonants described above explain many of the peculiarities of southern Hiberno-English articulation. Irish /v/ is normally realized as a bilabial fricative [β]; hence there is sometimes a confusion between English /v/ and /w/, particularly in unstressed positions, as in /ə hel əwə lɑt/ *a hell of a lot.* Irish /t, d/ are true dental stops; they share with English /θ, ð/ the dental articulation but not the fricative quality; the stop quality of SHE /ṱ, ḓ/ is a very characteristic feature of the dialect. In some districts, mainly in urban areas, /ṱ, ḓ/ have been further fused with /t, d/, so that there is no longer any distinction between such words as *thin* and *tin.* SHE /l/ is always 'clear' in quality; there is no trace of the 'dark' [ɫ] normal in RP in such words as *fill, field.* SHE /k, g/ are subject to more extreme allophonic variation than the corresponding English sounds, having a very marked palatal quality before and after front vowels (see chapter 7).

So far we have considered only differences in articulation; there are also a number of differences of distribution. Many of these are to be attributed to the influence of the Irish language. It is a rule of the Irish language that in any consonant group (with very few exceptions) all the consonants must be of the same quality; that is, all must be palatal or all must be non-palatal. The quality of the group is dictated by the quality of the final consonant of the group. As we have seen, some southern Hiberno-English consonants correspond to Irish palatal consonants, others to Irish non-palatal consonants; in particular, /t, d, ʃ, ʒ, n, l/ are 'palatal', and /ṱ, ḓ, s, z, r/ are 'non-palatal'. Any English consonant group which by Irish standards would mix the qualities would be difficult for a speaker of Irish to articulate, and so there is a tendency to substitute related consonants so as to preserve the same quality throughout the group; as in Irish, the quality of the last consonant is decisive.

The most widespread tendency affects the English groups /tr, dr/, which are replaced by /ṱr, ḓr/, as in /ṱrik/ *trick*, /ḓrap/ *drop*; the same replacement occurs when the /r/ is syllabic, as in /dɑːṱr/ *daughter*, /laḓr/ *ladder*. These pronunciations are almost universal, and in Anglo-Irish literature are often represented by such spellings as *thrick*, etc. No Irishman ever said */θrik/, of course; but since the phoneme used in /ṱrik/ is the same as the one used to replace English /θ/ in such a word as /ṱik/ *thick* it seems not unreasonable to use the spelling *th* to represent it. In the west of Ireland pronunciation is affected by a further wide-ranging series of changes of the same kind. Whenever in English the consonant /s/ is followed by one of the consonants equated with an Irish palatal consonant (that is, by /t, n, l/) it is replaced by /ʃ/, as in /ʃtap/ *stop*,

/ʃnoː/ *snow*, /ʃloː/ *slow*. The same change happens before final /t/ or vocalic /n, l/ as in /beʃt/ *best*, /liʃn/ *listen*, /reʃl/ *wrestle*. When English /s/ is followed by /tr/ this change does not, of course, take place, since English /tr/ is replaced bySHE /t̪r/ and the conditions for the change are not present: /st̪raŋ/ *strong*, /maːst̪r/ *master*. Though there is no /z/ phoneme in Irish, SHE /z/ follows the analogy of /s/ and is replaced by /ʒ/ when followed by /d n l/, as in /wenʒdi/ *Wednesday*, /biʒnəs/ *business*, /pɔʒl/ *puzzle*; these groups do not occur in initial position.

Other peculiarities of distribution are inherited from seventeenth-century English variants; in some cases such pronunciations are reinforced by a similar tendency in Irish. Perhaps the most important, and certainly the best known, survival of a feature of seventeenth-century pronunciation is the use of /eː/ instead of /iː/ as the reflex of ME *ẹ̄* in such words as /seː/ *sea*, /meːt/ *meat*, /rəˈseːv/ *receive*, /eːkwəl/ *equal*. Another common pronunciation is the use of /əu/ instead of /oː/ before /ld/ (and occasionally before /l/) in such words as /əuld/ *old*, /kəuld/ *cold*, /səul/ *soul*. These two pronunciations are avoided by educated speakers, but can be heard in all parts of the country. In the west of Ireland the vowel /e/ is commonly replaced by /i/ before a nasal consonant, and occasionally before other consonants, as in /d̪im/ *them*, /twinti/ *twenty*, /dəˈspinsəri/ *dispensary*, /vit/ *vet* 'veterinary surgeon'. A glide vowel tends to develop in the groups /lm, rm/, which become /ləm, rəm/; this type of pronunciation is common in all words, and in the word /filəm/ *film* it is universal, even among educated speakers.

Stress

Further peculiarities of southern Hiberno-English pronunciation are probably to be attributed to the hedge schoolmasters, who were partly self-educated. In the course of their extensive reading they came across many words which they had never heard pronounced, for which they had to invent a pronunciation; sometimes they guessed right, sometimes wrong, and their wrong guesses were transmitted to their pupils and passed into common use. The position of the southern Hiberno-English stress in polysyllabic words is often different from its position in English; in some words southern Hiberno-English merely continues the seventeenth-century stress, but in others there seems to be no historical justification for the position of the stress, and in these cases the hedge schoolmasters seem to be responsible. In general the stress falls one syllable later in southern Hiberno-English than in English: *defícit*, *díscipline*, *intégral*, *intrícate*, *antíquary*, *fragméntary*. However, if in English there is a syllable with secondary stress, the main stress in southern Hiberno-English falls on that syllable: *paralýse*, *architécture*, *speculátor*. The hedge schoolmasters had a good knowledge of Latin, and it is no doubt for this reason that many words of Latin origin are pronounced in southern Hiberno-English with Latin rather than with English vowels. Thus, *status* and *data* (in English /steitəs/ and /deitə/) are pronounced /staːtəs/ and /daːtə/; similarly *via* (in English /vaiə/) is pronounced /viːə/. There is a complex example in *a priori*: in English this is /ei praiˈɔːrai/, in southern Hiberno-English /aː priˈɔːri/.

Vocabulary

The vast majority of words used in southern Hiberno-English are Standard English words used in SE senses. A small proportion of the words used in southern Hiberno-English are nonstandard in one of two ways: either they are words which do not occur at all in SE, or they are words used in senses not found in SE. These words and senses are of two origins. On the one hand, a number of words which have become obsolete in SE, or which have never been current except in dialectal English, are current in southern Hiberno-English; on the other hand, a few Irish words, and a much larger number of English words used in nonstandard ways dictated by Irish usage, also form a significant part of the southern Hiberno-English vocabulary. As well as this direct influence, Irish has also had an indirect influence: a number of non-standard usages, undoubtedly of archaic or dialectal English origin, can be paralleled in Irish, and to this Irish influence they clearly owe (in part, at least) their survival.

It is very difficult to distinguish obsolete SE words from dialectal English words, since many obsolete words have survived in the dialects, and it is impossible to determine from which source they entered southern Hiberno-English. It is difficult, too, to determine the precise date at which a word became obsolete in SE: documentation is incomplete, and the issue may be confused by poetic and antiquarian usages. Among the words which were once standard, and appear not to survive to any large extent in dialects other than southern Hiberno-English, most have become obsolete since 1650. At least one, however, seems to have become obsolete about 1600: this is the verb *bring* in the sense of 'take', universally used in Ireland even by educated people in such contexts as *The injured man was brought to the hospital*. Probably the southern Hiberno-English usage is independent of the obsolete English usage: the same verb is used for both 'bring' and 'take' in Irish.

The following southern Hiberno-English words became obsolete in England from 1650 onwards (the date given is the approximate date of obsolescence):

1650: *cog*, the universal word for 'cheat (in an examination)';
1700: *airy* 'gay, light-hearted'; *bowsey* 'disreputable drunkard'; *latter*, in the common phrase *in the latter end*;
1750: *handsel* 'New Year's gift'; *mannerly* 'well-mannered'; *strand* 'beach';
1800: *crawthumper* 'ostentatiously devout person'; *cross* 'ill-natured' (the Irish *crosta* is derived from this, with the addition of the adjectival ending *-da*); *delph* 'crockery'; *shore* 'drain', perhaps originally a sub-standard pronunciation of *sewer*;

1850: *cock up* 'make a fuss of', based on the obsolete *cocker up*; *mearing* 'boundary', borrowed into Irish in the form *méirín*.

The following southern Hiberno-English words became obsolete in SE at the approximate dates given, but have remained current in many English dialects:

1650: *learn* 'teach'; *lief(er)* 'soon(er)'; *mitch*, the universal word for 'play truant from school'; *pismire* 'ant';

1700: *afeared* 'afraid'; *ail* 'be amiss with', in such a context as *What ails the child?*; *grain* 'prong of a fork'; *renegue* 'go back on one's word';

1750: *collogue* 'conspire together'; *great* 'friendly (with)', supported by Irish *mór le*; *lock* 'small quantity (of hay, etc.)', borrowed into Irish as *loca*;

1800: *dark* 'blind'; *draw* 'bring in (turf, etc.)', supported by Irish *tarraingt*; *mad* 'angry', supported by Irish *ar buile* 'insane, angry'; *rose* 'erysipelas';

1850: *galluses* 'braces'.

Among the dialectal words which seem never to have belonged to SE the most interesting group is the one consisting of words drawn from Scottish and northern English dialects. Some of these are used only in Ulster, where Scottish settlement was extensive (see chapter 7): *clarty* 'dirty'; *greet* 'weep'; *hap* 'wrap up'; *scunner* 'loathing, dislike'; *thole* 'endure'; *wee* 'small'. Other words have a much wider distribution, and can be heard in most parts of Ireland: *blather* 'talk voluble nonsense'; *cod* as a noun 'joke', as a verb 'make a fool of'; *dinge* 'dent'; *graip* 'dung-fork'; *kink* 'spasm (of laughing or coughing)'; *oxter* 'armpit'; *press* 'cupboard'; *whinge* 'whine, whimper'. The large number of such words in general use suggests that there must have been a sizeable Scottish and northern English element among the settlers in the three southern provinces. Other dialectal words in general use include the following: *butt* 'end'; *disremember* 'forget'; *ditch* 'bank'; *furze* 'gorse'; *peg* 'throw'; *sup* 'small quantity (of liquid)'; *tint* 'drop'; *widow-woman* 'widow', supported by Irish *baintreach mná*, literally 'widow of a woman'.

The number of actual Irish words used in southern Hiberno-English is small, even in rural areas; educated people do not use them at all, except by way of conscious rusticism. A substantial number of such words are terms of abuse: *ommadhawn* 'fool' (Irish *amadán*); *oanshagh* '(female) fool' (Irish *óinseach*); *bosthoon* 'clown' (Irish *bastún*); *sleeveen* 'sly fellow' (Irish *slíbhín*); *spalpeen* 'rascal' (Irish *spailpín* 'seasonal worker'). Many others refer primarily to rural life: *soogawn* 'hay rope' (Irish *súgán*); *gowlogue* 'forked stick' (Irish *gabhlóg*); *kish* 'basket' (Irish *cis*); *cleeve* 'basket' (Irish *cliabh*); *loy* 'narrow spade' (Irish *láighe*); *slane* 'turf-spade' Irish (*sleaghán*). In the west of Ireland the vocabulary of southern Hiberno-English has been much extended by the free use of the diminutive ending *-een*, from the Irish diminutive *-ín*. This ending may be added to any English word, but it is most common with words which already contain some suggestion of youth or smallness: *childreen*, *girleen, foaleen.* In Irish, when the diminutive is added to a word ending in non-palatal /s/, this phoneme is replaced by its palatal equivalent, and this phenomenon is sometimes reflected in southern Hiberno-English. Thus, *glass* gives the diminutive *glasheen*; and by an obvious analogy *breeze* gives *breezheen*.

Perhaps the most interesting group of southern Hiberno-English words consists of SE words used in a sense directly dictated, in one way or another, by Irish usage. One characteristic kind of usage can be illustrated by the word *let* in such a phrase as *I let a shout* – the universal usage in such a context. Irish *ligim* normally means 'I let'; idiomatically it also means 'I utter', in such a phrase as *ligim gáir* 'I utter a shout'. The Irish speaker learning English obviously learned a single equivalent, *I let*, for Irish *ligim*, and used it even when the English context required a different verb; hence to render *ligim gáir* he used *I let a shout*. In a sense we can say that SHE *I let a shout* involves a mistranslation from Irish into English. Another common instance of this kind of mistranslation is the general use of *bold* in the sense of 'naughty'; Irish *dána* can mean both 'courageous' and 'naughty', and the Irish speaker used his equivalent, *bold*, irrespective of the context.

Other instances of Irish influence are more complex, and may depend on mere errors. Irish *teilgim* 'I throw (out)' and *seilgim* 'I hunt' have past tenses *theilg* and *sheilg* respectively; these two forms have the same pronunciation, so that /hel'ig'/ may mean either 'threw (out)' or 'hunted'; in southern Hiberno-English one rendering may be substituted for the other, so that *He hunted his wife* means 'He turned his wife out of the house.' In rendering such an English expression as *I have had enough*, Irish uses a noun meaning 'sufficiency', either *dóthain* or *sáith* according to dialect, and this noun is preceded by a possessive, so that a literal translation of the Irish would be 'I had my sufficiency'. At some stage English *enough* was interpreted as *a nough*, and the supposed indefinite article was replaced by a possessive, so that southern Hiberno-English uses *I had my 'nough*. One very interesting instance of confusion depends on errors in both Irish and English. Irish has an obsolete word *Fiadha* 'God', identical in pronunciation with *fiadh* 'deer'; already in Irish the two words were confused, so that *dar Fiadha* 'by God' could be expanded to *dar fiadh is dar fiolar* 'by deer and by eagle'. This confusion was carried over into southern Hiberno-English, so that *God* could be replaced by *the deer*; in particular, *God knows* was replaced by *the deer knows*. No doubt under the influence of such English expressions as *Oh dear!* and *Dear me!*, deer was further replaced by *Dear*; *the Dear knows* is now always so spelt, and is understood as 'the dear one [i.e. God] knows.'

Finally, there are a few instances in which English words have undergone a development of meaning in southern Hiberno-English which cannot be explained in terms either of English dialects or of the Irish language; these seem to be instances of spontaneous development in Ireland. Two of the commonest of such words are *hames* and *yoke*. The word *hames* is plural, and is properly applied to the two curved pieces of metal placed on either side of the collar of a horse or an ass. In southern Hiberno-English *hames* is singular, and refers to a ludicrously unsuccessful attempt to perform some action: *He made a right hames of it*. The mechanism of this semantic change is obscure. The word *yoke* properly refers to a device by which two animals are coupled together for drawing a plough or a cart. In southern Hiberno-English *yoke* can be applied to anything for which the name is not known, or has been momentarily forgotten: *What's that yoke for?* Again the semantic development is obscure. It may be significant that in each case the proper context of the word is rural or agricultural.

The only specific study of vocabulary is Clark (1917), but see also Bliss (1972b). Joyce (1910) gives an alphabetic list of Hiberno-English words, and many regional word lists have been published in Irish newspapers and local journals – but these are not readily accessible.

Grammar

The 'tenses' of the English verb are partly tenses properly so called (placing an action in time, either absolutely or in relation to some specified event) and partly aspects (considering the nature of the action – instantaneous, repeated, habitual, completed, etc.). The 'tenses' of the Irish verb also have this dual function, but with a greater emphasis on aspect than in English. English has only two inflected tenses, present and past (*he writes, he wrote*). In addition it has a number of compound tenses formed with various auxiliaries: future and conditional (*he will write, he would write*), imperfect (*he used to write*), perfect and pluperfect (*he has written, he had written*). There are also the so-called 'progressive' tenses (*he is writing, he was writing*, etc.) The Irish verb has five inflected tenses, present, future, past, imperfect, conditional, but no perfect or pluperfect. The verb 'to be' has, in addition, a special consuetudinal present: *tá sé* 'he is', *bíonn sé* 'he is (usually)'. There is also a full range of 'progressive' tenses, formed with the verb 'to be' and the verbal noun, linked by the preposition *ag* 'at': *tá sé ag scríobh*, literally 'he is at writing'. There is a kind of progressive perfect and pluperfect, formed by substituting the preposition *tar éis* 'after' for the preposition *ag* 'at': *tá sé tar éis scríofa*, literally 'he is after writing'.

Southern Hiberno-English has precisely the same range of tenses as Irish has, but the forms are built up out of English material. Many of the tenses are, of course, the same as in SE. A study of the tenses can best begin with the verb 'to be', since in southern Hiberno-English, as in Irish, it has some distinctive forms. The consuetudinal present of Irish is reproduced in two ways: in the north of the country a common form is *I be, you be, he bees*, etc.; but the more general form is *I do be, you do be, he does be*, etc. This form is in very common use, though it is normally avoided by educated speakers. The future and conditional are formed as in SE, except that the auxiliary *shall (should)* is not used: *I will be, you will be, he will be*, etc.; *I would be, you would be, he would be*, etc. The imperfect is formed as in SE, but the preposition *to* is commonly omitted: *he used be*, instead of the standard form *he used to be*. The verb 'to write' may be taken as a typical example of verbs other than the verb 'to be'. The present tense of most verbs, including this one, is usually consuetudinal in aspect: *he writes (books)* means 'he is in the habit of writing (books)'. There is therefore no need for a special consuetudinal form, and there is none in Irish. Nevertheless, southern Hiberno-English often reinforces the consuetudinal aspect by the use of the form *he does write*. The future, conditional and imperfect are subject to the same qualification as those of the verb 'to be'. The progressive tenses include a consuetudinal present *he bees writing* or *he does be writing* 'he usually writes'. The progressive perfect and pluperfect are *he is (he was) after writing*. These tenses always imply recent action, and correspond fairly closely to SE *he has (had) just written*:

(1)   Amn't I after telling you? 'Haven't I just told you?'
      I was after getting married 'I had just got married'

In general, the progressive tenses are more widely used in southern Hiberno-English than in SE. In SE the progressive tenses are not used at all with certain types of verb, specifically those which do not denote duration in a limited time, like 'to believe', 'to see', 'to hope', 'to want'. In southern Hiberno-English there is no such limitation:

(2)   The door is facing to the East
      Who is this book belonging to?

Possibly the participle is here felt to be an adjective. The use of the progressive tenses sometimes makes it possible to express nuances of meaning which cannot readily be expressed in SE, e.g. 'I thought it was in the drawer [but in fact it wasn't]', but 'I was thinking it was in the drawer [and sure enough it was]'.

Though educated speakers use the SE perfect and pluperfect, these tenses do not exist in 'pure' southern Hiberno-English (except for the 'progressive' perfect and pluperfect described above). In some contexts other tenses are used. When in SE the perfect or pluperfect would be followed by an expression denoting duration in time, southern Hiberno-English uses the present or past:

(3)   She's dead these ten years 'She has been dead . . .'
      I know Tom about twelve or thirteen years 'I have known Tom . . .'
      We were there about half an hour when there was a knock on the door
      'We had been there . . .'

When in SE the perfect or pluperfect would not be followed by an expression denoting duration in time, southern Hiberno-English uses the past in either case (cf. chapter 7).

(4) I warned her before 'I have warned her ...'
     If he had his wits about him he would not have done it 'If he had had
     his wits ...'

Southern Hiberno-English further has two types of quasi-perfect, one used
with intransitive and the other with transitive verbs. In English the perfect and
pluperfect are always formed with the verb 'to have', but in many languages
verbs of motion, at least, form these tenses with the verb 'to be'. This
construction is used in Irish and in southern Hiberno-English:

(5) The sergeant is gone up to the barracks
     You were only gone out of sight when I came on your book

Possibly the participle is here felt to be an adjective. With transitive verbs
southern Hiberno-English uses tenses which superficially resemble the
English perfect and pluperfect, but are differently formed and have a different
connotation; where SE uses *he has (had) written it*, southern Hiberno-English
uses *he has (had) it written*:

(6) I have him persuaded at last
     The boots had her crippled, she said

Among the minor forms of the verb the most striking features of southern
Hiberno-English are to be found in the imperative. A common substitute for
the SE form is a construction with *let you ...*:

(7) Let you stay here till I come back
     Let you have a try at it, Michael

In Munster *let* is often replaced in this construction by *leave*. A kind of
progressive imperative is very common:

(8) Let you be listening to me, Joanna
     Let you be coming up and taking a look at it

In the negative imperative a progressive construction is very common, even
among educated speakers:

(9) Don't be talking like that
     Don't be troubling yourself

In common with many other dialects of English, some varieties of southern
Hiberno-English use nonstandard inflected forms of verbs. As in many dialects, the present participle ending *-ing* is generally pronounced /ən/; because
of this, in some verbs the present and past participles are pronounced the
same: /givən/ *giving, given*, /fɑːlən/ *falling, fallen*. Avoidance of ambiguity in
such cases has perhaps encouraged a tendency, already noticeable in seventeenth-century English, to use the past tense form also for the past participle,
as in *broke* 'broken', *rode* 'ridden', *tore* 'torn'. On the analogy of such verbs as

lead: *led*, *meet*: *met* there is a tendency to prefer a short vowel in the past tense instead of a historical long vowel: /bet/ *beat*, /ped/ *paid*, /kɑt/ *caught*.

For a discussion of the genesis of certain verbal forms see Bliss (1972a).

Sentence structure

In Irish, as in other Celtic languages, the verb normally stands first in the sentence. For the sake of emphasis, however, some other part of the sentence may stand there. In this case the word or phrase to be emphasized is moved forward and is preceded by the form of the verb 'to be' known as the copula, either in the present tense, *is*, or in the past tense, *ba*; the rest of the sentence is cast into the form of a relative clause. Since the copula is a verb, the rule that the verb stands first has not been broken; but since it is always unstressed, it does not interfere with the required emphasis. If the primary verb is in the past tense, the copula may be either in the present or in the past tense, with a difference of connotation: if the statement may be true of the present as well as of the past, the copula is in the present tense; if the statement is not true of the present, the copula must be in the past tense.

This Irish construction is very accurately imitated in southern Hiberno-English clefting, and is even more common there than in Irish: since the verb cannot well stand first in English, the construction is often used when there is no real need for emphasis. The present tense of the copula is replaced by *it is* or one of its contractions, the past tense by *it was*; the relative pronoun is usually omitted. Any part of the sentence may be emphasized. A simple sentence like *John saw Michael yesterday* might take any of the following forms:

(10)   It was John (that) saw Michael yesterday
        It was Michael (that) John saw yesterday
        It was yesterday (that) John saw Michael

If the subject of the sentence is emphasized, it may happen (as in the first example above) that the new sentence differs from the primary sentence only in so far as *it is* or *it was* is prefixed; but this is not always so. In Irish, if the subject is a pronoun the appropriate form is the disjunctive form, which is identical with the accusative form; in southern Hiberno-English the accusative form of the pronoun is often used, though there are exceptions. In Irish, the relative form of the verb is the same for all persons; in southern Hiberno-English the 3rd person singular of the verb may be used irrespective of the person of the pronoun. Both features are illustrated in the following sentence:

(11)   It's me has the good family that I ought to be proud of

Here *I have* of the primary sentence is replaced by *me has*.

If the primary sentence is negative or interrogative, the copula is made negative or interrogative, and the verb of the relative clause is positive:

(12) 'Tisn't ideas the like of you have, I'm thinking
     Is it out of your mind you are?

Any of the verbal forms described in the last section may be used with this construction, as in the following example:

(13) It's not after leaving it behind you anywheres you are?

Here the SE would be: *Did you leave it behind anywhere?* If the part of the sentence to be emphasized is an infinitive, difficulties may arise. In the following example the word *to* has been omitted in the course of transposition:

(14) Is it catch her you want?

In another example the word *do* has been added (here there are two instances of the construction in the same sentence):

(15) It's thinking I am that it's unyoke him we'd better do

The SE would be: *I think that we had better unyoke him.*
    Where English uses a subordinate clause, Irish often uses a kind of co-ordinate construction, introduced by *agus* 'and', and lacking a finite verb. A similar construction is often used in southern Hiberno-English: the 'clause' is introduced by *and*, has no finite verb, and normally contains a present participle, though an infinitive or an adjective is occasionally found. This kind of co-ordinate construction can be used as a substitute for any kind of subordinate clause, and the construction is in fact much less precise in its implications than any normal subordinate clause. Thus, in the following example it is clear that in English the clause would have *when* or *as*:

(16) It only struck me and you going out of the door

In the next example, however, it is not at all clear if the clause should have *when* or *if* or *seeing that*:

(17) How could you see me there and I to be in bed at the time?

The same construction may also be used when in SE a present participle would directly qualify a noun:

(18) There's a small path only, and it running up between two pools

Here SE would say *a path running up* . . .
    Another nonstandard substitute for a subordinate clause, also based on Irish idiom, uses an infinitive, corresponding to the Irish verbal noun. This construction may replace a noun clause:

(19) It's a pity you not to have left him where he was lying (SE: . . . that you did not leave him. . .)

Alternatively it may replace a conditional clause:

(20)   It would be no credit at all such a thing to be heard in this house (SE: ...
       if such a thing were to be heard ...)

A characteristic of southern Hiberno-English is concerned with the formation of indirect questions. Questions are of two kinds, simple questions that
can be answered 'yes' or 'no', and complex questions introduced by an
interrogative word. Direct questions of both kinds have inversion of verb and
subject. In SE, indirect questions are introduced by *if* or *whether* if they are
simple, or by the appropriate interrogative word if they are complex; in either
case there is no inversion. In southern Hiberno-English, as in Irish, indirect
questions have exactly the same form as direct questions (though the tense of
the verb may be changed); *if* and *whether* are not used in simple questions, and
inversion is retained. Thus, in the simplest case, after the verb *ask*:

(21)   She asked him were there many staying at the hotel
       They asked when would you be back

Indirect questions may also be used after a number of other verbs, such as
wonder, *know* (in the negative), *tell*, *see* (or its southern Hiberno-English
equivalent *try*):

(22)   I wonder does she honestly mean it
       I didn't know did anybody try to find out
       Tell me did you see them
       Go and see are they anyway ripe
       He had looked in to try would we give him a cup of tea

A similar construction may be used after the verb *think* in the interrogative,
though SE does not use an indirect question here:

(23)   Do you think would it be all right?

For further discussion of the syntax of southern Hiberno-English a useful
article is Van Hamel (1912); the syntax of one individual dialect is discussed in
great detail in Henry (1957).

Some idiomatic usages

Many rhetorical devices have been carried over into southern Hiberno-
English from Irish. In particular, the rhetorical question is in common use.
Such rhetorical questions are of two kinds: negative questions, and positive
questions followed by *but* or by its southern Hiberno-English equivalent *only*:

(24)   Amn't I the heart-broken woman?
       Now isn't he the fine-looking young fellow, indeed?
       Who has him enticed now but your own daughter?
       What did we want only to get our own?

As the first two examples show, it is normal in such rhetorical questions to use the definite article *the* where SE would use the indefinite article *a*. The definite article is similarly used in ejaculations and in general in sentences with a strong emotional colour:

(25) That's the grand morning, thank God!
      It was the sorry day I ever let you come into this house

The definite article is often used in contexts where SE would have no article at all. In particular, it is used with names of diseases, languages, counties, and certain festal seasons:

(26) He was taken bad with the jaundice
      She was a stranger with only the book Irish
      A lonely parish in the County Wicklow
      I had a few jars over the Christmas

The definite article is also used with names of relatives, where SE would have a possessive:

(27) I'll be going home, the mother will be expecting me

A number of idiomatic usages are connected with prepositions, and all of them are based directly on Irish idiom. One of the most prolific prepositions is *on*, used primarily of diseases and disagreeable sensations in general, and, by extension, to form a 'dative of disadvantage' designating the victim of any kind of unfortunate occurrence:

(28) It is not any common sickness that is on him
      Where's the use of talking to a man when the fear of death is on him?
      He was murdered on me one St Patrick's Day fair
      I was thinking they've took away my old brogues on me

The preposition *in* is very commonly used in the phrase *in it*, meaning 'in existence', 'there', but used in contexts where a considerable periphrasis would be necessary in SE:

(29) Sure there's no daylight in it at all now (SE: ... no daylight left ...)
      There was a good crowd here for the night that was in it (SE: ... seeing what night it was)
      He was a good footballer when he was in it (SE: ... before he gave up playing)

The preposition *of* is used in a number of related ways. In all these idioms *of* is followed by a noun and preceded by a noun, an adjective, a numeral or a numerical expression, or a quantitative interrogative. When *of* is preceded by a noun, that noun has a kind of adjectival function:

(30)   a blackguard of a Dublin cabman (SE: a blackguardly Dublin cabman)
        a soft fat slob of a girl

When *of* is preceded by an adjective, it is merely superfluous from the point of view of SE:

(31)   That's too big of a tree to cut down with a handsaw
        It won't be too bad of a day

When *of* is preceded by a numeral, SE would invert the order:

(32)   He is married and has three of a family (SE: ... a family of three)
        We finished up with 60,000 of an army (SE: ... an army of 60,000)

When *of* is preceded by a quantitative interrogative, the SE equivalents are various:

(33)   How many of a family has he? (SE: How many children .. ?)
        What age of a man was he when he died? (SE: How old was he .. ?)

There is no specific study of southern Hiberno-English idioms; however, there is valuable material collected by Hayden and Hartog (1909).

In the pronunciation and vocabulary of southern Hiberno-English it is possible to trace the influence both of older strata of the English language and of the Irish language; in grammar, syntax and idiom the peculiarities of southern Hiberno-English depend exclusively on the Irish language. Even in the parts of Ireland where Irish has long been extinct its unconscious influence still controls the usage of speakers of English.

REFERENCES

Barry, M. V. (ed.) 1981. *Aspects of English dialects in Ireland* vol. I. Belfast: Institute of Irish Studies, The Queen's University of Belfast.
Bliss, A. 1972a. Languages in contact: some problems of Hiberno-English. *Proceedings of the Royal Irish Academy* lxii C: 63–82.
———— 1972b. A Synge glossary. In S. B. Bushrui (ed.) *Sunshine and the Moon's delight: a centenary tribute to John Millington Synge.* Gerrards Cross: Colin Smythe; Beirut: American University.
———— 1979. *Spoken English in Ireland 1600–1740: twenty-seven representative texts assembled and analysed by Alan Bliss.* Dublin: The Dolmen Press.
Clark, J. M. 1917. *The vocabulary of Anglo-Irish.* St Gallen: Handels Hochschule, siebzehnter und achtzehnter Jahresbericht.
Hayden, M. and Hartog, M. 1909. The Irish dialect of English. *Fortnightly Review* N.S. lxxxv: 775–85, 933–47.
Henry, P. L. 1957. *An Anglo-Irish dialect of north Roscommon.* Dublin: University College.

—— 1958. A linguistic survey of Ireland: preliminary report. *Lochlann* i: 49–208.

Joyce, P. W. 1910. *English as we speak it in Ireland.* London: Longmans, Green and Co.; Dublin: M. H. Gill and Son Ltd. Reprinted (1979) with an Introduction by Terence Dolan. Dublin: Wolfhound Press.

Nally, E. V. 1971. Notes on a Westmeath dialect. *Journal of the International Phonetic Association* i: 33–8.

Van Hamel, A. G. 1912. On Anglo-Irish syntax. *Englische Studien* xlv: 272–92.

9

Highland and Island English

CYNTHIA SHUKEN

Introduction

Although this chapter is entitled 'Highland and Island English', it is principally concerned with English spoken in the northern Hebridean Islands of Lewis, Harris and Skye. Lewis and Harris are the names of the northern and southern parts, respectively, of the northernmost of the Outer Hebrides. Skye is the largest of the Inner Hebrides, and is very close to the mainland (see map 6.1 on page 110 for the geography of the region). Until recently these were primarily Gaelic-speaking areas, and Lewis and Harris are still among the greatest strongholds of Gaelic in Scotland. As such, scholars have given more attention to the Gaelic of these islands than to their English, and very little research has been done on English here or in the Highlands. This chapter will therefore concentrate on Hebridean English, for which the greatest amount of data is available.

The imposition of English (along with 'civilization' and Protestantism) and the elimination of Gaelic (along with 'barbarity' and Catholicism) in the Highlands and Islands was a definite policy of both the state and the religious institutions of the Lowlands from the seventeenth to the early or middle twentieth centuries. Statements of purpose and accounts of progress were often recorded. Detailed accounts of the history of English in Lewis can be found in Macdonald (1978); of English in the Highlands and particularly in Sutherland in Dorian (1981); and in the Highlands and Islands in general in Campbell (1950), Thomson and Grimble (1968) and MacKinnon (1974).

The elimination of Gaelic and the implantation of English was seen by official institutions as a key to social control of a geographically inaccessible and culturally distinct part of Scotland (and later, of Britain) over which governments found it difficult to exercise their authority. As far back as 1609, by imposing the Statutes of Iona on a group of island chiefs, the Scottish Government tried to ensure that at least their heirs would be educated in English. In 1616, Parliament ordered that schools be provided in order to replace Gaelic with English. These measures were not successful. No more successful were the English schools set up by the SSPCK (Society in Scotland for the Propagation of Christian Knowledge). As their primary aim was religious rather than linguistic, however, they eventually switched to Gaelic for the sake of comprehension. As late as 1812, a teacher in Lewis reported having pupils who had been to an English school, but who could not understand what they read (Macdonald, 1978). This seems to indicate that spoken English still had negligible influence in Lewis at that time. Increasing literacy in Gaelic seemed to lead to greater interest in learning English. It seems probable that English began to take a firm place in education no earlier than the mid-nineteenth century. Religious societies in Edinburgh, Glasgow, and Inverness sponsored schools, and their teachers were likely to have been educated Scottish Standard English speakers from the Lowlands, or Highlanders and Islanders who had gone to the Lowlands for a religious education in English. Macdonald presents some evidence to suggest that in Lewis some teachers were native Gaelic speakers who had studied in the Lowlands and had returned to Lewis to teach. These teachers would probably have spoken and taught a Gaelic-influenced variety of Scottish Standard English. Some form of Scottish Standard English was probably taught in the rest of the Highlands and Islands as well.

The fishing industry provided contact with English and Scottish fishermen, and particularly with the fishermen of the north-east of Scotland, and this may have had some influence on the English of the Highlands and Islands. However, since nearly all syntactic structures and lexical items in Hebridean English are also found in Scottish Standard English, the influence of vernacular Scots does not appear to have been very strong (see the discussion of syntax and lexicon on page 155).

In recent years outside influences have affected Lewis, Harris and Skye in very different ways. The influence of outsiders is much more important in Skye than in Lewis and Harris, where, even in the town of Stornoway, the number of resident outsiders (apart from the oil rig workers, who do not appear to mix with the local community very much) is relatively small. In contrast, there are many outsiders retired or working in Portree, Skye. The great majority of teachers in Portree primary and secondary schools are from outside the island, and many are from the Lowlands of Scotland, whereas in Lewis and Harris most of the teachers are local. As one might expect, the English accent of the younger generation in Skye, and especially in Portree, seems to be changing away from an Island towards a Lowland model, while this does not appear to be happening, at least at the same rate, in Lewis and Harris. The young Portree speakers frequently have velarized variants of /l/, glottalized post-vocalic and sometimes post-consonantal stops, and glottal stop variants of stop consonants. These features are all rare or non-existent in the English of Lewis and Harris.

The spread of English in the Highlands progressed at a faster rate than in the Islands. Economic forces, including the Highland clearances, played a part in this, as did increasing geographic accessibility. Clement (1980) points out that there is great variation within the Highland area both in terms of the

Gaelic dialects forming the 'sub- or adstratum' (i.e. a layer of Gaelic patterns which might be considered either to underlie or overlay the English), and also in the type and amount of English or vernacular Scots with which the communities were and are in contact. Gaelic remains the language of the community only in some parts of some of the Hebridean Islands and in a few of the more remote coastal mainland areas (and there only to a certain extent) where communication to the outside is primarily by sea. However, Gaelic was spoken more widely in the Highland areas until fairly recently. At the turn of the century 'there was Gaelic in every parish within the Highland Line ... and even as late as 1950 the Linguistic Survey of Scotland found local Gaelic speakers in most Highland parishes' (Clement, 1980; see also this volume, chapter 20).

Clement suggests that in the heart of the formerly Gaelic-speaking area, Gaels would have been exposed primarily to Scottish Standard English. Along what he terms 'frontier zones', the areas bordering the Highland Line, Gaelic speakers would have had vernacular Scots-speaking neighbours with whom to interact.

No systematic large-scale investigation of Highland English has ever been done, as most linguistic interest has been in Gaelic on one side of the Highland Line, and Scots and Scottish Standard English on the other. (A general review, however, has been given in Clement (1980); Grant (1914) does occasionally mention a few speech features of people from Gaelic-speaking areas, but does not distinguish between Highlanders and Islanders.) As a result, only random and tentative comments can be made here on Highland English, and these are based on four speakers who were recorded by Clement and transcribed by Shuken, in the course of research into Gaelic for the *Atlas linguarum Europae* (forthcoming). All are fluent bilinguals. Naturally, vowel systems could not be investigated. The speakers were from Embo, in east Sutherland, Assynt in west Sutherland, Loch Gair in Argyllshire and Killin in Perthshire. The Argyllshire and Perthshire speakers show more Lowland or Scots influence than the more northern speakers.

The only large-scale studies on Hebridean English have been of English in the northern Hebridean islands. Sabban (1981) is a study of the syntax of rural Gaelic/English bilinguals in northern Skye and in North Uist. Currently in progress is a phonetic, phonological, and sociolinguistic study funded by the Social Science Research Council and conducted by Shuken, under the direction of H. Speitel of the Linguistic Survey of Scotland. Speakers studied are from Lewis, Harris, and Skye. The bulk of the data used for analysis consist of word-lists, reading passages, and unstructured (but not casual) speech from sixty speakers of both sexes, and three adult age groups (15–25, 35–45, and 55+) in the three islands. Subjects are rural bilinguals from Harris, and rural bilinguals, urban bilinguals and monolinguals from Lewis (Stornoway) and Skye (Portree). Most of the data in this chapter are taken from this study.

Syntax and lexicon

Hebridean English is basically an accent of Scottish Standard English, i.e. that variety of SE which is spoken in Scotland. Speakers use very few syntactic structures and lexical items which would be considered nonstandard; they do use many structures which are typical of Scottish, rather than English, English. A few typically Scottish usages are the use of *will*, as in *Will I tick these?*, and of expressions such as *forever on about, Is that me finished?* Some but not all speakers also use the words *that* and *like* in the way described by Miller (forthcoming), e.g. *Do I fill this in, like?, Will I just put here where I met them like?, You have to consider the syllabus and that* (see chapter 6 for a fuller account of 'Scotticisms' in Scottish Standard English).

Gaelic influence would seem to be reflected in the following constructions: those in which items are focused by using clefting, e.g. *It was always Gaelic I spoke in the home, Is it this here you want me to read?*; sentences beginning *There is/was*, where the focused item is brought forward in the sentence, e.g. *There's not many in Invernesshire are Gaelic-speaking, There's that many English people here now, it's English you talk mostly*; non-conjugation of the verb 'to be' for person and number, especially in tag questions: *What do you do, just take that to Gaelic, is it?, I would say there was too few*; the use of the definite article where no article would be predicted from other varieties of SE, as in, *spoke the Gaelic/English, fishing with the long lines*; and the use of a few particular lexical items, like use of the verb 'to have' for speaking a language: *have (the) Gaelic/English*. Sabban (1981) also points out the relatively infrequent use of perfective verb forms, e.g. *I'm a widower now for six years*, instead of *I have been* ...

Hebridean English speakers use few particularly Scottish lexical items; most frequent seem to be *wee, aye, ach*. However, Stornoway has, or has had until recently, an extensive vocabulary of local words, some of which are of Gaelic origin, some from tinkers' cant, and some whose origin is more difficult to ascertain. Some of these are: *cove* 'man', *bloan* 'woman', *dirlo* 'hat', *hoof* 'steal', *skewped kadie* 'peaked hat', *dornag* 'stone for throwing', *hoyle* 'harbour', *hookit* 'come running', *wing* 'penny', *meek* 'halfpenny', *barts* 'shoes'.

There is not sufficient material to generalize about the syntax or lexicon of the Highland speakers. The two Argyllshire and Perthshire speakers studied did seem to show more Scots influence on their pronunciation, however, with pronunciations of /ɪ/ approaching [ɛ̈]; and used a few vernacular Scots words like *couldna, canna* (Argyllshire) and *wifie* (Perthshire). The east Sutherland speaker did use the phrase *wee stonies*.

Phonetics and phonology

Most discussions of English dialectology seem to centre around vowel systems and their phonetic realizations. However, many of the characteristics which make Hebridean English distinctive have to do with consonants, and many of these characteristics are paralleled in Gaelic. Abercrombie (1979) has said that 'it is possible to speak of a general English consonant system which is the same, with the occasional omission or addition of an item, for all standard English speakers' and Hebridean English fits this pattern very well, except that the voiced/voiceless distinction of stops and fricatives does not seem to be as consistently maintained as it is in many other accents of English. That some confusion exists was indicated by school teachers in Skye who reported that this distinction gave youngsters (rural ones at any rate) difficulty when they were learning to write. Some misspellings reported were *chust* (for *just*), *propaply* (for *probably*), and *thing* (for *think*). When reading a word-list, some informants pronounced *seal* and *zeal* identically, as [sil]. The amount of voicing used during stops and fricatives is variable, whether they are phonemically voiced or voiceless. However, it is likely that, in Hebridean English, perception of the reversed voicing characteristic especially of initial and final consonants is due more to a reversal of the duration and intensity of the period of friction characteristic of phonologically voiced and voiceless segments than to an actual reversal of voicing. The perceptual importance of friction in Gaelic consonants is attested to by Oftedal (1956: 161–2): 'There is a strong tendency to devoice otherwise voiced consonants when pre-pausal or utterance-final ... This devoicing doesn't cause any phonemic changes ... the phonetic difference consists in a much stronger friction on the part of the inherently voiceless phoneme.' In medial position it is likely that the reversal of characteristic voicing is perceptually important. In Gaelic, as in some varieties of English, initial and final stops are differentiated by aspiration (pre-aspiration in the case of final stops) rather than by voicing. Not only are phonemically voiced consonants often devoiced in Hebridean English, but phonemically voiceless consonants are often partially or completely voiced, especially in Lewis. Reversals of voicing can sometimes but not always be attributed to assimilation.

Consonants

Stops and affricates. Hebridean English has bilabial, alveolar, and velar stops like other accents of SE. It also has palato-alveolar affricates which, however, are often realized as (sometimes unaspirated) stops, especially in word-medial position. As has been mentioned above, the voicing contrast is not consistently maintained.

Dental variants of /t/ and /d/ sometimes occur, but only before /r/ or before a central retroflex vowel plus /r/ e.g. *wonder* [wän̪ːd̪ɚɹ]. Dentals were particularly frequent in /dr/ and /tr/ clusters, especially in Lewis and Harris, e.g. *tree* [t̪riː]. Considering that Gaelic has dental rather than alveolar stops, one would have expected dental stops in Hebridean English to be more wide-spread than they are (but cf. chapter 8, page 138).

/t/ and /d/ also have retroflex variants. These occur after /r/, and often occur before /r/ in clusters; but they also sometimes occur independently of /r/. Retroflexion appears to be a common but not consistent articulatory setting, and all the alveolar consonant phonemes have retroflex variants. Vowels in the environment of retroflex consonants tend to be retracted or r-coloured. (The terms 'retroflex' and 'retroflexion' are being used here to refer to the shape of the tongue, with the tip turned up; therefore, retroflex consonants can occur at a number of places of articulation.)

The palato-alveolar affricates are not always consistently differentiated, even in word-initial position. They are not always affricated word-medially. In fact, it is probably better to phonemicize these as clusters of palato-alveolar stops /t̠/ and /d̠/ plus homorganic fricative, since (1) the stops element can be optionally lengthened intervocalically, like other stops in clusters but unlike other intervocalic stops; (2) some speakers have a strongly affricated stop in *joke* [d͡ʒok] and *jewel* [d͡ʒʉəl], but a weakly or entirely unaffricated stop in *dual* [d̠ʉəl], *duel* [d̠ʉɛl], and *dew* [d̠ʉː] (where some accents of English have /dj/). Some speakers have a /j/-glide after the palatoalveolar stop in these words while others do not. Although the use of /tʃ/ instead of /dʒ/ (as in *just*) is a shibboleth, the frequency of occurrence of this feature appears from the data available to be overestimated. This may, of course, be due to the relatively formal nature of the interviews, or to the restriction of the data to the northern Hebrides.

/k/ and /g/ are generally velar, but tend to be palatal or at least slightly advanced before and after high front vowels (/iː/, /i/, and /ɪ/) e.g. *week* [wihk]. Especially in Lewis, vowels preceding phonemically voiceless stops, except for /t̠/, may have a breathy-voiced, voiceless, or frictional offset, as they do in Gaelic, e.g. *week* [wihk̟]. This is generally referred to as 'pre-aspiration'. Insofar as it occurs only before voiceless, and never before voiced, stops, it follows the Gaelic pattern. Apart from that, it is less predictable. As in Gaelic, it primarily occurs after stressed vowels. It is also influenced by the speed of utterance and by sentence stress, occurring more often in slow speech and in strongly stressed words. Stylistically, it is lengthened for emphasis, as are fricatives and the closures of stops in clusters e.g. *happen* [hahːpən], *discos* [dɪsːkos], *much* [mʌtːʃ]. Pre-aspiration is used more by rural Lewis speakers than by Stornoway speakers; more by Lewis than by Harris speakers; and more by Harris than by Skye speakers. In Skye speech pre-aspiration occurs most often after the diphthongs /aɪ/ and /au/ e.g. *bite* [bəɪht] or [bəɪçt], *about* [ɐbɛuʌt]. Because pre-aspiration after these diphthongs parallels the devoicing of sonorant consonants /l/ and /r/ e.g. *milk* [mɪl̥k], *cart* [kʰaɹ̥t], it is probably better to phonemicize these diphthongs as /a/ followed by /j/ and /w/, respectively, and to say that the approximants and sonorants can all be devoiced before voiceless stops. This parallels the occurrence of pre-aspiration in Skye Gaelic. Nasal consonants are normally devoiced before stops only in Lewis.

Some speakers glottalize post-vocalic stops rather than pre-aspirating them, e.g. *beat* [biʔt]. This occurs rarely in Lewis and Harris, and then mostly among young speakers, and among Stornoway speakers. It occurs much more frequently in Skye, especially among the young speakers, and most often among the young Portree speakers. Only in Skye do some speakers replace post-vocalic stops by glottal stops, e.g. *but* [bʌʔ]. This is likely to be due to growing mainland influence.

None of the four Highland speakers studied had pre-aspirated stops (though the east Sutherland speaker had a voiceless fricative /r/ in *working*). The Argyllshire and, more frequently, the Perthshire speaker, had glottalized medial and final stops. All four Highland speakers had some devoicing of final sibilants, but not as much consonantal devoicing as the Islanders. The west Sutherland speaker had some devoicing of nasals before voiceless consonants.

Fricatives. Voiced and voiceless fricatives occur at the labio-dental, dental, alveolar, palato-alveolar, and velar (voiceless only) places of articulation. Most speakers also have a voiceless or breathy-voiced labio-velar fricative. All speakers also have /h/. Fricatives show the same sorts of voicing inconsistencies as stops. The voiced sibilant fricatives /z/ and /ʒ/ seem to undergo more frequent devoicing than the other voiced fricatives, and are frequently devoiced in word-medial position (e.g. in *presume* [pɹɪsu̥m], *measure* [mɛʃə̥ɹ], etc.). Devoicing of all fricatives occurs irregularly in word-initial and especially in word-final position. Word-finally, /z/ is very frequently devoiced, /v/ is often devoiced, and /ð/ is sometimes devoiced, particularly before pause and before voiceless consonants, but even sometimes before voiced consonants. In the sequence *of the* [əf θə], /v/ and /ð/ were often partially or completely voiceless. Oftedal (1956: 161–2) mentions a similar phenomenon for the Gaelic of Leurbost, where phonemically voiced consonants are devoiced before pause and before voiced and even voiceless consonants across a word boundary. The difference between the frequency of occurrence of the devoicing of the sibilant, as opposed to the non-sibilant, consonants may be related to the fact that Gaelic has no /s/–/z/ contrast but does maintain an /f/–/v/ contrast; and in dialects where /ð/ occurs, it is voiced and is classified with the r-sounds (corresponding to a palatalized r-sound in dialects, such as Skye, which do not have /ð/).

/s/ and /z/ are usually retroflex after /r/ e.g. in *horse* [hɔ˞ʂ]. This is a feature sometimes mocked by outsiders, and some people appear to make an effort to eliminate it, with greater or lesser success (no attempt appears to be made to eliminate the, perhaps less noticeable, retroflexion of other consonants). Some of the more highly educated speakers sometimes have a gliding articulation, which begins more or less strongly retroflex and finishes non-retroflex (sometimes slightly retracted) e.g. *horse* [hɔ˞ʂs̱]. Some speakers use retroflexes nearly consistently in conversation, but use mostly alveolars or gliding-retroflexes when reading the word-list.

/s/ and /ʃ/ usually fall together as retroflex [ʂ] after /r/ (e.g. in *parcel* and *partial* [pʰaˑʂəl̩]), especially among rural speakers.

Most rural (and some urban) speakers have only /ʃ/ and never /s/ word-initially before /t̠ʃ/ (e.g. in *stewed* [ʃt̠ʃuːd]). This corresponds to a palatalization rule in Gaelic. However, a few speakers also have /ʃ/ rather than /s/ word-initially before /t/, as in *stop*.

The labio-velar fricative /ʍ/ is used by most speakers, although not with complete consistency. This phoneme occurs in some but not all of those accents which may have been used as models for Gaelic speakers learning English, and corresponds to no Gaelic phoneme. Its pronunciation varies from a breathy-voiced bilabial approximant to a labialized velar fricative e.g. *which* [w̤ɪt̠ʃ], [ʍɪt̠ʃ], [xɪt̠ʃ]. Some speakers occasionally use /ʍ/ where /w/ might have been expected.

Hebridean English also has /x/, as do Gaelic and Scottish Standard English. As in Scottish Standard English, it occurs primarily in names and in words of Gaelic origin (e.g. *loch*).

Approximants. Hebridean English has the voiced bilabial approximant /w/ and the voiced palatal approximant /j/. In Harris and Skye the second part of the sequences corresponding to the Lewis diphthongs /au/ and /aɪ/ are best interpreted as sequences of /a/ plus /w/ and /j/ respectively, (see 'Vowels', below, and 'Stops and affricates', above).

A /j/-glide occurs before /u/ after /p/ (*pure*), /b/ (*beauty*), /k/ (*cue*), /g/ (*argue*), /f/ (*feud*), /v/ (*view*), /l/ (in *failure*, but not always in *illuminate*), and /n/ (*new*). It often but not always occurs after /m/ in words like *music*, *community*; it sometimes occurs after /s/ in *assume* (but not *suit*), /z/ in *resume*, /θ/ in *enthuse*. /t/ and /d/ plus /j/-glide are occasionally used in words such as *tune, dew*; but more commonly a palato-alveolar stop or affricate (see 'Stops and affricates', above) is used.

Nasals. There are three nasals in Hebridean English, as in other accents of SE: /m/, /n/, and /ŋ/. The latter is usually advanced after high front vowels. Some speakers, especially in Stornoway, have /n/ instead of /ŋ/ in words ending in -*ing*. A stop is sometimes pronounced after /ŋ/ (as in *thing* [θɪŋg]); and conversely the stop is often omitted after /ŋ/ in words such as *language* [laŋwɪdʒ], *English* [ɪŋlɪʃ], and, sometimes, *think* [θɪŋ]. Nasals tend to be par-tially voiceless before voiceless stops in Lewis and sometimes in the other islands e.g. *ant* [ant̥]. They tend to be long word-finally, and are dental before dental stops (e.g. *wonder* [wʌn̪ːd̪əɹ].

Laterals. Hebridean English has one lateral phoneme, with several variants. The most frequently occurring variant is a fairly clear alveolar, not unlike the clear (neutral) lateral in Gaelic e.g. *seal* [si^dl]. After close or half-close vowels, there is often a very short voiced alveolar stop before /l/, especially in Lewis. Some speakers, primarily in Lewis, have a very clear variant. Some (particularly younger) speakers in Skye have a velarized variant [ɫ]. This is may be due to mainland influence. All speakers have a retroflex lateral [ɭ] after /r/, e.g. *pearl* [pʰëːɭ]. In addition, many speakers have a retroflex lateral variant independent of /r/ e.g. *call* [kɔːɭ], *stable* [steːbɭ]. This seems to occur most often word-finally, especially when /l/ is syllabic, and especially after back vowels; but it does occur in all positions and after all types of vowels. In the Gaelic of these islands, retroflex [ɭ] only occurs after /r/. /l/ is often wholly or partially voiceless before voiceless stops, especially in Lewis e.g. *milk* [mɪl̥k]. The laterals and r-sounds are voiceless in this environment in Gaelic. Some speakers have an epenthetic vowel between /l/ and a following nasal (e.g. in *kiln* [kʰɪlɪn], [kʰɪlən], *film* [fɪlɪm], [fɪləm]).

Among the Highland speakers studied, a neutral (not very clear or velarized) lateral was most common to the two Sutherland speakers, though the east Sutherland speaker also had quite a few occurrences of very clear [l]. The Argyllshire speaker had neutral to dark laterals; and the Perthshire speaker's laterals tended to be strongly velarized.

/r/ and retroflexion. The /r/ phoneme has a number of variants: it is usually a retroflex approximant or fricative word-initially; a tap intervocalically; a fricative, or an affricated tap (a tap followed by a fricative) word-finally, where it is also often voiceless. A tap, fricative or approximant can occur in releasing clusters. In arresting clusters, a voiceless fricative generally occurs before voiceless non-alveolar consonant phonemes; an approximant occurs before alveolar consonant phonemes (which are usually retroflex after /r/); and a tap or approximant occurs before non-alveolar voiced consonants. As in some Lowland varieties of Scottish English, some speakers have an epenthetic central vowel between /r/ and /m/ in words like *arm* [aːrəm], *warm* [wɔːrəm], although an approximant /r/ is equally common, [aːɹm], or [ɑːɹm], [wɔːɹm]. A vowel preceding an approximant variant is usually r-coloured.

Variants of /r/ for the Highlanders were similar to those of Hebridean English. The Sutherland and Argyllshire speakers had retroflexion of sibilants after /r/ and /d/. The Perthshire speaker had a tap [ɾ] followed by /d/. The Sutherland speakers also had retroflexion of /n/ after /r/. The Argyllshire and Perthshire speakers had a tap /r/ followed by non-retroflex /n/ in the words *horn, corn, barn*.

Consonant clusters. Hebridean English has the same cluster types as other forms of SE. As in many other forms of SE, clusters are often reduced in rapid speech (e.g. /dʒʌs/ for *just*, /lef/ for *left*, /wɒn/ for *want*). Speakers very frequently omit /d/ and /t/ in *wouldn't*.

Table 9.1. *Contrasting vowel systems influencing Hebridean English*

SSE			RP			Gaelic					
i		u	i		u	iː	i	ɯː	ɯ	uː	u
	ɪ	(ɔ)		ɪ	ɔ	eː	e	ɣː	ɣ	oː	o
e		o	eɪ		oɔ	ɛ/æː	ɛ/æ	aː	a	ɔː	ɔ
ɛ	ʌ	ɔ	ɛ	ʌ	ɔ						
	a	(ɑ)(ɒ)		a	ɑ	ɒ					

Table 9.2. *Vowels common to Hebridean English, Scottish Standard English, RP and Gaelic system*

i		u
e		o
ɛ	ɣ	ɔ
	a	

Vowels

Stressed vowels and diphthongs. The system of stressed vowels in Hebridean English seems to be variable, as it is in Scottish Standard English (Abercrombie, 1979; and see chapter 6). There appears to be variability not only among speakers, but within the speech of individual speakers, so that it is often difficult to tell whether certain contrasts exist or not. The phonemic inconsistency occurs where there are conflicts between the various English models, and between English and Gaelic. There is probably phonological instability in the system(s).

It seems reasonable to look at three potential models or potential sources of vowel contrasts: Scottish Standard English, RP and the Gaelic vowel systems of these islands (see table 9.1; cf. chapter 8). The Scottish, Standard English and RP models are taken from Abercrombie (1979). The Gaelic systems are taken from Borgstrøm (1940, 1941), and Oftedal (1956). In table 9.1, the items in parentheses in the Scottish Standard English description are those which occur in some but not all of its forms; in the Gaelic description, distinctive nasalization is omitted. It seems certain from the data that those items which Scottish Standard English, RP and Gaelic have in common are also present in the Hebridean English pattern shown in table 9.2. These vowels are generally monophthongal for most speakers. Occasionally /i/, /e/, /u/ and /o/ may show slight diphthongization. In Hebridean English, /ɣ/ (e.g. in the word *cut*) usually has a phonetic realization similar to that of the Gaelic short /ɣ/, [kʰɣt], [kʰÿt], or [kʰẍt].

In the front close vowel area, Hebridean English seems to have an unstable three-way contrast, between /iː/, /i/ and /ɪ/. Long /iː/ and short /i/ are usually distinguished in the minimal pair *weak* (long) /wiːk/ and *week* /wik/ (short), and are often distinguished in the pair *leak-leek* /liːk/, /lik/. Short /i/ and /ɪ/ are usually distinguished in *beat-bit* /biːt/, /bɪt/. Although speakers always distinguished these when reading the word-list, they do not always distinguish them in speech. Often /i/ is used in conversation and in reading where /ɪ/ might be predicted from Scottish Standard English, for instance, before /g/ in words ending -*ing*, (*milling* /mɪliŋ/, *sinning* /sɪniŋ/, etc.); in *six* /siks/, *picked* /pikt/, etc. In Gaelic, /iː/ contrasts with /i/ but there is no vowel which corresponds to /ɪ/. Long /iː/ ranges from Cardinal 1 in value to a fairly centralized articulation [ɪ] especially before /r/. Short /i/ has a similar range to long /iː/, although it is rarely as peripheral as Cardinal 1. /ɪ/ is generally quite centralized, often as retracted as [ɨ] and often approaching [ë]. In Skye, especially among young speakers, it is often [ë] and is difficult to tell from /ɛ/.

Length contrasts also probably occur for most speakers among the half-close vowels. Most speakers distinguish *great* (long) /greːt/ and *grate* (short) /gret/ when reading. Words like *take* and *make*, where /k/ follows, have a long vowel /teːk/, /meːk/. Long /eː/ is also used before /ʃ/ in words ending in -*ation*. /eː/ and /e/ range from closer than Cardinal 2 [e], to half-way between Cardinal 2 and Cardinal 3 [ẹ]. /eː/ is generally closer than /e/, and is especially close in Lewis [ẹ]. Hebridean speakers distinguish vowel length in *both*, *boat* (long) [boːθ], [boːt] from *coat* (short) /kot/ in reading, and in conversation *boat* and *both* are pronounced long. The pair *spoke* (n.) and *spoke* (v.) are distinguished by a number of people, with the noun usually having the long vowel /spoːk/. Those who have the contrast seemed quite certain about it, as they often corrected themselves when reading the word-list. The verb came up often in conversation and always had a short vowel. /oː/ and /o/ usually range between Cardinal 7 [o] and half-way between Cardinal 7 and Cardinal 8, [ọ].

While /ɛ/ shows no phonemic length contrast, it is generally pronounced long. It ranges from about half-way between Cardinal 2 and Cardinal 3, [ẹ], to about half-way between Cardinal 3 and Cardinal 4, [ɛ̣], and is often strongly centralized.

Most Hebridean English speakers have a contrast between two open unrounded vowels (as in *Sam* vs. *psalm* and *gather* vs. *father*). In Lewis, the contrast is primarily quantitative (with a short vowel /a/ in *Sam* and *gather* and a long one /aː/ in *psalm* and *father*), with both vowels having a wide range of variation along the front–back parameter. In Skye, the difference is mainly qualitative, with the vowel in *Sam* being farther forward, near Cardinal 4 [sa(ː)m], [sa̱(ː)m], and the vowel in *psalm* being central to back (though rarely as retracted as Cardinal 5 [sɐːm], [sɑːm]. In Harris, which is geographically between the other two, the vowels are contrasted both by quality and by quantity (*Sam* [sam], *psalm* [sɐːm]).

Most Hebridean speakers everywhere, except in Stornoway, distinguish *cot* from *caught* /kɔt/ ~ /kɔːt/, and most speakers apart from the Portree monolinguals also distinguish *don* /dɔn/ from *dawn* /dɔːn/ by quantity, with the first member of each pair being short and the second long. These vowels show a very wide range of variation, from a fully back and open rounded vowel to a variant half-way between Cardinal Vowels 6 and 7, e.g. [kʰɒ(ː)(h)t], [kʰɒ(ː)(h)t], [kʰɔ(ː)(h)t], [kʰɔ̈(ː)(h)t], [kʰɔ̞(ː)(h)t].

One sub-minimal pair (*feud–food*) was found to substantiate a contrast between a long and short close rounded vowel /fjuːd/ ~ /fud/. Most speakers contrasted this pair. No speakers contrasted the vowels in *pool* and *pull*, *suit* and *soot*; and this contrast may be of marginal importance. Lewis speakers generally have a central to front vowel (as in their Gaelic) [y] ~ [ʉ], while Harris and Skye speakers have a central to back articulation [u] ~ [ʉ]. Among the Highland speakers studied, the west Sutherland speaker had a fairly central articulation, while the others had a central to back articulation.

Long vowels tend to occur before voiced fricatives, word boundary, and syllable boundary. When followed by sonorant consonants, either the vowel or the consonant or both may be long.

Contrasts which do not occur in all the model systems seem to be maintained only inconsistently by most speakers, probably indicating that the vowel system of Hebridean English is in a state of flux.

Like most other accents of SE most Hebridean English speakers have three diphthongs: /aɪ/, /au/, and /ɔɪ/. In Skye and Harris, these are best considered as groups of vowel plus a /j/- or /w/-glide (see 'Stops and affricates' above). A few speakers from Portree distinguish long and short diphthongs in such pairs as *side* vs. *sighed* (e.g. /sʌid/ ~ /saɪːd/. This is probably due to Lowland influence; otherwise, longer /aɪ/ variants occur before voiced fricatives, sonorant consonants, syllable boundary and word boundary.

The first element in /aɪ/ varies over a wide area, from a fairly high, front [æ], to a strongly centralized [ʌ̈], though it is rarely fully backed. The higher fronter variants tend to be used in Skye, especially among rural speakers. When the diphthong is short, the first element tends to be strongly centralized or even central [ə], e.g. *bite* [bəɪ(h)t].

The first element in /ɔɪ/ tends to be a centralized or raised [ö] or [ɔ̞], but may be more open [ö], e.g. in *voice* [võɪs].

The final element in /aɪ/ and /ɔɪ/ varies over the whole range used for /ɪ/, usually being closer when the diphthong is long, and more centralized when the diphthong is short.

The first element of /au/ tends to be quite close in Lewis and Harris, and is often [ɛ] or [ë]. It tends to be more open in Skye, usually [æ] or [a]. It may, however, be a centralized [ʌ̈], [ɤ̈] or even [ə] in all three islands, e.g. *house* [hëʉs], [hæʉs], [haʉs] or [haʉs].

The final element tends to be quite fronted in Lewis, as is /u/ generally ([ʉ] or [y]). In Skye it is also quite fronted, usually around [ʉ] or [ʉ], more fronted than /u/ in the same speakers. In Harris, the final element in this diphthong is usually further back, around [u̟].

Vowels before /r/. Hebridean English has a fairly large number of contrasts before /r/, although some contrasts may be unstable. Vowels occurring before /r/ are /i/ (*hears* [hïːɹʂ̬]), /ɪ/ (*thirty* [θïɹ̥ʈï]), /e/ (*wear* [wëː(ə)ɾ] or [wëː(ə)ɹ̥]), /ɛ/ (*were* [wɛ̈ː(ə)ɾ] or [wɛ̈ː(ə)ɹ̥]), /a/ (*card* [kʰɐːʴɖ̥]), /ɔ/ (*horse* [hɔʴʂ̬]), /o/ (*hoarse* [hoʴʂ̬]), /u/ (*poor* [pʰʉːɹ̥] or [pʰʉːɾ]), /ɤ/ (*word* [wɤɹːɖ] or [wɤːɖ]). Vowels are long before /r/ unless /r/ is followed by a voiceless consonant, in which case the vowel is usually (but not always) short. The close and half-close vowels often diphthongize before /r/ (e.g. *here* [hiːɤɾ]). All vowels tend to be more or less centralized before /r/.

Again, not all of these contrasts are maintained consistently. Short /ɪ/ occurs fairly rarely before /r/, and occurs more often in some words (e.g. *thirty*) than in others (e.g. *fir*, *girl*). Some speakers do not seem to have /ɪ/ before /r/. The contrasts between /e/ and /ɛ/, and between /o/ and /ɔ/ are not always maintained, with the same person sometimes using one or the other of the pair in the same word at different times in conversation, although they do distinguish them when reading. These contrasts can perhaps be considered marginal.

Unstressed vowels. Unstressed vowels are generally reduced less in Hebridean English than they are in most other varieties of SE, often being neither very centralized nor very short. Thus, the first vowel in the word *about* is often a very open central vowel [ɐ] and is not particularly short. Sometimes, the unstressed vowel is actually longer in duration than the stressed vowel(s) in the same word. This length may be related to syllable division, as both stressed and unstressed vowels seem to be longer when syllable-final. At least in Harris, and in Skye, amplitude may be more important than duration for the perception of stress. A thorough investigation of rhythm and intonation in Hebridean English would be valuable, and would provide sufficient material for a separate research project.

As might be expected, there are no length contrasts among the unstressed vowels, nor do any of the more unstable contrasts exist. Thus, the system of unstressed vowels is that shown in table 9.3. Compare this with the stressed vowel system shown in table 9.4 and the system of vowels before /r/ shown in table 9.5.

Unstressed diphthongs may be reduced to fairly centralized monophthongs. /aɪ/ is often reduced to [ä] or even [ə]; /au/ is often reduced to [ɷ]. When diphthongized, the second element is often strongly centralized.

Conclusion

Hebridean English seems to be a variety of Scottish Standard English which is in a state of flux, probably for numerous reasons. It is the English of many

Table 9.3. *Unstressed vowels in Hebridean English*

i			u
	(ɪ)		
e			o
ɛ		ɤ	ɔ
		a	

Table 9.4. *Stressed vowels in Hebridean English*

iː	i			(uː)	u
		(ɪ)			
eː	e			oː	o
ɛ			ɤ	ɔː	ɔ
			a	(aː/ɑː)	

Table 9.5. *Vowels before /r/ in Hebridean English*

i			u
	(ɪ)		
(e)			(o)
ɛ		ɤ	ɔ
		a	

fairly isolated communities with varying concentrations of Gaelic speakers and varying proportions of Gaelic usage. The Gaelic dialects of each area differ. Although Scottish Standard English seems to have been the predominant variety of English imported into the area, Scottish Standard English is itself not a monolithic system, but is characterized by variation. The English of the media may also be having some influence and the speech varieties of Glasgow and other mainland areas seem to be having some effect, especially on young people. As might be expected, there is considerable inconsistency in Hebridean English and further analysis is likely to bring to light some interesting patterns. Further research on Hebridean English and a systematic study of Highland English are obviously needed.

REFERENCES

Abercrombie, D. 1979. The Accents of Standard English in Scotland. In A. J. Aitken and T. McArthur (eds.) *Language of Scotland*. Edinburgh: Chambers.
Atlas linguarum Europae Forthcoming. The Netherlands: Nimègue.

Borgstrøm, C. Hj. 1940. Dialects of the Outer Hebrides. Supplement 1 to *Norsk Tidsskrift for Sprogvidenskap*. Oslo: Norwegian Universities Press.

———— 1941. Dialects of Skye and Ross-shire. Supplement 2 to *Norsk Tidsskrift for Sprogvidenskap*. Oslo: Norwegian Universities Press.

Campbell, J. L. 1950. *Gaelic in Scottish education and life*. Edinburgh: W. and A. K. Johnston, for The Saltire Society.

Clement, D. 1980. Highland English. *Scottish Literary Journal*, supplement no. 12.

Dorian, N. 1978. *East Sutherland Gaelic*. Dublin: Institute for Advanced Studies.

———— 1981. *Language death*. Philadelphia: University of Pennsylvania Press.

Grant, W. 1914. *The pronunciation of English in Scotland*. Cambridge: CUP.

Macdonald, D. 1978. *Lewis: a history of the island*. Edinburgh: Gordon Wright Publishing.

MacKinnon, K. 1974. *The lion's tongue*. Inverness: Club Leabhar.

Miller, J. Forthcoming. Language variation and discourse. In J. Milroy (ed.) *Advances in the theory of language variation*. London: Edward Arnold.

Oftedal, M. 1956. The Gaelic of Leurbost Isle of Lewis. Supplement 4 to *Norsk Tidsskrift for Sprogvidenskap*. Oslo: Norwegian Universities Press.

Sabban, A. 1981. *Gälisch-Englischer Sprachkontakt*. Hudelberg: Groos.

Thomson, D. and Grimble, I. (eds.). 1968. *The future of the Highlands*. London: Routledge and Kegan Paul.

10

Manx English

MICHAEL V. BARRY

Introduction

Historically, the Isle of Man has had links with Ireland, Scotland and England but in the last two hundred years the strongest has been with north-west England, especially Lancashire.

The Celtic language of Man was of the Goidelic type, most similar to the Gaelic of the western isles of Scotland and of the north and north-west of Ireland (see Jackson, 1955; Adams, 1970 and this volume, chapter 15. Adams suggests that Manx Gaelic diverged from Scottish Gaelic from the fifteenth century because of the Anglo-Norman influence on the stress system.) The last speakers of Manx Gaelic died within the last twenty years, but no viable community of Gaelic speakers has existed since the 1940s. However, up to the early twentieth century Gaelic was strong and its influence is still noticeable in Manx English.

The Norsemen ruled the island for a time, eventually losing their hold in the thirteenth century but their influence upon Manx English is confined to place names, e.g. *Jurby, Kirk Michael, Foxdale, Snaefell,* and a few lexical items which might well have been imported from Lancashire dialects, e.g. *birk* 'birch', *bink* 'bench', *at* 'that' (rel. pronoun), *slake* 'put out tongue' (Wagner, 1958–69). Gelling, Nicholaisen and Richards (1970) suggest (p. 84, sub. *Douglas*) that a Norse-speaking population in Man was subsequently displaced by a new immigration of Gaelic speakers from south-west Scotland as late as the fourteenth century. Greene (1974) describes Manx as having 'a strong Scandinavian element', but offers no convincing evidence. Thomson (personal communication; see also this volume, chapter 15) comments 'the evidence for Norse influence is usually, in Scotland, the development of a system of consonants distinguished by aspiration rather than voice, but Manx (Gaelic) shows no signs of such a system and indeed tends in the opposite direction (since 1750 anyway), towards voicing medial voiceless consonants'.

The rise of English in Man, especially in the nineteenth century, and the predominance of Lancashire influence owes much to the growth of the tourist trade and sea links with Fleetwood and Liverpool. Lancashire influence was noted in Manx English from the seventeenth century (see Kneen, 1931; Kinvig, 1950). Ellis (1889) documents this more fully, though he may have overstated the similarities with Lancashire dialect and understated the Celtic substratum. He relegated Manx English to his dialect division D23 (i.e. a subdivision of the dialect of the Fylde district in the Blackpool region) on the basis of occurrence of *I am* (not northern English *I is*) and lack of northern English [uː] in *house, mouse*. Ellis also subdivided Man from the Fylde on account of the use in Man of the Standard English forms of *the* rather than the Lancashire 'suspended *t*', i.e. [t] or [θ] (Ellis, 1889: 351–63). He noted that Manx English was more similar to SE than the adjacent English dialects, a feature of many dialects in recent Celtic-speaking areas (Ibid.: 360). Wright (1905: 2, para. 1) concurred in general with Ellis's findings. Gill (1934: 3–4) noted that Manx English was a rather mixed dialect and was beginning to show Liverpool or south-west Lancashire influence in the Douglas area. The mid-east coast (as in the Pale area around Dublin in Ireland) seems to be an area of entry of new linguistic forms since it faces the mainland and is the site of the administrative 'capital' and three out of five of the remaining most significant towns. The Liverpool influence in the Douglas/Onchan area and amongst the younger generation is now very noticeable and seems to be spreading throughout the island. Manx Gaelic died first, traditional regional Manx English dialect seems to be following quite quickly.

Manx English was investigated by the present author for *The Survey of English Dialects* in 1958, and further data was collected by him in 1966. All examples cited below are from these two sources.

Phonology

The phonology of Manx English is a much standardized form of north-west English, influenced by Manx Gaelic, possibly with slight Scots elements.

Vowels

The system of vowels in stressed syllables is set out in table 10.1.

Table 10.1. *Vowel system of Manx English*

ɪ	ɛ	æ		ɒ		ʊ		
iː	æː		ɔː		uː		əː	
æɪ	əɪ		ɔɪ		æu		ou	
ɪə	uə			æɪə		æuə	eɪə	

/ɪ/   is realized as [ɪ] e.g. *difference, sink* (n.), *crib*. Lowered variants occur, e.g. [ɪ̞] *grip* (n.), *bin, pigs*, and [ɛ] *ring* (n.), *drink* (v.), *little*. Lowered forms are most common in the north of the island, and give rise there to some phonemic overlap with /ɛ/; they are most often found before velar or nasal consonants. [ɒ/ʊ] occurred in *which*. Jackson (1955) recorded /ɪ/ with [ɪ] as the main realization, and an occasional lowered [ɪ̞] variant in Manx Gaelic.

/ɛ/ is realized chiefly as [ɛ], e.g. *wealthy, very, heifer*. Off-glides to [ə] are very common in all contexts, as in *bed, breast, heather*. A lowered variant [æ] is quite common, notably in polysyllabic words, in the south of the island, in *getting, measured, never*. The lowered variant is sometimes followed by an off-glide [æə] *threshing, well*. The lowered variant gives rise to some phonemic overlap with /æ/. A few raised variants with [ɪ]/[ɪ̞] occur, especially in the south of Man *sled, plentiful, get*, giving rise to some phonemic overlap with /ɪ/. Jackson (1955) recorded /ɛ/ with two free variants [ɛ] and [e] in Manx Gaelic.

/æ/ is realized chiefly as [æ], e.g. *thatch, mallet, back*. Two raised variants [æ], as in *have, wagon, attract* and [ɛ], as in *slack, have, tag*, occur, with a slight tendency to greater frequency before velar consonants. Lengthening [æː] is quite common, especially before nasals, e.g. *man, sack, dams* (n.), and off-glides [æə] are quite frequently heard in the south of the island, as in *handle, rat, sand*; off-gliding is most commonly found before nasal consonants. Lengthening and off-gliding blurs the distinction between the two phonemes /æ/ and /æː/. Many words which have the phonemes /ɒ/ or /ʌ/ in RP have /æ/ in Manx English, e.g. *fox, not, body* and *one, crunching, another*. According to Jackson (1955) Manx Gaelic had the free variants [a] and [æ].

/ɒ/ is realized chiefly as [ɒ], as in *dog, trough, got, hopper, cod*. A fronted variant [ɒ̟'] occurs in words such as *knock, gone, got, tomorrow* and a somewhat unrounded and fronted variant [ɒ̞] in *donkey, wattles, doctor*, which might be a 'compromise' form resulting from the common relegation of words in the RP /ɒ/ category to the Manx English /æ/ category, qv. The majority of words with vowel phonemes which belong to the RP /ʌ/ and /ʊ/ categories prefer /ɒ/ in Manx English, e.g. *nuts, stump, done, cut*, and *butcher, put, wool, would*. Words with vowels in the RP /ʊ/ category which have initial labial consonants tend to prefer /ɒ/ in Manx English. Fewer words with the vowel phonemes /ʌ/ and /ʊ/ in RP are found with Manx English /ɒ/ in the north of the island than in the south.

In the north of Man, some words with vowels in the Manx English /ɒ/ category occasionally have a very close variant [o̞] as in *chop, lopping, was, knot*. *Horse* and other words with the RP phoneme /ɔː/ appear sometimes with /ɒ/ in Manx English. Jackson (1955) recorded an /ɒ/ derived from an older /æː/ in Manx Gaelic.

/ʊ/ The most common realization is [ʊ], e.g. *books, put, pull*. A closer variant [o̞] occasionally occurs in *took, could, full*, and, very occasionally, a lowered variety [o̞] as in *wooden, should*. A close, sometimes centralized form [u]/[ü] occurs in *mushrooms, good, educated, took* (*mushrooms* being stressed

on the second syllable). Words having the vowel phoneme /ʌ/ in RP may have
/ɒ/, /æ/ or /ʊ/ in Manx English. Words relegated to /ʊ/ in Manx English
include *muck* (v.), *up*, *much*, *butter*, *brush* and *gloves*, perhaps because of
influence of north English dialect speech. A few words with the RP vowel
phoneme /ɜ:/ have /ʊ/ in Manx English, e.g. *burnt, burst, worse* and *scurf* (with
metathesis of *r*). Jackson (1955) recorded /ʊ/ in Manx Gaelic.

/i:/   The chief realization is [iː] in all contexts, e.g. *swingle-tree, cleanings,
sheath, eat, weakling.* Occasionally an on-glide [ˡi]/[ɾi] occurs in *pieces, tea,
key.* Shortening in disyllables and compounds to [ɪ] was recorded in *swingle-
tree, sheep-skin, underneath* and to [ɛ] in *kneading. Fields* occasionally had an
off-glide [iə]. A number of words with vowels in the RP /eɪ/ and /aɪ/ categories
have /iː/ in Manx English, especially in the south of the island, e.g. *trades,
educated, way, rails, scale, gate, explain,* and *like, white, stile.* Jackson (1955)
recorded /iː/ in Manx Gaelic.

/æ:/   There are two main realizations:
    (1) [æː], e.g. *shaft, ask, half, calf, hard* (with the closer variants [æ̝ː], e.g.
farmer, basket, [æ̝ː] *cart,* [æː] as in *farm, calf*). Off-glides [æᵊ] occur in *shaft,
last, grass,* and [ɛᵊ] in *calf* (of leg), *laugh.* Shortened forms occur: [æ] in *pasture,
chaff,* and [ɛ] in *castle.* Since lengthened forms of /æ/ also appear in Manx
English, there is some phonemic overlap between /æ:/ and /æ/ – [æː] realizations are preferred before *s, f* and *th.*
    (2) [ɑ̟ː], e.g. *barn, harvest, bars, partridge* and [ɑː] as in *far, yarn* (= *thread*),
father. An off-glide was recorded in *arm-pit, starts* [ɑ̟ːᵊ]. These realizations
almost all occur before historical *r* (now usually lost), with or without a
following consonant. Some words with the vowel phoneme /au/ + *r* in RP
have [ɑ̟ː], e.g. *flowers,* [ɑ̟ːᵊ] *flour* or [æː] *flower* in Manx English. [ɑː] also occurs
in words which have the vowel phoneme /ɔ:/ in RP, e.g. *quarters, slaughter-
house, gorse, forty, walks, morning, caught.* Such words prefer [æː] in the north
of the island, especially after [w-]. Some words with the phoneme /ɜ:/ in RP
have /æ:/ in Manx English realized as [æː] in, e.g., *work,* and as [ɑː]/[ɑ̟ː] in,
e.g., *heard, dursn't.* Jackson (1955) recorded the free variants [aː] and [æː] in
Manx Gaelic.

/ɔ:/   The chief realization is [ɔː] in all contexts, e.g. *walk* (n.), *call, corn,
morning, halter, saw, mortar.* A more front variant [ɔ̟ː] also occurs in *all, fork,
almost, corpse, talk.* There is also a lower variant [ɔ̞ː] in *straw.* Off-glides [ɔːᵊ]
are quite common, e.g. *sorts, jawing, your.* A closer realization with off-glide
[oᵊ] is very common in *o + r, oa + r* and *ou + r* words such as *board, pork,
support.* A triphthongized form [ouə] also appears in *form, more, door, roar.*
An even closer form with off-glide [uə] was recorded in *door, more, shore.* A
few words with the phoneme /ɜ:/ in RP have /ɔ:/ in Manx English, e.g. *work,
turf, worst, word.* Shortened forms with [ɒ], [ɒˑ] occur in *gorse, worse.* Jackson
(1955) recorded /ɔ:/ in Manx Gaelic, realized [ɔː] or [oː].

/uː/ is realized usually as [uː], e.g., in *do, you, shoe, room, food, through*. Centralized realizations [üː] are common, especially in the south of the island, e.g., in *hoof, few, too, blue*. On-glides quite often occur before centralized variants [ᵊuː] in *hoof, stool, two, news*. There is therefore some phonemic overlap with the [ᵊu], [ᵊü] variants of /aʊ/. *Pool* has the off-glide [uːə]. A much more open variant [ou] has very occasionally been recorded in *too, you*. [oᵊ] occurs in *wound* 'womb'. This creates slight phonemic overlap with the [ou] variants of /aʊ/. In Manx English, words which have the /əʊ/ and /aʊ/ phonemes in RP occasionally have /uː/, e.g. *smoke, tadpoles*, and *about, ploughing, drought*. A few words which have the vowel phoneme /ʊ/ in RP have /uː/ in Manx English, e.g. *mushrooms, good, book*. Jackson (1955) recorded an /ʊː/ phoneme in Manx Gaelic.

/əː/ only occurs before historical *r*. The main realization is [əː] as in *girth, turn, perch, circle, learned* (v.). A number of words with /əː/ in RP have /ɑː/, /ɔː/, /ɛə/, /ɪə/, /ʊ/ in Manx English. There was no long central vowel phoneme in Manx Gaelic.

/æɪ/ The principal realization is [æɪ] in all contexts, e.g. *cow-tie, blind-teat, died, I, stride*. A wide range of variants occurs: [æːɪ] *dyke*, [æ̈ɪ] *pig-tie, bind*, [æ̈ɪ] *shy*, [æɪ] in *knife, time*. Shortening to [ɛ] or [ɪ] occurs in *like*. *April* has the off-glide [ɛə]. Many words with the vowel phoneme /ɔɪ/ in RP have /æɪ/ in Manx English, e.g. *join, soil, groin*. In fact the phonemic category /ɔɪ/ barely exists in Manx English. [ɛɪ] was recorded in *joiner*. In Manx Gaelic, Jackson (1955) recorded /ai/.

/eɪ/ The chief realization is [eɪ], e.g. *hay, name, haze, place, nailed*. A few glides occur, producing some phonemic overlap with /eɪə/, e.g. *paving stones, daisies, kale, gape*. Many words which have the vowel phoneme /aɪ/ in RP prefer /eɪ/ in Manx English, realized mostly as [eɪ], e.g. *fight, knife, bike, right, nice*. Some forms occur which could be regarded as a 'compromise' between the RP phonemic category /aɪ/ and the Manx English category /eɪ/ realized as [ɐɪ] in *child*, [ɛɪ] in *wife*, [ɐɪ] in *side*, [ɐɪ] in *white*. This suggests an increasing movement towards a distribution of /æɪ/ vs. /eɪ/, like that of RP /aɪ/ vs. /eɪ/. However, words which have the RP phoneme /aɪ/ + *ght* seem to be the ones most commonly to have /eɪ/ in Manx English. The 'compromise' forms do not occur in the north of the island, and words with RP /aɪ/ have the Manx English /eɪ/ very frequently indeed in that area. Words spelt with *ea* and a few other words which have the vowel phoneme /iː/ in RP frequently prefer /eɪ/ in Manx English, e.g. *beat, real, leaves, speak, convenient*. This occurs most frequently in the south of the island. Jackson (1955) recorded less distinction between closing diphthongs with open, front first elements in Manx Gaelic. Hence he has [ɐɪ] as the main realization of an /ɛɪ/ category, occasionally realized as [ɛ̈ɪ] or monophthongized to [iː]. It is notable that some English words with vowels in the RP /eɪ/ category have /iː/ in Manx English.

/ɔɪ/ This category has a low functional load and very many words which have the RP vowel phoneme /ɔɪ/ prefer /æɪ/ in Manx English. The most common realizations of /ɔɪ/ are, e.g. [ɒɪ] *boiling*, [ọ̈ɪ] *boys*. A 'compromise' form [æᶜɪ] appeared in *voice*. It seems likely that /ɔɪ/ is a new category in Manx English, emerging as a result of RP influence. Manx Gaelic had a rarely occurring /ɔi/ category according to Jackson (1955), and also an /öi/ category.

/æu/ There are two main realizations:

(1) [äü], e.g. *cowslip, now, ground, houses, out*. Many minor variants occur including [æu] in *ground, thousands, sow* (n.) [æʊ] *down*. Centralized second elements are more common in this diphthong than back ones. In the north of the island, the [æu] variant is the most common, and no centralization of the second element was recorded, whilst a more open first element sometimes appeared [au], [aʊ].

(2) [əu] occured in the south of the island only, in *cow-house, about, pound*. There are several minor variants, e.g. [ɛuː] *house*, [əuː] *stout* (adj.). In many cases the first element is reduced to a mere on-glide [ᵊuː] in *how, house*, causing some phonemic overlap with realizations of /uː/. Centralized second elements are extremely common. Metathesis produced [əːʲ] in *brown*.

Some words which have the vowel phoneme /əʊ/ in RP prefer the /æu/ phoneme in Manx English. This occurs in all *o + l(d)/l(t)* words, e.g. *cold, coltsfoot, rolling, mould*. Jackson has an /aʊ/ in Manx Gaelic realized as [æʊ], [aʊ] and, rarely, as [ɛu].

/ou/ The chief realization is [ou] in the south of the island, and [oʊ] in the north, e.g. in *no, nose, woven, home-made, roguery, those*. A few variants occur with a weak second element [oᵘ] e.g. *rope-twister, slope, toad*; and a small number with a very open first element [ɒu] in *throwing, mow*. In the north of Man, a monophthongal realization [oː] ocurs in *coal-rake, spokes, pole-cat*, or a monophthong and off-glide [oᵊ], [oə] in *boast, hip-bones, colt*. A more open [ɔː] variant occurs very occasionally in *poker*, or [ọː] in *slow*. Shortening to [ɒ] was recorded in *going, yoke, coulter*. Many words with vowels in the /aʊ/ category in RP have /ou/ realized [ou] in Manx English, e.g. *about, south, out, fowls, drought, without, blind-ploughman* (= mole). Jackson has an /ʌʊ/ phoneme in Manx Gaelic with 'the first element unrounded and advanced'.

/ɪə/ is realized mainly as [ɪə], e.g. in *here, shearling, years*. A variant with a closer first element is quite common, [iə] as in *here, clear, real*. On-glides [ʲiə] also occur in *ear-hole, ear-ring, two-shear*. Some words which have vowels in the /ɛə/ category in RP prefer /ɪə/ in Manx English, e.g. *rare, bare, fairs, theirs*. Centring diphthongs were not recorded in Manx Gaelic by Jackson (1955).

/eɪə/ The main realization is [eɪə] in, e.g. *wear* (v.), *hare, upstairs, affair, scare*. The variants [ẹɪə] as in *pears* and [ɛɪə] in *their, where, dare*, occur occasionally. Some words which have the vowel phoneme /ɪə/ in RP prefer /eɪə/ in Manx English, e.g. *beer, pier, ear, bier, hear, peering, dreary.* [ɑː] occurred in *scarecrow*.

/uə/   This category carries very little functional load in Manx English. [u̥ːə], [uə] occur as realizations of this phoneme in *suet, sure* and *gruel* respectively. [oə], [ouə] occur as realizations in *manures* and *poorly*, perhaps indicating some overlap with the realizations of /ou/.

/æɪə/   The main realizations are [æɪə], e.g. *byre, hire,* and [aɪə], e.g. *iron, fire.*

/æuə/   is realized as [auə] in one word only, *flour*, in the south of the island, but as [auə] in *our*, [auə] in *sour, scour* and [æuə] in *hour, ours* in the north. Many words which have the RP vowel phoneme /au/ + historical *r* prefer /æː/ in Manx English.

As far as vowels in unstressed syllables are concerned, the only feature worthy of note here is the widespread use of [ən] or [n̩] for the present participle, verbal noun and verbal adjective forms with *-ing*, e.g. *threshing, going, paving-stones, bedding* (n.). [ən] also occurs as the second syllable of *something, anything*.

Consonants

The system of consonants is shown in table 10.2. The following modifications and variations of the consonant phonemes are noteworthy:

Table 10.2. *Consonant system of Manx English*

p	b			t	d		k	g	ʔ
		f	v	s	z			x	h
				ʃ	ʒ				
				tʃ	ʤ				
				l					
	m			n			ŋ		
ʍ	w			ɹ		j			

/s/   may be dental occasionally, e.g. [s̪] in *solid*.

/z/   devoicing occurs quite frequently in final positions to [s] or [z̥], e.g. in *fields, was, roosters, potatoes, handles, rungs.*

/t/   (1) may be lost in final position in clusters, e.g. *best, loft, against, harvest, front door, coltsfoot*;
        (2) is heavily aspirated and dentalized in the initial combinations *tr-* and

str- [(s)]ţʰɾ-] e.g. in *trough. trace-horse, axle-tree, trestle, trimming,* and *street, stretcher, string, straw* (cf. chapters 7, 8 and 9).

(3) is also heavily aspirated and dentalized [ţʰ] in *coulter, master, better.* (In *Easter,* /t/ is realized as [θ].)

(4) is dentalized in final position, [ţ] in *street, weight, root.*

(5) is realized as [ʔ] when followed by [ṇ] in *forgotten, straighten, carting, spouting.*

/d/   (1) is lost in final position in *field, old, mould-board, pin-pound, land, ground* (n.), *bind* (= weed).

(2) is devoiced in word-final position both in pausa and before an initial voiceless consonant in the following word, e.g. *shepherd, inside, good, spade.*

(3) is devoiced when followed by plural *s* [ts/dẓ] *weeds.*

(4) is followed by voiced affrication and dentalized [d̪ᵟr] in *shandry* (= cart), *drills* (n. pl.), *dresser, ladder.* In *bladders, ladder* /d/ is realized as [ð].

/k/   is heavily aspirated [kʰ] e.g. in *kitchen.*

/g/   is devoiced occasionally in word-final position, e.g. *dig* (v.), especially at the close of a phrase or sentence.

/θ/   in initial position is often realized as a heavily aspirated dental stop [ţˢ/ţʰ], e.g. *thing, thistles, thin, thatch.* /θ/ + *r* is treated in the same way in *threshing, three, throwing.* This development, and the tendency to dentalize /t/, results in some homophonic clashes, e.g. *thin/tin, three/tree.* Manx Gaelic lacked a /θ/.

/x/   was recorded only in *trough* and in loan-words from Manx Gaelic such as *mucklagh* 'pig-sty' and *brashlagh,* the weed 'charlock'.

/h/   in initial position is usually preserved in the dialect, as it was in Manx Gaelic. It is occasionally lost in the unstressed second element of compounds, e.g. *dung-hill, bill-hook, court-house.*

/ʍ/   survives in the dialect *what, wheel, wheat.* However, it is often realized as [kʼʍ] *whip, wheel, whalebone brush.* Manx Gaelic *qu* (as in *quoi* [kwɛ:]) became [xwɛ/hwɛ:] when lenited (i.e. from initial [kw]). This may have caused native Gaelic speakers to assume the same mutation had taken place in English words with historical /ʍ/. By the time they realized there were no mutations of this kind in English, the pronunciation initial [kw] might have become fixed.

/r/   is often a short roll or flap, as in *rearing, prong, rungs, front door, mushrooms, street, threshing, ridges.* Occasionally r-colouring of vowels occurs no matter what the ensuing phonetic context might be, e.g. in *other*, *crupper*, *share* (n.), *mouldboard*. Ellis (1889) and Wright (1905) both indicate much more widespread occurrence of r-colouring than is found at the present time.

Lexical borrowings from Gaelic

Moore, Morrison and Goodwin (1924) indicated the use of over 750 Manx Gaelic words in nineteenth-century Manx English literature (chiefly in the poems of Brown and Rhydings). Gill (1934) recorded a further 250 in the poems of Quarries. The present author recorded a mere 126 during fieldwork for the *Survey of English Dialects* (Orton and Halliday, 1962–3) in 1958. Most of these appear in the earlier glossaries. Of these 126 words:

35 terms related to farming and farm animals:

> *saie* 'paddock'
> *collagh* 'stallion'
> *groabey* 'drain' (in cowhouse)

21 related to sailing or fishing:

> *becks* 'seats' (in rowing boat)
> *aley* a rough spot in sea where there is likely to be fish

21 related to human beings, relationships, behaviour, body, emotions:

> *ayr* 'father'
> *graney* 'feeling unwell', 'peevish'

15 related to the house, usually archaic items:

> *chiollagh* 'hearth'
> *slouree* 'crane' (over hearth)
> *jeush* 'pair of scissors'

9 related to wild plants:

> *bollan-doo* 'mug-wort'
> *brashlagh* 'charlock'

5 related to food:

> *braghtan* 'bread and butter'

5 related to folk traditions:

> *crosh-caoirn* ash twigs tied in shape of cross over door

2 were greetings:

> *kyns ta shiu* 'how are you?'

1 related to the weather:

  ard 'direction' (of wind)

1 related to insects:

  cregs 'beetles' (with English -*s* plural morpheme)

Just over 100 were nouns, 14 adjectives (some compounded with nouns). The largest number of Manx Gaelic words was given by an elderly lady from the south of the island who was one of the last speakers of the language; she provided 31 out of the 126 words. A great many of the words related to obsolete notions like the *slouree* and the *chiollagh*. Clearly the use of Gaelic expressions is likely to be reduced much further.

Syntactical influence of Manx Gaelic

The following are examples of Manx Gaelic structures, literally translated, used occasionally by native Manx English monoglot speakers today:

Manx Gaelic *ec* 'at' is used as a possessive personal pronoun:

  Coming back with English at them 'Coming back with a knowledge of English'
  They'd money at them 'They possessed (plenty) of money'

Manx Gaelic 'continuous' tense may be used where a habitual present or past occurs in English:

  What are we calling it? 'What do we usually call it?'
  They were getting a sap of straw 'They usually got a wisp of straw'

Also:

  (He) put a sight on us '(He) visited us'
  (Manx Gaelic: *cur shilley er* 'put a sight on')
  Them things wasn't in 'Those things didn't exist'
  (Manx Gaelic: *cha row ny reddyn shen ayn*)

Principal English dialects influencing Man

One hundred-and-twenty-five questions asked in the *Survey of English Dialects* (Orton and Halliday, 1962–3) revealed significant distribution patterns involving the Isle of Man:
31 showed correspondences with the dialects of the north of England generally;
30 showed correspondences with the dialects of the north-west of England;
4 showed correspondences with the dialects of the north north-west of England;

13 showed correspondences with the dialects of the west Midlands of England;
11 showed correspondences with the dialects of Lancashire only;
9 showed correspondences with the dialects of the north north-east of England;
19 proved to be 'standard' English forms occurring in Man;
8 revealed forms apparently peculiar to Man.

This data amply demonstrates the mixed nature of the Manx English dialect, but at the same time shows the principal influence to be the north and north-west Midlands. It seems likely that north-west Midland, (especially Liverpool) phonology and RP phonology will vie with one another for dominance in the pronunciation of English in Man during the next fifty years, so long as Liverpool remains the main port of access.

The distinctive intonation of Manx English is almost certainly derived from that of Manx Gaelic (not as yet described). It seems likely, as in most Celtic areas, to be the most durable aspect of the traditional dialect.

REFERENCES

Adams, G. B. 1970. Language and man in Ireland. *Ulster Folklife* 15/16: 174.
Brown, T. E. 1897. *Manx idioms.* Douglas: Broadbent. Reprinted from *The Isle of Man Examiner* 1897.
Ellis, A. J. 1889. *Early English pronunciation.* London: EETS, The Philological Society. pp. 351–63.
Gelling, M., Nicholaisen, W. F. H. and Richards, M. 1970. *The names of towns and cities in Britain.* London: Batsford. p. 84, sub. *Douglas.*
Gill, W. W. 1934. *Manx dialect words and phrases.* London and Bristol: Arrowsmith.
Greene, D. 1974. *Celtic languages.* In *Encyclopaedia Britannica* vol. 3, pp. 1064–8.
Jackson, K. 1955. *Contributions to the study of Manx phonology.* Edinburgh.
Kinvig, R. H. 1950. *A history of the Isle of Man.* Liverpool: Liverpool University Press.
Kneen, J. J. 1931. *A grammar of the Manx language.* Oxford: OUP; published for Tynwald by the Manx Museum and Ancient Monuments Trustees.
Lach-Szyrma, W. S. 1888. Manx and Cornish – the dying and the dead. *Journal of the British Archaeological Association* 44.
Moore, A. W., Morrison, S. and Goodwin, E. 1924. *Vocabulary of the Anglo-Manx dialect.* London: Humphrey Milford.
Orton, H. and Halliday, W. 1962–3. *The survey of English dialects (SED); Introduction* parts i–iii, The six northern counties and the Isle of Man. Leeds: E. J. Arnold.
Wagner, H. 1958–69. *Linguistic atlas and survey of Irish dialects.* Dublin: Institute for Advanced Studies.
Whittaker, I. B. 1953. The dialect of Dalby and Glen Maye. Unpublished undergraduate dissertation, University of Leeds.
Wright, J. 1905. *English dialect grammar.* Oxford: OUP. para. 1.

11

Welsh English

ALAN R. THOMAS

Introduction

The subject of Welsh English is inadequately documented, and it is not possible to decide how many of the varieties of English spoken in Wales are either structurally so differentiated that they might be considered as sub-varieties or dialects, or are felt to be differentiated in the consciousness of their speakers. Nor is it certain to what extent some bilingual speakers could be considered (or would consider themselves) to be speaking a totally functional variety of English – the range of situational roles for which speakers select the English language differs in a complex way, in terms of geographical location, social status and competence in writing and speaking it.

However, there are two distinctive models:

1. a 'southern' model, which is the more evolved. In the south – particularly in the industrial south, in Glamorganshire – and in the eastern counties which border with England, there are already indigenous English dialects which have strong affinities with the English dialects of the west Midlands and the south-west of England, superimposed on distinct substratal Welsh influences. These dialects are now independent of contemporary Welsh influence, and we must expect them progressively to shed indigenous Welsh characteristics, since their model is the same as that of other varieties of British English – Received Pronunciation and Standard English.
2. a 'northern' model, the structure of which is the more dependent on the structure of Welsh for its interpretation. Influences on northern Welsh dialects of English stem from the north-western counties of England, and we must expect the extraneous model to have the same influence on the development of those dialects, too. In the western parts of the country – where the Welsh language is at its strongest – less 'evolved' English dialects are found, with more evidence of interference from the contemporary Welsh language. Note the difference between these areas, in which the Welsh language is a living influence on the English accent of bilinguals, and those eastern areas in which the influence of the Welsh language is essentially substratal.

The description below will be based primarily on the 'evolved' southern model, since that is the variety spoken by the majority of the population of Wales, and since the majority of its speakers are by today monolingual speakers of English. Broadly speaking, we may think of the southern model as being representative of the final stage of the process of language shift (having principally monolingual English speakers), and the northern model as representing the transitional stage (having principally bilingual speakers).

I am well aware that this broad division is a gross one which conceals many sub-varieties: the south-west, for instance, has varieties which – though fundamentally southern in phonetic and grammatical structure – are spoken by bilinguals. Their English will be less 'evolved', in the sense in which I use this word, than that of speakers from the urbanized south-east.

In the following discussion, I have taken a dialect in south Wales (Upper Swansea Valley) as a model, and indicated departures from it, noting two primary variants – those of the rural south-west, and of the north (see Map 11.1). Detailed data on the English spoken throughout south Wales can be found in Parry (1977, 1979).

Pronunciation

Vowels

The pure vowels and diphthongs of the dialect under description are as shown in table 11.1. Note the following phonological differences from RP.

1. Corresponding to RP /eɪ/ in *late, sail* there are two contrasting vowels /e:/, which normally corresponds to orthographic *a. .e* and *ea* as in *great, late, made, sale*; and /ei/, which corresponds to orthographic *ai, ay, ei* and *ey* as in *eight, prey, maid, sail.*

2. The vowel /ɛ/ occurs in unstressed position in a number of cases where RP has /ɪ/ or /ə/:

helpless	/'ɛlplɛs/
ticket	/'tɪkɛt/
village	/'vɪlɛʤ/

3. The vowel /a/ corresponds not only to RP /æ/ as in *cat* but also to RP /ɑː/ in *bath, pass, craft, sample, branch.* (The vowel /aː/ does occur, however, in items such as *cart, calm, rather.*) /a/ also occurs for unstressed *a* where RP has /ə/:

   above   /a'bəv/   cf. RP /əbʌv/

4. The vowel /ɔ/ occurs for unstressed *o* where RP has /ə/:
   collect   /kɔ'lɛkt/   cf. RP /kə'lɛkt/

5. The vowel /oː/ corresponds to RP /əʊ/ in items such as *both, so,* but also to RP /ɔː/ where this is represented by stressed orthographic *ore, oor, oar, our.* In other cases WE /ɔː/ corresponds to RP /ɔː/. Moreover, Welsh English has a contrast between /oʊ/, corresponding to orthographic *ow, ou* and *ol,*

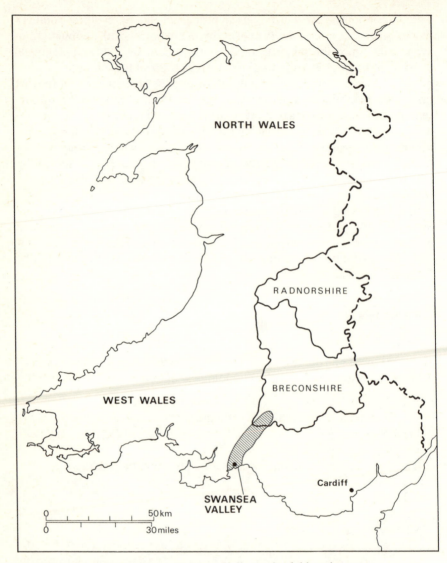

Map 11.1. South Wales: Upper Swansea Valley and neighbouring areas

Table 11.1. *Vowel system of the Upper Swansea Valley dialect of English*

Vowels:	/ɪ/	pit
	/ɛ/	bet
	/a/	hat
	/ʊ/	put
	/ə/	shut
	/ɔ/	lock
	/iː/	bee
	/eː/	late
	/ɛː/	fare
	/aː/	cart
	/ɔː/	bought
	/oː/	both
	/uː/	mood
	/əː/	girl
Diphthongs:	/eɪ/	sail
	/əɪ/	fly
	/ɔɪ/	boy
	/ɪʊ/	tune
	/əʊ/	louse
	/oʊ/	blow

and /oː/, corresponding to RP /əʊ/ for other spellings. Thus:

	Welsh English	RP
lawn	/lɔːn/	/lɔːn/
cord	/kɔːd/	/kɔːd/
hoard	/oːd/	/hɔːd/
door	/doː/	/dɔː/
so	/soː/	/səʊ/
both	/boːθ/	/bəʊθ/
slow	/sloʊ/	/sləʊ/
old	/oʊld/	/əʊld/

6. WE has no contrast between /ʌ/ and /ə/, thus:

	Welsh English	RP
rubber	/ˈrəbə/	/ˈrʌbə/

Diphthongs followed by /ə/
All the diphthongs may be followed by /ə/ in words like 'slower', 'employer':

fire	/-aɪə/
shower	/-əʊə/
player	/-eɪə/
slower	/-oʊə/
employer	/-ɔɪə/

In RP, the second element of the diphthong is frequently elided in such cases as these, with compensatory lengthening of its first element (see Gimson, 1965: 132–5). In Welsh English, however, no such elision occurs, probably because of the distribution of stress and pitch-prominence over the stressed syllable and any that follow it (see below). The post-stress syllable is not necessarily, as in RP, weak in relation to the stressed syllable, so that the second element of the diphthong (in all such cases, closing the stressed syllable) tends to be reinforced by the development of a semivowel glide which is homorganic with it, as onset to the following syllable containing /ə/. We thus get contrasts like the following between Welsh English and RP:

	RP		Welsh English	
fire	/faɪə/	→ [faːə]	/ˈfəɪə/	→ [ˈfəijə]
shower	/ʃaʊə/	→ [ʃaːə]	/ˈʃəʊə/	→ [ˈʃəuwə]
player	/pleɪə/	→ [pleːə]	/ˈpleɪə/	→ [ˈpleijə]
slower	/sləʊə/	→ [sləː]	/ˈsləʊə/	→ [ˈslouwə]
employer	/ɛmplɔɪə/	→ [ɛmplɔːə]	/ɛmˈplɔɪə/	→ [ɛmˈplɔijə]

Vowels followed by /ə/

RP has three centring diphthongs, /ɪə/, /ɛə/ and /ʊə/. The correspondent of /ɛə/ in this dialect is the pure vowel /ɛː/, but /ɪə/ and /ʊə/ have correspondents in the sequences /iːə/ and /uːə/.

These are not monosyllabic diphthongal glides like their correspondents in RP, however. They are disyllabic, and so we find the same tendency to the development of a semivowel glide as was described in the previous section, and for the same probable reason. The glide, in these cases, is homorganic with the stressed long vowel, and provides an onset for the following syllable which has /ə/ as a nucleus:

deer	/ˈdiːə/	→ [ˈdiːjə]
fear	/ˈfiːə/	→ [ˈfiːjə]
idea	/əiˈdiːə/	→ [əiˈdiːjə]
museum	/mɪʊˈziːəm/	→ [mɪʊˈziːjəm]
poor	/ˈpuːə/	→ [ˈpuːwə]
sure	/ˈʃuːə/	→ [ˈʃuːwə]

However, examples of /uːə/ are scarce, since most correlates of orthographic *ure* (a major source for the centring diphthong /ʊə/ in RP) have, in Welsh English, a sequence of diphthong /ɪʊ/ followed by /ə/:

pure	/ˈpɪʊə/
cure	/ˈkɪʊə/

They are amplified by a small set of forms with orthographic *ew* or *u* followed by a vowel:

jewel	/ˈdʒɪʊəl/
sewer	/ˈsɪʊə/

These forms develop a semivowel glide in the way described for /ʊə/ in the previous section, giving the forms:

['pɪuwə]   ['sɪuwə]
['kɪuwə]
['dʒɪuwəl]

Stress

In general, the stress system of Welsh English is not different in system from that of RP. Two distinctive features associated with Welsh English stress, however, derive from characteristics of the Welsh language. Long vowels, in the model we describe, occur only in stressed syllables – a feature of Welsh. Consequently words like *expert*, *export* which have a long vowel in the final syllable in RP, have a short vowel in Welsh English:

/ɛkspət/, /ɛkspɔt/

In rhotic dialects, they have the forms:

/ɛkspərt/, /ɛkspɔrt/

and even in the process of standardizing in which post-vocalic /r/ is lost, there is no compensatory lengthening of the preceding vowel when it is unstressed.

Again, the intonation system of Welsh differs from that of RP in that pitch-movement occurs on the syllables which FOLLOW a non-final stressed (tonic) syllable. Because of that, an unstressed syllable may have equal prominence with a preceding stressed one. This phenomenon is carried over into Welsh English, and is the source of the resistance of unstressed final-syllable vowels to reduce. At the same time, post-stress vowels in pre-final syllables resist elision for the same reason, so that Welsh English has:

/'tɔlərɛt/   rather than /'tɔlreɪt/   (tol*e*rate)
/'sɛpərɛt/   rather than /'seprɪt/   (sep*a*rate)
/dɪz'astərəs/ rather than /dɪz'ɑːstrəs/   (disast*e*rous)

Vowels in a pre-stress syllable tend to resist reduction in Welsh English (see above). No explanation can be offered for this, though it is tempting to suppose that investigation would reveal a connection with the phenomena of stress and intonation – possibly a lesser differential between 'weak' and 'strong' syllables (in terms of prominence) than there is in RP.

Consonants

The inventory of Welsh English consonants is identical with that of RP except that: (a) our Welsh English model has no /h/ and no /ʍ/; and (b) Welsh English has two additional fricative phonemes /ɬ/ and /x/, both of which have a highly restricted distribution.

Distinctive features of the Welsh English consonantal system include the following:

1. *Aspiration.* The plosives in Welsh English are accompanied by a much stronger aspiration feature than are those of RP. Indeed, the aspiration which accompanies VOICED plosives in Welsh English is almost as strong as that which accompanies VOICELESS plosives in RP. This feature is the source for one of the more common ways of caricaturing the phonetic characteristics of Welsh English speech in literature, in which voiceless plosives are made to substitute for voiced ones – thus reflecting the way in which an ear attuned to the relatively weakly aspirated voiced plosives of RP interprets the corresponding sounds in Welsh English. Examples are legion, and take the form of the following:

'Pring the pottle, Petty' (for 'Bring the bottle, Betty')

Indeed, the phonetic opposition between the so-called 'voiceless' plosive series and the corresponding 'voiced' one in Welsh English is less one of voice than of the relative strength of the aspiration features which accompany them.

Variations in the strength of aspiration, with both the voiceless and the voiced series, parallel those of the voiceless series in RP:

(a) aspiration is strongest initially as in RP, e.g.
    [pʰɪn] pin   [tʰɪn] tin   [kʰap] cap
    [bʰɪn] bin   [dʰɪn] din   [gʰap] gap
(b) there is frequently a strong release of a final voiceless plosive as well in Welsh English, e.g.
    [kapʰ] cap   [ratʰ] rat   [sakʰ] sack
    and, although aspiration is relatively weak, voiced plosives in final position are generally released, too, as in:
    [kabʰ] cab   [sadʰ] sad   [sagʰ] sag
(c) medially, between vowels, aspiration is relatively weaker for both series:
    ['tɔpʰə] topper   ['fatʰə] father   ['θɪkʰə] thicker
    ['rɔbʰə] robber   ['sadʰə] sadder   ['bɪgʰə] bigger
(d) a following /l, r, w, j/ is regularly devoiced after a 'voiceless' plosive, though not after a 'voiced' one:
    [pl̥iːz] please   [tr̥iːz] trees
    [kr̥iːm] cream   [kl̥əɪm] climb
    but:
    [bleːz] blaze   [briːz] breeze
    [griːn] green   [gliːn] glean
(e) following /s/ (and other voiceless continuants), the plosives are very weakly aspirated, and are perceived by the native speaker (for instance, the author) as being realizations of the 'voiced' series rather than of the voiceless series. Though the phones which occur after /s/ could be assigned to membership of either plosive series (they are always voiceless, and so could conveniently be interpreted as realizations of /p, t, k/ as is customarily done for RP), it seems to me that the awareness of the native

speaker offers a powerful argument for choosing to represent them as realizations of /b, d, g/, thus

/sbɪn/ spin   /sdɪŋ/ sting   /sgɪn/ skin

It is clear that one of the main considerations in choosing how to represent the plosives which occur after /s/ for RP is orthographic practice for English. Orthographic practice for Welsh similarly lends support to the interpretation offered here for Welsh English. The contrast between voiceless and voiced plosives in this context is neutralized in the Welsh language, as it is in English. The orthographic conventions of Welsh, however, handle the neutralizations differently. Welsh selects the symbols for the corresponding voiced phonemes for the labial and the velar ones, as in

/ˈsbiːo/   /ˈəsgol/
sbio 'to look'   ysgol 'school'

It seems evident that Welsh English retains this pronunciation feature from Welsh.

2. *Release.* As was stated earlier, it is relatively untypical of Welsh English for plosives not to be released in absolute final position, whereas it is common in RP for plosives to be either un-released or released only gently and relatively inaudibly.

In clusters of stop consonants, too, Welsh English differs from RP in respect of the release stage of the first plosive in a cluster of two plosives, or of a plosive and an affricate when they are not homorganic with each other. In RP, the first plosive has no audible release, a smooth uninterrupted transition from one point of articulation to the next being achieved as the speech organs adopt the posture for the second closure before the release of the first. In Welsh English audible (though often slight) aspiration occurs between the two stop consonants, as in:

[ˈakʰdə] actor   [wəitʰ poːst] white post
[tɔpʰ ʧein] top chain [ˈʧapʰdə] chapter

3. *Length.* Single consonants in medial position following a short stressed vowel are phonetically long in all varieties of Welsh English; this may be noted by doubling the appropriate consonant, as in:

[səppə] supper   [fillə] filler
[dɪnnə] dinner   [rəffə] rougher

It may well be that this feature is connected with the phenomenon of equalization of prominence over a stressed syllable and an unstressed one that follows it, in that a relatively prominent unstressed final syllable may require a stronger release of the medial consonants as onset to it.

4. *Glottal plosive.* The glottal plosive [ʔ] in Welsh English is not a phoneme, but is simply a non-significant phonetic phenomenon which occurs under predictable conditions. It serves two functions which it shares with RP:

(a) it may fill the hiatus between two vowels which belong to different
syllables, as in:
/rɪˈʔakʃən/ reaction   /rɪˈʔɔːdə/ re-order
(b) it may reinforce an accented vowel under emphasis, as in:
/ʃiːz ˈʔould/ she's old   /ɪts ˈʔɛvɪ/ it's heavy

Under no circumstances does /ʔ/ function, as it does in RP, to reinforce the
articulation of final voiceless stops (see Gimson, 1965: 162–3).
5. *The Welsh fricatives* /ɬ/ and /x/. All varieties of Welsh English (except those
of speakers whose speech has evolved to such a degree of similarity with RP
that they consciously anglicize indigenous Welsh forms which do not match
the RP phonetic system) have two additional fricative phonemes, /ɬ/ and /x/.
   Although [x] occurs in one idiomatic expression which has been taken over
from Welsh into Welsh English – the expression of disgust:

   [ax ə viː] ach a fu! (best translated, perhaps, as 'yuk!')

these two phones occur most commonly in Welsh-language proper names.
Examples are:

[ɬ]		[x]	
/ˈɬʊɛl/	*Ll*ywel	/ˈbrəxan/	Bry*ch*an
/ɬanˈsamlɛt/	*Ll*ansamlet	/kastɛɬˈkoːx/	Castell Co*ch*
/ɬəˈwɛlɪn/	*Ll*ywelyn	/kʊmˈgʊrax/	Cwmgwra*ch*

The only major restriction on the distribution of these two phones is that [x]
never occurs initially.
6. Unlike RP, /l/ always has a clear resonance in the variety of Welsh English
which we are describing. Dark [ɫ] in words like:

   [fiːɫ] feel   [puːɫ] pool

is heard only in the speech of those whose pronunciation is consciously
modelled on the pattern of RP and relatively free of local modification.

Accent variants

The model of pronunciation which we have outlined is representative of the
speech of an industrial community in the south of the country; more precisely,
the speech of a community in the western half of the urbanized south, in the
Swansea valley. We will now briefly identify the major variants to this accent
and note their principal pronunciation features.
   The most influential of the rival urbanized accents to our model is undoubtedly that centred on the capital city, Cardiff. Its most noticeable distinctive pronunciation feature – and the one usually chosen to caricature the
accent – is its fronted and raised realization of the phoneme /aː/, in words like

   [kæːt] cart   [ˈkæːdɪf] Cardiff

Both these dialects represent the most 'evolved' varieties of Welsh English, with their bases firmly established in extensive urbanized populations, where the Welsh language is spoken by a small minority of the population. Outside this urbanized area, there are two major accent-types which owe their distinctive features to the fact that most of their speakers are bilingual in Welsh and English.

In the rural communities of the south-west, the distribution of /r/ is extended regularly to post-vocalic position. Vowels other than /ə/ are usually long before a word-final /r/, as in:

/kaːr/ car   /boːr/ bore   /puːr/ poor

but:

/fər/ fur

Before clusters of /r/ + another consonant, a preceding vowel is usually short as in

/part/ part   /kɔrd/ cord

The occurrence of post-vocalic /r/ in these rural accents is clearly a feature of pronunciation which is carried over from the phonetic and phonological schema of the Welsh language, which is the first language of the majority who speak them. Another feature which is carried over from Welsh is the inclusion of the voiceless glottal fricative /h/ in the inventory of phonemes, as in:

/hat/ hat   /həɪd/ hide

Speakers who have /h/ as a phoneme also have an aspirated, voiceless labio-velar semivowel /hw/ ([hw̥]), so that they have minimal pairs like:

/wɪtʃ/ witch   /hwɪtʃ/ which
/wəɪ/ Wye   /hwəɪ/ why
/weːlz/ Wales   /hweːlz/ whales

Speakers of this variety also have an aspirated voiceless /rh/ ([r̥h]) in words like:

[r̥həin] Rhine   [r̥həim] rhyme   [r̥hɪðm] rhythm

This is an interesting example of spelling-pronunciation based on a characteristic of the indigenous language Welsh, which has an opposition between [r] and [r̥h], in which the two segments are orthographically *r* and *rh*.

Within the Welsh-speaking areas of Wales there are two major dialect-areas, the north and the south (see Thomas, 1973). The varieties we have so far discussed are all located within the southern area. The English accent of speakers of northern Welsh English (NWE), however, has distinctive features which, again, derive from features of the Welsh language.

Like the accent of the south-west, the northern one has /h/ and /hw/.

Another distinctive consonantal feature of northern Welsh English is its dental realization of the alveolar phonemes /t/, /d/, /n/, as in:

[t̪u] two   [d̪u:] do   [n̪əʊ] now

Another significant phonetic variant involves the realization of inter-vocalic plosives following a short stressed vowel. In all varieties of Welsh, consonants in this position are lengthened (another instance of interference from Welsh), but in northern Welsh English the release stage of voiceless plosives is more strongly aspirated: voiced plosives tend to be devoiced in their release stage:

[rɪppʰər] ripper   [vɪkkʰər] vicar
[rəbb̥ɪʃ] rubbish   [ləgg̊ɛdʒ] luggage

Perhaps the most distinctive consonantal feature of northern Welsh English, however, derives from the fact that the Welsh language has no voiced sibilant /z/. This gap in the system carries over into northern Welsh English, so that for speakers of northern Welsh English the following pairs are homophones:

seal, zeal   /si:l/
sink, zinc   /sɪŋk/
pence, pens   /pɛns/
use (n.), use (v.) /ɪʊs/

The affricates are not indigenous to Welsh, either, and the voiced affricate /dʒ/ is likewise interpreted in northern Welsh English as a voiceless phoneme, so that the following, again, are homophones:

chin, gin: /tʃɪn/
choke, joke   /tʃoːk/
rich, ridge   /rɪtʃ/

The principal vocalic difference between northern Welsh English and our model lies in the replacement of the diphthongs /ɛɪ/ and /oʊ/ by the pure vowels /eː/ and /oː/ respectively, so that whereas these two diphthongs have a restricted distribution in the model (southern Welsh English) in comparison with RP (see pages 179, 181), they do not occur at all in northern Welsh English.

So far, we have confined our attention to varieties of Welsh English in which the distinctive features can largely be attributed to interference from a substratal or co-existing Welsh language source.

There is one important instance, however, in which a local accent has affinities with regional accents within England. It concerns the areas of Wales which border directly on English counties like Herefordshire, Shropshire and Gloucestershire. The anglicization of these Welsh counties (notably Breconshire and Radnorshire) was essentially completed two hundred years ago. The dialects of the neighbouring English counties were an important formative influence on the English which is spoken today in these counties. There are two noteworthy vocalic features which can be connected with neighbouring dialects in counties of England:

1. a fronted realization [æ] of /a/ in:
   [æplz] apples   [kætʃ] catch
   Note that this is a different phenomenon from the fronted realization [æ:] of /a:/ previously referred to in the Cardiff area, which is restricted to the long vowel, and is probably to be connected with a similar feature in the indigenous Welsh dialects of that area. This fronted realization of the short vowel also occurs in the Cardiff area, though fronting of the long vowel does not occur in Radnorshire;
2. [r]-colouring (or retroflexion) of vowels, instead of the indigenous pattern, vowel + rolled [r]. Thus
   [əɹ:θ] earth   [bəɹ:d] bird
   [kaɹ:] car   [kɔɹ:n] corn

Accent and social class

The relationship of accent and class status is much the same for the community of speakers of English in Wales as it is for those in England. Standardization of a local accent entails proximation to RP, and speakers of regionally-modified RPs with a Welsh substratum will have some of the features we have described, to varying degrees and in different combinations.

Some general features of Welsh English, however, are clearly regarded as nonstandard, and are rejected early in the process of standardizing. The most obvious is the zero realization of /h/ for speakers in south-east Wales (the basic model): and as speakers adopt /h/, so do they also adopt /hw/, which is foreign to RP, and so becomes a mark of a regional accent.

Grammatical variation

As might be expected, the grammar of Welsh English is substantially like that of other varieties of British English: the written language and the media are a strong and pervasive unifying force. And frequently, of course, nonstandard forms are not specifically confined to varieties of Welsh English, but are more generally features of nonstandard usage (see chapter 2). My examples will be mainly from southern Welsh English.

A commonly occurring example in British English is that of the double negative, as in:

(1)   I 'aven't done nothin'
      I 'aven't seen no-one

Another example is the form which the reflexive pronouns 3rd singular masculine, and 3rd plural take in Welsh English, in which the possessive form of the pronoun is generalized throughout the paradigm: i.e.

his self, their selves

on the pattern of:

myself, herself etc.

Again, these are forms – ironing out irregularities in the paradigm – which occur in other dialects, too.

Strong verbs, in some cases, have adopted weak past tense forms, e.g.

bringed, catched, drawed, see-d, growed

and the past participle forms of some verbs, which in standard varieties form them with the suffix '-en', are standardized with those of the majority of verbs which have identical past tense and past participle forms, as in:

(2) It was all ate
     The window was broke
     Something was stole from the shop
     Not a word was spoke
     He was took ill

Fairly commonly, forms with 'some' occur where standard varieties have forms with 'any'; for instance in:

(3) I wonder if we've got some books
     (for '. . . . . any books')

and, with the negative:

(4) He hasn't got something to wear
     (for '. . . . . anything to wear')

The form of the indefinite article is of some interest: in the dialects of the south, the form 'a' is generalized, even before a vowel, e.g.

a apple, a orange

Also, the indefinite article can be used in a noun phrase denoting a sum of money, along with a demonstrative pronoun of SPECIFIC reference. This sentence was taken from a BBC news bulletin very recently:

(5) '. . . a warning to the government that you would use this a hundred million pounds'

There is also a tendency to use the strong form of the definite article where a weak form would be expected in other varieties. Again, in a sentence taken from a BBC news bulletin:

(6)   '... in an attempt to clear the [ði] dust from the [ði] ground'

The auxiliary verbs 'do' and 'have' have 3rd singular present forms *do* and *have* with the irregular forms again ironed out, e.g.

(7)   He do go to chapel
      They're coming to film what have been done

In the present tense paradigm of the full verb, however, the *s* ending of the 3rd singular has been generalized to all persons, giving forms like:

(8)   I knows that
      They plays football
      They wants us out of a job

(The paradigm of the verb 'to be' in the present tense is standard.)

The present participle with a prefix *a*- is common in southern Welsh English, as in

(9)   I'm a-going now
      What are you a-doing?

In both present and past tense forms, the verb can take the habitual rather than the expected simple forms, e.g.

(10)   I'm going to chapel every Sunday
       ('I go to ...')
       He was coming in before I was finishing
       ('He came in before I finished')

It is likely that this, again, is an instance of an indigenous Welsh verbal-group pattern emerging in Welsh English, since Welsh would have peri-phrastic verbal forms in such situations, which would involve a construction like:

Subject nominal + verb 'to be' + infinitive of verb ...

In some rural varieties of southern Welsh English (particularly in Brecon-shire and Radnorshire) the present and past tense forms of the previous paragraph are replaced by a construction which has the verb 'do' in appro-priate tense form, followed by an uninflected lexical verb, e.g.

(11)   I do go to chapel every Sunday
       He did come in before I did finish

Note that forms of 'do' carry weak stress in these examples. It is not clear whether this construction derives from Welsh-language interference; Welsh has an exactly parallel construction:

Inflected verb 'do' (+ subject nominal) + uninflected verb

but the construction with 'do' occurs also in neighbouring English counties (see chapter 5) where it might, of course, represent an older Celtic substratum.

The modal 'will' has a distinctive function in Welsh English when it serves as the future tense of 'be', as in:

(12) I've always been poor and I always will
      Is he ready yet? – No, but he will in a minute

In more standard varieties of British English, 'either' occurs as a tag to a negative sentence, as in:

(13) I can't do that, either
      Nor me, either

The function of *either* in such sentences is to express the speaker's solidarity with an addressee or a third party. In southern Welsh English, this function is carried by the adverb *too*, as in:

(14) I can't do that, too
      Nor me, too

Of fairly common occurrence in rural varieties of Welsh English is the generalization of the 3rd singular tag *isn't it* to replace the appropriate person reference, in forms like:

(15) You're going home now, isn't it?
      She came to see me yesterday, isn't it?

In varieties of northern Welsh English, the tag *yes* is used with a declarative sentence to form a question, as in:

(16) You're at university, yes?
      It's a lovely day, yes?

Again, this tag neutralizes the person reference which would occur in this context for other varieties, as in:

(17) You're at university, are you?
      It's a lovely day, isn't it?

The Welsh language has a frequently occurring syntactic device of inverting the constituents of a sentence, fronting (part of) the predicate for emphasis. Similar sentences have a high frequency of occurrence in southern Welsh English. Examples are:

(18) Coming home tomorrow he is
      Loud he was singing
      Sad she looked

In southern Welsh English the relative pronoun is frequently realized as *as*, e.g.

(19) The one as told me about it
      The school as closed last year

And often the relative pronoun is omitted, as in:

(20) There's no other place in South Wales have had to pay for the removal
      of tips

Notice the uninflected 3rd singular present form of 'have' in this sentence, heard during a radio interview.

Vocabulary and idiom

In this section, my aim is to illustrate the extent to which vocabulary and idiom in Welsh English are distinctive.

Most surprising, perhaps, is the fact that remarkably little has been borrowed from Welsh into Welsh English. The few examples of general occurrence include:

eisteddfod /əɪstɛðvɔd/ the name for a cultural institution, a competitive festival of the arts;
llymru /ɬəmrɪ/ a porridge-type dish;
tollut /tɔlət/ (W. *taflod*) 'hay-loft';
del /dɛl/, bach /baːx/ terms of endearment.

Isolated dialects have localized borrowings in greater numbers – for instance the dialect of Buckley in Flintshire has such borrowings as:

clennig /klɛnɪg/ (Welsh *calennig*, New Year's gift) an allowance of money;
dreven /dreːvɛn/ (Welsh *trefn*) 'untidiness';
glaster /glastə/ (Welsh *glastwr*) a drink made half of milk and half of water;
wackey /wakɪ/ (Welsh *gwachul*) 'feel unwell'.

In general, however, few indigenous Welsh words have entered the vocabulary of Welsh English.

There are some features of usage which are shared by neighbouring English dialects. Radnorshire has borrowed from the west Midlands the words:

askel	'newt'	cratch	'hay-loft'
hopper	'seed-basket'	lumper	'young teenager'

while south Welsh English words which come from the south-west of England include:

dap	'bounce'	pine-end	'gable-end'
pilm	'dust'	plud	'puddle'

Others have currency throughout both the south-west of England and the west Midlands:

oont	'mole'	quist	'woodpigeon'
sally	'willow'	clem	'starve'

Other words occur more commonly in the English dialects:

tup	'ram'	close	'paddock'
tundish	'funnel'	steam	'bread-bin'

Words which are regarded as being typical of southern Welsh English include:

delight 'interest', as in:
   He's got a delight in football
tidy (general purpose adjective of approval, and vague quantifier), as in:
   Nice car he's got. Very tidy
   He's got a tidy bit of money
off 'angry', as in:
   He was off!
lose 'miss', as in:
   He's lost the bus
rise (n. v.) 'raise', as in:
   I'll rise the tickets
   To rise money from the bank
   A rise in wages

A familiar feature of southern Welsh English is the use of repetition of an adjective for intensification, as in:

(21)   It was long, long i.e. 'very long'
       He was tall, tall i.e. 'very tall'

Distinctively southern Welsh English, too is the discontinuous adverb of place *where . . . to* as in:

(22)   I don't know where he's to 'Where he is'
       Where's the train to? 'Where is the train?',
           NOT 'Where is the train going to?'
       Where's he to? 'Where is he?'

REFERENCES

Gimson, A. C. 1965. *An introduction to the pronunciation of English*. London: Edward Arnold.
Parry, D. (ed.) 1977, 1979. *The survey of Anglo-Welsh dialects*; vol. 1, *The south-east*; vol. 2, *The south-west*. Swansea: University of Wales Press.
Thomas, A. R. 1973. *The linguistic geography of Wales*. Cardiff: University of Wales Press.

12

Cornish English

MARTYN WAKELIN

Introduction

The evidence lying behind this brief treatment of Cornish English is to be found in Wakelin (1975). No attempt is made here to deal with Scillies English, for which see Thomas (1979), and no account has been taken of intonation patterns, which still need investigation.

The Celtic dialect of Dumnonia, spoken in the south-western peninsula of England, underwent continual erosion from the time of the seventh-century Anglo-Saxon occupation of Devon, sources from the early eighth century onwards showing the West Saxon kings in sporadic conflict with the shrinking kingdom beyond the Tamar. This process of subjugation was completed by Athelstan, who also fixed the Tamar as the shire boundary. It is thus clear that by the early tenth century the present-day county of Cornwall, notwithstanding British enclaves for which there is evidence, had been thoroughly colonized, either by military or peaceful means. Cornish, as it had now become, continued its gradual decline: by 1100 English was apparently predominant as far west as Bodmin and by 1600 as far as Truro, whence it was pushed to the coast, English being spoken everywhere from c. 1700–50, leaving only one or two isolated Cornish speakers, the last of whom died in 1777.

The present-day dialect of east Cornwall is of basically the same stock as that of Devon and the western extremity of Somerset, having the typically rounded vowels [y:], [y] and [œy], the voicing of initial fricative consonants, reversal of pronoun order, and b- forms of the verb 'to be' (see chapter 5, page 84 and map 5.8). Features of the dialects of central and west Cornwall, however, show that a completely different type of English predominates here, probably owing its origin, as Bishop Gibson suggested in 1695 (p. 146), more to a form of early (sixteenth–seventeenth centuries) Standard English than to the dialectal speech of the south-west (there is no evidence whatever of influence from a Celtic 'substratum'). The selected features described below bear this out. In this synopsis 'SW' denotes east Cornwall, Devon and usually west Somerset, sometimes also territory to the east of this. It should be noted that this is necessarily a general statement, without defining isoglosses or citing exceptions (e.g. /v/ in *furrow* extends to the far west of the county).

Phonology

/a/ (<ME *a*) is [æ] in central and west Cornwall speech, contrasting SW
　　[a]:　[sæk]:[sak];

/aː/ (<ME *a* + *f*, *s*, *th*; ME *al* + *f*, *m*) is [æː], contrasting SW [aː]:
　　[kæːst]:[kaːst];

/ɷ/ (<ME *u*, *ọ̄*) is [ɷ], contrasting SW [ʏ]:　[bɷʃ]:[bʏʃ]; [gɷd]:[gʏd];

/uː/ (ME *ọ̄*) is [uː], contrasting SW [ʏː]:　[muːn]:[mʏːn];

/juː/, /uː/ (<ME *iu*) is [ɪɷ], contrasting SW [ʏː]:　[nɪɷ]:[nʏː];

/ɔː/ (<ME *al* + cons. or finally) is [ɔː], contrasting SW [aː], [a]:　[fɔːl]:
　　[fa(ː)l];

/aɷ/ (<ME *ū*) is [ɛɷ], contrasting SW [œʏ]:　[kɛɷ]:[kœʏ];

/ai/ (<ME *ī*) is [æɪ], contrasting SW [aː], [ɑː], etc.:　[næɪf], [naːf], [nɑːf];

/f, s, θ, ʃ/ (<ME initial *f*, *s*, *th*, *sh*) are [f, s, θ, ʃ], contrasting SW [v, z, ð, ʒ]:
　　[fɪʃ, siː, θʌm, ʃɪlɪn]:[vɪʃ, ziː, ðʌm, ʒɪlɪn];

/θr/ (<ME initial *thr*) is [θɾ], contrasting SW [dɾ]:　[θɾiː]:[dɾiː].

Morphology

(1) *Personal pronouns.* In central and west Cornwall speech:

We as subject contrasts SW *us*.
She as subject contrasts SW *her*.
They as subject contrasts SW *them, mun* ('them', of obscure origin, now
　　found only in Cornwall).

(2) *The verb 'to be' (cf. page 84 and map 5.8)*. In central and west Cornwall
speech:

I am; *am I?* contrast SW *I be*; *be I?*
I aren't; *aren't I?*, *ain't I?* contrast SW *I bain't*; *bain't I?*
We are contrasts SW *us be, we be, we'm*.
Art thee? contrasts SW *art?, be ye?*
Aren't ye/thee?, ain't thee? contrast SW *bain't ye?*
They are; *are they?* contrast SW *they be, they'm*; *be they/them/mun?*
They aren't/ain't; *aren't they?* contrast SW *they bain't*; *bain't they/them/*
　　mun?

(3) Zero is registered for SW *a-* (<OE *ge-*) + past part. for the whole of
central and west Cornwall, contrasting SW *a-found, a-broke*, etc.

(4) SW *a* (indef. art.) is absent before a numeral or the time in the whole of
central and west Cornwall, contrasting SW *about a six, about a four or five*, etc.

Lexicon

The struggle between English, as the dominant, and Cornish, as the 'lower',
language resulted, typically (Bloomfield, 1935: 26.1ff), in the lower language –

in so far as it survived – bearing off large numbers of English loan-words (cf. below) as well as being significantly influenced in orthography and phonology, while English assimilated few loan-words from Cornish. The English of west Cornwall does, however, still number some thirty such words in its lexical stock (many more have disappeared), though most of it, as Richard Carew said in 1602 (Halliday, 1953: 128), 'take[s] [its] source from the Saxon ...', including *mow-hay* 'stackyard', *studdle* 'tethering-stake', *crib* 'trough', *evil* 'muck-fork', *claw* 'fork-prong', *ditch* and *voryer* 'headlands' (the examples are from North and Sharpe, 1980).

   The following are examples of Cornish loan-words still surviving (note that many items have undergone modification, e.g. by adding -*s* of the English plural to a Cornish collective form, e.g. *muryon*):
Bannel 'a broom' (< Corn *banal* coll.); *bucca* 'scarecrow' (< Corn *bucca* 'hobgoblin, scarecrow'); *clunk* 'to swallow' and *clunker* 'windpipe' (probably < Corn *collenky* 'to swallow down'); *dram* 'swath' (< Corn *dram*); *fuggan* 'pastry dinner-cake' (< Corn *fūgen*); *gook* 'bonnet' (< Corn *cūgh* 'head-covering', etc.); *griglans* 'heather' (< Corn *gruglon* 'heather-bush'); *groushans* 'dregs' (< Corn *growjyon* pl.); *gurgoe* 'warren' (< Corn *gorgē*, pl. *gorgow* 'low hedge', etc.); *hoggan* 'pastry-cake' (< Corn *hogen*); *kewny* 'rancid' (< Corn *kewnÿek* 'mouldy', etc.); *muryans* 'ants' (< Corn *muryon* coll.); *padgy-pow* 'newt' (< Corn *peswar-paw* < *peswar* 'four' + *paw* 'foot'); *pig's-crow* 'pigsty' (< Corn *crow*, see Wakelin, 1969); *scaw* 'elder-tree' (< Corn *scaw* coll.); *stank* 'to walk, trample, step (on, in)' (< Corn *stankya*); *tidden* 'tender' (< late Corn *tidn* 'tight, rigid', etc.); *whidden* 'weakling' (of a litter of pigs) (< Corn *gwidden* 'white').

   The following examples were loan-words within Cornish, which, from an early period, showed itself susceptible to foreign (Latin, French, English) influence:
Bulhorn 'snail' (< Corn *bulhorn* < an English dialectal nickname for the snail); *bussa* 'salting-trough', 'bread-bin' (< Corn *bussa*, probably < ME *busse* < OF *buce*, *busse* 'barrel' and medieval Latin *bussa*); *croust* 'snack' (< Corn *crowst* < OF *crouste*, Latin *crusta*, probably *via* English); *hoggans* 'haws' (< Corn *hogan* [+ English pl. -*s*] < OE **hagga* + Corn singulative -*an*); *peeth* 'well' (cf. Latin *puteus*).
For further discussion of the lexicon see Colquhoun (1971) and Phillips (1976).

   From the above, we can see that aspects of the English of central and west Cornwall reflect a form of early SE (though there is influence to some extent from neighbouring dialects of east Cornwall, Devon and west Somerset). This emerges from a consideration of phonological and morphological features. In lexis, the dialect is again predominantly English, but a number of Cornish words remain.

REFERENCES

Bloomfield, L. 1935. *Language*. London: Allen and Unwin. American edn, New York: Holt, Rinehart and Winston, 1933.
Colquhoun, I. 1971. Cornish earth. *The Cornish Review* 18: 57–66.
Gibson, E. 1695. *Camden's Britannia, newly translated into English, with large additions and improvements*. London.
Halliday, F. E. (ed.) 1953. *Richard Carew of Antony: the survey of Cornwall*. London: Andrew Melrose.
Nance, R.M., ed. Pool, P.A.S. 1963. *A glossary of Cornish sea-words*. Marazion: Federation of Old Cornwall Societies.
North, D.J. and Sharpe, A. 1980. *A word-geography of Cornwall*. Truro: Institute of Cornish Studies.
Phillips, K.C. 1976. *Westcountry words and ways*. Newton Abbot: David and Charles.
Thomas, A.C. 1974. Dialect studies: 1. The Rablen collection and the establishment of an isogloss. *Cornish Studies* 2: 65–74.
——— 1979. A glossary of spoken English in the Isles of Scilly. *Journal of the Royal Institution of Cornwall* NS 8: 109–47.
Wakelin, M.F. 1969. *Crew, cree* and *crow*: Celtic words in English dialect. *Anglia* 87: 273–81.
——— 1975. *Language and history in Cornwall*. Leicester: Leicester University Press.
——— 1976–7. Norse influence in Cornwall: a survey of the evidence. *Cornish Studies* 4–5: 41–50.

13

Urban dialects in the British Isles

L. MILROY

Introduction

For many years now studies of various British urban dialects have been appearing, associated with different traditions of linguistic work. It is probably best to begin an account of this very heterogeneous body of scholarship by noting the general idealized descriptions of various accents (not all of them urban) by Wells (1970, and see chapter 4) and by Hughes and Trudgill (1979) who deal more broadly with a number of urban DIALECTS. Wells's study may be described as 'idealized' to the extent that he gives an account of the main phonological and phonetic characteristics of a range of Welsh and English accents without specifying the kind of speaker for whom his description is valid, or attempting to describe the kind of variation that occurs within the accent of an area. Although he sees the major task of people who describe urban accents as one of relating phonetic variables to various extralinguistic factors such as age, sex or social class, he himself concentrates on describing accent differences in purely linguistic terms, distinguishing between differences which are systematic (a matter of phonological structure) and those which are realizational – that is, purely phonetic. However, Wells's more recent work on British accents incorporates a general discussion on variability with attention to a range of extra-linguistic factors (Wells, 1982).

Hughes and Trudgill describe aspects of the phonology of ten urban areas of the British Isles (London, Norwich, Bristol, South Wales, West Midlands, Bradford, Liverpool, Tyneside, Edinburgh and Belfast). Although their accounts cover both systematic and realizational differences between accents, the framework of description is set out much less explicitly than that of Wells, probably reflecting the function of their book as a practical teaching tool for foreign learners who want to learn facts about the major kinds of variation within British English. They differ from Wells also in that they base their description on a series of comparable tape-recordings collected from each area, while the book as a whole discusses in a general way the main syntactic and phonological variables in urban varieties of British English. Neither of these studies is concerned with WHOSE speech is being described; both outline the major facts and sketch out the most important characteristics of differing phonological systems (it will become apparent that much of the work discussed here concentrates on phonology).

Early studies of British English dialects

We turn now to a large number of studies where the identity of the speakers on whose speech the linguistic descriptions are based is an important issue. Traditionally interest has focused on rural rather than urban districts when scholars have studied comparatively the dialects of different areas, and it should be noted that the theoretical basis of such studies was developed in the nineteenth century and has changed little since (Chambers and Trudgill, 1980: 18–23). Thus, such studies tend to be historical in orientation rather than attempting, as does Wells for example, to give a synchronic account of different phonological systems. Following this model, one recent publication (Orton, Sanderson and Widdowson, 1978) describes the sounds of different rural dialects not in terms of systematic and realizational differences, but as reflexes of the vowels of Middle English. This framework continues the nineteenth-century tradition of using dialectological data to reconstruct earlier forms of the language, rather than for synchronic comparative purposes. A recently published study of the phonology of Canton, a suburb of Cardiff, adopts this same framework (Lediard, 1977), while Wilson (1970) also describes an urban dialect (that of the Staffordshire Potteries) in terms of the ME vowel and inflectional system. Both of these are similar in design to the very early urban studies (Ellis, 1889; Wright, 1905).

A further consequence of this 'historical' approach is a preoccupation with what is variously described as the 'oldest', 'purest' or 'most genuine' form of the dialect. As a result, the informants selected for traditional studies were usually old (over sixty), male, and relatively uneducated, the assumption being that the 'genuine' form of the dialect can most easily be recovered from those speakers who will be relatively uninfluenced by more standard or non-local varieties, and that younger speakers, who have been exposed to the educational system, will be less genuine dialect speakers. The major difference between modern and these traditional urban dialect studies is that modern studies examine patterns of variation between ALTERNATIVE phonological, lexical or syntactic forms, rather than labelling one form as 'genuine' and focusing on that. However, a large number of relatively recent, and linguistically sophisticated, studies of British urban dialects retain this preoccupation with the 'genuine' form of the language in one way or another.

One example is Viereck's *Phonematische Analyse des Dialekts von Gateshead-upon-Tyne, Co. Durham* (1966), which is a substantial and clear synchronic phonological account and includes a good discussion of the relation between Received Pronunciation and 'local standards' (an idea derived from Wyld). There is also some detailed consideration of how dialect forms might interact with RP forms to produce such urban varieties as that of

Gateshead. However, although Gateshead's population is given as 100,000 and consists of persons of both sexes, all ages and varying social status, Viereck bases his description on the speech of 12 men, all retired manual workers, whose average age is 76.

Gregg's work in Larne, Co. Antrim, resembles Viereck's in that it contains a substantial and clear synchronic phonological account and shows similar theoretical interest in the emergence of local urban standards (Gregg, 1964). It is worth looking at it in detail. Gregg relates his findings in Larne to data on the local Ulster Scots dialect (see chapter 7), and notes that while Larne speakers have a similar phoneme inventory to rural hinterland speakers, they characteristically reorganize it in such a way that the available phonemic contrasts appear in different lexical items. This kind of systematic difference is what Wells describes as an 'incidential' difference in the distribution of phonemes.

Thus, for example, the item *butcher* falls into the /ü/ class in Larne, but into the /ʌ/ class in the hinterland dialect of Glenoe. Both systems contrast /ʌ/ and /ü/, but in Glenoe the vowels in the stressed syllables of *steady*, *wind* and *cinders* fall into the /ʌ/ class, while in Larne the vowels of *such* (Glenoe /sük/) and *rust* (Glenoe /rüst/) are analysed as /ʌ/. Thus, phoneme incidence appears to have been rearranged in Larne to reflect somewhat more closely the lexical sets of Standard English. This is an important study for anyone interested specifically in *urban* dialects, as evidence has appeared from elsewhere that such a reorganization of the system of phonemic contrasts which involves movement of lexical items from one phonemic class to another is characteristic of the relationship between urban dialects and the dialects of the rural hinterland (see page 214 below, and also Milroy and Milroy, 1978; Trudgill and Foxcroft, 1978; Petyt, 1980: 34). However, although Gregg's account is relatively sophisticated it resembles traditional dialect studies in its preoccupation with the 'genuine' speech of Larne as opposed to speech in which influence from nearby Belfast can be detected. Similar comments might be made about Sivertsen's *Cockney phonology* (1960). While recognizing that there are various kinds of Cockney which vary according to style and speaker, Sivertsen is explicitly interested in what she describes as 'rough Cockney', and her work is based mainly on the speech of four elderly female informants from Bethnal Green, selected for their relative social isolation, low social status, and lack of education. Although this is a substantial and clear synchronic account which includes a number of interesting observations (on, for example, sex-based differences in language) Sivertsen still reveals a preoccupation with the 'pure' form of the dialect, in her view obtainable only from uneducated, old, low-status speakers. The same preoccupation is revealed in a slightly different form in Weissmann's study of Bristol phonology (1970). Again we have a substantial and clear phonological account supplemented by both a phonemic and phonetic transcription of spontaneous speech. Weissmann's selected informants were all young men, partly because he felt more comfortable with men, but more importantly because he felt (probably correctly) that men would modify their characteristic Bristol speech less than women. Thus we see again a restriction in the type of informant selected with a view to producing a static description of some kind of 'extreme' phonological system.

Some problems

All of these synchronic studies (and others like them) provide valuable sources of data on the phonologies of various British urban dialects; however, they present two main problems, which can be exemplified by considering Sivertsen's study.

The first is one of representativeness. London is one of the largest cities in the world and has probably always been linguistically very heterogeneous; there are, for example, records of English creole speakers in London dating from Elizabethan times. Even if we confine our interest to working-class speech from the East End, we are still talking about hundreds of thousands of people, and so it seems inappropriate, without explicit acknowledgement, to limit the description to a single type of informant. Second, certain assumptions are inherent in the preoccupation with 'genuine' dialect, the most obvious being that young speakers, by virtue of access to education and modern communications networks, are more likely to be influenced by the standard. This assumption has not in general been borne out by empirical observation. For example, Hurford (1967), discussing the language of three generations of a London family, suggests that Cockney features are advancing among the youngest speakers at the expense of RP features. Beaken's study of the phonological development of 55 East London primary school children shows that the reality of age grading in language is simultaneously more complex and more interesting than had been traditionally assumed (Beaken, 1971). While children between five and seven years of age have begun to use many dialect features, the eight- to nine-year-olds have developed an additional formal (i.e. less localized) style which they use with the interviewer. At the same age, clear differences between the speech of boys and girls emerge, which Beaken is able to list.

Supporting evidence has appeared from elsewhere that children develop at primary school the capacity to vary their language stylistically and that the sexes are differentiated linguistically. For example, Reid documents the manner in which primary school boys systematically vary phonetic realizations of /t/ and inflectional /ɪŋ/ in Edinburgh, depending on whether they are reading aloud, participating in a relatively formal interview, or interacting with their friends (Reid, 1978). Romaine, in a detailed study of post-vocalic /r/ in Edinburgh, has shown that as early as ten years old, extremely sharp patterns of sex differentiation in the use of this phonological element have emerged. Boys are much more likely to delete /r/ than girls, and girls have a strong tendency to use [ɹ] rather than [r] (Romaine, 1978). Local (1983) documents equally sharp differences in the manner in which boys and girls use prosodic patterns in Newcastle-upon-Tyne.

Some recent quantitative studies suggest that the kind of age grading in language, noted by Hurford in London, is in fact rather general. For example, Trudgill shows clearly the manner in which a tendency to centralize vowels of the /ɛ/ class (as in *tell, well, better*) increases systematically in inverse proportion to the age of Norwich speakers (Trudgill, 1974: 105). As a result of findings like these, researchers now expect to find the most extreme form of an urban vernacular among young adolescent speakers. It is therefore dangerous to proceed on the basis of apparently commonsense assumptions which may, when investigated, turn out to be false.

Quantitative methods in urban dialect studies

Although these traditional studies may be criticized on various grounds, it must be conceded that the task of describing the speech of a city is a daunting one. Any investigator is immediately faced with such awkward facts as those noted by, for example, Sivertsen; individual informants vary in the extent to which they use a characteristic dialect feature (such as the glottal stop in Cockney), and speak noticeably differently according to situational context. How can these facts of intrapersonal and interpersonal variability be incorporated within a linguistic description? These questions were tackled by the American linguist William Labov in his innovatory urban study *The social stratification of English in New York City* (1966). I give in the following section only the briefest outline of Labov's contribution, concentrating on those aspects of his work which are particularly relevant to this chapter. For further details, readers are referred to Labov (1972a); Trudgill (1974); Chambers and Trudgill (1980); Petyt (1980).

Labov tackled the problem of representativeness by using a random sampling technique to obtain his informants. This meant simply that anyone within the sample frame had an equal chance of being selected. As in all samples of this kind, many of the originally selected informants were not interviewed for reasons such as death, illness, change of residence, non-local origin or simply refusal to co-operate, and it should be noted that Labov's final description was based mainly on 88 speakers out of an original sample of 340. Difficulties of this kind have led some scholars to query both the wisdom and the validity of a complicated sampling procedure which may not measure up to the standards demanded by disciplines outside linguistics (Knowles, 1974; Romaine, 1980). Nevertheless, Labov's procedure certainly assured representativeness in the rather weak and non-technical sense that he did not concentrate on a particular group of selected speakers; nor did he claim that any particular type of speech was 'typical' of New York City.

Further, Labov sampled a range of conversational and reading styles from each speaker. Altogether, five styles were distinguished in accordance with the amount of attention being paid to speech, and ordered along a single dimension of informal to formal. The styles were then examined compara- tively to give some insight into how people changed their language according to situation. It is likely that the single items elicited using the sentence frames favoured by traditional dialectologists correspond most closely to the formal end of Labov's stylistic continuum.

The key to direct analysis and systematic comparison of the very large amount of data obtained using these methods is the concept developed by Labov of the 'sociolinguistic variable'. This is a linguistic element, phono- logical usually, although syntactic variables have also been studied (see especially Cheshire, 1978, 1982; Petyt, 1978; Policansky, 1982) which co- varies not only with other linguistic elements but with social variables such as class, age and sex. Simple examples are [h] which is variably 'dropped' in much of England, and variable subject–verb agreement in Belfast: *the boys is coming* ~ *the boys are coming*. The concept of the sociolinguistic variable is important because it allows quantification of language use. Thus, speaker A may be said to use more or less of a particular variable than speaker B, rather than categorically to use it or not to use it.

We may demonstrate the manner in which the language characteristic of particular cities can be described in terms of sociolinguistic variables by considering data from two places, Bradford and Norwich. The figures in table 13.1 refer to the proportion of zero realizations of word-initial /h/ (in words like *hammer* and *heart*) recorded for five social-class groups in these cities, ranging from 'lower working class' to 'middle middle class'. It is clear that in both places speakers of relatively high status show a progressive tendency to approximate to the spoken standard of RP, which retains [h], although each social group in Bradford uses the zero variant more than the corresponding group in Norwich. This comparison of the distribution of [h] in the two cities may be interpreted as reflecting both the social function of variable linguistic elements to varying degrees in cities, and the tendency to retain relatively stigmatized dialect features throughout the social spectrum (which is greater in Bradford than in Norwich).

The basic method of presenting information on the speech communities' use of these variables was originally developed also by Labov in New York City. Table 13.1 shows how linguistic scores may be calculated for groups of speakers, divided according to their social-class characteristics, to reveal the systematic relationship between language use and social class. However, linguistic scores may be shown as in table 13.2 in relation also to other independent variables, such as age and sex, with stylistic variation being taken into account. Table 13.2 shows the distribution of the variable (ai) amongst working-class Belfast speakers in both interview style (in direct response to the fieldworker's questions) and in a more spontaneous speech style (not responding directly to questions, and often not addressing the fieldworker). The figures record the amount of fronting and raising to [ei] of the vowel in

Table 13.1. *(h) in Bradford and Norwich*

Social class	Bradford	Norwich
Middle-middle	12	6
Lower-middle	28	14
Upper-working	67	40
Middle-working	89	60
Lower-working	93	60

Source: after Chambers and Trudgill (1980: 69) and Petyt (1977)

Table 13.2. *(ai) in Belfast: IS = interview style; SS = spontaneous style*

Age	Men		Women
70+	173.0	IS	–
	194.0	SS	–
40–55	77.7	IS	62.7
	121.3	SS	126.0
18–25	74.0	IS	46.7
	133.7	SS	115.7

such words as *pipe* and *line*, and are shown separately for three age groups and both sexes. The maximum possible score is 200. Several facts are immediately apparent from the data presented here. First, the tendency to raise and front (ai) decreases systematically with the age of the speaker. Second, within each age group, women raise and front the vowel very much less than men; and finally, all speakers use raised and fronted variants very much more in spontaneous speech than in the relatively formal style of interaction appropriate to an interview.

The broad outlines of the findings suggested by tables 13.1 and 13.2 have been confirmed by other surveys, and for other consonant and vowel variables. Generally speaking, higher social-class groups have relatively high linguistic scores (that is, they approximate closer to standardized varieties); women score higher than men; and older speakers often score higher than younger, though the pattern may be complex here. For example, the Belfast data seem to show the gradual modification of a nonstandard pronunciation through three generations, while the Norwich data reported on page 203 above show a movement TOWARDS a nonstandard pronunciation. However, the tendency of speakers to shift away from nonstandard forms as they move in the 'formal' direction along a stylistic continuum seems to be very general.

There are many partial exceptions to these regularities; a sociolinguistic variable is not always evaluated in the same way by the whole community, and irregularities may provide evidence of linguistic change in progress (the direct observation and interpretation of facts of change is, in fact, a major theoretical interest of quantitative urban dialectology).

Labov's basic methods also allow language use to be seen as probabilistic rather than categorical, thus challenging the static models of linguistic competence which underlie modern linguistic theory (see Bailey and Shuy, 1973; Sankoff, 1978). The main effect of this development has been to move urban dialectology (and variation studies generally) closer to the central concerns of theoretical linguistics.

I have dwelt in a little detail on Labov's 1966 model here, showing how it has been applied to the analysis of British urban dialects, because in whole or in part it has been the basis of much subsequent research in Britain while other British scholars have been quite explicitly critical of it. However, we look briefly now at another group of studies which, although a considerable advance on the more traditional approaches, cannot be said to be much indebted to Labov in either a positive or a negative sense.

Recent studies of British urban dialects

Houck's work in Leeds was intended to provide a model for the study of urban dialects, and resulted, like Labov's, from a recognition of the inadequacy of an approach based on rural dialectology (Houck, 1968). Using an extremely sophisticated two-stage sampling procedure, he ended up with a sample of 115, representing a 75 per cent response rate – very much better than Labov's. Unfortunately however, Houck gives little indication of how he handled the speech of his 115 informants; his intention seems to have been to set up a phonological system using minimal pairs elicited by means of sentence frames.

Heath's survey of the urban dialect of Cannock, Staffordshire, carried out in the late 1960s is characterized by the same rigorous approach to sampling (Heath, 1980). However, the Labovian concept of a sociolinguistic variable is not used, nor are linguistic data quantified. The 80 informants are divided into five groups, depending upon the extent to which their speech is influenced by the 'extremes' of Cannock urban dialect on the one hand and RP on the other; thus, speakers are grouped linguistically rather than socially. The work contains also a useful discussion of the problems of applying some existing phonological models (phonemic analysis and generative phonology) to variable data. Although Heath has much more of interest, particularly a conclusion that the order in which Cannock vowels are 'corrected' to RP is implicationally predictable, the influence of traditional studies on his approach is shown by frequent references to the 'pure' Cannock speaker; the more neutral comparative approach of Labov's model is not adopted. Similar to Heath's general approach is that of Bowyer (1973) who studied the language of a South London suburb. We may also note here the work of Bertz

(1975) who classifies the Dublin speech of 132 informants into three types, 'educated', 'general' and 'popular', using a mixture of social and stylistic criteria which are not always clearly explained. This also is a non-quantitative study.

It is worth considering now in some detail two substantial British surveys which, unlike those discussed in the preceding sections, are quite explicitly critical of Labov's methods.

The Tyneside Linguistic Survey, begun in 1963 and still in progress, is characterized by a determination not to prejudge relationships between linguistic and social (not necessarily socioeconomic) factors, and the objection is raised by Pellowe (1976) that Labov's work is based on an underlying theory of social structure which is never made explicit (see also De Camp, 1971). Hence, the Tyneside Linguistic Survey has attempted to locate specific linguistic variants in a multidimensional 'variety space' (Pellowe, Nixon, Strang and McNeany, 1972), i.e. to associate a wide range of linguistic and non-linguistic factors. Much of the published work arising out of the Tyneside Linguistic Survey is devoted to the development of an accountable, explicit and ideologically unbiased methodology, and in the early stages of the project no speaker in the area, native Tynesider or not, was excluded from consideration. A further point is that the survey attempts to analyse data in accordance with the perceptions of hearers.

Although many would feel sympathetic to the aims of this ambitious project, the very punctiliousness of the Tyneside Linguistic Survey researchers has led to an imbalance in favour of methodology and theory and a relative weakness on results. Those results that have appeared are however frequently stimulating and innovatory. See, especially, McNeany (1971) for a generative analysis of vowel reduction rules; Pellowe, Nixon and McNeany (1972) for narrowly transcribed material on a range of variables; Pellowe and Jones (1978) and Local (1982) for excellent analyses of prosodic variables.

Knowles (1974) is also critical of Labov, although his original intention was to draw a sample of 100 persons divided equally between a working-class and an upper-middle-class area of Liverpool and from then on to follow Labov's general model. As a result of the same problems encountered by Labov in New York City his number of 'useful interviews' (Knowles's term) was reduced to 47 (see also Mees, 1977, for an account of the practical difficulties involved in random sampling for an urban dialect survey). Knowles concluded that his sampling procedure had been a 'timewasting exercise' of dubious value, although it is worth noting that his response rate was considerably better than Labov's. In fact, it is clear that Knowles is concerned with fundamental problems of linguistic description much more explicitly than Labov and others working in Labov's tradition; their tendency is to view variable data as a means of solving theoretical linguistic problems. Knowles wants to explain as accurately as possible 'what makes a Liverpudlian sound like one the minute he opens his mouth', and suggests that while Labov's

Table 13.3. *Realizations of /uə/, /oə/ in Liverpool speech (Scouse)*

	uə	oə
1 lax [u,o] before unstressed vowel:	uə	ɔə
or		
2 (a) diphthongize [u,o];	ɪúə,íuə	ɔ́uə
or		
(b) front [u]:	ʉə	
3 modify VVV to V + glide + V:	ɪwə	owə
4 front final [ə]:	uɛ, ʔuɛ	oɛ, ʔɔɛ
	ɪúɛ, íuɛ	ɔ́uɛ
	ʉɛ, ɪwɛ	ɔwɛ

Source: Knowles (1978: 85)

method of placing variants on a single social and phonetic dimension may make counting relatively easy, it also oversimplifies the real range of phonological choice open to the Scouse speaker.

Knowles demonstrates this point by showing the limitations of a single linear scale in relation to the realization of five phonological variables. One of them is an optionally merged variable, (uə) and (oə), as in *sure* and *shore* (cf. chapter 4). Some speakers keep /uə/ and /oə/ word-classes distinct, while others merge both with the /ɔ/ class (words such as *Shaw*). A Scouse speaker first has to choose whether to merge these classes or not, and then whether to apply a number of optional but low-level rules. Knowles characterizes the choices which are open to speakers in the way shown in table 13.3, pointing out that the second, third and fourth rules operate mainly in working-class speech. It is clear that when the aim is to describe the phonology of an urban dialect in this kind of detail, Labov's methods of characterizing social and linguistic variation on a single continuum are indeed quite inappropriate. Further, some very salient Scouse phenomena such as aspirated fricatives as in *bush* [buʃh] are probably best described not quantitatively, but qualitatively in terms of the articulatory setting peculiar to the dialect, which can account for a very large number of quite diverse phonetic characteristics.

Some preoccupations which characterize British work are apparent in Knowles's thesis. The value placed on coherent phonological description has already been noted several times in this chapter and Knowles's interest in the manner in which north-western and Anglo-Irish varieties of English are related to Scouse is reminiscent of the work of Gregg and Viereck on regional urban standards. With the Tyneside Linguistic Survey Knowles shares an interest in the sociolinguistic role of prosodic features (see also Gunn, 1983, for another such study), and a conviction that Labovian methods are too crude phonetically and phonologically for good urban dialectological description.

We turn now to a more detailed consideration of that British work which is most explicitly dominated by Labov's influence. By this I mean that it is quantitative: using the notion of the sociolinguistic variable, direct comparisons are made between one speaker and another and between language and a range of extra-linguistic factors. Despite problems associated with the notion of the variable (as we shall see, some British scholars have been particularly critical of this), quantitative analysis remains a powerful tool for this type of work. One of the most striking features emerging from the selection of work edited by Trudgill in 1978, which follows the quantitative tradition (and from British work published elsewhere), is the critical attitude adopted to various aspects of Labovian theory and methodology within a broad acceptance of the value of quantitative techniques. Accordingly, I will try to concentrate here, somewhat selectively, on the manner in which British work has diverged from the New York City paradigm, and refer the reader to Hudson (1980), Petyt (1980), Chambers and Trudgill (1980) and Romaine (1980), for more comprehensive accounts.

The first Labovian study to appear in Britain was Trudgill's survey of Norwich (1974). Although its design differs from Labov's in a number of details, the general principles (already exemplified above) of showing, and drawing conclusions from, systematic correspondences between language and a range of extra-linguistic variables, are followed. Unlike Labov, however, Trudgill attempts a relatively abstract phonology of the urban 'diasystem', that is, the full set of phonological rules available to a member of the Norwich speech community. Although this attempt is not entirely successful, it does reflect a more general British preoccupation with coherent phonological description. Macaulay's study of Glasgow (1977) was again carried out along broadly Labovian lines. It was found that five phonological variables corresponded closely to four social-class groupings.

(i)   the vowel in *hit, kill, risk* etc.
(u)   the vowel in *school, book, fool, full* etc.
(a)   the vowel in *cap, ban, hand* etc.
(au) the diphthong in *now, down, house* etc.
(ʔ)   the use of a glottal stop instead of [t] in *butter, get* etc.

The phonetic realizations of these vowels cover an extremely wide range; for example five variants of (i) are coded, as follows, in descending order of social prestige:

(i–1) [ɪ]
(i–2) [ɛ^] and [ɪᵥ]
(i–3) [ɛ ᶲ] and [ï_v]
(i–4) [ə^]
(i–5) [ʌ^]

Despite his adoption of the Labovian model, Macaulay is critical of a number of its standard techniques such as the practice of grouping both linguistic data and individual speakers. He himself presents data on individuals as well as groups, and subsequently checks the fit between individual and group scores. On the basis of breaks which emerge in his data between sets of ranked individual scores, he concludes that it is reasonable to describe the urban dialect of Glasgow as consisting of three major (but overlapping) social dialects (Macaulay, 1978).

Petyt's study (1978) of the urban dialect of West Yorkshire follows broadly Labovian lines also, but looks at structural types of phonological variable in some detail, in a manner related to Wells.

The notion of the sociolinguistic variable analysed on a single social and phonetic dimension is criticized by Hudson and Holloway (1977) in their study of working- and middle-class London children, and by Romaine (1978) who looks at the language of Edinburgh children. There are several reasons for these criticisms, the most important probably being the loss of information when phonological elements which may vary on more than one dimension (e.g. height and diphthongization) are in fact analysed as varying on a single dimension. Another problem is that an average score may reflect consistent use of the median value, or more variable use of extreme values. Moreover, as both Romaine, and Hudson and Holloway demonstrate, variants may sometimes not be analysable on a continuum at all. For example, three variants of (r), namely [ɹ], [r] and ø, distinguished by Romaine in Edinburgh, can hardly be placed in any kind of rationally motivated continuum and it is equally difficult to see how the nine variants of (th) (as in *moth*) distinguished by Hudson and Holloway, which include [θ] [f] [ɸ] [tθ] and [h] can be handled in this way.

A further criticism of the unidimensional variable is made by Milroy (1982), who reports results of a household survey carried out in Belfast (see also chapter 7). What appears to happen with words of the /a/ class as well as other phonological sets is that middle-class speakers most of the time converge relatively closely on the vowel space around the low front area while working-class speakers display a far greater range of phonetically conditioned allophonic variation, realizing /a/ as back-raised, front-raised and diphthongized variants. While data of this kind are clearly not amenable to analysis along a single phonetic dimension, Milroy demonstrates that they can be handled by other techniques, namely a range score and a bidimensional weighted index. This may be demonstrated by comparing the data in table 13.4, with that in table 13.5, which show the realizations of the /a/ vowel of a working-class and a middle-class speaker from the Belfast survey. The phonetic details have been considerably simplified here; for example, diphthongized tokens are not shown separately, so that realizations such as [mɔ ᵊn] *man* are shown in the [ɔ] column. Nevertheless, the general patterns are quite characteristic of the speakers' respective social groups.

Some British work has taken a little further the quantitative study of

Table 13.4. */a/ range for a working-class Belfast speaker: word-list style (from random sample survey)*

	ε	æ	a	ä	ɑ	ɔ
bag	+					
back		+				
cap			+			
map					+	
passage					+	
cab						+
grass						+
bad						+
man						+
castle				+		
dabble				+		
passing						+

Table 13.5. */a/ range for a middle-class Belfast speaker: word-list style (random sample survey)*

	ε	æ	a	ä	ɑ	ɔ
bag			+			
back			+			
cap			+			
map			+			
passage			+			
cab			+			
grass			+			
bad			+			
man			+			
castle			+			
dabble			+			
passing			+			

stylistic variation. Reid (1978) concludes from his work in Edinburgh that children have developed a capacity to manipulate the relevant variables while they are still of primary school age (see also the findings of Beaken, discussed on page 211 above). Reid is critical of a number of Labovian principles such as those of grouping informants and of analysing style shifting along a single dimension. Coupland's preoccupation is also with style shifting, and he examines quantitatively, from a number of perspectives, the speech of a single Cardiff speaker during a single day (Coupland, 1980).

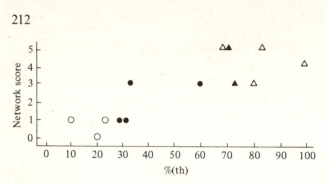

Figure 13.1. (th) and social integration in the Ballymacarrett area of Belfast

Most of the studies discussed in the preceding sections have been based on the speech of informants selected by some kind of random sampling procedure. However, we shall now look at two studies, one in Belfast and one in Reading, which are organized in terms of their goal of studying the speech of pre-existing social groups (see Labov, 1972b, and Blom and Gumperz, 1972, for discussions of the advantages of this technique).

One aspect of variation which was specifically investigated in the Belfast group study (restricted to working-class speakers) was the relation of the vernacular to 'hinterland' varieties (Milroy and Milroy, 1978; Pitts, 1982). The effect of internal group structure, characterized as 'network' structure, on the extent to which an individual adheres to a strongly nonstandard speech style, was also examined, using a range of statistical techniques, and found to be of some importance. Briefly, the most nonstandard speakers tended to have the strongest social ties with the local community. This is demonstrated particularly clearly in figure 13.1. Here, the scores of 13 speakers on the variable (th) – the voiced dental fricative in the intervocalic position in such words as *mother, brother, together* – are plotted against their personal network scores. This score is a measure of social integration into the local (low-status) community. The tendency of scores to cluster at the bottom left and top right corners of the graph suggests that the variables of language and network are associated with each other. The strong tendency is for high network scorers to delete the intervocalic consonant, and the correlation between the variables is in fact statistically highly significant (see Milroy, 1980, for details) These findings are interpreted in terms of the influence of solidarity-based factors on patterns of language use in cities, as opposed to the relationship between language and status which seems to emerge from surveys such as those in Glasgow and Norwich. Cheshire's study of the use made of a number of syntactic variables by adolescent groups in Reading explores similar kinds of relationship, and shows that those who occupy a central position in the vernacular culture tend to use the most extreme nonstandard language (Cheshire, 1978, 1982). This special kind of value attached to nonstandard speech is described by Trudgill (1972) as 'covert prestige' in his exploration of the manner in which middle-class men value characteristically working-class speech.

Like many other British studies, the Belfast project has attempted to include a coherent phonological description of a relatively idealized system (see Milroy, 1976, 1981). Work is also in progress on the quantitative analysis of phonological variation in terms of a large number of variants which cannot be analysed as lying on a single phonetic continuum. Means of formalizing this material and integrating it into a formal phonological theory other than by the use of a 'variable rules' format are being explored. See Sankoff (1978) for a discussion of variable rules methodology; and Milroy (1982) for comments on the limitations of the model. The implications of work on variation for phonological theory generally have also been explored by Milroy and Harris (1980) and by J. Milroy in several places. The Belfast study, along with several others, has specifically investigated the relationship between linguistic change and language variation (see, especially, Trudgill, 1974; Trudgill and Foxcroft, 1978; Romaine, 1978; J. Milroy, 1980). This aspect of quantitative work is clearly of great theoretical importance since, in revealing earlier stages of the language to be part of an individual's contemporary experience, it challenges the Saussurian dichotomy between synchrony and diachrony which underlies modern linguistic theory.

In view of changes in the ethnic composition of British cities over the last three decades and the consequent emergence of new language-contact situations, the work of John Wells (1973) on London Jamaican phonology should be noted. This work is Labovian only in that a small part of it makes use of quantitative techniques. On the other hand, Wells's use of sentence frames to obtain single-word responses reflects the influence of an earlier tradition and his own major preoccupation is with the phenomenon of hyper-adaptation, that is, the over-application or mis-application of a rule which a migrant speaker is attempting to adopt in his target language or dialect. For example, a common Jamaican Creole pronunciation of *needle* is [niːgl] as opposed to RP [niːdl], reflecting a rule of the form /d/ → [g]/-[l]. To correct this, speakers formulate an inverse rule of the type /g/ → [d]/-[l], which may then be over-applied, resulting in forms like [iːdl] for *eagle*. Wells notes the result of the same phenomenon in realizations of other phonological elements; *bed* is sometimes realized as [bɛð] for example, apparently an over-extension of the rule /d/ → [ð] which speakers formulate to correct such forms as [bɹʌdə] (RP [bɹʌðə]) for *brother*. This phenomenon of hyper-adaptation, often described as 'hyper-correction', has often been noted as significant in accounting for part of the range of choice open to speakers in cities (see for example Knowles, 1978; Petyt, 1977) and it seems likely that the principle is of general value in the study of urban dialects. This is because urban dialects characteristically involve the mixing (historically) of a number of linguistic systems, and a tendency for persons to adopt new systems, for social reasons.

Wells's conclusion is that phonetic adaptation is much easier for speakers than phonological adaptation, which involves acquiring new sets of oppositions or changing distributional constraints. The study also includes clear descriptions of a range of varieties – RP, Jamaican Creole and Cockney – which may be supposed to influence London Jamaican speakers, and as a whole it is a valuable addition to work on British urban dialects, particularly in view of Rosen's remark that a clear London Jamaican variety is now emerging (Rosen, 1980). We may note in passing that the design of Mees's study of Cardiff school children is very similar to Wells's in its combination of a limited quantitative analysis and a relatively sophisticated phonological description (Mees, 1977).

Towards a 'typology' of urban dialects

Finally, it is appropriate to ask whether urban dialects can be said to differ in any fundamental way from dialects generally. Most urban dialectologists would I think agree with Labov's view that very rapid mixing of a number of dialects from surrounding areas characteristically accompanies the growth of cities. Some scholars have attempted to disentangle the 'mix' – for example Knowles points out that traces of Northern English dialects, Irish dialects and RP can all be found in Scouse. Further, Milroy and Milroy (1978) have suggested that while urban dialects characteristically have phonological systems no closer than those of rural dialects to any nationally accepted standard, they do represent a closer approximation to the standard in that through time they re-classify particular lexical items into the vernacular phonological equivalents of 'standard' lexical sets. Thus for example the word *brick* in Belfast in 1860 apparently rhymed with *seek* but now all but the oldest speakers rhyme the word with *sick*. Gregg's work in Larne (see page 201 above) supports the suggestion that such a standardization of lexical sets may be characteristic of urban dialects generally.

The most obvious characteristic of urban dialects however, is what we might describe as their 'structured heterogeneity'. The quantitative studies have revealed clearly that phonological systems can vary very greatly within a single city, but that a great deal of variation, often associated with rapid change, is tied to the social characteristics of speakers. Those patterns of social differentiation which are reflected in differences in lifestyle, residence, income and education are also faithfully, and in great detail, reflected in patterns of linguistic stratification. It has been more recently suggested that the phonological systems characteristic of low-status urban speakers are TYPOLOGICALLY different from those of higher-status speakers in that they reveal much more phonetically conditioned allophonic variation (see Milroy, 1982 and page 211 above). The systematic relationship between linguistic variation and a range of extra linguistic factors revealed by the urban dialect studies has some important implications for linguistic theory which should be noted here. One very weak claim which may be made is that the so-called free variation of theoretical phonology is in fact often systematically constrained by a range of non-linguistic factors. The variable rule formalism first proposed by Labov (1972b) and developed further by Cedergren and Sankoff (1974) is an attempt to incorporate systematic variability, whether linguistically or socially constrained, into a formal grammar. This attempt is not limited to phonological variability; Labov's original article dealt with variable copula deletion in American Black English.

Some linguists, whose interests are mainly in constructing an adequate linguistic theory (rather than in studying urban dialects), have suggested that the systematic variations revealed by quantitative studies offer a considerable challenge to theoretical linguistics; for example, Sampson (1980) sees the breakdown of the synchronic – diachronic distinction as extremely important. Others argue, taking a more fundamental view, that the findings of quantitative studies indicate the need for a re-examination of core linguistic theory (see particularly Labov 1972c, 1975; Bailey and Shuy, 1973; Klein and Dittmar, 1979; Hudson, 1980). In particular, it is suggested that natural languages possess inherent properties such as vagueness, variability and context-boundedness which make a high degree of idealization within a static asocial model (such as Transformational Generative Grammar) inappropriate. Klein and Dittmar (amongst others) have argued that such a highly idealized model, relying as it does on relatively clear delimitations of what is or is not a grammatical sentence, is capable of handling only a small amount of actual language behaviour (the language of children and migrants acquiring a new code are picked out as linguistic phenomena which cannot be handled within a static framework).

Many theoretical linguists appear to regard objections like these, and those of Labov who queries the use of intuition in generative grammar (1975), as essentially trivial, or as referring to phenomena which are not part of 'linguistic knowledge' in the technical sense. Chomsky himself has argued strongly against the relevance of Labovian studies for linguistic theory, insisting (on the model of procedure in the physical sciences) that a high degree of idealization is the only rational approach to linguistic theory and that Labov's contribution is purely descriptive. The analyses of correspondences between linguistic and extra-linguistic factors (from which conclusions about linguistic change may be drawn) are likened to butterfly collecting (Chomsky, 1975). However, in view of the contrast emphasized in this chapter between the clearly descriptive approach of early urban dialectology and the determination of the later studies to address fundamental questions of linguistic theory raised by the facts of variability, it is hard to believe that Chomsky has taken account of all the relevant facts. Despite problems of *rapprochement* of this kind, it nevertheless seems likely that urban dialectological work in the future will continue to draw closer to the fundamental concerns of linguistic theory.

216

L. MILROY

REFERENCES

Bailey, C.J. and Shuy, R. (eds.) 1973. *New ways of analyzing variation in English.* Washington DC: Georgetown University Press.
Beaken, M.A. 1971. A study of phonological development in a primary school population of East London. Ph.D. thesis, University of London.
Bertz, S. 1975. Der Dubliner Stadtdialekt. Ph.D. thesis, Freiburg: Albert Ludwigs Universität.
Blom, J.P. and Gumperz, J. 1972. Social meaning in linguistic structures: code switching in Norway. In J. Gumperz and D. Hymes (eds.) *Directions in sociolinguistics.* New York: Holt, Rinehart and Winston.
Bowyer, R. 1973. A study of social accents in a south London suburb. M.Phil. thesis, University of Leeds.
Cedergren, H.J. and Sankoff, D. 1974. Variable rules: performance as a statistical reflection of competence. *Language* 50: 333–55.
Chambers, J.K. and Trudgill, P.J. 1980. *Dialectology.* Cambridge: CUP.
Cheshire, J. 1978. Present tense verbs in Reading English. In Trudgill (1978).
——— 1982. *Variation in an English dialect.* Cambridge: CUP.
Chomsky, N. 1975. *Language and responsibility.* Sussex: Harvester Press.
Coupland, N. 1980. Style shifting in a Cardiff work setting. *Language in Society* 9: 1–13.
De Camp, D. 1971. Towards a generative analysis of a post-creole continuum. In D. Hymes (ed.) *Pidginization and creolization of languages.* Cambridge: CUP.
Ellis, A.J. 1889. *On early English pronunciation, part V: the existing phonology of English dialects.* London: Trübner.
Gregg, R.J. 1964. Scotch-Irish urban speech in Ulster. In G.B. Adams (ed.) *Ulster dialects: an introductory symposium.* Holywood, Co. Down: Ulster Folk Museum.
Gunn, B. 1983. Aspects of intonation in the speech of the Cork urban area. Thesis, University College Cork.
Health, C.D. 1980. *The pronunciation of English in Cannock, Staffordshire.* Oxford: Blackwell.
Houck, C.L. 1968. Methodology of an urban speech survey. *Leeds studies in English* NS II: 115–28.
Hudson, R.A. 1980. *Sociolinguistics.* Cambridge: CUP.
Hudson, R.A. and Holloway, A.F. 1977. *Variation in London English.* Report to the Social Science Research Council.
Hughes, A. and Trudgill, P. 1979. *English accents and dialects.* London: Edward Arnold.
Hurford, J.R. 1967. *The speech of one family.* Ph.D. thesis, University of London.
Klein, W. and Dittmar, N. 1979. *Developing grammars.* Berlin: Springer.
Knowles, G.D. 1974. Scouse: the urban dialect of Liverpool. Ph.D. thesis, University of Leeds.
——— 1978. The nature of phonological variables in Scouse. In Trudgill (1978) pp. 80–90.
Labov, W. 1966. *The social stratification of English in New York City.* Washington, DC: Centre for Applied Linguistics.
——— 1972a. *Sociolinguistic patterns.* Philadelphia: Pennsylvania University Press.
——— 1972b. *Language in the inner city.* Philadelphia: Pennsylvania University Press.

—————— 1972c. Where do grammars stop? In R. W. Shuy, (ed.) *Sociolinguistics: current trends and prospects*. Washington DC: Georgetown University Press.

—————— 1975. *What is a linguistic fact?* Lisse: The Peter de Ridder Press.

Lediard, J. 1977. The sounds of the dialect of Canton, a surburb of Cardiff. In D. Parry (ed.) *The survey of Anglo-Welsh dialects*. University College, Swansea: University of Wales Press.

Local, J. 1982. Modelling intonational variability in children's language. In Romaine (1982).

Macaulay, R. K. S. 1977. *Language, social class and education: a Glasgow study*. Edinburgh: Edinburgh University Press.

—————— 1978. Variation and consistency in Glaswegian English. In Trudgill (1978) pp. 132–43.

McNeany, V. 1971. Vowel reduction in localized Tyneside and RP speech. Mimeo, Department of English Language and Linguistics, University of Newcastle-upon-Tyne.

Mees, I. 1977. Language and social class in Cardiff. M. A. thesis, University of Leiden.

Milroy, J. 1976. Length and height variations in the vowels of Belfast vernacular. *Belfast Working Papers in Language and Linguistics* 1, 3.

—————— 1980. Lexical alternation and the history of English. In E. Traugott (ed.) *Current issues in linguistic theory, vol. 14*. Amsterdam: Benjamins.

—————— 1981. *Regional accents of English: Belfast*. Belfast: Blackstaff.

—————— 1982. Probing under the tip of the iceberg: phonological 'normalization' and the shape of speech communities. In Romaine (1982) pp. 35–47.

Milroy, J. and Harris, J. 1980. When is a merger not a merger? the MEAT/MATE problem in a present-day English vernacular. *English World-Wide* 1, 2: 199–210.

Milroy, J. and Milroy, L. 1978. Belfast: change and variation in an urban vernacular. In Trudgill (1978).

Milroy, L. 1980. *Language and social networks*. Oxford: Blackwell.

Orton, H., Sanderson, S. and Widdowson, J. 1978. *Linguistic atlas of England*. London: Croom Helm.

Pellowe, J. 1976. The Tyneside Linguistic Survey: aspects of a developing methodology. In W. Viereck (ed.) *Sprachliches Handeln – soziales Verhalten*. Munich: Fink.

Pellowe, J. and Jones, V. 1978. On intonational variability in Tyneside speech. In Trudgill (1978).

Pellowe, J., Nixon, G. and McNeany, V. 1972. Defining the dimensionality of a linguistic variety space. Mimeo, Department of English Language and Linguistics, University of Newcastle-upon-Tyne.

Pellowe, J., Nixon, G., Strang, B., and McNeany, V. 1972. A dynamic modelling of linguistic variation: the urban (Tyneside) linguistic survey. *Lingua* 30: 1–30.

Petyt, K. M. 1977. Dialect and accent in the industrial West Riding. Ph.D. thesis, University of Reading.

—————— 1978. Secondary contraction in West Yorkshire negatives. In Trudgill (1978).

—————— 1980. *The study of dialect: an introduction to dialectology*. London: Andre Deutsch.

Pitts, A. 1982. Urban influence in Northern Irish English: a comparison of variation in two communities. Ph.D. dissertation, University of Michigan.

Policansky, L. 1982. Grammatical variation in Belfast English. *Belfast Working Papers in Language and Linguistics* 6: 37–66.

Reid, E. 1978. Social and stylistic variation in the speech of children: some evidence from Edinburgh. In Trudgill (1978).

Romaine, S. 1978. Post-vocalic /r/ in Scottish English: sound change in progress? In Trudgill (1978) pp. 144–57.

——— 1980. A critical overview of the methodology of urban British sociolinguistics. *English World-Wide* 1, 2: 163–98.

——— (ed.) 1982. *Sociolinguistic variation in speech communities*. London: Edward Arnold.

Rosen, H. 1980. Linguistic diversity in London schools. In A. K. Pugh, V. J. Lee and J. Swann (eds.) *Language and language use*. London: Heinemann and Open University Press.

Sampson, G. 1980. *Schools of linguistics*. London: Hutchinson.

Sankoff, D. (ed.) 1978. *Linguistic variation: models and methods*. New York: Academic Press.

Sivertsen, E. 1960. *Cockney phonology*. Oslo: Oslo University Press.

Trudgill, P. 1972. Sex, covert prestige and linguistic change in the urban British English of Norwich. *Language in Society* 1: 179–95.

——— 1974. *The social differentiation of English in Norwich*. Cambridge: CUP.

——— (ed.) 1978. *Sociolinguistic patterns in British English*. London: Edward Arnold.

Trudgill, P. J. and Foxcroft, T. 1978. On the sociolinguistics of vocalic mergers: transfer and approximation in East Anglia. In Trudgill (1978).

Viereck, W. 1966. *Phonematische Analyse des Dialekts von Gateshead-upon-Tyne, Co. Durham*. Hamburg: Cram, de Gruyter.

Weissmann, E. 1970. Phonematische analyse des Stadtdialekts von Bristol. *Phonetica* 21: 151–81, 211–40.

Wells, J. C. 1970. Local accents in England and Wales. *Journal of Linguistics* 6, 2: 231–52.

——— 1973. *Jamaican pronunciation in London*. Oxford: Blackwell.

——— 1982. *Accents of English*. 3 vols. Cambridge: CUP.

Wilson, D. 1970. The phonology and accidence of the North Staffordshire Potteries. M. A. thesis, University of Birmingham.

Wright, J. 1905. *The English dialect grammar* (published as an appendix to the *English dialect dictionary*). London: Frowde.

14

British Black English and West Indian Creoles

DAVID SUTCLIFFE

Introduction

The language complex described in this chapter came to the British Isles with the post-war migration from the Caribbean. English-based West Indian Creoles are vernacular languages, used mainly by people of African origin in the Caribbean and, as a result of this migration, in Britain. They differ markedly in their structure from English, although they are lexically related to it. However, much of the distinctive speech of the younger black community in Britain cannot properly be called Creole: 'British Black English' (BBE) is adopted here as a convenient label for a range of language phonologically and grammatically more or less close to the local white norm, and generally referred to as 'English' by its speakers, which yet remains distinctively 'black'.

It is well known that, both in the Caribbean and this country, speakers frequently shift back and forth between Creole and English (in Britain, British Black English) and that the intermediate forms of speech so created can be viewed as a continuum of dialects stretching between the two languages. In Britain the younger generation speakers generally control a very large span of this continuum, as they are drawn linguistically in two directions. There are, it is true, a number of named speech varieties in or around black communities: broad Jamaican, Bajan (Barbadian) and other Caribbean varieties including French Creoles, local 'white' English, BBC English, as well as gradations in between, and this does not immediately suggest a simple unidimensional continuum. However, probably the most salient aspect of a British black speaker's language at any moment, for both speaker and audience, is the degree to which that language is overtly Creole. The situation is made less complicated also by the fact that, for the younger generation, the Creole element is nearly always Jamaican. For most speakers, therefore, regardless of other varieties in their repertoire, it makes sense to speak of a continuum existing between their Creole and their English (British Black English). In this chapter we look, first, at Jamaican Creole as spoken in Britain, and then at British Black English and the continuum that spans the range between the two varieties. Note that in example word-forms and sentences below the orthography is normally that developed by Cassidy (1961); items in modified English orthography are prefixed by †.

British Jamaican Creole

The original migrants came from widely scattered areas of the Caribbean, and their various strands of influence can be detected in the emergent British black language and life-styles. Very clearly, however, Jamaican influence has dominated. For the younger generation, broad Creole (or 'Patois', the community's usual word for it) is a variety of Jamaican Creole (JC) in terms of structure, phonology and intonation, not only in London but also in such centres as Bedford, Birmingham, Bristol, Luton, Manchester, Peterborough, Swindon and Wolverhampton (Leitch, 1980; Sutcliffe, 1982). (There are pockets of resistance – Bajan in Reading, for instance, and French Creole in parts of London.)

The language of parents and older relatives or family friends continues to provide an important model for British-born black speakers. Yet the Patois of these younger people, which we could term 'British Jamaican Creole' (BJC), does differ from that of the older generation. The differences, as its speakers see them, are lexical more than grammatical – many conservative, mostly African words have fallen out of use, and new words have come in. There are also, undoubtedly, some differences brought about by the discontinuation of certain rural/conservative variants, mainly function words. Thus *laka* ('like' in comparisons) has generally been superseded by *laika* and *laik*. A purely phonological feature of conservative Jamaican Creole, the use of /b/ for English /v/ as in *riba* 'river' is similarly shunned by British Jamaican Creole speakers. London-born native speaker Marcia Smith (personal communication) explains the differences in the following way:

I think the main difference is that the Jamaican of my generation relies heavily on slang. For example:
   (1) *dunseye* meaning 'money'.
   (2) *banacheck* describing a black person who goes out with a white person.
   (3) an *edge* a 50p coin.
Also it changes and shifts constantly. For example, (2) is already out of date. I would say the language of my generation is closer to the Rastafarian language than the native patois of my parents' generation. For instance my parents would *not* say 'farwud I di dunseye,' meaning 'give me the money', but 'gi mi di moni'.

Grammatical characteristics of British Jamaican Creole

Adjectival verbs and other stative verbs. Predicate adjectives in the Creoles function as a type of verb. Thus *blak*, as an adjectival verb, predicates directly from the subject, without need of copula, as in the following example from a British-born speaker recorded in London:

(1)   Im blak im blak im kyaan don! Im blak im blak im blak im blak so til im kyaan blak no muor
      'He's exceedingly black'; or 'He's black until he can't be any more black'
      (†*kyaan don* lit. 'can't finish')

What is more surprising is that *blak*, here at least, behaves like an active verb rather than a stative one. The iterated verb in Jamaican Creole expresses either intensity or continuing action, but the latter reading is reinforced in this case by *kyaan don* (which the speaker later glosses as 'wont stop') and *kyaan blak no muor*. This suggests an inexhaustible and active quality to the blackness. Normally predicate adjectives are not 'active' in this way although still verbs, syntactically. Their un-iterated form denotes a completed state, so that in a sense *im blak* is a present tense form, a reference to the present. Very occasionally one finds adjectival verbs given a continuous form: *im a blak* 'he is/was becoming black' – literally, 'he is/was blacking' (*a* marks the verb as continuous). Adjectives incidentally appear in non-verbal positions, too:

As abstract noun, in the proverb:

(2)   Hongri-hongri an ful-ful no travl siem paas
      'hunger and plenty do not travel the same path'

As noun modifier, as in the following example from a British-born speaker from London:

(3)   wan kaina red sompn
      'a really red thing!'

As adverb, in the following example from 'Ballad for you' (Johnson, 1978 a):

(4)   Is dem a control di middle a di room an' a rave strong, strong
      'They were dominating the middle of the room and were 'raving' really strongly'

There are a few important stative verbs which are not adjectival. They are transitive (or transitive with deletable objects) and refer to states of mind and relationships:

nuo 'know'; lov 'love'; laik 'like'; gat, av 'have'; fieva 'resemble'

Their basic reference is to the present (which the use of stem form *mi nuo* etc., designates). They can be marked for tense but generally not for continuous aspect – compare **I am knowing* in English.

Action verbs. These can be subdivided:

(a)   ± Transitive:
      mek 'make'; nyam 'eat'; tek 'take'; shout, fiks 'fix'; etc.

Equivalent verbs in English are transitive only (or transitive with deletable objects). Creole intransitive use has the force of a passive or past participle (in English terms), demonstrated in the following example from 'Park bench blues' (Johnson, 1978 b):

†(5)   ... di pack fiks
       'The pack of cards is/was "fixed"'

This intransitive form can be classed with the adjectival verbs already described. Like them it can be ambivalently stative/non-stative.

(b) Intransitive only: these include verbs of locomotion, and changes of
    bodily state:
    ron 'run'; jomp 'jump'; laaf 'laugh'; ded 'die'; etc.

A simple stem form of ANY action verb denotes a completed action and therefore refers to a (single) action in the past as in this example from 'Ballad for you':

†(6)   Well di Satdey nite *come* an' is one piece a ting *gwaan*
       'Well Saturday night came and things certainly happened!'

Extended or repeated action is expressed through iteration (particularly if dramatized) as in example (7), recorded in the Bedford survey from a Jamaican-born speaker:

(7)   An kyach di kyat an wi biit di kyat. Wi biit dem wi biit dem we biit dem,
       wi tai dem op an wi biit dem wi biit dem wi biit dem. Mi anti se: 'we y'a
       biit di kyat faa?'
       'And (we) caught the cats and we beat them. We tied them up and we
       went on beating them. My auntie said "Why are you beating the cats?"'

If this continuing action is summarized, rather than dramatized, it is expressed as a continuous (or, in the terms of this analysis, non-completive). That is: *a* + stem verb:

(7b)   we y'a biit di kyat faa?

This form can have past or present continuous reference (in English terms) though more frequently the latter. The distinction between complete and incomplete actions and states is most important in Jamaican and other Creoles. As we shall see, modality and aspect generally are more important than tense.

BJC also uses the stem form of action verbs to express habitual actions. Other Creoles use a variety of forms, but most have a separate habitual marker *does* /doz/. The lack of this in Jamaican Creole and British Jamaican Creole contributes to the fact that the stem form occurs extremely frequently – giving casual observers the impression that the verb in Creole is just the 'simple' verb, as in (8) for example, recorded from a British-born speaker in London:

(8)   Mai mom kaal bluu blak an blak bluu
       'My mum calls ...'

Tense. Tense marking of the verb in British Jamaican Creole is more the exception than the rule. Once the time reference for a paragraph of a story, for instance, is established, neither the completive nor non-completive action verbs carrying the story normally carry past tense markers. If, however, the sequence of actions is disrupted by flashback, an anterior marker is used with the flashback verb: *en* or *ben* in conservative Jamaican Creole, *di(d)* in other varieties including British Jamaican Creole. Adjectival and other stative verbs, on the other hand, are marked for tense (by *did* etc.) if they refer to states which are definitely past and finished. This *did* particle can be prefixed to *a* to express an action emphasized as past continuous, as in the following example, taken from 'Ballad for you':

†(9)   One by one di man whey Chalice *did a* dance wid woman an' she fr'en dem a tiptoe outside
'The woman with whose man Chalice had been dancing, and her friends, were tiptoeing outside'
Lit. 'One by one the man (rel.) Chalice (+ past incomplete markers) dance with woman and her friend (plural marker) (incomplete marker) tip-toe outside

Did + stem is obligatory in the first half (the condition) of a past conditional construction as in example (10) from a British-born speaker in Bedford:

(10)   If dat man *did* eva *kien* mi, im wuda fain-out sompn tidie
'If that man had ever caned me he would have found out "what for"'

The conclusions of such past conditionals feature *wuda* + stem. For present conditionals – referring to hypothetical cases which may be realized in the future – *wi* + stem is used as in the following, recorded in Bedford from a Jamaican-born speaker:

(11)   Ef im ron, graastraa wi kot-aaf im fut
'If he runs/should run, grass will cut off his legs'

Jamaican Creole is rich in auxiliary and modal verbs. The following list is not exhaustive:
Modal verbs. In addition to *wi* and *wuda* there are *fi* 'should', 'in order to', *mosa* 'ought to', 'appears to', *mós* 'must' (= be obliged to), *haffi* 'be obliged to', *shuda* 'should', *kyan* 'can', *kuda* 'could', *maita* 'might'. Two or more modals can be combined together, and/or combined with the tense marker, according to certain constraints (Bailey, 1966).
Lexical verbs functioning as auxiliary. These include: *a go* (future marker, variants: *gwain, gon*), *don* 'finish', *get, kyach* ('catch' as in 'catch fraid') *waan(t), go, kom, gaan, staat, begin, trai, mekfi,* etc.
Of these verbs, *a-go* and *don* are quite clearly to be considered aspectual markers. *Don* emphasizes the completion of a state. It is not at all certain that

verbs towards the end of the list are auxiliaries at all (that is, subordinate to a
main verb in the same clause) since, although they do link with the 'main' or
lexical verb, it is possible that this link should be analysed as constituting a
serial verb construction – a string of verbs sharing the same subject and expressing one composite event (see below). In fact ALL these modals and auxiliaries
could be considered as linking in this way. A large number of permutations of
these auxiliary verbs and particles is in theory possible; in practice there are
semantic and grammatical constraints. To find out more about possible
combinations of verbs and particles marking tense, aspect or mood in British
Jamaican Creole, we have tested various permutations of the following,
together with the verb *waak* 'walk', for acceptability with a native speaker:

wi, wuda, di(d), a, a go, don, and zero (ø).

Something about the acceptable order of combination was known at the time,
since some combinations are common or have been described by Bailey
(1966), Voorhoeve (1973) and others. Tense – mood is ordered before aspect:

$$
\begin{Bmatrix} \text{wi} \\ \text{wuda} \\ \text{di(d)} \\ \text{ø} \end{Bmatrix} \quad + \quad \begin{Bmatrix} \text{a} \\ \text{a go} \\ \text{don} \\ \text{ø} \end{Bmatrix} \quad + \quad \text{stem verb}
$$

Zero [ø] prefix, in tense – modal or aspect position, is significant in this system –
it takes part in the permutations. The native speaker's intuitions on acceptable
combinations and their meanings were firm, and she was well able to communicate them. She wrote down the meanings in English, together with
examples of actual usage, as in these instances:

(†) mi did a walk   'I was walking'   'mi did a walk an di
                                                     police stop mi'

     mi woulda done   'I would have   'mi woulda done walk by
          walk   finished walking'   now if I never tek wrong
                                                     turning'

     *mi done a walk   'No meaning'

Don cannot precede *a* + verb stem since one cannot have a continuing
completed action. Thus English *I finished walking* is *mi don waak*. On the
other hand *I started walking* can be either *mi (s)taat waak* or *mi (s)taat a
waak*. Table 14.1 shows the verb paradigm which these findings suggest for
British Jamaican Creole. This paradigm is for action verbs. Stative verbs are
more limited in that forms with *a* are rare with adjectival verbs and cannot
occur with transitive stative verbs: **mi a nuo*.

Lone stem verbs form the negative by prefixing *no*, as in *mi no waak*. The
negatives of *a* and *a go* are *naa* and *naa go*; *did* can become *din* in British
Jamaican Creole (contrast the conservative equivalent *(b)en* which becomes
neen or *na ben*); *wi* and *wuda* become *wuon(t)* and *wudn*.

Table 14.1. *An analysis of the British Jamaican Creole verb system*

Mood	Completive	Non-completive	Reinforced completive	Future**	Tense
Real (indicative)	ø ———	a ———	don ———	a go ———	Untensed
	di(d) ——	dida ——	di(d) don —	did a go——	Past (anterior)
Unreal (hypo-thetical)	wi ———	wi a —	wi don ——	wi a go ——*	Untensed
	wuda ——	wudaa —*	wuda don —*	wudaa go —*	Past

*These (rarely occurring) forms have been checked with other British Jamaican Creole speakers.
**Perhaps 'projective' would better describe the range of forms based on *a go*, although the basic form *a go* is a pure future marker.

One more verb form, at least, should be noted, used mainly with adjectival verbs. This is the intensive *tú*, usually with high pitch (or tone) followed by the adjectival verb marked by low pitch (or tone): *yu tú fuùlish* 'You're so silly'.

Consecutive and sequential serial verbs. Serial verb constructions are common in British Jamaican Creole, as in a number of West African languages. They may even be fundamental to the major part of the Creole verb and clause structure in a way which has not yet been fully described. Verbs sharing the same subject are strung together in such constructions without conjunctions, to express consecutive or simultaneous actions. There are various constraints on the way these verbs can combine. Most obviously they must come in order of actual chronological occurrence. In true serial verbs (sequentials) the actions represented by the verbs must merge into one overall composite action. This is not true of example (15) below, *ron doun/tel se*, which would be better described as a consecutive:

†(12) 'Dat will teach dat gal fi *come try mash up* my scene,' Chalice seh, an' di addahs agree
'That will teach that girl to come and try to ruin my scene ...' (from 'Ballad for you')

(13) Mi *kyari* mi aki *go* a Linsted maakit
'I took my ackees to Linstead market' (Traditional song)

(14) *Tek* rieza blied *kot* it aaf
(*tek* 'take' = instrument marker)
'Cut it off with a razor blade' (British-born speaker from London)

(15)   Im *a ron* mi *doun tel* mi *se* ...
       (*a* = uncomplete marker, *ron* 'run')
       'He was arguing with me and saying ...' (British-born speaker from
       London)

The copula. In British Jamaican Creole the copula takes various forms,
according to the type of predicate with which it links. Before a nominal it is *a*
or *iz*:

(16)   Im se *a* wan kain a daak sompn
       'He says it's really dark thing' (British-born speaker from London)

In locative constructions the copula is *de*. This is optionally deletable except in
certain cases, notably in clause final position:

†(17) No man! You stay where you *deh*
       '... You stay where you are' (from 'Park bench blues')

Copulas are not needed when predicating adjectives: *im blak*, *shi sik*. However
did or *woz* (conservative JC *en* or *ben*) appear as past tense markers, in, for
example, *im woz sik*.

   The forms *stan* or *ste* are used as copula (or, more exactly, as a substitute for
an unexpressed adjective). This occurs with *so*, or in clauses introduced by *hou*
(how):

†(18) I wonder *is* soh all Peckham people *stay*?
       (*is* = focus marker; *stay* 'be')
       'I wonder whether all Peckham people are like that?' (from 'Ballad
       for you')

Note that in example (18) the normal Creole word order of SVO (+ adjunct)
is rearranged for emphasis, a very common occurrence. The emphasized
item is moved to the front of the clause and prefixed by a focus marker
which takes the same form as the nominal copula – *a* or *iz*. Subject can be
focused on, with of course no inversion, since it is already at the front of the
clause:

†(19) '... *is dem* a control di middle a di room ...'
       (*is* = focus)
       '*They* were controlling ...' (from 'Ballad for you')

Focused verbs (including adjectival verbs) are reduplicated in a strikingly un-
English fashion:

(20)   A *ful* mi beli *ful*!
       (*A* = focus)
       'My belly is really full', or 'the explanation is that my belly is full'
       (Jamaican-born speaker in Bedford survey)

Question words are, optionally, prefixed with the focus marker as in this example from 'Park bench blues':

†(21) Gal, you bring di tune dem?
       Yes man; *is whey* y'u tek mi fah?
       (*is* = focus)
       'Did you bring the records? Yes; what do you take me for?

Note, incidentally, that the yes/no question (in its unemphasized form) does not show inversion. It is marked only by intonation: a level and high, or slightly descending, contour with final upturn. The *wh-* question, in contrast, has a pronounced descending contour with no upturn.

Tonality

Much more research needs to be done on Creole tonality. It must be made clear that findings at this stage are tentative. There are indications, however, that Jamaican Creole and British Jamaican Creole may be comparable to a degree with the tone languages of sub-saharan Africa whence the ancestors of modern Creole speakers came. It is certainly possible (and instructive) to transcribe them as if they were (Carter, 1979).

English-based Caribbean Creoles commonly have high pitch where the equivalent English word has stress, and this conveys the impression of stress to English ears. In fact, though, these languages are lightly stressed, being syllable-timed, and all short vowels are of approximately equal duration, while long vowels last approximately twice as long. Stress (perhaps better defined as intensity) does not necessarily coincide with high pitch, and probably does not distinguish meaning. Thus in Jamaican Creole one finds stress and pitch patterns which are un-English:

"Màntígò "bíè 'Montego Bay'

" = stress ´ = high pitch ` = low pitch

Stress and *low* pitch fall together on the first syllable here, as they may do on the second syllable of the famous trickster's name:

Á"nànsí

Low pitch is relative only, and 'lows' gradually get lower towards the end of a sequence, in a phenomenon known as 'downdrift'. 'Highs' are similarly high relative only to adjacent low tones. They descend in a series of steps towards the end of a sequence (clause or sentence), except in yes/no questions and exclamations. Downdrift is reminiscent of African languages such as Igbo and Hausa with two tone levels (see figure 14.1).

For a language which lexically is based on English there are a surprising number of minimal pairs which may possibly be distinguished by pitch. The examples listed below are offered tentatively:

(a) *Jamaican Creole*   (b) *Igbo (Nigeria)*

‾   ‾   ‾   ‾

‾   ‾

‾   ‾

‾   ‾ ‾

á wé dí 'bákrà dé`?
'Where is the white man?'   gí'ní̧ kà ó mèrè?
                                       'What did he do?'

´ = high pitch   ` = low pitch   ' = downstep
A downstep occurs where a high is lower than an immediately preceding high.

Figure 14.1. Downdrift of sentence pitch pattern

î̧ dé`	'He is there'
î̧ dé`	'in there'
mí díèr	'my dear'
mì díèr	'I am there'
míèrì bróùn	'Mary is brown'
míeřì bróùn	'Mary Brown' (Lawton, 1963)
únú píknì	'your children'
únù píknì	'you children'

Allsopp (1972) has further examples of this kind. Pitch appears to be important both lexically and grammatically as certain of the examples above
suggest. In the (British) Jamaican Creole personal pronoun system there may
possibly be case distinctions marked by pitch, with oblique pronouns taking
high pitch (compare Krio, as discussed in Fyle and Jones, 1980: xxi; and
Saramaccan in Voorhoeve, 1961: 161–2). If so, the personal pronoun system
and the rules for its use are considerably more complex than previously
thought, and at least as complex as the English system.

There are a set of emphatic/disjunctive pronouns which also take high
pitch: *mí, yú, im* and so on. A variant of the first person singular nominative
emphatic is *áí* 'I', as used in this example from *Ballad for you*:

†(22)   Man, you shoulda did dey deh fi see it, but seen as you wasn't, *I* a go
        tell you 'bout it,
            'You should have been there to see it, but as you were not, *I* shall tell
            you about it'

The Rastafarians have taken up emphatic 'I' to replace 'mi' for all cases, as a
symbol of the freeing of their consciousness. It is notable that *I-an-I* (an
extension of the first person to include God and one's fellows) is not only
'I-er' as Rastas would say, it is literally higher, since its pitch pattern is characteristically *áí n áí*.

It is crucial, of course, that the pitch features noted above are understood as part of an overall system which may or may not be tonal in the African sense. At present our evidence is ambiguous although it is, I think, already clear that Creoles are different (and probably systematically different) from English on this level (see Carter, 1979, 1980; Lawton, 1968).

The continuum

Linguistic variation

South-eastern British English			*Jamaican Creole* (Cassidy orthography)
say,	day	/eɪ/	*e* /ɛ/ se
			ie /ɪə/ die
	man	/æ/	*a* /a/ man, tap
gone,	top	/ɒ/	
	part	/ɑː/	*aa* /aː/ gaan, baan, paat
born,	four	/ɔː/	
			uo /uə/ fuor, nuo
go,	know	/əu/	
	bird	/əː/	*o* /ɔ̃/ go, bod, ron
	run	/ʌ/	
	noise	/ɔɪ/	*ai* /aɪ/ naiz, fait
	fight	/aɪ/	
	shout	/au/	*ou* /ɔ̈u/ shout

Figure 14.2. Phonological changes involved in shifting between a common variety of south-eastern British English and Jamaican Creole (vowel system only)

The connection between British Jamaican Creole and English, including British Black English, is first of all lexical, and therefore phonological. A word in Jamaican Creole will be related to any equivalent (cognate) English word, and this will differ to a lesser or greater extent in its pronunciation, in a predictable way. The vowel values at either end of the language spectrum (specifically in southern England) are shown in figure 14.2. There are, to be sure, different geographical dialects in Jamaica, but they differ mainly in intonation and vocabulary. The Jamaican Creole vowel system shown is basic to most, if not all, geographically-determined Jamaican varieties. The concerted grammatical changes which accompany this phonological changeover along the continuum are too complex to be described in any detail here – but see Bickerton (1975) and Sutcliffe (1978, 1982). Bickerton provides an account of changes along the Guyanese continuum. By way of illustration, however, table 14.2 shows realizations for two sets of grammatical features along the Bedford Jamaican–English continuum, for black speakers aged 8–16 years. The terms 'first quarter', 'fourth quarter' refer to increasing

Table 14.2. *Grammatical variation along the Bedford Jamaican–English continuum*

Texts		Past tense uninflected* %		Jamaican Creole pronouns realized** %
A – L	1st quarter	79.3	Patois	78.6
M – Q	2nd quarter	80.6		18.4
R – Y	3rd quarter	33.7		4.8
Z – FF	4th quarter	13.0	English	1.8

*That is, stem form as a reflex for the English simple past and perfect forms
** *mi, im, wi, unu, dem, fi-mi* etc. – tokens were scored only where contrastive with English; had *shi* been counted as a Jamaican Creole pronoun the A – L score would have averaged close to 100 per cent.

English and decreasing Creole phonology according to a phonological count (see Sutcliffe, 1978). To produce a measured continuum range, 32 texts taken from tapes were phonetically transcribed and then placed in order on this basis. Each text was in a relatively homogeneous piece of dialect – that is, it contained no obvious switch.

There is, it seems, a widespread and consistent tendency all over Anglophone Afro-America for black language to appear superficially more English than is true when its underlying grammaticality is considered. This has been shown for Trinidadian Creole (Pyne-Timothy, 1977). It is so even for varieties which are labelled 'English', such as black English in America (cf. the quite UNEnglish analysis of its tense–aspect system provided by Fickett, 1970). Simply by comparing the different Creole vernaculars throughout the Caribbean we gather a general sense of the so-called less 'broad' varieties (Grenadian, for instance, or Trinidadian) dropping more English-seeming lexical 'fillers' into the same grammatical slots as Jamaican, so that the Creole format of the grammar, the syntactic structures and the verb paradigm tend to be retained despite surface changes as in this example from Le Page (1972: 129):

(23) Jamaican: ef yu ben haks mi, mi wuda shuo yu fi ar
    St Vincentian: if yu did aks mi, a wuda shoo yu fu shi
    Grenadian: if yu did aks mi, a wuda sho yu hez
    'If you (had) asked me, I would have shown you hers'

However, this is a simplification of what actually happens. For a more detailed exposition of such a process see Pyne-Timothy (1977). The same phenomenon occurs within the British Jamaican Creole–English system, so that a great deal of distinctively black language, while being black ENGLISH rather than Patois, is capable of a Creole grammar interpretation.

Despite this continuum variation, (British) Jamaican Creole has its own grammatical stability and separate integrity, and John Richmond's summary (1979) of language use in the play *Brixton Blues* could hardly be improved upon on this point:

... identifiable forms from Standard English, to 'black South London', to almost impenetrable (to the white ear) patois, are used with skill and precision and a sense of the appropriate ... I don't mean that the forms are always distinct and separate. Speech patterns and conventions of syntax merge and remerge constantly ...

(It is worth noting here that this play was orally composed by senior pupils in a south London school, videotaped, then transcribed by the actresses themselves for publication.)

Patterns of selection

Individual members of the younger generation vary greatly in their attraction towards Patois and its associated culture, but it is safe to say that a majority of pre-adolescents and adolescents speak Patois at least occasionally. Sutcliffe (1978, 1982: 151–2), in structured group interviews, found that only 4 per cent of a sample of 47 black pupils in Bedfordshire, aged from 8 to 16 years, claimed to speak no Patois ('West Indian' was the term used) while 78 per cent claimed that they sometimes spoke Patois as broad as:

(24)   mi aks di man fi put mi moni iina im pakit
       'I asked the man to put my money in his pocket'

Hadi (1976) used the same diagnostic sentence with twenty pre-adolescents in the West Midlands, and she found that 72 per cent claimed that they sometimes spoke like that. Tomlin (1981), British black herself, found that all but one of her sample of 120 claimed to speak Creole – she interviewed black people in the street in Dudley, West Midlands. Finally, Palmer (1981) used the Sutcliffe methodology with black pre-adolescents in Manchester and found that only 6 per cent saw themselves as not using Creole, while 50 per cent saw themselves as using Creole as broad as the diagnostic sentence.

Evidence from the highly informative Survey of Linguistic Diversity (Rosen and Burgess, 1980) indicates that out of the 682 London children in their sample who could speak in a distinctively 'black' way 79 per cent were described as 'basically a London (or Standard) speaker but occasionally deepen[ing] overseas dialectal features', and 17 per cent as speaking 'the dialect regularly in certain contexts'. These findings can be reconciled with the others (and with my own and others' informal observation) if one takes it that 'the occasional deepeners' can deepen right into Creole, that is, into (British) Jamaican Creole. The metaphor is certainly very apt, and Rosen and Burgess bring to our attention the important observation that black language use is markedly fluid and subtle. Another notable finding of the survey was that about 20 per cent of these black Londoners expressed a desire to be able to read and write in Jamaican Creole.

British Black English

In this part of the chapter the English end of the continuum is examined and I list some of the salient features of British Black English. Observations are offered tentatively since their generality is not established in every case. British Black English, as opposed to British Jamaican Creole, allows its speakers to talk 'black' while remaining within what can reasonably be called 'English'. At the same time, it sometimes gives the impression that Creole is scarcely suppressed below its surface, and it can be used interchangeably with British Jamaican Creole in certain culturally-important verbal performance styles. In view of this it is interesting that the younger generation in Britain are not abandoning the Creole end of their linguistic range. Commentators have described Jamaican Creole (Patois or 'dialect') as a reference point for black youth. Without reference to it, other cultural and linguistic forms cannot be properly understood.

There is a significant difference, too, between British Black English and black English in the USA. The latter represents the nonstandard extreme in most localities and, despite evolution over the years, has preserved some highly divergent syntax. British Black English, on the other hand, is best understood relative to the much broader Creole varieties in the background, which in most cases British Black English speakers also use. The syntax and tense–aspect features of British Black English approximate quite closely to those of SE, but the situation is fluid and difficult to characterize.

At one end of its range British Black English merges into local forms of white English – Standard/Cockney in London, and so on. But the evidence which we have so far suggests that, even in very English speech, a few distinctive features remain, in what might be termed 'minimal' British Black English. The following example comes from a British-born speaker in the Bedford survey:

†(25)   Then he come back, and he *seh*: shutcha face you!
         And they started fightin

The whole impact of the story from which this example is taken, is 'white'. *Come* (like *see, give*) is zero-marked for the past tense in white dialects too. But *seh*, unvarying for person as well as tense, is distinctive to British Black English – and of course British Jamaican Creole – and is one of the last features to disappear in the move to standard.

The phonology of minimal forms of British Black English tends to show its incipient relationship to Creole phonology in that the diphthongs for /eɪ/ in *day*, for /əu/ in *nose*, and /aɪ/ in *fight* are generally narrower than is usual for Midland or southern English white working-class accents. In fact British Black English phonology, overall, has a middle-class quality which merges into a Jamaican accent along the continuum. But in minimal British Black English there are few occurrences of fully Creole vowel values except for sporadic /ɔ/ for standard /ʌ/ in *run*, etc.

There are also some interesting lexical differences. Even when speakers seem intent on converging on white English, lexical items can occur which may not be known by outsiders. The following are actual speech data used in such situations:

†(26) You just have to be *extra*   'extraverted', 'bossy'
       ... with no shoes *and all* socks   'or even'
       Just me *one* and John   'alone'
       Was he *red*?   'light-skinned West Indian'

Other items are more consciously used, and some of these have been adopted by non-West Indian speakers attracted by black performance style:

†(27) He *tiefed* Angela's pen
       They're *poppin'* their *style, ennit*?
       He was *badly shamed-up, guy*!
       Wickèd!

'Popping' or 'cutting' style ('showing off', 'being fashionable', etc.) are just two of a number of cultural terms made up of verb + noun: *cut-eye* (give an insolent eye gesture in which one catches another's eye and then pointedly looks away), *skin-teet*(*h*) (give a 'plastic' smile), *suck-teet*(*h*) (place tongue behind teeth and make a sucking noise which indicates off-handedness, disdain, or displeasure). *Ennit?/innit?* is used as a universal tag. There are other similar tags in Jamaican Creole, but this one is more typical of usage in the eastern Caribbean. *Badly* occurs very commonly, on the Creole model, where *bad* is used adverbially as an intensifier. *Guy* and *man* feature very frequently as tags, addressing either sex, but really used more as interjection than address. These tags, together with exclamations such as *wickèd*! usually invoke a Jamaican Creole type of intonation. All of the above, except the cultural terms, are used by young whites (see also Hewitt, 1982), and universal *ennit* may be in the process of becoming fully integrated into white speech.

Morphology and syntax

Standard morphology is pervasive but is, obviously, less prevalent in more Creole-influenced, 'maximal' British Black English. Third person singular present/habitual verb forms variably drop -*s*, preterites and present perfect equivalents variably appear as lone uninflected stem forms: *I told/tell*. Some speakers make frequent use of the marker *did* before the verb stem. This is obviously a carry-over from British Jamaican Creole, but in British Black English it may be purely a past tense form, rather than having its more narrow Creole function, for example, in sentence (27) uttered by a British-born speaker in the Bedford survey:

†(28) He *did sèe* this shape of this duppy
       (*duppy* 'ghost')

Uninflected possessive nouns and plural nouns also occur. However, with most speakers all these uninflected forms have a low incidence in their 'English'. In fact it should be made clear that many of the younger generation can eliminate them altogether from their speech and writing when they choose to do so.

Morphology signals the operation of deeper levels of the grammar, and it is the interpretation of these in British Black English which poses considerable problems for analysis. The occurrence of both Creole and English morphology in British Black English in itself suggests grammatical ambiguity or duality. Ambiguities begin in Jamaican Creole, where word-order, and even phonological shape can closely match English:

(29) *mi no nuo* ~ *ai duon nuo*
      'I don't know'

Mi no nuo is the 'older' form (older still would be *mi no sabi*). Where on the continuum does *ai duon nuo*, integrated into Creole grammar, become *I don't know*, grammatically integrated into English? (cf. Le Page's remarks on *de/there*, 1977).

Other ambiguities involve surface coincidences that mask possible syntactic divergence in British Black English, as in the following example from a British-born speaker in the Bedford survey:

†(30) Boy! *what you doin'* theh?

Here it is difficult to decide whether to assume an underlying English syntax interpretation (with elision of *are*): 'Boy! What are you doing there?', or to assume a Creole type of syntax. In British Jamaican Creole this would have no copula and no inversion:

(31) Bwai! *wa yu ø duin* de? or *wa yu ø a-du* de?

However it is often possible to see clear 'calquing' or carry-over from British Jamaican Creole to British Black English; again the examples are from British-born speakers:

†(32) Look at him, he's *easy to cry*!
       'Look at him, he cries easily'
       JC: *Im iizi fi krai*

†(33) ... and *don't make* her see
       '... and didn't let her see'
       JC: *no mek shi si*

†(34) Them boys, *when they came in*, they stepped on my bag, and all my sandwiches broke-up

Temporal clauses precede main clauses in Jamaican Creole. When the subject of the main clause is shifted to sentence-initial position for emphasis, the temporal clause intervenes between this and the rest of the sentence, thus the Jamaican Creole equivalent the last example would be: *dem bwai, wen dem kom in, dem (s)tep aan mi bag, an aal mi sangwij-dem brok-op.*

In Jamaican Creole indirect commands are introduced by a verb of obligation, so that *go huom* is reported as *dadi tel mi (mi) mos go huom, dadi se mi mos go huom,* or *dadi tel mi fi go huom,* where *fi* is interpretable as 'should' (see page 223, above). Note also that in both indirect commands (36), and other indirect speech, for example (35), the verbs of the reported clauses in Jamaican Creole-influenced speech retain the tense they would have had before embedding, in contradistinction to the pattern in SE where *can't climb the tree* becomes *said she couldn't climb the tree.* (*Kudn* is available as a past tense form in Jamaican Creole, but would not not used here.)

†(35)   The old lady said she *can't* climb the tree
        '... said she couldn't climb the tree'
†(36)   And then my dad said that I *must go* home
        'And then my dad told me to go home/said that I had to go home'

Since this invariant verb pattern also occurs in many African languages, between direct and reported speech, this may be one of the apparently large number of African syntactic patterns which were carried over into the Caribbean Creoles.

The following example (37) of British Black English features a serial verb construction which is also a British Jamaican Creole-derived tense–aspect form:

†(37)   When you *finish wash* you(r) hair ...
        'When you finish washing your hair/have finished washing your hair'

(For *don* = 'finish', see page 223.)

There are, finally, syntactic features, such as double or multiple negatives, which occur in both white nonstandard English and (British) Jamaican Creole, and so can plainly be derived from either or both when they occur in British Black English.

Discourse and style

Certain discourse phenomena involved in the unfolding of lengthy passages of speech, such as narratives, seem to be especially persistent in all Afro-American varieties, from Saramaccan (in Surinam) to American Black English. Such a feature is linkage through recapitulation; in British (Jamaican) Creole and British Black English this most often takes the form of a temporal clause that recapitulates the meaning, not necessarily using the same words, of the previous narrative clause. Even where there is no clause recapitulation, temporal clauses may be used markedly more often than in SE, as the following example, from a Jamaican-born speaker in the Bedford survey, illustrates:

†(38)   *And when she came back*, she took the bag, and she were goin' home.
        And when she were goin' home she felt something wet comin' down on
        her. She said: Well, yuh a pi-pi on mi? Well I'll find out about you when
        you get home. *And when she came home ...*

These, and other, features of cohesion and construction of discourse are more
or less optional components of style. It is in the style of certain selfconscious
speech performances that British Black English can be most strikingly distinctive. Prosodic features are important here. Particularly in tags and exclamations there is a tendency towards syllable-timing and Jamaican Creole-
like intonation. Black performance style requires an uninterrupted flow of
words, with the proviso that speakers frequently elicit feedback from their
audience with tags such as: *okay? right? yeah? you know wha(t) I mean?* This
last phrase can also be used by responsive listeners, meaning 'I know what *you*
mean', as can *seen!*, the British Black English equivalent of *right on!* To
maintain flow, fillers are often used, not only *mm* and *a-em*, but those which
cover rather than express hesitation, e.g. *like* with low 'tone' or pitch, and *you
know* demonstrated in these final examples from British-born speakers, recorded in south London:

†(39)   A: Well, when two sounds [sound systems] are playin', yeah, it's
            kinda like one a dem wanna show the other one that they really
            rubbish. And seh like they run each other different cuts of the
            records, and things like if somebody should play a really good cut
            den the next one would seh *dem saaf* [Cassidy orthography 'they
            are soft']
        B: An play another cut, you know?
†(40)   Like anytime you were young, yeah? and you like kinda when other
        people were talking or arguing, right? You wait somewhere nearby,
        like, right? And you *kwabz-op* [Cassidy orthography 'edge up'].

REFERENCES

Allsopp, R. 1972. *Some suprasegmental features of Caribbean English and their rele-
vance in the classroom.* Cave Hill: University of the West Indies.
Bailey, B. 1966. *Jamaican Creole syntax: a transformational approach.* Cambridge:
CUP.
Bickerton, D. 1975. *Dynamics of a Creole system.* Cambridge: CUP.
Carter, H. 1979. *Evidence for the survival of African prosodies in West Indian Creoles.*
Society for Caribbean Linguistics, Occasional Paper no. 13.
——— 1980. *How to be a tone language: theoretical considerations involved in the
classification of Creole languages as tonal (or otherwise).* Society for Caribbean
Linguistics third biennial conference, Aruba.
Cassidy, F. 1961. *Jamaica talk.* Basingstoke: Macmillan.
Fickett, J. 1970. *Aspects of morphemics, syntax and semology of an inner-city dialect
(Merican).* New York: Meadowood Publications.

Fyle, C. and Jones, E. 1980. *A Krio-English dictionary*. London: OUP.

Hadi, S. 1976. Some language issues. Unpublished paper on a survey undertaken as part of the Schools Council/NFER 'Education for a multiracial society' project.

Hewitt, R. 1982. White Adolescent Creole Users and the Politics of Friendship. Paper given at 'Language and Ethnicity' seminar held by Linguistic Minorities Project/ British Association of Applied Linguistics, University of London.

Johnson, J. 1978a. Ballad for You. *Race Today* January/February issue. [Also in Sutcliffe, 1982, with glosses.]

——— 1978b. Park bench blues. *Race Today* January/February issue.

Lawton, D. L. 1963, 1978. Suprasegmental phenomena in Jamaican Creole. Ph.D. thesis, Michigan State University. Published (1978) on microfilm. Ann Arbor and London: Microfilms International.

Leitch, J. 1980. *A perspective on Caribbean language and dialect*. Occasional Paper no. 1: on Caribbean language and dialect. London: Caribbean Communications Project/Arawadi.

Le Page, R. B. 1972. *Sample West Indian texts*. York: University of York.

——— 1977. Processes of pidginization and creolization. In A. Valdman (ed.) *Pidgin and Creole linguistics*. Bloomington: Indiana University Press.

Palmer, P. 1981. An investigation into the language use of children of Jamaican origin, in Manchester. M. A. dissertation, University of Reading.

Pyne-Timothy, H. 1977. An analysis of the negative in Trinidad Creole English. *Journal of Creole Studies* 1, 1.

Richmond, J. 1979. *Jennifer and 'Brixton Blues'; language alive in school*. Supplementary Reading for Block 5, PE232 Language Development. Milton Keynes: Open University Press.

Rosen, H. and Burgess, A. 1980. *Languages and dialects of London school children: an investigation*. London: Ward Lock.

Sutcliffe, D. 1978. The language of first and second generation West Indian children in Bedfordshire. Unpublished M.Ed. thesis, University of Leicester.

——— 1982. *British Black English*. Oxford: Basil Blackwell.

Tomlin, C. 1981. The extent to which West Indian linguistic differences hinder or enhance learning. Unpublished dissertation, Dudley College of Education.

Voorhoeve J., 1961. Le ton et la grammaire dans le Saramaccan. *Word* 17, part 2.

——— 1973. Historical and linguistic evidence in favor of the relexification theory in the formation of Creoles. *Language and Society* 2.

Part II

Celtic languages

Introduction

As we have noted in the Introduction to Part I, the Celtic languages in the British Isles have been contracting for the last fifteen hundred years, in the sense that they have been spoken natively by a progressively smaller proportion of the total population. This decline is chronicled in chapter 15 in this section, *The history of the Celtic languages in the British Isles*. Two of the languages, the subjects of chapter 17, *Cornish*, and chapter 19, *Manx*, no longer have any native speakers. And the subjects of the other chapters, chapter 16, *Welsh*, chapter 18, *Irish*, and chapter 20, *Gaelic*, formerly the native languages of almost the entire populations of, respectively, Wales, Ireland and the Scottish Highlands, have suffered very considerable setbacks indeed over the last two hundred years. Some writers (see chapter 15) are pessimistic about their survival. However, as is explained in some detail in Part IV of this book, all three languages now receive institutional support, and there are definite and encouraging signs of a revival in certain areas (see especially chapter 28). There has also been a considerable upsurge of interest in the languages themselves on the part of academic linguists. It is hoped that this section of the book will contribute to this upsurge by bringing the results and traditions of Celtic scholarship before a wider audience.

15

The history of the Celtic languages in the British Isles

R. L. THOMSON

Introduction

The Celtic languages constitute one family within the Indo-European group of languages, distinguished from the other families of the group by a complex of features, some of which individually are shared with other families: such are the loss of IE *p*, the presence of an *-ī* suffix in the genitive singular of *o*-stems, the retention of an *r*-element in the passive or impersonal of verbs, the regular agglutination of simple prepositions with personal pronouns, and a shifting of the articulation of medial consonants while initial consonants undergo the shift or retain their original form according to the closeness of their contact with the ending of the preceding word. This last feature, mutation, at first formed a barrier to the recognition of Celtic as Indo-European. A number of these Celtic features are also found in the Italic group, of which Latin is the best known representative, and some dialectal divisions within Celtic are paralleled within Italic, so that some have posited an intermediate Italo-Celtic stage, but this view is not generally accepted.

The Celts extended, or migrated, across a broad band from the south-east to the mid-west of Europe, to France and at least some of Spain, and eventually to the British Isles, which are named from their inhabitants, Gk *Pretannikai nēsoi* (OW *Priten*, OI *Cruithni* 'Picts'), or Latin *Britannia*, a modification influenced by the tribal name *Brittones*. The ancients knew also the name of Ireland, Gk *Ierne* (Welsh *Iwerddon*, OI *Ériu*), Latin *Hibernia*, influenced by *hibernus* 'wintry', whereas St Patrick latinizes directly as **Hiberio*. The date of the arrival of the Celts in Britain is not known, nor for certain the part of the continent from which they crossed. Of the language of the pre-Celtic inhabitants, which probably survives in some geographical names, nothing else is known. Earlier speculation assumed the Celts had crossed at the narrowest point and in successive waves, so that the earliest settlers found their way to Ireland and the later ones stayed in Wales and England. This view was apparently supported by Caesar's reference to recent migration into south-eastern England. However, it is now generally believed that Ireland was celticized directly from Gaul, though it had perhaps already been partly settled from Britain. In general the arrival of the Celts is associated with the Iron Age, but archaeological evidence is necessarily silent about language in the pre-literate period. By the beginning of the Christian era the whole of Britain was probably predominantly Celtic in speech except for the Pictish areas in the north and north-east of Scotland, where a Celtic minority may have ruled and been culturally assimilated by an earlier population.

Celtic was current in two forms which were to grow increasingly apart; their first traceable distinction is in the treatment of IE *k^w, which in the east became *p*, while in the west it first remained and then lost its labial element, e.g. OI *cia*, Welsh *pwy* (Latin *quis*), the interrogative pronoun; OI *cóic*, Welsh *pump* (Latin *quinque*) 'five'. Similarly IE *s*, e.g. OI *sen-*, Welsh *hen* (cf. Latin *senex*) 'old'; IE *w*, e.g. OI *find*, MW *gwynn* 'white'. The western branch is named Goidelic or Gaelic, and the eastern Brythonic or British, the earliest and principal representatives of which are Irish and Welsh respectively.

During the Roman period each branch was confined to its own island (except for possible Brythonic settlements in Ireland (see page 241), but from about the fourth or fifth century Goidelic expansion planted colonies in the extreme west of North and South Wales and in north Cornwall. The expansion was permanent in the Isle of Man, and in Scotland, where the colonization began in Argyll and spread gradually north and east to include the islands and the northern half of the mainland, largely at the expense of the Picts, but producing conflict also with the Brythonic speakers to the south and east. Much later there was also substantial Gaelicization of the south-west of Scotland (probably tenth century), and to a lesser extent in the south-east (see chapter 29). At the coming of the Saxons, England, Wales, and southern Scotland were purely Brythonic except insofar as Latin, the language of education, administration and culture, was familiar, at least as an acquired accomplishment, to the native aristocracy and most town-dwellers, as well as being the common tongue of settlers in Britain from all over the Empire.

The expansion of the Angles and Saxons from the fifth century onwards gradually altered this linguistic distribution. The Goidelic expansion continued in Scotland but was absorbed in Wales and Cornwall; Brythonic was gradually reduced in area, first becoming the language of a subject population and then disappearing over most of England, until by the end of the Old English period it was confined to approximately modern Wales and Cornwall or, in the sixth century, had sought a new home in Brittany. Scandinavian raids and later settlements affected the Western Isles, Man and Ireland, as well as Wales, but in none of these areas did they have any permanent linguistic effect beyond the deposit of a limited number of loan-words and a rather more substantial influence on placenames. The Gaelic-speaking nations retained a strong sense of community throughout the Middle Ages, and Cornish and Breton remained in close contact, but as the languages developed the two major groups lost any sense of a common identity so that when the underlying linguistic unity was rediscovered in the eighteenth century a unifying term 'Celtic', which had no existence in the individual languages, had to be sought in Classical sources.

The beginnings

The earliest written record in both Goidelic and Brythonic is epigraphic, for Brythonic in Latin letters, but for Goidelic in the ogam character, an alphabet of strokes and notches. Such ogam inscriptions begin in the fourth century; there are about 300, mainly in the southern half of Ireland. They are generally memorials of the dead (similar monuments in Gaulish are found on the continent in Latin or Greek letters), and very brief, mainly personal names. In their earliest period they suggest, however, that both branches of Celtic were at similar stages of development, possessing a fullness of inflection similar in range and form to Latin or Greek.

The manuscript record of Irish begins with eighth-century interlinear glosses and commentary on Latin religious and grammatical texts, made by Irish monks resident on the continent; similar work was no doubt produced in Ireland and Gaelic Scotland but under conditions less favourable to its preservation. The habit of writing was first applied, when introduced from Britain in association with Christianity, to the purposes of clerical education, but was extended to the recording of secular learning, notably in law and literature, thus supplementing, but only very gradually displacing, an oral tradition of learning, from a period at least as early as the surviving religious record. This secular material, though of very great antiquity, particularly in the case of law, as attested by the form of its language, survives only in manuscripts of a later period.

The remains of early Welsh are of about the same period but less extensive: they consist of glosses and memoranda, the glosses on Latin literary or educational texts, the memoranda including a legal note, a fragment of a computational commentary, and two short pieces of verse. Other texts were no doubt written down in the Old Welsh period, notably the poetry of Aneirin and Taliesin, which relates to events *c*. 600, but the surviving manuscript evidence is later, though bearing traces of copying from an earlier ortho-graphy. Cornish and Breton are similarly first known from numerous glosses of the ninth century. The similarity in the oldest orthographic conventions of all three Brythonic languages suggests that the system had been devised and diffused before they became dialectally differentiated; the substantially similar early Irish spelling was created on the same Brythonic model.

Phonology and orthography

The language termed Old Irish is based primarily on the evidence of the eighth- and ninth-century glosses, and is differentiated from the highly in-flected polysyllabic stage represented by the earliest inscriptions by several major changes. (i) The accent, which in the prehistoric stage is likely to have been fixed as in Greek and Latin in relation to the length of the word and perhaps the quantity of certain syllables, became fixed on the first syllable (with certain exceptions), and took the form of a strong dynamic stress. This produced a reduction in the length of polysyllabic words by the syncopation of the vowel element in alternate syllables, followed by simplification of the resulting consonant groups, thus reducing the similarity between forms etymologically related but differently accented. (ii) Single medial and final consonants (i.e. medial before the loss of final syllables) underwent a shift of articulation, the Celtic voiceless stops *k* and *t* becoming [x] and [θ], and the voiced stops *b*, *d*, *g* the voiced fricatives [β], [ð], and [ɣ], while geminated consonants remained unaffected. This is the process known as lenition. Nasals assimilated to the position of a following stop and the resulting homorganic group was then simplified. When the stop was voiceless, it simplified to the corresponding voiced stop without a nasal, and when the stop was voiced it was absorbed by the preceding nasal, i.e. *nt* becomes [d], *nk* becomes [g], and *mb*, *nd*, *ng* become [m], [n], [ŋ]. This process is known as nasalization. (iii) All consonants, in whatever position, became subject to the influence of adjoining vowels and retained these modified qualities even when the vowel had disappeared by syncope or loss in final position: they thus distinguished a palatal quality when influenced by adjoining *e* or *i*, and a neutral quality when influenced by adjoining *a* or *o*, also, in the earlier stages at least, a velar quality when originally followed by *u*, though this later merges into the neutral quality.

A single consonant of Common Celtic, therefore, may assume four or six forms in Old Irish, e.g. [k] neutral, [k′] palatal, [kʷ] *u*-quality, and [x], [x′], [xʷ] (the same lenited), and this is true of the liquids and nasals as well as of the stops. The Latin alphabet was clearly inadequate to provide symbols for all these distinct sounds, all potentially and many actually phonemic (see page 247). The orthography was based on the British pronunciation of Latin, a language whose spelling was regarded as fixed, so that when sound-changes akin to lenition affected the pronunciation of medial consonants, the effect was to modify the relationship between sound and symbol. Thus, while, for example, *t* represents [t] initially, it stands for [d] medially, and similarly *b* is [b] initially, but [β] or [v] medially; medial [k], [t] occurred only when long or geminate, so they could quite properly be written *cc*, *tt*; the voiceless spirants produced by lenition, [x] and [θ], were written *ch* and *th* following the analogy of Greek loan-words in Latin. Each consonant is understood to take its quality from the following vowel; in final syllables, when the preceding vowel's quality is different from that of the final consonant, a digraph is written. The system is not fully developed in Old or Middle Irish: for example, *e* is understood to be followed by a neutral consonant unless otherwise indicated. In early Modern Irish, however, the system is elaborated towards the modern usage whereby every medial consonant is flanked by vowels of the same quality, and initial and final consonants take their quality from the vowel immediately adjoining. In later usage the lenited consonants, too, are more precisely indicated in accordance with general European usage, e.g. *c* for [k], *ch* for [x], *g* for [g], and *gh* for [ɣ]. This clarification, however, was undermined by several phonetic changes: *th* passed from [θ] to [h], and *dh* from [ð] to identity with *gh*, i.e. [ɣ] when neutral and [j] when palatal; lenited *s*, written *sh*, was always [h], and lenited *f*, written *fh*, is zero; lenited and unlenited *m*, earlier *m* and *mm/mb*, respectively became *mh* and *m*, and *mh* with *bh* tending frequently to vocalize and form *u*-diphthongs with a preceding vowel, have all combined to leave the Gaelic orthography historically based (until the recent reforms) and internally consistent – but full of conventions unfamiliar to the non-Gaelic reader. Marking the length of vowels by the use of the acute accent, sporadic in early sources, gradually becomes standard. Historical quantity in vowels is fairly well preserved in stressed syllables in Goidelic, though there is some lengthening in monosyllables before particular consonants or groups; length in unstressed syllables, generally derivative affixes, is also preserved in some forms of Gaelic, but in Manx and some Irish dialects such long syllables tend to attract the accent, while in Scottish Gaelic and other Irish dialects the accent is unaffected and such long syllables are reduced in quantity, not necessarily in quality. Movement of the accent on to suffixal syllables is frequently associated with reduction of length or quality, even to zero, in root syllables. (On spelling, see also page 289.)

In Brythonic the accent retained or adopted the penultimate position and the final syllables of Common Celtic were lost, so that the stress fell on final syllables in Old Welsh. About the eleventh century, however, the stress moved back once more to the penult and has remained there, except for a few words which have final stress because of an earlier hiatus in the final syllable. Historical quantity is not preserved in Brythonic; except in monosyllables all vowels are relatively short, though longer in stressed open, than in closed, syllables; in open monosyllables the vowel is long, in closed syllables length depends on the nature of the consonant, consonant groups and voiceless stops being associated with shortness in the vowel. The consonants in Old Welsh etc. are written as described above for Old Irish, but Middle Welsh and Cornish show a prolonged transition between this logical, if unusual, system and one in which the sound-values would be conveyed with less regard to history and more to general European conventions. Lenition and nasalization affected Brythonic as well as Goidelic, but with some differences in the results. In Brythonic the lenition of Celtic voiceless stops produced voiced stops, and the nasalization of voiceless stops produced voiceless nasals. Middle Welsh expressed the voiceless stops initially as *p*, *t*, *c* (before consonants and back vowels), *k* (before front vowels), medially *pp*, *tt*, *cc/ck*; the voiced stops initially as *b*, *d*, *g*, medially as *b/p*, *t/d*, *g*, and finally as *b/p*, *t*, *c*; the voiced fricatives medially (initially they occur only as mutated forms (see page 246)) are *u/v/f*, *d* (sometimes *t*), while lenited *g* is zero; the voiceless fricatives are *ph/f/ff*, *th*, *ch*; lenited *m* shares the spelling of lenited *b*. Certain features of this stage betray the influence of Anglo-Norman in the distinction of *c* and *k*, and the use of *u/v/f* for [v]. Modern Welsh has regularized this system chiefly by removing the numerous ambiguities and positional variants: voiceless stops *p*,

Table 15.1. *The Celtic article*

Singular	Masculine	Neuter	Feminine
Nominative	*sindos	*sindon	*sindā
Accusative	*sindon	*sindon	*sindān
Genitive	*sindī	*sindī	*sindās
Dative	*sindō	*sindō	*sindā

t, *c*; fricatives *ff* (*ph* as mutation of *p*), *th*, *ch*; voiced stops *b*, *d*, *g*; fricatives *f*, *dd*; lenited *m* is *f*; added to the medieval distinction of voiced and voiceless in *l*, *ll*, is that of *r*, *rh*. (On spelling, see also page 274.)

Consonant mutations

The lenition, nasalization, and other consonant changes in medial and final position occurred also in initial consonants when these were treated as being medial, i.e. when they formed part of a group of words treated as a single unit (as is evidenced by such groups being written as single words in Old Irish). Nominal phrases are a common example of such groups, e.g., article + noun + adjective: the Celtic article was declined for gender, number, and case as indicated in table 15.1. Similar endings are associated with the first two declensions of nouns, masculine and neuter *o*-stems, and feminine *ā*-stems, and with *o*- or *ā*-stem adjectives. After a final vowel the following consonant within the group was lenited, and after a final nasal the following consonant was nasalized; after final -*s*, however, no change occurred. So in the article + noun + adjective group in the nominative masculine there would be no mutation of noun or adjective, in the feminine lenition of both, in the neuter nasalization of both; in the accusative, nasalization of both in all genders; in the genitive, lenition of both in the masculine and neuter, no mutation in the feminine; in the dative, lenition of both in all genders; in the nominative plural, lenition of both in the masculine and neuter (though even in Old Irish there seems to be no lenition associated with the neuter nominative/accusative); in the accusative, no mutation in masculine and feminine; in the genitive, nasalization of both in all genders; and in the dative, no mutation. With the *i*- and *u*-stems and the consonant-stems, which have identical forms of declension for masculine and feminine nouns, we should expect identical mutations in the adjective, but even the earliest evidence shows that the mutations, properly dependent on the declensional type, have become controlled by gender and case only, the patterns being generalized very largely from the *o*- or *ā*-stems. Nasalization in Goidelic also involves the prefixing of *n*- to initial vowels, and in some cases where the inflection ends in -*s*, *h*- is prefixed to the following vowel, e.g. after the genitive feminine singular and the nominative/ accusative feminine plural of the article. The process of lenition may be inhibited when it brings homorganic consonants together, e.g. the *-n* of the article and a following dental consonant.

The mutations in Brythonic, where the case distinctions disappeared earlier than in Goidelic, became controlled solely by considerations of gender as regards lenition; they also reflect the different course of Brythonic lenition. For example, Welsh has three mutations: (i) the 'soft' (i.e. lenition), involving the voicing of the voiceless stops and *ll, rh*, and conversion of the voiced stops and *m* into the corresponding fricatives (*g* becoming zero); (ii) the nasal, by which the six stops are converted into the corresponding nasals (voiceless and voiced); and (iii) a spirant mutation, converting only the three voiceless stops into the corresponding fricatives. In Cornish and Breton only (i) and (iii) occur, but there is in addition an unvoicing of voiced stops.

Lenition is everywhere the principal mutation, reckoning by the number of circumstances in which it can occur, with the others confined to a much more restricted set of positions. During the medieval period written expression of the mutations remained optional, though they were no doubt supplied in reading aloud; any history of the rules of mutation in this period has therefore to be based on positive, not negative, evidence.

Morphology

Celtic inherited a version of the Indo-European morphology of nouns and adjectives. Nouns might be of one of three genders: masculine, feminine and neuter. The neuter loses ground early to the other two in Irish, and seems to have disappeared from Brythonic before the earliest texts; it can be traced in later Goidelic chiefly in the eccentric behaviour in gender or declension of a small number of former neuters. Nouns distinguish three numbers, singular, dual and plural, but even in Old Irish, adjectives have no separate dual forms but use the plural instead. The dual in nouns occurs only with the numeral '2'; in the later language it is distinguished by being identical with some form of the singular. The cases distinguished are nominative, vocative (chiefly *o*-stems), accusative, genitive and dative; the dative, with some early exceptions, is used only with a preposition. Both the vocalic (*o, ā, i, u*) and consonantal (velar, dental, nasal, *r, s*) stems continue into Celtic. The reduction or loss of final syllables generally leaves only the base intact, while modifications of internal vowels and the quality of final consonants represent the lost endings. For example, an *o*-stem, with singular endings *-os, -e, -om, -ī, -ō*, gives proto-Goidelic *-as, -i, -an, -ī, -ū*, so that the cognate of Latin *vir* appears as nom. *fer* (implied neutral quality in *-r*, much later explicitly as *fear*); voc. *fir* (implied palatal quality in *-r*, raised root vowel before lost final front vowel); acc. *fer n-* (neutral *-r* as in the nominative, and *n-* of the lost inflection prefixed to a following vowel or nasalizing a following consonant); gen. *fir* (implied palatal *-r*); dat. *fiur* (raised root vowel and explicit *u*-quality in *-r*). In the plural the endings are *-ī, -ōs* (historically nominative), *-ons, -om, -obhis* (instrumental), yielding proto-Goidelic *-ī, -ūs, -ŭs, -an, -abis*, whence OI nom. *fir* (as for genitive singular), voc., acc. *firu*; gen. *fer n-* (as for accusative singular); dat. *feraib*. The dual forms are nom., acc., gen. *dá fer*, dat. *díb feraib*. (For following mutations, see page 246, above.) It is notable that fourteen different functions are here conveyed by only six distinct forms of the noun (five if the following nasalization is disregarded), and of these forms only one, *fiur*, is confined to a single function. A velar stem will serve to illustrate the consonant stems: nom. *cathir* 'city', **katrik-s*, with loss of final syllable, and *-r* becoming syllabic; acc. *cathraig n-*, **-k-em* becoming *-in*, with nasalizing *n-* as in *fer n-* above; lenited *k* yields [x] but this, when palatal and unstressed finally, is voiced, i.e. [j]; gen. *cathrach*, **-k-os*; dat. *cathraig*, **-k-i*, cf. accusative, or *cathir*, as nominative; plural nom. *cathraig*, **-k-es* becoming *-is*, cf. accusative and dative singular; acc. *cathracha*, **-k-ās*; gen. *cathrach*, **-k-om* becoming *-an*; dat. *cathrachaib*, **-k-obhis* becoming *-aib*. The vocative singular is like the nominative, and the vocative plural, following the example of the *o*-stems, is like the accusative plural.

In Old Irish, adjectives of the *o*- or *ā*-stem type follow almost exactly the same declension as the corresponding nouns, apart from lacking the dual, though *io*-stem, *iā*-stem, *i*-stem, and *u*-stem adjectives differ in having only a single form for the plural in all three genders. The Celtic languages all have three degrees of comparison beyond the positive, i.e. equative, comparative, superlative. In Old Irish these are marked by the suffixes *-ithir, -iu, -em* respectively; in Middle and early Modern Irish the equative suffix gives way to the prefix *com-* 'equally' + positive, and the superlative is displaced by the comparative, resulting, inflectionally-speaking, in a single degree of comparison (see page 254, below). A number of common adjectives have irregular, i.e. suppletive, comparison, as OI *maith* 'good', comparative *ferr*, superlative *dech*, but more usually with comparative and superlative on the same stem, as *olc* 'bad', *messa, messam; becc* 'small', *lugu, lugam*.

This system of declension has survived remarkably well with the following qualifications: (i) the earlier distinct endings, *e, i, iu,* and *a, o, u,* are reduced in late Old and early Middle Irish to *-e* and *-a* respectively, i.e. a single [ə] vowel after palatal and neutral consonants according to their quality, but without syllabic loss until a much later period; (ii) the distinct masculine plural in *o*-stem adjectives yields to the feminine/neuter ending, which also accords with the form of the other stem-formations, and at a much later date the distinction of case in plural adjectives will disappear, except for the genitive; (iii) in nouns the historical plural formations are felt to be insufficiently distinctive and a number of single and multiple suffixes, some of rather obscure origin, gain widespread currency in the Modern Irish period; (iv) the distinction of nominative and accusative disappears in early Modern Irish, and there is considerable confusion between accusative and dative as the case appropriate after particular prepositions.

The Brythonic languages evolved more rapidly in morphology than the

Goidelic, and when first known to us have already shed the neuter gender, the dual number (other than as a compound of the numeral and a singular noun, chiefly for things naturally occurring in pairs), and all but a few traces of a case system. The variation in the form of nouns and adjectives is therefore confined to the expression of the singular/plural contrast (apart from a very limited distinction of gender in singular adjectives in Welsh only). Plurality in nouns is marked either by internal vowel change (in original *o*-stems, from the nominative plural *-ī* ending), or, much more frequently, by the addition of a syllable, with or without modification of the singular by the form of the suffix; these plural suffixes are in origin the full form of the stem (*u*- and consonant stems), the whole final syllable being lost in the singular, but only the nominative *-es* in the plural, e.g. **cat-u-s* 'battle', MW *cat*, pl. **cat-ou-es, cadeu; *car-ant-s* 'friend, relative', MW *kar* (OI *carae*), pl. **car-ant-es, karant*, also *kereint* (with mutation), OI *carait*; cases in which these plural suffixes are etymologically correct are only a very small minority. It follows that the formation of the plural in Brythonic, except of nouns formed with a derivative suffix, is unpredictable. A third type of noun, generally denoting a mass-word or countable item more usually met with in numbers than individually, takes its simple form as plural or collective, and adds a singulative suffix to denote the individual item, e.g. *tywarch* 'turf', *tywarchen* 'a sod', *plant* 'children' (cf. Irish *clann* fem. sing.), *plentyn* 'a child'.

Brythonic adjectives form a plural primarily for use as nouns, either by the *o*-stem mutation type, or by a single suffix; the lenited plural form is found early with dual nouns, but with plural nouns it occurs in Middle Welsh chiefly in translation literature, and seems to have disappeared in Middle Cornish and Middle Breton. As in Goidelic, the Brythonic comparison proceeds in three degrees: the equative has either a prefix, MW *kyn-*, Middle Breton *quen-*, with, in Middle Welsh, a suffix **set*, or more frequently *mor*, Cornish and Breton *mar*, + positive; the comparative has the suffix Welsh *-ach*, Breton *-och*, superlative **sam*; the *-s-* of the equative and superlative, becoming *-h-*, unvoices the preceding consonant, later analogically extended to the comparative; in Cornish the loss of [v] in the superlative and the weakening of [x] in the comparative caused the two degrees to fall together as a final vowel *-a* or *-e*. A few common adjectives have irregular comparison, the comparative and superlative generally being on the same stem and the comparative often lacking the characteristic suffix, e.g. MW *da* 'good', *kystal, gwell, goreu; drwg* 'bad', *kyndrycket, gwaeth, gwaethaf; bychan/bach* 'small', comparative *llei*, superlative *lleiaf*.

Adverbs derived from adjectives are formed in Old Irish only with *in(d)* + dative neuter singular of the adjective, but subsequently with the preposition *co* ('to' in other contexts) + adjective; *ind* may occur with the compared forms but *co* does not. Brythonic similarly has the prepositions MW *yn, y*, Cornish *yn*, Breton *en* + adjective, and these may or may not occur with the compared forms according to their position in the sentence.

Conjugation: the Goidelic group

The system of conjugation in Old Irish is extremely elaborate. In the indicative mood there are present and imperfect tenses, future and secondary future or conditional, preterite and perfect (the latter generally a modification of the former); in the subjunctive, a present and past; and a single-tense imperative. Non-finite parts are the 'verbnoun' (see chapter 16 for the verbnoun in Welsh), a verbal adjective/passive participle, and a closely related verbal of necessity. The present and imperfect are formed on the present stem; the secondary future with the endings of the imperfect on the future stem, which may be an *f*-future, reduplicated future, *é*-future or *s*-future (with reduplication), is formed from the verbal root; the preterite and perfect may be *s*-preterite, *t*-preterite, reduplicated or ablaut preterite. The present and imperfect subjunctive are formed either as an *ā*-subjunctive or an *s*-subjunctive. In addition to active verbs there are deponents with distinctive inflections, except in the imperfect and past subjunctive, which are common to both. The inflections of the verb correspond to three persons each singular and plural, of which the 3rd singular and plural (and in the present and future, the 1st plural) also have relative forms except in the imperfect.

This range of inflectional forms is effectively doubled since each personal form may occur affirmatively in a principal clause (the 'absolute' or 'independent' form), or be preceded by a 'preverb', e.g. of negation or interrogation, or by a subordinating conjunction (the 'conjunct' or 'dependent' form); the conjunct generally appears as a shortened or reduced form of the absolute; attempts to explain these two kinds of inflection as continuing the contrasting Indo-European primary and secondary endings have had only limited success. Many verbs are compounded with one or more preverbs or prefixes (usually related to prepositions) which modify the meaning. The accent, which is on the first syllable, the root syllable, in uncompounded and weak verbs, falls immediately after the first preverb in compound verbs (the 'deuterotonic' form) in the absolute position, but on the first preverb (the 'prototonic' form) in the conjunct position. For example, 3rd sing. present absolute *berid* 'bears', conjunct (negative) *ní beir*; compound absolute and deuterotonic *as-beir* 'says', conjunct and prototonic (negative) *ní epir*. The accent in the imperative is always prototonic, 2nd sing. *epir*. The effect of this movement of the accent, and its consequences for succeeding syllables, is to impair the transparency of the paradigm so far as compound verbs are concerned.

This opaqueness is presumably the reason for the great simplification which set in in Middle and early Modern Irish, generalizing the most regular types of formation and leaving only a very small group of irregular verbs and a scattering of isolated survivors of earlier formations. The major change was to abandon the contrast between deuterotonic and prototonic forms in favour of the latter (except in the few irregular verbs); all uncompounded verbs had this accent already and in compounded ones it was the accent of the imperative, the verbnoun and verbal adjectives, and of all the conjunct forms. The stem formation of the verb was stabilized by abandoning examples of the contrast between present stem and root, and of reduplication. The *f*-future (with some use of the *é*-future, particularly in weak verbs) and the *ā*-subjunctive were generalized at the expense of the *s*-formations, and the *s*-preterite (historically perfect) was already dominant over the numerically insignificant reduplicated, ablauting, and *t*-preterites. The scope for the absolute–conjunct division was much reduced: the imperfect had always had conjunct forms only, and the perfect, formed from the preterite by the use of a preverb, was also found only with conjunct flexion; the two subjunctives and the conditional naturally occurred chiefly in subordination and so were conjunct in form, and the imperfect indicative and subjunctive became identical; only in the present and future was the contrast partially maintained, but even here the originally conjunct 3rd sing. *-ann* (of uncertain origin, and replacing an older zero suffix, maintained in Scottish Gaelic and Manx) has eventually taken over from the absolute *-idh*. A further simplification, carried to different lengths in the various dialects, involves the substitution of the 3rd singular form with subject pronouns for the separate inflections.

The passive True passive forms were restricted in Old Irish to the 3rd person singular and plural; for other persons the 3rd singular was used with pronoun object, thus effectively converting it into an impersonal construction; e.g. *marbfidir* 'he will be killed', *marbfitir* 'they will be killed', but *no-m-marbfaider* (conjuct 3rd sing.) 'I shall be killed' (= one will kill me). The impersonal construction gradually ousted the passive and by early Modern Irish the 3rd plural forms had disappeared, and the surviving old 3rd singular required a pronoun object in all persons.

The verb 'to be' Celtic distinguished two forms of the verb 'be': in Old Irish, *is* (cognate of Latin *est*) as the copula, linking subject and nominal or adjectival predicate, in the syntax of comparison, and to bring an element of the sentence into prominence; and *atá* (cognate of Latin *stat*) as the substantive verb of existence. Though the substantive verb has gained some ground from the copula, especially in Manx, the division of functions has remained remarkably stable. The substantive verb was used as early as Old Irish with the preposition *oc* 'at' and the verbnoun to convey a durative or iterative aspect (which otherwise found expression only in the substantive verb's consuetudinal present). This type of formation became more important in Scottish Gaelic and Manx since there the future forms of the verb were replaced by the inflected present, and this formation took over as a new present, in all aspects. At all periods it was also possible to replace the inflected tenses by the corresponding part of the verb 'do' with the verbnoun as its object – though only in Manx was this option developed into a complete double conjugation.

Conjugation: the Brythonic group

In the Brythonic group most of the complications seen in Old Irish had been removed before the record begins. The distinction of absolute and conjunct forms had disappeared except for rare examples of MW 3rd sing. present indicative -*id* (absolute) against zero (conjunct); the different system of accentuation (see page 245, above) did not favour special status for the first preverb, though some examples of it are found in the early poetry; the formations of the subjunctive are reduced to the *s*-type, but the more striking combinative changes this induces are quickly levelled out, leaving only the unvoicing effect of *s* before *h*; the formation of the preterite is overwhelmingly of the *s*-type with even fewer survivors of the reduplicated, ablaut, and *t*-preterites than in Irish.

The tenses of the indicative are present-future (shifting to future or habitual present), imperfect, preterite and pluperfect (sometimes regarded as formed in imitation of Latin, though no more alien than the Irish secondary future, for which no such model can be adduced). The subjunctive has a present, imperfect and pluperfect (though in the medieval period the imperfect is more common even in unfulfillable conditions, while more recently the pluperfect has tended to oust the imperfect). The imperative has no variation of tense. Each tense has six personal forms (except the imperative, which lacks 1st singular), one for each of the three persons singular and plural, and one impersonal form. The group of irregular verbs is very small, and their irregularity consists chiefly in having several stems instead of one, in sometimes distinguishing preterite and perfect, and in being partially assimilated to each other and to the verb 'be'. Both the copula and the substantive verb are found, but the scope of the former is more restricted than in Irish, being almost confined to conferring prominence; in this use it is usually unexpressed when affirmative, and is extant only in a single (present) tense; when required for this purpose in other tenses and moods the substantive verb does duty. The substantive verb has two distinct forms to serve as present and future or habitual present, and two forms of the imperfect, the second denoting habitual action and the conditional. To a greater extent than in Irish the periphrasis 'be' + *yn* + verbnoun is used to express the actual present and continuous imperfect. The impersonal forms are used to express the passive.

The situation in Middle Cornish and Middle Breton is generally similar to that in Middle Welsh. Some major differences are: in the periphrastic present a different preposition, Cornish *ow*, Breton *ouz* (= Welsh *wrth*), is used; both freely use auxiliary 'do' with the verbnoun to form any tense, whereas Middle Welsh confines this to the narrative past; the impersonal forms are much less used in Cornish and Breton in expressions equivalent to the passive, both having retained a verbal adjective (Cornish -*ys*, Breton -*et*) with the value of a passive participle, and this is used in combination with 'be' in the Anglo-French manner. All three languages lack a normal verb for 'have' and supply this in various ways: Welsh uses *y mae gennyf* 'is with-me', while Cornish and Breton continue the use of the infixed pronoun with dative force (see page 253, below) combined with 'be', Cornish *am bes*, Breton *am eux* (occasionally MW *a'm oes*) 'to-me is'; Breton develops this further with the verbal adjective to form the perfect as in Anglo-French 'has seen, a vu'.

The Celtic pronoun

All the Celtic languages share one further class of inflected words, the pronominal prepositions, i.e. combinations of the simple prepositions (all also have numerous phrasal prepositions based on nouns) with the seven personal pronouns (3rd singular masculine and feminine). Although these formations, presumably originating in the generalization of the preposition + personal pronoun group with stress on the preposition (the neutral or non-contrastive type), are common to recorded Celtic, parallel forms differ sufficiently as between Goidelic and Brythonic, to make the reconstruction of Common Celtic archetypes impossible, and they must therefore be regarded as a common parallel innovation. Within the Brythonic group the parallelism is much closer, though there are apparent differences when Cornish and Welsh agree against Breton about the membership of the three paradigmatic classes of inflection, while Cornish and Breton agree against Welsh on the inflected forms (or lack of some of them in Welsh) of the preposition Cornish *the*, Breton *da*, OW *di*, MW *y* 'to'.

The Celtic personal pronouns are only marginally an inflected word-class, their variety of forms being positional rather than a matter of case. In modern Goidelic the nominative and accusative are identical, but in earlier times the nominative forms were used only independently or as predicate with the copula or an interrogative, while the accusative object was represented either by suffixes to the verbal form (a practice which died out early), or infixed elements in the verbal complex after the first preverb (or, when the verb was uncompounded, after an 'empty' preverb). Such an infixed pronoun is normally accusative, but it earlier occurred, less frequently, as a dative. When infixation was given up as part of the simplification of the verbal system (see page 250, above), the pronouns were used as direct objects, and in the dialects in which some of the personal inflections of the verb were given up they serve as subjects also. Associated with the personal pronouns in Goidelic are the *augentia*, a set of suffixes emphasizing a preceding pronominal element and attached to the personal pronouns, to the pronominal prepositions, to nouns preceded by a possessive particle, to verb-forms without expressed object to stress the subject inflection, and to verb-forms with infixed object pronoun to stress that object.

The second principal form of the personal pronoun is conveniently termed the possessive or objective; with a noun it is the former, but with a verbnoun usually the latter. It should be observed that Celtic generally prefers to take the genitive as objective rather than subjective. As the periphrastic verb-forms with auxiliary 'be' and 'do' develop, the pronominal object of an inflected tense becomes the object of a verbnoun and as such assumes the possessive or objective form before it.

The position in the Brythonic languages is generally parallel but with the following differences: the suffixed pronouns are not found, and infixed pronouns in the Irish sense occur only in early verse examples; the *augentia* are not present but the simple pronouns are freely used in all the same positions (except, naturally, that they cannot be attached to the pronouns); the infixed pronouns are included in a verbal group (e.g. placed between a relative or conjunction and the verb) rather than incorporated within a verbal form. Particularly in Welsh a larger, triple series of independent personal pronouns developed, including a conjunctive/disjunctive formation 'I too/I on the other hand'. The genitive forms, as in Goidelic, appear as possessive with nouns, and as objective when found in association with verbnouns, in the periphrastic conjugation with 'be' and 'do'.

Syntax

Some features of interest are the following: in the nominal phrase the article is not used (except sporadically in early Irish) with a noun upon which a noun in the genitive depends – in Brythonic and some advanced forms of Gaelic it is this feature of syntax which marks the second noun as having the genitive function; the demonstratives, originally enclitic in Goidelic, but later accorded independent status, as always in Brythonic, follow their noun and require it to be preceded by the article; the numerals, followed throughout by a singular noun in Brythonic, take the plural from '3' onwards in Goidelic, while the decades '20' to '90', and '100', declined as nouns, are followed by the genitive; in compound numerals the smaller component comes first, followed by the noun, then the larger; although Old and Middle Irish had names for the decades '20' to '90', all the modern languages as well as Brythonic operate on a vigesimal base, repeating the sequence 1–19 with 20, 40 (2 × 20), 60 (3 × 20), 80 (4 × 20) up to 99, or in some cases (including Manx) up to 199 (nine score and nineteen); compared adjectives in Goidelic appear only in a miniature relative clause introduced by the copula when attributive, or by a relative particle and the copula when predicative or adverbial, the tense and mood of the copula varying with the context; some examples of this construction are found in Middle Welsh but generally the compared forms in Brythonic behave like the positive.

In the verbal phrase the Celtic order is Verb–Subject–Object in all subordinate clauses, and in principal clauses (except for those containing an interrogative, which always has initial position), except that, in Middle Welsh, the subject (or object) frequently stands first in affirmatives; this became the normal practice in Cornish and Breton, though later displaced in Welsh by the normal order; the order with the copula differs in that after the verb in initial position the second place is taken by the predicate, with the subject last. Despite these provisions, however, there is a great freedom to convey emphasis on any part of the clause (for example, subject, objects, prepositional phrases, adverbs) by placing them in initial position preceded by the copula (omissible if present affirmative), and introducing the following verb as if in a relative clause; the verb itself may be emphasized by making its verbnoun the object of the verb 'do', or placing it initially with auxiliary 'be'. The initial position of the verb is subject not only to the priority of interrogatives, but also of affirmative, negative, interrogative and relative particles, and all co-ordinating and subordinating conjunctions. Concord between the verb and its subject is always complete in the 1st and 2nd persons (though emphatic personal pronouns may be treated as nouns and so 3rd person), but from an early period in Brythonic, more slowly in Goidelic, the practice has been to use the 3rd singular verb with a plural noun subject; a similar usage has developed in Goidelic after the loss of 3rd plural relative forms and in those dialects in which the verbs abandon separate inflected forms for a single inflection (invariably 3rd singular) with subject pronouns.

Relative clauses fall into three types, in consequence of Celtic treating the nominative–accusative relative relationship (the 'direct' relative) differently from others (the 'indirect' relative). Brythonic has one relative particle, MW *a*, for (i) the direct relative, another, MW *y*, for the indirect, which may be subdivided into (ii) the relative governed by a preposition, and (iii) the relative in the genitive (where *a* is also found). In (i) the particle alone marks the relationship, though without specifying case, number, or gender. In (ii) and (iii) the particle is further defined: in (ii) by the occurrence in the relative clause of the appropriate pronominal preposition, i.e. 'the man to whom I gave it' is '... that I gave it *to-him*', and in (iii) by the presence of the appropriate possessive, i.e. 'the man whose wife is ill' is '... that *his* wife is ill'. Similar constructions occur in the modern Goidelic languages. Although the case of the relative in (i) is not indicated with an inflected verb, a periphrastic one does so by inserting the possessive/objective pronoun before the verbnoun, i.e. 'the thing I see' is '... that I am in *its* seeing'. In certain circumstances this is possible in Goidelic too, particularly in Manx. The earlier Goidelic usage in relative clauses, however, is very different: in (ii) the preposition combines with a relative element before the verb, and in (i), apart from the specifically relative forms of the verb, there is nothing corresponding to the relative pronoun except lenition (whether the relative is subject or object), or nasalization (when it is object, including cognate accusative and accusative of extent, or an adverb of quality or manner). The later relative particle *a* is a reduction of the commonest preverb, *do-* (which had ousted *ro-* as preverb of the perfect, and *no-* as preverb of the imperfect or conditional), which was extracted from deuterotonic verbal forms with relative function, and re-interpreted. Corresponding to the superlative adverb in the relative clause in English, Celtic has the corresponding adjective attached to the antecedent, a usage maintained in Goidelic, though lost in Welsh after the medieval period.

All the Celtic languages, though to varying degrees, retain the nominal function of the verbnoun, using it governed by prepositions (with its object in the possessive/objective form, and the subject/agent preceded by a pre-position) as an alternative particularly to temporal and causative clauses; the time-reference in such constructions is to be interpreted in the light of the context. Similarly the verbnoun may often be used as an alternative to a finite verb-form in all but the first of a series of co-ordinate clauses. Furthermore the verbnoun provides a substitute for subject and object noun clauses having a superficial similarity to English *I want him to do it.*

The lexicon

The vocabulary of the Celtic languages consists of basic stock inherited from the Indo-European parent (as yet incompletely explored etymologically), with, no doubt, non-Indo-European material acquired in the course of migra-tion and settlement. The first traceable foreign element is Latin, in Brythonic as a result of incorporation in the Roman Empire, and in Goidelic from the introduction of Christianity, first from Gaul, then from Britain. This source continues to be exploited throughout the Middle Ages, but its oldest Brythonic stratum provides the readiest exemplification of the changes under-gone in the transition from Common Brythonic to the beginnings of the separate languages.

Welsh, and to a lesser extent Irish, borrowed from Anglo-Saxon; and Irish, and to a lesser extent Welsh, acquired some new vocabulary from Viking Norse. Anglo-Norman is clearly the source of much of the French element in Irish and Manx, but this is less evident in Welsh and Scottish Gaelic, where it is harder to distinguish such borrowings from French material already adopted into Middle English or Middle Scots. In Middle Cornish the extent of borrowing from English and French, and in Middle Breton the extent of borrowing from French, is very great. In the modern period English is the proximate source of almost all borrowing in insular Celtic.

For the alternative process of coining neologisms based on native material Welsh is well equipped, but the Gaelic languages less so, for the technical reason that they have generally abandoned close compounds, with conse-quent loss of flexibility in shifting from one part of speech to another. There is also the difficulty of getting new coinages into circulation once the corre-sponding loanword has become established. The use of Irish as an official language and of Welsh as a language of equal validity has encouraged the development of both to meet contemporary demands, though anxiety over the consequences of not saying or implying exactly the same in each version of a bilingual document can easily lead to an official style even further removed from natural Celtic than officialese is from normal English. Even under more favourable conditions, however, bilingualism renders it impossible for idiom entirely to resist the pressure to assimilate to English.

The decline of Celtic

After being first the sole, and then for a long period the predominant, media in their respective areas all the Celtic languages are now in decline. Cornish was so from the Anglo-Saxon conquest in the tenth century, but more especially from the sixteenth, dying out about the end of the eighteenth and now revived. Manx began to decline in the eighteenth century, and formally ended on 27 December 1974 with the death of the last native speaker, but there has been sufficient overlap with the last generation to secure a tenuous continuity for the future. In Scotland, Ireland and Wales, the decline in numbers of speakers (or in Wales their decline as a proportion of the population) has been accompanied by a retreat: in Scotland from the mainland Highland area to the Isles and adjoining coastline; in Ireland from all but the far west and a number of other small areas isolated from one another; in Wales from the south-east and the border counties. Native speakers of Scottish Gaelic in 1971 were about 90,000, and of Welsh a little over half a million; speakers of Irish, as a result of its place in the educational system and its official position, numbered about three-quarters of a million, but estimates of the number of native speakers, or persons using Irish as their first language, are as low as 30–35,000. Figures for Breton are not available, but estimates place the number of speakers at least as high as Welsh. None of these languages, however, is sustained by a reservoir of monoglot speakers, and the effect of bilingualism on Celtic, from Gaulish onwards, has so far always proved fatal.

FURTHER READING

The brevity of the foregoing account has entailed severe compression and the omission of many qualifications and reservations; it should not be relied upon for more than a general outline of the subjects dealt with, and for details the reader should consult references to other chapters in Part II, and the works named below.

GENERAL

Pedersen, H. 1909–13. *Vergleichende Grammatik der keltischen Sprachen*. 2 vols. Göttingen: Vandenhoeck and Ruprecht.
Lewis, H. and Pedersen, H. 1937. *A concise comparative Celtic grammar*. Göttingen: Vandenhoeck and Ruprecht. Reprint with Supplement, 1961.

GOIDELIC

Dottin, G. 1913. *Manuel d'irlandais moyen*. 2 vols. Paris: Champion.
Greene, D. 1966. *The Irish language*. Dublin: Cultural Relations Committee.
——— 1913–75. *Dictionary of the Irish language*, [subsequently] *Contributions to a Dictionary of the Irish language*. Dublin: Royal Irish Academy.
Thurneysen, R. 1946. *A grammar of Old Irish*. 2 vols. Dublin: Institute for Advanced Studies.

BRYTHONIC

Evans, D.S. 1964. *A grammar of Middle Welsh*. Dublin: Institute for Advanced Studies.

Hemon, R. 1975. *A historical morphology and syntax of Breton*. Dublin: Institute for Advanced Studies.

Jackson, K.H. 1953. *Language and history in early Britain*. Edinburgh: Edinburgh University Press. [A similar treatment of the history of Goidelic is in preparation.]

Lewis, H. 1931. *Datblygiad yr iaith Gymraeg*. Cardiff: University of Wales Press.

―――― 1943. *Yr elfen Ladin yn yr iaith Gymraeg*. Cardiff: University of Wales Press.

―――― 1946. *Llawlyfr Cernyweg Canol*. 2nd edn. Cardiff: University of Wales Press.

Parry-Williams, T.H. 1923. *The English element in Welsh*. London: Cymmrodorion Record Series.

1950– . *Geiriadur Prifysgol Cymru: A dictionary of the Welsh language*. Cardiff: University of Wales Press.

16

Welsh

G. M. AWBERY

So far as syntax is concerned, there is a fair consensus with respect to the present-day language as to what counts as 'Standard Welsh'. There is however no one accent which counts as a prestige norm. Regional accents vary widely and no single accent based on the usage of a particular social class can be seen as overlying this diversity, providing a model for speakers from all parts of Wales. Accordingly, the treatment of syntax below refers to accepted standard forms, but it is necessary in the sections on phonology to make frequent references to dialectal variation.

Syntax

In this brief outline of Welsh syntax a few topics only can be touched on; first and most typically the initial mutations, then the more basic issues of word order and inflection, and finally back to two characteristically Welsh syntactic features, the use of the 'verbnoun' and of sentence particles. The account given here of the standard language holds in the main for the various spoken dialects of Welsh. These differ from each other only in minor morphological matters, such as the precise form of inflections, the details of where agreement rules apply, and the use of initial mutations.

Initial mutations

Undoubtedly the most striking thing about Welsh for those unfamiliar with the Celtic languages is the set of alternations known as initial mutations (see chapter 15). As in all the Celtic languages the initial consonant of a word varies according to the syntactic environment in which it appears. In some contexts the consonant of the isolation form is retained, but in others it changes. Take as an example the noun *ci* 'dog':

(1)   ein ci 'our dog'
(2)   ei chi 'her dog'
(3)   fy nghi 'my dog'
(4)   dy gi 'your (sing.) dog'

Following the possessive *ein* 'our' we find the isolation form *ci*, but elsewhere it appears as *chi*, *nghi* and *gi*.

Table 16.1. *Initial mutations in Welsh*

Isolation form	Aspirate Mutation	Nasal Mutation	Soft Mutation
p /p/	ph /f/	mh /mh/	b /b/
t /t/	th /θ/	nh /nh/	d /d/
c /k/	ch /χ/	ngh /ŋh/	g /g/
b /b/		m /m/	f /v/
d /d/		n /n/	dd /ð/
g /g/		ng /ŋ/	zero zero
m /m/			f /v/
ll /ɬ/			l /l/
rh /r̥/			r /r/

These alternations can be grouped into three sets, known traditionally in Welsh studies as the soft mutation (SM), the nasal mutation (NM) and the aspirate mutation (AM). The AM converts voiceless stops into the corresponding voiceless fricatives, while the NM nasalizes all stops, and the SM carries out a mixture of changes (see table 16.1). Some of those environments that trigger the AM also require the addition of *h* to words with initial vowels, as *afal* 'apple' but *ei hafal* 'her apple'.

Each mutation is associated with specific environments. Following the possessive *ei* 'her', for instance, a noun must appear in its AM form; initial *p, t* and *c* shift to *ph, th* and *ch*. *Ci* becomes *chi* as in (2), and *tŷ* 'house' and *pen* 'head' undergo similar changes:

(5)   ei thŷ 'her house'
(6)   ei phen 'her head'

These same AM forms are required following the numeral *tri* 'three':

(7)   tri chi 'three dogs'
(8)   tri thŷ 'three houses'
(9)   tri phen 'three heads'

Elsewhere it is the NM or SM forms that are required.

There are basically two kinds of triggering environment. The first of these is illustrated by the examples already given. A particular lexical item such as *ei* 'her' or *tri* 'three' requires the item immediately following it to appear in a mutation form. The actual mutation involved is an idiosyncratic feature of the lexical item concerned; *tri* triggers the AM but *dau* 'two' the SM:

(10)   dau gi 'two dogs'
(11)   dau dŷ 'two houses'
(12)   dau ben 'two heads'

The second type relates to rather more general features of the syntactic envi-

ronment, and here for some reason it is always the SM that is involved. The
object of the verb for instance undergoes SM as long as it is not preceded by
a determiner:

(13)   Gwelodd y bachgen gi 'The boy saw a dog'

Initial mutations first developed as straightforward phonological alternations, sensitive to the phonological environment in which a word appeared.
Gradually however this original motivation has been obscured. The phonological environments which once triggered the alternations have been eroded,
and re-analysing them in terms of lexical and syntactic features has led to
considerable analogical reshuffling. As a result, in the modern language there
are phonologically identical environments with quite different requirements.
For instance, following the determiner *y* 'the' a masculine singular noun such
as *bachgen* 'boy' retains its isolation form but a feminine singular noun such
as *merch* 'girl' undergoes SM.

(14)   y bachgen 'the boy'
(15)   y ferch 'the girl'

Word-order

Welsh sentence structure is characterized by rigid word-order. The pattern for
simple sentences is V + S + O + PP + Adv. The verb appears in initial
position and is followed first by the subject and then by the direct object:

(16)   Gwaeddodd y bachgen
            V   S
       'The boy shouted'
(17)   Darllenodd y dyn y llyfr
            V   S   O
       'The man read the book'

If the sentence contains a prepositional phrase it must follow the core
constituents:

(18)   Taflodd y ferch y bêl dros y gwrych
            V   S   O   PP
       'The girl threw the ball over the hedge'

Adverbial phrases normally come last:

(19)   Rhedodd y plant at y tŷ neithiwr
            V   S   PP   Adv
       'The children ran to the house last night'

Within the noun phrase too the constituents are rigidly ordered: Det +
Num + N + Adj + Dem. Note that there is no indefinite determiner in
Welsh: 'Det' in this context will always refer to a definite determiner. A

demonstrative such as *hon* may not occur alone without an accompanying determiner; a form such as *merch fach hon is not acceptable. It is unusual to find all of the above constituents in any one noun phrase, but those that are present observe this ordering:

(20)   y ferch fach hon
         Det N   Adj Dem
         'this little girl'
(21)   y   tri dyn dall
         Det Num N   Adj
         'the three blind men'

A very few exceptional adjectives such as *hen* 'old' must precede the noun. They can co-occur freely with adjectives in the normal position:

(22)   yr hen ddyn cyfoethog
         Det Adj N   Adj
         'the rich old man'

Possessive noun phrases are unusual in that the order varies according to whether the possessive is a noun or a pronoun:

(23)   llyfr y dyn
          N   Poss
         'the man's book'
(24)   ei lyfr ef
         clitic N Poss
         'his book'

If the possessor is a noun it follows the head noun. If it is a pronoun we find a clitic preceding the head noun, and the pronoun possessor either follows it as in (24) or is optionally dropped as in (25):

(25)   ei lyfr
         clitic N
         'his book'

Copula sentences are a little more flexible, with two different word-orders being equally possible in some cases:

(26)   Mae Elwyn yn athro
         be   S   Pred
         'Elwyn is a teacher'
(27)   Athro yw Elwyn
         Pred be   S
         'Elwyn is a teacher'

The second is almost a complete reversal of the first. Not all copula sentences, however, may appear freely in both forms. Only the first is possible with a predicative adjective:

(28) Mae Elwyn yn dawel
    be   S   Pred
    'Elwyn is quiet'

And with a definite predicative noun only the second type of word-order is possible:

(29) Yr enillydd yw Elwyn
    Pred   be   S
    'Elwyn is the winner'

Inflection and agreement

The structure of the simple sentence is further clarified by patterns of inflection and agreement. The verb, for instance, agrees with a pronoun subject in person and number:

(30) Gwelais i'r ddamwain
    'I saw the accident'
(31) Gwelodd ef y ddamwain
    'He saw the accident'
(32) Gwelsant hwy y ddamwain
    'They saw the accident'

If the subject is a noun then the position is rather different; all nouns, singular and plural alike, take the same inflection as 3rd person singular pronouns.

(33) Gwelodd y ferch/y merched y ddamwain
    'The girl/the girls saw the accident'

These inflections in fact serve a dual purpose in that they convey tense and aspect; the examples given here all refer to a specific event in the past.

It is normal in many languages for a verb to agree with its subject, but it is very unusual to find, as in Welsh, that a preposition is inflected to agree with its object. Where the object of a preposition is a pronoun the preposition agrees with it in number and person:

(34) amdanaf i 'about me'
(35) amdanat ti 'about you (sing.)'
(36) amdanoch chwi 'about you (pl.)'

In the case of a 3rd person singular pronoun agreement extends to gender:

(37) amdano ef 'about him'
(38) amdani hi 'about her'

If the object of the preposition is a noun, however, then there is no agreement at all:

(39)   am y dyn 'about the man'.

In neither of these contexts does the pronoun add new information not already conveyed in the inflection on the verb or preposition, and it is hardly surprising therefore that the pronoun may be omitted, though dropping the 3rd person singular subject pronoun *ef* 'he' or *hi* 'she' will result in the loss of some information, as the verbal inflection does not indicate the gender of the omitted subject. Sentences (30) and (34) alternate freely with (40) and (41).

(40)   Gwelais y ddamwain
       'I saw the accident'
(41)   amdanaf 'about me'

Stylistically the forms where the pronoun is present are less formal than those where it is omitted.

Nouns in Welsh are not inflected to show their role in the sentence, as subject or object. It is rather the inherent features of number and gender that are important. Singular and plural are regularly distinguished; usually, but not always, the singular is the isolation form and the plural is marked by a suffix:

(42)   llyfr/llyfrau 'book'/'books'

All nouns are grammatically masculine or feminine, but it is not often that this is overtly marked.

(43)   athro/athrawes 'teacher'/'female teacher'

The form of most nouns does not immediately reveal their grammatical gender; for instance there is no obvious indication of the fact that *toes* 'dough' is masculine while *coes* 'leg' is feminine.

These two features, number and gender, trigger agreement in other elements of the noun phrase. The adjective may agree with the noun in number:

(44)   y dyn arall 'the other man'
(45)   y dynion eraill 'the other men'

And, in the singular only, it may agree with the noun in gender:

(46)   y plentyn tlws 'the beautiful child'
(47)   y ferch dlos 'the beautiful girl'

This is by no means common however. Many adjectives resemble *da* 'good' which indicates neither number nor gender:

(48)   y dyn da 'the good man'
(49)   y dynion da 'the good men'
(50)   y ferch dda 'the good girl'

The demonstrative also agrees with the noun in number and, in the singular only, in gender. Very few numerals agree with a following noun in gender:

(51)   dau ddyn 'two men'
(52)   dwy ferch 'two girls'

Note that it is the singular form of the noun *dyn* rather than the plural form *dynion* that appears with a numeral.

It is perhaps worth making the point that the determiner does not agree with the noun. The different forms it takes are all conditioned purely by the phonological environment:

(53)   i'r tŷ 'to the house'
(54)   yn y tŷ 'in the house'
(55)   yn yr ystafell 'in the room'

Following a vowel we find *'r*; otherwise we find *y* before a consonant and *yr* before a vowel.

The 'verbnoun'

The verb of a simple sentence is inflected for tense and aspect; so too is the verb in various kinds of subordinate clause:

(56)   Gobeithiai Siân y byddai Ifan yno
                        V   S   Adv
       'Sian hoped that Ifan would be there'
(57)   Gwelais i y dŷn a ddygodd yr arian
                 relS V   O
       'I saw the man who stole the money'
(58)   Aeth Wyn adre pan welodd ef y dyrfa
                       when   V   S O
       'Wyn went home when he saw the crowd'

In other contexts however we find a verb which carries no inflections and is known traditionally as the 'verbnoun'. Its syntactic behaviour differs from that of the normal inflected verb in several interesting ways.

The verbnoun appears, for instance, as the main verb of an embedding functioning as the subject or object of a sentence:

(59)   Bwriadai'r athro i'r plant ddarllen llyfr arall
                      for S   VN   O
       'The teacher intended the children to read another book'

On comparing the subordinate clause of (59) with the corresponding simple sentence (60) several characteristic points strike one immediately.

(60)   Darllenodd y plant lyfr arall
       'The children read another book'

The subject of the verbnoun precedes it and is itself the object of the preposition *i* 'for'; the verbnoun undergoes SM; and the object of the verbnoun is not mutated.

Another difference, but one not immediately apparent from this example, concerns pronoun objects. In a simple sentence the pronoun object appears quite straightforwardly in the same position as the noun object:

(61)   Darllenodd y plant ef
       'The children read it'

With a verbnoun however the position is different. The pronoun object does indeed appear in the normal position following the verbnoun, but also as a clitic preceding it:

(62)   Bwriadai'r athro i'r plant   ei   ddarllen ef
                            for S   clitic VN   O
       'The teacher intended the children to read it'

It is in fact quite possible to omit the object pronoun:

(63)   Bwriadai'r athro i'r plant   ei   ddarllen
                            for S   clitic VN
       'The teacher intended the children to read it'

The similarity of this pattern to that of the genitive noun phrase described on page 262 is striking, and is further highlighted by the fact that the pronouns and clitics are identical in form and trigger the same mutations.

Where the subject of the verbnoun is identical to the subject of the main clause it is simply omitted:

(64)   Bwriadai'r athro ddarllen llyfr arall
                            VN   O
       'The teacher intended to read another book'

It is in examples of this type that we find one of the central uses of the verbnoun, in the periphrastic forms of the verb.

Not all tense and aspect combinations can be expressed by a simple inflection on the verb; in some cases a rather more complicated structure is needed:

(65)   Mae'r plant wedi darllen llyfr arall
       be   S   after VN   O
       lit. 'The children are after read another book'
       i.e. 'The children have read another book'

One can see (65) as a complex sentence (figure 16.1) where the lexical content has been separated out from the information about tense and aspect. The main clause conveys the latter, the subordinate verbnoun clause the former. The subject of the verbnoun is dropped as it merely repeats information already present in the main clause.

Sentence particles, questions and answers

The verb of a simple statement may appear in sentence-initial position as in the examples presented so far, or it may instead be preceded by a particle. (66)

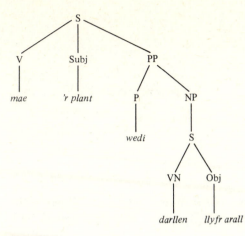

Figure 16.1.

and (67) are semantically identical:

(66) Gwelodd Wyn ef yn yr ardd
       'Wyn saw him in the garden'
(67) Fe welodd Wyn ef yn yr ardd
       'Wyn saw him in the garden'

The particle merely marks overtly the fact that this is a positive state-ment. Similar particles mark sentences as negative statements or as yes/no questions:

(68) Ni welodd Wyn ef yn yr ardd
       'Wyn did not see him in the garden'
(69) A welodd Wyn ef yn yr ardd?
       'Did Wyn see him in the garden?'

Only the positive particle is optional; the negative and interrogative particles are obligatory.

But if forming a yes/no question is a simple matter, it is not so easy to find the right answer. There is in Welsh no equivalent of 'yes' which can be used as an appropriate response to any question. The answer must be tailormade in each case and consists of a bare verb inflected for the same tense and aspect features as the verb of the question:

(70) Q: A gaf i fynd?
          'May I go?'
       A: Cei
          'You may'

Where the question contains an auxiliary verb as in (70) it is this which appears in the answer. Where the question contains a full lexical verb then the answer consists of an inflected form of *gwneud* 'do':

(71)   Q: A ddoi di yfory?
            'Will you come tomorrow?'
       A: Gwnaf
            'I will do'

Negative responses are formed in the same way except that the verb is preceded by a negative particle:

(72)   Q: A fydd Wyn yno?
            'Will Wyn be there?'
       A: Na fydd
            'He will not'

There is one further complication. Where the question has a full verb in the past tense the response is either *do* 'yes' or *naddo* 'no', regardless of both person and number:

(73)   Q: A welais ti'r llyfr?
            'Did you see the book?'
       A: Do/Naddo
            'Yes/No'

Phonology

The discussion below of Welsh phonology falls into three core sections and one addition. The core sections deal in turn with word-stress, the segmental phonemes of the language, and the restrictions on their distribution. The final section looks at how the phonological system is reflected in the orthography.

Word-stress

Primary stress is normally on the penultimate syllable of the word, and this regardless of its morphemic structure. Consider for instance the following sets of forms:

(74)   /əs'kriven/ 'writing'
(75)   /əskri'venið/ 'secretary'
(76)   /əskrive'nəðes/ 'female secretary'

As additional inflections are added, so the stress shifts to the right, and in the last example it is no longer on the basic morpheme but rather on that inflection which happens to occupy the appropriate position in the overall word. A small number of forms only have stress exceptionally on the final syllable:

(77)   /ɬux'bɛn/ 'above'

Monosyllables carry full word-stress in a straightforward way. Only a few grammatical items fail to do so; the definite article, for example, functions as a clitic and is always unstressed:

(78)   /ə 'tiː/ 'the house'

Segmental phonemes

It is in north Wales that we find the greatest number of distinct segmental phonemes. The south operates with a slightly reduced set of consonants and vowels, and a much simpler set of diphthongs. Here then first is the northern system.

The consonantal system is straightforward and is set out in table 16.2. There are two points of interest. Alongside the voiced lateral /l/ we find /ɬ/, the voiceless lateral fricative well known from such names as /*ɬaŋ'gɔɬen/ 'Llangollen'. The roll /r/, though normally voiced, has a voiceless allophone in word-initial position as in ['r̥iːð] 'free'.

Table 16.2. *The consonants of north Wales*

	Bilabial	Labio-dental	Dental	Alveolar	Palato-alveolar	Palatal	Velar	Uvular	Glottal
Voiceless stops	p			t			k		
Voiced stops	b			d			g		
Voiceless fricatives		f	θ	s, ɬ	ʃ			χ	h
Voiced fricatives		v	ð						
Nasals	m			n			ŋ		
Liquids				l, r					
Glides	w					j			

The simple vowels are as described in figure 16.2; they fall clearly into pairs, a long vowel and a short one in each position. The only exception to this is the short central vowel /ə/ which has no long equivalent.

There are three sets of diphthongs, as shown in figure 16.3. In set A the diphthong closes towards a high front position and the first element is always short. In set B the diphthong closes towards a high back position. Here the length of the first element is never contrastive but it does figure as an allophonic alternation – the first element of /eu/ and /au/ is short if there is a following consonant but long otherwise:

(79)   ['mɛun] 'in'; ['kaus] 'cheese'
(80)   ['teːu] 'fat'; ['ɬaːu] 'hand'

In set C the diphthong closes towards a high central position and the length of the first element varies in significance. In /eɨ/, /oːɨ/ and /uːɨ/ it is predictable

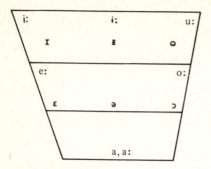

Figure 16.2. The simple vowels of north Wales

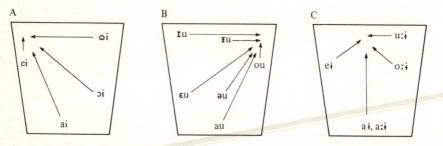

Figure 16.3. The diphthongs of north Wales

but since /ai/ and /aːɨ/ differ only in this one particular it is here contrastive.

The Welsh of south Wales is characterized by the loss of some of the phonemic distinctions still current in the north. For the native speaker of Welsh perhaps the difference between north and south is marked most clearly by the loss of the high central vowels /iː/ and /ɨ/. Items such as /diːn/ 'man' and /bɨr/ 'short' are realized in the south with high front vowels as /diːn/ and /bɪr/. But if this is the most well-known change in the vowel system it is not the only one. In the south-west, in Pembrokeshire, there is a strong tendency to drop another vowel, the short central /ə/. Items having this vowel in other parts of Wales here replace it with one of the high vowels; for instance /ˈkənar/ 'early' becomes /ˈkɪnar/ and /ˈbəguθ/ 'to threaten' becomes /ˈbʊguθ/.

Only one consonant is dropped, the glottal fricative /h/. As one moves towards the south-east /h/ becomes progressively less stable, alternating more and more freely with zero, as in /ˈheːn/ ∼ /ˈeːn/ 'old', until a point is reached where it can no longer be said to have distinctive phonemic status. It functions rather as a prosodic marker of stress, appearing if an item is stressed but not otherwise. In this same area the voiceless allophone [r̥] is replaced by [r].

It is the diphthong system that is most radically affected, with two major differences between north and south. The diphthongs of south Wales are

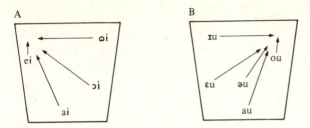

Figure 16.4. The diphthongs of south Wales

described in figure 16.4. The south has no diphthongs closing towards a high central position, and no /ɪu/, a gap which is no doubt related to the loss of the high central vowels /ɨː/ and /ɨ/ already mentioned. Secondly, in south Wales the first element of a diphthong is always short.

On the whole the mapping from the fuller system of the north on to the reduced system of the south is straightforward. Where a high central element appears in the north it is replaced by a high front element in the south:

(81)   north /'krei̯/, south /'krei̯/ 'to create'

Where the first element is long in the north it is short in the south:

(82)   north ['teːu], south ['tɛu] 'fat'

There are two exceptions only to this pattern, which undergo quite different developments in the south, northern /oːɨ/ and /aːɨ/. Throughout most of the south each of these is realized by a long vowel, with /oːɨ/ becoming /oː/ and /aːɨ/ becoming /aː/.

(83)   north /'oːɨr/, south /'oːr/ 'cold'

In formal contexts southerners realize these diphthongs as /ɔi/ and /ai/ respectively. Locally in the south-west we find not /oː/ but /oːe/, /uːe/ or /weː/.

This brief account has been limited to the systematic differences holding between north and south. The exact realization of individual phonemes varies considerably from place to place, but this cannot be explored in any detail here.

Three consonants and one vowel appear in loans from English only – /ʧ/, /ʤ/, /z/, /ɔː/. (/ʤ/ and /ʧ/ do occur, though only marginally, in native Welsh forms; in certain circumstances the sequence /dj/ alternates with /ʤ/ and this is devoiced to /ʧ/ in the south-east.) In addition one new phonemic distinction has arisen where loans from English disregard Welsh patterns of allophonic alternation. It is normal for the roll /r/ to be voiceless in word-initial position, but on the whole loans fail to observe this rule. As a result voiceless /r̥/ and voiced /r/ are now seen to be in contrast at least in this one position:

(84)   /'r̥iːð/ 'free'; /'raːs/ 'race'

Restrictions on phonemes

The phoneme system is not realized in full all the time; contrasts holding in one context are neutralized elsewhere. Take the vowel system. It was claimed earlier that vowel length in Welsh is contrastive. This claim must now be toned down a little. In north Wales this contrast is confined to monosyllables, and monosyllables of a specific kind at that – where the vowel is followed by a single nasal or liquid consonant:

(85)   /ˈtaːn/ 'fire'; /ˈman/ 'place'

Not all nasals permit this contrast; before /m/ and /ŋ/ only short vowels are possible. In the south this contrast is found in all stressed syllables, mono-syllables and penultimates alike, though again only if the vowel is followed by a single nasal or liquid:

(86)   /ˈaːraɬ/ 'other'; /ˈkareg/ 'stone'

Elsewhere vowel length is predictable from the context, the details varying as between north and south.

These restrictions have a close parallel in the diphthong system. All north-ern diphthongs, long and short alike, appear freely in monosyllables:

(87)   /ˈoːin/ 'lamb'; /ˈr̥ɔi/ 'to give'

In all other contexts diphthongs are predictably short. So far the pattern is very similar to that found with simple vowels; the only difference is that with diphthongs there is no need to take into account what immediately follows in the monosyllable. In the south of course no such parallelism with simple vowels is possible since all diphthongs are uniformly short.

There are very few instances in Welsh of specific restrictions on particular vowels or diphthongs. The mid-central vowel /ə/ is found, with a very few monosyllabic exceptions, only in nonfinal syllables, and must be followed by a consonant or a consonant cluster:

(88)   /ˈkənar/ 'early'
(89)   /kənˈheiav/ 'harvest'

The diphthong /əu/ is also confined to nonfinal syllables but there is no need here for a following consonant or cluster:

(90)   /ˈtəuið/ 'weather'

Three other diphthongs, /ai/, /ai/ and /aːi/, are confined to word-final syllables:

(91)   /ˈgair/ 'word'
(92)   /ˈdamwain/ 'accident'

Clusters of consonants are formed very freely, subject to two restrictions. A nasal and a following stop must be homorganic:

(93) /ˈkəntav/ 'first'
(94) /ˈdaŋgos/ 'to show'

And a sequence of two obstruents must agree in voicing:

(95) /ˈkɔpsi/ 'top of corn stack'
(96) /ˈr̥agvir/ 'December'

The full range of cluster types may not however appear freely in all positions in the word. Initial and final clusters in particular are restricted, and to some extent form mirror-image patterns, though this is not always the case. For instance, a cluster formed of a stop and a following liquid may appear in word-initial position but not finally:

(97) /ˈblaud/ 'flour'

In final position we find the reverse, a liquid followed by a stop:

(98) /ˈtalp/ 'lump'

Single consonants too are affected by where they appear in the word. If we ignore /h/ and the glides for a moment, the pattern that emerges is quite simple. There are no constraints on medial and final position, but initially in the word a rather motley selection of consonants, /ŋ/, /ð/ and /x/ is ruled out (/θ/ and /v/ are rare initially but do occur in a few items). These consonants do not form a natural class and there is no apparent explanation for why they should be restricted in the same way.

As was implied above, /h/ is exceptional. It may appear in initial position:

(99) /ˈhiːr/ 'long'

And it may appear medially if it immediately precedes a stressed vowel and follows either another vowel or a nasal consonant or /r/:

(100) /oˈhɛrwið/ 'because'
(101) /brɛnˈhines/ 'queen'

No other consonant displays this preference for initial position and no other consonant takes any notice of stress.

The glides /j/ and /w/ are also exceptional, but it seems likely that this is a function of the phonemic analysis adopted. It is established practice in structuralist accounts of Welsh to assign phonemic status to diphthongs; a sequence consisting of a vowel and a following glide is on this view one phoneme:

(102) /g + ai + r/ 'word'

This leaves those glides which precede vowels to be analysed separately as consonantal phonemes with a highly skewed distribution:

(103) /j + aː + r/ 'hen'

An alternative account can be suggested however, which removes this imbalance very simply. On this revised view a diphthong is a sequence of two phonemes, a simple vowel and a consonantal glide. The glide is grouped with the phonetically similar pre-vocalic glide to form one phoneme, which now appears freely both before vowels, as in /'jaːr/, and after vowels, as in /'gajr/.

There are two cases where regional differences in phonotactic restrictions strike the native speaker with particular force. The first of these splits off the north from the south again. We have seen that the voiceless uvular fricative /χ/ cannot appear alone in initial position in the word; in the north, however, it appears freely in a cluster with /w/. In the south this cluster is ruled out and /χ/ is replaced by /h/:

(104)   north /χweːχ/, south /'hweːχ/ 'six'

The second instance of regional variation concerns the south-east. There, and there alone, voiced stops may not appear medially in the word following the stress, and instead we find the corresponding voiceless stops:

(105)   general /'eːbol/, south-east /'eːpol/ 'foal'

Orthography

The orthography of Welsh is almost completely phonemic, reflecting the full northern system of contrasts, as can be seen from table 16.3, where the correspondences are set out. There are, however, a number of points where the relation between phoneme and orthographic representation is not quite so simple.

So far as the consonant system is concerned the orthography twice goes further than is necessary for the preservation of phonemic distinctiveness. The voiced and voiceless allophones of /r/ are differently represented as *r* and *rh* respectively. And there are two different symbols, *ff* and *ph*, for /f/. Of these *ph* is used in one context only, when /f/ results from the aspirate mutation of a basic /p/:

(106)   /ei fɛn/ *ei phen* 'her head'

In all other contexts *ff* is used, and nowhere else does the orthography take account of whether a consonant is basic or the result of initial mutation.

One distinction only is not reflected in the orthography; /ŋ/ and /ŋg/ are both written *ng*:

(107)   /'aŋen/ *angen* 'need'
(108)   /*'baŋgor/ *Bangor*

Turning to the vowel system we find that the orthography takes no account of length distinctions; the same symbol serves for both the long and short vowel of a pair, with *i* for instance representing both /iː/ and /ɪ/. There is no problem where vowel length is predictable. Where it is contrastive two

Table 16.3. *The orthography of Welsh*

Consonants:	/p/	p	/t/	t	/k/	c
	/b/	b	/d/	d	/g/	g
	/m/	m	/n/	n	/ŋ/	ng
	/f/	ff, ph	/θ/	th	/s/	s
	/ɬ/	ll	/ʃ/	si	/χ/	ch
	/h/	h	/v/	f	/ð/	dd
	/l/	l	[r]	r	[r̥]	rh
	/w/	w	/j/	i		

Vowels:	/iː/, /ɪ/	i		
	/eː/, /ɛ/	e		
	/aː/, /a/	a		
	/oː/, /ɔ/	o		
	/uː/, /ʊ/	w		
	/ɨː/, /ɨ/	u, y		
	/ə/	y		

Diphthongs:	/ei/	ei	/ɪu/	iw	/ei/	eu
	/ai/	ai	/ɛu/	ew	/ai/	au
	/ɔi/	oi	/au/	aw	/aːɨ/	ae
	/ʊi/	wy	/ou/	ow	/oːɨ/	oe
			/ɨu/	yw, uw	/uːɨ/	wy
			/əu/	yw		

different strategies are adopted. In a monosyllable the long vowel is marked with a circumflex accent while the short vowel is left plain:

(109)   /ˈtaːn/ *tân* 'fire'; /ˈman/ *man* 'place'

In a stressed penultimate syllable the short vowel is marked by doubling the following consonant, and it is the long vowel that is left plain:

(110)   /ˈaːraɬ/ *arall* 'other'; /ˈkareg/ *carreg* 'stone'

Only *n* and *r* are in fact doubled. As was noted above, there is no length contrast before /m/ and /ŋ/, and doubling *l* would give *ll*, leading to confusion with the digraph *ll* which represents /ɬ/.

In displaying length contrasts in penultimate syllables the orthography follows the south rather than the north. This is the only point where the south preserves a distinction lost in the north, and it is the only point where the orthography diverges from northern usage.

The symbol *y* is used for both /ə/ and the high central vowels /ɨː/ and /ɨ/:

(111)   /ˈkənar/ *cynar* 'early'
(112)   /ˈdɨːn/ *dyn* 'man'

One might expect this to cause some confusion but in fact this does not happen as the use of *y* for high central vowels is limited in an interesting way. It is used only for those instances of /i̇/ or /ɪ/ which appear in a monosyllable or the final syllable of a longer form and which convert to /ə/ when an inflection is added.

(113)   /ˈdiːn/ *dyn* 'man' ∼ /ˈdənjon/ *dynion* 'men'

All other instances of /iː/ and /ɪ/ are represented by *u*:

(114)   /ˈpi̇ːr/ *pur* 'pure' ∼ /ˈpi̇ːro/ *puro* 'to purify'

One problem affecting the whole system is that the orthography does not clearly distinguish between high vowels and glides. The one symbol *i* is used for all high front elements – the glide /j/, the vowels /iː/ and /ɪ/, the first element of a diphthong as in /ɪu/ and the second as in /ai/:

(115)   /ˈjaːχ/ *iach* 'healthy'
(116)   /ˈtiːr/ *tir* 'land'
(117)   /ˈnɪul/ *niwl* 'fog'
(118)   /ˈgair/ *gair* 'word'

In the same way *w* is used for all high back elements, and *u* or *y* for all high central elements.

Normal penultimate word stress is not marked:

(119)   /ˈplɛntɪn/ *plentyn* 'child'

Where stress is exceptionally on the final syllable this can be shown by means of the diacritic ′, but this is not always done:

(120)   /gwaˈkai̇/ *gwacáu* 'to empty'
(121)   /paraˈtɔi/ *paratoi* 'to prepare'

English segment types are absorbed without difficulty by the orthography. In English loans the symbols *j* and *z* are used for /ʤ/ and /z/, and *tsi* is used for /ʧ/. The English symbol *sh* for /ʃ/ is often used to symbolize dialectal usage where /ʃ/ occurs in word-final position; for instance, /miʃ/ 'mouth' is written *mish*. The vowel /ɔː/ is represented by *ô*. It might be expected that this would cause some confusion as *ô* already stands for /oː/. In practice there is no problem as examples of /ɔː/ are very few.

BIBLIOGRAPHY

The account of the Welsh language given in this chapter has necessarily been very restricted. Two general and easily accessible descriptions of Welsh syntax are Jones and Thomas (1977) and Williams (1980); Williams is traditional in approach while Jones and Thomas adopts an informal transformational style. Awbery (1976) is more technical and covers a more restricted field. Different viewpoints on initial mutations may be found in Hamp (1951), Allbrow (1966) and Awbery (1975). Jones and Ball (forthcoming) contains a useful range of papers on different aspects of Welsh phonology. Most studies of dialect phonology are in the form of unpublished University of Wales theses, but Fynes-Clinton (1913) and Sommerfelt (1925) are classics whose value has not diminished with time. For lexical dialectal variation the main source is Thomas (1973).

Those who are able to read Welsh may also find it useful to consult Richards (1938) on syntax, and Morgan (1952) on mutations. Watkins (1961) provides a very useful general introduction to the linguistic study of Welsh.

Two journals, *The Bulletin of the Board of Celtic Studies* and *Studia Celtica* (both published by the University of Wales Press in Cardiff), regularly publish articles on various aspects of Welsh linguistics; *Bibliotheca Celtica* (published by The National Library of Wales, Aberystwyth) lists publications in the field; Davies (1973) lists relevant theses. Supplementary bibliographies and lists of theses are published from time to time in *Studia Celtica*.

REFERENCES

Allbrow, K. H. 1966. Mutation in spoken north Welsh. In C. E. Bazell *et al.* (eds.) *In memory of J. R. Firth*. London: Longman.
Awbery, G. M. 1975. Welsh mutations: syntax or phonology? *Archivum Linguisticum* 6: 14–25.
—— 1976. *The syntax of Welsh: a transformational study of the passive*. Cambridge: CUP.
Davies, A. E. 1973. *Welsh language and Welsh dissertations accepted by British, American and German universities 1887–1971*. Cardiff: University of Wales Press.
Fynes-Clinton, O. H. 1913. *The Welsh vocabulary of the Bangor district*. Oxford: OUP.
Hamp, E. 1951. Morphophonemes of the Keltic mutations. *Language* 27: 230–47.
Jones, G. E. and Ball, M. J. (eds.) Forthcoming. *Readings in Welsh phonology*. Cardiff: University of Wales Press.
Jones, M. and Thomas, A. R. 1977. *The Welsh language: studies in its syntax and semantics*. Cardiff: University of Wales Press.
Morgan, T. J. 1952. *Y treigladau a'u cystrawen*. Cardiff: University of Wales Press.
Richards, M. 1938. *Cystrawen y frawddeg Gymraeg*. Cardiff: University of Wales Press.
Sommerfelt, A. 1925. *Studies in Cyfeiliog Welsh: a contribution to Welsh dialectology*. Oslo: I Kommission Hos Jacob Dybwad.
Thomas, A. R. 1973. *The linguistic geography of Wales: a contribution to Welsh dialectology*. Cardiff: University of Wales Press.
Watkins, T. A. 1961. *Ieithyddiaeth*. Cardiff: University of Wales Press.
Williams, S. J. 1980. *Welsh grammar*. Cardiff: University of Wales Press.

17

Cornish

ALAN R. THOMAS

Historical background

Tradition has it that the Cornish language died with the passing of Dolly Pentreath, its last known native speaker, in December 1777. Though it is now believed that Dolly was survived by a scattered handful of elderly people who also knew the language, it is unlikely that any of them lived beyond the end of the eighteenth century.

Originally a dialect of Brythonic, Cornish began its independent development when the Tamar became the effective boundary between England and Cornwall in the tenth century. From then on, there was no land contact with the dialects which ultimately developed into Welsh, nor of course with Breton (itself an offshoot of the Brythonic dialect spoken in the south-west of Britain in the sixth century (see chapter 15)).

Three historical periods are attributed to the Cornish language: Old Cornish is dated to the end of the twelfth century, Middle Cornish from then until the seventeenth, and Late Cornish for its final century or so of existence. There were no literary texts in Cornish before the fifteenth century; the division between the earlier historical periods was made on the sparse evidence of glosses and proper names in Latin manuscripts of the time. Those texts which do exist are mainly miracle plays, translated from English. One result of this paucity of literary texts is that the orthography of Cornish is extremely inconsistent, with multiple representation of almost every sound, vowel and consonant alike: so much so, that contemporary language revivalists have – with considerable opposition – devised a new orthography as a model of pronunciation (R. Morton Nance's 'Unified Spelling'). The vowel /ə/, for instance, is variously represented as orthographic *e, eu, ue, u, uy, o, ey*, so that the word with the phonological structure /mər/ 'big' appears as *meur, mur, mer, meyr*; and that with the phonological structure /ləv/ 'hand' as *leff, leyf, luef*. There is no means of knowing whether some of the variations in spelling reflect dialectal variation. In describing the phonology and morphophonology of Cornish, I will give the phonological structure which can be deduced from analysis of the written forms, with comment on its orthographic representation only where it would be excessively confusing to omit it. It goes without

Table 17.1. *Vowel system of Cornish*

	Front	Central	Back
Close	i	ɨ	u
Mid	e	ə	o
Open		a	

saying that, with no spoken record available, we can do no more than set up an abstract configuration of contrasting units, though we have for guidance Edward Lhuyd's description of the sounds of Cornish as they were spoken in the early eighteenth century (Lhuyd, 1707: 222–53).

Phonology

Word stress

Cornish, like Welsh and Breton, has primary stress regularly on the penultimate syllable of polysyllabic words, as in /'arluð/ *arluth* 'lord' /'maru/ *marou* 'dead'. There is no evidence of weakening of the vowel in a final unstressed syllable – for instance, *redya* /'redja/ 'read' is made to rhyme with *da* /'da/ 'good'; so it is likely that Cornish, like Welsh, separated rhythmic stress (on the penultimate syllable) from pitch movement (which occurs on the post-stress syllable, giving it prominence, often greater prominence than the stressed syllable has, thus inhibiting any weakening in vowel quality).

Vowels

The vowel system is of the 3-3-1 type shown in table 17.1.

There is no evidence of restrictions on the distribution of the vowels, even /ə/ occurring freely in monosyllables (contrast Welsh). The vowels can be exemplified thus:

/i/: /ði/ *the* 'to' /gwiskɨs/ *gweskis* 'dressed'
/e/: /dre/ *dre* 'through' /jesɨ/ *ihesu* 'Jesu'
/a/: /mab/ *mab* 'son' /skians/ *skyans* 'wisdom'
/o/: /bos/ *bos* 'to be' /kolon/ *colon* 'heart'
/u/: /gur/ *gour* 'husband' /maru/ *marou* 'dead'
/ɨ/: /tɨ/ *tu* 'side' /davɨð/ *dauyth* 'Dafydd'
/ə/: /ləv/ *leff* 'hand' /brəder/ *broder* 'brother'

There are also two semivowels,

/j/: /koljek/ *coljek* 'cockerel'
/w/: /war/ *war* 'on'

The vowel /ɨ/ is interesting on two scores. It appears to be the typical Brythonic 'high' mixed' vowel – central with lips spread (written *y* in Welsh). Brythonic also had a central vowel with lips rounded (written *u* in Welsh and by today merged with that written *y*): it may well be that this vowel was still extant in late Cornish, since forms like *jhesu* 'Jesu' and *dev* (a spelling variant of *du* 'God') are made to rhyme with the Norman French loan-word *vertu* 'virtue', which may have retained the original frontness and rounding of the final vowel. Certainly, as in Welsh, there are two distinct representations for the close central vowel region.

Rhyming evidence, again, suggests that the vowels /e/ and /ɨ/ were in free variation, possibly on account of their phonetic similarity: for instance the word for 'faith' appears as the doublet *feth* /feð/, rhyming with *dyweth* /diueð/ 'end', and *fyth* /fɨð/ rhyming with *fyllyth* /filɨð/ 'fail'.

Vowel length

Since it is hazardous to give precise information on vowel length, I have left it unmarked. However, what evidence there is indicates that Cornish followed the same basic indigenous pattern as Welsh: long vowels occur in stressed syllables only; those in open stressed monosyllables are invariably long, while those followed by consonant clusters or voiceless stops are invariably short; vowels before voiced stops are long, while before fricatives and resonants long and short vowels are in contrast. Vowel length is marked in the spelling only irregularly, and in one of three ways:

(i) by placing a *y* after the long vowel, as in [taːz] (*tays* 'father'), [moːz] (*moys* 'go');

(ii) by doubling the vowel letter, as in [graːs] (*graas* 'grace'), [miːn] (*myyn* 'edge');

(iii) by writing an *e* in final position after a consonant, to show that the vowel preceding the consonant is long, as in [skoːl] (*scole* 'school').

This latter convention is borrowed from English, and is one of many instances of the influence of English spelling on the Cornish orthographic system. The evidence is too scanty for us to be able to demonstrate to what extent word-borrowing from English may have led to the length patterns of English words penetrating and disturbing the indigenous system (though it surely must have done, as happened in Welsh, where extensive borrowing from English has led to the growth of length contrasts in almost all those contexts noted as being without in the basic system).

Place-name evidence and that of Cornish dialects of English suggest that the peripheral long and short vowels differed phonetically much as they do in Welsh, so that we can contrast them schematically thus on the open–close parameter:

/i/: [iː] ~ [ɪ]
/e/: [eː] ~ [ɛ]
/o/: [oː] ~ [ɔ]
/u/: [uː] ~ [ʊ]

It seems, too, that long /a/ may have been raised and fronted to approximate [eː] or the diphthongized [eə], as in:

glas 'blue', 'green': [gleːz], [gleəz]

This would form a striking parallel with the neighbouring Welsh dialect of Glamorgan, which has the cognates:

[glæːs], [glæʌs]

Diphthongs

Cornish has few diphthongs, and none closing to /i/ in the indigenous system. They can be exemplified as follows, though the vagaries of the orthography, coupled with the scarcity of the evidence, make authentic identification of any but /ou/ in unstressed syllables extremely perilous. There are plentiful examples of the latter because of its frequent occurrence as a noun plural suffix:

/ei̯/:	/mei̯n/	*meyn* 'stone'
/oi̯/:	/moi̯/	*moy* 'more'
/iu/:	/liu/	*lyw* 'colour'
/i̯u/:	/di̯u/	*dyw* 'two' (fem.)
/eu/:	/eun/	*evn* 'right'
/ou/:	/krous/	*crous* 'cross'
	/lavarou/	*lauarow* 'words'
/au/:	/nau/	*naw* 'nine'

Again, rhyming patterns suggest either free variation or dialectal variation in the phonetic realization of the diphthongs /eu/, /iu/ and /ou/: /deu/ *deu* 'God' rhymes with /livrjou/ *lyfryou* 'books', while its spelling variants *deu*, *du* can both rhyme with the Norman French loan *vertu*; and *vertu*, in turn, can rhyme with *lyw* /liu/ 'colour'. If our previous suggestion of the retention of rounding in the final vowel of the borrowed *vertu* is right, it seems that the combination of high or mid tongue position with rounding, whether simultaneously or in sequence, gives rise to considerable uncertainty about the precise phonetic values involved.

It seems, too, that English loan-words filled out the gap in the indigenous system to some extent; a form such as *paynys* 'pains' was clearly borrowed before the Great Vowel Shift altered the value of orthographic *ai*, *ay* in English: so we can predict a realization approximating /painis/; and a form such as *ioy* 'joy' would have had a realization approximating /dʒoi/.

Table 17.2. *Consonant system of Cornish*

	Labial	Alveolar	Palato-alveolar	Velar	Glottal
Plosives	p	t		k	
	b	d		g	
Fricatives	f	θ s	ʃ	x	h
	v	ð (z)	—	—	—
Nasals	m	n		ŋ	
Affricates	—	ʧ		—	
	—	ʤ		—	
Lateral	l				
Trill	r				

Consonants

Cornish has a contrast of voiceless and voiced consonants at labial, alveolar and velar positions, with an extension of alveolar contrasts as shown in table 17.2. Most of the consonants occur freely in word-initial position, medially and in word-final position; they can be exemplified thus:

Plosives

|pen| *pen* 'head' |bara| *bara* 'bread'
|apert| *apert* 'obvious' |neb| *neb* 'no-one'
|ketel| *kettel* 'as' |tas| *tas* 'father'
|ketep| *ketep* 'every' |dov| *dof* 'tame'
|karadou| *caradow* 'loved' |golou| *golow* 'light'
|agan| *agan* 'our' |kig| *kyg* 'meat'

Fricatives

|fals| *fals* 'false' |ləv| *ləuf* 'loved'
|vil| *vyl* 'vile' |avel| *avel* 'like'
|arluð| *arluth* 'lord' |ði| *the* 'to'
|beð| *beth* 'grave' |temtaʃon| *temptasyon* 'temptation'

Nasals and |r|, |l|

|mam| *mam* 'mother' |anel| *anel* 'breath'
|neb| *neb* 'no-one' |aŋou| *ancou* 'death'

A few consonants have restricted distributions: /h/ occurs only at word-initial position: /haval/ *haual* 'like'; /x/, which is considered to be only lightly frictionalized, occurs only medially and word-finally:

|axos| *ahos* 'cause' |brex| *bregh* 'arm'

The orthography makes no distinction between [s] and [z], which are in complementary distribution as realizations of /s/. [s] occurs initially, following a short vowel, and word-finally following a consonant, thus

[soːn] *son* 'noise'   [axos] *ahos* 'cause'
[sans] *sans* 'saint'

When /s/ follows /n/ in medial position, intervocalically, or at word-end following a long vowel, it is realized as [z], thus [glaːz] *glas* 'blue'; [penzans] *Pensance*; [keuzel] *keusel* 'speak'. Cornish differs from Welsh in this respect, in that the indigenous Welsh system had no voicing opposition between sibilants, even at the level of phonetics. The affricates are rare, occurring mainly in word-initial position, e.g. /ʧif/ *chyf* 'chief', /ʤaul/ *iaul* 'devil'.

Clusters of two consonants are very common. Initially, they are typically composed of (i) a plosive or fricative followed by /l/, /r/ or /n/:

/*bl*amjux/ *blamyough* 'blame' (imp.)	/*dr*e/ *dre* 'through'
/*br*as/ *bras* 'big'	/*kl*os/ *clos* 'praise'
/*kn*es/ *cnes* 'flesh'	/*kr*esi/ *kresy* 'believe'
/*θr*on/ *thron* 'throne'	

(ii) /s/ followed by a plosive, as in /*sk*ians/ *skyans* 'wisdom'; /*sp*eris/ *speris* 'spirit'.

In final position, clusters of two consonants are typically composed of /r/ or /l/ followed by a plosive, fricative or a nasal, or of /s/ or /N/followed by a plosive:

/ku*rt*/ *curte* 'court'	/ki*rx*/ *kyrgh* 'attack'
/fa*ls*/ *fals* 'false'	/wo*rθ*/ *worth* 'by'
/a*rv*/ *arv* 'tool'	/ko*rf*/ *corf* 'body'
/be*st*/ be*st* 'beast'	/be*rn*/ *bern* 'worry'
/in mi*sk*/ *yn mysk* 'among'	/he*rn*/ *hern* 'iron'
/jo*ŋk*/ *yonk* 'young'	/pi*mp*/ *pymp* 'five'

Medially, any of the above two consonant cluster types can occur:

/ko*rt*es/ *cortes* 'courteous'	/go*lx*i/ *golhy* 'wash'
/he*lm*a/ *helma* 'this'	/me*rs*i/ *mersy* 'mercy'
/te*rm*en/ *termen* 'time'	/bi*st*el/ *bystel* 'bile'
/ke*fr*is/ *keffrys* 'also'	

Additionally, there are sequences of two plosives, as in /ba*pt*ist/ *baptist* 'baptist'; of a nasal and a plosive, as in /gwa*nd*er/ *gwander* 'weakness'; and of /rl/, as in /a*rl*uð/ *arluth* 'lord'.

Initial sequences of /s/ + plosive did not develop a prosthetic vowel, as happened in Welsh, so that we have

Cornish /skol/ *scole* 'school', Welsh *ysgol*

Also, in final homorganic clusters which had **lt*, **nt* in British, the final /t/ developed as /s/ in Cornish, giving

/als/ *als* 'hill', Welsh *allt*
/dan*s*/ *dans* 'tooth', Welsh *dant*

The same development gives Cornish final /s/ (phonetically [z]) as compared with Welsh final /d/ in words like /bos/ *bos* 'to be', Welsh *bod*; /taːs/ *tays* 'father', Welsh *tad*. Final /-nt/ clusters in English loans retained their final plosive, however, as in

/tormont/ *tormont* 'torture'

Clusters of three consonants are rare, consisting of /s/ + plosive + /r/ or /l/ initially, as in

/stretʃa/ *streccha* 'delay'   /skriva/ *scryve* 'writing'

and of the same or similar types medially:

/mei*str*i/ *meystry* 'authority'   /ken*tr*ou/ *kentrow* 'nails'
/lo*sk*van/ *loscvan* 'a burning'

Initial mutations

There are three types of initial consonant mutation: they occur in a variety of lexical and syntactic environments, which will be only briefly exemplified. *The soft mutation* (SM) involves voicing of the voiceless plosives /p, t, k/ > /b, d, g/; frictionalization of the voiced stops /b, m/ > /v/, /d/ > /ð/ (the SM of /g/ has passed through a historical /ɣ/ to 0). Thus, in a singular feminine noun after the definite article /an/, as in

/an *v*ro/ 'the area' (< /*b*ro/)
/an *v*oran/ 'the maiden' (< *m*oran)
/an *d*us/ 'the people' (< *t*us)

The spirant mutation involves frictionalization of the voiceless plosives /p, t, k/ > /f, θ, x/; for example, in a noun after the 3rd singular feminine possessive adjective, as in

/i *θ*ir/ 'her land' (< /*t*ir/)
/i *x*olon/ 'her heart' (< /*k*olon/)

Provection involves: (a) devoicing of the voiced plosives /b, d, g/ > /p, t, k/; for example, in the verbnoun after the aspectual particle /ou/, as in

/ou *p*eue/ 'living' (< /*b*eue/)
/ou *t*os/ 'coming' (< /*d*os/)

(b) a set of secondary segmental changes to segments which were themselves the historical products of soft mutation: /v/ > /f/, /ð/ > /t/, ø > /h/, for example, in an adjective following the predicative particle /ən/, as in

/ən *ta*/ 'good' (< /*d*a/ via */ən *ð*a/)
/ən *h*aru 'rough' (< /garu/ via */ən (ɣ)aru/)

The environments for (b) overlap with those for SM only in respect of the one exemplified; and, of course, in that environment they displace the 'regular' SM alternations for voiced plosives /b, d, g/ > /v, ð/ ø.

Grammar

The noun phrase

Nouns contrast singular and plural forms, by alternation of the vowel of the base, by suffixation and by a combination of the two, as in

margh 'stallion' ~ *mergh*
corf 'body' ~ *corfow*
mab 'son' ~ *mebyon*

They also contrast masculine and feminine gender. The attributive adjective typically follows the noun, as in *benen vras* (lit. woman big, 'big woman'), and ·has homographic derivational variants to denote comparative and superlative forms, as in

Radical	Comparative	Superlative
bras 'big'	*brassa*	*brassa*

The homograph is disambiguated by the fact that the comparative is followed by a conjunction *ages*:

(1) brassa ages kyns
     'bigger than before'

The equative is represented analytically with the particles *mar* or *maga* preceding the radical form of the adjective:

(2) mar ver nerth
     'such big strength'
(3) maga fuer drok
     'such big wickedness'

The personal pronouns contrast three persons in singular and plural, with a gender contrast at 3rd singular:

Singular: 1st person *my*, 2nd person *ty*, 3rd person masc. *ef*, fem. *y*
Plural: 1st person *ny*, 2nd person *why*, 3rd person *y*

There is a matching series of possessive adjectives,

Singular: 1st person *ow*, 2nd person *the*, 3rd person masc. and fem. *y*
Plural: 1st person *agan*, 2nd person *agas*, 3rd person *aga*

The form of the relative pronoun is *a*:

(4) gans diodydd *a* relle agis sawye
     lit. 'with drinks which may make you cure'
     'with drinks which may cure you'

The yes/no interrogative particle is also *a*:

(5) *a* glewsyugh why?
     lit. '(particle) heard-you you'
     'did you hear?'

The interrogative pronominal forms are based on the particle *py* 'which':

(6) *pyw* a whyleugh?
     lit. 'who (rel. pro) seek-you'
     'who do you seek?'
(7) *pyth* yw the gallos? 'what is your power?'
(8) *pe* feste? 'where were-you?'
(9) *prag* na ðons?
     lit. 'why not come-they'
     'why don't they come?'

They have the related adjectival forms, as in *py dol* 'what hole?'; *py nyl* 'which one?'; *pan pyn* 'what pain?'.

The numerals follow the Brythonic pattern, running in series from 1–10, with gender contrasts in some cases:

1. *un*; 3. *try*, *teyr* (masc., fem.)

After 10 *dek*, a new series starts, predicated on 10:

11. *unnek* (lit. 'one-ten'); 15. *pymthek* (lit. 'five-ten')

After 20 *ugens* a further series begins, predicated on 20 preceded by the preposition *war* 'on', and incorporating the previous 11–19 series:

30. *dekwarnugens* (lit. 'ten on twenty')
31. *unnekwarnugens* (lit. 'one-ten on twenty')

This is repeated for each further unit of 20 up to 180, after which units of 100 *cans* take over, incorporating the previous series from 1 to 99. After 1000 *myl* the basic unit is *myl*, incorporating the previous 100 and 1–99 series.

The verb phrase

The inflected lexical verb has three contrasts of mood – indicative, subjunctive and imperative – an impersonal form for each tense, and a past participle. Though each tense contrasts three persons in both singular and plural, the paradigm is illustrated in table 17.3, with the 3rd singular only in each case, for the verb *care* 'love'.

Table 17.3. *Inflected lexical verb in Cornish*

	Present	Imperfect	Perfect	Pluperfect
Indicative				
3rd singular	*car*	*care*	*caras*	*carse*
Impersonal	*keryr*	*kerys*	*caras*	?
Subjunctive				
3rd singular	*caro*	*care*		
Impersonal	*carer*	?		
Imperative				
3rd singular	*cares*			
Past participle	*kerys*			

Periphrastic constructions

Cornish has a number of periphrastic constructions which partly mirror those which occur in Welsh:

1. The verb *bos* 'to be' is followed by the progressive aspect marker *ow* and the uninflected verb or verbnoun, as in
   Yma ow kelwel ely
   lit. 'He-is progressive call Elias'
   'He is calling Elias'
2. The passive is expressed in a relative construction which has the 3rd singular of an appropriate tense of the verb *bos* 'to be' followed by the past participle, as in
   The voth *a vyth gurys*
   lit. 'Your wish relative particle will-be done'
   'Your wish will be done' i.e. 'Thy will be done'
3. Inflected forms of the verb have an alternative realization in an inflected form of an auxiliary verb *gruthyl* 'do' followed by the uninflected form of the lexical verb, as in
   Pan *wruk* an bara *terry*
   lit. 'When did-he the bread break'
   'When he broke the bread'

The verb *bos* 'to be' extends the semantics of the verb further by adding to the basic paradigm, in the first of the periphrastic constructions above and independently, a habitual present and habitual imperfect in the indicative mood.

Sentence structure

Cornish is a VSO language, as in

(10)   *gallas henna thy ken tyr*
       lit. 'went-he that-one to another land'
       'that one went to another land'

There is a frequent variant in which the subject is fronted and followed by the relative pronoun and a verb in the 3rd person singular:

(11)   *My a gyrgh* an guas
       lit. 'I rel. pron. will-get the servant'
       'I will get the servant'

Negation is achieved by placing the negative particle *ny* before the inflected verb:

(12)   *ny* evaf
       'I do not drink'

There is no direct negative correlate of the fronted-subject sentence type, though there is a similar construction in which a pronominal subject is followed by the negative particle *ny* and an inflected verb in agreement with the person of the subject pronoun:

(13)   Wy ny woðough
       lit. 'You neg. part. know-you'
       'You do not know'

On the general history of Cornish Thomas (1973), Wakelin (1975) and Ellis (1974) are especially useful, while Lewis (1946) and Gregor (1980) give a lot of information on the structure of the language and its relations with the other Celtic languages. On recent attempts to provide pedagogic materials for language revival see Nance (1929) and Gendall (1972).

REFERENCES

Ellis, B. 1974. *The Cornish language and its literature*. London: Routledge and Kegan Paul.
Gendall, R. 1972. *Kernewek bew*. Cornish Language Board.
Gregor, D. B. 1980. *Celtic: a comparative study*. Cambridge: The Oleander Press.
Lewis, H. 1946. *Llawlyfr Cernyweg Canol*. New edn. Cardiff: University of Wales Press/Gwasg Prifysgol Cymru.
Lhuyd, E. 1707. *Archaeologia Britannica*. London.
Nance, R. M. 1929. *Cornish for all*. St Ives: James Lanham Ltd.
Thomas, C. 1973. *The importance of being Cornish*. Exeter: University of Exeter Press.
Wakelin, M. F. 1975. *Language and history in Cornwall*. Leicester: Leicester University Press.

18

Irish

CATHAIR Ó DOCHARTAIGH

Spelling system

The spelling system of Irish derives from an adaptation of the Roman alphabet made after the introduction of Christianity into the country in the fifth and sixth centuries. This orthography was modified to an extent in the course of the Old and Middle Irish periods until it reached a fairly standardized form by the thirteenth century. This Classical Gaelic standard was promulgated through the literate classes and accepted in both Ireland and Gaelic Scotland until the break-up of traditional Gaelic society in the course of the seventeenth century, when the orthographic systems of the two languages began to diverge somewhat. The letter forms derive from an Insular version of Latin half uncials and remained more or less unchanged throughout the whole period of Irish manuscript writing, a tradition which, in the relative absence of printing in Irish, survived on a large scale down to the mid-nineteenth century.

In the twentieth century two major developments have affected this traditional orthographic system. Firstly, the adoption of the so-called 'Roman script' – that is, the common Western European print fonts together with English cursive forms – in place of the Gaelic script – and secondly, an extensive reform of the spelling. This latter was necessary mainly on account of the large number of non-initial voiced fricatives (*bh*, *dh*, *gh* and *mh*) which had been lost in the course of the Classical Gaelic period with varying types of compensatory lengthening or diphthongization of preceding short vowels, e.g. *adhbhar* 'cause' → *ábhar* /aːwər/; *beannughadh* 'blessing' → *beannú* /bʹaNuː/ (the capitalized consonant in phonemic representation indicates a long consonant, often a doubled consonant in the orthography). Generally speaking, where the vocalization of a fricative has given rise to a diphthong, the original fricative is still written, e.g. *Tadhg* /taig/, otherwise the fricative is dropped with the new long vowel being indicated by the acute accent, as in the examples above.

A fundamental distinction within the consonant system is that opposing broad, or neutral, consonants to palatalized varieties. This is shown in the orthography by means of the abutting vowels: thus a consonant followed by *e* or *i*, or preceded by *i*, is palatalized; otherwise (i.e. with the vowels *a, o, u*) it is neutral, e.g. *bó* /boː/ 'cow'; *beó* /bʼoː/ 'alive'; *greann* /gʼrʼaN/ 'humour'; *grinn* /gʼrʼiNʼ/ 'humour' (gen. sing.). This rule implies that an intervocalic consonant or cluster redundantly requires congruence of quality marking vowels both before and after it. This requirement gives rise to a considerable number of vowel digraphs where only one member marks the actual phonetic quality of the syllabic peak and the second is used to indicate the quality of a preceding or following consonant, e.g. *cailín* /kalʼiːnʼ/ 'girl', where the *i* preceding the *l* has no implications for pronunciation apart from marking the *l* as palatalized, a fact also indicated by the following *í*, which thus has the dual role of indicating both vowel quality (and length here) and the palatalized quality of the *l* and the final *n*.

Consonantal lenition, either within a word or in initial position (morphophonemic lenition) is marked by the presence of a following *h* – apart from the letters *l*, *n* and *r*, which in initial position are not distinguished in the orthography as regards unlenited versus lenited. In non-initial position these three segments are written doubled to indicate the unlenited variety: *beann* /bʼaN/ 'cliff' vs. *bean* /bʼan/ 'woman'; *geall* /gʼaL/ 'bet' vs. *geal* /gʼal/ 'white'. Other consonant digraphs are found in initial position where the combinations *bp*, *dt*, *gc*, *mb*, *nd*, *ng* and *bhf* indicate eclipsed or nasalized varieties (see page 296 for a discussion) with the pronunciations /b, d, g, m, N, ŋ, w/.

There are five vowel graphs (*i*, *e*, *a*, *o*, *u*) together with the acute accent to mark length, and the digraph combination *ao* represents a long monophthong, /ɯː/ or /eː/ depending on the dialect. Short vowels in unstressed syllables can be variously written but are usually pronounced as a schwa-type vowel, higher or lower depending on whether the quality of the neighbouring consonants is palatalized or neutral, e.g. *gasta* /gastə/ 'quick', *níos gaiste* /Nʼiːs gasʼtʼə/ 'quicker'.

Sentence structure

The basic order of elements in the Irish sentence is Verb + Subject + Object + Indirect Object + Adverbial, with the only major exception to this occurring when the direct object is a pronoun, when it usually appears at the end of the clause. Any departure from this normal order usually involves topicalization, where a particular element (noun, adjective or adverb) is fronted to appear in a copula phrase with the remainder of the sentence in a relative clause. Modifiers such as the negative, interrogative or question particles appear directly in front of the verb.

The copula is defective in tense-forms and serves to link a subject with a noun or pronoun complement in sentences of the type:

(1) Is é Seán an dochtúir
     lit. 'Is him John the doctor'
     'John is the doctor'

or, with an indefinite complement:

(2) Is dochtúir é
     lit. 'Is a doctor him'
     'He is a doctor'

Similarly, in a topicalization:

(3) Is é an dochtúir atá ag an dorus
     lit. 'Is him the doctor who is at the door'
     'The doctor (emphatic) is at the door'

The stative verb *tá*, which has a fuller tense system than other verbs, including as it does both a simple and a habitual present tense, is used to link a subject with adjective, adverb or prepositional phrase complements. This last includes those situations where the combination of the verb *tá* with various prepositions in conjunction with non-finite verbal forms is used in order to generate aspectual forms:

(4) Tá Seán ag imeacht
     lit. 'Is John at leaving'
     'John is leaving'
(5) Tá Seán i ndiaidh imeacht
     lit. 'Is John after leaving'
     'John has left'

As there are no simple words for 'yes' and 'no', responses are formed by repeating the verb of the question in the positive or negative as appropriate and without any accompanying subject. In a number of northern dialects there appears to be an increasing use of the auxiliary 'to do' in responses, presumably as a calque on the English auxiliary in this position.

Subordinate clauses

Subordinate clauses dependent on a verb are introduced by the particle *go* (past tense *gur*) if positive, and *nach* (past tense *nár*) if negative, followed in each case by the dependent form of the verb (see page 294).

Relative clauses are introduced by a relative particle, the form of which varies with differing relationships between the noun or pronoun antecedent and the verb of the subordinate clause. In 'direct' relatives, the antecedent is either subject or object of the underlying relative sentence; with 'indirect' relatives, the antecedent occurs in either genitive or prepositional case in the underlying clause. In addition, the relative pronoun varies in a similar way to the subordinating particle above, depending on whether the clause is positive or negative, present or past:

(6) Chunnaic mé an duine a cheannaigh an teach
     lit. 'saw I the man who bought the house'
     'I saw the man who bought the house'

(7)   Chunnaic mé an duine ar ceannaíodh a theach
        lit. 'saw I the man (rel.) was bought his house'
        'I saw the man whose house was bought'

Noun phrases

The noun phrase consists of the following elements:

definite article $\Big\}$ + numeral + noun + adjective + demonstrative
possessive pronoun

Of these, only the noun is obligatory and other possible optional elements are
adjectival modifiers which precede the noun, and adverbial modifiers preceding any of the adjectives. In addition the whole phrase may be preceded by
a preposition, which can take a special form before the definite article. There
is no indefinite article. The demonstrative element requires the presence of the
definite article in most instances and occurs as a three-way system with *seo*
'this', *sin* 'that' and *siúd* 'yonder'. The ordering of adjective subclasses is:
size + quality + colour.

(8)   leis na trí coin móra gránna fíor-dhubha sin
        lit. 'with the three dogs big ugly very black those'
        'with those three big ugly very black dogs'

   Where a noun in a phrase dominates a second following noun, the latter
appears in the genitive case and the whole phrase is marked for definiteness or
indefiniteness by the presence or absence of the article before this second
noun. In such phrases the article normally cannot occur before the first noun:

(9)   bean tí
        lit. 'a woman of a house'
        'a housewife'
(10) bean an tí
        lit. 'a woman of the house'
        'the housewife'.

Morphology

The verb

Apart from some fourteen verbs which are in varying degrees irregular in
their conjugation, the paradigm of the Irish verb is highly regular, with all
tenses and personal forms being based on the root. Although the spelling of
these endings may vary (broad or slender) with the quality of the final consonant of the root (neutral or palatalized) the basic forms are the same and
are illustrated in table 18.1 for a monosyllabic verb ending in a neutral
consonant. (Certain disyllabic verbs of the 'second conjugation' form the
future and conditional tenses with an -ó- morpheme instead of the -f- as here.)

Table 18.1. *Morphology of 'tóg' 'lift'*

Tense	Singular	Plural
Present	1 tógaim	tógamaoid
	2 tógair	tógann sibh
	3 tógann sé	tógaid
	Impersonal tógthar	Relative thógas
Imperfect	1 thógainn	thógamaois
	2 thógthá	thógadh sibh
	3 thógadh sé	thógadaois
	Impersonal thógthaoi	
Past	1 thógais	thógamar
	2 thógais	thógabhar
	3 thóg sé	thógadar
	Impersonal tógadh	
Future	1 tógfad	tógfamaoid
	2 tógfair	tógfaidh sibh
	3 tógfaidh sé	tógfaid
	Impersonal tógfar	Relative thógfas
Conditional	1 thógfainn	thógfamaois
	2 thógfá	thógfadh sibh
	3 thógfadh sé	thógfadaois
	Impersonal thógfaí	
Imperative	1 tógam	tógamaois
	2 tóg	tógaidh
	3 tógadh sé	tógadaois
	Impersonal tógtar	

The range of forms given here represents the maximum system of morphological variants, a system only found in a number of dialects of Munster Irish. In the other dialects the various personal endings have been replaced in varying degrees by personal pronouns separate from the verb, giving the distinction between synthetic and analytic verbal forms. The paradigm of the verb *bheith* 'to be', which is used as an auxiliary verb in various aspectual constructions, is given in table 18.2, and shows an additional tense in the form of a present habitual, a system which has been widely adopted in various Hiberno-English dialects.

The major differences between the conjugational forms of the irregular verbs and the regular paradigm lies in the use of different roots in order to form at least some of the various tenses. Generally speaking, these differences have their origins in the massive series of morphological simplifications which affected the language during the course of the Middle Irish period, simplifications which were only partially carried through in the case of the irregular verbs. In addition to the use of different roots, another important difference

Table 18.2. *Morphology of 'bheith' 'to be' (only 3rd singular forms are given)*

	Absolute	Dependent (used after preverbal particles)
Present	tá	fuil
Habitual	bíonn	bíonn
Imperfect	bhíodh	bíodh
Past	bhí	raibh
Future	beidh	beidh
Conditional	bheadh	beadh

is found in the distinction between absolute and conjunct verbal forms, where the former is used in the absence of any preverbal particle. For example, in the conjugation of the verb *téigh* 'go' we have: *chuaigh mé* 'I went', *an deachaidh tú?* 'did you go?', *rachaidh sé* 'he will go'.

Nouns and adjectives

Within the classical description of the paradigm the noun is declined for four cases in both singular and plural – nominative, genitive, dative and vocative. However, as illustrated in table 18.3, the actual patterns of morphological differentiation are somewhat simpler than might be suggested by the traditional description. In general, the changes involve the opposition between neutral and palatalized consonants in word-final position to indicate case-marking in the singular, with plurals showing in the main the addition of various plural morphs or morph combinations to the singular form. In addition to these final changes, there is also the possibility of various initial mutations – lenition, nasalization or *h*-provection – affecting both the noun and any following adjectives (see below, under 'Initial mutations'). Table 18.3 gives paradigms of article + noun + adjective phrases for a number of different combinations of genders and declensional types.

There are various plural morphs in the language. With masculine first declension nouns (corresponding to Indo-European *o*-stems or the Latin second declension in -*us*), the nominative and prepositional case plurals are formed by palatalizing the final consonant of the word (genitive plural is identical to the nominative singular). In the other declensions plurals are usually formed by the addition of a morph or morphs, which represent the modern reflexes of earlier consonantal (as opposed to vocalic) stem plurals. In a number of instances these modern morphs may represent a combination of several distinct earlier morphs. In general, different dialect areas tend to favour particular plural formatives as productive morphs, for example:

Table 18.3. *Some examples of noun and adjective declension in Irish*

	Singular	Plural
Nominative	an fear mór	na fir mhóra
Genitive	an fhir mhóir	na bhfear mór
Prepositional	an fhear mhór	na fir mhóra
	an fear mór 'the big man' (masc.)	
Nominative	an bratach dubh	na bratacha dubha
Genitive	an bhrataigh dhuibh	na mbratach dubh
Prepositional	an bhratach dhubh	na bratacha dubha
	an bratach dubh 'the black flag' (masc.)	
Nominative	an fhuinneog bheag	na fuinneogaí beaga
Genitive	na fuinneoige bige	na bhfuinneogaí beaga
Prepositional	an fhuinneoig bhig	na fuinneogaí beaga
	an fhuinneog bheag 'the little window' (fem.)	
Nominative	an toitín fada	na toitíní fada
Genitive	an toitín fhada	na dtoitíní fada
Prepositional	an toitín fhada	na toitíní fada
	an toitín fada 'the long cigarette' (masc.)	
Nominative	an léine gheal	na léinte geala
Genitive	na léine gile	na léinte geala
Prepositional	an léine ghil	na léinte geala
	an léine gheal 'the white shirt'	

fuinneog 'window'	pl. *fuinneogaí*
ubh 'egg'	pl. *uibheacha* or *uibhe*
braon 'a drop'	pl. *braonta*
bratach 'flag'	pl. *bratacha*

Pronouns

The pronominal system is outlined in table 18.4, showing for a number of persons a distinction between subject and object forms. The distinction between *muid* and *sinn* in the first person plural is a matter of dialect only, with *muid* being the usual northern version. The superscript letters with the possessive adjectives indicate the type of initial mutation which follows each (see below for a fuller discussion). The particles given under the heading of 'emphatic forms' represent suffixes which normally appear as clitics to personal endings in verbs and prepositional pronouns. In addition, they may also occur as suffixes to nouns or noun phrases, in combination with possessive adjectives, e.g. *mo chat-sa* 'my cat', *a n-athair mór-san* 'their grandfather'. As suffixes to the personal pronouns these emphatic particles give rise to forms which may be used either for simple emphasis, for contrastive purposes, or in

Table 18.4. *Pronominal system of Irish*

			Singular	Plural
Subject	1		mé	muid/sinn
	2		tú	sibh
	3	masc.	sé	siad
		fem.	sí	
Object	1		mé	muid/sinn
	2		thú	sibh
	3	masc.	é	iad
		fem.	í	
Possessive	1		mo^L	ár^N
	2		do^L	bhur^N
	3	masc.	a^L	a^N
		fem.	a^H	
Emphatic				
(a) suffixed	1		-sa	-ne
	2		-sa	-sa
	3	masc.	-san	-san
		fem.	-sa	
(b) subject	1		mise	muidinne/sinne
pronouns	2		tusa	sibhse
	3	masc.	seisean	siadsan
		fem.	sise	
(c) object	1		mise	muidinne/sinne
pronouns	2		thusa	sibhse
	3	masc.	eisean	iadsan
		fem.	ise	
Prepositional	1		orm	orainn
	2		ort	oraibh
	3	masc.	air	orthu
		fem.	uirthi	

order to form independent pronouns which appear when no verb is present. One example is also given of pronominal combinations with prepositions, in this case with *ar* 'on'.

Initial mutations

As indicated in table 18.4, three types of initial mutation are found in Irish (see also chapter 15). Of these, the most widespread is lenition (or, in traditional terminology, aspiration = L), followed by nasalization (or eclipsis = N) and with h-provection (prefixing /h/ to an initial vowel = H) the least common. Historically, the system of mutations has changed little since the period of Old Irish, with the exception of h-provection which in the earlier period caused gemination of certain initial consonants in addition to the effects on initial vowels. In general these mutations must be interpreted as triggered by the word (including its grammatical specifications of case and gender) immediately preceding the word in which the initial mutation actually occurs. In diachronic terms the mutations are the result of purely phonological processes which appear in word-internal position (e.g. normal historical consonantal lenition phenomena) also being allowed to operate as sandhi phenomena across certain close junctures (e.g. preverb + verb, article + noun + adjective or possessive pronoun + noun). Synchronically the initial mutations must be taken as having a number of diverse origins. Thus they may be introduced lexically where, for instance, the particle *a* /ə/, may be /əL/, /əH/ or /əN/, representing 'his', 'her' and 'their', respectively. Other examples of this category are the preverbal interrogative particle *an* /əN/ or the negative particle *ní* /N'iːL/. These types of lexically introduced 'intrinsic' mutations cover the category of h-provection and most of the examples of nasal mutation. Although some occurrences of lenition are to be included here, a number appear as the result of the operation of various derivation rules in the syntax. Thus, in the noun phrase, with the noun as the dominating category, the feature of lenition is introduced in the singular with the feminine nominative, the genitive masculine and in the prepositional case of both genders with definite article. From the noun head, the /L/ is then transferred to a preceding article and to any following adjectives by means of concord rules within the noun phrase, for example:

/boː/	[+ fem] 'a cow'	→ /boːL/
/ə/	definite article	→ /əL/ article + feminine noun
/moːr/	'big'	→ /moːrL/ 'big' [+ fem]
/duh/	'black'	→ /duhL/ 'black' [+ fem]

hence:

/əL + boːL + moːrL + duhL
[ə   voː   voːr   ɣuh]

'the big black cow' where, in the absence of a suitable environment (i.e. no furthur following adjectives), the /L/ of /duhL/ is simply dropped.

Phonology

Syllable and word structure

The phonemic inventory of the language is given in table 18.5 and shows an almost complete parallel series of neutral and palatalized consonantal segments (see also chapter 8), together with a fairly small number of vowels, though the phonetic realizations of these latter do show wide allophonic

Table 18.5. *Phoneme inventory of Irish*

	Labial	Dental/Alveolar	Palatal/Velar	Glottal
		Consonants		
Stops	p p′	t t′	k k′	
	b b′	d d′	g g′	
Fricatives	f f′	s s′	x x′	h h′
	v v′	— —	ɣ ɣ′	
Nasals	m m′	N N′ n n′	ŋ ŋ′	
Laterals		L L′ l l′		
Trills		R r r′		

Vowels

iː i		u uː	
	ə əː		
eː e		o oː	
	aː a		

Diphthongs

ia   ua

variations. There is no accepted standard pronunciation of Irish and the system indicated here can be regarded as a maximal one which is subject to various simplifications in the individual dialects. For instance, the opposition between unlenited and lenited laterals and dental nasals has been almost completely lost in Munster dialects and appears to be undergoing rapid decay in a number of Donegal dialects, though the resulting simplifications are not necessarily the same in the two areas.

The structure of the syllable is indicated in table 18.6, showing generally a pattern of increasing openness as one moves through the onset towards the peak and corresponding decreasing openness through the coda. The only exception in onset clusters is found with the combinations of /s/ followed by a stop (with neutralization of the voiced – voiceless distinction in the stop in this position) and with these should probably also be put the cluster /sm-/ which tends to behave more like a combination of /s/ plus a stop than /s/ followed by a continuant. There are also certain restrictions within the syllable structure insofar as the combination of a long vowel (but not necessarily a diphthong) followed by a long consonant (e.g. /L, N, R, m, ŋ, p, t, k/) is concerned. It would appear to be the case that the basic syllabic unit can be either long or short, with the exponents of length being found either in the nucleus or in the coda.

Words can consist of up to four syllables, with disyllables being the most common; compared with English, there are relatively few monosyllabic words.

Table 18.6. *Basic syllable structure of Irish*

$$S \Rightarrow (C_1)\,(C_2)\,(C_3)V_1\,(V_2)\,(C_4)\,(C_5)$$

	C_1	C_2	C_3
(a) *Onset*	s	$\left\{\begin{matrix}p\\k\end{matrix}\right\}$ t	$\left\{\begin{matrix}1\\r\end{matrix}\right\}$ r
	s	$\left\{\begin{matrix}p\\t\\k\\l\\t\\m\\n\end{matrix}\right\}$	—
	—	$\left\{\begin{matrix}p\\t\\k\\b\\d\\g\\f\end{matrix}\right\}$	$\left\{\begin{matrix}1\\r\end{matrix}\right\}$
	—	$\left\{\begin{matrix}t\\k\\g\\m\end{matrix}\right\}$	n

Single C = any consonant from table 18.5 with the exception of /x, x′, ɣ, ɣ′, n, n′, h, h′/

(b) *Nucleus* V_1V_2: any vowel short or long ($V_2 =$ /ː/) or diphthong from table 18.5

	C_4	C_5
(c) *Coda*	r	$\left\{\begin{matrix}p\\t\\k\\b\\d\\g\\m\\n\end{matrix}\right\}$
	l	$\left\{\begin{matrix}p\\t\\k\\b\\g\\m\end{matrix}\right\}$
	Homorganic nasal + s	$\left\{\begin{matrix}p\\t\\k\end{matrix}\right\}$
	x	t

Single C = any consonant from table 18.5

In general, word stress falls on the initial syllable, though in Munster dialects it may be attracted to a non-initial long syllable, where the first syllable is not itself long.

In the matter of phonetic and phonological symbolization, most dialect studies of Irish have used either the system of Sweet or that of the IPA. Some peculiarly Irish modifications of the international system are to be found in the use of the upper case letters /L, N, R/ to represent 'strong' or unlenited varieties of these sounds, and in the appearance of the symbol /'/ following a consonant to represent a palatalized variety, with the neutral consonant being unmarked.

Neutral and palatalized consonants

The articulatory phonetic realizations of the underlying feature of palatalization vary with the point of primary articulation involved, but in the main palatalization involves some movement of the body of the tongue in the direction of the palate. With articulatory retiming, this action of the tongue may be separated out from the primary segmental articulation to appear as a following segment [j]. This is particularly true of the labials, which in most dialects of the language now show a j-glide (or a full segment) to a following back vowel, with complete loss of the distinctive palatalization within the segment itself. With the velars, palatalization is realized by means of a shift in the point of primary articulation, from a true velar for the neutral consonant to a palato-velar for the palatalized variety. In the dental stops, we find a distinction between a blade dental with fairly velarized articulation for the neutral, and a blade alveolar stop, usually accompained by an affricated off-glide, as the realization of the palatalized segment. With /s/ and /s'/ the distinction is between a blade dental [s] with neutral tongue position behind the primary articulation and a blade dental variety with a secondary articulation of palatalization. In the dental lateral and nasal the distinction is carried by the difference between dental (or alveolar) segments for the neutral consonants and palatal or alveo-palatal with the palatalized members. In terms of phonological interpretation, there is some argument as to whether the glottal fricative can be considered to show both neutral and palatalized varieties. In my opinion, northern dialects can be most reasonably interpreted as having both /h/ and /h'/, with the phonetic realizations of the palatalized variety tending to show the presence of an i-like segment intercalated before the [h'], in close parallel to the occurrence of j-like off-glides from palatalized labials mentioned above.

Lenition

The sets of neutral radical and mutated initial segments are given in table 18.7 (the same general patterns of change applying, *mutatis mutandis*, to the corresponding palatalized consonants). Of these initial mutations, the most widespread is lenition, both in terms of the number of consonants affected and

Table 18.7. *Initial mutations in Irish*

Radical															
Orthographic		p	t	c	b	d	g	m	n	l	r	s	f		Vowel
Phonemic	/	p	t	k	b	d	g	m	N	L	R	s	f			/
Lenition																
Orthographic		ph	th	ch	bh	dh	gh	mh	n	l	r	sh	fh	—		—
Phonemic	/	f	h	x	v	ɣ	ɣ	ṽ	n	l	r	h	∅	—		/
Nasalization																
Orthographic		bp	dt	gc	mb	nd	ng	—	—	—	—	—	—	bhf	n-Vowel	
Phonemic	/	b	d	g	m	N	ŋ	—	—	—	—	—	—	v	n	/
h-provection																
Orthographic		—	—	—	—	—	—	—	—	—	—	—	—	—	h-Vowel	

of the syntactic environments in which it occurs. For the stops, the change is one which takes the segment to the corresponding homorganic fricative, apart from the dentals, which show lenited varieties which are fricative but shifted as regards point of articulation. In historical terms, this is an innovation in the language, with the modern spelling still showing the historical forms with, presumably, dental fricatives to represent /t, d/ under lenition. The further development of these to the modern realizations can be taken as extensions of lenition where the articulatory information in the oral cavity has been deleted, leaving only the glottal fricative to represent the de-articulated [θ], on a par with the change of [t] to a glottal stop in a number of dialects of English. The corresponding voiced dental fricative, which would have given a voiced glottal fricative under this scenario, has now become indistinguishable from the voiced velar fricative, as the articulatorily closest fricative to the, relatively unusual, presumed target of the voiced glottal fricative. A similar change is found with the lenition of /s/ appearing as [h], where once again the supra-glottal information has been deleted to leave only the glottal fricative as the exponent of the lenited segment.

The lenited varieties of the dental laterals and nasals are perhaps the most interesting in that they involve a number of articulatory adjustments. The area of contact between the articulators in the primary articulation is reduced for the lenited segments – thus a dental becomes an alveolar segment and a palatal, or alveo-palatal, is weakened to an alveolar. In addition, the secondary articulations are made more open: with the neutral segments, a relatively high back tongue position in the unlenited varieties is opened to a much more neutral secondary articulation behind the primary closure. With the palatalized consonants, we again find that the secondary articulation is opened from a high front position to a much lower front colour. It seems likely that we are seeing in these a vocalic parallel to the de-articulation of [θ] discussed above, in that the resulting glottal fricative bears the same relationship to fully articulated consonants as the neutral vowel does to those vowels with full colour.

Long syllables

In the historical development of the language, long syllables consisting of a short vowel followed by a long lateral or nasal consonant have shown a number of interrelated developments. Basically these have involved some transfer of the syllabic length from the consonant in the coda, either into the preceding nucleus, with the development of a long vowel or diphthong or, where the syllable ended in a cluster containing a liquid, the length may be written out in an epenthetic vowel intercalated between the consonants of the coda cluster to give a new phonetic disyllable. Synchronically the language is divided between dialects in the southern part of the country which show this diphthongization or lengthening, and dialects which preserve the older system with a short vowel and long consonant (mainly Donegal Irish, though even in Donegal there appears to exist a strong tendency for a movement in the direction of transfer of the length from the coda to the nucleus). On the other hand, the development of an epenthetic vowel has affected more or less all dialects equally, with the only exceptions being in some of the more north-eastern parts of the country. It seems reasonable to link such re-assignments of length with the relative syllabicity of the consonantal segments involved, and on this basis, though the evidence from Irish is sparse (Scottish Gaelic dialects give a much clearer picture in this matter), we must posit the order /R/, /L/, /N/ and /m/ for decreasing syllabicity. Additionally, there is evidence from another part of the phonology – the lenition rules affecting the first member of an initial cluster – which would suggest that the segment /m/ is to be taken as more on a par with the stops than with the other liquids.

Variation

Regional variation

Due to the increasing fragmentation and disintegration of the *Gaeltacht* communities over the past two hundred years, and to the lack of any sort of widely accepted central educational standardization, present-day dialects of Irish present a picture of marked regional variation, even within a comparatively small area. This is most obvious in the phonetics and phonology, and also in the lexicon, whereas differences in the morphology and syntax are much less marked. A major distinction can be drawn between dialects of Munster Irish on the one hand and those of Connacht and Ulster on the other. Within the northern group of dialects, the most obvious re-partition is between dialects of Connacht and of Ulster Irish. The presumption is that the earlier boundary between these two major areas would have roughly divided the country in two on a line from Dublin to Galway, though any serious attempt to try to locate isogloss patterns accurately is no longer possible given the current situation of the language with its isolated ilots surrounded by a sea of English speech. Usually the best that can be done is to examine fairly large-scale patterns of differentiation, and attempt by reasonable extrapolation to relate these to presumed earlier states within a more flourishing linguistic community.

In the realm of phonology, the most striking difference between the two major dialect areas lies in the patterns of word-stress. Northern dialects, in common with Scottish Gaelic, preserve the (presumed) historical situation where (with very few exceptions) every word which can appear as a citation form is stressed on the first syllable. In Munster and some South Connacht dialects certain polysyllables ending in a long vowel (or in -*(e)ach*) show stress on the long syllable, providing the first syllable of the word is short. However this pattern of word-stress may be affected by sandhi effects of phrase stressing to shift the stress back to the initial syllable, e.g. *cailín* /ka'l′iːn′/ 'girl' but *cailín mór* /ˌkal′iːn′ 'moːr/ 'a big girl'. Within the northern dialect area, the Irish of Connacht appears to have best preserved the historical system with initial stress and with original long vowels in unstressed syllables receiving full length. In Ulster dialects there appears to be a cline of increasing quantitative and qualitative reduction of unstressed historically long vowels as one moves from the south-west of the province to the north and east, until we find dialects of East Ulster which appear to have reduced all unstressed vowels in closed syllables to a schwa.

In the morphological sphere the chief differences are between those Munster dialects which show morphologically complex verbal forms with subject endings, and more northern dialects, which generally have separate subject pronouns. It has been estimated that West Munster dialects make use of 34 different verbal forms where Donegal dialects use only about half that number (O'Rahilly, 1972: 219). In addition, particular dialect areas tend to favour one type of plural morpheme over another, though there are no absolute and clear-cut rules to cover usages here.

In addition to the above, there is considerable variation in the non-core lexicon, although it is not possible in the present state of dialect studies to provide any more than this impressionistic statement of the situation.

Age differentiation

The differences between the speech of the younger generation and that of their parents and, even more so, of their grandparents, are very obvious and, on casual observation, would appear to have become even more marked in the course of the past twenty or thirty years. Given the massive adstratum effects of the English language upon Irish, particularly over the past century, it is not surprising that English lexis for new ideas and technologies has been taken over wholesale. However, in addition to this, use of English has spread into areas of the language where there exist common and, one would have thought, readily available native equivalents. The reasons for this are presumably to be sought in the bilingual *milieu* in which every Irish speaker exists, with the constant presence of the media and the surrounding English-speaking world.

As most traditional dialect studies of Irish have tended to look for their informants to the oldest stratum of conservative speakers, contrasts with the younger generations made on the basis of such studies are even more marked than they might otherwise be. A recent small study of a dialect of Donegal Irish (Ó Dochartaigh, 1982) has revealed interesting patterns of inter-generational differentiation which can be correlated, to some degree, with isogloss patterns of geographical differentiation within Ulster as a whole. Moreover, the apparent rate of change in the language, as seen through the viewpoint of the artificial time depth provided by the study, shows an increase as one moves down through the generations.

BIBLIOGRAPHY

There is no grammar of Modern Irish available in English. A useful and detailed teaching course with accompanying grammatical materials is Ó Siadhail (1980) and for those with some acquaintance with the language Ó Huallacháin and Ó Murchú (1976) provides a convenient reference grammar. On morphology, Lucas (1979) is a detailed study of one particular Donegal Irish dialect organized on fairly 'traditional' linguistic lines, and Wigger (1970) provides a generative approach to noun morphology in a Conamara dialect. A transformational treatment of a fairly wide range of topics in syntax and semantics is provided by Stenson (1981), and McCloskey (1979) treats in detail of the syntax of relative and interrogative structures in Irish, together with a formal statement of the syntax of these in terms of a Montague grammar.

Initial mutations have been extensively studied, both from the phonological point of view and as regards their position within the grammar of the language – see Hamp (1951), Oftedal (1962), Cram (1975) and Ó Dochartaigh (1979, 1980 with the references noted therein). On the question of palatalized segments, particularly labials, see Jackson (1967) and Gleasure (1968).

Regional variation is dealt with extensively in various dialect monographs – there is no comprehensive listing available, though dialect materials have been published in varying formats for most dialect areas. The *Linguistic atlas and survey of Irish dialects* (Wagner, 1958–69) is an atlas based on a non-structuralist approach to the dialects. For a generative approach to some aspects of dialectal variation see Ó Murchú (1969) and for an extended Transformational Generative phonology (in Irish) see Ó Siadhail and Wigger (1975). Two excellent dictionaries are available – De Bhaldraithe (1959, English-Irish) and Ó Dónaill (1977, Irish-English).

Cram, D. F. 1975. Grammatical and phonological conditioning of initial mutations in Scottish Gaelic. *Leuvense Bijdragen* 64: 363–75.
De Bhaldraithe, T. 1959. *English-Irish dictionary*. Dublin: Stationery Office.

Gleasure, J. 1968. Consonant quantity in Irish and a problem of segmentation. *Studia Celtica* 3: 79–87.

Hamp, E. P. 1951. Morphophonemics of the Keltic mutations. *Language* 27: 230–47.

Jackson, K. 1967. Palatalisation of labials in the Gaelic languages. In W. Meid (ed.) *Beiträge zur Indogermanistik und Keltologie*. Innsbruck. pp. 179–92.

Lucas L. W. 1979. *Grammar of Ros Goill Irish, Co. Donegal*. Belfast: Institute of Irish Studies.

McCloskey, J. 1979. *Transformational syntax and model theoretic semantics*. Dordrecht: D. Reidel.

Ó Dochartaigh, C. 1979. Lenition and dependency phonology. *Éigse* 17: 457–94.

—— 1980. Aspects of Celtic lenition. In J. M. Anderson and C. J. Ewen (eds.) *Studies in dependency phonology*. Ludwigsburg Studies in Language and Linguistics. pp. 103–38.

—— 1982. Generational differences in Donegal Irish. *Belfast Working Papers in Language and Linguistics* 6: 67–103.

Ó Dónaill, N. 1977. *Foclóir Gaeilge Béarla*. Dublin: Stationery Office.

Ó Huallacháin, C. and Ó Murchú, M. 1976. *Irish grammar*. Coleraine: New University of Ulster.

Ó Murchú, M. 1969. Common core and underlying forms. *Ériu* 21: 42–75.

O'Rahilly, T. F. 1972. *Irish dialects past and present*. Dublin: Institute for Advanced Studies. Reprinted from 1932 publication.

Ó Siadhail, M. 1980. *Learning Irish*. Dublin: Institute for Advanced Studies.

Ó Siadhail, M. and Wigger, A. 1975. *Córas fuaimeanna na Gaeilge*. Dublin: Institute for Advanced Studies.

Oftedal, M. 1962. A morphemic evaluation of the Celtic initial mutations. *Lochlann* 2: 92–102.

Stenson, N. 1981. *Studies in Irish syntax*. Tübingen: Gunter Narr.

Wagner, H. 1958–69. *Linguistic atlas and survey of Irish dialects*. 4 vols. Dublin: Institute for Advanced Studies.

Wigger, A. 1970. *Nominalformen in Conamara-irischen*. Hamburg: Hardmutd Lüdke.

19

Manx

R. L. THOMSON

Introduction

Manx is one of three Celtic languages of the Goidelic group (see chapter 15). It was introduced into the Isle of Man, then probably Brythonic-speaking, by the fourth-century Irish expansion into Britain, and it seems that it took root there successfully, as in Scotland, and became the majority language of the island. Attempts have been made to demonstrate, on toponymic evidence, that it was extinguished or reduced to negligible importance during the period of Norse overlordship (tenth century to mid-thirteenth century), and that its dominant position until the end of the eighteenth century was the result of a reintroduction from the adjoining mainland of Galloway; but the balance of scholarly opinion inclines to favour continuity from the first introduction.

Apart from Irish, the Goidelic group is poorly attested until the sixteenth century, but reconstruction suggests an almost uniform development for all the branches until the thirteenth century, followed by a further period of parallel development in Scottish Gaelic and Manx from the thirteenth century to the fifteenth.

Continuous text in Manx in contemporary manuscripts begins only in the seventeenth century, and during the nineteenth and twentieth centuries the language has been undermined by bilingualism; the language described in this chapter is that of the Classical period, the eighteenth century (see also chapters 10 and 15). Comparison with early Scottish Gaelic suggests that after their separation the evolution of Manx was more rapid, and that this was encouraged by the social and political factors which cut Manx off from the conservative influence of the Irish literary tradition and the form of language that conveyed it. Throughout its short attested history Manx has been notable for the variety of alternative constructions available for the same purpose, a variety which reflects an historical series of innovations, but one in which the new does not entirely displace the old, but rather may limit its scope to some degree, and which writers exploit to avoid repetition. Hence the appearance of some degree of complication in the following account, though the language is the most evolved of all the Celtic languages in the direction of formal simplicity. Its analytic tendency (apart from the verbal system, for

306

which see below) is most marked in the number of verbs composed with prepositions, e.g. *cur* 'give, put, send', *cur er* 'cause', *cur gys* 'add', *cur lesh* 'bring'; and of verb + noun + preposition groups, e.g. *cur fys er* 'send for', *cur graih da* 'love'.

Orthography

Separation from the Irish tradition caused Manx to be written not in the Gaelic orthography but in a system based on Middle and Early Modern English conventions, broken (and then only in part) by the spelling adopted in the 1610 translation of the *Book of Common Prayer*, in which the simple vowels have 'continental' values – a practice which contemporary criticism suggests was an unwelcome innovation. The English conventions mean that the radical and lenited or nasalized consonants lack the visible connection shown in Gaelic spelling, but the spelling has the advantage for the linguistic historian of showing the vocalization of fricatives and such new developments as svarabhakti vowels, and lengthening or diphthonging in monosyllables before unlenited liquids and nasals when these are not shown in the traditional orthography. The system is rather weak on the indication of palatalization, though better in this respect than the similar nonstandard orthography of Scottish Gaelic, based on Middle Scots usage. The conventions of English and Manx orthography have, however, grown apart, and it by no means follows that Manx pronunciation is immediately apparent to the English reader. The spelling, moreover, has developed an iconic element, in that words of similar or identical pronunciation but different meaning are as far as possible deliberately spelt differently.

Syntax

The normal order of elements in the simple sentence and in the clauses of a complex sentence is Verb + Subject + Direct Object + Indirect Object; adverbial elements are more mobile and may occur at the beginning or the end of this series, or within the verb itself when it is complex (see page 309). The verb is in absolute initial position only in isolated affirmative single-clause sentences; otherwise it is preceded by co-ordinating conjunctions, the negative, interrogative and similar particles and, in subordinate clauses, by the various subordinating conjunctions. The placing of other elements in initial position in the clause is a stylistic or rhetorical variant, except in the case of interrogatives, which always take position before the verb.

   With the substantive verb the normal order is Verb + Subject + Complement (e.g. adjective, prepositional phrase, adverb); when used absolutely without predicate, the predicate position is filled by the 3rd singular masculine prepositional pronoun *ayn* 'in it'. The indefinite predicate noun appears generally with the substantive verb, the predicate being preceded by a combination of the preposition 'in' and the appropriate possessive personal pronoun, 1st sing. *my*, 2nd sing. *dty*, 3rd sing. *ny*, pl. *nyn* (e.g. *t'eh ny ghareyder* 'he's a gardener'). With the copula (which, apart from its primary functions of emphasis and in the formation of compared adjectives, is much less used and lacks a full range of tense-forms), the order is Verb + Complement + Subject. In the affirmative present (but not elsewhere) the copula is omitted before a demonstrative or personal pronoun, though not in the earliest period. Zero copula is also found, though with declining frequency, when two nominal groups are equated.

In the absence of words corresponding to 'yes' and 'no', an affirmative or negative response is conveyed by repeating the verb of the question in the affirmative or negative in its minimal form, i.e. in a simple verb, without subject pronoun, and in a complex verb, by repetition of the corresponding minimal form of the auxiliary.

Subordinate clauses are introduced by their various conjunctions, some of which are followed by simple or relative verb-forms, e.g. *my* 'if', *tra* 'when', *derrey* 'till'; others by dependent forms, e.g. *dy* 'that', *nagh* 'that not', either alone or as the final element in phrasal conjunctions such as *er-yn-oyr dy* 'because'.

Relative clauses observe a division into proper (or direct) relatives, in which the relative is nominative or accusative, and improper (or indirect) relatives, in which the relative is an oblique case. In direct relative clauses the affirmative form of the relative is zero for almost all purposes, and the negative form is *nagh*. In indirect relative clauses in which the relative is governed by a preposition the appropriate form of the pronominal preposition is used, either before the verb or at the end of the relative clause, with zero affirmative relative particle, negative *nagh*. When the relative is genitive, the appropriate possessive occurs in the relative clause.

Noun phrase

The subject and objects and many adverbs and prepositions may be formally noun phrases: the sequence of elements in the noun phrase is preposition + article or possessive + numeral + adjectival prefix + noun + adjective modifier + adjective + demonstrative. There is a definite article only; the numeral may be split, part before and part immediately after the noun; the adjectival prefixes are few: *ard-* 'high, chief', *drogh-* 'bad', *reih-* 'choice', *shenn-* 'old'; the adjective modifiers are also limited: *feer* 'very', *lane* 'quite', *ro* 'too'; the demonstratives, in three degrees of proximity: *shoh* 'this', *shen* 'that', *shid* 'yon', require the article before the noun; an alternative to the possessive particles before the noun is the article before and the appropriate person of the preposition *ec* after, e.g. *my hie*, or *yn thie aym* 'my house'. In addition to definite or previously mentioned nouns the article is used with some abstracts; it is not used with a noun upon which another noun, definite or indefinite, depends in the genitive (which may be marked by mutation or inflection or be totally indistinguishable from the nominative), e.g. *jerrey'n skeeal* 'the end of the story', *jerrey skeeal* 'the end of a story'. The noun itself, the only indispensable element, exemplifies the noun phrase at its minimum extent; its function may be filled alternatively by a pronoun or a noun clause.

Verb phrase

The verb phrase similarly may be a single item (the least common situation), or else a phrase in which the verbal form conveys the tense but the person is indicated by a pronoun, or in which the tense is conveyed by an auxiliary verb. The inherited distinction between independent and dependent verbal forms is well preserved in the auxiliaries and in the small group of irregular verbs, but only slightly in the regular verb.

Inflected tenses are the future (the dependent of which also functions as present subjunctive), the conditional or past subjunctive, the preterite, and the imperative. The future 1st singular is inflected, *-ym*, the remaining persons have *-ee* (indep.), zero (dep.) with pronouns (1st pl. *mayd* only, not *shin*, see page 313, below); the relative form (otherwise always identical with the independent form) has *-ys*: e.g. 1st sing. *troggym* 'I'll lift', other persons *troggee* + *oo, eh, ee, mayd, shiu, ad*; dependent *cha droggym, cha drog* + *oo, eh*, etc.; relative *hroggys*. The conditional 1st sing. *-in*, the other persons *-agh* + pronouns (1st pl. *shin* only), with permanent lenition in the independent and nasalization in the dependent, e.g. 1st sing. *hroggin*, the other persons *hroggagh oo*, etc., dependent *cha droggin, cha droggagh oo*, etc. The preterite has no personal inflections, no independent–dependent contrast, and is permanently lenited, e.g. *hrog mee, oo*, etc., *cha hrog mee*, etc. The imperative exists in the 2nd person only, the singular with zero inflection, the plural with the suffix *-jee* (with some competition from *shiu*) e.g. *trog, trog-jee*; there are a few ambiguous traces of 1st pl. *-mayd*. In the 3rd signular and plural, and usually in the 1st plural, the corresponding construction is *lhig* 'allow, let' (always singular imperative in this context) + 3rd sing. masc. *da* 'to him', fem. *j'ee*, 1st pl. *dooin*, 3rd pl. *daue* + verbnoun, e.g. *lhig dooin troggal* 'let us lift'.

The auxiliary *ve* 'be' has inflected forms similar to those outlined above, i.e. future indep. 1st sing. *bee'm*, 1st pl. *beemayd*, all other persons *bee oo, eh*, etc., future dep. *cha bee'm* etc. (the nasal mutation in verbs affects only the voiceless consonants); conditional indep. 1st sing. *veign*, other persons *veagh oo*, etc., conditional dep. *cha beign, cha beagh oo*, etc.; preterite indep. *va mee, v'ou, v'eh*, etc., preterite dep. *cha row mee, cha r'ou, cha row eh*, etc.; imperative 2nd sing. *bee*, 2nd pl. *bee-jee*. In addition there is an uninflected present indep. *ta mee, t'ou, t'eh*, etc., and present dep. *cha vel mee, oo*, etc.

The present and preterite of *ve* are used to form the present and imperfect of other verbs by means of the preposition *ag 'at' (reduced to *g-* before vowels, and zero before consonants) and the verbnoun, e.g. *ta mee troggal* 'I lift, I am lifting', *v'ad troggal* 'they were lifting'. The perfect, future perfect, past conditional and pluperfect of the verb are formed with the preposition *er* in place of *ag and the present, future, conditional and preterite of *ve*, e.g. *t'eh er droggal* 'he has lifted', *tra veesmayd er droggal* 'when we (shall) have lifted', *dy beagh ad er droggal* 'if they had lifted', *dy row eh er droggal* 'that he had lifted'. All these tenses of the perfect series are found in frequent use.

The second auxiliary *jannoo* 'do', like *ve*, also has an independent existence. Future indep. 1st sing. *nee'm*, 1st pl. *neemayd*, other persons *nee oo, eh*, etc.; future dep. 1st sing. *cha jeanym*, 1st pl. *cha jeanmayd*, other persons *cha jean oo*, etc.; conditional indep. 1st sing. *yinnin*, other persons *yinnagh oo*, etc.; conditional dep. *cha jinnin, cha jinnagh oo*, etc.; preterite indep. and dep. *ren mee, oo*, etc.; imperative 2nd sing. *jean*, 2nd pl. *jean-jee*.

As an auxiliary *jannoo* provides a free alternative to the four inflected tenses, its own forms grammatically governing the verbnoun as their object, though in practice, except in the earliest period, the usage with auxiliary *ve* prevails and *g-* is prefixed to an initial vowel. Examples are: *nee'm troggal = troggym; nee eh girree = irree eh* 'he will rise'; *cha jinnagh eh troggal = cha droggagh eh; dy ren ad troggal = dy hrog ad; jean-jee troggal = trog-jee* (see above, page 309).

There is thus no compulsion to utilize the inflected tenses of any verb except the two auxiliaries, and the preference for this analytical form increases steadily to an almost exclusive use of it in late Manx; at all periods a few verbs seem not to form inflected tenses. Auxiliary *jannoo* may be used with *jannoo* itself (e.g. *nee'm jannoo = nee'm* 'I shall do'), but not with *ve*.

Only one inflected passive form survives, *ruggyr* 'is born', used also as a preterite. Otherwise the passive is an analytical construction combining auxiliary *ve* with the passive participle or its equivalent. The participle is formed with the suffix *-it* (sometimes *-t*); the equivalent, preferred in this construction in the early and middle period, consists of *er* + the appropriate possessive pronoun in concord with the subject (but tending to become fixed in the 3rd singular masculine form) + the verbnoun; e.g. *ta mee er my hroggal* 'I am lifted', future *bee oo er dty hroggal*, conditional *veagh eh er ny hroggal*, preterite *v'ee er ny troggal*, imperative *bee-jee er nyn droggal*. The perfect series: *va shin er ve er nyn droggal, bee shiu er ve* ... , *veagh ad er ve* ... , is less common, the present series being often an adequate replacement. An alternative construction uses the conjugation of *goll* 'go' + *er* + verbnoun, e.g. future 1st sing. *hem er troggal*, conditional 2nd sing. *ragh oo er troggal*, preterite 3rd sing. masc. *hie eh er troggal*, present 3rd sing. fem. *t'ee goll er troggal*, imperfect 1st pl. *va shin goll er troggal*; no imperative.

Nouns and adjectives

The traditional declensions according to stem-formations are reflected in Manx only in the contrast of two types of plural, by internal change, and by suffixation, the former continuing or imitating the *o*-stems, the latter the rest, occasionally with continuation of original consonant-stem formation as an infix before the common plural suffix -*yn*. There is only one common case in the plural, apart from vestiges of a genitive plural like the nominative singular (*o*-stems again) and of the dative plural in -*oo* in phrasal prepositions or adverbs; in the singular the nominative, accusative and dative have fallen together, generally under the old nominative, but sometimes under the old accusative or dative; the vocative is the common case, lenited. The genitive singular survives in a limited number of words, chiefly with the suffix -*ey* (*a*-, *i*-, and *u*-stems) and generally of the feminine gender, but occasionally masculine and formed by vowel change as in the plural, the largest group here being nouns in -*agh* and verbnouns in -*ey*, both with genitive in -*ee*. The genitive, however, is not used, even when it can be formally conveyed by inflection or mutation (see page 313), in all the contexts in which grammatical analysis suggests it is called for. A major exception here is the regimen of a verbnoun (see page 312), where the genitive is extremely rare in nouns, and then only by mutation, hardly ever by inflection. In general the genitive is used only in a traditional collocation such as *folt e ching* 'the hair of his head', or as an indefinite genitive in a quasi-adjectival function, as *siyn cloaie* 'stone vessels', *dooinney-mooinjerey* 'relative', and commonly in *fer* + genitive of a verbnoun to express an agent, as *fer-coonee* 'helper' (= person of helping), *fir-choyrlee* 'advisers' (= persons of counselling).

Nouns may be divided into two gender classes, masculine and feminine, of which the former is the unmarked, the latter the marked member of the pair, and nouns can effectively be regarded as masculine unless there is evidence to suggest they are not. The gender distinction appears in the 3rd person singular personal pronouns but discrepancies between these and other indicators of gender are frequent as the non-personal notion 'it' becomes indistinguishable from the masculine 'he' or 'him' in almost every instance.

Adjectives are normally invariable as to gender and case, and only a handful of common, mainly monosyllabic, adjectives optionally form a plural, invariably in -*ey*, in attributive use only. Adjectives in -*agh* and a few other *o*-stem types form a plural by vowel change, but only in nominal use, as *baccagh* 'lame, a lame person', *ny baccee* 'the lame', *marroo* 'dead, a dead person', *ny merriu* 'the dead'. The nominalized plural of other adjectives is expressed by attaching them (in the plural form if there is one) to plural or collective nouns, as *fir*, *deiney*; *sleih*, *mooinjer*, *feallagh*, *cloan*.

The inflection of adjectives for comparison is also restricted. The main indicator is the syntactical context, with inflection playing a much smaller and dispensable role. The syntactic framework is a relative clause introduced by the copula *s'* (rarely *by*) when attributive, or relative *ny* + copula when predicative, + adjective, usually without any modification of form except that adjectives in -*agh* generally substitute -*ee*, and some irregular comparatives occur. There is no distinction between comparative and superlative, the former being indicated when *na* 'than' follows, the latter when the noun qualified by the compared adjective is definite. Adverbs formed from adjectives prefix *dy* to the positive form; the compared adverb is the same as the predicative form of the adjective, except that in relative clauses the compared adverb may be replaced by the compared adjective attached to the antecedent, e.g. *yn fer share ren eh* 'the one who did it best' (instead of *yn fer ren eh ny share*).

Direct object

The varied structure of the verbal phrases (see pages 309–10) generates a variety of treatments of the direct object. (i) The simple verb treats nominal and pronominal objects alike, placing them after the verb and subject (inflection or pronoun), e.g. *hrog eh yn thie* 'he built the house', *hrog eh eh* 'he built it'. (ii) With auxiliary *ve* the order is as in (i) with a noun object, e.g. *v'eh troggal yn thie* 'he was building the house'; the pronoun object can choose an older construction *v'eh dy hroggal eh* (where *eh* supports the included pronoun in *dy* 'at its'), and similarly in the plural *dyn droggal ad* 'building them' (or *dy nyn droggal*, with re-analysis of *dyn* 'at their'), or it can choose the noun pattern *v'eh troggal eh*, which is the more common type. The alternative with *dy* is most common when the object precedes the verb either by rhetorical re-arrangement of the sentence, as *shoh ta mee dy ghra* 'this I say', or in relative clauses when the relative is accusative, as *cha vel mee toiggal ny t'eh dy ghra* 'I don't understand what he's saying'. In the perfect series of tenses both noun and pronoun follow the verbnoun (as *t'ad er droggal yn thie, t'ad er droggal eh*), except that in a relative clause when the object precedes, early Manx includes the object pronoun, as *shoh'n thie t'eh er ny hroggal* 'this is the house he has built' (lit. 'is after its building'). However the ambiguity with the more frequent *t'eh er ny hroggal* (see page 310) led to the disuse of this option when subject and object are of the same person; it continues most freely with objects of the 1st and 2nd singular, as *v'eh er my hroggal seose* 'he had lifted me up'. (iii) With auxiliary *jannoo* and other auxiliary verbs the noun object has the choice between position after the verbnoun or inclusion before it, as *nee eh troggal yn thie* or *nee eh yn thie y hroggal*; in a relative clause with preceding object the *y* is found as in the inclusive construction, e.g. *shoh'n thie ren eh y hroggal* 'this is the house he built'. The pronoun has three choices: (a) it may take the possessive form before the verbnoun, e.g. *ren eh y hroggal eh* (with supporting *eh* as in *v'eh dy hroggal eh* in (ii) above); this option is found chiefly in the 1st and 2nd singular, as *ren eh my hroggal seose* 'he lifted me up', less commonly in the other persons; (b) it may be included in the same way as the noun, e.g. *ren eh mee* (or *mish*) *y hroggal seose*, and this is very common; and (c) it may follow the verbnoun, e.g. *ren eh troggal eh*, the normal usage in the later period.

Pronouns

The personal pronouns occur in simple and emphatic forms, the latter used for emphasis, contrast, or as the antecedent of a relative clause: 1st sing. *mee*, *mish*, 2nd sing. *oo, uss*, 3rd sing. masc. *eh, eshyn*, 3rd sing. fem *ee, ish*; 1st pl. *shin, shinyn*, 2nd pl. *shiu, shiuish*, 3rd pl. *ad, adsyn*; these function both as subjects and direct objects. The possessive forms are: 1st sing. *my*, 2nd sing. *dty*, 3rd sing. *e* (masculine and feminine distinguished by mutation) 1st, 2nd and 3rd pl. *nyn*. With the simple prepositions the personal pronouns combine as seven inflections for person, e.g. 1st sing. *rhym* 'to me', 2nd sing. *rhyt*, 3rd sing. masc. *rish*, and fem. *r'ee*; 1st pl. *rooin*, 2nd pl. *riu*, 3rd pl. *roo*; in the phrasal prepositions the personal element is conveyed by the possessive forms, e.g. (*er*) *son* 'for', 1st sing. *er my hon*, 2nd sing. *er dty hon*, etc.

The suffixes added to the personal pronouns, above, to form the emphatic can also be added to the prepositional pronouns, for example, in *rhym's, rhyt's, rishyn, r'eeish, rooinyn, riuish, roosyn*; and the *'s* of the 1st and 2nd singular may be added to the nominal element in phrasal prepositions and to other nouns following the possessive, for example, in *er my hon's, ayns dty hie's* 'in your (sing.) house'; they are attached also to the verbal inflections of 1st singular and plural future, and 1st singular conditional, as in *-ym's, -in's*, while *-mayd* has emphatic *mainyn* and early Manx *meidjyn*. The demonstratives (see page 308) and the marker of identity *hene* 'self' may be attached to all the pronominal forms listed above (*hene* becomes *pene* after *-m*, as *rhym pene*). The demonstratives serve also as pronouns in the non-personal sense in the singular, but for the plural require the 3rd plural pronoun, as *ad shoh* 'these', *roo shen* 'to those'; *hene* following a possessive equates with 'own', as *my hie hene* 'my own house'. The imperatives do not take the suffixes and the emphatic forms are 2nd sing. *trog uss*, 2nd pl. *trog-jee shiuish*.

Mutation

Manx preserves the two inherited consonant mutations, lenition and nasalization; the third type, the prefixing of *h-* to a vowel, is fairly regularly shown in the oldest orthography but its indication thereafter becomes sporadic. Lenition – the shift of the voiceless stops (and *s, f*) to the corresponding fricatives or their further developments – is the commonest mutation. It occurs in nouns (except in dental consonants) after the singular article in the nominative or accusative of feminine nouns, the genitive of masculines, and the prepositional case of both genders; in the vocative (also adjectives), and in the genitive of proper names; after the possessive or object particles of the 1st, 2nd and 3rd person singular masculine, and elements containing them, and the prepositions *dy* 'to' (with verbnouns) and *dy* 'of'. In adjectives it occurs after a feminine singular noun and sometimes after a vowel-change plural. In verbs it is normal in relative future forms, in the preterite, and the independent conditional, and common in verbnouns after *er* 'after', as an alternative to the once universal nasalization.

Nasalization – the conversion of voiceless stops and *f* into the corresponding voiced sounds, of voiced stops to the corresponding nasals, and the

Table 19.1. *The consonant system of Manx*

		Labial	Dental	Velar
Voiceless stop:	neutral	p	t	k (c, k, q)
	palatal	[p′]	t′ (ch)	k′ (ki)
Voiced stop:	neutral	b	d	g
	palatal	[b′]	d′ (j)	g′ (gi)
Voiceless fricative:	neutral	f	—	x (ch-, -gh)
	palatal	[f′]	—	x′ (chi)
Voiced fricative:	neutral	v	ð (t, d, ss)	ɣ (gh)
	palatal	[v′]	—	ɣ′ (y, ghi)
Voiced nasal:	neutral	m	n	ŋ (n + velar)
	palatal	[m′]	n′ (ni)	ŋ′ (n + velar)

prefixing of *n-* to initial vowels – follows the plural possessive or objective particle and elements incorporating it, and occasionally occurs after the genitive plural of the article (with fossilized examples in place names). In verbs it affects only the voiceless sounds after a variety of particles, e.g. the zero sign of the interrogative, *cha* 'not', *dy* 'that', *nagh* 'that not', *mannagh* 'if not, unless', *my* 'before', *dy* (conditional) 'if', *dy* 'of those that'.

The prefixing of *h-* occurs in nouns after the genitive feminine singular and the plural of the article, and after the 3rd singular feminine possessive and elements containing it; less commonly it may be found in adjectives used as adverbs after the particle *dy*. As mutation rarely carries any semantic distinction (except 3rd singular possessive and some verbal forms) writers and speakers have increasingly neglected it.

Phonology

The consonant system is marked by the opposition between the neutral and palatal articulation of each consonant, though this contrast is largely lost in the labials. Most consonants also exhibit a contrast between voiceless and voiced, and between explosive and fricative articulation. This network of oppositions produces the system given in table 19.1 (spellings in round brackets). The absence of [θ] is to be explained historically by its falling in with [h], and [ð] originally fell in with [ɣ] both as neutral and palatal, but a new [ð] has been created by modified articulation of [t, d, s] in medial position in some words. In addition there are the voiced liquids /l, l′, r, r′/, the voiceless sibilants /s, s′/ and their voiced partners /z, z′/, the semivowels /j, w/ and the aspirate /h, h′/.

The distribution of some of these is limited: /f, v, ð, ɣ, x′/ do not occur in word-final position: /ð, z, z′/ do not occur in word-initial position, and /ɣ, ŋ, w, v, h/ do so only in mutation conditions or in loan-words, except that /h/

sometimes occurs in permanent lenition with no radical alternative. There has been a general tendency, probably since the second half of the eighteenth century, to relax the articulation of single intervocalic stops and fricatives and/or to voice them: hence /z/ from earlier /s/, /z′/ from /s′/ or /d′/, /ð/ from /t, d, s/, /ɣ/ from /x/; and a further tendency, at a somewhat later date, for these new /z′/ and /ɣ/ sounds to become /j/ and zero respectively. Most of these changes are not recognized by the orthography except in substandard spelling. The double opposition, unlenited–lenited, neutral–palatal, which produced four distinct *l*, *r* and *n* phonemes in earlier Gaelic, is in Manx reduced to the single opposition of neutral–palatal in each of the three, with a late tendency to neutralize even this contrast in the case of *r*; pre-consonantal and word-final *r* in recent times show a weakened articulation verging on loss.

Initial consonant groups consist of the unlenited consonants (and their lenited equivalents) followed by the two liquids, but the earlier clusters /kn, gn, tn, dl, tl/ fell in by the end of the seventeenth century with /kr, gr, tr, gl, kl/ and /mn/ became /mr/; while /kd/ (by syncope) also yields /kr/. The stops may be preceded by *s*, but in that event the voiceless–voiced contrast is neutralized, as shown by standard spelling *scoan* 'scarcely' (from *goaun*), and the occasional spellings *speg*, *stierree* beside etymological *s'beg* 'little' (does he know ... etc), *s'jerree* 'last'. In the group /s′t′/ the orthography has never indicated the palatal quality in both consonants; the older spelling *sch* marks it only in the second, while the standard *sht* does so only in the first. Original *sr* has fallen in with *str*; medial /sk, s′k′/ with some exceptions falls in with /st, s′t′/ by the beginning of the eighteenth century. Final /t/ tends to be lost after /s/ and /x/, the latter as early as the seventeenth century, the former perhaps during the eighteenth, though the standard spelling generally conserves both. The original length in unlenited *l*, *r*, *n*, *m* is, in monosyllables, transferred to the preceding vowel either as an increase in length or as a *u*-diphthong. Miscellaneous modifications include the development of a weak version of the corresponding voiced stop before final *m*, *n*, and *ŋ*, in stressed monosyllables, and the tendency of *g-* in proclitics to become *d-*, as *dy*, earlier *gy* 'that', *gys*, *dys* 'to', *gyn*, *dyn* 'without'.

The vowel system includes long and short vowels and diphthongs; long vowels and diphthongs are confined to stressed syllables and historically long vowels in unstressed syllables have become short or indeterminate. The vowels may be represented by figure 19.1. Of these /e/ and /o/ are only long (apart from occasional shortening), the remainder long or short; the quality of the long and short members of each pair is not necessarily identical. The vowels /a, ɛ, ə/ form both *i-* and *u*-diphthongs, /ɔ, u/ only *i*-diphthongs, while /i, u/ form *ə*-diphthongs. These last are inherited and subject to monophthonging in recent times; the *i-* and *u*-diphthongs, except in monosyllables before /l, r/ (see above), are the product of the vocalization of palatal and labial (sometimes also of dental) spirants; in monosyllables final /ɣ/ seems spontaneously to become /ɣ′/.

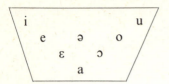

Figure 19.1. The vowel system of Manx

The vowels of unstressed words, and of the unstressed syllables of stressed words, are restricted to /ə, a, u, i/, of which the last is usually long and morphologically significant; the adjective and verbnoun suffix -agh(-) generally retains /a/ despite some early evidence for /əx/. Unstressed short pretonic and proclitic initial vowels have tended to disappear altogether, and long vowels in a similar position are generally shortened. The quantity of stressed syllables is generally historical but there is extensive lengthening of /a/ and /ɔ/ in monosyllables and in disyllables with open stressed syllable.

Stress

The normal position for the stress is on the first syllable in words that can be stressed. This usage is disturbed by various factors. (i) Derivative suffixes containing originally long vowels may attract the accent to themselves, as (nouns) -ane, -aag or -age or -eig, -eyr, and (verbnouns) -ail or -eil, with consequent shortening, not always shown in the spelling, of the root syllable. The reverse process obtains when the accent remains on the root and the vowel of the suffix is shortened to give (nouns) -an, -ag, (verbnouns) -al. (ii) The vocalization of labial spirants in medial position when the accent did not immediately follow (as in (i) above) produced long vowels by crasis in originally unstressed syllables to which the accent was attracted, as *thálloo*, genitive *thallóoin* (Gaelic *talamh*, *tal(a)mhain*) 'earth', *tarróogh* 'industrious, busy' (Gaelic *tar(a)bhach*), and the adjectival suffix -oil (Gaelic -amhail). (iii) Loan-words, in the first instance from Anglo-Norman, show final stress associated with length, as *vondéish* 'advantage, profit', *preachóor* 'preacher', and this element has been seen as the trendsetter imitated by native words with long syllables not originally under the accent; if so, the historical order of development would be (iii), (i), (ii).

FURTHER READING

Thomson, R. L. 1969. The study of Manx Gaelic. *Proceedings of the British Academy* 55: 177–210. A critique of the earlier scholarship, including the dictionaries of Cregeen (1835), Kelly (1866) and the grammars of Kelly (1804) and Kneen (1931).

HISTORICAL LINGUISTICS

O'Rahilly, T. F. 1932. *Irish dialects past and present*. Dublin: Institute for Advanced Studies (reprint 1972).

Thomson, R.L. 1960. Svarabhakti and some associated changes in Manx. *Celtica* 5: 116–26.

PHONOLOGY

Jackson, K.H. 1955. *Contributions to the study of Manx phonology.* Edinburgh: Nelson.
Thomson, R.L. 1976. The stressed vowel phonemes of a Manx idiolect. *Celtica* 11: 255–63.

EARLY TEXTS, IN CHRONOLOGICAL ORDER

Thomson, R.L. 1962–3. The Manx traditionary ballad. *Études celtiques* 9: 321–48; 10: 60–87.
Moore, A.W. and Rhŷs, J. 1893–4. *The Book of Common Prayer in Manx Gaelic* (1610, 1765). Douglas: The Manx Society.
Ifans, D. and Thomson, R.L. 1980. Edward Lhuyd's *Geirieu Manaweg* (*c.* 1700) *Studia Celtica* 14/15: 129–67.
Wilson, T. 1707. *The principles and duties of Christianity.* London. Bilingual. Reprint Menston, 1972.
Thomson, R.L. 1954–7. A glossary of early Manx (1610). *Zeitschrift für Celtische Philologie* 24: 272–307; 25: 100–40, 264–308; 27: 79–160.

PEDAGOGY

Goodwin, E. 1966. *First lessons in Manx.* 3rd rev. edn. Douglas: Yn Cheshaght Ghailckagh.
Thomson, R.L. 1981. *Lessoonyn sodjey 'sy Ghailck Vanninagh.* A linguistic commentary on the translations of St John's Gospel. Douglas: Yn Cheshaght Ghailckagh.

20

Gaelic

R. D. CLEMENT

Introduction

The 1981 Census reports 79,307 Gaelic speakers (1.6% of the population). Scottish Gaelic was once the language of the great majority of Scots. Under the first Gaelic kings of united Scotland, Duncan, Macbeth and Malcolm Canmore, it was probably spoken in every part of present mainland Scotland, though not, of course, by everyone. Until the sixteenth century it continued to be spoken by at least half the population. Thereafter it disappeared from the south-west of Scotland and from the lower-lying country of the east coast (Nicholson, 1974: 274).

Twenty years after the Education Act brought compulsory schooling in English, the 1891 Census reported 43,738 monoglot Gaelic speakers out of a Gaelic-speaking population of a quarter of a million, and even as late as 1951 it was still possible to collect Gaelic questionnaires or tapes from almost every parish within the old Highland Line – approximately the boundary of Gaelic speech and culture in 1746.

In 1981 the Gaelic-speaking communities are now mainly in the islands and on the western seaboard. Comhairle nan Eilean, the Western Isles regional authority set up after the 1974 reorganization of local government, has an avowed bilingual policy in education and public life. It remains to be seen whether this will be sufficient to stem the decline. The 1981 Census figures show very little decrease in the number of speakers in the Western Isles compared with 1971 (for more background, see Lockwood, 1975; Romaine and Dorian, 1981; Durkacz, 1983).

Phonology

Consonants

All dialects of Gaelic are characterized by a large inventory of phonemes, with the distinction palatalized versus neutral or velarized being universal. The number of phonemic distinctions made varies from dialect to dialect: this is particularly true of the liquids and nasals.

The stops of Gaelic are as follows:

p	t	t′	k	k′
pʰ	tʰ	t′ʰ	k′ʰ	kʰ

These are normally voiceless in all positions in the word, except after nasals. If we allow, for the purpose of minimal pairs, 'words' including the proclitic article, we may recognize a further series:

b   d   d′   g   g′

with full voicing. Of course, if the nasal of the article survives, these are only positional variants. In many dialects, at least for the conservative speakers, there may be a further series: /bʰ/ etc. (Ternes, 1973; Dorian, 1978) corresponding to the aspirated voiceless stops; in others, /b/ etc. is the nasal mutation of both the voiceless series.

Of the other stop phonemes, /t/ and /tʰ/ are dental; /t′/ and /t′ʰ/ are palatalized, and in many dialects strongly affricated: [t′ʃ] and [t′ʃʰ]; /k′/ and /k′ʰ/ are medio-palatal; /k/ and /kʰ/ are velar.

The fricatives and frictionless continuants are as set out in table 20.1. It may be necessary to recognize in some dialects an opposition between a semivowel /j/ and a voiced fricative (Oftedal's /ĵ/ as in *ionnsaich* /jũːsiç/ 'learn' and *dh'ionnsaich* /ĵũːsiç/ 'learned'; see Oftedal, 1956).

Table 20.1. *Fricatives and frictionless continuants in Gaelic*

Labio-dental	Dental	Palatal	Medio-palatal	Velar	Glottal
f	s	ʃ	ç	x	h
v			j		

Note: In addition, some dialects have [z]. For its morphophonemic status see below, under 'Initial mutations'.

As far as liquids and nasals are concerned, most of the Hebridean dialects have three l-phonemes, three r-phonemes and three nasal phonemes (apart from /m/). Some have fewer; some such as Uig (Lewis) and Scarp (Harris) have four lateral phonemes. No dialect seems to have four n- or four r-phonemes. Each of the dialects having a '3 × 3' system has a velarized member /L, N, R/, an alveolar /l, n, r/ and a palatalized /L′, N′, r′/. The last-mentioned /r′/, in particular, has widely varying phonetic implementations: on Lewis it is a voiced interdental fricative; on the mainland generally it is a palatalized alveolar /r/ (Borgstrøm, 1940, 1941; Oftedal, 1956; Ternes, 1973; Shuken, 1980).

Vowels

Almost all the dialects appear to have an 8- or 9- vowel system, with length distinctions on all vowels. A typical Hebridean system would be:

i	ɯ	u
e	ə	o
ɛ	a	ɔ

In this system, /i, e, ɛ/ are front unrounded; /a/ is mid to front unrounded; /ə/ and /ɯ/ are mid to back unrounded. /u, o, ɔ/ are back rounded.

Most dialects have phonemic nasality. In Barra the system of nasal vowels (Borgstrøm, 1937) is:

ĩ	ɯ̃	ũ
ɛ̃	ã	ɔ̃

Only the high and low vowels can be nasalized. This is not universal in Gaelic, however; in east Sutherland there is an 8-vowel system (Dorian, 1978):

i		u
e	ə	o
ɛ	a	ɔ

All these vowels can be nasalized. In Argyll we find both 8- and 9-vowel systems, though the former predominate. In the south-west dialects there seems to be no phonemic nasality.

Diphthongs

All the dialects have diphthongs. Probably the greatest variety is found in the Hebrides. Most numerous are the i-diphthongs, which are distinct from vowel + /j/ : /ai, ei, əi, ui, ɔi/. There is also /au, ɔu, ɛu/, /iə, uə/ and /ia, ua/. These are found in virtually all Hebridean dialects, but each dialect has one or two extra of its own. The functional yield is very low (see Borgstrøm, 1937, 1940, 1941; Oftedal, 1956). Examples of diphthongs, distributed over lexical items, are as follows (on Gaelic orthography, see pages 244–5 and 289–90):

/ai/	dhaibh	'to them'
/ei/	beinn	'mountain'
/əi/	coilltean	'woods'
/ui/	dhuibh	'to you'
/ɔi/	coimhead	'watching'
/au/	ann	'there'
/ɔu/	donn	'brown'
/ɛu/	ceann	'head'
/iə/	grian	'sun'
/uə/	duan	'poem'
/ia/	fion	'wine'
/ua/	uan	'lamb'

Pre-aspiration

One of the most characteristic features of Scottish Gaelic is pre-aspiration. It is unknown in Irish and Manx, and indeed only seems to occur within Europe in a few Scandinavian languages. It is not found in Scotland in the dialects of the north (Caithness and Sutherland), south-east (east Perthshire) or south-west (south Argyll and Arran). It has developed in the original (geminate) voiceless stops, now spelled *p*, *t*, *c*, as in *tapaidh* 'clever', *cat* 'cat', *muc* 'pig'. The voiced stops of Old Irish are now voiceless in almost all the Scottish dialects (not in Sutherland) so that pre-aspiration has an important distinctive function.

The phonetic realizations in the modern dialects vary greatly: from breathy voice in Lewis to an /h/ (with /ç/ and /x/ before palatals and velars) in the other islands. North Argyll and west Perthshire have fricatives: /x/ or /ç/ according to the preceding vowel. Most dialects have fricatives before the velar and medio-palatal stops (spelled *c*). Examples are as follows:

	cat 'cat'	*muc* 'pig'
Lewis:	/kʰaʰt/ (breathy voice)	/muʰk/
Harris, Uist etc.:	/kʰaht/	/muxk/
N. Argyll, W. Perth:	/kʰaxt/	/muxk/

For further details, see Thomson (1983); and on the possible Norse origin, see Borgstrøm (1974).

Svarabhakti

The development of an epenthetic vowel within certain consonant groups is common to all the Gaelic languages, but in Scotland there are some special developments in the north-west dialects, i.e. those of the Hebrides and the western seaboard as far south as north Argyll. Instead of an unstressed /ə/ developing, as in the other dialects (and Ireland), there is a fully stressed vowel, usually a replica of the vowel in the first syllable.

The principal environments for svarabhakti are between one of the lateral or r-phonemes and a lenis stop or voiced fricative, or /m/: *fearg* /fjarak/ 'anger'; *falbh* /faLav/ 'go away' and *arm* /aram/ 'army'. It does not arise between r-phonemes and homorganic consonants such as /s, L, N/, nor the corresponding stops (see Oftedal, 1956).

In most of the Hebridean dialects we have level stress here; in Wester Ross (cf. Ternes, 1973, 1980) the svarabhakti vowel is perceptibly longer than the original stressed vowel. In Lewis the words consisting of $(C)V_1CV_2C$, where V_2 is the svarabhakti vowel, have the tonal contours of the original monosyllable, i.e. they are like *bó*, rather than *bodha* (cf. below, under 'word tones'). It does not arise after long vowels: thus *mìorbhailteach* does not contain a svarabhakti vowel.

Word tones

This feature has not been widely reported in Scots Gaelic and seems to be absent from Irish and Manx. We have descriptions from Lewis and Sutherland (Oftedal, 1956; Dorian, 1978) vouching for its existence, but it seems to have a very low functional yield in both dialect areas. As described for Leurbost, it bears a very close resemblance to the Scandinavian tones, with a complex tone in contrast with a simple tone. The former is used in original polysyllables, and the latter in original monosyllables. Hiatus in Lewis Gaelic is not marked by a glottal stop, but it is marked by the complex tone, e.g. *bodha* 'underwater rock' /po-o/ ≠ *bó* 'cow' /po:/. Conversely, the simple tone of *ainm* 'name', with a svarabhakti vowel, marks it off from *anam* 'soul' with the complex tone appropriate for polysyllables.

Stress

In all words of native origin Scottish Gaelic has initial stress. Apart from very recent loan-words, only *tombaca* 'tobacco' and *buntàta* 'potato' have failed to conform. In some dialects the words containing svarabhakti may form a special class as far as stress is concerned; otherwise level stress or strong secondary stress is confined to compounds.

Hiatus

The loss of Old Irish hiatus in the Middle Irish period is well documented for Ireland. It does not seem, by and large, to have occurred in Scotland. Thus, we have minimal pairs like *fitheach* /fi-əx/ 'raven' vs. *fiach* 'debt' /fiəx/. The number of words with hiatus in Scottish Gaelic has been swelled by the loss of medial consonants, particularly voiced fricatives, since the medieval period.

How hiatus is marked varies from dialect to dialect. The most common way is by a glottal stop between the vowels. In many dialects, particularly in Argyll, the glottal stop occurs even when a consonant is present, provided that that is derived from a Common Gaelic lenis consonant. Thus Common Gaelic /b, d, g/, also lenited /l, r/ and their palatalized equivalents, have concomitant glottal stops, though never in words containing svarabhakti vowels, nor after long vowels.

Morphophonology

Initial mutations

Various proclitics are affixed to forms beginning with a vowel, e.g. the article, the past tense marker *dh'* and the aspectual particle *ag*. These exhibit palatal or non-palatal forms according to the vowels.

As far as the written language is concerned there is only one consonantal mutation, lenition, but most dialects also have a nasal mutation ('eclipsis').

Lenition is a fundamental characteristic of Gaelic. There is very little dialect variation, at least among the stops and fricatives, as to the form it takes, and it is a unifying factor among the Gaelic languages (cf. Irish and Manx). There is also a similarity to Welsh which has been obscured by subsequent changes in the two branches of Celtic.

/m/ and lenis stops alternate with voiced fricatives:

m	p	t	t′	k′	k
v	v	ɣ	j	j	ɣ

Fortis (aspirated) stops alternate with voiceless fricatives:

p^h	t^h	t'^h	k'^h	k^h
f	h	h	ç	x

Fricatives alternate with zero or /h/:

f	s	ʃ
zero	h	h

In the more conservative Hebridean dialects there is also alternation among the liquids and the remaining nasals:

L′	R	N	N′
l	r	n	n

In those dialects with four l-phonemes, we also find an interdental /L/ alternating with a post-dental /ɫ/.

sl, *sn* and *sr* also lenite, but there is considerable variation as to the phonetic realizations of those and *shl* etc. Some initials are immutable: *sg*, *st*, *sp*, *sm*.

The nasal mutation, or 'eclipsis', which is a feature of most dialects, is quite different in its manifestation from Irish and Manx, though it has some domains in common; there are two types. In the 'Lewis' type, found in Lewis and the nearby territories of Assynt (Sutherland) and Trotternish (Skye) the lenis stops alternate with the corresponding nasals:

p	t	t′	k′	k
m	N	N′	ŋ′	ŋ

and the fortis (aspirated) stops alternate with the corresponding nasal + /h/:

p^h	t^h	t'^h	k'^h	k^h
mh	Nh	N′h	ŋ′h	ŋh

There is no alternation involving the fricatives.

There is also the voicing type where, in some dialects, we find an alternation between voiceless stops and the corresponding voiced stops. Most commonly both /p/ and /p^h/ will alternate with /b/, but in some dialects we have voiced aspirates /b^h/ etc. alternating with /p^h/.

The treatment of the fricatives /f/ and /s/ is threefold: (i) in the islands there is no eclipsis of the fricatives; (ii) in a crescent-shaped area stretching from

Braemar in the extreme north-east through Perthshire to Loch Fyne there is an alternation of /f/ ~ /v/ and /s/ ~ /z/, e.g. *fear/am fear, samhradh/an samhradh*; (iii) west of Braemar in east Inverness-shire and Ross-shire /f/ alternates with /b/ (cf. Watson, 1974: 58).

Non-initial mutations

'Palatalization' is a term applied both to vocalic and consonantal mutations. In the case of the consonants, it means that there is a set of non-palatals corresponding to palatals:

t	ʰt	k	ʰk	ɣ	x	h	s	N	n	L	L	r
t′	ʰt′	k′	ʰk′	j	ç	j	ʃ	N′	N′	L′	l	r′

The labials and /R/ do not participate in these alternations. A typical example of this mutation would be *cat* (nom. sing.) vs. *cait* (gen. sing. or nom. pl.).

There are vocalic mutations, often in combination with these consonant mutations, but also before labials. Apart from closely similar phenomena in the other Gaelic languages, there are similar developments in Welsh, and also in the Germanic languages, where it is called 'umlaut'. The alternations are extremely numerous; it will suffice to mention a few:

fear nom. sing.	fir gen. sing. or nom. plur.	'man'
seòl	siùil	'sail'
eun	eòin	'bird'
grian	gréine	'sun'

There is another vocalic mutation – that of quantity – involving liquids and resonants:

geàrr	imperative	gearradh	VN	/aː/ ~ /a/	'cut'
cam	sing.	cama	pl.	/au/ ~ /a/	'crooked'
donn	sing.	donna	pl.	/ɔu/ ~ /o/	'brown'
seall	imperative sing.	seallaibh	imperative pl.	/ɛu/ ~ /a/	'book'

Preverbal particles

Negation, yes/no questions and many other functions are expressed by a preverbal particle + the dependent form of the verb. These include *cha/chan* 'negative' *an/am* 'interrogative' *nach* 'negative interrogative' *mun/mus* 'before'. A small number of particles are followed by the relative, e.g. *a* 'relative' *na* 'what', *ma* 'if' *mar a* 'as' *nuair a* 'when'. Note that the relative is distinguished from the independent form of the verb only in the future of the regular verbs.

Bhith 'to be'. The four simple 'tenses' are traditionally referred to as present, past, future and conditional. The last two may express habitual aspect:

	Neutral	Habitual
Non-past:	tha	bithidh (unstressed bidh)
Past:	bha	bhitheadh (bhiodh)

The 'future' has a special relative form *bhitheas* (unstressed *bhios*). All these forms are invariable as to person and number, except for the conditional, where we find a 1st person sing. *bhithinn* and 1st person pl. *bhitheamaid* (*bhiomaid*).

The forms given above are the independent ones, i.e. those found when the verb is not preceded by any preverbal particle; the relative particles may be followed by *tha*, *bha* or *bhitheadh*; after the preverbal particles, most of which are nasalizing (see 'Initial mutations') we find the following forms:

	Neutral	Habitual
Non-past:	(a) bheil/eil	(am) bi
Past:	(an) robh	(am) bitheadh

eil is used after leniting particles (e.g. *cha/chan*) or particles that do not nasalize or lenite (e.g. *nach*).

Except for *bhithinn* and *bhitheamaid*, all of the forms listed above may have a noun or pronoun as a subject. As *bhith* is an auxiliary as well as a verb in its own right (see below, under 'Verbal noun'), it has a full set of impersonal endings:

	Neutral	Habitual
Non-past:	thathas/thathar	bithear
Past:	bhathas	bhithte

The same endings are attached to the corresponding dependent forms: *a bheilear*, *chan eilear* etc.

Unlike the forms given above the imperative has a full paradigm of personal endings:

Singular	Plural
bitheam	bitheamaid
bi	bithibh
bitheadh e/i	bitheadh iad

The imperative has no dependent forms, but may be preceded by a special negative particle *na*, which neither nasalizes nor lenites.

The regular verb. This characteristically has three simple 'tenses' and the imperative, all derived from one stem. The verbal noun *cur* has the stem *cuir*:

		Independent	
		Neutral	Habitual
Non-past:		—	cuiridh
Past:		chuir	chuireadh

The endings of the conditional, relative and imperative are as for *bhith* 'to be':

	Dependent	
Non-past:	—	(an) cuir
Past:	(an) do chuir	(an) cuireadh

The impersonal endings for all regular verbs are:

Future: -(e)ar   *Past*: -(e)adh   *Conditional*: -te

There is an increasing tendency for -*ar* to spread to the past and, less commonly, to the conditional. Impersonal forms are mainly found with transitive verbs, but such forms as *dh'fhalbhadh* 'they went', 'people went' occasionally occur. The impersonal form of the imperative is *cuirtear*.

The irregular verb. There are about a dozen irregular verbs in Gaelic and they are approximately the same verbs in all dialects, and also in Manx and Irish. Characteristically they are formed with more than one stem, often by suppletion. They have no irregular endings, but lack the endings of the future and relative given in the description of regular verbs, above. The conditional is entirely regular in its ending, but the dependent may have a different stem from the independent form. More often the independent conditional has the same stem as the independent future, and similarly the dependent conditional. The forms of irregular verbs are summarized in table 20.2.

Defective verbs. These have no verbal noun and only one or two tenses. For example, in *feumaidh* 'must' the future is used as present and future; the conditional is used as the past: *dh'fheumainn* 'I had to'; and there is an impersonal form, *feumar, dh'fheumte*.

The verb *faodaidh* 'may' also uses the future as present and future: *faodaidh tu smocadh* 'you may smoke'; the past tense is *dh'fhaodadh* and the impersonal *faodar*. The impersonal conditional *dh'fhaodte* is used to mean 'perhaps': *dh'fhaodte gu robh* 'perhaps it was', *dh'fhaodte gu bheil* 'perhaps it is'.

The verb *theab* '(I) nearly' has only a past form, *theab mi tuiteam* 'I nearly fell', with the impersonal *theabadh mo bhàthadh* 'I nearly drowned'.

The verb *arsa* '(he) said' also has a past form only '*Tha mi a' falbh,*' *ars' e* 'I'm leaving,' he said. It is always unstressed.

The verbs *trobhad* 'come' and *siuthad* 'go on' occur in the imperative form only.

The copula. The copula is a unique defective verb: it has two tenses, present and past (the latter also serves as conditional); it has no verbal noun and no imperative. It has no stressed forms: in one-word replies (responsives) it has to be extended by the addition of a personal pronoun or *ann*. It has three distinct types of usage:

(i)   In equative sentences, where both the subject and predicate are nominal

Table 20.2. *The irregular verb in Gaelic*

	Verbal noun	Imperative 2nd sing.	Future		Conditional		Past	
			Dep.	Indep.	Dep.	Indep.	Dep.	Indep.
'make, do'	dèanamh	dèan	(an) dèan	nì	(an) dèanadh	dhèanadh	(an) do rinn	rinn
'come'	tighinn	thig/na tig	tig	thig	tigeadh	thigeadh	tàinig	thàinig
'get'	faighinn	faigh	faigh	gheibh	faigheadh	gheabhadh	d'fhuair	fhuair
'see'	faicinn	faic	faic	chì	faiceadh	chitheadh	faca	chunnaic
'give'	toirt	thoir/na toir	toir	bheir	toireadh	bheireadh	tug	thug
'say'	(g)ràdh	abair/na h-abair	abair	their	abaireadh	theireadh	tuirt	thuirt
'give birth, lay eggs'	breith	beir	beir	beiridh	beireadh	bheireadh	do rug	rug
'hear'	cluinntinn	cluinn	cluinn	cluinnidh	cluinneadh	chluinneadh	cuala	chuala
'reach'	ruighinn	ruig	ruig	ruigidh	ruigeadh	ruigeadh	do ràinig	ràinig
'go'	dol	rach	téid	théid	rachadh	rachadh	deach(aidh)	chaidh

breith, *cluinntinn* and *ruighinn* are regular in the future and conditional. *Rinneadh, thugadh, thuirteadh* and *rugadh* have the regular endings in the past impersonal, while *fhuaras, facas/chunnacas* and *chualas* have *-as*.

in form, we find *'S e sin an duine* 'That's the man'; *An tusa am fear?* 'Are you the one?' (Answer: *'S mi* or *Cha mhi.*)

(ii)   The copula is used in a number of very common idioms: *'S urrainn dhomh* 'I can'; *'S eudar dhomh* 'I must'; *'S toigh leam* 'I like'; *Bu math leam* 'I would like'; *'S leamsa e* 'it is mine!' None of these is now productive as a structure.

(iii)   The copula appears in emphatic sentences, including sentences of classification: *'S e dotair a tha ann an Iain* 'John is a doctor', as opposed to *Tha Iain na dhotair* 'John is a doctor (now)', a form which implies a change of status.

	Independent and relative	*Dependent*
Non-past	's (as)	zero
Past and conditional:	bu* /b'	bu* /b'

where *bu** lenites labials and velars and *b'* before *fh* and vowels. (Throughout this chapter * indicates a leniting item.) There is a special form of *gu* 'that' in the non-past, viz. *gur: tha mi a' smaoineachadh gur tusa an duine* 'I think you are the man'. In addition to the above forms, there is a special wish form *gu ma*, e.g. *Gu ma fada beò sibh* 'May you live long'.

The responsive. Only a small number of verbal forms contain the subject. Except with the impersonal forms, the subject is always expressed by a noun or pronoun. However, in replying to questions, or in confirming or modifying a statement, it is usual to omit the subject in the reply:

(1)   Ciamar a tha sibh? Tha gu math
       'How are you?' 'Fine'
(2)   Am faca sibh Sim an raoir? Chunnaic
       'Did you see Simon last night?' 'Yes'

There is no general word for 'yes' and 'no' in Gaelic, so that the reply may be a one-word response, consisting only of the verb in the appropriate tense, in the case of the negative preceded by the negative particle.

The omission of the subject pertains even where the subject would be expected to be contained in the verbal form:

(3)   Am bitheadh tu toilichte ...? Cha bhitheadh
       'Would you be pleased?' 'No (I wouldn't)'

Bhitheadh does not contain any subject, and is always used instead of *bhithinn* or *bhitheamaid* in responsives.

Participles

There are no participles in Gaelic, active or passive, but what is often called the past participle survives as an adjective:

(4)   Tha an dorus fosgailte
       'The door is open'

Verbal noun

The Verbal noun (VN) is used with an auxiliary – usually the appropriate form of *bhith* 'to be' – to form the compound tenses of the verb:

tha mi ag ithe	bithidh mi ag ithe
'I am eating'	'I will be eating' or 'I habitually eat'
bha mi ag ithe	bhithinn ag ithe
'I was eating'	'I used to eat' or 'I would be eating'

It retains many nominal characteristics – it may itself be in the genitive after another noun: *oran luaidh* 'a walking song' or it may govern as its object a noun in the genitive: *Tha mi ag ionnsachadh na Gàidhlig* 'I am learning Gaelic'. (For pronoun objects see under 'Possessive pronouns', below: *Tha mi ga h-ionnsachadh* 'I am learning it'.) However, the genitive is not usual with indefinite objects: *Tha mi ag iarraidh deoch* 'I want a drink', as opposed to *tha mi ag iarraidh an dibhe* 'I want the drink'.

There is no regular formation of the verbal noun. By far the commonest ending is *-adh*, which is generally used with loan-words from English. Palatal stems are depalatalized before *-adh* is added, as in *buail*: *bualadh* 'strike'; *toisich*: *toiseachadh* 'begin'.

There are several other common endings:

-eil/-ail: *leig*: *leigeil* 'let'
          gabh: *gabhail* 'take'
-t: *freagair*: *freagairt* 'answer'
-e: *ith*: *ithe* 'eat'
-d: *foighnich*: *foighneachd* 'ask' (with depalatalization)
zero: *cuir*: *cur* (with depalatalization)
          òl: *òl*
-amh: *seas*: *seasamh* 'stand'
-inn/-tinn/-sinn: *faic*: *faicinn* 'see'
          cluinn: *cluinntinn* 'hear'
          tuig: *tuigsinn* 'understand'

Case

The case system in Scottish Gaelic is in the process of breaking down. There has been a certain amount of erosion over the centuries, but only one case – the accusative – has been lost completely between the earliest recorded Old Irish and the conservative speakers alive today.

The nominative is used for subject or object, after certain prepositions and to express duration of time; the vocative is used with the vocative particle *a** in addressing people; the genitive is used after certain prepositions and after nouns to express possession or relationship and the dative is used only after certain prepositions.

The dative masculine has completely fallen together with the nominative in the noun though the article and attributive adjectives still maintain the distinction. Of the feminines, only nouns of type 2 maintain the distinction (see below, pages 330–4 for the types of Gaelic noun).

Only masculine nouns of type 1 have a special vocative form. A number of men's names belong to this class. It is identical with the genitive in the singular. A new vocative plural has developed for some nouns in this class, derived from the old dative plural, now obsolete.

The genitive is the best preserved case: four of the five declensions (and most of the irregular nouns) have a special genitive.

Four of the five declensions usually make the noun indeclinable in the plural; but initial mutations or the article may help to distinguish the genitive plural.

Number

There are three numbers in literary Gaelic: singular, dual and plural. Dual number is vestigial – it only occurs in connection with the word *dà* 'two'. Nominative and dative dual are like the dative singular, genitive is like the genitive singular. That means that the dual is only distinct in the feminine and then only in dialects that distinguish dative singular from nominative. The plural in all nouns is distinct from the singular.

Gender

There are two genders in Gaelic: everything is masculine or feminine: with animate beings, gender normally follows from male or female sex – but *boireannach* 'woman' is masculine. There are some general rules: grains, metals, seasons, days of the week, diminutives in *-an* and words ending in *-as*, *-ear*, *-aire*, *-iche*, and *-adh* are masculine. Names of countries, musical instruments, heavenly bodies, illnesses and words in *-ag* and *-achd* are feminine. A few words are masculine in the nominative, feminine in the genitive, e.g. *am muir* 'the sea', gen. *na mara* (*na* is the feminine article).

The article

There is only one article in Gaelic. It varies according to number, case and gender. It is involved in initial mutations, both pre-vocalic and pre-consonantal (lenition and eclipsis – see above, under 'Morphophonology'). Some sample paradigms (based on Oftedal, 1956) are given in tables 20.3–20.8.

The noun

The case distinctions given here are still largely maintained in the more conservative Outer Hebridean dialects. On the mainland and with the young people in the islands, the trend is towards one form for the singular and one for the plural.

There are five main paradigms and a residue of irregular nouns:

Type 1.   Masculine nouns only. The nominative ends in a non-palatal, voca-

Table 20.3. *The Gaelic article: non-dental stops*

	Singular	Plural	Singular	Plural
Nom.	an ceann 'head' (masc.)	na cinn	am bòrd 'table' (masc.)	na bùird
Dat.	a'cheann		a'bhòrd	
Gen.	a'chinn	nan ceann	a'bhùird	nam bòrd
Nom.	a'chlach 'stone' (fem.)	na clachan		
Dat.	a'chloich			
Gen.	na cloiche	nan clach/clachan		

Table 20.4. *The Gaelic article: dental and pre-palatal stops, nasals and liquids*

	Singular	Plural	Singular	Plural
Nom.-dat.	an taigh 'house' (masc.)	na taighean	an tobair 'well' (fem.)	na tobraichean
Gen.	an taighe	nan taighean	na tobrach	nan tobraichean
Nom.-dat.	an duine 'person' (masc.)	na daoine	an nàbuidh 'neighbour' (masc.)	na nàbuidhean
Gen.		nan daoine		nan nàbuidhean
Nom.-dat.	an latha 'day' (masc.)	na lathaichean	an ràmh 'oar' (masc.)	na ràimh
Gen.		nan lathaichean	an ràimh	nan ràmh

Table 20.5. *The Gaelic article: /m/*

	Singular	Plural	Singular	Plural
Nom.	am mìos 'month' (masc.)	na mìosan	a'mhàthair 'mother' (fem.)	na mathraichean
Dat. Gen.	a'mhìos	nam mìosan	na màthar	nam màthraichean

Table 20.6. *The Gaelic article: s + vowel, l, n, or r*

	Singular	Plural	Singular	Plural
Nom.	an samhradh 'summer' (masc.)	na samhraidh	an t-snàthad 'needle' (fem.)	na snàthaidean
Dat.	an t-samhradh		an t-snàthaid	
Gen.	an t-samhraidh		na snàthaide	nan snàthaidean

Table 20.7. *The Gaelic article: f + vowel*

	Singular	Plural	Singular	Plural
Nom.	am fear 'man' (masc.)	na fir	an fhaoileag 'seagull' (fem.)	na faoileagan
Dat.	an fhear		an fhaoileig	
Gen.	an fhir	nam fear	na faoileige	nam faoileagan

Table 20.8. *The Gaelic article: vowels*

	Singular	Plural	Singular	Plural
Nom.	an t-each 'horse' (masc.)	na h-eich	an oidhche 'night' (fem.)	na h-oidhcheannan
Dat.	an each			
Gen.	an eich	nan each	na h-oidhche	nan oidhcheannan

tive and genitive in a palatal. Apart from initial mutations there are only two forms in the singular:

	Singular	*Dual*	*Plural*
Nom.	fear 'a man'	dà fhear	fir
Voc.	a fhir	—	a fhearaibh
Gen.	fir	dà fhir	fhear
Dat.	fear	dà fhear	fir

This is the only declension where the vocative is distinct from the nominative in its ending. The vocative plural is derived from the, now obsolete, dative plural, which is attested in the Bible translation of the late eighteenth, early nineteenth century. The vocative dual is not attested. The nominative-dative plural is like the genitive singular.

Type 2.   Feminine nouns with non-palatal final consonant:

	Singular	*Dual*	*Plural*
Nom.	cearc 'hen'	dà chirc	cearcan
Gen.	circe	dà chirce	chearcan
Dat.	circ	dà chirc	cearcan

Type 3.   Masculine and feminine nouns with genitive in *-a* or *-e*. The dative form is like the nominative; the dual is like the singular; the plural form varies.

Nom./dat. fiodh 'wood' ⎱ No pl.   sgeir 'reef' ⎱ Pl. sgeirean
Gen.   fiodha   ⎰ forms   sgeire   ⎰

Type 4.   Feminine nouns ending in a palatal in the nominative case, forming the genitive by depalatization (and syncope if disyllabic) and adding *-ach*. The dual is like the singular; the plural usually ends in *-aichean*.

Nom./dat. iuchair 'key' ⎰ Pl. iuchraichean
Gen.   iuchrach   ⎱

Type 5.   Nouns indeclinable in the singular (and dual) e.g. *oidhche* 'night' (see table 20.8.). There are various plural forms.

There are a number of irregular nouns of various kinds. For example, there is a group of kinship terms with some features in common:

Nom.		Gen.		Pl.	
athair 'father'		athar		athraichean	
màthair 'mother'		màthar		màthraichean	
bràthair 'brother'		bràthar		bràithrean	
seanair 'grandfather'		seanar		seanairean	
seanmhair 'grandmother'		seanmhar		seanmhairean	

More anomalous are the following:

	Singular	*Plural*
Nom.	piuthar 'sister'	peathraichean
Gen.	peathar	pheathraichean
Dat.	piuthair	peathraichean

	Singular	*Plural*
Nom./dat.	cù 'dog'	coin
Gen.	coin	chon

	Singular	*Plural*
Nom.	bó 'cow'	bà
Gen.	bà	bó
Dat.	boin	bà

	Singular	*Plural*
Nom.	bean 'wife'	mnathan
Gen.	mnatha	bhan
Dat.	mnaoi	mnathan

	Singular	*Plural*
Nom.	leaba 'bed'	⎧ leabthannan
Gen.	leabtha	⎨
Dat.	leabaidh	⎩

To summarize the plural forms: the commonest ending is -*an*, found in all declensions, though in type 1 it is confined to a few polysyllabic forms in -*ach*. From type 4, -*ichean* has spread to types 3 and 5; it is also used with loan-words. A less common variant -*achan* is used after palatal consonants, e.g. *àite/àiteachan*. Words ending in -*le* and -*ne* favour -*tean*, e.g. *baile/bailtean* 'village'. Words of type 3 ending in -*m* take -*annan*, e.g. *àm/amannan* 'occasion', as do some from type 5, e.g. *oidhche* 'night', *cupa* 'cup'. Type 1 forms its plural by palatalization; the nominative/dative plural have the same endings as the genitive singular. Apart from the irregular nouns given, there are some irregular plurals of otherwise regular nouns: *duine/daoine* 'man, person', *gamhainn/gamhna* 'stirk', *caora/caoraich* 'sheep', *long/luingeas* 'ship'.

Adverbs

A certain number of adverbs are formed from adjectives with the prefix *gu*, as in *gu math* 'well', *gu h-obann* 'suddenly'. *Gu* is not used when one adjective precedes (modifies) another, e.g. *anabarrach math* 'wonderfully good' or 'wonderfully well'.

There are various adverbs of location and direction:

Repose		*Movement*
thall	'over there'	a null/a nunn
a bhos	'over here'	a nall
a staigh	'in'	a steach
a muigh	'out'	a mach

The adverbs *shuas* and *shìos* ('up' and 'down') require special comment. The most common system is:

Repose		*Movement away from speaker*	*Movement towards speaker*
shuas 'up'	suas		a nuas
shìos 'down'	sìos		

However, a small number of dialects preserve the full system, whereby 'up towards the speaker' is *a nìos* and 'down towards the speaker' is *a nuas*.

Adjectives

Predicative adjectives are invariable. Attributive adjectives agree in gender, case and number with the preceding noun. A small number of very common adjectives are preposed, e.g. *droch-* 'bad', *deagh-* 'good'. They are themselves invariable, and cause lenition of the following noun. If they have (semantic) equivalents among the predicative or (postposed) attributive adjectives, there is usually no phonetic similarity: cf. *dona* 'bad', *math* 'good'. *Seann-* 'old' seems to be an exception: cf. *sean* 'do'.

The paradigm of adjectival declension of a very conservative speaker might be:

| | | *Singular* | |
	Masc.	Fem.	
Nom.	mór	mhór*	[Forms marked* lenite following adjectives.]
Voc.	mhóir*	mhór*	
Gen.	mhóir*	móire	[*Móire* tends to be replaced by *mhóir**.]
Dat.	mhór*	mhóir*	[The dative is only used after noun with article.]

Plural

All cases. móra (mhóra)   [The lenited form occurs only after type 1 nouns.]

Adjectives of more than one syllable are invariable except for the initial mutations. This is true of the comparative and superlative, which are formed by palatalization and the addition of a suffix *-e*. The comparative and superlative forms are preceded by *nas* or *as*, which contain the copula: if the main verb is in the past or conditional, we find *na bu/a bu* being used instead:

(5)   Tha Iain nas sine na Seumas
      'John is older than James'
(6)   Bha e na b'fhuaire an dé na tha e an diugh
      'It was colder yesterday than today'

There is a small number of irregular comparatives:

mór	(nas) motha	'big'
beag	lugha	'small'
furasda	fhasa	'easy'
goirid	giorra	'short'
math	fheàrr	'good'
dona	miosa	'bad'
teth	teotha	'hot'

Numerals

There are two sets of cardinal numbers, according to whether they are followed by a noun or not: these are described in table 20.9.

From these examples it can be seen that the number of the noun depends on the numeral immediately preceding it: *dà* requires the dual; 3–10 the plural, and all the other numbers the singular.

In literary Gaelic and in conservative dialects, the above numbers are not used when counting people; for this there is a special set of personal numbers covering 2–10:

dithis
triùir
ceathrar
cóigear/cóignear
sianar
seachdnar/seachdar

ochdnar/ochdar
naoinear
deichnear

These are nouns and may be used by themselves or followed by another noun in the genitive plural: *triùir bhraithrean* 'three brothers'.

Table 20.9. *Cardinal numbers in Gaelic*

Alone		With noun	Remarks
a h-aon/aonan	1	aon* chearc 'one hen'	Lenites labials and velars
a dhà	2	dà* chearc	Followed by dual (see under 'Nouns')
a trì	3	trì chearcan	May lenite /k^h/ and /k$'^h$/
a ceithir	4	ceithir chearcan	May lenite /k^h/ and /k$'^h$/
a cóig	5	cóig chearcan	May lenite /k^h/ and /k$'^h$/
a sia	6	sia cearcan	
a seachd	7	seachd cearcan	
a h-ochd	8	ochd cearcan	
a naoi	9	naoi cearcan	
a deich	10	deich cearcan	
a h-aon deug	11	aon fhear deug/aon chearc dheug	*Deug* 'teen' follows the noun and is treated as
a dhà dheug	12	dà fhear deug/dà chirc dheug	an adjective as far as the initial mutations are
a trì deug	13	trì fir dheug/trì chearcan deug	concerned
.	.	.	
.	.	.	
.	.	.	
a naoi deug	19	naoi ... deug	
fichead	20	fichead cearc	Singular
	21	cearc air fhichead	
	30	deich cearcan air fhichead	Plural after *deich*
	40	dà fhichead cearc	
	50	lethcheud cearc	
	60	trì fichead cearc	
	80	ceithir fichead cearc	
	100	ceud cearc	
	300	trì cheud cearc	
	1000	mìle cearc	

The ordinal numbers precede the noun, but with the exception of *a' cheud* 'first' they do not cause lenition. They do not vary according to the gender of the noun that follows, but usage varies within and between dialects:

Table 20.10. *The personal pronouns of Gaelic*

	Singular	Plural	Singular	Plural
1st	mi	sinn	mise	sinne
2nd	thu	sibh	thusa	sibhse
3rd masc.	e	iad	esan	iadsan
fem.	i		ise	

Table 20.11. *The possessive pronouns of Gaelic*

	Singular		Plural	
	Before consonants	Before vowels	Before consonants	Before vowels
1st	mo*	m'	ar	ar n-
2nd	do*	d'/t'	ur	ur n-
3rd masc.	a*	' ⎫		
fem.	a	a h- ⎭	an/am	an

1st a' cheud* fhear (lenites labials and velars)
2nd an darna/an dara fear
3rd an treas fear
4th an ceathramh/a' cheathramh fear
5th an cóigeamh/a chóigeamh fear
6th an siathamh/an t-siathamh fear
7th an seachdamh/an t-seachdamh fear
8th an t-ochdamh/an ochdamh fear fear
9th an naoidheamh fear
10th an deicheamh fear
11th an aona fear deug
12th an darna fear deug
13th am ficheadamh/an fhicheadamh fear

Pronouns

The personal and possessive pronouns are as demonstrated in tables 20.10 and 20.11. The personal pronouns *sibh, sibhse* can also be used in the singular when addressing a person requiring respect or formality (cf. French *vous*). All these pronouns can be used interchangeably as subject or object of the verb. *Thu/thusa* are replaced by *tu/tusa* after conditional, future and relative forms ending in *-adh, -idh* and *-as* respectively, and in combination with all forms of the copula. *Tu* and *tusa* do not occur as object pronouns:

(7) Có chuireas tu?
     'Whom will you send?'
(8) Có chuireas thu?
     'Who will send you?'

Possessive pronouns are used mainly with nouns denoting relationship or parts of the body: *mo mhàthair* 'my mother', *mo cheann* 'my head'. To signify temporary possession of objects or animals a periphrastic construction is used involving the preposition *aig* 'at', e.g. *an taigh agam* 'my house' (article + noun + prepositional pronoun). Possessives are also used when a pronoun is the 'object' of a verbal noun: (i) in impersonal constructions:

(9) *Chaidh a bhàthadh* 'He was drowned'

(ii) in conjunction with a particle:

(10) *gam mharbhadh* 'killing me' (ag + mo)
(11) *dham mharbhadh* 'in order to kill me' (do + mo)

Prepositions

Prepositions in Scottish Gaelic may govern nominative, genitive or dative. Only a few take the nominative, e.g. *eadar* 'between', *gu* 'until', *gun* 'without'.

All the compound prepositions take the genitive: e.g. *an déidh* 'after', *mu dheidhinn* 'about', *as aonais* 'without', *os cionn* 'above'; most but not all of these consist of preposition + obsolete noun. Some simple prepositions take the genitive: *thun* 'to', *bharr* 'from, off', *fad* 'throughout'.

The great majority of the simple prepositions take the dative. For preposition + noun, see the description of cases of the noun phrase above, page 330. For preposition + pronouns, see 'Prepositional pronouns', below. We may find *eadar thusa agus mise* 'between you and me', but otherwise simple prepositions cannot be used with ordinary pronouns. In the case of compound prepositions, the pronoun is infixed in the form of a possessive: *na dhéidh* 'after him', *na déidh* 'after her'.

Prepositional pronouns. Most of the simple prepositions combine with pronouns to give a fused form, which can be arranged like a verbal conjugation in inflecting languages such as Latin or Hebrew. Thus for *a* 'out of' we have:

	Singular	Plural
1st	asam	asainn
2nd	asad	asaibh
3rd masc.	as	} asda
fem.	aisde	

And for *air* 'on':

	Singular	Plural
1st	orm	oirnn
2nd	ort	oirbh
3rd masc.	air	orra
fem.	oirre	

These in turn have an emphatic form, corresponding to *mise, thusa* etc. The 1st singular ending is always *-sa*, otherwise they are identical to these pronominal endings:

Singular	Plural
ormsa	oirnne
ortsa	oirbhse
air-san	orrasan
oirrese	

The prepositions which are thus conjugated: *a* 'out of', *air* 'on', *aig* 'at', *ann* 'in', *mu* 'about', *ri* 'to', *roimh* 'before', *troimh* 'through', *fo* 'under', *o/bho* 'from', *le* 'with', *do* 'for', *de* 'of' all take the dative; of the others, only *gu/thun* 'to' has a full conjugation:

Singular	Plural
thugam 'to me'	thugainn
thugad	thugaibh
thuige	thuca
thuice	

In most dialects, *eadar* 'between' has plural forms only:

eadarainn
eadaraibh
eatorra

Syntax

The order of the sentence in Gaelic is (Pre-verbal particle) + V + S + O. The usual place for adverbs or prepositional phrases is at the end of the sentence, but some may occur in sentence-initial position. A pronoun object generally comes at the end. Nothing may separate the verb and its subject. If the verb is the auxiliary verb *bhith* linked by the continuous particle *ag* or the perfective *air* to the verbal noun, we have the following possibilities: V + S + *ag* + VN   or   V + S + *air* + VN.

If the verbal noun has an object the treatment is quite different for the two types of sentence: with the structure *ag* + VN, the noun follows; definite nouns (i.e. with article or possessive pronoun) are in the genitive, indefinite nouns usually in the nominative. The pronoun is infixed between the particle and the verbal noun as a possessive pronoun:

(12)   Tha mi ga ghabhail
        'I am taking it'
(13)   Tha mi a' gabhail mo bhithidh
        'I am taking my food'
(14)   Tha mi a' gabhail biadh
        'I am taking food'

With the structure *air* + VN, the pronoun object is also prefixed to the verbal
noun, but it does not blend with the particle; noun objects come between the
air and the verbal noun, but are in the nominative:

(15)   Tha mi air a ghabhail
        'I have (just) taken it'
(16)   Tha mi air mo bhiadh a ghabhail
        'I have taken my food'
(17)   Tha mi air biadh a ghabhail
        'I have taken food'

   The two constructions (postposition with the genitive, prefixation with the
nominative) are found elsewhere in the grammar:

(18)   Thàinig mi an seo a ghabhail mo bhithidh
        'I came here to take my food'

as opposed to:

(19)   Tha mi ag iarraidh mo bhiadh a ghabhail
        'I want to take my food'

Purpose clauses have the first construction, noun complement the other. This
also applies to negative sentences:

(20)   Dh'iarr e orm gun biadh a ghabhail
        'he asked me not to take food'

Emphatic sentences ('Fronting')

These are formed in Gaelic with the copula + a relative clause. The form of
the copula depends on the part of speech which is to be highlighted. The
unextended *is* (*'s*) is only used with personal pronouns (with or without
emphatic particle):

(21)   'S mi a tha a' dol dhachaidh
        I'm going home
(22)   'S tusa a bhios a' fuireachd
        It is you who is staying

'S e is used before nouns, pronouns with emphatic particles and demonstrative pronouns:

(23) 'S e Iain a bhios a' tighinn
      John's coming
(24) 'S e mise a bhios a' tighinn
      I'm coming
(25) 'S e sin a tha mi ag iarraidh
      That's what I want

In all these sentences the *'s e* may be omitted.
 'S ann is used before all other parts of speech:

(26) 'S ann an diugh a thàinig mi
      I came *today*
(27) 'S ann air a' bhord a tha am peann
      The pen is *on the table*
(28) 'S ann fuar a tha e
      It's *cold*
(29) 'S ann agadsa a tha an t-airgead
      You have the money
(30) 'S ann ag ithe a tha mi
      I'm *eating*

The prepositional pronouns are treated in the same way as prepositional phrases. In sentences involving the past or conditional, *b'e* or *b'ann* may be used instead of *'s e*, *'s ann*, but the latter seem to be more common.

REFERENCES

Borgstrøm, C. Hj. 1937. The dialect of Barra. *Nord Tidskrift for Sprogvidenskab* (*NTS*) VIII: 71–242. Oslo: Aschehoug.
——— 1940. Dialects of the Outer Hebrides. *NTS*. Supplementary vol. I.
——— 1941. Dialects of Skye and Ross-shire. *NTS*. Supplementary vol. II.
——— 1974. On the influence of Norse on Scottish Gaelic. *Lochlann* VI (*NTS*. Supplementary vol. XI): 91–107. Oslo: Universitetsforlaget.
Dorian, N. C. 1978. *East Sutherland Gaelic*. Dublin: Institute for Advanced Studies.
Durkacz, V. E. 1983. *The decline of the Celtic languages*. Edinburgh: John Donald.
Lockwood, W. B. 1975. *Languages of the British Isles past and present*. London: André Deutsch.
Nicholson, R. 1974. *The later Middle Ages. Edinburgh History of Scotland*, vol. 2. Edinburgh: Oliver and Boyd.
Oftedal, M. 1956. The Gaelic of Leurbost Isle of Lewis. *NTS*. Supplementary vol. IV.
Romaine, S. and Dorian, N. C. 1981. Scotland as a linguistic area. *Scottish Literary Journal* supplement no. 14: 1–24.
Shuken, C. R. 1980. An instrumental investigation of some Scottish Gaelic consonants. Unpublished thesis, University of Edinburgh.
Ternes, E. 1973. *The phonemic analysis of Scottish Gaelic*. Hamburg: Helmut Buske.

———— 1980. Scottish Gaelic phonemics viewed in typological perspective. *Lingua* 52: 73–88.

Thomson, D. S. (ed.) 1983. *A companion to Scottish Gaelic studies.* Oxford: Blackwell.

Watson, J. 1974. A Gaelic dialect of N. E. Ross-shire. *Lochlann* VI (*NTS.* Supplementary vol. XI): 9–90. Oslo: Universitetsforlaget.

Part III

Other languages

Introduction

Very many languages are spoken in the British Isles in addition to English and Celtic languages. Most of these are languages brought to Britain in the last hundred years or so by refugees and immigrants: Hungarian, Italian, Yiddish, Polish, Bengali, Panjabi, Greek, Maltese – and so on. We are, however, only just beginning to obtain information about the sociolinguistic position of these languages (see Part IV) and we know almost nothing at all about their linguistic characteristics. There are, of course, many descriptions available of, say, Bengali, but we know nothing about the nature of Bengali as it is spoken IN BRITAIN. There are exceptions: for example, Agnihotri (1979) is a very interesting study of Panjabi in Leeds (see chapter 25). But for the most part it is true to say that a wealth of fascinating and important linguistic data as yet has gone untouched. This is why the languages spoken by the newer minorities are discussed in this book only in Part IV. In the present section, Part III, we confine our attention to the linguistic characteristics and sociolinguistic position of languages whose British Isles varieties have been the subject of detailed study by linguists. Chapter 21, *Channel Island French*, describes the dialects of French and their sociolinguistic situation in the Channel Islands. Chapter 22, *Orkney and Shetland Norn*, discusses what is known about the variety of Scandinavian formerly spoken in the Northern Isles. Although Norn is now no longer extant as such, it has had a very considerable effect on the English/Scots now spoken there (see also chapter 6). Chapter 23, *Romani and Angloromani*, and chapter 24, *Shelta and Polari*, look at linguistic varieties spoken by Travellers and other itinerant and fringe groups in the British Isles. Romani is an Indo-Aryan language originally related to Panjabi and Bengali, and very recessive in the British Isles although alive and very well in the USA and continental Europe. The other three varieties, Angloromani, Shelta and Polari, may not, as Ian Hancock explains, truly qualify for the label 'a language', since they are more in the nature of in-group jargons. They are, nevertheless, of very considerable linguistic interest, and have been very little studied hitherto. One other variety that is used in Britain and assuredly DOES qualify for the label 'a language' has been excluded from the present volume. This is British Sign Language, as employed by the British deaf community. This has been omitted from this book solely on the grounds of its employment of a different medium.

344

21

Channel Island French

N. C. W. SPENCE

Norman French dialects are still spoken – if by steadily reducing numbers of people – in three of the Channel Isles: Jersey, Guernsey and Sark. In Alderney, although the island is mainly rural and relatively inaccessible, the local *patois* appears to have died out soon after the turn of the century. Its early disappearance can plausibly be attributed to the presence throughout the nineteenth century of large numbers of civilian and military personnel from Britain who built or manned extensive fortifications on the island (the military garrison was not withdrawn until 1930). In Sark (only two square miles and thus an even smaller island than Alderney), on the other hand, the Sark-born were nearly all dialect speakers until quite recently. Interestingly, although Sark is much closer to Guernsey than to Jersey, its dialect is more akin to Jersey-French than to Guernsey-French. This is because the island was colonized from Jersey in the sixteenth century, after Elizabeth I granted it as a fief to the Jerseyman Malet de Carteret on condition that at least forty men took up residence on the island.

My data for Jersey-French derive mainly from my own research, while my information about the phonology and morphology of Guernsey- and Sark-French is primarily based in the case of the former on Sjögren (1964), and in the case of the latter on the rather less reliable entries in Gilliéron and Edmont's *Atlas linguistique de la France*. The number of dialect speakers in the islands has never been established precisely (e.g. by census inquiries), and any estimate is little better than a guess. In 1960 I put the number of *patoisants* in Jersey at about 10,000 out of the then population of 60,000 (Spence, 1960: 11). The number is certainly lower today, for young people are not joining the ranks of the dialect speakers. Most of the southern coastal area has been urbanized, and even in the rural northern parishes of Jersey many residents are not native-born. In Guernsey the geographical distribution of dialect speakers is different since it is the east of the island that has been urbanized, while the dialect was widely spoken until comparatively recently in the west and south-west. Guernsey has received fewer English immigrants than Jersey and the number of dialect-speakers is estimated to be still over 10,000. However, according to Mrs Marie de Garis of the Société Guernesiaise, 30–40 year-olds hardly ever use the dialect, so that their children are barely aware of its existence.

The relationship of the Norman dialects of the Channel Isles to the standard language is different from that of the Norman dialects of the French mainland, in the sense that there are far fewer gradations from a broad dialect (assuming that anyone in France or England ever speaks 'pure' dialect) to as close an approximation to the standard as a given speaker can achieve. The Channel Islander switches to English when he feels that the use of a dialect is inappropriate (e.g. with strangers). There will therefore often be a switch of language, but there will not be a progressively greater approximation to Standard English – or to Standard French, since the latter is not the cultural language of the islands.

Some twenty-five years ago, I contrasted the dialects of mainland Normandy with that of Jersey, which I saw as maintaining its individual characteristics where the mainland dialects were undergoing piecemeal assimilation to the regional form of Standard French (Spence 1957: 90). The mainland dialects are clearly still very much at risk; what seems to have changed is the position of Channel Island French, the vitality of which has deteriorated dramatically since the end of the Second World War. It is still no doubt true that the last speakers of the island dialects will be speaking *patois* that are phonetically and grammatically still relatively 'pure' – but the indications are that those last speakers are already alive, and probably middle-aged. It is difficult to state categorically that none of the younger generation still use dialect in everyday life, but my informants in the islands felt that there are now few, if any. Mr Beaumont, the Seigneur of Sark, for instance, believes that 'the cut off point is about the age of 25 above which the patois is progressively more fluent and below which it is not spoken but understood and in the very young not even understood' (personal communication).

The reasons for the decline of the Channel Island dialects are no doubt largely similar to those that have applied elsewhere. The language of the media, of school, of most places of work and of monoglot friends and acquaintances is English. The dialects are rural, and although the material situation of the farming communities is not inferior to the urbanized inhab-itants – on the contrary – many people are obviously ashamed of their dialect. There are other factors that have had a cumulative effect. Given that all Channel Islanders speak English, and have done so for generations, there has long been no need for immigrants to learn the *patois*. The children of immi-grants from France have tended to reject their parents' language in favour of English, as the mass of second-generation immigrants has done in the United States and elsewhere. The most important single reason for the decline of the dialects, however, is probably that in a society where knowledge of the dialect is no longer a significant asset, the children of a dialect speaker and a non-dialect speaker are inevitably brought up as monoglot English speakers. Mr Beaumont informs me that of the forty children in Sark's primary school, only two have parents who are both Sark-born. The result is the same whether the non-dialect speaker is an immigrant or is Channel Island-born: let us recall that the dialect has not been spoken in the town of St Helier (with half the population of Jersey) in living memory, and add that the position of St Peter Port and St Samson in Guernsey is similar.

The Channel Island dialects share a number of features that are not found on the Norman mainland, and which are largely explained by the fact that English, not French, is the standard language of the islands. This is most evident at the lexical level. Many anglicisms have come into use over the centuries – cf. the widespread use in the dialects of forms based on *blacking* (= shoe polish), *cook*, *kiss*, *shop* and so on – and as individual islanders' knowledge of the dialects becomes less secure, so they use more and more anglicisms. All recent technical vocabulary is inevitably English, so conversations about motor vehicles, modern machines and techniques are copiously sprinkled with English words (cf. [ɑː ty frymɛ le tɒplaits d la griːnhaus?] *Have you closed the toplights of the greenhouse?*). Since the spontaneous development of the dialects has not been inhibited by the normative influence of Standard French, phonological and grammatical features are characterized by a greater consistency than exists in the mainland dialects, both in the survival of archaisms and in the spread of innovations. However, there does seem to have been a significant influence of English not only on the vocabulary of the dialects, but also on their pronunciation, if mainly by accentuating developments that are also found on the Norman mainland. Thus, the secondary palatalization of /k/ and /g/ before front vowels is widespread in Normandy, but the fact that English-type [tʃ] and [dʒ] affricates regularly replace them in the island dialects may be due to the contact with English (but Lechanteur (1948: 121) regularly found [tʃ] on the mainland as well). Similarly, although secondary diphthongs are quite common in the mainland dialects, the consistency with which [ei] and [ou] (for instance) have replaced lengthened close vowels seems to reflect the accentuation of a 'Norman' laxness in the articulation of vowels. The use of alveolar [t] and [d] rather than the French dentals is even more clearly due to the co-existence of the dialect and English speech systems.

The similarities between the island and mainland dialects are, however, more remarkable than the differences between them, and parallels are observable even in respect of features, such as the assibilation of intervocalic *r*, that are not common to all the island dialects. Let us first take some of the features that go back to the medieval period (cf. Pope, 1952: 487f and 501ff), and distinguished Norman from Francian (the dialect of the Île de France round Paris). These are, among others:

(i) The 'Normano-Picard' development of Latin /k/ before front vowels /e/, /ɛ/ and /i/ and semi-vowel /j/: cf. [ʃɑ̃] Fr *cent* [sɑ̃] 'one hundred'; [ʃimɑ̃] Fr *ciment* 'cement', etc.

(ii) The 'Normano-Picard' non-palatalization of Latin /k/ and /g/ before

Latin /a/: cf. [ka] Fr *chat* [ʃa] 'cat'; J,S [gɑ̃:b] G [gɑ̃:p] Fr *jambe* [ʒɑ̃:b] 'leg'. ('French' forms are also found (cf. [ʃɑ̃:br] 'bedroom', [ʃæ:n] 'chain', etc.), and there are many cases of secondary palatalization, e.g. [ʧɑ̃] Fr *chien* [ʃjɛ̃] 'dog' < Latin *canem*.)

(iii) The Norman and west French treatment of OF /ei/: cf. J,S [drɛ] Fr *droit* [drwa] 'straight'; J,G,S [me] Fr *moi* [mwa] 'me'; J [vɛl], G [veil] Fr *voile* [vwal] 'sail'.

(iv) A divergent development of Latin ĕ and ŏ (V Lat /ɛ/ and /ɔ/): cf. J [aɲɛ] G [ɔɲɛ], [aɲɛ] 'today' (OF *anuit*); J [jɛ] G [jɛt] S [λɛt] Fr *lit* [li] 'bed' (< Latin *lĕctum*), etc.

The dialects also preserve many of the features that were attributed to Norman by the French grammarians of the sixteenth and seventeenth centuries, and also parallel the mainland dialects in many of their more recent secondary developments:

(v) In east Jersey and south-west Guernsey at least, the [au] diphthong deriving from Latin *a* + *l* + C has been retained (cf. Thurot, 1881: vol. 1, 429): cf. east J, south G [kau] Fr *chaud* [ʃo] 1. 'hot' (< Latin *calidum*), 2. 'lime' (< Latin *calcem*), etc. An [au] diphthong from other sources is also heard in Guernsey: cf. [nau] Fr *nœud* [nø] 'knot' (< Latin *nōdum*); [nvau] Fr *neveu* [nəvø] 'nephew' (< Latin *nepōtem*).

(vi) In Guernsey and Sark, the nasality of pre-nasal vowels has often been preserved (or restored?) before front vowels: cf. G,S [fɑ̃:m] Fr *femme* [fam] 'woman'; G [lœ̃:n], [lɛ̃:n] Fr *lune* [lyn] 'moon', etc. (Cf. Hindret, 1696: 305.)

(vii) OF [ɔ], [o] have closed to [u] before retained nasal consonants: cf. J,G,S [kum] Fr *comme* [kɔm] 'how', 'as'; [um] Fr *homme* [ɔm] 'man', etc.

(viii) The aspiration of Germanic *h* has survived: cf. J,G [humar] Fr *homard* [ɔmaʀ] 'lobster'; J,G,S [haʃ] Fr *hache* [aʃ] 'axe', etc.

(ix) /k/ and /g/ have undergone secondary palatalization before front vowels, (including [y], [ø], [œ], etc.), and [tj] and [dj] have also become the affricates [ʧ] and [ʤ]: cf. J [ʧ ɥi] Fr *cuir* [kɥiʀ] 'leather'; [ʤeil] 'gale' (< Eng *gale*); [ʧɛd] Fr *tiède* [tjɛd] 'tepid'; [ʤɑ:bj] Fr *diable* [djabl] 'devil', etc.

(x) In Jersey and Guernsey, [λ] developed in exactly the same way as in the mainland Bessin dialect (cf. Joret, 1881: 25), i.e. it has simplified to [j] in medial position as in Standard French, but to [l] in final position in words like [fil] Fr *fille* [fi:j] 'daughter'; [famil] Fr *famille* [fami:j] 'family' and [butɛl] Fr *bouteille* [butɛ:j] 'bottle'. In Sark, according to the *ALF* readings, [λ] has often survived (*ALF* maps *ail, ailleurs, que j'aille, caillé*, etc.) but is tending to de-palatalize to [l] in word-final position (*ALF* maps *bouteille, chevreuil* and *vieille*). A rarer development of [λ] before earlier flexional *s* in some words is also matched in certain mainland dialects: cf. J,G [jɛr] 'eyes' and *ALF* maps 932 and 933 showing similar plurals at two points in Normandy (points 387 and 395); J,G,S [vjɛr] Fr *vieux* [vjø] 'old' (< Latin *vĕtulos*), etc.

(xi) As in mainland dialects (cf. Guerlin de Guer, 1898), [l] in C + *l* groups has undergone secondary palatalization: cf. J,G [kjou] S [kλoː] (cf. Fr *clos* [klo]) 'field'; J,G [bjã] S [bλã] Fr *blanc* [blã] 'white', etc.

(xii) Assimilation of voice has been extended in the islands and many mainland dialects to voiceless consonants such as /k/ and /ʃ/ brought into contact with following voiced consonants by the slurring of [ə]: cf. J [ʒvœ] G,S [gvœː] Fr *cheveu* [ʃəvø] 'hair'; J,G [ʒva] Fr *cheval* [ʃəval] 'horse' and *ALF* map *cheveu*.

(xiii) The secondary diphthongization of vowels that is very characteristic of the Channel Island dialects, particularly of Guernsey-French, is also found in mainland dialects; for example, [u] has been replaced by [wɔ] ([wɛ] in Haguais) in many – though not always the same – words in the islands and in the Bessin, the Calvados Department, etc. Close [e] and [o] have tended to diphthongize to [ei] and [ou], particularly in the Manche. Lengthened [œː] has been variously replaced by secondary [ai] in Jersey, and by [ei], [aø] or [øy] in Lower Normandy (cf. *ALF* map *deux* and Lechanteur, 1948: 114); Guernsey-French [ai] comes rather from /eː/ – cf. G [amair] Fr *amer* [amɛr] 'bitter'; [bɔtai] 'goodness', etc., (see Fleury, 1886 for similar development in Haguais). Guernsey's nasal diphthongs are (or were) paralleled by similar diphthongization in the La Rocque area in south-east Jersey.

(xiv) Final long vowels deriving from earlier V + [s] or V + [ə] have been preserved both in the island and mainland dialects, the difference between singular and plural (or masculine and feminine) often being marked by an opposition between short and long (e.g. J,G [pi ~ piː] 'foot ~ feet'). There is in the islands at least a distinction between short and long diphthongs as well: the Jersey word for 'rooster' is [koʉ], with two short elements compared to the plural [kou], in which both elements are normally longer.

(xv) The weakening of intervocalic *r* in Jersey is manifest in its assimilation to other consonants (e.g. in [lɛttiː] Fr *laiterie* [lɛtri] 'dairy' or [maʃunniː], Fr *maçonnerie* [masɔnri] 'masonry'). Its assibilation to [ð] ([t͡ʃɛðyː] Fr *charrue* [ʃary] 'plough'; [frɛð] Fr *frère* [frɛːr] 'brother', etc.) or to [z] (J [pit͡ʃœːz] G [pit͡ʃœːr] Fr *piqûre* [pikyr] 'sting') is paralleled, not in the other islands (unless S [md͡ʒuːk] 'stinking mayweed' derived from Latin *amarusca*, with its substitution of [d͡ʒ] for etymological *r*, is taken as evidence), but in mainland Normandy, in Haguais (Lechanteur, 1948: 120) and elsewhere (cf. Romdahl, 1881: 13 and Maze, 1903: 31).

(xvi) Morphological and syntactical similarities between the island and mainland dialects are too numerous to mention. This is perhaps less surprising than the convergence in phonetic developments occurring in areas that are not in any direct contact with each other, and which can only be explained in terms of some common articulatory traits and of the general dynamic of a common structure. The morphological similarities are largely due to relative conservatism of grammatical structures, rather than to common innovation. A feature that is common to the islands, but rare or non-existent on the mainland, is the extension into the imperfect and conditional of 1st and 2nd person plural forms in [eim] and [eit] parallel with the [i] or [y] + [m] and + [t] endings of the past historic: cf. [pɑːleim] Fr *parlions* '(we) were talking', [paːlleim] Fr *parlerions* '(we) should talk'. Fleury (1886: 76) notes the existence of forms like *étioumes* and *avioumes* with a different vowel + *m*, probably by analogy with *soumes* (= Fr *sommes*). This goes back to a much older tradition (cf. Pope, 1952: 503).

Having stressed the points of similarity between the island and mainland dialects, it is necessary to point to the other side of the coin, and note that there are remarkable variations not only between the dialects of the separate islands, but within the dialects of Jersey and Guernsey themselves. Since the total area of Jersey is 45 sq. miles and that of Guernsey under 30 sq. miles, the existence of such marked variation is surely unusual. In French, one would refer to *les parlers jersiais* (or *guernesiais*), and the use of the plural is certainly justified. Even an unobservant Jerseyman would identify a speaker as being from either east or west Jersey, and indeed would recognize the pronunciation of someone from St Ouen in the north-west as different from that of other west Jersey speakers. A language-conscious observer could probably place a speaker within a mile or so of his or her birthplace. The same is no doubt true of Guernsey.

Guernsey-French differs from Jersey- and Sark-French in a number of ways, the most obvious being in its nasal vowels. Along with some of the dialects of the Manche, it is characterized by the fact that the reflex of Latin *an* + C has remained distinct from that of Latin *en* + C, paradoxically through the development of the former to [ɛ̃ː]: cf. G [grɛ̃] Fr *grand* [grɑ̃] 'big'; [hɛ̃ːk] Fr *hanche* [ɑ̃ːʃ] 'hip', etc. The frequent development of nasal diphthongs has already been mentioned, and nasal vowels are often still followed, as in the French of the Midi, by a residual nasal consonant. There is a strong tendency for final voiced consonants to devoice, a trend which, to judge from the *ALF* map *auge*, appears to have existed in Alderney-French as well. According to Sjögren (1964: xx), final *b*, *d* and *g* regularly devoice to *p*, *t* and *k*, although this is not entirely confirmed by Sjögren's own notations. Both Guernsey and Sark have been more conservative than Jersey about the retention of final consonants: cf. G,S [byt] J [by] Fr *bout* [bu] 'end'; G,S [tʃœr] J [tʃø] Fr *cœur* [kœʀ] 'heart'. The conservatism of the Sark dialect is further attested by the retention of [ʎ], lost in the other islands, and above all by the retention of the affricate [dʒ] in the equivalents of Fr *argent*, *auberge*, *auge*, *bougeait*, *cage* and *changer* (cf. the corresponding *ALF* maps). As in Jersey-French, earlier *-ier* and *-ié* have reduced to [i]: cf. [kraʃi] Fr *cracher* [kʀaʃe] 'to spit'; J [ʃãʒi] S [ʃãʤi] Fr *changer* [ʃãʒe] 'to change'; and in Sark [ie/je] has often reduced to [i] even before a retained consonant: cf. S [koːdiːr] east J [ʃauʤɛð] Fr *chaudière* [ʃodjɛʀ] 'cauldron', etc.

It is sad to think that what has been a fundamental component of local culture in the Channel Isles should be threatened with rapid extinction, but one feels that unless there is a miracle, the local vernaculars will have disappeared completely within fifty years, and probably even earlier.

REFERENCES

Fleury, J. 1886. *Essai sur le patois normand de la Hague.* Paris: Maisonneuve and Leclerc.
Gilliéron, J. and Edmont, E. 1900–1912. *Atlas linguistique de la France (ALF).* Paris: Champion.
Guerlin de Guer, C. 1898. *Essai de dialectologie normande: la palatalisation des groupes initiaux gl-, kl-, fl-, pl-, bl-.* Paris: Champion.
Hindret, J. 1696. *L'art de prononcer parfaitement la langue française.* Paris: L. d'Houry.
Joret, C. 1881. *Essai sur le patois du Bessin.* Paris: Société de Linguistique.
Lechanteur, F. 1948. Nos enquêtes de l'Atlas Linguistique: de l'enquête en Basse-Normandie. *Le français moderne* 16: 109–22.
Maze, Abbé C. 1903. *Etude sur le langage de la banlieue du Havre.* Paris: Dumont.
Pope, M. K. 1952. *From Latin to Modern French.* 2nd edn. Manchester: Manchester University Press.
Romdahl, A. 1881. *Glossaire du patois du Val de Saire (Manche).* Linköping: Ridderstad.
Sjögren, A. 1964. *Les parlers bas-normands de l'île de Guernesey,* ɪ: *Lexique français-guernesiais.* Paris: Champion.
Spence, N. C. W. 1957. *Jersiais* and the dialects of the Norman mainland. *Bulletin de la Société Jersiaise* 17: 81–90.
——— 1960. *A glossary of Jersey-French.* Oxford: Blackwell.
Thurot, C. 1881. *De la prononciation française depuis le commencement du XVIe siècle.* 2 vols. Paris: Imprimerie Nationale.

22

Orkney and Shetland Norn

MICHAEL BARNES

The term *Norn* (noun and adjective, spelt in different ways but clearly derived from Old Norse *norrænn* 'Norwegian, Norse', *norræna* 'Norwegian, Norse language'), first recorded in 1485, has been used to denote a form of Scandinavian, closely related to Faroese, Icelandic and Norwegian, that was spoken in various parts of Scotland by the descendants of the Viking settlers. Today it is applied exclusively to the Scandinavian language that existed in Orkney and Shetland until the eighteenth century, and to remnants of this language in the modern dialects. Relatively little is known of Scandinavian speech elsewhere in Scotland (cf., however, Werner's annotated bibliography published in 1968), and for this reason as well as for lack of space, only the linguistic situation in Orkney and Shetland will be treated in this chapter (see map 22.1).

The origins and decline of Norn

Historical, archaeological and place-name evidence combine to suggest that the Scandinavian settlement of Orkney and Shetland began around 800 A.D. The settlers, the majority of whom apparently came from the coastal areas of western Norway (see map 22.2), arrived in great numbers, and by the end of the ninth century, if not before, their form of Scandinavian must have become the dominant language in the islands. Of the earlier inhabitants few linguistic traces survive. Scandinavian appears to have remained linguistically dominant in Orkney until the succession to the earldom of the Scots-speaking Sinclairs in 1379. In Shetland its position was unchallenged until well after the pledging of the Northern Isles (Orkney in 1468, Shetland in 1469) to King James III of Scotland. Our knowledge of Orkney Norn during its period of dominance is very slight. Scaldic verse was composed in the islands and some of it, mostly from the twelfth and early thirteenth centuries, is preserved, though in Icelandic MSS. Over thirty runic inscriptions have been found, the majority scribbled on the walls of Maeshowe, a prehistoric chambered mound, probably in the latter half of the twelfth century. Beyond this all we have are four documents from the period 1329–*c.* 1426. From Shetland some five runic inscriptions are known. They are fragmentary and

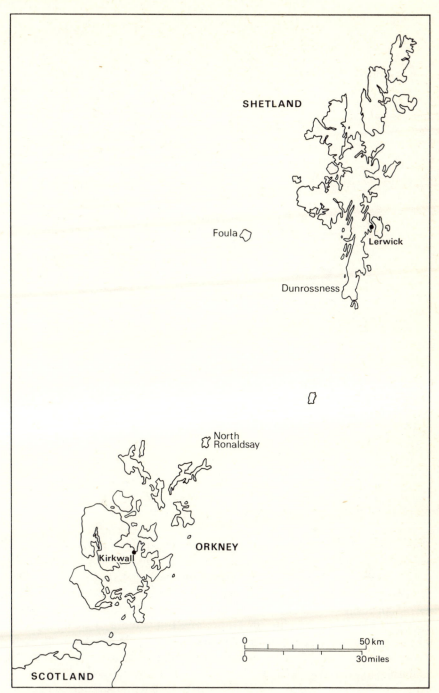

Map 22.1. Orkney and Shetland

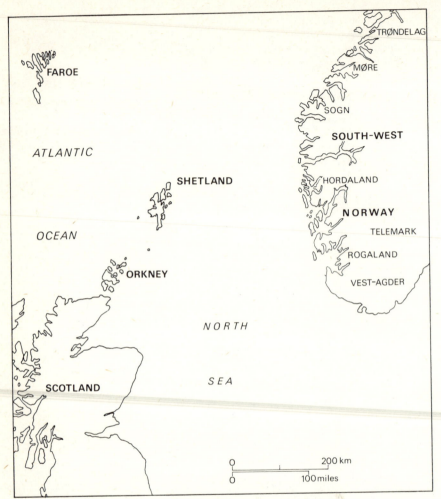

Map 22.2. Norway and Faroe in relation to Orkney and Shetland

difficult to date, but probably belong to the period 1000–1200. Nine documents have also been preserved, the oldest dated 1299 and the youngest 1509. The first surviving document in Scots from Orkney is dated 1433, and in 1438 we find the native Lawman of Orkney using the new language on internal Orcadian business. It is clear that Scots had replaced Norn as the language of prestige in Orkney before the impignoration. In the more isolated Shetland change did not come so quickly. The first surviving Scots document from these islands is dated 1525, but until the beginning of the seventeenth century Danish seems to have been used as well (the last document in this language is dated 1607). Of the fate of spoken Norn after 1500 we have a fair number of contemporary reports. It seems that it was the first language of most native Orcadians up to the end of the sixteenth century, and of most native

Shetlanders until well into the seventeenth. The reasons for the change from Norn to Scots are several. (i) Between 1379 and 1560, the date of the Reformation in Scotland, Scots became the language of the economic and social upper class, the administration, the courts and the Church. It therefore grew necessary for Orkneymen and Shetlanders to know something of the new language in order to deal effectively with authority. (ii) After the Reformation Scots (and English) gradually became the medium of religion. (iii) Considerable numbers of Scotsmen (apparently chiefly lowlanders from Angus, Fife and the Lothians) began to settle in the islands after 1400 (although immigration into Shetland was in general later and less intense). (iv) Trade with Scotland increased and Scots merchants established themselves in Orkney (especially) and Shetland in growing numbers. At the same time contact with Norway declined, although extensive trading links and family ties continued to exist at least until the end of the seventeenth century. (The bulk of Shetland's trade seems to have been with Norway and Germany until well into the eighteenth century.) (v) Schools established by the Society for Promoting Christian Knowledge are also said to have contributed to the disuse of Norn, although there were no such schools in Shetland until the eighteenth century.

The mechanics of the change from Norn to Scots are not entirely clear. What sources we have point to a high degree of bilingualism in the sixteenth and seventeenth centuries, with the bilingual element constantly increasing among the native Norse population and decreasing among the Scots. Hand in hand with this bilingualism, we must suppose, went considerable linguistic borrowing, especially from Scots to Norn. By the latter half of the seventeenth century there can have been few monoglot speakers of Norn left, and those still using the language had doubtless adopted a wider or narrower range of Scots features, depending on geography, age, place and topic of conversation and general inclination. Scots influence on Norn may in part underlie the references of contemporary (mainly eighteenth-century) writers to the language's being 'worn out'. So-called Norn speakers in the latter half of the eighteenth and first half of the nineteenth century probably represented the next stage in the process of change: their phonological and grammatical structure was basically Scots, but they used so many Norn words and phrases that to most, particularly younger people, their speech was largely unintelligible. It has been estimated (probably over-generously) that as late as 1850 nearly two-thirds of the total vocabulary of the Shetland dialect was still Norn in origin. Since then the Norn share of the vocabulary has declined greatly, though not always at the same speed. Under the letter *h* Jakobsen's dictionary of Norn (1928–32) contains 720 words. By his own general estimation only half of these were in common use in the 1890s. In 1949 J. J. Graham, now headmaster of a school in Lerwick, recognized a mere 107 of them, while in 1979 a 21-year-old Shetlander could still identify 65 (Graham, 1979: xix).

Although what we appear to see is a gradual change from pure Norn to Scots (and more recently English), it is unlikely that there were ever speakers who mixed the two languages up so inextricably that a trained linguistic observer would have been unable to determine which language they were speaking. If an individual's grammatical, and, above all, phonological structure were Scots, that person was no longer speaking Norn, however many Norn words or phrases his or her language contained. A number of fragments in what is or is alleged to be Norn survive, almost all from Shetland. One can only hazard an informed guess about the phonological system that underlies any one of them, but about the grammatical system there is often less doubt, as the following examples illustrate.

(1)   Nu fac an Iarlin dahuge
      Dar min de an engin gro
      An cast ans huge ei
      Fong ednar u vaxhedne mere nio.

      Di lava mir gugna
      Yift bal yagh fur o landi
      Gipt mir nu fruan Hildina
      Vath godle u fasta bande.

      (Now the earl received his death stroke,
      no one there could heal him;
      he [Hiluge] threw his [the earl's] head into her arms
      and her mood grew fiercer still.

      'You promised me a bride
      if bold I left the country;
      now give me the lady Hildina in marriage
      with gold and betrothal vows.')

(2)   Fy vor o er i Chimeri. Halaght vara nam dit. La Konungdum din cumma. La vill din vera guerde i vrildin senda eri chimeri. Gav vus dagh u dagloght brau. Forgive sindorwara sin vi forgiva gem ao sinda gainst wus. Lia wus ekè o vera tempa, but delivra wus fro adlu idlu for doi ir Konungdum, u puri, u glori, Amen.

(3)   to lag de kjøren
      'to move the cows'

(4)   Jarta, bodena komena rontena Komba
      'My dear, the boat (a boat) has come round Komba'

   Example (1) is stanzas 22–3 of a ballad about the Earl of Orkney and the King of Norway's daughter, Hildina, recorded on Foula, Shetland, in 1774 (ed. Hægstad, 1900). The ballad as we now have it contains 35 stanzas and is the only extant text of any length in Norn. Grammatically the two stanzas (which are typical of the ballad as a whole) are Scandinavian. They contain the suffixed definite article in *Iarl-in* and *dahug-e*. The distribution of morphological cases is as in those varieties of Scandinavian that have or had a four-case system, e.g., *an* (nom., subj.), *an* (acc., direct obj.), *ans* (gen.) 'he', 'him', 'his' (ON *hann, hann, hans*); *ednar* (gen.), *hedne* (dat., ind. obj.) 'her', 'to her' (ON *hennar, henni*); *yagh* (nom., subj.), *mir* (dat., ind. obj.) 'I', '(to) me' (ON *ek, mér*); *ei Fong* (accusative after a preposition denoting motion) 'into [her] arms' (ON *i fang*); *o landi* (dative after the preposition *o* which seems only to have governed this case) 'from the country' (ON *ór landi*). The verbal forms are Scandinavian, e.g. the past tense endings *-de, -a* in *minde, lava*. The word-order: head + modifier in *Fong ednar* is typically West Scandinavian. Vocabulary and usage are entirely Nordic except for the Scots loan-word *Yift*; indeed, lines very similar to some of these can be found in a number of ballads from various parts of Scandinavia.

Example (2) is a version of the Lord's Prayer, also recorded on Foula in 1774 (ed. Hægstad, 1900). Of the 63 words it contains, 9 are of Scots or English origin (as against *c.* 12 : 500 in *Hildina*), but they are used in a Scandinavian grammatical context, and have been assigned appropriate positions and endings, e.g. *vill din* (head + modifier), *forgiva* (pl. pres. verb ending), *tempa* (past part. ending), *puri* (weak noun ending). Other grammatical features that mark the Prayer as Scandinavian are, for example, the suffixed definite article (*vrild-in*), retention (at least in part) of the four-case system (*fro adlu idlu*, dative after the preposition *fro*), agreement in case, number and gender between adjective and noun (*Halaght vara nam dit*: both *Halaght* 'holy' and *dit* 'your, thy' are neuter singular nominative in agreement with *nam*), and various verbal endings such as the infinitive in *-a* (*cumma*), the imperative in *-a* (*delivra*), and the present indicative singular in *-r* (*er* 'are, is', *iir* 'own').

Example (3) is a 'fragment of conversation' recorded by Jakobsen in the 1890s (1928–32: xcii). It is too brief to allow the drawing of any far-reaching conclusions, but grammatically it clearly is not a 'fragment of Norn' as suggested by Jakobsen. Two of the words are of Norn origin (*lag, kjøren*), but the grammatical structure is Scots (or English): infinitive marker *to*, infinitive without ending (*lag*), prepositional def. art. (*de*). The ending *-en* is in origin a Norn definite article, but it no longer seems to function as such since *de* has been supplied. The status of the Norn words here is no different from that of the Scots (English) words in (2).

Example (4) is another of Jakobsen's 'fragments of conversation' (1928–32: xcii). Here the 'grammatical system' is neither Norn nor Scots. The piece offers a good example of the levelling of endings under *-(en)a* characteristic of many of the so-called Norn fragments, especially those in verse. Lexically (4) is Norn, and on that basis it could be classed as Scandinavian in its ultimate stage of decline in the Northern Isles.

The phonological and grammatical structure of Norn

Since written texts are our only guide, we can be more positive about the grammatical than about the phonological structure of Norn. It seems certain,

Table 22.1. *The vowel phonemes of twelfth-century Icelandic*

	Front		Non-front	
	Unrounded	Rounded	Unrounded	Rounded
High	iː ĩː i	yː ỹː y		uː ũː u
Mid	eː ẽː e	øː ø̃ː ø		oː õː o
Low	ɛː ɛ̃		aː ãː a	ɔː ɔ̃ː ɔ

In addition there were three diphthongs /ei/, /ey/, /au/ and an unstressed vowel sub-system /i/, /u/, /a/.

Table 22.2. *The consonant phonemes of twelfth-century Icelandic*

	Labial		Dental		Velar		Glottal
Stop	p/b	pː/bː	t/d	tː/dː	k/g	kː/gː	
Fricative	f	fː	θ s	sː			h
Nasal	m	mː	n	nː			
Trill			r	rː			
Lateral			l	lː			

A number of consonants must have had two or more allophones; /θ/, for example, had a voiced allophone [ð], while /g/ was [g] before non-front vowels, but almost certainly [ɟ] before front vowels, and [ɣ] in intervocalic and final postvocalic position.

however, that the linguistically dominant settlers in Orkney, Shetland, the Faroes and Iceland hailed mainly, if not exclusively, from the coastal areas of western Norway (between modern Nord-Trøndelag and Vest-Agder, see map 22.2). It is doubtful whether the language spoken in these areas in the ninth century was homogeneous, but there is much to suggest that it was a fairly uniform type of Scandinavian, possibly resembling most closely the Norwegian dialects of the south-west (modern Hordaland, Rogaland and Vest-Agder), that eventually became established in the islands of the north Atlantic. The phonological system of twelfth-century Icelandic, of which we have a fairly clear picture, probably differed very little from that which operated in the earliest 'island Scandinavian', and I therefore include tables (22.1, 22.2) of the vowel and consonant phonemes of that Icelandic system.

  How long this system (or an almost identical one) lasted in Orkney and Shetland cannot be gauged with certainty. The few extant Scandinavian texts which originated in the islands while Norn was still the principal or at least the majority language there show few if any traces of specifically Orcadian or Shetlandic features. The Scaldic verse apart, their language seems more or less identical with that current in contemporary writings in Norway. Even the replacement of Norwegian as a written language by Danish in the sixteenth century is faithfully reflected in the last Scandinavian documents from Shetland. However, taking into account the developments which occurred in the closely related dialects of Iceland, Faroe and western Norway, as well as what can be gleaned from the fragments of spoken Norn that have been recorded, we are safe in assuming that by the seventeenth century the following changes at least had affected the system outlined above. (i) Vowel length had ceased to be a distinctive feature and was regulated by the length of the following consonant(s). (ii) The nasal phonemes had merged with their oral counterparts. (iii) The high front rounded vowels had disappeared, /y/ having merged with various other phonemes in the system. (iv) The diphthongs had (in most words and varieties of speech at least) been replaced by one or other of the existing monophthongs. (v) The unstressed vowel system had been or was in the process of being reduced from three units to two (/a/ vs. some other vowel). (vi) /θ/ had, for the most part at least, merged with /d/, /t/ or /h/. (vii) A new phoneme, /ʃ/, had developed. Many other changes must also have taken place, but the evidence for them is often slight or contradictory and their effect on the phonological system uncertain. The following may be mentioned. (i) It is possible that /e/ and /ε/, and /o/ and /ɔ/, had merged. (ii) There are indications that certain of the original long vowels were diphthongized, but firm conclusions about the nature and status of this diphthongization cannot be reached on the basis of the available evidence. (iii) A range of palatal consonants apparently developed, but their phonemic status is uncertain; it does seem, however, that /lː/ and /nː/ must have disappeared from the system, at least in most varieties of speech, being replaced either by [l̩] and [n̩] or the clusters /dl/ and /dn/. (iv) /p/, /t/ and /k/ seem to have merged with /b/, /d/ and /g/ in intervocalic and final post-vocalic position, but although the *Hildina* ballad offers clear evidence of this development, it is by no means always found in the Norn vocabulary surviving in the nineteenth- and twentieth-century dialects. (v) There is some evidence for the development of affricates.

The grammatical structure of early Norn clearly did not differ materially from that of contemporary Icelandic and Norwegian, which in the Viking Age and medieval period were the main representatives of the western branch of Scandinavian or North Germanic. Early Norn thus possessed most of those grammatical features which characterize or characterized Germanic and Scandinavian languages as a whole, as well as a number which were typical of the western Scandinavian of the period (often called Old West Norse). A detailed rehearsal of these features here would be pointless since they can be readily ascertained from any grammar of Old Norse (e.g. Gordon, 1927 and later editions). A brief summary will suffice.

In common with all Germanic languages, Norn had two basic tenses of the verb (present and past), and three moods (indicative, subjunctive, imperative). It also distinguished between strong and weak verb conjugations (dependent on whether the past tense was formed by vowel alternation or a dental suffix). As in all the earliest Germanic languages three genders and four cases were marked in nouns, pronouns and adjectives, a distinction was made between a strong and weak adjective declension (a difference in form depending on function), and there was personal inflection in the verb. In common with virtually all varieties of Scandinavian, Norn had a suffixed definite article, and in common with all a verbal form in /-sk/ (later /-st/, East Scandinavian /-s/) which had reflexive, reciprocal and passive functions. Like all other Old Norse dialects, Norn often represented case, number and tense morphemes by alternations in the root vowel instead of, or as well as, by endings (a more common feature in Old Norse than in other Germanic languages). It also shared with other varieties of Old Norse an infinitive in /-a/ (or some other vowel), and vowel endings in virtually all forms of the weak adjective. Peculiarly West Norse were certain nominal and verbal forms (e.g. dat. pl. def. art. /-unum/, 2nd pl. ending /-Vþ/, vowel change in the present singular and past subjunctive of strong verbs), as well as the forms of a number of personal pronouns (e.g. *ek* 'I', *vér* 'we', *þit* 'you two', *(þ)ér* 'you' pl.).

Most of this system can be found intact in the *Hildina* ballad (which probably represents seventeenth- rather than eighteenth-century Norn), and seemingly in the Lord's Prayer, although this is too short to allow detailed conclusions about its grammatical structure to be drawn. Nevertheless, considerable simplification of the verbal paradigms has taken place: personal inflection has disappeared and been replaced in some verb types and tenses by a singular–plural distinction (based mainly on the 3rd person forms) and in others (as far as can be judged) by a single ending. There are also signs of an incipient breakdown in the case system of nouns and adjectives, but here the Old Norse pattern for the most part still prevails. Analogical levelling seems in some cases to have affected the representation of number, case and tense morphemes by root vowel alternation. Thus, while we still have *tegar*, pres. sing. of *taga* 'take', and *londen*, dat. pl. of *land* 'country', there is reason to think that the forms *buthe* (ON *bœtr*, pl. of *bót* 'compensation') and *cumi* (perhaps ON *kœmi*, 3rd sing. past subjunct. of *koma* 'come') no longer had front vowels in the stressed syllable. The personal pronouns too have undergone changes. For OWN *ek* 'I' we find *yach*, *yagh* and *a*, for *vér* (or *vit*) *vi* 'we', and for *þér* 'you' pl. (or *þit* 'you' dual) *di*. These forms could all be native developments, but *yach* (or *yagh*) and *vi* could also be due to the influence of Swedish and Danish which is evident in Scandinavian language documents emanating from Orkney and Shetland from the fifteenth century onwards. The use of the dative form *dem* (OWN *þeim* 'them') for the accusative, which occurs in the ballad, could be due to influence from Scots *them*, but is paralleled in numerous Scandinavian dialects.

In a number of important respects the grammatical system of seventeenth-century (Shetland) Norn is reminiscent of present-day Faroese. In Faroese the verbal forms have been simplified in much the same way: there are signs of a breakdown in the case system and analogical levelling of root vowel alternation has taken place in many forms. In terms of its grammatical structure Faroese has sometimes been classified as a relic of 'Middle Scandinavian'. This classification could probably also be applied to Norn in the last centuries of its existence as a natural and everyday language.

The relationship of Norn to other varieties of Scandinavian

That the linguistic origins of Norn, as well as those of Faroese and Icelandic, lie in western Norway has already been stressed. Many have argued that Norn was most closely related to the dialects of south-western Norway, but this is far from clear. 'South-western Norway' is a vague term. To some it means western Norway from Trøndelag to Agder, to others nothing much outside Rogaland (see map 22.2). Most people (including myself) take it to mean Hordaland, Rogaland and Vest-Agder. The earliest form of Norn may in fact have been based on the north-west Norwegian of the eighth and ninth centuries. Recent research on Shetland farm names suggests that they show very close affinities with those in north-west Norway, especially Møre and Sogn. On the other hand, the vocabulary of Norn, as preserved in the nineteenth- and twentieth-century dialects of Orkney and Shetland, seems to compare most closely with that of the dialects of Hordaland, Rogaland, Vest-Agder, Sætesdal and western Telemark. The phonetic evidence is contradictory. Pointing most clearly to south-west Norway are (i) the general retention of unstressed /a/, (ii) /ptk/ > /bdg/ in intervocalic and final post-vocalic position, (iii) /rn/ > /dn/, (iv) /nː/ > /dn/, and (v) /lː/ > /dl/. However, changes (iii)–(v) are only found in western areas of Shetland, especially Foula. Elsewhere in Shetland we find /rn/ and /nː/ > [n̩] and /lː/ > [l̩], and in Orkney /lː/ > [l̩], a development which in Norway seems to have its centre in Trøndelag. The change /fn/ > /mn/, regular in Orkney and Shetland Norn, is found in most parts of Norway outside the south-western area. The monophthongization of /ei/, /ey/ and /au/, regular in Shetland, more sporadic in Orkney Norn, is a strictly east Norwegian feature, though the form it takes in Norway (and east Scandinavia in general) is somewhat different from that found in Norn. Feature for feature the varieties of Scandinavian most closely related to Norn are Faroese and Icelandic, in that order. Both have undergone changes (i)–(v) above, either in all or some dialects. In addition Icelandic and Faroese have lost /y/, though in both languages, unlike Norn, it merges with /i/ (as it does in a few very small areas of Norway – none of which are in the south-west). ON initial [xw] appears in the south of Iceland as [xw], elsewhere as [kv]; in the latter area it is not distinguished from original [kw]. In Shetland Norn there seems to have been an east–west split, original [xw] and [kw] appearing as [kw] in the west and [hw] in the east. In Orkney Norn ON [kw] > [ʍ] (occasionally [w]), though many words still preserve [kw], perhaps suggesting an earlier dialectal split. In Faroese and Norwegian ON [xw] regularly > [kv] (merging with original [kw]), although in some eastern areas of Norway we find [xw] > [gv] or [v]. Three features are found in Shetland and one in Orkney Norn that otherwise only occur in Faroese. (i) The inter- calation of /g/ (Faroese /gv/) after the reflexes of ON /oː/ and /uː/ when in final position or followed by a vowel, e.g. ON *sjór* > **sjóur* 'sea', Faroese *sjógvur*, Foula Norn *sheug*. (ii) /m/ > /n/ in weakly stressed final position, e.g. ON *honum* (dative of *hann* 'he'), Faroese *honum* /honɔn/, Foula Norn *honon*. (iii) /θ/ > /h/ sporadically in initial position, e.g. ON *þetta* 'this', Faroese *hetta*, Foula Norn *ita* (< **hitta*); 'Thurstainshow' (Orkney rental of 1492) > 'Hurteso' (Rental of 1595, also the modern form of this name).

Differences between Orkney and Shetland Norn

It has been suggested that there were considerable differences between Orkney and Shetland Norn, and this may indeed have been the case, but few are observable now. Most of the differences noted above concern phonetic fea- tures found in eighteenth-century Foula Norn. We must remember, however, that we do not have records equivalent to those from Foula from any other part of Shetland or Orkney, so no proper comparison is possible. If we restrict ourselves to the late nineteenth and early twentieth centuries when Norn existed only as a powerful substratum in Orkney and Shetland Scots (and English), the following differences can be seen. (i) The change /ptk/ > /bdg/ was more regular in Orkney. (ii) The voiced allophone of /θ/, which except in Dunrossness was lost in Shetland (often merging with /d/), was apparently retained in a number of words in Orkney, e.g. ON *mið* 'fishing ground' > Shetland /mid/, Orkney /miþ/. (iii) Monophthongization of ON /ei/, /ey/ and /au/ was less consistent in Orkney than in Shetland, e.g. ON *skreið* 'swarm, multitude' > Shetland /skre/, Orkney /skrei/. On the different development of ON /rn/, /nː/ and /lː/ and of initial [xw] and [kw], see above.

There are considerable differences between the Norn word-stocks of Orkney and Shetland as they appear in the principal collections made between *c*. 1890 and 1930. This is explained partly as a result of the earlier and more radical Scotticization of Orkney (far fewer Norn words were recorded there), partly with reference to the different mode of life on the two groups of islands. While Orkneymen are primarily farmers, Shetlanders are fishermen, and Shetland speech was (and is) much richer in traditional words and expressions to do with the sea and fishing, many of which come from Norn. Orkney speech did not reveal a corresponding stock of traditional farming terms because by the time collecting started agriculture there had undergone considerable modern- ization. Similarly, for example, the practice of common grazing preserved the names of sheep ear-marks in Shetland, many of which stem from Norn, while the survival of the original native type of sheep ensured the continued use of many Norn adjectives describing their various colourings. In Orkney (except in North Ronaldsay), on the other hand, common grazing went out early in the nineteenth century, and the native sheep were replaced by white breeds imported from Scotland. Nevertheless there were, and to some extent still are, numerous words of Norn origin in regular use in Orkney which were rarely used or obsolete in Shetland. It should also be noted that the Scandinavian place names of Orkney and Shetland show certain differences of frequency and type, but this of course has more to do with topography and the naming habits of the settlers than with the Norn dialects that eventually became established in the islands.

Traces of Norn in the modern dialects of Orkney and Shetland

There exists no proper description of the modern dialects of Orkney and Shetland, or of the dialects of Scotland as a whole (though *The linguistic atlas of Scotland*, when complete, should go some way towards remedying this situation). The fundamental work on Norn was done 50–100 years ago by scholars whose main aim was to record as many words as possible that were or might be of Norn origin. The phonetic and grammatical information these scholars give is largely incidental and the presentation entirely unsystematic. Nor is any attempt made to place the lexical, phonetic or grammatical information recorded in the context of the Orkney or Shetland dialect of the period (about which we know very little). Those who wish to capture the Norn substratum in the modern dialects of Orkney and Shetland therefore have the unenviable task of trying to establish a plausible connection between the tantalizingly incomplete information offered by earlier scholars and what is known about the linguistic situation in the Northern Isles and Scotland today. Until more work is done on the latter, results can only be tentative and no firm pronouncements should be made. It is essential too to maintain a clear distinction between one's interpretation of earlier evidence and the features recorded in present-day speech. With all these reservations, I append the following list of what may be traces of Norn in the modern dialects of Orkney and Shetland.

Prosody

Many claims, often contradictory, have been made about affinities in intonation between Shetland (and to a lesser extent Orkney) speech and various Norwegian dialects. In the absence of proper measurements and contrastive studies, such assertions have no linguistic value.

Phonology

It is generally thought that the use in Shetland of /d/ and /t/ in nearly all cases for standard /ð/ and /θ/ is due to the loss of /θ/ in Norn. (In Orkney, too, it seems that in both Norn and Scots words original /θ/ appeared as /t/, but this is no longer the case.) It is also likely that Norn speech habits underlie the lack of distinction between initial [hw] and [kw] in Shetland (see page 361 above). In words of both Norn and Scots origin [kw] is (or was until very recently) used in the west, while [hw] prevails (or prevailed) in the east. (An eighteenth-century writer resident in Orkney reports the widespread use of initial *wh* – probably [ʍ] – for [kw], as in *wheen, whestion* 'queen, question', but this does not appear to be a feature of the modern dialect.) The occurrence of [l̥], [n̥] and other palatalized consonants, about which there is much conflicting information, and the use of which may have declined rapidly over the last 100 years, is paralleled in many Norwegian dialects and may be a Norn survival. It seems to be generally accepted that [l̥] and [n̥] do not occur in other dialects of Scotland. Reports that the syllable structure of closed stressed monosyllables in modern Shetland dialect is either VC̄ or V̄C remind one of the structure of all stressed syllables in most varieties of Scandinavian outside Denmark. The vowel systems of modern Orkney and Shetland dialects are Scots. (It has been suggested that Norn speakers with their rich vowel system but relatively small number of consonant phonemes could more readily imitate the vocalic than the consonant distinctions of Scots.) Nevertheless, it is sometimes argued and widely believed that the [ø] and [øː] sounds of these dialects (there is disagreement about their phonemic status, and no clear indication is offered, owing to different systems of notation, about the exact shade or shades of sounds that occur) are a Norn relic.

Morphology

Shetland speech distinguishes between familiar *du* and formal *you*. Such a distinction is not apparently found elsewhere in Scotland, not even in Orkney, but is general in Scandinavia. Orkney dialect is said to distinguish between the present participle and the verbal noun which end in /-ən/ and /-in/ respectively. The same distinction is apparently also to be found in some dialects of Scots, but it is claimed that in both cases the participial ending goes back (independently) to ON *-andi*. Nothing similar seems to be reported from Shetland. Many fossilized case-endings and suffixes occur in the surviving Norn vocabulary.

Syntax

The extensive use of 'preposition-adverbs' is put down to Norn influence, e.g. Shetland *come at* 'touch', Orkney *lay off* 'chatter, talk volubly'. Such usage is certainly far more common in Scandinavian than in English or Scots generally. The use of *he* to describe meteorological phenomena, e.g. Orkney *He's gaan tae blaw, I doot*, also has parallels in Scandinavia, especially in the Faroes and certain parts of Norway. It is variously claimed or suggested that, in Orkney *the're* or *de'r*, Shetland *der* 'there is, there are', the verb and possibly the pronoun too are of Norn origin (perhaps /de er/ < ON *þat er* 'it is, there is'). A recent article on Shetland dialect states that constructions such as *Minds du?* 'You remember?', *Kens du?* 'You know?' are 'obviously Norn'

(Melchers, 1981: 259–60), but no evidence is offered in support of this contention.

Lexicon

It is in the lexicon that the Norn substratum is clearest in both Shetland and Orkney Norn. For details the reader is referred to Jakobsen (1928–32) and Marwick (1929), but it should be remembered that these works list all the Norn words and phrases their authors were able to elicit 50 to 100 years ago. If we were to extend Graham's figures for the letter *h* in Jakobsen's dictionary (see page 355) to the whole work we would conclude that a Shetlander of the older generation might now recognize about 1,500 of the original 10,000, while a member of the younger generation would perhaps be familiar with *c*. 900. Similar calculations about Marwick's 3,000 words are unfortunately impossible since they were collected a generation later and he does not tell us how many were then in common use. Nevertheless, it is clear that the modern dialects of both Orkney and Shetland still contain a sizeable body of words of Norn origin. These tend to be restricted to certain areas of vocabulary and many writers attempt a rough categorization. The categories that emerge, however, seem often to be based chiefly on the Norn word-stocks of Jakobsen and Marwick, and much has happened in Orkney and Shetland society over the last 50–100 years which makes a categorization based on this material invalid for the modern dialects. It would be wrong to think, for example, that an important area of Shetland speech for the preservation of Norn words is the taboo language of fishermen, since this system of oblique references is now no longer in use. Melchers (1981: 260b), writing about the present-day dialect, lists the following areas of vocabulary as being particularly rich in Norn words: types of wind and weather; flowers and plants; animals; seasons and holidays; food; tools; materials and colours; movement; whims, ludicrous behaviour, unbalanced states of mind, qualities.

In conclusion it should be noted that the vast majority of place names of all types in Orkney and Shetland are of Norn origin. A recent study of the place names of Foula showed there to be about 80 Scots or hybrid names to 800 Norn. It is likely that the proportion would be similar throughout the Northern Isles.

REFERENCES

Gordon, E. V. 1927 and later editions. *An introduction to Old Norse.* Oxford: OUP.
Graham, J. J. 1979. *The Shetland dictionary.* Lewis: Thule Press.
Hægstad, M. (ed.) 1900. *Hildinakvadet.* Videnskabsselskabets Skrifter II: Historisk-filosofiske Klasse, 2. Christiania.
Jakobsen, J. 1928–32. *An etymological dictionary of the Norn language in Shetland.* London: David Nutt; Copenhagen: Wilhelm Prior.
Marwick, H. 1929. *The Orkney Norn.* Oxford: OUP.

Melchers, G. 1981. The Norn element in Shetland dialect today – a case of 'never accepted' language death. In E. Ejerhed and I. Henrysson (eds.) *Tvåspråkighet.* Umeå: Acta Universitatis Umensis. pp. 254–61.

Werner, O. 1968. Die Erforschung des Inselnordischen. *Zeitschrift für Mundartforschung* Supplement, NS 6, 2: 459–519.

23

Romani and Angloromani

IAN HANCOCK

The historical background

The total population of Gypsies throughout the world is somewhere between six and ten million, over half of whom speak dialects of the Gypsy language, Romani. In Britain, two distinct varieties of Romani are spoken, the inflected (Romnimos) and the creolized (Angloromani), the latter by perhaps 80,000 people, not all of whom are ethnically Gypsy, and the former by between two and five hundred people, perhaps more, primarily in north central Wales. These estimates do not include the small number of more recently arrived speakers of different Continental dialects.

The name 'Gypsy' is a misnomer, and not much liked by Gypsies themselves, whose self-designation is *Kɔlo* (Romnimos) or *Romničal* (Angloromani), or often 'Traveller' in English. The name 'Gypsy' is the result of Europeans believing Gypsies to be "gypcians' from Egypt; Gypsies are in fact of northern Indian origin, and left that part of the world some time in the first millennium, reaching southern Europe by about AD 1100. This exodus, the details of which are still not clearly understood, has been amply discussed elsewhere (Soulis, 1961; Vaux de Foletier, 1971).

It is convenient to discuss the migrations within Europe in terms of two waves, or diasporas, the first at the time of initial entry and the second after the abolition of more than five hundred years of slavery in the Balkans, in 1864 (Hancock, 1982). The traditional Gypsy populations in Spain, Scandinavia, Scotland, England and elsewhere arrived in those places during the Middle Ages, and have little in common now with those who have settled in the same countries over the past hundred years.

The Romani language is today fragmented into about sixty dialects, which fall into a number of groups. Work on their classification is still in progress, and this differs from scholar to scholar (Hancock, 1975; Wentzel and Cherenkov, 1976; Kaufman, 1979), but it appears broadly to be the case that there is a major division into the northern and the southern European dialects. The less extensively any dialect has been influenced by the non-Gypsy languages around it, the more it is likely to be understood by speakers of other conservative dialects.

British Romani belongs to the northern branch, and is historically most closely related to the Sinte dialects spoken in Germany and elsewhere. In the five hundred years of separation from the continental dialects, Romnimos has not appreciably altered, and there is still 75 per cent or greater mutual intelligibility with speakers of some other European (and American) varieties of the language. Angloromani, which has grown out of, but away from, Romnimos, cannot be understood by speakers of any other dialect.

The earliest reference to Gypsies in the British Isles is dated about 1452, when 'a company of Saracens or Gipsies from Ireland infested the country of Galloway' in Scotland (MacRitchie, 1894: 20; see also McPeek, 1969: 252:5); specific references mentioning Gypsies by name turn up again in 1470, 1505 and 1512. There are descriptions of people who may well have been Gypsies but who are not specifically identified as such, dating from the early fourteenth century, though Bercovici (1929: 263) is probably wrong in believing that the first Gypsies in Britain 'arrived in the isles in the eleventh or twelfth century'.

The small number of French words in British Romani suggest by their form that entry into Britain was via Belgium or northern France; there is also evidence that there was a certain amount of trafficking between the British Isles and Scandinavia at this time; a similar linguistic development has taken place in the latter countries among the Gypsy population there (Hancock, 1977: 14–15).

Romnimos

The first sample in print of inflected British Romani (and in fact of any dialect anywhere in the world) appeared in 1547, and was collected by Andrew Boorde, apparently in a tavern. This is given below in the sample texts. For several centuries it was believed by non-Gypsy scholars that the inflected dialect had become extinct. George Borrow, who explored all of Wales and who wrote a book about it, remained unaware of the language despite his enthusiasm for Angloromani. The first outsider to learn that the inflected language was indeed still alive in Wales was Crofton in 1874 (Smart and Crofton, 1875), in Bettws-y-Coed (in Gwynedd). This was reconfirmed in 1876 by Francis Hinde Groome who met a man, John Roberts, in Y Dref Newydd (in Powys), who could not only speak the language but who could read and write it as well. Groome later published samples of this, in 1879 and 1880. It was John Sampson, however, who must be remembered for systematically collecting folktales and linguistic data from Kɔle all over Wales (but particularly in the neighbourhood of Tal-y-Llyn in Gwynedd), culminating in his magnificent *Dialect of the Gypsies of Wales* (1926). Reviews of the book, such as those of Gilliat-Smith (1927) and Collinson (1927) add a little to the available sources on the language; the latter writer published an article on

Welsh grammatical interference in Romani a year later (Collinson, 1928). Hutchison (1976) has edited a collection of children's writing.

A sketch of the structure of the language actually appeared 16 years earlier (Bourgeois, 1910), though this had been gleaned from the texts of some Welsh Romani folktales which Sampson had already published. The next important discussion of the state of the language was that of the late Derek Tipler in 1957; no major first-hand treatments have appeared since, though Lockwood (1975) presented a grammatical outline based entirely on Sampson's earlier work. Lockwood believed that the language had become extinct: of its speakers, he said, 'there are none surviving today' (1975: 243). In 1977 an article on Welsh Romani place names appeared by Fowkes but, again, based wholly on Sampson's data. In 1954 the late Dora Yates of the Gypsy Lore Society in Liverpool supervised a short tape-recording at Bettws-Gwerfil-Goch of a conversation in Romnimos, for a long time available only through the BBC sound archives, but now commercially available in cassette form, together with samples of Romani music and song (Wood, *et al.*, 1975). In 1979 a book appeared by Jarman and Jarman, in Welsh, which deals with the history and life of the Welsh Gypsies, but the whole book, including chapter 6, which deals with language, is derived from secondary sources, and once more, from Sampson in particular. Although historically related to them, the *Kɔle* in Wales regard the 'English' Gypsies, whom they refer to as *Hotchiwitchies* (Angloromani for 'hedgehog', the Romnimos word being *určos*), as quite a distinct group. Sampson's informants remembered that their ancestors came to live in the Principality from Frome (in Somerset) in the eighteenth century, so the inflected language was still current in England at that time.

Romnimos has two genders, two numbers and three cases in the nominal, pronominal and adjectival systems, and four tenses of the verb. Its lexicon is overwhelmingly of central and north-western Indian origin, with layers of accreted vocabulary from Persian, Armenian, Greek, Balkan, German, French, English and Welsh, in that order, reflecting the chronology and migratory route of the ancestors of the Gypsies in Britain.

There are several classes of nouns, verbs and adjectives, each with slightly differing paradigms. No attempt has been made here to give examples of them all; these may be found in Sampson (1926).

Nouns, adjectives, pronouns, adverbs

Masculine nouns usually end in *-o* or a consonant, and feminine nouns in *-i* or a consonant, when they are in the singular subject (nom.) case form. When they are the object of a sentence, these endings become *-es* and *-ya* respectively. The object form is sometimes called the 'oblique' case in Romani linguistics, because as well as being the accusative, it is the form to which a number of postpositions may be suffixed. Some grammars of Romani treat these postpositional forms as distinct cases. The complete set of endings (for one type of masculine and one type of feminine noun), together with the corresponding article and adjectival forms, is as set out in table 23.1. *Raklo* and *rakli* apply only to a non-Gypsy (*gɔdžikano*) boy and girl; a Gypsy boy is a *čavo* or *čɔvo*, and a Gypsy girl is a *čai*, both declined slightly differently. The genitive form also functions adjectivally, and takes the appropriate endings,

Table 23.1. *Declension of nouns in Romnimos*

(1) Masculine singular, *raklo* 'boy':

Nominative	*o bɔr-o rakl-o*	the big boy (subj.)
Oblique	*i bɔr-e rakl-es*	the big boy (obj.)
genitive	*i bɔr-e rakl-es-k(er)o*	of the big boy
dative	*i bɔr-e rakl-es-ki*	to/for the big boy
ablative	*i bɔr-e rakl-es-te*	from the big boy
instrumental	*i bɔr-e rakl-es-sa*	by/with the big boy
prepositional	*i bɔr-e rakl-es-ti*	(prep. +) the big boy
Vocative	*bɔr-e rakl-aya!*	oh big boy!

(2) Masculine plural, *rakle* 'boys':

Nominative	*i bɔr-e rakl-e*	the big boys (subj.)
Oblique	*i bɔr-e rakl-en*	the big boys (obj.)
genitive	*i bɔr-e rakl-eŋ-(er)o*	of the big boys
dative	*i bɔr-e rakl-eŋ-i*	to/for the big boys
ablative	*i bɔr-e rakl-en-de*	from the big boys
instrumental	*i bɔr-e rakl-en-sa*	by/with the big boys
prepositional	*i bɔr-e rakl-en-di*	(prep. +) the big boys
Vocative	*bɔr-e rakl-ɔle!*	oh big boys!

(3) Feminine singular, *rakli* 'girl'

Nominative	*i bɔr-i rakl-i*	the big girl (subj.)
Oblique	*i bɔr-e rakl-ya*	the big girl (obj.)
genitive	*i bɔr-e rakl-ya-k(er)o*	of the big girl
dative	*i bɔr-e rakl-ya-ki*	to/for the big girl
ablative	*i bɔr-e rakl-ya-te*	from the big girl
instrumental	*i bɔr-e rakl-ya-sa*	by/with the big girl
prepositional	*i bɔr-e rakl-ya-ti*	(prep. +) the big girl
Vocative	*bɔr-i rakl-i!*	oh big girl!

(4) Feminine plural, *raklya* 'girls'

Nominative	*i bɔr-e rakl-ya*	the big girls (subj.)
Oblique	*i bɔr-e rakl-yan*	the big girls (obj.)
genitive	*i bɔr-e rakl-yaŋ-(er)o*	of the big girls
dative	*i bɔr-e rakl-yaŋ-i*	to/for the big girls
ablative	*i bɔr-e rakl-yan-de*	from the big girls
instrumental	*i bɔr-e rakl-yan-sa*	by/with the big girls
prepositional	*i bɔr-e rakl-yan-di*	(prep. +) the big girls
Vocative	*bɔr-e rakl-ya-le!*	oh big girls!

thus *i bɔre rakleskero kher* 'the big boy's house', but *i bɔre rakleskeri skamin* 'the big boy's chair', *i bɔre rakleskere khera* 'the big boy's houses', *i bɔre rakleskere skaminya* 'the big boy's chairs', etc. The prepositional form is the one which follows certain prepositions, though its use is inconsistent, speakers often using the simple nominative in such constructions instead. Like the dative, it may also stand for the 'to' or 'for' form of the object. Prepositions requiring this nominal form include *avri* 'out of', *maskal* 'between', *opre* 'over', *pɔše* 'near', *tala* 'under', etc.

There is no superlative construction for adjectives, but there is a comparative which is made by adding *-eder* to the root:

(masc.) o bɔro kher   'the big house'   o bɔreder kher   'the bigger house'
(fem.)   i bɔri skamin 'the big chair'   i bɔreder skamin 'the bigger chair'
(pl.)   i bɔre khera 'the big houses' i bɔreder khera 'the bigger houses'

'Than' is *nor*, from English: *bɔreder nɔ man* 'bigger than me'.

Many nouns can produce adjectival forms by adding various suffixes to their root; one of the commonest is *-ano* (masc.), *-ani* (fem.), *-ane* (pl.):

Rom   'Gypsy (man)'   Romani čib   'Gypsy language'
gɔdžo   'non-Gypsy (man)'   gɔdžikano xɔben 'non-Gypsy food'
bal   'hair'   balane hera   'hairy legs'

Adverbs derived from adjectives are formed from the latter by the addition of *-es* to the stem:

Romanes   'Gypsily', 'in the Gypsy manner'
gɔdžikanes   'non-Gypsily', 'in the non-Gypsy manner'
balanes   'hairily'

The comparative forms of such adverbs are the same as those of the corresponding adjectives, thus:

žɔž   'power'
žɔžvalo   'powerful'
žɔžvales   'powerfully'

but:

žɔžvaleder   'more powerful; more powerfully'
mus te thiles les žɔžvaleder   'you must hold it more firmly'

There is in a few words the remnant of another adverbial form, possibly once a locative postpositional ending, thus:

kher 'house'   khere   'in the house', 'at home'
rat 'night'   rati, rate 'at night', 'nightly'

The subject and oblique forms of the personal pronouns are *me/man* 'I/me', *tu/tut* 'you', *yov/les* 'he/him/it', *yoi/la* 'she/her/it', *ame/amen* 'we/us', *tume/*

tumen 'you' and *yon/len* 'they/them'. These follow the general pattern for nouns, thus *man-de* 'from me', *amen-sa* 'with us', etc. The possessive forms, which must agree in their various endings in number, case and gender, are, in the masculine nominative singular, *miro* or *mo* 'my', *tiro* or *to* 'your' (sing.), *lesk(er)o* 'his', *lako* 'her', *pesko* or *po* 'his own/her own', *amɔro* or *'mɔro* 'our', *tumaro* 'your' (pl.), *leŋ(er)o* 'their' and *peŋo* 'their own'. These may also take nominal endings, thus *tumarende* 'from yours', etc.

Verbal forms

There are four indicative tenses of the verb, plus a past participle and an imperative, though there is no infinitive. The present indicative endings for the commonest class of verb are

(me)	dikh-av (dikh-a, dikh-ava)	'I see'
(tu)	dikh-es(a)	'you see'
(yov)	dikh-el(a)	'he sees'
(yoi)	dikh-el(a)	'she sees'
(ame)	dikh-as(a)	'we see'
(tume)	dikh-en(a)	'you see'
(yon)	dikh-en(a)	'they see'

In the present tense, either the long or the short forms (i.e. with or without the final *-a*) can be used, while the long form alone is used to express the future tense, and the short form alone, when it follows *te* (or *me*) is used to express what would be the infinitive in English:

dikhas i bare džukles	'we see the big dog'
dikhasa i bare džukles	'we see/we will see the big dog'
trašasa te dikhas i bare džukles	'we are scared to see the big dog' (lit. 'we fear that we see . . .')

The perfect tense is usually formed by affixing an *-l-*, *-n-*, *-d-* or zero to the verb stem, followed by the personal endings thus:

(me)	dikh-om	'I saw', 'I have seen'
(tu)	dikh-an	'you saw', 'you have seen'
(yov)	dikh-as	'he saw', 'he has seen'
(ame)	dikh-am	'we saw', 'we have seen'
(tume)	dikh-an	'you saw', 'you have seen'
(yon)	dikh-e	'they saw', 'they have seen'

The imperfect and the pluperfect tenses are both constructed by suffixing *-as* to the present and the perfect paradigms respectively:

(me)	dikh-av	'I see'
(me)	dikh-av-as	'I was seeing', 'I used to see'
(me)	dikh-om	'I saw', 'I have seen'
(me)	dikh-om-as	'I had seen'

This last tense is not commonly used in Romnimos, its place being taken by the perfect.

The past participle, like the perfect tense to which it is related, is also formed from the verb root plus an *-n-*, *-l-*, *-d-* or zero followed by *-o* (masc.), *-i* (fem.) or *-e* (pl.). This usually functions as an adjective, for example:

o phago udar   'the broken door'   (< phag- 'break')
i mardi kaini   'the slaughtered chicken' (< mar- 'slaughter')
i thodile rivibena   'the washed garments'   (< tho- 'wash')

With the 'be' verb, the past participle is used in passive constructions:

čindo šomas   'I got cut'
čordi sas i grasni 'the mare was stolen'
ride si   'they are dressed'

The 'be' verb has the following forms:

(me)	šom	'I am'	(ame)	šam	'we are'
(tu)	šan	'you are'	(tume)	šen	'you are'
(yov)	si	'he is'	(yon)	si	'they are'

(me)	šomas	'I was'	(ame)	šamas	'we were'
(tu)	šanas	'you were'	(tume)	šenas	'you were'
(yov)	sas	'he was'	(yon)	sas	'they were'

The same verb in combination with the prepositional form of the noun or pronoun translates 'have', thus *si mandi bɔro kher* 'I have a big house'; *sas i rɔnyati rinkeni raxuni* 'the lady had (a) beautiful dress'.

The future of 'be' is translated by the verb *av-* (*'v-*) 'come' or 'become': *tu 'ves bɔro rai* 'you'll be a great man'.

Verbs are negated with *na* (or *ne* before *te*):

na dikhava la   'I don't see her'
wɔntsava ne te 'vel pɔle 'I want him not to come back'

The third person present tense of the 'be' verb has its own negative, *nai*:

nai lesti lovo   'he has no money'
o gono nai phardo   'the sack isn't full'

The negative imperative is *mɔ*; the imperative itself is generally the verb stem alone in the singular, and the stem plus *-en* in the plural:

mɔ per!   'don't fall!'
mɔ kuren! 'don't fight!'

Angloromani

In order to understand why Romani in Britain has become what are essentially two mutually unintelligible languages – or rather, extremities of a continuum – one must understand the social situation Gypsies met upon their arrival.

The transitional period between the Middle Ages and the Renaissance was a time of great social change. When Gypsies came into the British Isles during this time, they found a very considerable population of native 'sturdy beggars', i.e. healthy and often skilled, though unemployed, men who were obliged to support themselves through petty crime because of the breakdown of the guild system. There were also a great many 'real' beggars, forced on to the roads because of the dissolution of the monasteries (which traditionally took care of the poor) and as a consequence of the ending of the Hundred Years' War and the War of the Roses in the fifteenth century, which brought thousands of ex-soldiers back to burden the job market (Chamberlin, 1965). Gypsies who remained aloof from the native population were able to maintain the language intact; those who interacted with the English outlaws developed, over a period of time, a restructured contact language, Angloromani, which has gradually supplanted Romnimos almost entirely.

There are two hypotheses regarding the origins of Angloromani, namely that it is either the result of comparatively recent decay of the inflected speech (Kenrick, 1971, 1979), or that it began developing alongside Romnimos as a consciously-disguised means of communication in the sixteenth century, gradually supplanting the latter almost entirely save in Wales, where the Welsh language environment hindered the massive influence from English (Hancock, 1970, 1971, 1977). There are arguments for both hypotheses, and perhaps the existence of Angloromani is a result of both. Inflected Romani in Wales today is beginning to crumble in the face of the increasing use of English there; in the 1950s Tipler recorded such calques and misinterpretations as *šomas uštilo* 'I was lifting' instead of *azeravas* (lit. 'I was' + 'raised') and *šom beravav* 'I am combing', instead of *buravav* or *xulavav*, (lit. 'I am' + 'I comb'). The present writer heard similar constructions in Llanidloes in the mid-1960s, and noted especially lexical loss and misapplications of case and gender assignations. Whether Romnimos is becoming what Angloromani was in its formative stages, however, is not easy to say. A study of the demise of inflected Romani in Britain along the lines of Dorian's recent work on the death of Gaelic in Sutherland (1981) would be most valuable.

The principal characteristics of Angloromani, which is sometimes called *pɔgədi džib* 'broken language' or *pɔš-ta-pɔš* 'half-and-half' by its speakers, are the almost wholesale loss of the grammatical features of the inflected language, and their replacement by English morphological and syntactic rules, and by a number of linguistic characteristics which seem to have generated themselves independently of either English or Romnimos.

Phonology

Angloromani phonology is English phonology. The only non-English sound to remain for some speakers is the uvular fricative /x/, and even this has frequently become /h/ or /k/:

R: xɔben   A: hɔbən   'food'
R: xoxano   A: hʌkəno   'deceitful'

The phonetic and phonemic distinction between aspirated and non-aspirated stop consonants has been lost, or else has become a voiced – voiceless contrast:

R: ker-   A: kɛr   'do'
R: kher   A: kɛr   'house'
R: tud   A: dud   'brightness'
R: thud   A: tud   'milk'

Angloromani has also acquired various non-Romani secondary vowels of English (ʌ, ə), and the stress pattern typical of that language.

Nouns and pronouns, adjectives and adverbs

Nouns follow the regular English pattern of pluralization and formation of the possessive (Romani items are in roman type, English-derived morphemes are in italics):

R: džukel   A: *a* džuk   'a dog'
R: dui džukle   A: dui džuk*s*   'two dogs'
R: i džuklesa   A: *wi' the* džuk 'with the dog'
R: i džukleskero A: *the* džuk'*s* 'the dog's'

There remains in common use the ending -*bən*, which may combine with verbs, adjectives, etc., to produce nouns: *džin* 'know', *džinəbən* 'knowledge'; *kɔni* 'blind', *kɔnibən* 'blindness', etc. Less frequently employed is the suffix -*məs*, with the same function: *hɔinə* 'angry', *hɔinəməs* 'anger'.

Although the function of the nominal possessive endings has been taken over by English -'*s*, some of these have remained as frozen forms, or else have been reapplied as a means of expanding the vocabulary. Since nearly everything EXCEPT the vocabulary in Angloromani is of English derivation, it is only by maintaining the latter that the language retains its distinctiveness. These endings may be attached to items which are historically of either number or gender, and they have no possessive function of their own, thus:

kur   'to fight'
kurəmɛskrə 'boxing glove'
kurəmɛngrə 'boxer, fighter'
kurəmɛngri 'tambourine'

The same word-forming process occurs in Romnimos (and other northern dialects), but far less extensively.

All distinctions of gender and case have been lost in the Angloromani pronouns. This may be illustrated by the 1st person singular:

R: me	A: mandi	'I'
R: man	A: mandi	'me'
R: maya	A: mandi	'me' (emph.)
R: mandi	A: mandi	'me' (prepositional)
R: maɲi	A: *to, for* mandi	'to, for me' (dat.)
R: mansa	A: *wi'* mandi	'with me' (instr.)
R: mande	A: *from* mandi	'from me' (abl.)
R: miro	A: mandi'*s*	'my' (masc. sing.)
R: miri	A: mandi'*s*	'my' (fem. sing.)
R: mire	A: mandi'*s*	'my' (oblique)

While Romnimos has both prepositions and postpositions, only the former have been retained in Angloromani; similarly most plural personal pronouns, and the 'his/her own', 'their own' forms are wanting. Those which remain in use are *mandi* 'I', *tuti* 'you', *yʌv* or *lɛsti* 'he', *yɔi* or *yuwi* 'she'. Other personal pronominal forms (such as *lɛdi* or *lɛndi* 'they', *lis* 'it', etc.), are known to some older speakers and in some families. The commonest Angloromani pronouns derive from oblique forms in the inflected language.

Adjectives conform to the English pattern in their comparative and superlative forms:

yɔk*y*, yɔk*ier*, yɔk*iest*   'clever', 'cleverer', 'cleverest'
wafədi, *more* wafədi, *most* wafədi   'bad', 'worse', 'worst'

'Than' is expressed by *dən* or *ən* (< English *than*), *nə* (< *nor*), or sometimes *tə* (< *to*):

kʌvə'*s much more* šilənə '*n Reggie's* tan
'this is much colder than Reggie's place'

Adverbs derived from adjectives retain the same adjectival form. Some items contain the frozen adverbial ending *-is*, though this is no longer a productive morpheme in the language:

she gil*ies right* šukə   'she sings very prettily'   (šukə 'nice, sweet, quiet')
stɔl *actin'* lubənis   'stop acting wantonly'   (lubni 'whore, whorish')
he ridəs rʌmnis   'he dresses Gypsy-fashion'   (rʌmni 'Romani')

Verbal forms

Verbs in Angloromani usually correspond to the singular imperative or the 3rd person singular in Romnimos; these are unanalysable forms which follow the English pattern:

R: dav	A: mandi del*s*	'I give'
R: del	A: *he* dels; lɛsti dels	'he gives'
R: les	A: tuti lel*s*	'you take'
R: činasa	A: *we* čin*s*	'we cut'

R: mɔŋ! (sing.)   A: mɔŋ!   'beg!' (sing. and pl.)
R: dikhen! (pl.)   A: dik!   'look!' (sing. and pl.)

Other verbal constructions are similarly patterned on English:

R: šundom len   A: mandi's šuned 'em   'I've heard them'
R: dikhan les tu?   A: did tuti dik it?   'did you see it?'
R: avena marde   A: lɛdi'll get mɔred   'they'll get killed'
R: xoxado sas o Luther A: Luther had been čived   'Luther had been
                                                     cheated'
R: činesas   A: tuti was činin'   'you were cutting'

The 'be' verb is usually English, although some families of speakers retain the singular present tense native forms, i.e. *šom, šan, si*, though this last most frequently serves for all persons and numbers: *mandi si the šerengrə*, 'I'm the boss' (*the* is English). The past tense is the regularized 3rd person singular native past, *mandi sas, tuti sas* (Rom *šomas, šanas*) 'I was', 'you were'. Sometimes the 'be' verb is omitted altogether in copula constructions:

əkai tuti's patərans   'here are your pages' (lit. 'leaves')
tuti rinkəni rɔni   'you are a beautiful lady'
tuti kušti dikin' muš   'you're a fine looking man'

Negation is indicated by the word *kɛk* or *kɛkə*; the negative imperative is *mɔ*, 'don't':

mandi *can* kɛk ker lis   'I can't do it'
tuti kɛk'*ll be able to* dik *the* muš   'you won't be able to see the man
  from əkoi   from here'
mɔ rɔkə *you* div, *the* gɔdžə's šunin' 'don't talk, you fool, the non-
                                         Gypsy's listening'
There's kɛkə pani dre kʌvə kuri   'there's no water in this bucket'

Lexicon

It is in its internally-generated vocabulary that Angloromani shows its greatest inventiveness. Speakers show remarkable skill, when necessary, in keeping it as free from English, or recognizable English, as possible. Even where items in the source language did not exist, such as e.g. 'aeroplane', 'television', etc., equivalents for these have been formed from the existing stock of words to expand the lexicon. This is also true for items which, although occurring in inflected Romani, have been lost in Angloromani, e.g. 'gun', 'wheel', 'sand', etc. Several processes of expansion are employed, the most usual being incoining, whereby new words are created by joining existing morphemes in original combinations having no exterior models (i.e. in either English or Romnimos):

dikin' muktə   'television'   (lit. 'looking box')
dur-dikəmɛngrə   'telescope'   (lit. 'far-see' + -mɛngrə)

lolə-čam	'copper'	(lit. 'red tin')
lon-čik	'sand'	(lit. 'salt dirt')
naš*in*' pani	'waterfall'	(lit. 'running water')
prastər*in*' sastə	'bicycle'	(lit. 'running iron')
rɔkəšunɛngri	'telephone'	(lit. 'speak listen' + -ɛngri)
rʌmni-rɔkər*in*'-čeriklə	'parrot'	(lit. 'Romani-speaking-bird')
sasti-čɛriklə	'aeroplane'	(lit. 'iron bird')
sasti-groi	'locomotive'	(lit. 'iron horse')

A number of items originate in the fact that their primary English interpretations have homonyms in that language which provide secondary interpretations in Angloromani; thus *drʌm* means 'way' or 'road' in all dialects of
the language, but on the basis of the additional meaning of *way* in English,
also means 'way' or 'manner' in Angloromani. Similarly *hev* means 'hole',
while *hevy* (-y is English) means 'holy', *šil* means 'cold, chilly' and also 'cold,
catarrh', *tulo* is 'fat, overweight', as well as 'fat, grease', and so on. Clearly
an intimate knowledge of English is necessary for these pun-like extended
interpretations to be used and understood. Some of these techniques (others
are discussed in Hancock, 1977: 26–32 and 1980: 63–88) are applied spontaneously, sometimes as a kind of linguistic exercise or game, and the resulting
creations may never be heard again; but those listed here, and dozens of others
similarly formed, have gained widespread currency throughout England. The
social function of such Angloromani language skills, as well as a discussion of
other socio-linguistic aspects of the British Romničal population, has been
well described in Kenrick (1979).

Texts

1.   The earliest recorded text in inflected Romani (from anywhere), collected
in England *c*. 1547. The modern Romnimos form is given in square brackets
after Boorde's original text:

Lach ittur ydyues!	[lači tuti dives!]	'good morrow!'
Cater myla barforas?	[kater *maila* k'o foros?]	'how far is it to the next town?'
Maysta ves barforas	[mišto aves k'o foros]	'you are welcome to the town'
Mole pis lauena?	[mol piyes, levinɔ?]	'will you drink some wine?'
A vauatosa	[avava tusa]	'I will go with you'
Hyste len pee	[beš tele *and* pi]	'sit down and drink'
Pe, pe, deue lasse!	[pi, pi, Develeste!]	'drink, drink for God's sake'
Achae, da mai manor la veue	[av, čai, de ma mɔro ta (?)]	'maid, give me some bread and wine'

Da mai masse!	[de ma mas!]	'give me some meat!'
Achae, a wordey susse!	[av, čai, *a word*i tusa!]	'maid, come here; a word with you!'
Da mai paba la ambrell!	[de ma phaba ta 'brol!]	'give me some apples and pears!'
Iche misto!	[ač misto!]	'much good may it do you!'
Lachira tut!	[lači rat tut']	'good night!'

2. The Lord's Prayer in Romnimos:

Amɔro dad, ka šan ar'o ravnos, t' avel Tiro nav parikedo.
Our father who art in-the heaven, that become Thy name esteemed.

T' avel Tiro krališesko them; t' aven kede Tire lava
That comes Thy kingly land; that become done Thy words

ar' o them odža-sar ar' o ravnos. De amen kedives amɔro
in the land same-as in the heaven. Give us today our

divesesko mɔro, tha atav amen amɔre basibena odža-sar
daily bread, and forgive us our evils same-as

atavas ame odolen ka keren ameŋi. Mɔ muk amen te
forgive we those who do to-us. Don't let us that

wɔnčasa but-but, *on* riger amen avr' i basibenasti.
we want too much, but (< Welsh ond) guide us out-of-the evil.

Si Tuti o krališesko them th' o žɔž th' o ravliben
Is to-you the king land, and the power and the glory

sɔr o čeros. Amen.
all the time. Amen.

3. Part of a folktale in Romnimos (Sampson, 1911: 40–1):

Sas yekhar dui bɔre filišina. Are yekh *o'* lende
Was once two great castles. In one of (< English) them

sas phivli rɔni, tha phivlo rai 're i vaver. Sas i
was widow woman, and widower gentleman in the other. Was- (to) the

phure rɔnyati čai, tha čai i phure resti pɔpale. I phure
old lady (a) daughter and daughter (to) the old man as-well. The old

rɔnyaki čai bita uglimen yekh tha dumeskri sas.
woman's daughter bit ugly one and hunch-backed was.

I phure reski čai raikani rɔni sas-li. Romerde pen
The old gentleman's girl (a) pretty lady was. Married themselves

o phivlo tha i phivli. Džidile sɔr kitanes
the widower and the widow. They lived all together

ar'e   reski   filišin.
in the gentleman's castle.

4.   Contemporary inflected Romani, adapted from Tipler (1957):

Nai man kek paramisi; 'kova sɔr si man. Me šom
Is-not to-me any story;   that all is to-me. I am

khino 'kanɔ, tha džava   khere. Uštava rani i 'sarla;
tired now, and I'm going home. I'll rise early the morrow;

    džava k' i Lonesko   Gav.   Kamav te   uriav,
I'm going to the   Salty   Town [= Pwllheli]. I want that I (could) fly,

uriava [odoi]. 'Verdo pakhyensa' si so me phenav
I'd fly there. 'waggon with-wings' is what I   call

                                  bavalesko – verdo   si   fededer.
[an aeroplane, but perhaps]   wind   – waggon [= car] is [a] better [word].

5.   The Lord's Prayer in Angloromani (English-derived items in italic):

Midivəl kon bešes dre *Your* tan, *we* lels Tiro nav
  God who sits in your place, we take your name

šukər*ly. Thy** kralisipən *'ll* wel,   so *that* Tuti koms *'ll*
nicely. Thy kingdom will come, what that You want will

be kɛr*ed here on earth* pensə dre *Your own* tan. Del *us*
be done here on earth like in Your own place. Give us

sɔ:kən divəs *our* mɔrə, *and for*del *our* bengəli kɛrəpən*s*
every day our bread, and forgive our evil   doings

*same as we for*del*s them as* kɛr*s them* kɛrəpən*s to us*.
same as we forgive them as does them doings to us.

  Mɔ: lel *us* dre wafədipən, *but* handər *us* əvri *from it*,
Don't take us into badness, but lead us out from it,

 'cause Tuti'*s the right* ruzlipən *and* sɔ: kʌvəs *that's*
because You're the right power and all things that's

kušti, sɔ: *the* čirəs, *forever. Amen.*
good, all the time, forever. Amen.

*Thy here because of its presence in the English version.

6.   Personal letter, written in 1977 (with adjusted orthography):

mandi sikər*ed it to the* gɔ:džo. *He* pɛn*ed that* miro tikno
   I   showed it to the non-Gypsy. He said that my small

  lil   sas kušti, *but I'd* kɛr*ed some* bongo wafədi lav*s*
book was good, but I'd made some wrong bad words [= mistakes]

in it. Then with his kokəro vast *he* čin*ed* mandi *a*
in it. Then with his own hand he wrote me a

translation ədre Rʌmnis *of an* angitrakəri gili, *but* mandi'*s*
translation in Romani of an English song, but I'm

atrašed *as it's* kɛk but kušti.
afraid as it's not much good.

7. Passage from Luke xvi (Bible Society, 1981: 5), in existing orthography:

There was a rich mush with kushti-dicking purple togs.
There was a rich man with good-looking purple clothes.

Every divvus his hobben was kushti. By his jigger suttied a
Every day his food was good. By his door slept a

poor mush called Lazarus. Lazarus dicked wafedi, riffly as
poor man called Lazarus. Lazarus looked   bad,   dirty as

a juk. He was ready to scran anything he could get his vasters
a dog. He was ready to eat anything he could get his hands

on or kur it from the rich mush's table. One divvus he
on or steal it from the rich man's table. One   day   he

mullered, and angels kurred him opre to besh by Abraham in heaven.
  died,   and angels called him up to sit by Abraham in heaven.

8. Text of traditional song (from LP record, Yates, 1975):

Now all through me rakli	girl
Kicking up a goudli	fuss, noise
Like me dear old dadus boy	father
I'll leave her in the tan.	(camping) place
Mandi went to t' wesh one night	I; woods
To chin a bit o' cosh;	cut; wood
'long come a baulo	pig [= policeman]
Lelled mandi opre.	took me up [= arrested me]
Mandi's lifted up the mush	I; man
And delled him in the pur,	gave [= punched]; stomach
Says 'like me dear old dadus boy,	father
You can kor well!'	fight

REFERENCES

Acton, T.A. (ed.) 1971. *Current changes amongst British Gypsies and their place in international patterns of development*. Oxford.
Bercovici, K. 1929. *The story of the Gypsies*. London.
Bible Society. 1979. A kushti lav: good news for you. London.
——— 1981. More kushti lavs. London.
Boorde, A. 1547. *The first boke of the introduction of knowledge*. Reprinted in F.J. Furnival (1907).
Bourgeois, H. 1910. Esquisse d'une morphologie du Romani gallois. *Revue de Linguistique et de Philologie Comparée* xliii: 179–90.

Chamberlin, E. R. 1965. *Everyday life in renaissance times.* New York: Capricorn Books.
Collinson, W. E. 1927. Review of J. Sampson, *The Dialect of the Gypsies of Wales. Modern Language Review* XXII: 114–15.
——— 1928. Some Welsh parallels to Welsh Gypsy. *Journal of the Gypsy Lore Society* VII (314).
Dorian, N. C. 1981. *Language death: the life-cycle of a Scottish Gaelic dialect.* Philadelphia: Pennsylvania University Press.
Fowkes, R. A. 1977. Onomastic sophistication of the Gypsies of Wales. *Names* XXV (2): 78–87.
Furnival, F. J. 1907. *The rogues and vagabonds of Shakespeare's youth* London and Cambridge.
Gilliat-Smith, B. 1927. Notes on Sampson's *Dialect of the Gypsies of Wales. Journal of the Gypsy Lore Society* VI (1): 22–32.
Groome, F. H. 1879. Gypsies. In *Encyclopaedia Britannica* (9th edn.).
——— 1880. In Gypsy tents. Edinburgh:
Hancock, I. 1970. Is Angloromani a creole? *Journal of the Gypsy Lore Society,* XLIX (1–2): 41–4.
——— 1971. [Rejoinder to Kenrick (1971).] In Acton (1971).
——— 1975. *Problems in the creation of a standard dialect of Romanes* Social Science Research Council Working Paper No. 25. Austin, Texas.
——— 1977. *The social and linguistic development of Angloromani* Sociolinguistic Working Papers No. 38. Austin, Texas: Southwest Educational Development Laboratory.
——— (ed.) 1979. *Romani sociolinguistics.* The Hague: Mouton.
——— 1980. Lexical expansion in creole languages. In Valdman and Highfield (1980) pp. 63–88.
——— 1982. Land of pain: five centuries of Gypsy slavery. *Roma* VII (1): 7–21.
Hutchison, J. (ed.) 1976. *The travelling man and other stories: an anthology of Gypsy and Traveller children's writing* London: National Gypsy Education Council.
Jarman, E. and Jarman, A. O. H. 1979. *Y Sipsiwn Cymreig* Cardiff: Gwasg Prifysgol.
Kaufman, T. 1979. Review of W. R. Rishi, *Multilingual Romani dictionary.* In Hancock (1979) pp. 131–44.
Kenrick, D. 1971. Anglo-Romani today. In Acton (ed.) (1971) pp. 5–14.
——— 1979. Romani English. In Hancock (1979) pp. 111–20.
Lockwood, W. B. 1975. *Languages of the British Isles past and present.* London: Andre Deutsch.
MacRitchie, D. 1894. *Scottish Gipsies under the Stewarts.* Edinburgh: Constable.
McPeek, J. A. S. 1969. *The black book of knaves and unthrifts.* Storrs, Conn.: Connecticut University Press.
Sampson, J. 1908–11. Welsh Gypsy folktales. *Journal of the Gypsy Lore Society,* NS I, 26–30, 149–56, 258–70, 314–18; II, 53–61, 141–9, 231–41, 372–6; III, 17–19, 40–7.
——— 1926. *The dialect of the Gypsies of Wales* Oxford: Clarendon Press.
Smart, B. C. and Crofton, H. T. 1875. *The dialect of the English Gypsies.* London: Asher & Co.
Soulis, G. C. 1961. The Gypsies in the Byzantine Empire and the Balkans in the late middle ages. *Dumbarton Oaks Papers* XV Cambridge, Mass.

Tipler, D. 1957. Specimens of modern Welsh Romani. *Journal of the Gypsy Lore Society* XXXVI (1–2): 9–24.

Valdman, A. and Highfield, A. (eds.) 1980. *Theoretical orientations in Creole studies.* New York: Academic Press.

Vaux de Foletier, F. 1971. *Milles ans d'histoire Tsigane.* Paris: Fayard.

Wentzel, T. W. and Cherenkov, L. N. 1976. Dialektij tsiganskogo jazika. *Jazika Aziji i Afriki* 1: 15–26. Moscow.

Wood, H., Wood, M. and Richards, N. 1975. Harps and hornpipes: traditions of the Welsh Romany. Folktracks Recording FSA 053. Dartington Ciderhouse. Totnes, Devon.

Yates, M. 1975. Songs of the open road: Gypsies, Travellers and country singers. LP record, Topic 12T253. London: Topic Records, Ltd.

24

Shelta and Polari

IAN HANCOCK

Introduction

Both Shelta and Polari may be treated together typologically, and to a very limited extent socially, but they have few shared vocabulary items, and their histories are very different.

They are both widely spoken, in Britain and overseas; Shelta by as many as 15,000 in England and Wales alone (Acton and Davies, 1979: 102); Bewley (1974: 16) puts the population in the Irish Republic at 'about 6,000'. Those who have a corpus of Polari words in their ordinary speech, and who are aware that their use constitutes a discrete linguistic register, probably amount to something more than that.

Shelta speakers form what has repeatedly been referred to in the literature as a 'caste' of people – today we'd more fashionably call them an ethnic group; whether this is justifiable or not, Shelta at any rate has all the characteristics of an ethnic language which Polari, spoken by a variety of social and professional groups, does not. Even though each is essentially a collection of ingroup words used in the framework of English, Shelta is perceived of by its speakers as a distinct language; Polari is not. Many of the Polari items listed below have fallen out of use, to the extent that one hesitates to equate a knowledge of, say, twenty Polari words with a knowledge of Polari itself. Shelta has status among nearly all groups of Travellers – Polari does not. Leland learnt this when he was first introduced to Shelta in 1876 by an itinerant whom he met in Somerset, who told him (Leland, 1882: 354–5) that

Back slang an' cantin' and rhymin' is grown vulgar, and Italian always *was* the lowest of the lot; thieves' *kennick* is genteel alongside of organ-grinder's lingo, you know.

In terms of their synchronic characteristics, both Shelta and Polari are vestigial languages; that is, they each give evidence of having once been 'complete' linguistic entities.

384

Shelta

Origins

The name 'Shelta' has become well-established for those who have studied it, but it does not seem now to be current amongst the speakers of the language, who use, however, a variety of other names such as 'Gammon', 'Tarri', or simply 'The Cant' (< Irish *caint* 'speech'). The name Shelta was no doubt more current at an earlier time, since three different scholars recorded it at first hand during the same ten-year period. Leland (Barrère and Leland, 1889: xviii) suggests an origin for 'Shelta' in the word *Celtic*, though this does not seem likely.

There are, broadly speaking, two divisions within the language, probably best labelled the Gaelic and the English, i.e. spoken in Ireland (and Scotland), and in England (and Wales) respectively. The latter variety contains considerably fewer non-English words. Sampson (1891) remarked on these two kinds of Shelta nearly a century ago, and the situation still obtains – see Clement (1981: 18), who was unable to find Gaelic Shelta in Ireland:

Shelta is widely known in Ireland to this day, but embedded in English, as none of the Irish travellers seem to know Irish. In Scotland, as far as it is spoken at all, it is used in a Gaelic framework.

The process of lexical replacement – English for Shelta – is a continuing one; Harper and Hudson (1971: 82) noted an 80 per cent loss of non-English items across an eighty-year period in American Travellers' Cant (originally Shelta); such loss does not seem to be so drastic in Britain. There are other differences between Gaelic and English Shelta too: the occurrence of non-English grammatical features, the frequency of use of items from Angloromani and from British Cant, and so on. However, all Shelta dialects have a core vocabulary which they share, and which is demonstrably of Irish derivation. Taken altogether, the supposedly Irish element in the language probably amounts to between 2,000 and 3,000 words, which are spoken in an almost entirely English grammatical mould. Like Clement, Maher (in L'Amie, forthcoming) notes that very few Shelta speakers in Ireland can speak Irish, which may account for this.

Shelta first appeared in print over 170 years ago, in an article on Irish by McElligott in which he referred to a 'Fenian' dialect of that language, Berla Feine, used by the old poets and which 'underwent some little alteration, whereby it is impossible even for natives to read' (McElligott, 1808: 10), and to

another dialect spoken in the county of Cork, and a little in Limerick, Clare and Kerry, called Berlagar na Sær or Mason's Jargon, which seems to me to be a remnant of some of the languages or dialects above mentioned ... it will appear to be ancient and worth preserving. (Ibid.)

He followed this with a list of words, some of which are found in modern

Shelta. In 1859 Edward Fitzgerald published a list of about 250 words and sentences in the same Berlagar na Sær, the secret language of stonemasons (1858–9: 384ff.). Berlagar na Sær is a professional jargon similar to Shelta, though without the extensive lexical disguise (discussed below) and with greater grammatical retention from Irish. An American variety of this dialect has been discussed by Arnold (1898). Another word-list, supposedly collected in the 1850s, was that of Norwood, published in 1887. But the 'discovery' of Shelta is usually credited to Charles Godfrey Leland, who first wrote about it in the *New Quarterly* in 1880, and who believed that he was 'the only man who has collected or published a word or a vocabulary of it' (Savage, 1895: 436). Because of its obvious Celtic content, and because of the Irish connection of its speakers (Leland did not encounter the language in Ireland itself), and no doubt because of his penchant for the romantic, Leland believed, rather like McElligott, that it was very old – a previously unknown Goidelic language, kept alive in secret by its speakers, who were themselves, he suggested, the descendants of a distinct prehistoric population of bronzeworkers.

The debate surrounding the origins and affinities of Shelta is an ongoing one (Harper, 1969, 1972, 1973; Hancock, 1974; Cash, 1977; Seaholm, 1977; Butler, 1979), and useful bibliographies have been compiled for further research (Reinecke *et al.* 1975: 622–31; Gmelch and Gmelch, 1977: 159–69; L'Amie, forthcoming). John Sampson, who collected most of the available texts of Gaelic Shelta during the late nineteenth century, was able to discern a number of phonological modifications of original Irish words, some of which he believed to predate 1000 AD. These modifications included, e.g. pronouncing the word backwards, adding extra prefixes or suffixes, and so on (see below).

An early origin for Shelta was also proposed by Kuno Meyer, who worked with the same informant that Sampson used, and who cited by way of support a number of rules for 'the manufacture of artificial language' (1909: 243) taken from a ninth-century Irish manuscript, some of which apply to Shelta. Meyer believed that Shelta must have been created by scholars, possibly monks or poets, because the mechanisms for its creation were too ingenious for illiterate people to have devised. This point of view was maintained by Macalister (1937), whose study remains the most complete to date, despite its subjectivity and a certain lack of linguistic sophistication. Seaholm (1977: 12) sees the origin and perpetuation of the language rooted in the asocietal status of its speakers, and points out that earlier scholars have arrived at false conclusions because of their lack of familiarity with minority-group psychology. This lacuna has been filled in part by the more recent work of Acton and Davies (1979: 91–110).

The various studies by Harper on the English Shelta-based Cant spoken in the southern United States reiterate that Leland, Sampson and Meyer were wrong in believing that Shelta descended from an ancient tongue, and in his M.A. thesis (1969) he gives convincing evidence for a much more recent origin which, in a later, unpublished paper he puts at *c.* 1700 AD (1973: 12). The hypothesis of an early origin, he said, has come about partly because of romanticism and partly from an incomplete understanding of the historical phonology of Irish. He also disagreed that it could not have been created by illiterates, arguing that 'the evidence points to the contrary' (Harper and Hudson, 1971: 82). On the other hand, Cash, himself of Traveller stock and a speaker of the language, DOES find it 'difficult to believe that an itinerant, fragmented people could have invented such a complex, in many ways sophisticated, and internally-consistent, language' (1977: 180). He believes also that 'there are far more Shelta words than have ever been recorded' (loc. cit.), and gives random examples of a number of these not listed anywhere previously. Thomas Acton, of the Thames Polytechnic School of Social Science, who has considerable acquaintance with Shelta, estimates that some speakers he has met have a working knowledge of over 2,000 Shelta words, and says that new items are constantly being recorded from contemporary speakers (personal communication).

Some observations worth considering about Shelta's origins have been made more recently by Sinead Shuinear Butler (1979), who believes that Shelta in fact does have an ancient, even pre-Celtic, origin, overlain with 'Oghamizations', i.e. intentionally crypticized, pre-Christian druidic Irish forms, at a very early date. She points out that too much has been made of the techniques of word-disguise, that these techniques are not extensively applied in terms of the whole available lexicon, and that over half of the, *c.* 900 items collected by Macalister (from other people's works) cannot be satisfactorily etymologized in terms of Irish or any other known language. She refers to, but does not pursue, Stokes's suggestion (1872) that some of the cryptic vocabulary in Irish, and hence in Irish secret languages, may be of Pictish origin.

One must agree with Butler's scepticism regarding lexical sources; it may be that the very fact that the words are not all of Irish origin has caused such elaborate suggestions to be made to explain their forms. While some items are clearly relatable to specific Irish sources, many of them could equally well be derived from any language using the same techniques and a little inventiveness: thus *gop* 'kiss' (< Irish *póg* with reversal) might also be explained by taking the English word and applying initial voicing, medial vowel retraction and final desibilantization. With the exception of one or two of the processes listed by Macalister, such as reversal, the distribution of these supposed modifications is quite random.

Lexicon and phonological disguise, grammar

According to Macalister's analysis, the following occur in Shelta (examples include all of those which appear in the texts on pages 389–90).

(i) Reversal: *Ayən* 'nine' < *naoi*; *gɔp* 'kiss' < *póg*; *kam* 'son' < *mac*; *nɔp* 'white' < *bán*; *ɔd* 'two' < *do*; *rɔg* 'car' < *carr*

(ii) Reversal with substitution: *Greydi* 'make, do' < *deinim*; *nʌp* 'neck' < *muineal*; *sɔlk* 'take' < *glac*

(iii) Reversal plus suffixation: *Niydyeš* 'no, not' < *ni ead*; *turpowg* 'rag' < *ceirt*

(iv) Prefixing plus suffixation: *Gaːtər* 'father' < *athair*; *graniy* 'understand' < *aithním*; *sluwn* 'Monday' < *Luain*

(v) Substitution of prefix plus suffixation: *Taːdyiraθ* 'strength' < *láidir*

(vi) Loss of syllable plus substitution. *Mʌnik* 'name' < *ainm*; *skɔp* 'open' < *oscailt*

(vii) De-nasalization: *Bin* 'good' < *mín*; *labərt* 'exchange' < *malairtaigh*

(viii) De-aspiration (= spirantization): *Skɔp* 'open' < *oscailt*

In addition to these phonological modifications, the language is further disguised by the inclusion of archaisms (e.g. *bin* 'good' < *mín*; *karb* 'grandmother' < *frac*); items from Romani (*goštə* 'enough' < *dosta*; *kani* 'hen' < *kaini*) and English Cant e.g. *čeyt* 'thing', *wɔdlə* 'duck' (< *cheat*, *waddler*). English Cant has in turn acquired from Shelta such items as *monicker* 'name' (< Shelta *mʌnik* < Irish *ainm*) and *gammy* 'bad' (< Shelta *gyamyaθ* < Irish *cam*).

Metaphor is also apparent in *glɔχ* 'man', from Irish *glacaim* 'hero, champion', and semantic shift: *gyami* 'bad' < Irish *cam* 'crooked, bent'; *getul* 'tremble' < Irish *scáth*, or *eagla* 'fear'; *tribliy* 'crowd' < Irish *teaghlach* 'family'. The lexicon has been expanded by means of nominalizing enclitics (*tadyi* 'strong' > *tadyiraθ* 'strength'; *gyami* 'bad' > *gyamiaθ* 'badness, evil'; *mʌnyi* 'good' > *mʌnyaθ* 'goodness'), which are also employed for semantic extension (*guk* 'old man' > *gukra* 'old beggar'; *yuk* 'man' > *yukra* 'beggar'; *gladər* 'skin' > *gladəriy* 'half-naked beggar', etc.). Incoined forms include *kadyɔg nap* 'lime', lit. 'white stone', *byowr skeyv* 'fishwife', lit. 'woman fish', *nyak regləm* 'brass', lit. 'rogue iron', *gety grimšər* 'summer', lit. 'hot time', *gwɔp grimšər* 'winter', lit. 'cold time', *liː nedyas* 'bed', lit. 'lie place', *nedyas gyɔr* 'brothel', lit. 'place penis', *kunya kyena* 'latrine' lit. 'shit house', *Skai Gruwt* 'America', lit. 'water new', *skai šural* 'river' lit. 'water run(ning)', etc. Among calques on English are found *skai'd* 'be transported (to the American and Australian penal colonies)', lit. 'watered', *gladər* 'skin', both anatomical, and as a verb meaning 'to swindle', and *lʌš swʌrt*, lit. 'drink up'. Further examples of some of the processes employed to enlarge the vocabulary in Shelta are found in Hancock (1980: 63–88); similar techniques in a secret variety of American English (unrelated to Shelta) are found in Adams (1971).

Grammatically, Shelta structure is basically that of English, with certain characteristics reflecting Irish syntax, such as occasional post-nominal adjectives. Sentence-final verbs are also characteristic of the language:

(1)   Have you the feen's dorah nyocked?
      'Did you take the man's bread?'

This differs from the usual SVO order of English and the VSO order of Gaelic sentences. Articles are seldom used and there is often relativizer deletion:

(2) niydyəs greydi gyamyaθ mwiylšə
'people [who] do badness [to] me'.

The locative/existential verb is *steyš*, which also means 'yes', but there is no copula:

(3) Dwiylšə munyi tariər
'You [are] [a] good talker'

All of these features alternate with constructions more closely approximating those of English, while some varieties, such as that mentioned by Clement (1981), are characterized by greater influence from Gaelic.

The nature of Shelta may be seen from the following four passages, the first of which has been analysed. This is the Lord's Prayer as collected by Sampson in the 1890s and reproduced by Macalister (1937: 139–40). It is the same as the 'Gaelic Shelta' in the rest of his texts. The second is a song (Connors and Acton, 1974: 11–12) which, like the third and fourth examples (Moran, 1980; Casey, 1980) is representative of contemporary 'English' Shelta. The first was recorded in Liverpool and is given both in Sampson's own orthography, and in a phonemic approximation based on that of Macalister. The last three were recorded in London.

1. Mŭílsha's gather, swŭrth a mŭnniath, mŭnni-graũa-kradyi
   mwiylšə's ga:tər swʌrt ə mʌnyaθ   mʌnyi grɔ ə kradyi
   I 's   father above in goodness luck   at standing

   dhŭílsha's mŭnnik. Gra be grēdhi'd shedhi ladhu, as aswŭrth
   diylšə's   mʌnik   grɔ *be* greydi'd šeydi la:du *as* ɑswʌrt
   you's   name   love be make -ed upon earth as above

   in mŭnniath. Bŭg mŭílsha thalosk-minŭrth goshta dhurra. G[e]tul
   in mʌnyaθ bʌg mwiylšə talɔsk minyʌrt gɔštə   duwrɔ getyəl
   in goodness give I/me   day   now   enough bread forgiveness

   our shakū, araík mŭílsha getyas nīdyas grēdhi gamiath mŭílsha.
   our ša:kuw əreyk mwiylšə getyəs niydyəs greydi gyamyaθ mwiylšə
   our sin   same I   forgive-s person-s do   badness I/me

   Nijesh solk mwī-īl stŭrth gamiath, but bug mŭílsha achim
   niydyeš sɔlk mwiyil stʌrt gyamyaθ *but* bɔg mwiylšə aχim
   not   take I/me into   badness but take I/me   out of

   gamiath. Dhī-īl the srīdug, thardyūrath, and mŭnniath gradhum a gradhum.
   gyamyaθ diyil *the* sriydug ta:dyiraθ   *and* mʌnyaθ gradum ə   gradum.
   badness you   the kingdom strength   and goodness life   and life.

2. As I was a-krushing through the town   'going'
   one day,
   A bold young buffer boy passed my way;   'non-Traveller'
   I korbed him so hard, I broke his pi,   'hit'; 'head'

ing I knew, the shades   'police'

li-oorali-ay,
li-oorali-ay.
ard   'hit'
pt,   'head'
nd the next thing I knew,
The shades had bogged me.   'police'; 'taken'
Now I sit in the sherrig   'jail'
By night and by day,
Eating mouldy potatoes
And rotten old feah.   'meat'
Now all you bold Travellers
Take warning here too,
Don't you get to korbing   'fighting'
Or the shades'll take you;   'police'
Whoa for that!

3. Sooblik inorsha in a shop, lakeen
wids 'galyune, the feen's gloaking'.
Lakeen and sooblik mistle out the
door. The shopkeeper calls the
shades. The shades mistle up the
mauli. The byuer wids 'galyune,
hide the gohorrah'. The feens
mistle up to the shades. 'We
think you have a little boy here
stole some sweets from the shop'.
A feen wids 'I'm very sorry, I
won't let my gohorrah do it again'.
The shades mistle away.

A boy is here in a shop. The girl
says 'hey pal, the man's looking'.
The girl and the boy go out the
door. The shopkeeper calls the
police. The shades come up the
street. The woman says 'hey pal,
hide the child'. The men
go up to the police. 'We
think you have a little boy here
who stole some sweets from the shop'.
The man says 'I'm very sorry, I
won't let my child do it again'.
The policemen go away.

4. The byuer inorsha is mistling
to the market. She mistles down
to the stall with the crorts.
She bogs a crort for the lakeen.
The lakeen runs. The byuer on
the stall gloaks her bogging the
crort. She says 'Hey, you come
back!' The byuer hides herself
in a garden. The byuer on the
stall comes gloaking around. She
couldn't find her. The traveller
byuer mistles off home.

The woman here is going
to the market. She goes down
to the stall with the coats.
She takes a coat for the girl.
The girl runs. The woman on
the stall sees her taking the
coat. She says 'hey, you come
back!' The woman hides herself
in a garden. The woman on the
stall comes looking around. She
couldn't find her. The traveller
woman goes off home.

Polari

Unlike Shelta, Polari was probably not consciously created, but is either the
result of gradual language loss or decay, or else of large-scale interference

from another language upon an already existing English cant. It survives only as a lexicon of between 80 and 100 words, and it is extremely unlikely that any single speaker today is familiar with them all. Some Polari items have become current outside of the register: *ponce, scarper, mankey, carsey, charver,* etc.; the name of the register, also spelt Parliaree, Palarie, etc., is probably derived from Italian *parlare* 'to speak'.

Today, words which may have an origin in Polari turn up in the language of the theatre, the circus, in show business and in the speech of certain male homosexual communities, especially those with connections with show business and with life at sea. Its sources are unclear; it is certainly lexically Romance-based, in particular Italian, and this – together with its nautical connection – suggests an origin in the Lingua Franca, a fact to which Partridge has already alluded (1948: 122). Modern Polari is more likely, however, to be of composite origin, having elements from the Lingua Franca, Italian, and Cant – 'Cant' here referring to the speech of road people, criminals, etc., generally, rather than to Shelta, which is also known as the Cant. The former, according to Wilde (1889: 306), originated in the eleventh century:

At the time of the Conquest, under Norman oppression, many of the Saxons became outlaws and thieves. The language of these vagabonds was the language of the conquered, because they knew no other speech, and generation after generation simply continued this, with little or no change ... this is English Cant.

Lingua Franca

Until the turn of the twentieth century Lingua Franca was spoken in the major ports along the Mediterranean coast. Its origins are usually thought to date from the time of the Crusades (Hadel, 1969; Coates, 1971; Collier, 1977) although this has been disputed by Whinnom (1977), who points out that no concrete evidence exists for this supposition. Another hypothesis links Lingua Franca with the 'Commercial Latin' of the previous millennium (Hancock, 1977). Whatever its origins, existing texts show that it was typologically a pidgin, being native to nobody, having a very much reduced structure, and with a lexicon which was primarily Italian and southern Romance, indicated by such forms as *lingo, sabir,* but which differed from place to place reflecting the languages of its surroundings.

Its main structural characteristics included invariable nominal and verbal forms, though morphological interference from the various native languages of its speakers was consistently apparent, with e.g. plurals and tenses marked by enclitics. Only one bound morpheme really became stabilized in the language, which served to show past tense. All grammatical relationships were otherwise indicated syntactically, with free morphemes. Plurality and gender were not regularly shown, and possession was expressed by following the noun with *di* plus the appropriate invariable nominal:

mi sabir	'I know'	butia di mi	'my bottle(s)'
ti star	'you are'	kadera di ti	'your chair(s)'
elu avir	'(s)he has'	lingo di elu	'his/her language(s)'

As in a number of other Romance-related pidgins and creoles (e.g. Papiamentu, Papia Kristang, etc.), the object noun phrases of transitive verbs were marked with a particle, which in Lingua Franca was *per*:

(4)   Ti mirar per mučera di Eduardo
      'You're looking at Edward's wife'
(5)   Voi amar per noi
      'You (pl.) love us'

The unmarked verb has no tense reference, this being assumed from the context. Where it was necessary to specify tense or aspect, intention ('future') came to be indicated by placing *bizonyo* before the subject, though there is no record of this construction before the nineteenth century:

(6)   Bizonyo ti lavorar kon mi
      'You will work with me'
(7)   Bizonyo il mučaču jokar aki
      'The boy(s) will play here'

Past action was indicated by suffixing *-to* to the verb minus its final *-r*, and recently completed action by inserting *ja* between these:

ti mirato	'you saw'
ti ja mirato	'you've already seen'
elu volito	'(s)he wanted'
elu ja volito	'(s)he has already wanted'

A great deal has been written about the Lingua Franca, which is the earliest recorded European pidgin known to us, and which (it has been suggested) served as the model for subsequent European-lexicon creoles now spoken throughout the world by millions of people, including many of the inhabitants of Britain of West Indian origin. Such a connection is, however, a tenuous one at best. It was certainly known to sailors from many European nations including England, on the Mediterranean run, and references to it have occurred from time to time in western literature since the late Middle Ages. Molière has a Lingua Franca-speaking Turk in his *Bourgeois Gentilhomme*, and Cervantes before him refers to it in *Don Quixote* as the language spoken 'between slaves and Moors all over Barbary, and even in Constantinople . . . neither Moorish nor Castilian, nor the tongue of any other country, but a mixture of every language, in which we can all understand each other'. No indication was given at that early date of a specific Italian component in Lingua Franca.

Coelho (1880: 187) has already suggested that sailors returning to England from the sea may well have interspersed their talk with nauticisms and Lingua Franca words and expressions not only unconsciously, but also as a means of creating what Halliday has called an 'anti-language', a means of keeping oneself and one's community insulated from the establishment and the law. However, since Polari survives today as a lexicon specifically associated with theatrical, circus and homosexual environments, we are still obliged to explain how these different social contexts are related.

If a thread can be said to connect them, it is probably a nautical one. Sailors home from the sea, unused to a static means of livelihood, were drawn to the Road for a living, joining troupes of players, sideshows and hiring-fairs (Ribton-Turner, 1887: *passim*; Salgãdo, 1977: 138). Perhaps the circus tradition of tattooing originated with these same sailors. Sometimes they became travelling peddlers and merchants; in the seventeenth and eighteenth centuries, when Polari seems to have developed in England, this kind of transient population was very common, having its origins in the Middle Ages (see chapter 23). Mayhew, writing in 1851, was certainly wrong when he said that Italianisms had been introduced 'but lately' into showmen's cant; possible examples of these turn up in earlier decades: *bever, bene, fake, commission, lingo, gad-so, gambs*, etc., for example, are listed in Grose (1785). Although Leland was unaware of Polari as such, he did acknowledge an Italian element in English slang, putting the introduction of Italian words into the language in the sixteenth century (Barrère and Leland, 1889: xix):

During the reign of Queen Elizabeth many Italian words found their way not only into English literature but also into slang, and additions have occasionally been made since then from the same source.

Homecoming seamen were sometimes obliged to take to the roads against their will, and became a part of the wandering population as a result. In 1601 the 'Acte for the necessarie Reliefe of Souldiers and Mariners' (*43 Elizabeth I c.3*) was passed, which confirms that sailors returning to England were often put ashore very far from where they were to be paid off:

Whereas it must needes fall out that many of suche hurte and maymed Souldiers and Marriners doe arrive in Portes and Places far remote from the Counties whence they are by Vertue of this Acte to receive their yeerlie Annuities and Pensions; as also they are prescribed by this Maister or Receiver Generall of the Muster Rolles, who is commonlie like to abide aboute the Courte of London, so that they shall neede at the firste provision for the bearing of their Charges to such places.

Such individuals, wounded and not able to receive their pay at once, had to make their way across England as best they could, joining the post-Renaissance masses of rogues and sturdy-beggars for the protection they afforded, living off their wits and frequently running afoul of the law. In 1713 an act (*13 Anne c. 26*) was passed which operated against such road people, but which specifically exempted sailors, probably in recognition of the legitimacy of their plight:

All persons ... wandering abroad ... (except Soldiers, Mariners or Seafaring Men licenced by som Testimonial) are Persons to be deemed rogues and vagabonds, and who, if found wandering and begging, are to be punished as such.

Needless to say, a whole class of beggars pretending to be sailors sprang up, leading to the repeal of that law in 1792 (*32 George III c. 45*) during the reign of George III:

The permission formerly accorded to soldiers and mariners is highly improper, and those of them who beg shall be deemed rogues and vagabonds.

This road contact, then, can be considered to have been the cause of the earliest introduction of Lingua Franca into Britain.

Influences on Polari and its current use

Eric Partridge is the only person to have written about Polari at any length, referring fleetingly to its connections with the Lingua Franca, the circus and the theatre. Like R. Compton Rhodes, whom he refers to in Partridge (1948: 116), he believed that it 'existed among itinerant actors and showmen through-out the 18th century'. Circus slang, he says, is '... little more than a mixture of Cockney and Romany (with a few words from Lingua Franca and the under-world), and lacks individual character except in its vestiges, which resemble ghosts rather than survivors' (Partridge, 1970: 247). He goes on to say that it is 'a slang that has much in common with Parlyaree', and more specifically (Ibid.: 249) that it '... in the 19th century detached itself from the moribund Parlyaree'. Regarding its link with the acting profession, he notes that 'until about the end of the eighteenth century, actors were so despised that in self-protection, they had certain words that should properly be described as cant and were actually known as Parlyaree' (Ibid.: 223). But despite these observa-tions, his sections on sailors' and theatrical slang say no more about Polari, nor do they list any words from it – all of which are given in his discussion of circus life. The shortcomings of Partridge's etymological excursions are amply dealt with by Legman (1966: lxxxiii–xc).

The connection with male (and not, apparently, female) homosexual speech is also through the sea and the theatre, milieux which have tradition-ally been comfortable ones for homosexuals. Little linguistic research has been done in this area, though a social comment is made by Chesney (1972: 328–9), who briefly discusses the connection between sailors and homo-sexuality and who suggests that 'it was probably in the great ports that the most genuinely professional male prostitution was to be found'. Polari items have been confirmed by the writer (Hancock, 1973) in the speech of homo-sexuals from London, Sydney and San Francisco, none of whom are con-nected with either circus or theatrical life. An ex-seaman with an extensive knowledge of Polari writes (in personal communication, courtesy of Dr John Holm), that

Having served for a number of years in the British Merchant Navy I thought I would drop you a line with as many examples of ship-board slang as I could remember. I never thought of the words as being remnants of Lingua Franca, but rather as bastardized Italian ... they seem to have derived from the wit and imagination of the gay sailors themselves.

Peter Burton, who lectures on Polari in London and who has written on the dialect, believes that it is, in part at least:

derived from foreign words which were brought into this country by various influxes of refugees – from the days of the Huguenots fleeing from the wrath of Catherine de Medici to the Jews flying from the pogroms in Russia and Poland ... Polari has always seemed a curiously English phenomenon ... it was a secret language born out of repression. It owed allegiance to and was curiously linked with the curious argots developed by the 'underworld' groups – the Gypsies, the blacks, the drug sub-culture, the criminal, the racing fraternity (Burton, 1979: 23).

Burton's labelling of Gypsies and Blacks as 'underworld' peoples speaking 'curious argots' is scarcely justifiable. His hypothesis that Polari words were introduced by outsiders coming into Britain, however, might be upheld as being more in keeping with some of the facts we have – though there is nothing clearly Gypsy or Black in Polari, and Sephardic immigrants would more likely have contributed Romance words to the dialect than would have Ashkenazim from Russia and Poland.

   Two other sources of Italianisms need to be acknowledged, since they may well have helped to reinforce the currency of some of the items listed below, and to have given at least some of them a more specifically Italian form, besides contributing words of their own. Firstly, many Italian Punch and Judy men, monkey trainers, organ grinders and peddlers of crucifixes, buttons, ribbons, etc., came into Britain during the 1840s, and naturally had close association with showpeople. Frianoro (1627) and Lacroix (1874: 475–7) provide some discussion of the *Bianti* or *Ceretani*, those who comprised the 'argotic kingdom' in Renaissance Italy and who spoke Gergo or Italian cant. Secondly, though perhaps less likely, were the 'great number of Italian children' Ribton-Turner describes (1887: 303–4):

Persons known as *padroni*, acting generally two together and working alternate six months in Italy and England, obtained the children from their parents in the Neapolitan districts ... they were then placed in depôts in London, whence they were distributed throughout the country in suitable groups under experienced members of the fraternity. They were sent into the streets by day to play, or to pretend to play, a musical instrument, singing and dancing in time to it, and at night they performed in like manner in public houses. In recent years the importation of Italian girls has much increased; they slept in the same room as their padroni and, sad to say, were used, under various pretences, for the most immoral purposes . . . [because of] . . . their total ignorance of our language, and the general ignorance of their own language in England, these poor children are thus completely cut off from verbal intercourse with our people . . . this system has all the characteristics of a slave trade and slavery. (Taken from the Report to the Committee of Inquiry of the Charity Organization Society, London, 1887).

Hotten (1864: 22–3) acknowledges the nautical introduction of Lingua Franca-derived items into English, but clearly attributes cant of Italian origin to a separate source. Of the former he says:

Lingua Franca, or bastard Italian [is] spoken at Genoa, Trieste, Malta, Constantinople, Smyrna, Alexandria and all Mediterranean seaport towns. The ingredients of this imported cant are many. Its foundation is Italian, with a mixture of Modern Greek, German (from the Austrian ports), Spanish, Turkish and French. It has been introduced to the notice of the London wandering tribes by the sailors, foreign and English, who trade to and from the Mediterranean seaports, by the swarms of organ-players from all parts of Italy, and by the makers of images from Rome and Florence, all of whom, in dense thoroughfares, mingle with our lower orders.

And of the latter:

Many of the Cant terms, again . . . are Italian, got from the wandering musicians and others; indeed, the showmen have but lately introduced a number of Italian phrases into their Cant language.

Like Hotten, Baumann, in his book on British slang and cant (1887: cviii) believed that Lingua Franca and Italian items in English came into the language via separate origins.

There are no texts in Polari, and it does not now seem to be spoken in connected sequences. Hotten gave as an example *scarper with the feele of the donna of the cassey* ('run off with the landlady's daughter'), but this may well have been contrived by himself. Today, constructions of this length would be quite unusual, though a similar passage is given by way of illustration, below – also a non-spontaneous sample. In any case, the function of Polari is not to provide a completely separate lexical system from English, but rather a pool of 'secret' words sufficient to make cryptic any utterance that needs to be kept from outsiders. It also serves as a factor of social cohesion for those who use it. Like Shelta – though unlike its ancestor, Lingua Franca – Polari functions to erect barriers between people, rather than to break them down.

Polari is a lexicon. While Shelta exhibits some grammatical and syntactic features of its own (discussed above), there is nothing un-English about the structure of Polari, although like Shelta it continues to generate new words from original combinations of its existing morpheme stock: e.g. *ogle-riahs* 'eyelashes', lit. 'eye hairs', and *omie-pollone* 'gay person', lit. 'man woman'.

The following samples of Polari include (text 2) a short text taken from Burton (1979), and (text 3) a list of lexical items recognized as Polari collected from all available sources, both printed (listed in the bibliography) and at first-hand. No attempt has been made to indicate the different social or professional areas for which each item has been recorded, and only those of Romance origin, or possible Romance origin, are listed. They appear in a broad phonemic representation based upon my own hearing of the items in speech and my own reading of the written form assumed from English spelling conventions. The suggested etymologies are tentative at best.

The first sample is the Lord's Prayer in Lingua Franca (cf. the same text in Shelta, Romani and Angloromani, above):

1. Padri di noi, ki   star in syelo, noi volir ki nomi
   Father of us, who be in heaven, we want that name

   di ti   star saluti. Noi volir ki il paisi di ti   star
   of You be saluted. We want that the land of You be

   kon noi, i ki ti lašar ki tuto il populo fazer volo
   with us, and that You let that all the people do wishes

   di ti   na tera, syemi syemi ki nel syelo. Dar noi
   of You in earth, same way that n-the heaven. Give us

   sempri pani di noi di kada jorno, i   skuzar per noi
   always bread of us of every day, and excuse us

   il kulpa di noi, syemi syemi ki noi skuzar kwesto populo
   the sins of us, same way that we excuse DEM people

   ki fazer kulpa a noi. Non lašar noi tenir katibo
   that do sins to us. NEG let us have bad

   pensyeri, ma tradir per noi di   malu, perke ti tenir
   thoughts, but lead   us from bad, because You have

   sempri il   paisi e   il fortsa e il gloria. Amen.
   always the land and the strength and the glory. Amen.

2. As feely homies, when we launched   young men
   ourselves on the gay scene, Polari
   was all the rage. We would zhoosh   fix
   our riahs, powder our eeks, climb   hair; faces
   into our bona new drag, don our   nice, clothes
   batts and troll off to some bona   shoes; wander; nice
   bijou bar. In the bar, we could   small
   stand around polarying with our   chatting
   sisters, varda the bona cartes on   gay acquaintances; look at; nice; genitals
   the butch homie ajax who, if we   'male'; man; nearby
   fluttered our ogle riahs, might   eyelashes
   just troll over to offer a light.   wander

3. ǽkwə (*aqua, acqua*) n. 'water'. It *acqua*, LF *akwa* 'water'.
   ǽsprow (*aspro, aspra*) n. 'male prostitute'. LF *aspro* 'money'.

bæt (*bat*) n. 'shoe'; v. 'shuffle or dance on stage'. See next item.

bǽtriy (*battery*) v. 'knock' or 'strike'. It *battere* 'beat, strike'.

bǽtriy kɑːziy (*battery carsey*) v. 'knock at a door'.

báːkiy (*barkey*) n. 'a sailor'. It *barca* 'boat'.

béviy/bíviy (*bevvy, bivvy*) n. 'a drink'; v. 'to drink'. It *bev-* 'to drink'.

béviy owmiy (*bevvy omee*) n. 'a drunkard'.

bədéygə (*bodega*) n. 'shop'. Spanish *bodega*. It *botteca* 'shop'.

bəgǽjə (*bagadga, bagaga*) n. 'penis'. It *bagaggio* 'baggage'.

bímbow (*bimbo*) n. 'a dupe, a sucker'. It *bimbo* 'kid, infant, child'.

bínkow (*binco*) n. 'a kerosine flare'. It *bianco* 'white'.

biyn (*bene, ben*) adj. 'good'. It *bene* 'well'.

bíynə (*benar*) adj. 'better'.

bównə/bównow (*bona, bono*) adj. 'good'. It. *buono*; LF *bonu*.

bównə nowčiy (*boner nochy*) 'good night'.

byǽnək/byown (*beyonek, beone, beyong*) n. 'shilling'. It *bianco* 'white'.

čáːpə (*charper*) v. 'seek'. It *cercare* 'seek'.

čáːpərin kɑːziy (*charpering carsey*) n. 'police station'.

čáːpərin owmiy/šáːpə (*charpering omee; sharper*) 'policeman'. Cf. preceding items
    and English 'sharp'.

čáːvə/čóːvə (*charver, chauver*) v. 'have sexual intercourse'. Cf. Spanish *chava* 'girl',
    chabacanada 'a very vulgar expression'.

čáːvərin dɔnə (*charvering donna*) n. 'whore'.

čínkə/číkwə (*chinker, chikwa*) number 'five'. It *cinque* 'five'.

dǽčə/déjə (*dacha, deger*) number 'ten'. It *dieci* 'ten'.

dáwriy (*dowry*) adj. 'a lot of' e.g. *a dowry of acqua*. It *dare* 'give'.

díynə (*deaner*) n. 'shilling'. See next item.

dínəliy/dínəley (*dinarly, dinarlā, dinaly*) n. 'money'. Spanish *dinero* 'money'.

dóliy/dɔl (*dolly, doll*) n. 'smart and attractive young woman'. It *dolce*.

dɔnə (*dona, donna, doner*) n. 'lady, landlady'. It *donna* 'woman'.

dúwi (*dooe, duey*) number 'two' e.g. *duey saulty* '2d' [two old pence]. It *due* 'two'. See
    sóltə, below.

fæb/fǽbl (*fab, fabel*) adj. 'marvellous'. Spanish *fabuloso*, English *fabulous*.

fǽčə (*fatcha*) n. 'face' e.g. *fake the fatcha* 'shave or apply make-up'. It *faccia*.

feyk (*fake*) v. 'make, do'. It *faccio* 'I make'.

féykmənt (*fakement*) n. 'thing, doing, action'. See preceding item + English *-ment*.

fɛrikədúwzə (*ferricadooza, ferricadouzer*) n. 'a knock-down blow'. It *ferire*.

fíyliy/fíylyə (*feele, feelier, feelia*) n. 'child'. It *figlie* 'children'.

fiyliyówmiy (*filiome*) n. 'youth legally underaged'. It preceding item + *owmiy*.

fláwriy (*flowery*) n. 'lodgings, accommođation; house entertainment'.

fówgəl (*fogle*) n. 'handkerchief'. It *foglia* 'leaf'; 'handkerchief' (slang).

gæm (*gam*) n. 'leg'. LF *gamba* 'leg'.

jɛnt (*gent*) n. 'money'. It *argento* 'silver'.

jŏgə (*jogar, jogger*) v. 'play, sing, entertain'. It *giocare* 'play'.

jógərin-owmi (*joggering omee*) n. 'entertainer'. See preceding item.

júwzay (*Jew's eye*) n. 'anything of value'. It.

kæmp (*camp*) v., adj. 'be excessive or showy', 'affect mannerisms of the opposite sex'.

kǽtivə/kəːtivə (*catever, kerterver*) adj. 'bad'. It *cattivo* 'bad'.

káːniš (*carnish*) n. 'meat, food'. It *carne* 'meat'.

káːniš-kɛn (*carnish ken*) n. 'eating house'. See preceding item + *ken* 'house'.

káːtsow (*cartzo*) n. 'penis'. It *cazzo* 'thrust'.

káːziy/káːzə (*carsey, karzy, carser*) n. 'house', 'lavatory', 'brothel'. It *casa* 'house'.

kəmísə/kəmíšən/miš (*camisa, comission, mish*) n. 'shirt'. It *camisa* 'shirt'.

kəpélə (*kapella*) n. 'hat, cap'. It *capella*.

kəpélow (*kapello*) n. 'cloak'. It *capello*.

kɔ́ːtivə-kɑːtsow (*kerterver cartzo*) n. 'venereal disease'. It, see kætivə, kætsow.

kwətríyn/kwɔ́ːtərin (*quartereen*) n. 'a farthing'. It *quattrino*.

kwɔ́ːtə (*quater, quarter*) number 'four'. It *quattro* 'four'.

lǽliy/layl (*lallie, lyle*) n. 'leg'.

létiy (*letty*) n. 'bed'. It *lette*.

létiyz (*letties*) n. 'lodgings, accommodation'. See preceding item.

líŋgow (*lingo*) n. 'language', esp. 'foreign language'.

lɔ́ŋ-dɛjə (*long dedger*) number 'eleven'. It *undici*.

mænjáriy/mʌ́njəliy/nənyáriy/nəmyáriy/jˊáriy (*manjarie* etc.) n., v. 'eat', 'food'.

mǽnkiy (*manky*) adj. 'bad, poor, tasteless'. It *mancare* 'lack, want for'.

mæzəríyn (*mazarine*) n. 'mezzanine, platform below stage'. It *mezzanino*.

médzə/mǽdzə (*madzer, medzer*) n., adj., 'half'. It. *mezzo* 'half'.

médzə-kərúwn/mǽd-zǽkəruwn (*madzer caroon*) n. '2/6d' [two shillings and six-pence]. It *mezzo corona*.

médzəz/mǽdzəz/mɛ́žəz (*medzers, measures*) n. 'money'. See preceding item.

mʌk (*muck*) n. 'stage make-up'. It *macchia* 'stain'; English *muck*.

mʌ́ltiy (*multy*) n., adj. 'many, a lot'. It *molto*.

nǽntiy/nǽntə (*nanty, nantee*) 'no, nothing, not, don't'. It *niente*.

niks (*nix*) 'no, not, don't'. German *nichts*.

niks-mʌ́njəliy (*nix mungarlee*) 'nothing to eat', 'no food'.

nówčiy (*nochy*) n. 'night'. It *notte*, Spanish *noche*, LF *note*.

nóbə (*nobber*) number 'nine'. It *nove*.

ówgəl/úwgəl (*ogle, oogle*) n. 'eye'. It *occhio* 'eye', English *ogle*.

ówmiy (*omee, omy*) n. 'man', 'landlord'. Creole *omi*, Portuguese *homem*, It *uomo*.

ówmiy-pəlówniy (*omee-paloney*) n. 'male homosexual'. See ówmiy, pəlówn.

ɔ́tə (*otter*) number 'eight'. It *otto* 'eight'.

pǽnəm (*pannam, pannum*) n. 'bread'. It *pane*, Latin *panem*.

páːkə (*parker*) v. 'pay'. It *partire* 'pay out'.

pəláriy (*polari, parlaree, parlary, palarie, parlyaree, panarly*) v. 'speak'; n. 'speech', 'language'. It *parlare* 'to speak'.

pəláːvə (*palaver*) n. 'talk, argument'; v. 'to argue, discuss'.

pəlówn/-iy (*polone, palone, paloney, pollone*) n. 'girl, young woman'. It *pollone* 'chick' (?).

pówgiy (*pogy, pogey*) n., adj. 'small, a little'. It *poco* 'little'.

pówgiy-akwə (*pogey acqua*) 'a little water'.

pɔnt/pɔnts (*pont, ponce*) n. 'a pimp'. Cf. Fr *pont* 'prostitute' and English *punk*.

pɔ́ntiy (*ponte*) n. 'pound sterling'. It *pondo* 'weight' (calque).

púwnə (*poona*) n. 'pound sterling'. See preceding item.

pʌnk (*punk*) n. 'male homosexual'. Spanish *punto, puto* 'male prostitute'. See also pɔnt, above.

ráyə/réyə (*raih, riah*) n. 'hair'. Spanish *raya* 'parting in the hair'. Also possibly English backslang.

sǽviy (*savvy*) v. 'know, understand'. LF *sabir*, 'know', 'understand'.
sey (*sa, say*) number 'six'. It *sei*.
sey-dúwiy (*say dooe*) number 'eight'.
sey-ówniy (*say oney*) number 'seven'.
sey-trey (*say tray*) number 'nine'.
sétə (*setter*) number 'seven'. It *sette* 'seven'.
skáːpə/skáːpiy/skáːpəliy (*scarper, scarpy, scapali*) v. 'flee'. It *scappare*.
skriyv (*screeve*) v. 'write', n. 'written material'. It *scrivere* 'write'.
sóltə/sóltiy (*salter, saltee, salty, saulty*) n. 'one penny'. It. *soldi*.
sápələ (*suppelar*) n. 'hat'. It *suppellettile* 'household goods, fittings'.
stril (*strill*) n. 'musical intrument'. It *strillare* 'cry out, shriek'.
towbər-owmiy (*tober omee*) n. 'landlord'.
tɔšərúwn/tɔsərúwn (*tosheroon, tusheroon, tusseroon*) n. '2/6d' [two shillings and
   sixpence].
trey (*tray*) n. 'three'. It *tre; tray saultee* '3d' [three old pence].
úwnə (*una*) number 'one'.
vǽjəriy (*vaggerie*) v. 'go, leave, travel'. It *viaggiare*.
váːdə/váːdiy (*vardo, vardy*) n. 'a look'; v. 'see'. Venetian *vardia* 'a look'.
vówčiy (*voche*) n. 'voice'. It *voce*.
wɔ́ləp (*wallop*) v. 'dance on stage'. It *gallopare*.
wɔ́ləpə (*walloper*) n. 'a dancer'. See preceding item.

REFERENCES

Acton, T. and Davies, G. 1979. Educational policy and language use among English
   Romanies and Irish Travellers (Tinkers) in England and Wales. In Hancock (1979)
   pp. 91–110.
Adams, C. C. 1971. *Boontling, an American lingo*. Austin and London: The University
   of Texas Press.
Arnold, F. S. 1898. Our old poets and tinkers. *Journal of American Folklore* XI, 42:
   210–20.
Barrère, A. and Leland, C. G. 1889. *A dictionary of slang, jargon and cant, embracing
   English, American and Anglo-Indian slang, Pidgin English, Tinkers' jargon and other
   irregular phraseology*. 2 vols. London: The Ballantyne Press.
Baumann, H. 1887. *Londinismen: Slang und Cant*. Berlin and Schöneberg: Langen-
   scheidtsche Verlagsbuchhandlung.
Bewley, V. (ed.) 1974. *Travelling people*. Dublin: Veritas Publications.
Bonaparte, L. L. 1877. [Exchange of correspondence on the Lingua Franca], see
   Clarke.
Burton, P. 1979. The gentle art of confounding naffs: some notes on Polari. *Gay News*
   CXX: 23.
Butler, S. S. 1979. *Commentary on Macalister*. Privately-circulated essay. Dublin.
Casey, D. 1980. A Gammon story. *Traveller Education* XV: 10–11.
Cash, A. 1977. The language of the Maguires. *Journal of the Gypsy Lore Society* 4th
   series, 1, 3: 177–80.
Chesney, K. 1972. *The Victorian underworld*. New York: Schocken Books.

Clement, D. 1981. The secret languages of the Scottish travelling people. *Grazer Linguistische Studien: Sprachliche Sonderformen* XV: 17–25.

Coates, W. A. 1971. The Lingua Franca. Papers from the Fifth Annual Kansas Linguistics Conference. Lawrence.

Coelho, F. A. 1880. Os dialectos romanicos ou neolatinos na África, Asia e America. *Boletim da Sociedade de Geographia de Lisboa* II, 129–96.

Collier, B. 1977. On the origins of Lingua Franca. *Journal of Creole Studies* 1, 2: 281–98.

Connors, M. and Acton, T. 1974. Have you the feen's gread nyocked? London: Romanestan Publications.

Farmer, J. and Henley, W. 1890. *Slang and its analogues, past and present.* Reissued by University Books, New York, 1966.

Fitzgerald, E. 1858–9. On ancient mason marks at Youghal and elsewhere: the secret language of craftsmen in the middle ages in Ireland. *Journal of the Kilkenny Archaeological Society* N.S., II: 67, 384, 390ff.

Frianoro, R. 1627. *Il vagabondo, overo sferza de' Bianti e vagabondi.* Venice: Signor R. F. Publ.

Gmelch, G. and Gmelch, S. 1977. Ireland's travelling people: a comprehensive bibliography. *Journal of the Gypsy Lore Society* 4th series, 1, 3: 159–69.

Grose, F. 1785. *Classical dictionary of the vulgar tongue.* London.

Hadel, R. E. 1969. Modern creoles and Sabir. *Folklore Annual of the University Folklore Association* I: 35–43. Austin.

Hancock, I. 1973. Remnants of the Lingua Franca in Britain. *The University of Southern Florida Language Quarterly* XI, 3–4: 35–6.·

———— 1974. Shelta: a problem of classification. In DeCamp & Hancock (eds.) (1974) pp. 130–7.

———— 1977. Recovering pidgin genesis: approaches and problems. In Valdman (ed.) (1977) pp. 277–94.

———— 1980. Lexical expansion in creole languages. In Valdman and Highfield (eds.) (1980) pp. 63–88.

Harper, J. V. 1969. *Irish traveler Cant: an historical, structural and sociolinguistic study of an argot.* Unpublished M. A. thesis, Department of Linguistics, University of Georgia, Athens.

———— 1972. 'Gypsy' research in the South. Proceedings of the Southern Anthropological Society IV: 16–24.

———— 1973. Irish traveler Cant: its evolution and classification. Unpublished paper, privately circulated MS.

———— and Hudson, C. 1971. Irish traveler Cant. *English Linguistics* V: 78–86.

Hotten, J. C. 1864. *Slang dictionary.* London: Charles Camden Hotten.

Lacroix, P. 1874. *Manners, dress and customs during the Middle Ages and during the Renaissance period.* London: Chapman and Hall, Ltd.

L'Amie, A. (ed.) Forthcoming. *The Irish travelling people: a resource collection* (especially vol. VI, *Shelta, the secret language*, with a foreword by Séan Maher). Newtownabbey: Ulster Polytechnic.

Legman, G. (pseud.) 1966. Introduction to Farmer and Henley (1890) pp. xxx–xciv.

Leland, C. G. 1880. Shelta. *New Quarterly Magazine* N.S. III: 136.

———— 1882. *The Gypsies.* Cambridge: Houghton Mifflin and Co.

Macalister, R. A. 1937. *The secret languages of Ireland.* Cambridge: CUP.

Maher, S. Forthcoming, In L'Amie.

Mayhew, H. 1851. *London labour and the London poor* III (43), October. London: G. Woodsall.

McElligott, P. 1808. Observations on the Gaelic language. *Transactions of the Gaelic Society of Dublin* I: 1–40. Dublin.

Meyer, K. 1909. The secret languages of Ireland. *Journal of the Gypsy Lore Society* N.S. II: 241–6.

Moran, M. 1980. The sooblik not bogged by the shades. *Traveller Education* XV: 9.

Norwood, W. 1887. Tramp's language. *The Academy* 1 January: 11–12.

Partridge, E. 1948. Parlyaree, Cinderella among languages. From his *Here, there and everywhere.* London: Hamish Hamilton. pp. 116–25.

———— 1970. *Slang today and yesterday.* London: Routledge and Kegan Paul.

Reinecke, J., *et al.*, (eds.) 1975. *Bibliography of pidgin and creole languages.* Honolulu: University of Hawaii Press.

Ribton-Turner, C. J. 1887. *History of vagrants and vagrancy, and beggars and begging.* London: Patterson Smith.

Salgādo, G. 1977. *The Elizabethan underworld.* London: J. M. Dent and Sons.

Sampson, J. 1890. Some words of thief talk. *Journal of American Folklore* II, 7: 301–6.

———— 1891. Tinkers and their talk. *Journal of the Gypsy Lore Society* II: 204–21.

———— 1908. A hundred Shelta sayings. *Journal of the Gypsy Lore Society* N.S. 1: 272–7.

Savage, E. B. 1895. Shelta. *Notes and Queries* 8th series, VIII: 435–6.

Seaholm, P. 1977. Shelta and the creole classification device. Unpublished MS. Austin, Texas.

Stokes, W. 1872. *Goidelica.* London.

Valdman, A. (ed.) 1977. *Pidgin and creole linguistics.* Bloomington and London: Indiana University Press.

Valdman, A. and Highfield, A. 1980. *Theoretical orientations in creole studies.* New York: Academic Press.

Whinnom, K. 1977. The context and origins of Lingua Franca. In Meisel (ed.) (1977), pp. 3–18.

Wilde, W. C. 1889. Some words of thief talk. *Journal of American Folklore* II, 7: 301–6.

Since many readers may be unfamiliar with Shelta and Polari, some additional sources are given below as an aid to further study.

Allingham, P. 1934. *Cheapjack: a novel.* London: Heinemann.

Anon. 1830. *Dictionnaire de la Langue Franque ou Petit Mauresque.* Marseilles: Feissat and Demonchy.

Clarke, H. 1877. [Exchange of correspondence with Lucien Bonaparte on the Lingua Franca] *Athenaeum* no. 2583: 545; no. 2585: 607–8; no. 2586: 640; no. 2587: 671–2 and no. 2588: 708.

Coates, W. A. 1969. The German pidgin Italian of the 16th century Lanzichenecchi. *Papers from the Fourth Annual Kansas Linguistics Conference*, Lawrence.

Connors, M. and Acton, T. 1974. *Mike's Book.* London: Romanestan Publications.

DeCamp, D. and Hancock, I. (eds.) 1974. *Pidgins and creoles: current trends and prospects.* Washington: Georgetown University Press.

Emerson, P.H. 1893. *Signor Lippo: burnt cork artiste: his life and adventures*. London: Sampson and Low Co.

Frost, T. 1875. *Circus life and circus celebrities*. London: Privately printed.

Gmelch, S. and Langan, P. 1975. *Tinkers and travellers*. Montreal: Queen's University Press.

Gordino, P. 1969. The walloper's polari. *TV Times* October 18th–25th. London.

Greene, P. 1931–4. Irish tinkers or 'travellers'. *Béaloideas* III: 171–86 (1932–1933); Further notes on tinkers' 'cant'. *Béaloideas* IV: 290–303 (1933–1934); Some notes on tinkers and their cant. *Béaloideas* IV: 259–63 (1933–1934).

Hancock, I. (ed.) 1979. *Romani sociolinguistics*. The Hague: Mouton.

Harper, J.V. and Hudson, C. 1973. Irish traveler Cant in its social setting. *Southern Folklore Quarterly* XXXVII, 2: 101–4.

Hindley, C. 1876. *The life and adventures of a cheap Jack*. Brighton: Charles Hindley.

Leland, C.G. 1886. A prehistoric language yet surviving in Britain. *The Academy* 759, 20 November, p. 346.

——— 1891. Shelta. *Journal of the Gypsy Lore Society* II: 321–3.

——— 1907–8. Shelta and the 'tinkers'. *Journal of the Gypsy Lore Society* N.S., II: 73–82.

MacRitchie, D. 1901. *Shelta, the caird's language*. Inverness: Publications of the Gaelic Society.

Manning, R. 1952. *English circus*. London: W. Laurie and Co.

McCormick, A. 1906. *The Tinkler Gypsies of Galloway* [pp. x–xxiv, Cant vocabulary]. Dumfries: J. Maxwell and Son.

Meisel, J.M. (ed.) 1977. *Pidgins-creoles: languages in contact*. Tübingen: Gunter Narr.

Merrill, C. 1976. On the origin of the Lingua Franca. Privately circulated unpublished. MS.

Meyer, K. 1891. On the Irish origin and the age of Shelta. *Journal of the Gypsy Lore Society* II, 5: 257–66.

Rodgers, B. 1972. *The queen's vernacular*. San Francisco: Straight Arrow Books.

Russell, A. 1914–15. Scoto-Romani and tinkers' cant: twenty sources arranged and edited. *Journal of the Gypsy Lore Society* 2nd series, VIII: 2–86.

Seago, E. 1933. *Circus company: life on the road with the travelling show*. London: Putnam.

——— 1934. *Sons of sawdust: with Paddy O'Flynn's circus in Western Ireland*. London: Putnam.

Sinclair, A.T. 1909. The secret language of masons and tinkers. *Journal of American Folklore* XXII, 86: 353–64.

Smith, E.F. 1931a. *Flamenco*. London: Victor Gollancz.

——— 1931b. *Satan's circus and other stories*. London: Victor Gollancz.

——— 1936. *Red wagon, a story of the tober*. London: Victor Gollancz.

——— 1948. *British circus life, with additional material supplied by John Hind*. London: Hutchinson and Co.

Ware, J.R. 1909. *Passing English of the Victorian era: a dictionary of heterodox English, slang and phrase*. London: George Routledge and Son.

Whinnom, K. 1977. Lingua Franca: historical problems. In Valdman (ed.) (1977), pp. 295–310.

Wicks, H.W. 1938. *The prisoner speaks*. London: Jarrolds.

Wiedel, J. and O'Fearadhaigh, M. 1976. *Irish tinkers*. London: Latimer Press.

Part IV

The sociolinguistic situation

Introduction

This final section of the book deals not with the languages of the British Isles themselves but with the social, cultural, demographic and political situations in which the languages find themselves. The first two chapters, 25 *The newer minorities: spoken languages and varieties* and 26 *The newer minorities: literacy and educational issues*, are concerned with languages that, as noted earlier, are not otherwise discussed in this volume. This is because more or less nothing is known about the linguistic characteristics of the newer minority languages as they are spoken in Britain. Indeed, as will be apparent from chapters 25 and 26, very little is actually known about their sociolinguistic situations either, and most of what information we do have has been obtained relatively recently. These two chapters arise out of pioneering work in the field by the Linguistic Minorities Project which, as a result of initiatives by the European Economic Community, has been financed by the British Department of Education and Science, at the London University Institute of Education. Their results are still at the preliminary stage, but the work is clearly very promising and vitally important, and it is to be hoped that this first serious attempt to carry out research into, and produce information on (and for), speakers of these minority languages will continue to receive support and funding. (Similarly, it is also to be hoped that more finance will be forthcoming to support work on the West Indian linguistic minority: it is distressing and disquieting to note that, at the time of writing, the authors of chapters 14 and 33 in this book, two of the leading British authorities on West Indian language issues, are without full-time employment.)

Chapters 27–29 look at the bilingual sociolinguistic situations involving the main indigenous minority languages, and their relationships with English. Chapter 27 *Welsh and English in Wales* and chapter 29 *Scottish Gaelic and English in the Highlands*, unlike the chapters on the newer minority languages, are able to make good use of British census data, while chapter 28 *Irish and English in Ireland* can rely on a certain amount of research data from the Republic of Ireland. Nevertheless, it is clear that in these cases, too, more detailed information would be very welcome. All three chapters necessarily deal with political as well as cultural issues, and will therefore doubtless be found controversial by some readers with a particular commitment or with different perspectives. They do represent, however, serious attempts to present balanced accounts of complex issues.

The last four contributions, chapter 30 *Scots and English in Scotland*, chapter 31 *The sociolinguistic situation in Northern Ireland*, chapter 32 *Indigenous nonstandard English varieties and education*, and chapter 33 *British Black English and education*, deal with varieties of English in monolingual (though often bidialectal) situations. In spite of some impressive research, relatively little is known about the complicated sociolinguistic situation in Northern Ireland in general, and most of our information on Scotland, too, is based on informal (though informed) rather than systematic observation. Chapters 32 and 33 are focused mainly on England, about which perhaps rather more is known (and which has also received some sociolinguistic attention in this book in chapters 3, 13 and 14). The emphasis in these two chapters is particularly on education, and it is clear that their conclusions should be of considerable relevance for English speakers in Wales, Scotland and Ireland too. But perhaps the most important point is to note that, though speakers of nonstandard varieties of English form the great majority of the population of England, they too, like many of the speakers of the minority languages dealt with in other chapters in this section, suffer in British society from considerable linguistic discrimination and disadvantage.

25

The newer minorities: spoken languages and varieties

EUAN REID

The pattern of settlement

The British Isles have for long been an area of greater cultural and linguistic diversity than is sometimes recognized. The histories of the Celtic languages, and of the interaction of Anglo-Saxon dialects and the languages of the later Scandinavian and Norman French invaders have been relatively well documented. Yet in almost every period there have also been migrations and settlements of speakers of other languages whose stories are much less well known. For example, Dutch-speaking Flemings settled in England in the fifteenth century, and French-speaking Huguenots in the sixteenth. Spanish- and Portuguese-speaking Jews arrived principally in the seventeenth and eighteenth centuries (the earliest minutes of the Board of Deputies of British Jews, dating from 1760, are in Portuguese). From the Russian Empire in the nineteenth and early twentieth centuries came mostly Yiddish-speaking Jews, to be followed in the 1930s by German-speaking refugees from Austria, Czechoslovakia and Germany itself. These settlers were all motivated by some combination of economic, political and religious disadvantage in the countries they came from, and a view of Britain as offering them greater opportunity to live and work as they chose.

The newer linguistic minorities arrived in the British Isles for a similar mixture of economic and political reasons. They came from east and central Europe in the immediate postwar period during the upheaval caused by the collapse of Nazi Germany and the establishment of Soviet control over eastern Europe; and from Italy at the same time, partly in continuation of an already well-established tradition of migration to Britain (see, for example, King, 1979). The numbers coming from the Indian sub-continent increased greatly in the 1950s, partly as a consequence of the 1947 Partition into India and Pakistan, which particularly affected the Panjab and Bengal, but also to some extent because of economic conditions in, for example, Gujerat and Sylhet. Considerable numbers came also from Hong Kong and from Singapore. In fact as long as immigration legislation allowed it, which was for as long as there was a demand for cheap labour in Britain, people from Commonwealth and other countries took advantage wherever they could of the opportunity to improve economic prospects for themselves and for their families, in just the same way that millions from these islands have gone over the last few centuries to North America and to Australasia.

In the last twenty years or so there have been additional, specific developments which have led to further settlements. The pressure from the Africanization movements which have followed decolonization, particularly felt by Asians in the East African countries, has led to an increase in particular in the numbers of Panjabi and Gujerati speakers in Britain. The exacerbation of Greek-Turkish tensions in Cyprus, climaxing in the Turkish invasion and partial occupation of the island in 1974, added to the already considerable numbers of Greek and Turkish speakers, particularly in north London. Most recently the acceptance as part of an international programme of 'Vietnamese boat-people', some actually Vietnamese speakers, but a high proportion ethnic Chinese, boosted the numbers of speakers of Cantonese and other Chinese languages.

Language statistics

National censuses

Except for Welsh, Irish or Gaelic in their home areas, there has never been any comprehensive source of language statistics for minority languages in the British Isles. However, information relating to country of birth in the ten-yearly national censuses does offer some pointers to the distribution of such languages. Table 25.1 is based on data from the 1971 British Census. One can be fairly confident, on the basis of such figures, that there are, for example, sizeable numbers of residents in Britain who speak or understand Italian or Polish or German, since Italy, Poland or Germany were the birthplaces given for the people concerned, and these are all relatively homogeneous countries from a linguistic point of view. Of course even in cases like these, where there is likely to be a one-to-one relationship between country and language, we have no way of being sure that people born in the country were at any point speakers of the national language – and even if they once were, they may no longer consider themselves speakers of their original languages. Some of the Jews who settled in England in the late nineteenth century, for example, and for whom Yiddish translations of the census questions were produced up to 1921, had abandoned Yiddish as a spoken language within a generation (Kosmin, Bauer and Grizzard, 1976).

Even a birthplace like Cyprus is more difficult in terms of predicting language spoken, since, as well as the Greek-speaking majority (of about 80 per cent in the 1960s), there is a sizeable Turkish-speaking minority, and smaller Armenian and other groups. People from all these Cypriot communities have settled in Britain, and not necessarily of course in the same proportions of the population as they represented in Cyprus. Neither does the

Table 25.1. *Overseas-born population of Great Britain by selected countries of birth, according to the 1971 Census*

Country of birth		Number resident in Great Britain
Total population of Great Britain		53,978,540
Total born in Great Britain		50,388,690
Total overseas-born population (UK)		3,088,110
of which:		
Total Europe		*677,300*
of which:	Germany	157,680
	Italy	108,980
	Poland	110,925
	Spain	49,470
	Malta and Gozo	33,840
Other countries in Europe		216,405
Total NC Africa*		*164,205*
of which:	Ghana	11,215
	Kenya	59,500
	Nigeria	28,565
	Tanzania	14,375
	Uganda	12,590
Other countries in Africa		37,960
Total NC Asia and Oceania*		*638,285*
of which:	Ceylon	17,040
	Cyprus	73,295
	Hong Kong	29,520
	India	321,995
	Malaysia	25,685
	Pakistan	139,935
	Singapore	27,335
Other countries in Asia and Oceania		3,480
Total NC America*		*304,070*
of which:	Barbados	27,055
	Guyana	21,070
	Jamaica	171,775
	Trinidad and Tobago	17,135
Other countries in America		67,035
Other countries	China**	*13,495*

*New Commonwealth countries
**Mainland and Formosa
Source: Campbell-Platt (1978).

fact of having been born in Malaysia or Singapore point clearly to a single language: people born there may speak Malay, Chinese languages or South Asian languages, for example. Even the apparently culturally homogeneous Hong Kong is linguistically far from simple, given the several Chinese languages, principally Cantonese and Hakka, which are widely spoken there. (With reference to Chinese communities in Britain, research for librarians has produced some very useful linguistically-oriented estimates of the current demographic position: see Chin and Simsova, 1981.)

The biggest difficulties in predicting language from birthplace arise of course with reference to people recorded in the census as born in India, Pakistan or the East African countries, all of them sources of substantial immigration to the British Isles in the postwar period, and all of them obviously multilingual. As far as Pakistan is concerned, an added difficulty in using 1971 Census figures comes from the fact that the term 'Pakistan' in 1971 embraced not only the country now called Pakistan, but what was then West Pakistan, but is now Bangladesh. There is therefore no systematic way of estimating from birthplace figures even the number of speakers of Panjabi or Pushtu or Urdu as compared with the numbers of Bengali speakers.

The lack of simple correspondence between country of birth and language spoken is probably most widely recognized with respect to people from India. More than 1,600 mother tongues were recorded in the 1961 Census of India, with twelve of these claimed by more than six million speakers each (Pandit, 1977) and substantial bilingualism. Without taking other sources of information into account, all that one can say on the basis of India and Pakistan as birthplaces is that there were likely to be not less than 450,000 speakers of South Asian languages in Britain in 1971. Given that a high proportion of the immigrants from East Africa were also of South Asian origin, the true figure was probably in excess of half a million.

Possibly the greatest weakness of birthplace statistics is that they give no linguistic information at all about the British-born descendants of speakers of other languages who have settled here from abroad. For some groups at least there are as many such people as there are actual immigrants, and the transmission of languages to this 'second generation' is certainly widespread. The 1971 Census figures were already misleading in this respect: the 1981 figures are now available and they are even less satisfactory as a reliable source of statistical information on linguistic minorities.

Electoral registers

The other major sources of systematic, publicly available information that has some value in terms of indicating the distribution of adult speakers of different languages, especially at local level, are personal names on electoral registers. The Linguistic Minorities Project based at the University of London Institute of Education from 1979 to 1983 made use of such sources in its surveys in Coventry, Bradford and London, and table 25.2 derives from work

Table 25.2. *South Asian languages in Coventry: ambiguities of language group designation from South Asian names*

(a) Estimates of numbers of adult speakers of the main South Asian languages made by the Coventry City Planning Department on the basis of intuitive knowledge of the relationships of names to language. The italicized figures represented their more confident attributions; the others, it was recognized, might be speakers of either the language at the beginning of the line or of the language at the head of the column.

	Urdu	Panjabi	Gujerati	Hindi	Bengali
Urdu	*1102*				
Panjabi	56	*7012*			
Gujerati	20	128	*2016*		
Hindi	0	412	839	*532*	
Bengali	333*				*88*

Note: *This group was thought most likely to be either Bengali-speaking or Urdu-speaking, but a proportion might also turn out to be Gujerati-speaking Muslims.

(b) Re-estimates of numbers of adult speakers of the main South Asian languages in Coventry in 1980–81, corrected from the above on the basis of fieldwork for the Linguistic Minorities Project's Adult Language Use Survey.

Language	Approximate number of speakers
Panjabi	8,000
Gujerati	3,000
Panjabi-Urdu	1,000
Bengali	300
Hindi	200

Source: Smith (1982).

done before and during the Coventry Adult Language Use Survey. It will be seen from this table that the correspondence between personal name and language is far from perfect for all languages; it may be relatively easy to identify Muslim names, for example, but not easy to decide if the individuals concerned are likely to be speakers of Bengali, of Panjabi, of Turkish, or of Arabic (or even of Caribbean varieties of English, since families from Guyana or Trinidad are in some cases descended from Muslim 'East Indians'). It is difficult too to estimate the degree to which different populations are accurately registered for electoral purposes: studies done at the time of the 1974 and 1979 General Elections in Britain (Anwar, 1980) suggest considerable variation in different parts of England in the degree of under-registration among ethnic minorities. Furthermore, only British subjects (who included, under legislation in force at least until 1982, citizens of all Commonwealth countries) and Irish citizens should appear on the electoral registers, so that quite sizeable groups of people who have settled in Britain from, for example, Poland or Italy, or more recently Pakistan, but who are not naturalized, will not be identified by this approach.

Although, then, information on birthplace and on personal names can be helpful pointers to certain of the newer linguistic minorities in the British Isles, there are evidently very serious limitations on these indirect approaches, and the figures produced on such bases have to be treated with great caution.

Language surveys in schools

A more direct approach to the establishing of numbers and distribution of speakers of minority languages is available where it is possible to put direct questions to pupils in schools. The pioneers in this respect were the Inner London Education Authority's Research and Statistics Division, who conducted their first language census in late 1978 (ILEA, 1979), and a further such enquiry early in 1981 (ILEA, 1982). The main function of the original exercise, which was carried out in every class in every Inner London primary and secondary school, was to establish the degree of need perceived by teachers for further teaching of English as a second language. However, teachers were asked at the same time to indicate the numbers of speakers in their classes 'for whom English is not a first language' (1978), and 'with a home language other than, or in addition to, English' (1981), along with the names of those languages.

Nearly 45,000 pupils, representing about 14 per cent of ILEA's rolls, were recorded in 1981 as having a home language other than, or in addition to, English. More than a hundred languages were represented and the list included languages from every continent and from most countries of the world; however, in both 1978 and 1981 12 of the languages were recorded for more than 1,000 speakers, as indicated in table 25.3. In 1978 these top 12 languages accounted for more than three-quarters of the pupils not having English as a first language, and in 1981 for more than four-fifths of those with a home language other than, or in addition to English. The 12 most frequently reported languages hardly changed between 1978 and 1981, although 'French' displaced 'West Indian', probably because of the different guidance given to teachers about the treatment of both English-based and French-based Creole varieties. The rank order of the other languages changed slightly, with Bengali and Arabic apparently showing the most marked increases.

The Linguistic Minorities Project, unlike ILEA, aimed to enquire only about languages other than English. It undertook the first of its Schools Language Surveys in late 1980 in the Peterborough Division of Cambridgeshire, and by early 1982 had also produced basic data on the linguistic

Table 25.3. *Twelve most frequently reported languages among Inner London schoolchildren*

Languages reported by more than 1,000 pupils (as percentage of total number of pupils reporting a language other than English)

1978		1981	
Greek	3802 (11)	Bengali	5377 (12)
Turkish	3587 (10)	Turkish	4418 (10)
Bengali	2954 (8)	Greek	3859 (9)
Spanish	2674 (8)	Spanish	3436 (8)
Gujerati	2344 (7)	Gujerati	3377 (8)
Italian	2272 (6)	Panjabi	2879 (6)
Panjabi	1926 (5)	Italian	2808 (6)
Urdu	1892 (5)	Urdu	2778 (6)
Cantonese/Chinese	1712 (5)	Chinese	2237 (5)
West Indian/Jamaican	1638 (5)	*French	2133 (5)
Portuguese	1439 (4)	Arabic	1968 (4)
Arabic	1038 (3)	Portuguese	1858 (4)
(Other languages 23 %)		(Other languages 17%)	

*French in 1981 included all pupils reporting a French-based creole.
Source: ILEA (1979 and 1982).

composition of the school-age populations of Coventry, Bradford and the London borough of Haringey. Surveys in several further local education authority areas, including the London boroughs of Waltham Forest and Brent, took place in 1982.

In the Schools Language Surveys teachers were asked to put to each pupil, wherever possible individually, the following basic question:

(1) Do you yourself ever speak any language at home apart from English?

For those pupils giving a positive answer to this question, responses were recorded to these further questions:

(2) What is the name of that language?
(3) Can you read that language?
(4) Can you write that language?

The basic picture that emerges for Coventry, Bradford and Haringey is set out in table 25.4.

When more than one in eight of pupils in several of our largest conurbations report some knowledge of languages other than English, this is surely a fact of considerable social and educational importance, particularly when linked to some degree of literacy among 40 to 50 per cent of these pupils. It will be seen too, from the languages listed in tables 25.3 and 25.4, that the term 'newer

Table 25.4. *Linguistic Minorities Project: Schools Language Survey data, 1981*

	Coventry	Bradford	Haringey
(1) Local Education Authority			
(2) Age-range comprehensively surveyed*	6–16	6–15	6–15
(3) Total number of pupils on rolls of classes surveyed	55,444	81,043	27,104
(4) Number of pupils recorded as speaking a language other than English at home	7,174	14,207	7,383
(5) (4) as percentage of (3)	13	17.5	27
(6) Percentage of pupils reporting some degree of literacy in one of the spoken languages given, or in another language of literacy	41	52	50
(7) Number of different languages reported	64	78	115
(8) Most frequently reported languages (as percentage of (4))**	Panjabi (59)	Panjabi (52)	Greek (34)
	Gujerati (15)	Urdu (19)	Turkish (15)
	Urdu (7)	Gujerati (8)	English-based creoles (8)
	Hindi (3)	Bengali (3)	Gujerati (6)
	Italian (2)	Pushtu (3)	Italian (6)
	Bengali (2)	Italian (3)	Bengali (3)
	Polish (2)	Polish (1)	French-based creoles (3)
	Chinese (1)	Hindi (1)	Urdu (2)
	English-based creoles (1)	Chinese (1)	Panjabi (2)
	German (1)	Ukrainian (1)	Spanish (2)
Cumulative percentage of (4)	93	92	81

*In the 3 places reported in this table the distribution of children reporting a language other than English was fairly evenly spread over the age-range investigated.
**These general terms for language names in some cases represent groupings of finer subdivisions.
Source: Summary of data to appear in Linguistic Minorities Project (1983) *Working Paper 3: Schools Language Survey: summary of findings from five LEAs* (available from Information Room, University of London, Institute of Education).

minority languages' is not simply a synonym for South Asian languages. Although these are predominant in many areas, particularly outside London, South and East European, Middle Eastern and East Asian languages are also reported for young people covered by these surveys, and by implication are also used by larger numbers among the adult population.

However, in interpreting the data from these Schools Language Surveys, it is important to bear in mind the possibilities of distortion arising from the way in which such information is collected and analysed. The figures presented in table 25.4 derive from teachers' written reports of pupils' oral answers. Although maximum possible standardization of the wording of the questions is asked for, it may not always be achieved, and individual pupils' perceptions of the meaning and motivation of the questions will certainly have affected the answers given. Moreover, teachers' attitudes to such surveys, the degree of exactness with which they record answers, and their general understanding of language and languages also vary enormously.

It is important then to regard this type of 'language census' data as offering an indication only of the general shape of linguistic diversity in an area. Detailed, smaller-scale sociolinguistic studies are needed, in which more reliable information on actual language use can be assembled and analysed. Nevertheless, if future national population censuses continue to omit reference to language, an approach to the documenting of minority languages through school-based censuses, regularly updated, may be the least problematic way of building up the full account of the newer minority languages in Britain which is still needed for educational purposes. Continued over a sufficient period of time, this approach would also provide some indication of patterns of language shift.

Language names

Some of the names for languages which have been used, so far with very little qualification, are worth examining rather more closely. As will be evident from many of the other chapters in this book a conventional term for a language, for example, 'English', is highly problematic in itself. Different people offering the answer 'English' in response to the question 'What language do you speak at home?' are likely to mean very different things by that answer. The different varieties represented by the common term 'English' relate partly to the geographical and social origins of the speakers, but also to the current context within which speakers are operating, and to their personal and social aspirations.

The same factors are involved for most of the newer minority languages under discussion here, and for them too it seems to be the case that only a minority of speakers habitually use the high prestige standard varieties of the languages concerned, with the majorities speaking nonstandard, lower prestige varieties. Within this broad similarity across languages, however, there are detailed differences which need to be borne in mind.

To begin with an example close to home, it is clear that quite a high proportion of people of Italian origin who have settled in the British Isles come from the southern regions of Italy, speaking, for example, Sicilian or Neapolitan dialects (King, 1979). In the Bedfordshire-EEC 'Mother Tongue Teaching' pilot project in the late 1970s (see also chapter 26), which was partly concerned with the teaching of Italian to children from families of Italian origin, one of the major tasks faced by those charged with producing appropriate teaching materials was to relate the spoken Italian dialects, of which the children had varying degrees of understanding, to the standard written Italian which was one of the goals of the teaching (Tosi, 1982a). Tosi has compared the Italian now spoken by southern Italian families who came to Britain in the early 1950s and through the 1960s with the variety now spoken by their contemporaries who remained in southern Italy. He suggests that when the British Italians return on holiday to their regions of origin, their ability to transfer from dialect to standard, both in coding and decoding, is limited, since their experience is almost exclusively of dialect. The explanation proposed is the relative lack of exposure to the contemporary standard language as used by, for example, the national broadcasting media and the national education system, as well as by civil servants and local administrators (Tosi, 1982b).

There are probably similar factors relating both to other Romance languages in Britain, such as Spanish and Portuguese, and to Cypriot Greek and Cypriot Turkish (although the presence of these languages results on the whole from later migrations) and British forms of the languages are even less well documented than Italian. Nor would it be surprising to find a similar phenomenon in the Panjabi and Gujerati spoken by those who learned these languages in the Asian communities in East Africa, and who were also out of day-to-day contact with linguistic changes in the sub-continent, and therefore not subject to the same influences as their contemporaries in the Panjab or in Gujerat.

The situation of some of the five most widespread South Asian languages in Britain now is, at least from a Eurocentric point of view, even more complex. 'Hindi' and 'Urdu' are the terms now used for the closely-related official languages of India and Pakistan respectively. They have displaced almost entirely the term 'Hindustani', used in pre-Partition times to refer to the spoken *lingua franca* of northern India by those who wished to stress intercommunal unity rather than the differences between Hindus and Muslims. As far as their spoken realizations are concerned, mutual intelligibility between everyday Hindi and Urdu is more or less complete. It is only in their more elaborate spoken styles, and in their written forms, when they draw respectively on the Sanskritic and Perso-Arabic lexicons and writing systems, that

Hindi and Urdu begin to diverge significantly: in fact the term 'Hirdu' has been proposed to signal the linguistic closeness of the two varieties (Kelkar, 1968), and Pandit (1977) suggests that the 'rules of grammar' of the two are identical, with the important differences lying in the 'rules of speaking' which convey social meaning (see also chapter 26).

Khubchandani's (1979) discussion extends to Panjabi too, which has some-thing of the same function in India for the Sikhs that Hindi has for Hindus and Urdu for Muslims. In an older written form Panjabi is the language in which the holy scriptures of Sikhism are preserved, and the language was also the major basis for the formation of the smaller, unilingual Panjab state in India which in 1966 was carved out from the larger post-Independence Panjab, where both Hindi and Panjabi had been state languages. Khubchandani in fact suggests that a large part of north India and Pakistan can be treated as a unified Hindi-Urdu-Panjabi communication region, and that mother tongue census returns in the Panjabi region at least have more to do with religious affiliation than with linguistic difference. He writes:

At the expense of slight statistical inaccuracy one can say that the Sikhs in the region generally tend to report Panjabi as their mother tongue ... the Hindus show preference for Hindi, and the Muslims for Urdu, although one does not notice any sharp distinction in the speech these three religious groups actually use for primary com-munication (Khubchandani, 1979: 193)

It is against this historical background and contemporary situation in the sub-continent that self-report of mother tongues and the relationship between Hindi, Urdu and Panjabi in the United Kingdom now have to be understood. Muslim people of Pakistani or East African origin, many of whom will have as their everyday spoken language some variety of Panjabi, will quite commonly report Urdu as their mother tongue. The same is true of some Indian Muslim families originating in the Panjab. Similarly, Hindu families from Panjab or East Africa may report Hindi as their mother tongue. Both Hindi and Urdu then assume an importance going beyond the numbers of actual speakers of the languages: to use Khubchandani's term, they represent the 'ideal stan-dard' of mother tongue held by different groups.

An interesting small-scale study (Mobbs, 1981) has been made of the vocabulary used in a broadcast of the BBC television magazine programme aimed at speakers of Hindi and Urdu, *Nai Zindagi – Naya Jeevan*. The lexical content of the broadcast was analysed according to etymological origins, on the basis that a high incidence of words of Persian or Arabic origin would indicate Urdu style, likewise Sanskritic origin would indicate Hindi style. To check the validity of this approach, a sample of viewers was asked to rate selected words from the broadcast as 'Hindi', 'Urdu' or both. The significant finding was that users of Hindi-Urdu, whose backgrounds were Hindu, Indian Muslim and Pakistani, regularly mis-attributed lexical items of Perso-Arabic or Sanskritic origin to the Hindi and Urdu 'styles' (as Mobbs prefers to refer to them) respectively. It seems clear then that, in the United Kingdom too, 'Religious, educational and national norms ... influenced people in their judgements' (Mobbs, 1981: 209), and that the basis for speakers deciding whether the linguistic items they use are Hindi or Urdu is at least as likely to be their own Muslim or Hindu, Pakistani or Indian affiliation as anything 'objective' – such as the historical origins of the particular linguistic element.

The close relationships between the three spoken languages, Hindi, Urdu and Panjabi, do not mean that in making provision for the teaching of the languages in Britain, they can simply be treated as a single target. The writing systems at least are clearly distinct, and it is the written forms of the standard languages that are usually the subject of 'mother tongue' classes. However, there may be some room, at the oral level, for the encouragement of some common teaching, assuming that a mutual interest exists or can be developed by speakers coming from the three language traditions.

With reference to the three more regionally-specific South Asian languages spoken quite widely in Britain now, it is important to remember that 'Panjabi speakers', 'Gujerati speakers' and 'Bengali speakers', like 'Italian speakers', include some who speak the standard languages, but also large numbers who speak only or also nonstandard dialects regarded with varying degrees of disparagement by the educated elites of the areas and communities concerned.

The term 'Panjabi', quite apart from the major distinction already noted between speakers whose families come from Indian Panjab and those whose families come from Pakistani Panjab, covers, for example, a wide range of spoken varieties within Pakistan and, by extension, in several parts of Britain. These were eventually grouped under the general heading of 'Panjabi' in the presentation of the findings of the Linguistic Minorities Project's Schools Language Surveys, but it is important to bear in mind that all such language labels conceal very considerable diversity.

With Gujerati, the major variant encountered with any frequency in Britain seems to be Kutchi, but there is some uncertainty about whether this would be more appropriately grouped with Sindhi, whose speakers are mostly now located just across the international frontier in Pakistan. Certainly most who claim to speak Kutchi appear to be Muslims whose origins lie in the border areas of the Indian state of Gujerat.

As far as Bengali is concerned, the major distinction to be made is between the middle-class minority in Britain, deriving from both Bangladesh and from India, who speak something close to Standard Bengali, and the very high proportion of 'Bengali speakers' whose families have come from Sylhet in the far north-eastern corner of Bangladesh, and who therefore speak Sylhetti, referred to by Ray, Hai and Ray (1966) as 'highly deviant' from Standard Bengali. Certainly the answers to questions in the Linguistic Minorities Project's Adult Language Use Survey of Bengali speakers in East London, about the range of languages known, elicited answers from a significant proportion of the Sylhetti respondents which suggested a perception of 'Bengali' and 'Sylhetti' as two separate entities.

Reference to 'speakers of Chinese' is a shorthand of another kind, since it has been suggested that Chinese is best seen as 'an assemblage of several separate languages intertwined in an endless network of dialects' (Voegelin and Voegelin, 1977: 114). The feature that relates this group of languages most closely is the common system of written characters drawn on by all of them, a unifying force throughout Chinese history. As far as spoken Chinese languages in Britain are concerned, the most widespread seems to be Cantonese, followed by Hakka and Hokkien. Cantonese is also the spoken language most widely known among the ethnic Chinese from Vietnam who settled in Britain during 1980 and 1981, and is the spoken medium generally used in the classes organized by various communities in Britain where children learn written Chinese.

What this emphasizes once again is the desirability of getting away from the widespread use of the term 'mother tongue' when referring to the languages being learned by large numbers of minority children in voluntary classes throughout Britain (Saifullah Khan, 1980). There are good reasons, both educational and social, for encouraging the study of the languages of minority communities (National Congress on Languages in Education, 1982), but these do not all depend on the languages chosen for study being identical with the languages of the home.

Functions and forms

Until the results of the Linguistic Minorities Project's Adult Language Use Survey (covering ten spoken languages in three different areas of England) are analysed there is not a great deal of evidence to draw on in attempting to answer an important series of related questions about the functions served by the spoken languages of the newer minorities in Britain. It is clear that, in the absence of the kind of statutory support given rather belatedly to the indigenous Celtic minority languages of the British Isles (see chapters 27–29), there are no official roles available for these languages: citizens cannot apply in Panjabi for a driving licence, or write in Italian to a civil servant and expect an answer. The use of English (or of Welsh or Gaelic in certain areas and circumstances) is still required for all official purposes, as it is also to a great extent in the workplace, the exceptions to this latter generalization occurring in the kind of work environments which are entirely staffed by a single language group, for example Bengali-speaking clothing workers in the London borough of Tower Hamlets, Italian-speaking brickworkers in Bedfordshire, Cantonese- or Hakka-speaking catering workers in Chinese restaurants almost everywhere.

Apart from these, probably transitional, situations, the main continuing extra-domestic role for minority languages is likely to be in the religious

Table 25.5. *Language choice in the home among South Asians in Leicester*

(a) Main language spoken in the home, by respondents' first language

Language spoken in the home	First language of respondents					
	Gujerati		Panjabi		Kutchi	
	no	%	no	%	no	%
Gujerati	184	92	–	–	1	9
Panjabi	2	1	97	96	–	–
Kutchi	–	–	–	–	6	55
Urdu	1	–	–	–	1	9
English	8	4	4	4	3	27
First language and English	5	3	–	–	–	–

(b) Main language used with different family members

Language used	with spouse		with children		with parents/ parents-in-law	
	no	%	no	%	no	%
First language	284	93	225	73	240	98
English	5	1.5	21	7	1	–
Both	12	4	58	19	2	1
Other	5	1.5	2	1	2	1
Total	*306*	*100*	*306*	*100*	*245*	*100*

Source: Wilding (1981: 23–4, tables 6.2–6.5).

sphere. There are, for example, church services held in Polish, Ukrainian, German and Italian wherever there are even quite small communities of speakers of these languages, and some of these services have a continuous history since the 1930s at least. Similarly, Panjabi and Urdu, Koranic Arabic, Gujerati, Bengali and Hindi are widely used in various combinations in *gurdwaras*, mosques and temples in most large centres of population in industrialized Britain now. The continued association of the languages with religious practices, and with communal activity going beyond the religious, as in Polish parish clubs or Panjabi Sikh *gurdwaras*, seems likely to guarantee the survival of some forms of the languages in this domain. This may come in some ways to parallel the use of Hebrew by the longer-established Jewish communities, now much more widespread than Yiddish, the language originally brought from eastern and central Europe.

The key domain for the wider future use of the newer minority languages is likely, however, to be the home. The survey of about 300 mainly Panjabi-speaking and Gujerati-speaking parents in Leicester (Wilding, 1981) carried out in 1979 gives some indication of what adults there say they do: some findings from that study are reproduced in table 25.5. Possibly the most striking feature of table 25.5 is the very much lower figure reported for use of first language with respondents' children as compared with spouses and parents. The Leicester survey did not ask, unfortunately, about children's choice of language for use with parents, but in work with London schoolchildren (Rosen and Burgess, 1980) there are indications of non-reciprocal language use with parents. That is to say that, even when parents address children in, for example, Greek, the response from the children is often in English. The Linguistic Minorities Project hopes, from its Adult Language Survey data from Coventry, Bradford and London, and from its Secondary Pupils Survey, in which school pupils are asked about their own language use at home, to be able to offer clearer answers to questions in this area.

The extent to which more recent settlers in the British Isles will follow the example of their predecessors in terms of language shift to English is not yet clear. The pressure of the dominant language in the British Isles is now even stronger than before, since it is also at the moment the dominant world language. Its native speakers may for this reason be especially liable to undervalue knowledge of other languages in themselves and in others, and current language education policies have so far had little success in counterbalancing this.

However, there is evidence (Saifullah Khan, 1977; Wilding, 1981) of a strong wish on the part of adult members of many linguistic minority communities to maintain their languages, and to see that their children have the opportunity and encouragement to learn them too. Technological developments too make it more feasible than it was for most immigrants to the United States in the early twentieth century to keep living contact with languages which originated in quite distant areas of the world. To mention only two; relatively cheap air travel is much used by immigrants to Britain now to allow regular visits 'home' to and with their families, and video-recorders are widely used for the viewing of minority language films in the home. Although there are very strong pressures towards linguistic and cultural anglicization, there are also countervailing forces which make the eventual patterns of use for the newer minority languages far from certain.

One of the most important areas of remaining ignorance is about the nature and results of the interaction of English and other languages under discussion here. Few of the children of the migrants and refugees who brought these languages to the British Isles are likely to use them as their parents did, and sometimes even these parents used quite highly anglicized forms of the languages if they came from countries where English was used extensively. Yet there have been almost no substantial studies of the contact varieties which have resulted in Britain – British Polish, British Italian or British Panjabi for example.

The most significant contribution so far to this important topic in the British context has been made by an Indian scholar visiting England, Rama Kant Agnihotri. In a study of Leeds teenagers from a Panjabi Sikh background he points to 'the emergence of a mixed Panjabi-English code being increasingly influenced by English', and claims that 'The use of un-adulterated Panjabi has nearly ceased to exist among Sikh children in Leeds. It is the mixed code and not Panjabi which must be recognized as the medium of intra-group communication as against English as the medium of inter-group communication' (Agnihotri, 1979: 255–6).

More detailed sociolinguistic and ethnographic studies are needed to in-vestigate the extent and nature of contact varieties between English and the newer minority languages, as well as the ways in which teaching of the standard varieties in 'mother tongue' classes inside and outside schools may interact with contact varieties that are developing in the world outside the classrooms.

Saifullah Khan's observation (1979) that the superordinate, and originally purely majority, category of 'Asian' is now used in certain circumstances by South Asians themselves alongside more specific sub-ethnic categories (at least in south London), suggests that it may be worth watching out for further linguistic reflections of changing ethnicities.

REFERENCES

Agnihotri, R.K. 1979. Processes of assimilation: a sociolinguistic study of Sikh children in Leeds. Unpublished D.Phil. dissertation, University of York.
Anwar, M. 1980. *Votes and policies: ethnic minorities in the General Election 1979.* London: Commission for Racial Equality.
Campbell-Platt, K. (revised S. Nicholas) 1978. *Linguistic minorities in Britain.* London: Runnymede Trust.
Chin, W.T. and Simsova, S. 1981. *Information sheets on Chinese readers.* London: British Library R and D Report.
Inner London Education Authority (ILEA) 1979. *Report on the 1978 Census of those ILEA pupils for whom English was not a first language.* London: ILEA.
——— 1982. *1981 Language Census.* London: ILEA.
Kelkar, A.R. 1968. *Studies in Hindi-Urdu I: introduction and word phonology.* Poona: Deccan College.
Khubchandani, L. 1979. A demographic typology for Hindi, Urdu and Panjabi speakers in South Asia. In W.C. McCormack and S.A. Wurm (eds.) *Language and Society.* The Hague: Mouton.
King, R. 1979. Italians in Britain: an idiosyncratic immigration. *Journal of the Association of Teachers of Italian* 29: 6–16.
Kosmin, B. Bauer, M. and Grizzard, N. 1976. *Steel City Jews: a study of ethnicity and social mobility in the Jewish population of the city of Sheffield.* London: Board of Deputies of British Jews.
Mobbs, M. 1981. Two languages or one? The significance of the language names 'Hindi' and 'Urdu'. *Journal of Multilingual and Multicultural Development* 2, 3: 203–11.
National Congress on Languages in Education (NCLE). 1982. *Report of the Working Party on the Languages of Minority Communities.* London: Centre for Information

on Language Teaching and Research.

Pandit, P. B. 1977. *Language in a plural society: the case of India*. New Delhi: Delhi University Press.

Ray, P. S., Hai, M. A. and Ray, L. 1966. *Bengali language handbook*. Washington DC: Center for Applied Linguistics.

Rosen, H. and Burgess, T. 1980. *Languages and dialects of London school-children* London: Ward Lock Educational.

Saifullah Khan, V. 1977. *Bilingualism and linguistic minorities in Britain*. London: Runnymede Trust.

———— 1979. Work and network: South Asian women in south London. In S. Wallmann (ed.) *Ethnicity at work*. London: Macmillan.

———— 1980. The 'mother tongue' of linguistic minorities in multicultural England. *Journal of Multilingual and Multicultural Development* 1, 1: 71–88.

Smith, G. P. 1982. *Locating populations of minority language speakers*. Linguistic Minorities Project, Working Paper 1. London: Institute of Education.

Tosi, A. 1982a. Between the mother's dialect and English. In Davies, A. (ed.) *Language and learning at home and in school*. London: Heinemann.

———— 1982b *Immigration and bilingual education* Oxford: Pergamon.

Voegelin, C. F. and Voegelin, F. M. 1977. *Classification and index of the world's languages*. New York: Elsevier.

Wilding, J. 1981. *Ethnic minority languages in the classroom? – a survey of Asian parents in Leicester*. Leicester: Council for Community Relations and Leicester City Council.

Note: Some of the findings of the Linguistic Minorities Project's surveys are published in their series of Working Papers available from the Information Room at the University of London Institute of Education. A book, provisionally entitled *Linguistic minorities in England*, will appear in the *Language, Education and Society* series from Routledge and Kegan Paul in 1983 or 1984.

26

The newer minorities: literacy and educational issues

MARILYN MARTIN-JONES

Patterns of immigration and settlement

Largely as a result of the patterns of immigration to Britain in the postwar period, a range of quite different languages has become part of the overall sociolinguistic fabric of urban British society in the 1980s. Many of the industrial cities of northern England, the Midlands and London itself now have multilingual populations including speakers of languages from Southern and Eastern Europe, Africa and South and East Asia (see chapter 25).

In one or two communities, the history of migration to Britain goes back several hundred years. The Italian community, for example, was already well established in the Clerkenwell area of London over a century ago (Sponza, 1981). In London and in other urban areas of Britain, there have been distinct patterns of settlement. In the Greater London area, Cypriot settlement has, for the most part, been in and around the boroughs of Camden and Islington, and, more recently, in Haringey and Hackney (Alkan and Constantinides, 1982). Greek and Turkish are widely used in the day-to-day lives of people in these two Cypriot communities. In the same way, Panjabi has become one of the principal community languages in Southall, and, similarly, Bengali in Tower Hamlets, Gujerati in Brent, Cantonese in Soho and, in the Portobello area of West London, Portuguese, Spanish and Moroccan Arabic.

In other industrial cities in Britain, there is a similar clustering of linguistic communities. Many postwar migrants from Italy found work in the brick factories of Bedford and Peterborough and settled there with their families. There are also long-established Italian communities in Glasgow, South Wales and in the Midlands. Polish refugees who arrived in Britain in the 1940s and 1950s settled in Ealing, Slough and Reading as well as in the cities of northern England and the Midlands. There are also other small communities of eastern European origin, such as the Ukrainian communities in Bradford and Coventry.

The oldest established Chinese communities are in London and Liverpool. In recent years, however, because of their specialization in the fast food business, individual Chinese families have tended to settle in many different areas of the British Isles, not only in the larger industrial conurbations.

Among the most recent groups of Chinese immigrants to Britain are refugees from Vietnam, who arrived during the late 1970s.

The Panjabi Sikhs in Coventry, London, Leeds and other major industrial cities, are among the oldest established South Asian communities in Britain (Ballard and Ballard, 1977). Panjabi is the language people still prefer to use at home with their families, and with friends and relatives at the Sikh Temple. Many children are taught to read and write Panjabi at home and in classes organized by the community. One of the main areas of settlement for Pakistani Panjabis in Britain has been in West Yorkshire. In Bradford, Urdu and Arabic are now widely taught to Panjabi-speaking children at home and in the local mosques. Panjabi is the language people generally use to converse with at home, at the corner shop and, to some extent, at work. Quite a large number of people, men and women, in this community work in the woollen mills in the Bradford area. Other people of Pakistani Panjabi origin, mostly those of an urban, educated background, may use Urdu as a community language. Urdu is also a *lingua franca* amongst speakers of different South Asian languages.

The other South Asian language which is widely used in Britain today is Gujerati. Many of the Gujerati-speaking families in the Midlands, in northern England and in the London area, came to Britain from East Africa in the late 1960s and 1970s. During this period Gujerati became established as one of the principal community languages of cities like Leicester and Coventry, as well as in some of the outer London boroughs such as Brent and Harrow in north-west London.

The right to minority language literacy

Over the last decade there has been a growing debate about the place of these newer minority languages in British society and, in particular, in British schools. This chapter will focus on one dimension of this debate, namely the right to 'mother tongue' or 'community language' literacy. (Definitions of these terms are given in the glossary. The term 'mother tongue' is only adopted in this chapter when referring to contexts where it is conventionally used and understood.)

Urban Britain of the 1980s has become a multilingual, multi-literate society. The communicative repertoires and language resources of different linguistic communities in Britain include a range of written languages, alphabets and scripts, yet it is still only literacy in English that is recognized as having any value in British society. While languages such as Greek, Turkish, Bengali, Urdu and Chinese have a very different status elsewhere, in the British context they are minority languages. In England, in particular, English is the majority language not only in terms of numbers of speakers and users, but, more importantly, in terms of legitimized power and control. The relationship between English and many minority languages in Britain, new and old, is embedded in a long history of colonization, with English as the language of rule. In Britain in the 1980s, English remains the dominant language of literacy in education, in the media, in the workplace, in government and in all aspects of British life. The ability to read and write Standard English is regarded as a crucial measure of educational performance, and as such it also serves as a means of discrimination in the labour market. Minority languages and literacies only have a legitimized place within minority institutions such as the home, the temple, church, mosque or the local community association. They also have a place within the marginalized sectors of the economy, such as the 'rag' trade or in small family businesses: the corner shop or the fast food business.

Minority languages are also defined as such by the perceptions of the majority community. In the English-speaking world, linguistic and cultural diversity has long been perceived as a 'problem'. This is reflected in the assimilationist educational policies that have shaped English education in the postwar years (Saifullah Khan, 1980). Long before this, English was imposed as the sole medium of instruction in schools throughout Britain, to the cost of the indigenous minority languages such as Welsh and Gaelic. This intolerance is not limited to the monolingual English-speaking majority in England: Romaine and Dorian (1981) have remarked on the fact that most Anglophone nations fail to exhibit much enthusiasm for additive bilingualism. Given this predominant attitude, the reference point for the minority language and culture outside Britain takes on all the more significance. In most parts of the world it is, of course, considered to be quite natural to be able to speak or write more than one language. In India, for example, linguistic pluralism is supported and developed through mother tongue education at the primary school level (Pattanayak, 1981). Moreover, this often involves the acquisition of more than one script.

The debate about the use and development of minority language literacy in the British context has to be interpreted in the light of the status accorded to English literacy. Broadly speaking, there are three kinds of issues involved. First and foremost, there is the educational issue. There is a growing concern among parents from linguistic minorities about the teaching of their languages, and literacy in those languages, to their children. This issue has also been taken up by educational organizations and individuals concerned with the education of children from linguistic minorities. Secondly, it is generally argued that there should be more general institutional support for the newer minority languages in Britain, including more media access and adequate library resources, as well as a place in all sectors of mainstream education. Thirdly, and perhaps belatedly, it is coming to be recognized that there should be more provision of translation and interpreting services in the principal community languages in the various local authority areas.

The broad picture of the distribution of literacy skills in English remains elusive, but there is still an urgent need for bilingual information leaflets, documents and forms in places such as the social services offices, in hospitals, dental clinics and law centres. In an attempt to meet this need, directories documenting the availability of information materials of this kind in centres throughout Britain have recently been compiled (National Association of Citizens' Advice Bureaux and Commission for Racial Equality, 1980; London Voluntary Service Council's Migrant Services Unit, 1981). Another promising new development has been the production of multilingual resources linked with broadcasting back-up. The Broadcasting Support Services produced a booklet in 1982, entitled *Your right to health* which has been translated into twelve community languages. This project was funded by the Health Education Council. The booklet was then advertised, in the twelve languages, on BBC television (Broadcasting Support Services, 1982).

The educational issue

The educational policy response to the increasing linguistic diversity in British schools in the 1950s and 1960s was to step up provision and resources for the teaching of English as a second language. It was not until the mid-1970s that there was any discussion of institutional support for bilingualism or for the teaching of the newer minority languages. The issues that began to emerge at this time have been documented in detail by some of those who were directly involved in the debate (Saifullah Khan, 1977; Tosi, 1979; Rosen and Burgess, 1980).

The first landmark in the development of attitudes at this time was the publication of the long-awaited report *A language for life* (Department of Education and Science, 1975) by the Bullock Committee of Enquiry, first commissioned in 1972 to look into the use of English in schools and the teaching of English literacy. The report made a number of recommendations regarding the education of children from the newer linguistic minorities (DES, 1975: ch. 20). Those recommendations that aroused the most interest and discussion at the time were the following:

No child should be expected to cast off the language and culture of the home as he crosses the school threshold and the curriculum should reflect those aspects of his life. (20.5)

Every school with pupils whose original language is not English should adopt a positive attitude to their bilingualism and wherever possible help maintain and deepen their knowledge of their mother tongue. (20.17)

There should be further research into the teaching of their own language to children of immigrant communities and into the various aspects of bilingualism in schools. (20.17)

In retrospect, the wording of the recommendations seems cautious and imprecise. They were general statements of principle and, at a time when little else was being said or done about the newer minority languages, they were very welcome. But there were no guidelines for action. It was not possible to assess what kind of curriculum changes or language education policy was envisaged. There was also no reference to the implications of linguistic diversity for the school community as a whole, not just for the bilingual children. The most far-reaching statement was perhaps that bilingual children should be able to 'maintain and deepen their knowledge of their mother tongue'.

In the mid-1970s some support for the concept of bilingual teaching came from one or two organizations concerned with the education of children from ethnic minority communities, organizations such as the National Association for Multiracial Education and the National Association of Teachers of English. In 1976, a conference on 'Bilingualism and British education: the dimensions of diversity' was convened by the Centre for Information on Language Teaching and Research, in association with Leicestershire Local Education Authority and with the support of a number of other local authorities. The focus of the conference was on three aspects of bilingualism in Britain: bilingualism in Welsh education, bilingualism in minorities and bilingualism and foreign-language teaching. In evaluating the outcome of the conference, Saifullah Khan (1977) points to the contrast between the experience and commitment of bilingual teachers and educators from Wales and those participants whose concern was with the language education of the children from the newer linguistic minorities. She concludes that 'it clearly indicated the limited impact that developments in the Welsh education system have had in the rest of the UK' (1977: 5)

In 1975 and 1976 there were some concrete developments in England at the local authority level. In November 1975, the Council of Europe funded a pilot scheme in Birmingham for the teaching of Panjabi. This was the first of its kind and ran until July 1976. In the same year, the EEC allocated direct funds to Bedfordshire Local Education Authority to set up an experimental bilingual education project where Panjabi and Italian were to be taught to junior and middle school children as part of the regular school timetable. The Bedfordshire experience has been documented in some detail (Tosi, 1982).

In mid-1976, the National Association of Asian Youth and *Yuvak Sangh*, a Gujerati association which organized community language classes on a voluntary basis, held two joint conferences for teachers of South Asian languages. The first conference focused on the need to separate language teaching from religious instruction. After the second conference, the participants called for a co-ordinated campaign for educational provision within the mainstream school system for the teaching of minority languages and for financial support wherever communities opted to organize classes themselves. One eventual outcome of this conference was the setting up of a joint Co-ordinating Committee for Mother Tongue Teaching along with members of a group of teachers of European minority languages.

The EEC Directive

By this time, a draft Directive on the 'Education of migrant workers' children' had been issued by the commission of the European Communities. One of the clauses of the original draft Directive called for 'tuition in the mother tongue and culture of the child within the normal school curriculum'. The British government tabled a number of objections to the draft Directive, some of which were voiced in the debates in both Houses of Parliament in June 1976. The principal objections were that:

(1) The term 'migrant' was quite inappropriate in the British context. Unlike other member states where 'guestworkers' lacked fundamental rights of citizenship, in Britain most linguistic minority children had either been born here or had parents with British nationality. The numbers of children whose parents were migrant workers from member states were very small in comparison. It was argued that there should be no discrimination between provision for these children and the children of immigrant workers from non-EEC countries. In March 1980, at an EEC colloquium on the Bedford project the then Secretary of State for Education, Mark Carlisle, underscored this point in his opening remarks:

We intend to apply the Directive without regard to the country of origin of the children concerned. That means that we will be concerned about provision for about 650,000 pupils, only a small proportion of whom will be from Community countries. (Commission for Racial Equality, 1980)

(2) The Directive contradicted the fundamental principle in British education that central government should not impose mandatory policies on local education authorities or on individual school heads. Thus it could not be enforced without a change in the legal system.

(3) There were not enough resources or qualified teachers in Britain to entertain provision on the scale proposed in the Directive. Fred Mulley, who was Secretary of State for Education at the time, reflected the overall response to the Directive when he spoke in Parliament of the 'intolerable burdens' this would put on the educational system in the current economic situation (*Hansard*, 10 June 1976).

The draft Directive was circulated to local authorities and teachers' associations by the Department of Education and Science, but there was no direct consultation with minority organizations or parents' groups. The only representation for minority organizations was through the Community Relations Commission, which welcomed most of the proposals in the draft Directive, but insisted that instruction in English should remain the first priority. Responses from teachers' unions and local authorities were guardedly negative and, overall, objections were based on legal and administrative criteria without due consideration for the linguistic and educational arguments in favour of statutory support for the teaching of community languages.

Eventually a new version of the Directive was adopted by the Council of the European Communities on 25 July 1977. Article 3 of the Directive, which pertained specifically to community language teaching, was rephrased so that the mandatory force of the Directive was removed. It now called for the teaching of the 'mother tongue' and culture of the children of migrant workers 'in accordance with national circumstances and legal systems'.

The EEC Directive came into effect on 25 July 1981, four years after it was first adopted. On 31 July 1981, the Department of Education and Science and the Welsh Office sent out a joint circular to all local education authorities with the text of the Directive attached (DES, Circular 5/81; Welsh Office, Circular 36/81). This circular sets out guidelines for interpretation and compliance with the requirements of the Directive. Article 3 of the Directive which called for the promotion of the mother tongue and culture of the child's country of origin is interpreted as follows:

For local education authorities in this country, this implies that they should explore ways in which mother tongue teaching might be provided, whether during or outside school hours, but not that they are required to give such tuition to all individuals as of right. (DES, 1981: 2)

It is unlikely that there will be any significant change in local education policy, especially in the light of the views reflected in this circular.

The implications of the Directive have been commented on at length from very different standpoints (Saifullah Khan, 1977; Brook, 1980; CRE, 1980). What has been noticeably absent in the debate conducted at the national level and in academic circles is, above all, the view of the minorities themselves regarding their language rights. There is strong evidence from surveys conducted at local level in different areas that parents favour the teaching of their languages to their children. For example, in a study carried out in Leicester, 75 per cent of the South Asian parents interviewed said they were either already sending their children to classes to study their languages or expressed an interest in doing so, while 60 per cent said they would like their children to take a public examination in those languages (Wilding, 1981).

Between the autumn of 1980 and the winter of 1981, the Linguistic Minorities Project conducted a series of sociolinguistic surveys in ten different linguistic minority communities, including speakers of both European and South and East Asian languages: Bengali, Cantonese, Greek, Gujerati, Italian, Panjabi, Polish, Portuguese, Turkish and Ukrainian. The surveys were based in three different urban areas: Coventry, Bradford and London. Adults of all ages were asked about the ways in which they used the languages they knew in their daily lives here in Britain and about their views on the teaching of their languages to their children. The project is still at the field-work stage at the time of writing, but the overwhelming impression from the fieldwork experience is that there is a great deal of concern with language teaching and language maintenance in minority communities.

The educational response

In some schools and local authorities, there has been a perceptible shift away from the exclusive emphasis on the teaching of English as a second language to a broad acknowledgement of the linguistic and educational value of developing a child's home language or community language. In practice, this new approach is reflected in efforts to support the existing voluntary classes organized by the communities themselves, either by providing free classroom facilities or direct financial support. The Inner London Education Authority (ILEA) has, for example, sponsored ten voluntary schools and classes teaching different languages. ILEA has also specifically formulated a multi-ethnic education policy (in October 1977) and has taken the lead in involvement and consultation with ethnic minorities at all levels of education. A modern languages inspector has recently been appointed with special responsibility for minority community languages. Bilingual materials have also been devised for the secondary school level and are available to teachers through the Centre for Urban Educational Studies (Wright, 1980).

Other local authorities have taken some initiatives in support of linguistic minority children in their schools: in Leicester, five bilingual teachers have been recruited to work in the primary sector. In the Peterborough division of Cambridgeshire, both Italian and Urdu have for some time now been taught by specialist teachers. Nottinghamshire has recently appointed an inspector for multicultural education who, as part of his brief, will be co-ordinating the development of community language teaching in local schools. Three 'team leaders' have also been appointed, along with a number of Panjabi and Urdu teachers, for the primary, secondary and voluntary sectors. The City of Coventry has a well established Minority Support Group Service with a 'mother tongue' specialist. In Birmingham, an eight-session course on 'mother tongue teaching' has been organized and working parties have been set up to look into the production of teaching materials and teacher education with special reference to Panjabi and Urdu. Nearby Walsall and Dudley also have specialist staff dealing with the teaching of community languages.

The City of Manchester now has a team of six teachers of Urdu. This 'mother tongue' team forms part of the overall Multicultural Development Service. A national working party for the development of Urdu teaching materials has been meeting in Manchester on a regular basis. Further north, in Bradford, there has been considerable interest and discussion in local educational circles about the nature and type of support for community language teaching that should be made available by the local authority. Two advisers for multicultural education had been appointed by 1981 and plans made to recruit teachers of South Asian languages.

Some of the outer London boroughs have also begun to introduce classes in some local community languages. Four South Asian languages, Panjabi, Urdu, Hindi and Gujerati are currently taught in schools in Ealing. In north-west London, the borough of Brent has two Gujerati teachers, one Hindi and one Urdu teacher. The borough of Haringey, in north London, has recently introduced support for Greek classes in two secondary schools. This support is the outcome of close collaboration between a local Greek Cypriot parents' association and the local authority. In north-east London, four Urdu teachers are now supported by Waltham Forest Local Education Authority. However, despite these recent developments at the local authority level, the teachers of minority community languages still face enormous difficulties since they often have to divide their time between teaching their languages and other subjects. They are also often obliged to hold their classes in the lunch hour or after school. More often than not, new initiatives come from individual teachers and heads within a local authority. For example, in north London Greek classes were offered at Stationer's school as far back as the 1960s and a Turkish class was also instituted at Archway during the same period. In Highgate school in Birmingham, a mode 3 CSE syllabus in Panjabi has recently been introduced. And in the outer London borough of Brent, a local 'mother tongue' project, focusing on issues of materials development, was set up in 1980 by local community language teachers and a modern language teacher at Alperton school, in conjunction with the Community Librarian. However, the lack of a coherent overall policy on community language teaching in most local authorities has resulted in the emergence of very different types of provision and different degrees of support in each area, and, often, individual schools.

The most obvious outcome of the EEC Directive has been, perhaps predictably, the funding of a series of research projects, echoing the caution of the third recommendation of the Bullock report of 1975. These projects are briefly described below:

1977–78 *Linguistic Diversity in London Schools:* a research project based at the Institute of Education, London University. Harold Rosen and Tony Burgess carried out a survey of the languages and dialects of London schoolchildren in collaboration with teachers from 28 comprehensive schools.

1978–80 *Mother Tongue and English Teaching Project*: a two-year research project monitoring a one-year Panjabi–English bilingual education programme. The research was conducted by Olav Rees and Barré Fitzpatrick at Bradford University.

1979–83 *Linguistic Minorities Project*: a research project based at the Institute of Education, London University. Work in progress is described in this chapter and in chapter 25.

1981–84 *Schools Council Mother Tongue Project*: a project based at the Centre for Urban Educational Studies (an ILEA teachers' centre). The project team is developing materials and resources for the teaching of two of the community languages widely spoken in the Greater London area: Bengali and Greek.

A number of key educational bodies have now also issued explicit policy statements on the teaching of the newer minority languages. In April 1981, the National Association for Multiracial Education appointed a working party to draft a policy statement which spelt out a series of 'practical measures' to be taken to ensure that minority languages 'take their rightful place in the British education system' (NAME, 1981). The Commission for Racial Equality have also become increasingly concerned with the promotion of the 'mother tongue' debate. In 1980, for example, they co-sponsored a conference on 'mother tongue teaching' with Bradford College. In September 1981, the Schools Council held a conference which focused on one particular area of the debate about educational issues, namely examinations (Bardell and Denyer, 1981). This brought together groups concerned with multicultural education and the status of minority languages in the school curriculum with representatives of examination boards. Commissions for the study of examinations in Hindi and Urdu have now been set up. Other seminars and workshops have been organized locally and nationally, for example, in November 1981 and February 1982 the Centre for Information on Language Teaching and Research ran two seminars on 'The education of the bilingual child': these seminars drew teachers and administrators in both the voluntary and mainstream education sectors, from different regions in the British Isles.

In November 1980, the National Congress on Language in Education set up a working party on the 'Languages of minority communities'. Over a period of two years, this working party has been investigating and reporting on some of the following: teacher training needs, examples of existing good practice in language teaching, criteria for developing teaching materials, assessment and examinations in a number of different languages (NCLE, 1982).

In the autumn of 1981, the BBC produced a series of documentary films on multicultural education for teacher training. One of these films ('Language for life') focused on the current debate about community language teaching and showed a number of classes in different languages, including Italian, Panjabi and Urdu.

More recently, the National Union of Teachers adopted a favourable stance towards 'mother tongue teaching' and published a policy statement (NUT, 1982) which makes quite specific recommendations for different levels of education in a positive but realistic way. At the primary level, the statement defines mother tongue teaching as 'instruction for part of the day in the pupil's home or community language, preferably by a bilingual teacher, in the ordinary classroom' (1982: 3). At the secondary school level, the statement calls for parity with other subjects in the mainstream school curriculum for the minority languages taught in preparation for public examinations: 'Pupils studying languages such as Urdu or Gujerati for GCE examinations should ideally have the subject timetabled in the normal way and not be expected to study the language in their spare time or at the expense of other subjects' (1982: 4).

The original Co-ordinating Committee for Mother Tongue Teaching gradually became established as the principal forum for the exchange of ideas and information about the teaching of community languages. It brought together representatives of voluntary agencies, community organizations, local education authorities and individual teachers concerned with 'mother tongue' education. In 1980, under a new constitution, it became known as the National Council for Mother Tongue Teaching and it received a grant from the Department of Education and Science. In addition to maintaining an increasingly wide information network and publishing a newsletter, the NCMTT has been active in promoting discussion about the different issues related to the teaching of specific mother tongues. In addition to its annual general meetings, a series of national conferences have been convened by the NCMTT. Since 1979 there have been six such conferences, five dealing with the teaching of a South Asian language used here in Britain: Urdu, Panjabi, Hindi, and Bengali; and one on the teaching of Greek. The focus of other conferences organized by the NCMTT over this period has been on the following themes: biliteracy, assessment and examinations in mother tongue teaching and bilingualism and education: policies and politics.

Nature and extent of existing provision

In the debate about provision for the teaching of community languages in mainstream education in Britain, a distinction is made between the nature of provision at the primary and secondary school level. At the primary level, it is argued that as much support as possible should be given to the child's home language on entering school so as to ensure continuity of linguistic and cognitive development. Discussions about the appropriate nature of provision tend to vary from the introduction of activities (such as story telling) in the home language and the need to recruit more bilingual teachers, to various bilingual approaches and the use of the community language as the medium of instruction. At the secondary level, it is the actual teaching of the language as a subject within the curriculum that is debated from different standpoints. Those concerned with support for minority languages argue that, in each area, community languages should have a place alongside French and German in the school timetable. Commenting on this aspect of the educational debate, Bhiku Parekh has called for the teaching of a much wider range of languages and literacies in British schools (in his keynote address at the Annual General Meeting of the NCMTT, November 1981). He argued that the newer British languages such as Greek, Gujerati and Arabic should be integrated into the mainstream curriculum as languages for all children instead of the usual narrow choice of European languages now offered. He suggested that demand for provision of this kind should be formulated in precisely the same terms that have always been used in demanding provision of the so-called 'modern' and 'classical' languages. The persistence of terminology of this kind in British education is indicative of a lack of awareness of the changing sociolinguistic patterns of British society. The existing compartmentalization of language teaching activities within the educational system needs to be carefully reassessed. Bhiku Parekh's argument reflects a view which is widely endorsed by proponents of multicultural education in Britain, namely that language and literacy education have to be more broadly conceived as part of a multicultural curriculum that reflects and responds to the linguistic and cultural diversity of contemporary Britain.

Some quite practical proposals as to ways in which teachers of different languages could collaborate and define ways of developing language awareness among children have been put forward (Hawkins, 1981). A number of schools and groups of teachers have already taken their own initiatives along these lines: they have designed language teaching materials and courses which reflect the linguistic composition of their schools and draw on the linguistic resources of the bilingual children. A wider range of languages can also now be studied as subjects for public examinations, although there are a number of problems with the ways in which the examinations were originally designed and the candidates they were designed for. A survey of the availability of the examinations from the various examination boards in twelve languages (Arabic, Bengali, Chinese, Greek, Gujerati, Hindi, Panjabi, Polish, Portuguese, Turkish, Ukrainian and Urdu) has been carried out by the NCLE working party on 'Languages of minority communities' (Reid, 1982).

Despite the efforts of individual teachers and schools, the overall picture of provision within the mainstream education system is discouraging. The bulk of provision for the teaching of the newer minority languages in Britain, including preparation for public examinations, is organized outside the education system. This provision has been steadily growing along with the increasing demand. The classes, mostly held in the evenings or at weekends, are organized for a range of different languages throughout the British Isles. Sometimes referred to as 'Saturday' or 'Sunday' schools or 'mother tongue' classes, they are set up with a variety of different goals in mind: political, religious and cultural (Saifullah Khan, 1976, 1977; Russell, 1980; Elliott, 1981). The organizers of these classes and schools have differing views regarding the possibility of provision within British schools. Some religious establishments, such as the Greek and Ukrainian Orthodox churches, the synagogues, temples and mosques, combine language teaching and religious instruction. Parents and community organizations rent local premises, often at considerable cost, and recruit teachers to provide the preferred kind of language instruction for their children. These community organizations often cater for considerable numbers of children: one of the oldest Saturday schools in Britain – the Polish school in Ealing – had 300 pupils on the roll in 1980

(Elliott, 1981). In the same year, a Gujerati Sunday school in Coventry had 285 children on its roll (NCMTT newsletter, December 1980). A Greek Cypriot parents' organization in north London has its own office and staff and runs nearly a hundred different classes and youth clubs in different premises across this area of London.

Some embassies and high commissions provide support for the teaching of different languages of southern European origin. The Italian, Spanish and Portuguese governments organize instruction in their respective languages and recruit native speakers who are trained teachers to teach in their classes. The Greek Cypriot High Commission and the Turkish Federated State of Cyprus also recruit teachers and pay their salaries. The Council of Europe recently funded a successful two-year project in collaboration with the Portuguese and Spanish governments in a West London school, where Portuguese and Spanish classes were integrated into the school timetable (NCMTT newsletter, Spring 1982). At the local level, a number of studies of existing language provision outside the mainstream curriculum have been carried out. More recently, because of the need to obtain a broader picture, NCMTT set up a working party which is currently surveying the mother tongues and community language teaching going on in different areas. This work is being carried out in collaboration with members of the Linguistic Minorities Project research team. The aim is to set up a systematic national directory of mother tongue teaching.

The growing demand for provision for community language teaching points to an urgent need for teacher training facilities; both in-service training and initial teacher training courses will have to be developed for teachers at all levels. The Royal Society of Arts has set up a working party on 'The training of teachers of minority languages' and specific recommendations have been made regarding the content and focus of this kind of teacher education by other individuals and educational organizations (Broadbent, 1982).

Library provision and resources in community languages

A survey of library authorities in Britain carried out in 1979 indicated that most areas make some provision available for adult readers among linguistic minorities (Cooke, 1979). There is a range of literacy resources in the different languages, including books, periodicals and newspapers, some of which are published here in Britain (Clough and Quarmby, 1978). There is increasing demand for this kind of support for minority language literacy. In October 1980 the School of Librarianship at the Polytechnic of North London held a conference on 'Library Provision in the Mother Tongue'; and work on the library needs of specific linguistic minorities, as well as groups within those minorities is also being carried out at the same School (Gundara, 1981; Chin and Simsova, 1982).

Attention has also been turned to the library needs of linguistic minority children (Taylor and Hurwitz, 1979; Elliott, 1981). In January 1982 a three-year research project into the reading habits and interests of children in an urban multicultural community was set up at Middlesex Polytechnic. The work of this project will focus on north London. A survey of 'mother tongue' schools carried out in the London area focused in particular on their library needs and the children's level of literacy and reading preferences (Elliott, 1981). Elliott's account of her work gives us the first qualitative insight into the educational contribution and experience of voluntary schools and classes; she documents in detail the effort that goes into organizing classes, the kinds of difficulties faced by individual schools and communities in obtaining appropriate teaching materials and in recruiting teachers.

Sociolinguistic perspectives on community language teaching

While the debate about mother tongue or community language policy hinges on questions of language rights and status relative to English, decisions about the actual content of language curricula have to take into account the specific sociolinguistic situation of the different linguistic minorities. The series of conferences organized by NCMTT about the teaching of different community languages has served as a valuable sounding board for those aspects of language use and language change that are in issue for the different linguistic minorities here in Britain and for defining teaching priorities. A range of different issues has been discussed. The focus here will be on those socio-linguistic issues that have a direct bearing on the teaching of literacy in community languages. Traditional beliefs and attitudes about the relationship between spoken and written language are fundamental to our understanding of language and literacy use and teaching in individual linguistic communities. As Stubbs (1980) has observed, literacy has a social primacy which spoken language does not have, although the latter has chronological primacy.

The first question that comes up again and again in discussions about the teaching of community languages is what, in fact, is to be taught? Is it the language or language variety spoken at home? Is it a standard language associated with formal schooling in the country of origin? Is it a written language traditionally associated with religious practices? The diglossia that characterizes the sociolinguistic situation of several different linguistic minorities in Britain raises the question of what target norms to follow in teaching the language. In some cases, as with Kutchi speakers from Gujerat or East Africa, or Panjabi speakers from the Pakistani Panjab, there is virtually no tradition of writing in these languages in linguistic communities from these regions of South Asia. Literacy is associated with the standard regional language which, in the case of most Kutchi speakers would be Gujerati, or with the national language of Pakistan, namely Urdu. People mean different things when they talk about 'mother tongues'. For example, when asked the question: 'What is your mother tongue?', a Panjabi speaker of Pakistani origin is just as likely to answer 'Urdu' as 'Panjabi', Urdu being the preferred language in more formal settings. It is also Urdu that is taught to children in classes organized by the communities themselves or, occasionally, in local schools.

Besides Urdu, children whose parents came from the Pakistani Punjab may be learning to read and write Qur'anic Arabic at the local mosque. Religion plays a significant role in the development of children's literacy repertoires in a number of different communities. Urdu, along with Pushtu and Sindhi, was one of the Indo-European languages which came to be written in the Persian-Arabic script under Moghul rule in north India. The written form of the language thus has close associations with Islam and with Islamic literature. What is particularly significant is the value attached to calligraphic skills: because of the reverence attached to the Islamic scriptures and because pictorial representation has been discouraged under Islam, calligraphy has become an art form in itself and an important means of subjective expression and self-discipline. In the context of Urdu and Arabic instruction in Britain today, part of this calligraphic tradition and this view of literacy is being passed on to the younger generation.

Other alphabets, scripts and written languages taught to linguistic minority children in Britain have the same sort of symbolic value for different social and historical reasons, be it the Chinese system of written characters, the Greek or Cyrillic alphabets or the different South Asian scripts: Panjabi in the *Gurmukhi* script, Hindi in the *Devanagari* script, Bengali or Gujerati. The use of a distinctive writing system is emblematic of ethnic and cultural identity and shared linguistic heritage. It is part of the social history of a particular linguistic community. It is important to bear this in mind in discussions of community language and literacy teaching in the British context. In Britain, the Industrial Revolution and the subsequent promotion of mass literacy led to an association of English literacy with technology, science and trade. Writing English by hand has come to be most highly valued as a skill or tool rather than as a medium of subjective expression. Typewritten and printed text is held in higher esteem than calligraphy.

There are other diglossic situations among linguistic minorities in Britain that have implications for language and literacy teaching. In the Greek Cypriot community, for instance, the spoken variety of Cypriot Greek is significantly different in terms of phonology and lexis from the spoken Athenian variety (Roussou, 1981). The traditional language of literacy is *Katharévusa*. It is only associated with very formal varieties of written language and with the teaching of religious texts. In recent years, a written standard based on the Athenian Demotic variety of Greek has been coming into general currency. In this emerging standard there is a substantial amount of lexical borrowing from *Katharévusa* in, for example, journalistic texts (Ferguson, 1959). This lack of fit between the spoken Cypriot Greek of the home and the spoken and written standards used in Greece is a source of considerable difficulty for Cypriot children in Britain learning to read and write, and has to be taken into account in the preparation of teaching materials (Roussou, 1981).

In the Italian communities in Britain, the term *dialetto* is commonly used to refer to the spoken varieties or home languages associated with different regions of Italy. The teaching of standard Italian to children in Britain who have acquired these spoken varieties and regional languages at home, presents a number of problems, notably in the preparation of teaching materials. Some of the difficulties arising from this discrepancy between home and target language have been documented with specific reference to the context of the Bedford project (Tosi, 1982).

Qur'anic Arabic is widely learned and used in Moslem communities throughout Britain. Children who speak Bengali, Panjabi, Gujerati or some spoken variety of Arabic at home may well attend the local mosque to learn to read and recite aloud the Islamic scriptures. In many cases, Qur'anic Arabic will be taught in this way to children who have already acquired literacy in a community language and/or English. Arabic is also the secular language of literacy for North African and Middle Eastern communities in Britain. Since there are considerable differences between the regional varieties of spoken Arabic and the standard written forms (Ferguson, 1959), this again has implications for children who have learned spoken varieties such as Moroccan Arabic at home in Britain, but who have had little or no exposure to the standard forms they encounter in the classroom. Teachers of Arabic as a community language need to take this diglossia into account in their teaching and in the development of teaching materials.

Another sociolinguistic phenomenon which has consequences for the teaching of community languages in Britain is what Dale (1980) has described as 'digraphia'. This is defined as 'the use of two (or more) writing systems for representing a single language (or varieties thereof)' (1980: 5). Two examples from the South Asian context are pertinent here because they include languages which are also widely used and taught in Britain (including at the university level), namely Hindi and Urdu. Dale recalls how, during the era of Moghul rule in north India, Hindustani was written in the 'politically predominant' Persian-Arabic script. Towards the end of this period, the *Devanagari* script – long associated with Sanskrit, the scriptural language of Hinduism – came to be more and more widely used to write the same language, Hindustani. Two rival varieties of written language have thus emerged. In their most formal styles, they have a characteristically high frequency of loan-words from Persian and Sanskrit respectively. Neither Hindi nor Urdu are widely spoken languages in the British context, but play a significant role as *lingua francas* and languages of literacy: in direct contact between members of different South Asian communities or in local radio or television programmes in South Asian languages (Mobbs, 1981). While Urdu is widely taught in the Pakistani Panjabi community, Hindi (written in the *Devanagari* script) is often the preferred language of literacy for Panjabis in Britain who are practising Hindus, particularly when it comes to literacy instruction for their children. A considerable number of Gujerati Hindus also read and write Hindi as well as Gujerati and teach it to their children here in Britain. Gujerati Moslems, on the other hand, prefer their children to read and write Urdu in the Persian-Arabic script.

A further example of the role of religion in script choice is the case of the Sikh community from the Indian Panjab. In contrast to Hindu Panjabis from East Africa and from the Indian state of Haryana, Sikh Panjabis write Panjabi in the *Gurmukhi* script. This was the script first adapted in the sixteenth century to write the *Granth Sahib*, the sacred hymns of Sikhism. *Gurmukhi* now has secular as well as religious status in the Panjab. In Britain, Panjabi in the *Gurmukhi* script is used as much for personal correspondence and community transactions as for religious purposes. Panjabi children in Britain learn to read and write in the *Gurmukhi* script at the local *Gurdhwara* (Sikh temple) or, where provision is already available, at their local school.

Turkish is taught in Britain to children of both Turkish Cypriot and Turkish origin, mostly in the north London area. The alphabet that is currently used is the Roman alphabet with a number of distinctive diacritic and accent markings. This alphabet was brought into use in 1928 following a movement for linguistic reform that accompanied the westernization programmes of Kamal Attatürk. For centuries before this the Arabic script was used to write Turkish. This particular case of diachronic digraphia now only has relevance for the oldest members of these linguistic communities who received their education in Turkey or Cyprus during the early part of this century.

In one British minority community the debate about choice of a written standard for community language teaching originates from political and cultural differences. A new dilemma emerged in overseas Chinese communities as the balance of international diplomacy changed and the People's Republic of China began to establish links with the West. There are now two rival forms of standard written Chinese: (1) the traditional Taiwan or overseas norm, known mostly as *Guoyu* in its spoken form and modern *Baihuawen* (vernacular or colloquial writing style) in exclusive reference to the written form; and (2) the Mainland norm, known as *Putonghua* or Modern Standard Chinese, which comprises a set of about 2,000 simplified characters adopted by the People's Republic in 1956. 'Mandarin' is a European term first coined in 1727 to refer to *Gwanhua*, i.e. the language spoken by the Mandarin scholars. With the establishment of the Republic in 1911 and the disappearance of the Mandarins, the term *Gwanhua* was abolished, but 'Mandarin' is still used loosely to refer to either *Guoyu* or *Putonghua* (Hsü, 1979: 120). Hsü summarizes the situation in the following way:

The Chinese language is at present going through a transitional period during which two major norms, while being mutually exclusive in their primary spheres of influence, can under certain circumstances actually coexist. (1979: 117)

In addition to these two major norms, other mixed varieties of the written language have developed in other regions where Chinese is widely used and taught, for example, in Hong Kong, Singapore and Malaysia.

The choice of one norm over another in literacy classes for overseas Chinese children has particular significance because of the time invested in learning the written characters. Chinese children are generally introduced to about 2,000 characters in the first four years of primary school (Taylor, 1981). Classes for Chinese children in Britain are organized up and down the country from Aberdeen to Surrey. In the London area, for example, approximately 585 Chinese children attend classes at the four schools run by the Overseas Chinese Education Centre. The schools are based in Shepherds Bush, Euston, Hounslow and in Reading, Berkshire. The classes meet for two hours a week, usually on Saturdays and Sundays, and, in a year, they cover the language syllabus for half of a school year in Hong Kong (Lue in NCMTT newsletter, 1982). Another class in north London caters for almost 200 children and, in Soho itself, the Chinese school run by the Chinese Chamber of Commerce has over 800 pupils. Several other classes in central and east London have been established for some time.

Other sociolinguistic issues that are discussed in relation to the teaching of community languages originate from the changes that are taking place in both the spoken and written varieties of the languages through contact with the dominant language, English. Broadly speaking, two immediate concerns are voiced by community language teachers. First, there is the question of how much lexical borrowing from English should be acceptable in the classroom. Second, there is the related question of the degree to which teaching materials and strategies should be adapted to the linguistic and cultural experience of children who have learnt their own community languages at home here in Britain. These are complex issues and can only be resolved through time and through experience with different teaching approaches which take into account the specific sociolinguistic situation of individual groups.

Minority children and literacy

A great deal has been said and written about the teaching of community languages and literacy in those languages to minority children. Yet very little is known about the distribution of language skills among children in different linguistic minorities (see chapter 25). Still less is known about literacy.

Rosen and Burgess (1980) carried out a survey of the linguistic diversity in London schools between 1977 and 1978. In close collaboration with teachers they surveyed 4,600 pupils in 28 comprehensive schools. The findings reported

Table 26.1. *Survey of linguistic diversity in London schools: proportions of pupils estimated as reading and writing in a language other than English*

Language spoken by more than 14 pupils	Reads and writes %	Reads but does not write %
Cantonese	64	12
Spanish	66	6
Bengali	30	31
Urdu	40	20
French	53	6
Arabic	50	6
Portuguese	43	11
Turkish	42	12
Greek	37	16
German	37	7
Gujerati	24	12
Hindi	13	23
Italian	21	4
Panjabi	17	5
Yoruba	11	11
French creoles	3	18

Source: Rosen and Burgess (1980: 76).

for literacy are itemized by language in table 26.1. Fifty-five languages were recorded in all; for 16 of these languages the number of speakers was over 14 pupils and these 16 languages accounted for over three-quarters of the bilingual pupils.

Most of the survey evidence available so far is from work based in schools and hence on teachers' accounts of children's literacy. The constraints on the interpretation of this sort of survey data have been outlined in chapter 25 of this volume, and elsewhere, for example, Rosen and Burgess (1980), Smith (1982). Nevertheless, provided those limitations are taken into account, survey work can provide the first step towards an overall picture of the broad distribution of language and literacy skills throughout schools in a particular local authority area. It can also be argued that the actual process of involving teachers in asking pupils about their language and literacy skills is as valuable as the survey results themselves. As Rosen and Burgess (1980) have observed in their commentary on their own survey work:

Our figures are an indication of the massive change which has altered the linguistic profile of the schools in a very short space of time. It is without precedent in the history of compulsory schooling ... It does not require any kind of survey to make people, especially teachers, aware of the language variety in schools. However, the precise nature of the variety was something of a surprise! ... The survey can bring home both quantitatively and qualitatively the multilingualism of our schools. (1980: 97)

Since 1980, the Linguistic Minorities Project has been carrying out a Schools Language Survey in a number of different local education authority areas (see chapter 25). The overall literacy profile for languages other than English in three of these areas, Coventry, Haringey and Bradford, is set out in table 26.2. Teachers were asked to record all levels of literacy reported by their pupils, including instances when pupils said they could read and write 'only a little'. Table 26.2 incorporates the overall figures for different types and degrees of literacy skills recorded: not only those cases where children reported literacy in the language spoken at home but also the diglossic and digraphic situations such as those described in this chapter. The overall literacy profile for boys and girls is also given.

Those languages which were most frequently reported tended to be different in these three local authority areas (see chapter 25: table 25.4) The number of pupils reporting some degree of literacy in each of these languages is indicated in table 26.3. Three separate categories are given for Panjabi: first, those cases where pupils clearly reported literacy in Panjabi with reference to the *Gurmukhi* script; second, those cases which reflected the diglossic situation in the Pakistani Panjab, that is where pupils reported speaking Panjabi at home but gave Urdu as their language of literacy; and, third, those cases where the teachers did not specify the pupils' language of literacy.

For South Asian languages such as Panjabi, Urdu and Pushtu, children's full literacy repertoire is best represented with reference to several different written languages, including Urdu and Arabic. Table 26.4 gives the percentage of children reporting some degree of literacy in the language or language variety spoken at home and/or in Urdu and/or in Arabic. The same broad grouping of returns for Panjabi is adopted here as in table 26.3. The figures for Panjabi, Urdu and Pushtu are compared with those for two other South Asian languages: Gujerati and Bengali. In the majority of these cases, the reporting of Urdu and Arabic reflects religious affiliation.

This kind of survey data gives us a broad picture of the literacy repertoires of school children in a particular local authority area. However, insights into children's actual use and perception of literacy and their fluency in reading and writing can only be obtained through observation in context. The uses to which they put their literacy repertoires also has to be assessed in the light of attitudes and beliefs about literacy held in different linguistic communities – and, more importantly, in terms of the status assigned to English literacy. Awareness and appreciation in the schools of the child's own language and literacy resources can meanwhile go a long way toward tilting the balance. In the words of the 1982 NUT policy statement on mother tongue teaching: 'Respect for ethnic minority pupils in our schools can be fostered by the status accorded to their home and community language.'

Table 26.2. *Linguistic Minorities Project Schools Language Survey: percentage of bilingual/multilingual children with some degree of literacy in one or more languages other than English*

	Coventry %	Haringey %	Bradford %
boys and girls	41	52	50
boys	38	53	47
girls	45	52	54

Source: Linguistic Minorities Project (1982) *Working Papers* (University of London, Institute of Education).

Table 26.3. *Linguistic Minorities Project Schools Language Survey: percentage of children with some degree of literacy in one or more languages other than English (not necessarily the language or language variety spoken at home)*

	Coventry %	Bradford %	Haringey %
Panjabi			
unspecified	35*	54	37
Urdu script	56	52	—
Gurmukhi script	35	39	—
Urdu	62	59	52
Gujerati	37*	34	25*
Bengali	50	56	50
Hindi	37	30	24
Chinese	61	56	69
Italian	63	72	59
Greek	—	—	60*
Turkish	—	—	49*
Polish	79	66	—

* In these groups there are statistically significant sex difference in literacy rates. In all cases, a smaller proportion of boys than of girls reported literacy in a language other than English.
Source: Linguistic Minorities Project (1982) *Working Papers* (University of London, Institute of Education).

Table 26.4. *Linguistic Minorities Project Schools Language Survey Bradford* *(March 1981)*

Language group	Total no. of pupils in each lang. group	% of pupils with literacy in lang. spoken at home	% of pupils with Urdu as a lang. of literacy	% of pupils with some knowledge of written Arabic
Bengali	449	50	4	13
Gujerati	1,251	28	4	6
Panjabi (*Gurmukhi* script)	588	34	—	—
Panjabi (Urdu literacy)	2,419	22	27	24
Panjabi (script not specified)	4,474	35	24	13
Pushtu	415	25	18	22
Urdu	2,700	55	—	13

Note: (a) Total number of pupils surveyed in Bradford in 1981 = 79,758; (b) Total number of pupils recorded as speaking a language other than English at home = 14,197 (17.8%).

Source: Linguistic Minorities Project (1982) *Working Papers* (University of London, Institute of Education).

REFERENCES

Alkan, F. and Constantinides, S. 1982. *Cypriots in Haringey*. London: Haringey Borough Council.

Ballard, R. and Ballard, C. 1977. The Sikhs: the development of South Asian settlements in Britain. In J. Watson (ed.) *Between two cultures: migrants and minorities in Britain*. London: Blackwell.

Bardell, G. and Denyer, J. 1981. *Examining in a multicultural society*. London: Schools Council.

Broadbent, J. 1982. *Toward a programme of in-service teacher training for minority languages*. London: NCLE/CILT.

Broadcasting Support Services, 1982. *Your right to health*. London: Health Education Council.

Brook, M. 1980. The 'mother tongue' issue in Britain: cultural diversity or control? *British Journal of the Sociology of Education* 1, 3: 237–55.

Chin, W.T. and Simsova, S. 1982. Library needs of Chinese in London. School of Librarianship, Polytechnic of North London.

Clough, C. and Quarmby, J. 1978. *A public library service to ethnic minorities in Great Britain*. London: The Library Association. pp. 299–301.

Commission for Racial Equality. 1980. *The EEC's directive on the education of the children of migrant workers*. London: CRE.

Cooke, M. 1979. *Public library provision for ethnic minorities in the UK*. Report of a study carried out on behalf of the BNBRF. Leicestershire Library and Information Service.

Dale, I. 1980. Digraphia. *International Journal of the Sociology of Language* 26: 2–13.

Department of Education and Science. 1975. *A language for life* ('The Bullock report'). London: HMSO.

Department of Education and Science and the Welsh Office. 1981. Joint circular No. 5/81 (DES)/ No. 36/81 (Welsh Office) *Directive of the Council of the European Community on the education of the children of migrant workers*. London/Cardiff, July 1981.

Elliott, P. 1981. *Library needs of mother tongue schools*. Research report No. 6. School of Librarianship, Polytechnic of North London.

Ferguson, C. A. 1959. Diglossia *Word* xv: 325–40.

Garner, M. (ed.) 1981. *Community languages: their role in education*. Applied Linguistics Association of Australia. Melbourne/Sydney: River Seine Publications.

Gundara, J. 1981. *Indian women in Britain: a study of information needs*. School of Librarianship, Polytechnic of North London.

Hawkins, E. 1981. *Modern languages in the curriculum*. Cambridge: CUP.

Hsü, R. S. W. 1979. What is standard Chinese? in R. Lord (ed.) *Hong Kong language papers*. Hong Kong University Press.

Lue, A. S. T. 1982. The Overseas Chinese Education Centre. *NCMTT Newsletter* Spring 1982.

Migrant Services Unit. 1981. *Directory of information material in non-Asian languages*. London: Voluntary Service Council.

Mobbs, M. 1981. Two languages or one? The significance of the language names: 'Hindi' and 'Urdu' *Journal of Multilingual and Multicultural Development* 2, 3: 203–11.

National Association of Citizens' Advice Bureaux and the Commission for Racial Equality. 1980. *Community information: Asian languages directory*. London: CRE.

National Association for Multiracial Education. 1981. *Policy statement: mother tongue and community languages in education*. London: NAME.

National Congress on Languages in Education. 1982. *Report of the working party on 'Languages of minority communities'*. London: CILT.

National Union of Teachers. 1982. *Linguistic diversity and mother tongue teaching: policy statement*. London: NUT.

Pattanayak, D. P. 1981. *Multilingualism and mother tongue education*. Delhi: OUP.

Reid, E. 1982. *Availability of public examinations*. Report for the Working Party on 'The languages of minority communities'. London: NCLE/CILT.

Romaine, S. and Dorian, N. C. 1981. 'Scotland as a linguistic area' *Scottish Literary Journal* language supplement 14: 1–24.

Rosen, H. and Burgess, T. 1980. *Languages and dialects of London schoolchildren*. London: Ward Lock Educational.

Roussou, M. and the Schools Council Mother Tongue Project, 1981. Issues in mother tongue teaching. Talk given at a conference on 'Mother tongue teaching' organized by NCMTT.

Russell, R. 1980. *Ethnic minority languages and the schools (with special reference to Urdu)*. London: The Runnymede Trust.

Saifullah Khan, V. 1976. Provision by minorities for language maintenance. In *Bilingualism and British education*. London: CILT.

—— 1977. *Bilingualism and linguistic minorities in Britain: developments, perspectives*. Runnymede Briefing Paper, 422. London: The Runnymede Trust.

—— 1980. The 'mother tongue' of linguistic minorities in multicultural England *Journal of Multilingual and Multicultural Development* 1, 1.

Smith, G.R. 1982. The geography and demography of South Asian languages in England. Linguistic Minorities Project Working Paper 2. London: Institute of Education.

Sponza, L. 1981. The unification of Italy and the beginning of mass migration to Britain. Paper presented at the Italian Day at Coventry organized by the Association of Teachers of Italian, March 1981.

Stubbs, H. 1980. *Language and literacy: the sociolinguistics of reading and writing*. London: Routledge and Kegan Paul.

Taylor, I. 1981. Writing systems and reading. *Reading Research: Advances in Theory and Practice* 2.

Taylor, M.R. and Hurwitz, K. 1979. *Books for under fives in a multicultural society*. London: Islington libraries.

Tosi, A. 1979. Mother tongue teaching for the children of migrants. *Language Teaching and Linguistics: Abstracts* 12, 4.

—— 1982. Between the mother's dialect and English. In A. Davies (ed.) *Language and learning at home and school*. London: Heinemann Educational.

Wilding, J. 1981. *Ethnic minority languages in the classroom? A survey of Asian parents in Leicester*. Leicester Council for Community Relations and Leicester City Council.

Wright, J. 1980. *Bilingualism in Education*. London: Centre for Urban Educational Studies (Occasional papers).

27

Welsh and English in Wales

WYNFORD BELLIN

Welsh: death or new vitality?

The prophecy in the dark ages was that Wales would lose everything but its language and religion. In a Saunders Lewis poem, a mysterious mentor disappears when asked:

'Eu hiaith a gadwant a oes coel ar frud?'
'Their language they will keep': is there credibility in the prophecy?

Today, terms like 'Welsh-speaking' refer to a bilingual situation. Even the terminology 'Welsh as a first language' refers to simultaneous acquisition of both languages (see Bellin, 1984). During the 1960s it became a widespread assumption that confining Welsh to particular domains of usage and to particular locales would lead to the disappearance of the language. Hence dramatic campaigns by Cymdeithas yr Iaith Gymraeg (The Welsh Language Society) and intensive lobbying, which led in turn to changes in the status of Welsh. The Welsh Language Act of 1967 in particular (see Cyngor yr Iaith Gymraeg/Council for the Welsh Language, 1978) gave equal validity to Welsh in law and administration. However, equal validity is not equal status (see Davies, 1973), and bilinguals who make extensive use of Welsh receive constant reminders of the ease with which rapid language shift can take place. Mass media in English, moreover, seem increasingly to intrude on the hitherto most stable domain of usage, the home. The campaign for a television channel on which Welsh language programmes could be concentrated and given a share of prime time remains to be chronicled.

Also during the 1960s, popular awareness of the dramatic decline in the proportion of Welsh speakers in Wales over the century sharpened. In popular parlance, Welsh was 'dying' and English was too strong for it. However, at the same time, and in spite of the prevalence of the death metaphor, a new cultural vitality came to be acknowledged (see Jones, 1973). Social analyses substantiate this popular awareness and indicate a tension between the possibility of the death of Welsh on the one hand, and the viability of the language on the other. Successive Censuses document the decline of Welsh, while various surveys point to the emerging cultural vitality of the language.

449

Table 27.1. *Landmarks in British constitutional history directly affecting Wales*

1284	Wales conquered. English law established (Statute of Rhuddlan). Legal use of Welsh retained.
1485	Battle of Bosworth. Welsh nobles follow Tudor monarchs to London.
1536 and 1542	Statute of Wales (Acts of Union) unites Wales and England, excluding Welsh language from officialdom.
1746	Wales and Berwick Act. England deemed to include Wales.
1886	Foundation of Cymru Fydd (Wales of the future) with home rule aims.
1914	Welsh Disestablishment Act. Anglican church disendowed in Wales.
1925	Plaid Genedlaethol Cymru/Welsh National Party, later Plaid Cymru, founded.
1963	First direct action by Cymdeithas yr Iaith Gymraeg/Welsh Language Society.
1964	James Griffiths appointed first Secretary of State for Wales.
1966	Gwynfor Evans, leader of Plaid Cymru, first elected to the Westminster parliament.
1967	Welsh Language Act. Equal validity for the Welsh language in Wales. Wales no longer deemed to be part of England.

Williams (1980) describes two kinds of factor that always underlie a language shift: aggregate structural factors, like in-migration of non-Welsh-speaking population; and behavioural-evaluative factors, like the perceived utility of the language. The tension in the Welsh language situation can be seen as a result of the tension between and within these two kinds of factors.

Historical background

As is noted elsewhere in this volume (see especially chapters 1, 11, 12, 15, 17 and 30), modern Welsh is the descendant of what was the original language of most of Britain. Outside Wales, the British language survived the Anglo-Saxon conquest longest in Cornwall, Devon, the Lake District and south-western Scotland, but by late medieval times, the only strongly surviving descendants were Cornish and Welsh. For the last 200 years, Welsh in Wales has been the only survivor, and even there it is spoken by a minority of the population (although there are also communities of native speakers in Argentina).

In the history of Wales, after English rule was established in 1284, both political and cultural events have influenced the status of the Welsh language. Table 27.1 shows some landmarks in British constitutional history which have had direct effects on Wales. Most events before the late nineteenth century served to submerge Welsh identity on a political level, but in the late nineteenth century Wales began to assume more of a distinctive identity.

Morgan (1981) discusses why nationalist feeling subsided as soon as the Anglican church was disestablished in Wales in 1914. The unifying influences of the two world wars militated against separatist tendencies and expanded widening spheres of influence for central government. The reason for listing the beginning of direct action campaigns in the language cause in table 27.1 is because Rees (1973) and Jones (1973) emphasize the break between the language movement and movements with separatist aims. Morgan (1981) and previous commentators agree on the importance of the way in which Cymdeithas yr Iaith Gymraeg (The Welsh Language Society) went its own way after its foundation in 1962, even to the extent of damaging the electoral prospects of Plaid Cymru candidates (see also Williams, 1977). After the break, political pressures were exerted on elected representatives and existing institutions without waiting for major political changes, and language issues were addressed more directly.

It should be noted that historically and politically the Welsh situation has differed, from early on, from those in Scotland and Ireland. Wales was very thoroughly conquered by the Normans, and indeed archaeological evidence shows how systematically urban settlement and population movement were used to lay the foundations for a common fate for Wales and England. Acts of union between Wales and England preceded unifying legislation for both Scotland and Ireland. When the possibility of a measure of devolution of government was put to a referendum in Wales in 1977, only 11 per cent of the electorate (one-fifth of the votes cast) were in favour; there was a majority against devolution even in areas with high proportions of Welsh speakers (in Scotland a majority voted for devolution).

Table 27.2 lists cultural and educational events, from the sixteenth century to the present, which have had consequences for the Welsh language.

It seems that the Tudor keenness to have the Bible translated into Welsh (see table 27.2) came from a desire for religious uniformity. Incidentally however, a great service was rendered to the standardization of Welsh. From Tudor times the Anglican church accommodated to the speech of the parishioners. After successive religious revivals accommodation became necessary because of competition with nonconformist denominations. Pryce (1978a, 1978b) has been able to use church records to chart the territorial domains of the Welsh language from the early eighteenth century, when bishops first required returns from their clergy concerning the use of Welsh and English in their services. Pryce shows that a shift from speaking only Welsh to bilingualism was followed by the demise of Welsh even before the industrial revolution. 'Once a community moved towards a bilingual status then almost inevitably English was to gain an overwhelming dominance in the next generation' (Pryce, 1978b).

Table 27.2. *Some events in the history of culture and education in Wales*

1547	Salesbury (translator of the New Testament and prayer book) warns of the demise of the Welsh language.
1584	Last part of Gruffydd Robert's grammar of Welsh is published.
1588	Bishop Morgan's translation of the Bible into Welsh is published.
1736	Griffith Jones, Llanddowror, launches circulating schools.
1743	William Williams, the prolific hymnwriter, is refused ordination and joins the Methodists.
1779	Death of Madame Bevan (Griffith Jones' colleague and benefactor) and end of circulating schools.
1789	Thomas Charles of Bala begins the Sunday Schools movement, spreading ability to read the Welsh Bible.
1835	David Rees starts *y Diwygiwr* a radical nonconformist magazine.
1847	Brad y llyfrau gleision/treachery of the Blue Books (see pages 453, 461).
1856	Evan James and James James of Pontypridd compose 'Hen wlad fy nhadau' ('Land of my Fathers').
1893	University colleges at Aberystwyth, Cardiff and Bangor are federated to form the University of Wales.
1900	Owen M. Edwards begins a children's magazine entitled *Cymru'r Plant*.
1922	Urdd Gobaith Cymru (League of Welsh Youth) founded by Ifan ap Owen Edwards.
1937	New constitution for the National Eisteddfod with Welsh as the official language (Machynlleth).
1939	First primary school to teach through the medium of Welsh founded (privately) in Aberystwyth.
1950	National Eisteddfod adopts the all-Welsh rule (Caerffili).
1956	First secondary school to teach through the medium of Welsh founded (Glan Clwyd, Rhyl).
1967	Gittins report (DES, 1967) gives a new place to the Welsh language in education.
1971	Mudiad yr Ysgolion Meithrin (Welsh preschool education movement) founded.
1974–79	Cyngor yr Iaith Gymraeg/Council for the Welsh Language set up to advise the Secretary of State on matters concerning the language.
1980	Government averts a fast to the death by Gwynfor Evans, leader of Plaid Cymru, by honouring election pledges on a fourth television channel.
1982	Welsh language programmes concentrated on a fourth television channel.

Industrialization, moreover, did not inevitably speed up language shift. As Stephens (1976) emphasizes, initially the iron-smelting and coal-mining areas drew labour from the Welsh-speaking counties. But later in the nineteenth century, increasing labour needs and an expanding scale of production brought about a large scale in-migration of non-Welsh-speaking population, especially in the south.

At the time of these dramatic population changes, the influence of education was at work. Education movements till the middle of the nineteenth century (see table 27.2) favoured Welsh, but then came the reports of government commissioners (the 'blue books') notorious for general anti-Welsh prejudice, as well as educational recommendations (see Coupland, 1954; Jones, 1966; Le Calvez, 1970; Gwynfor Evans, 1975; Khleif, 1980; this volume: table 27.4). 1870 saw the first act of parliament concerning elementary education placed on the statute book, and from the end of the nineteenth century a very anglo-centric education system worked against the Welsh identity, which had been forged by affection for the language, nonconformist religion and a distinctive brand of radicalism.

The influence of the education system took some time to take effect (see the percentages of Welsh-only speakers of school age in the bottom two graphs of figure 27.1 on page 475). But other factors working against the language took effect rapidly. The biggest percentage drops in the Welsh-speaking population were between 1911 and 1921, and 1931 and 1951 (see table 27.10, page 474). Nevertheless, as Morgan (1981) suggests, there was considerable complacency in 1921, because the overall number of Welsh speakers was the highest ever, and the Welsh language seemed secure around the hearth, in religious institutions and voluntary cultural activities like the *eisteddfodau*.

The periods of biggest decline coincided with massive population disruptions, as economic depression and war led to rural-urban migration, international migration and a selective loss of young and well-educated people. However, the list of events in table 27.2 reflects the activity of a variety of groups and individuals in continually extending the domains where the Welsh language could be used. Such activity did not always take a spectacular form. Le Calvez (1970) documents the struggles for an education policy within local authorities by people who understood what could be achieved with existing institutions.

A particular view of the historical background to the linguistic situation in Wales, which accounts for both the 'colonialist' kind of event which submerged the status of Welsh, and the concessions towards Welsh which have been recently wrested from the initially unsympathetic authorities, is put forward by Aull (1978) in a 'state bureaucracy' model. As the state bureaucracy expanded its political and administrative apparatus, there was increasing encroachment on local concerns and organizations in Wales. Thus the eagerness in the nineteenth century to have all of Wales as an English-speaking area was more a matter of bureaucratic convenience than colonialist intervention; the death metaphor never seems to shade into a murder metaphor. However, there comes a point in any area of centralist concern where it is simpler to hand the problem down, and at such a point the role of people like directors of education in local authorities, or influential figures in broadcasting takes on a new importance. Hence the current situation where, after a number of concessions have been secured, the cultural vitality of the

Welsh language is acknowledged in spite of the pervasiveness of the 'death' metaphor.

Demographic characteristics

Bowen and Carter (1974, 1975) provide invaluable maps showing the percentage of Welsh speakers in wards and parishes as at 1971, and the relative percentage change since 1961, given the overall reduction for the whole of Wales. They speak of anglicization spreading from towns and coastal areas along the valleys, breaking up and splintering territories in Dyfed, Powys and Gwynedd, where Welsh had been spoken by the large majority of inhabitants (map 27.1 shows the administrative counties since 1974). Williams (1981) claims a continuity between the 1971 Census and previous ones, with anglicization as an 'innovation' spreading through a hierarchy of urban centres. Over successive censuses, progressively fewer urban centres remain in the category of having a high proportion of Welsh speakers.

Map 27.2, the map provided by Bowen and Carter, suggests a division of Wales into three kinds of area: (i) Welsh-speaking areas (y Fro Gymraeg) with a high proportion of speakers of the language, (ii) mixed language areas (without a clear majority either way) and (iii) anglicized areas. Advances have been made in characterizing social areas on the basis of census data. Carter and Williams (1978) and Williams (1979), using one set of multivariate techniques (principal components analysis of measures for 51 aggregated spatial units) to examine areas with a high percentage of Welsh speakers, conclude that 'the Welsh language is essentially a rural phenomenon ... It is lodged in an environment of limited economic potential.' Bracken (1980), with a different blend of techniques and concentrating on one county (Powys), identified three types of area with a high percentage of Welsh speakers. Their characteristics by contrast with all other types are listed in table 27.3. Again, limited economic potential emerges, but some declining industrial settlements are included along with rural areas.

Changes in population between censuses have a notable effect on Welsh speaking areas. The 1961 Census showed effects of rural depopulation, and the 1971 Census showed suburbanization robbing these areas of population still further. A study of migration (Y Swyddfa Gymreig/Welsh Office, 1979) showed a net immigration into Dyfed, Powys and Gwynedd of the oldest and youngest age groups. By 1971, rural Wales was established as a resort and retirement area, with considerable numbers of second homes owned mainly by permanent residents in England. Map 27.3 shows the proportions of second homes in 1980 in the districts within the administrative counties.

As an echo of a wider secular trend (the rural-urban turn-round in other countries) rural Wales showed small net increases in population in the 1970s. Map 27.4 shows changes in population between 1971 and 1981 (based on

Table 27.3. *Three social areas with high percentages of Welsh speakers in Powys: characteristics relative to eight types in all (from Bracken, 1980)*

	Social area		
	Type 5	Type 7	Type 8
Population			
% of old people	balanced	high	high
Outmigration	high	low	high
Inmigration	low	low	low
% of large households	high	average	low
Housing			
% of vacant dwellings	high	average	low
Occupancy level	high	average	average
% of council tenants	low	low	low
% with no inside lavatory	average	high	low
Occupations			
Predominant social class	self-employed	E	C
Unemployment	high	high	high
Employment for wives	very low	very low	very low
% in agriculture	high	high	very low
Own account farmers	very low	very low	very low
% in manufacturing	very low	very low	high

Office of Population, Censuses and Surveys, 1982). The continuation of trends apparent in the 1979 migration study meant that Gwynedd and Clwyd drew population from the north-west of England, and Dyfed drew people from the south-west of England. Given that rural Wales was sparsely populated anyway, small net changes in population can have a considerable impact on the language situation.

Bowen and Carter (1975) and Carter and Williams (1978) see great significance in the shrinkage of an integral *bro Gymraeg* and its probable split-up in the 1981 Census. Their account of negative symbolic values becoming prevalent as the proportion of bilinguals diminishes can be linked with studies of the importance of social networks for language shift. Boissevain (1974) describes certain key figures in small communities as 'brokers'. Change of ownership in a garage or tavern makes an impact on a village in providing a new pivot for social networks. Gal (1979) describes how bilingualism, when associated with a vanishing way of life, can decline as social networks loosen and migration removes community members who might have held them together. Population increases in Welsh-speaking areas can have a dramatic effect when large by comparison with the 2.2 per cent for the whole of Wales.

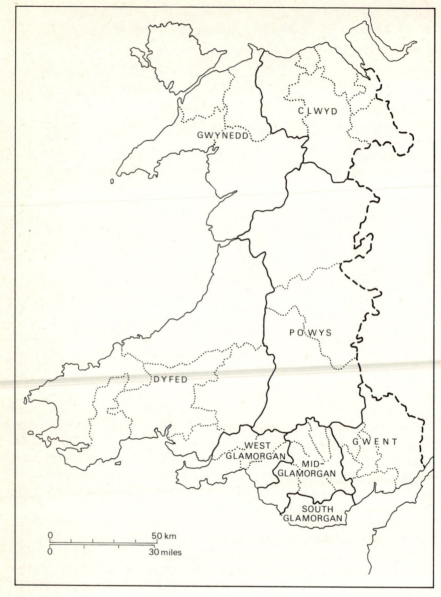

Map 27.1. Administrative counties of Wales since 1974

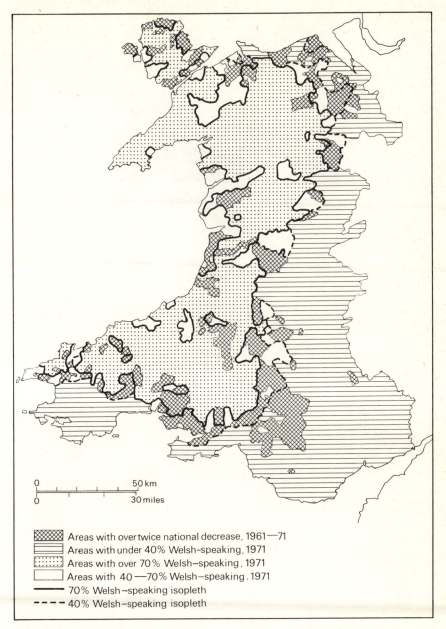

Map 27.2. The relation between Welsh-speaking areas 1971 and the decrease in Welsh speakers 1961–71 (with permission of Professor H. Carter and the Royal Geographical Society)

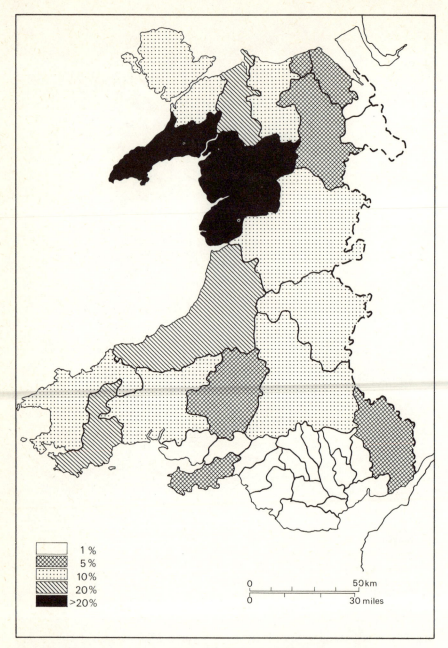

Map 27.3. Proportion of second homes in Wales in 1980 (drawn using figures collated by Cymdeithas yr Iaith Gymraeg/the Welsh Language Society)

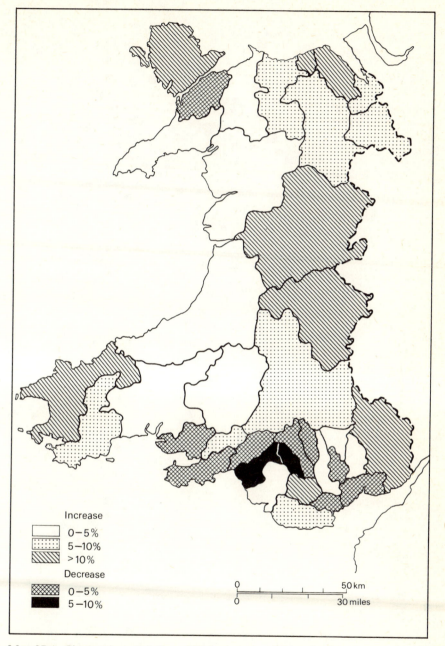

Map 27.4. Changes in population of Wales between 1971 and 1981

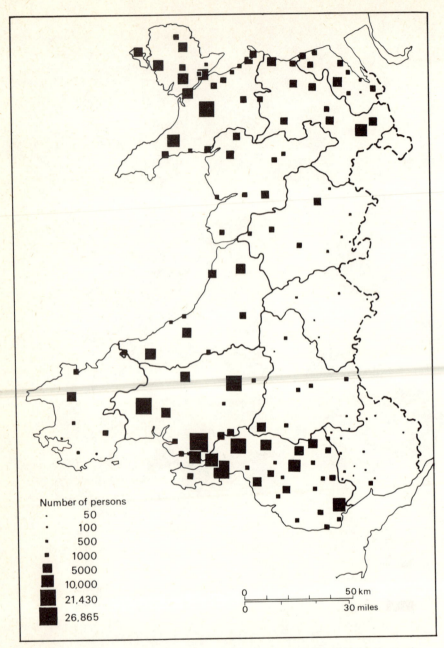

Map 27.5. Distribution of the numbers of people over the age of 3 able to speak Welsh, 1971 (with permission of the University of Wales Press)

But how important is an integral area with a high proportion of Welsh speakers? In the *National atlas of Wales* (Carter and Griffiths, 1981) Carter himself lists risks in mapping proportions of speakers. Some of the spatial areas are sparsely populated. Cardiff, the capital of Wales, had less than five per cent of its population assessing themselves as Welsh speakers in 1971, but that small percentage nevertheless numbered 12,930. Betts (1976) describes stereotypes of Welsh speakers in anglicized areas which hardly square with being rural and having limited economic potential.

Map 27.5 is reproduced from the *National atlas* and shows the numbers of speakers in different areas, rather than the proportions. In 1971, places with large numbers were already split off and separated by areas with sparse population and small numbers.

Ambrose (1980) believes in 'micro-scale mapping', using census data only as a way of selecting areas for investigation. In an area near the English border where the isopleth for 70 per cent of Welsh speakers had not been pushed back till 1971, he found massive proportional drops in sparsely populated hilly areas. But he could also show movement of Welsh speakers across the border into the town of Oswestry. Such speakers would never be counted in the census (the language question being asked only in Wales). From his research an important corrective to the impression given by proportional changes must not be overlooked. Separated in the rural heartland, there was little opportunity for Welsh speakers to form cultural associations and support religious institutions on the scale made possible by concentrating in the English town. The monolinguals (speakers of English only) now possessing the hilly areas had taken part in 'overarching immigration'. Their small numbers could still have an impact. It would no longer be taken for granted in the area that conversations might be initiated in Welsh. Nevertheless, 'micro-scale' mapping upsets the uniform appearance presented by map 27.2. It is important, too, to remember how small Wales is in comparison with countries where language situations are discussed in terms of territoriality. For most of the 1970s and later Aberystwyth would be only a five-hour drive from London, even though passing through *y Fro Gymraeg* would slow progress because of its terrain.

Welsh and English in education

The most radical changes in the status of the Welsh language have taken place in education (see Jones, 1966; Le Calvez, 1970; Centre for Information on Language Teaching, 1976; Khleif, 1980). The contrast with the past can be appreciated by comparing selected statements from the nineteenth century concerning the Welsh language and institutions (set out below) with the various official statements of the 1980s. First consider these extracts from the (1847) Report of the Commissioners, the 'Blue Books' (similar sentiments were expressed in an article published by the weekly *New Statesman* in July 1981):

a peculiar language isolating the mass from the upper portions of society . . . the Welsh element is never found at the top of the social scale . . . his language keeps him under the hatches

(living) in an underworld . . . and the march of society goes completely over his head

the Welsh language is a vast drawback to Wales and a manifold barrier to the moral progress and commercial prosperity of the people . . . it bars the access of improving knowledge to their minds

(English is) in the process of becoming the mother-tongue of the country

no book on geography, history, chemistry, natural history or any of the useful arts or sciences owes its origins to an Eisteddfod except for two or three treatises on agriculture

and the London *Times* of 1866:

the Welsh language is the curse of Wales

an eisteddfod is one of the most mischievous and selfish pieces of sentimentalism . . . a foolish interference with the natural progress of civilization and prosperity

The story of the Commission is told by Coupland (1954), Jones (1966) and Gwynfor Evans (1975). Consider now the following statements on Welsh in the school curriculum and in schools, issued on behalf of the Secretary of State for Wales (Y Swyddfa Gymreig/Welsh Office, 1980, 1981):

issues relating to the Welsh language generate strong and conflicting feelings

most authorities in Wales have already formulated Welsh language policies for their schools

it is no longer possible to count on vigorous Welsh-speaking communities alone to safeguard pupils' ability to speak Welsh whatever the medium of their education

for effective bilingual education the Welsh language should be accorded an appropriate place in the community life and not be confined to the classroom

Welsh is now used as a medium in a number of schools over most areas of the curriculum, including mathematics and science

fortunately the once common practice of offering a straight choice between Welsh and French in secondary schools has largely been discontinued

the encouragement given to the Welsh language provision by successive governments has had a significant impact in schools in recent years

studies undertaken of schools which follow bilingual policies have shown that children's general education does not suffer as a result

a number of studies suggest that learning through the medium of a second language enhances achievement in the mother tongue and may assist in the understanding of concepts

Table 27.4. *Changes in education in Wales over years*

(a) Primary school pupils fluent in Welsh (headteachers' assessment) expressed as a percentage for the whole of Wales

1975	1976	1977	1978	1979
10.6	10.6	12.8	13.5	13.7

(b) Designated bilingual schools or departments in English-speaking areas (Ysgolion Cymraeg)

	1950	1960	1970	1977	1978	1979	1980	1981
Primary	7	28	46	52	52	53	53	53
Secondary	0	1	4	8	8	11	11	13

(c) Numbers of pupils in bilingual schools or departments in English-speaking areas

	1970	1980
Primary	6253	9550
Secondary	2017	7860

(d) Numbers of Welsh medium entries in examinations for the 16+ and 18+ age groups

	1974	1980
Advanced Level GCE		
Entries	102	319
Subjects	6	19
Ordinary Level GCE		
Entries	829	2861
Subjects	14	30
CSE		
Entries	786	2047
Subjects	17	33

Source: Welsh Office, *Statistics of Education in Wales* vols. 1–5.

The statements about bilingual education are made in the light of figures such as those in table 27.4, and large-scale research projects such as that undertaken by the Schools Council (1978). As Le Calvez (1970) records, none of the educational changes were achieved without assiduous defence of policies by education authorities as well as more dramatic campaigns.

The results of education policies are important for challenging the claim that the decline of Welsh is somehow inevitable. The local authority with the most consistent education policy is Gwynedd. The declared aim is bilingual education in spite of the in-migration of the 1970s and 1980s apparent on the map showing population changes (map 27.4). In the mid-1970s a report by the inspectorate gave cause for alarm to supporters of such policies (Swyddfa Addysg Cymru/Welsh Education Office, 1977). The percentage of bilingual children in the primary school age-range was sinking fast. The inspectorate used teachers' assessments with a five-fold classification. Children were categorized as 'initially Welsh-speaking', 'initially English-speaking now considered fluent in Welsh', 'initially English-speaking with a developing command of Welsh', 'initially English-speaking with a very restricted command of Welsh' and there was a category for no knowledge of Welsh. Oral fluency was considered for infants, and written work entered into the classification for juniors.

Monitoring teachers' assessments using these categories satisfied the inspectorate that they were adequate for purposes such as judging suitability for receiving bilingual secondary education – a resource which was by then in demand. A number of educational innovations were aimed at increasing the proportion of bilingual primary school children. To improve provision for Welsh as a second language, *athrawon bro* (area teachers) were appointed to look after more than one school without being attached to any particular school. Besides mobility, the possibility of co-ordinating provision was catered for. Table 27.5 gives data from Gwynedd which was the basis for evaluating the success of *athrawon bro* in four parts of the county.

Table 27.5(a) shows percentages of children who were 'initially Welsh-speaking' in the primary schools of four areas. In spite of a drop in enrolment, percentages stay the same between 1979 and 1980 after rounding. So there was a relative increase in the proportion of children in that category. For the whole county the overall percentage of children speaking Welsh on entering school rose from 44.6 per cent to 44.9 per cent between 1979 and 1980. Table 27.5(b) shows pupils for whom Welsh was a second language. A rise in the percentage in the 'now fluent' category and a fall in the 'restricted command' category was the basis for attributing success to the educational innovation. But the question for the sceptic is whether the changes in the percentages merely reflect proximity to high percentages of Welsh-speaking children, rather than any achievement attributable to educational methods.

The classification of children for whom Welsh is a second language is an ordered scale. The districts can be ranked according to the percentage of children initially speaking Welsh, so scores can be assigned to rows and columns of the original tables of frequencies for each year (recoverable from the 1979 and 1980 columns in table 27.5). It is possible to calculate what the percentages would be in each year, if there was a simple linear trend on the percentage of first-language children in a district. (See Fienberg, 1977 and references in Singer, 1979, section L1.)

Table 27.6 shows how the actual percentages differ from those expected according to a linear trend on the percentage of first-language children. The table indicates that Meirionydd did worse than would be predicted from the number of first-language children in 1979, while East Gwynedd did better than would be predicted. The 1980 differences in table 27.6 show that *athrawon bro* succeeded in improving the situation in Meirionydd and Anglesey, while exploiting the advantages of West Gwynedd more fully. The table shows how they raised the percentage of fluent children overall.

Table 27.5. *Primary school pupils in four parts of Gwynedd*

(a) Percentages of pupils with Welsh as a first language, over two years

| | 1979 | | 1980 | |
	Total pupils	Welsh as L1 (%)	Total pupils	Welsh as L1 (%)
West Gwynedd	6225	75	6151	75
Meirionydd	3371	52	3218	52
Anglesey	8201	39	7807	39
East Gwynedd	7675	24	7365	24

Note: Since the totals decrease, stable percentages represent a relative increase.

(b) Pupils with Welsh as a second language in primary schools in four areas of Gwynedd, over two years

	Now fluent %	Developing command %	Restricted command %	Little knowledge %
1979				
West Gwynedd (1558)	43	31	14	12
Meirionydd (1627)	28	34	28	10
Anglesey (5034)	13	51	23	12
East Gwynedd (5855)	14	41	32	13
1980				
West Gwynedd (1558)	47	32	13	8
Meirionydd (1555)	30	38	24	8
Anglesey (4792)	15	50	25	10
East Gwynedd (5618)	16	42	31	11
Change				
West Gwynedd	+4	+1	−1	−4
Meirionydd	+2	+4	−4	−2
Anglesey	+2	−1	+2	−2
East Gwynedd	+2	+1	−1	+2

Note: Numbers in brackets are percentage bases.

Source: Reports of Gwynedd Local Authority.

Changes in language provision since 1975 succeeded in raising the percentage of fluent children in primary schools for all Wales from 10.6 per cent in 1975 to 13.7 per cent in 1979. But educational changes have been made hand in hand with changes in parental aspirations. According to surveys conducted for the Gittins report (Department of Education and Science, 1967; Le Calvez, 1970), there was demand for bilingual primary education but not secondary education. In the survey for Cyngor yr Iaith Gymraeg/Council

Table 27.6. *Differences between observed percentages (O) of second-language children and percentages expected (E) if there were merely a linear trend on the percentage of L1 children in each district (Gwynedd)*

	Second-language category			
	Now fluent (O–E)	Developing command (O–E)	Restricted command (O–E)	Little knowledge (O–E)
1979				
West Gwynedd	4	−3	−3	2
Meirionydd	−2	−4	8	−2
Anglesey	−3	7	−4	−1
East Gwynedd	2	−4	2	0
1980				
West Gwynedd	6	−3	−2	1
Meirionydd	−4	−1	5	0
Anglesey	−4	6	−2	0
East Gwynedd	2	−4	1	1

Note: Although percentages and percentage differences are used to summarize, statistics for significance testing were calculated with the frequencies in original contingency tables.

for the Welsh Language (see Harrison *et al.*, 1981), conducted ten years later and after increased provision of bilingual primary education, 70 per cent of mothers whose children could not speak Welsh nevertheless wanted bilingual secondary education for their children. (The figure for those with bilingual children was 90 per cent).

It must not be thought that the mothers' aspirations were necessarily realistic, since the overall situation in schools is very variegated. It is still possible to come from a Welsh-speaking home and attend a school where the language has very little place, or where it is confined to use in religious instruction. It is also possible to come from such a home and be educated partly through the medium of Welsh and partly through the medium of English (with English implicitly associated with science and technology). The fully bilingual education pattern is much scarcer than might be expected from the success attributed to it. Then there are children from monolingual (English only) homes in all the varied patterns of school practice, and large numbers for whom Welsh is a lesson once or twice a week.

What has been shown in the changed education systems in Wales is that there is no inevitability about the decline of the language. If school and community could exert a combined influence, further language decline could be arrested if not reversed.

Table 27.7. *Ceredigion, Dyfed: percentages of children in primary schools with only English as their first language, and for whom Welsh was a second language, according to parental linguistic status* (Percentage bases in brackets)

	1949 survey %
Parents:	
Both Welsh-speaking (3463)	5
One Welsh-speaking (709)	58
Neither Welsh-speaking (598)	89
	1961 survey %
Parents:	
Both Welsh-speaking (2612)	8
One Welsh-speaking (771)	81
Neither Welsh-speaking (1037)	97
	1967 survey %
Parents:	
Both Welsh-speaking (2641)	10
One Welsh-speaking (989)	85
Neither Welsh-speaking (1147)	99
	1973 survey %
Parents:	
Both Welsh-speaking (2633)	10
One Welsh-speaking (997)	82
Neither Welsh-speaking (1864)	100

Source: Reports of Dyfed Local Authority.

Social structure and the transmission of Welsh

A crucial question for the future of a language is whether older people will speak it with children. In this respect, demographic changes which are out of the control of speakers seem to influence factors within the control of speakers in the way that Bowen and Carter (1975) and others, notably Lewis (1971, 1973) suggest. Table 27.7 comes from surveys of schools in Ceredigion, a district of Dyfed. In 1949, it seemed possible to acquire Welsh before school in spite of having parents who could not speak the language, even though only 11 per cent of children did so. By 1961, the community could not provide conditions for acquisition. A child from a non-homogeneous marriage (linguistically speaking) was very unlikely to acquire Welsh. The size of the percentage for that category means that many mothers who spoke Welsh were not transmitting the language, even though they lived in an area with a high percentage of speakers. There is some slowing in the trend which may have been due to the changes in the status of the language in the 1960s. But choice of language with children is something that is within the control of bilingual mothers. A survey of such mothers was commissioned by Cyngor yr Iaith Gymraeg/Council for the Welsh Language, and conducted in ten towns where over 60 per cent of the population spoke Welsh, according to the 1971 Census (see Cyngor yr Iaith Gymraeg/Council for the Welsh Language, 1978; Harrison et al., 1981). The sampling was purposive, in that bilingual mothers not transmitting Welsh were sought out for comparison with those that had bilingual children. However, the questionnaire was presented as a general inquiry into the role of mothers in upbringing.

One of the main findings was that geographical location was much less important than socioeconomic status. The highest status mothers showed greater language loyalty in terms of transmission than any other group.

Two questions can be answered from the results: 'Are elites turning round and giving a lead back to language loyalty?' 'Does a fall in the proportion of speakers in the community inevitably break up social networks?'

The possibility of elites giving a lead in language loyalty would have repercussions for the claim by Khleif (1980) that loyalty to minority languages poses a dilemma for social mobility. The survey used the Registrar General's classification of occupations (as used in the Census), and mothers with experience of class 4 or 5 occupations were nearly as likely to transmit Welsh as those with experience of professional occupations. The mothers who were least likely to have bilingual children were those with experience of class 3 occupations. Given the likelihood of transmission at either end of the social scale, it would be an oversimplification to claim that elites were setting a countervailing trend to that followed by the most numerical occupational group (see Harrison et al., 1981: 32–8).

The associations between socioeconomic status and transmitting Welsh confirmed the observation that speaking Welsh cuts right across social-class differences. Roberts and Williams (1980) summarize by describing bilinguals in Wales as members of a 'status group' in the Weberian sense – a social movement which cuts across other social differences. Boissevain (1974) would want to pit analysis in terms of social networks against analysis in terms of social stratification, but stratification was relevant to the way social networks seemed to operate.

Mothers were asked about how many Welsh speakers they would be likely to encounter in various locales, and what were their language preferences with peers. Those with bilingual children gave higher estimates of the number of Welsh speakers they might encounter. Differences in language preferences with peers were complicated by fluctuations according to social status. Most of the mothers had received an amount of education consistent with a class 3 occupation and a potential for social mobility upwards. Among that most numerous group, a shift to preferring English with peers seemed to precede bringing children up to speak only English. That association would be predicted by social network analysts, but in the same social category mothers with bilingual children tended to have an absence of a preference for Welsh or English with peers, rather than a preference either way. Nevertheless, lower on the social scale a preference for Welsh was associated significantly with having bilingual children, as if there were low status social networks sustaining language with peers and in transmission. The high status mothers followed the low status pattern, but associations were much weaker, as if they were less dependent on social support (see Harrison *et al.*, 1981: 39–42).

Such a kaleidoscope of social influences cannot be reconciled with a view of the language situation as an inevitable historical process moving in the direction of anglicization, whether the analysis is in terms of the spread of innovation, social structuring, or social networks. There is sufficient lack of determinacy, and enough countervailing tendencies, to require room for language stabilization as well as shift.

Mass media

Even when the language situation in Wales was very stable, ambivalence could be detected. The poet Gwenallt complained 'Dy iaith ar ein hysgwyddau megis pwn' ('Your language on our shoulders like a burden'). And language loyalty certainly also went together with conserving old ways and values. However, changes in domains of use for Welsh in the 1960s led to a wide variety of forms of cultural expression. Besides the volumes edited by Jones (1972) and Stephens (1973) there are also descriptions of lively youth subcultures like that described by Emmett (1978), in which Welsh is an in-group language even though trends from outside Wales are being adopted.

The response to changes in technology for communication is also indicative of a new situation. There has never been a daily paper in Welsh, but there have always been weeklies. The 1970s saw a new printing technology (web-offset production), and Betts (1976) describes how seven monthly publications in Welsh were launched between 1974 and 1975. These were popular presentations of local news – *papurau bro* (lit. 'local newspapers'). By July of 1981, the National Library of Wales could list 46 such publications. The numbers of *papurau bro* for each county, and for Liverpool and Cardiff are as follows (taken from the National Library of Wales list, July 1981):

17 Gwynedd
14 Dyfed
 5 Clwyd
 4 Powys
 2 West Glamorgan

1   South Glamorgan
1   Cardiff
1   Liverpool

Changes in broadcasting in the 1970s also allowed radio programmes in Welsh to be moved from the medium wave-band to the VHF wave-band. News and current affairs could then be broadcast in Welsh, with a much fuller service than when Welsh and English might compete from being on the same wave-band. From the mid 1970s Welsh speakers, even when a minority, could hear international news in Welsh and read about local events without any great expense. Cultural participation with consistent use of Welsh was made available on a new scale. (See Betts, 1976, for problems encountered when social or cultural usage aims at including both languages.) Audience research shows the extent of participation with mass media. Table 27.8 gives results from research commissioned by BBC and the IBA. The survey, conducted in 1980, used a quota sample intended to represent Welsh speakers from all over Wales. At the time of the survey, there were severe constraints on the timing of television programmes in Welsh, so the figures for viewing Welsh programmes are impressive.

Table 27.8. *Figures from self-estimates of listening and viewing behaviour, made by 891 Welsh speakers (BBC/IBA survey)*

Activity	%
Hearing	
a radio programme in Welsh at least once a day	45
a play in Welsh, competing with Sunday prime viewing time, once a month or more	14
Watching in either language	
a TV programme five or six days of the week	96
a TV programme every day of the week	90
Watching TV programmes in Welsh	
five or six days of the week or more	64
at least once a day	55
a BBC programme in Welsh every day of the week	53
an ITV programme in Welsh every day of the week	48

An incidental finding illustrates the usefulness of putting survey data alongside census data. The language question used for the 1971 Census was as follows:

(a) Do you speak Welsh? Tick the appropriate box.
(b) If so, do you:
   Speak English?
   Read Welsh?
   Write Welsh?

Obviously there has to be some cause for concern about the simple use of 'yes' or 'no' in the self-assessment. However, the BBC/IBA survey allowed for three categories of response: 'fair' (able to follow two popular programmes but not using the language), 'moderate' (following conversations as well as programmes) and 'excellent' (using the language every day at home or at work). The numbers in these categories were:

   fair: 3
   moderate: 67
   excellent: 820

These numbers suggest that a simple categorization into Welsh-speaking is, in fact, probably not misleading. A survey conducted for the Gittins report (see Department of Education and Science, 1967) included an intermediate category 'speak a little'. Only 5 per cent of the 1,222 informants considered themselves in that group. Harrison *et al.* (1981) abandoned intermediate categories for their sample. Recent censuses can thus be assumed to give counts that would not be improved on by including an extra category of speaker.

Changing symbolic values

What does ability to speak Welsh mean to the bilingual person? The changes in the status of the language, and educational changes, mean that the answer will depend on whether the person comes from one of the areas of limited economic potential, whether Welsh is a second language acquired at school, whether there are plenty of other speakers around – and a host of other complicating factors. (A controversial caricature of social life in Cardiff by Jones, 1978, includes people with all these different characteristics along with monolinguals who are at various stages of learning Welsh, portrayed in terms of their ability to join in a social situation where Welsh is being used.) Sharp *et al.* (1973) report on a large-scale survey of attitudes in children learning Welsh at school. They found that favourable attitudes to Welsh declined sharply between the ages of 11 and 15. Roberts and Williams (1980) criticize the level of aggregation in the study, and suggest that factors like the level of institutional support need to be taken into account, but their own surveys suggest that reliance on any one kind of institution for maintenance (whether school, family or religious institutions), leads to less use of Welsh and less favourable attitudes than when a number of institutions give mutual encouragement. Harrison *et al.* (1981) also face the fact that attitudes in the mothers they interviewed were inconsistent.

Table 27.9. *Reasons for learning Welsh in Further Education classes: reasons ticked by 182 evening-class students in Clwyd, 1980*

Number ticking	Reason given
122	because I have come to live in Wales
111	to understand and communicate with neighbours
109	to get involved/integrate into social life
107	to ensure survival of the language
101	to understand radio/TV programmes
71	to learn a new language
64	because I am Welsh/Welsh descent
63	because I am interested in languages
50	to help my children
22	because my spouse speaks Welsh
20	to improve my job prospects

Note: Multiple answers were allowed.

Gal (1979) regards symbolic values as of secondary importance to forms of association, since they alone did not explain language shift in the community she studied. However, they are important for the relations between Welsh and English in Wales in the monolingual majority. Why should a monolingual want to learn Welsh? Giles and Powesland (1975) comment on the remarkable movement for learning Welsh in adults which began in the early 1970s. They link the movement with a rise in ethnic feeling. However, this does not seem necessarily to be the case, especially as monolinguals (English speakers) moving into Wales often show considerable enthusiasm for learning Welsh. Table 27.9 gives results from surveys among adults learning Welsh in Clwyd. What is striking is the sheer 'integrative motivation' (cf. Harrison, 1980) even though Clwyd has few areas with very high percentages of Welsh speakers: there is no real need of the language for plain communication with neighbours. However, if these answers are linked with the acknowledged cultural vitality of modern Wales, the motivation may well be a desire to participate in what is going on. If speaking Welsh is in fact associated with cultural vitality rather than economic failure, then clearly symbolic values have changed over the period between the last two censuses. Favourability to the Welsh language cuts across social differences and even across origins, inside or out of Wales.

Trends indicated by censuses and surveys

This chapter claims, as far as the Welsh language situation is concerned, that a tension exists in popular awareness between adherence to the 'death' metaphor and acknowledgement of cultural vitality. A similar tension emerges in

informed discussion in evaluating the relative merits of data from censuses and surveys. It is easy to dismiss survey evidence as over-interpreting unrepresentative samples, and indeed the evidence quoted here has been collected for special purposes unrelated to the argument of this chapter. On the other hand, it is possible to accuse those who rely heavily on census data alone of the ecological fallacy. Can the tension be resolved?

One of the breakdowns in the census results is according to age and sex. Figures for different age groups are given in a way that can be summarized in table 27.10, table 27.11 and figure 27.1. Changes in the composition of the total population in successive censuses are important because of the way they reflect the major social movements described by Williams (1980) and Morgan (1981). Figure 27.1 provides the overall picture for what happens to the reported linguistic abilities in the different age groups at each census. There is an age gradient for all Welsh speakers, but a nonlinear relationship between age and the proportion of people recorded as able to speak only Welsh. Now if the death metaphor was a good guide, it is clear what to expect. As the overall percentage of speakers declines, there should be more and more reliance on old people to keep numbers up. The age gradient should become steeper over the decades.

The techniques for investigating trends in tables of frequencies which were applied to the figures for schools in Gwynedd (table 27.5 and table 27.6) can be used to compare the age gradients in the table from successive censuses. The gradient does get steeper till 1961, and it provides a further indication of decline. For example, although the overall percentage of speakers did not drop between 1911 and 1921, the decline of the language showed up in the extra steepness of the gradient for 1921. From 1921 till 1961 the gradient continued to get steeper while the overall percentage of speakers kept dropping. But in 1971, despite a further drop, there was a flattening in the best fitting linear trend for the census counts depicted in the top graph of figure 27.1.

What was more important, the 1971 Census yielded further indications of a distinctive situation. Fitting a linear trend is, to put it informally, finding a principled way of holding a ruler over each of the graphs in figure 27.1, to even out the irregularities. But in the original tables the breakdown is by both age and sex. So it is important to realize how much is lost by looking only at the simplifying trend. In terms of age, a truer representation of what is in the figures would be a linear rise until the 15–24, or young working age group, then a levelling (or dip in 1971) and then another rise until there are more old speakers than would be expected from just smoothing out the graphs in figure 27.1. (Informally, two shorter rulers should be used over the graphs to appreciate the relation with age.) In terms of age breakdowns alone, successive censuses appear much like each other.

Since the totals for the categories in table 27.11 are very large, it is worth refining the appreciation of lack of fluctuations around fitted gradients even

Table 27.10. *Percentages of Welsh speakers according to age and sex, at successive censuses*

Age (years)	Sex	1971 %	1961 %	1951 %	1931 %	1921 %	1911 %
3–4	m	11	13	14	22	27	30
	f	11	13	15	22	27	30
5–9	m	14	16	20	26	29	36
	f	15	17	20	27	29	36
10–14	m	16	19	22	30	32	39
	f	18	20	23	31	32	40
15–24	m	15	20	22	33	34	40
	f	16	21	23	33	34	41
25–44	m	18	23	28	38	37	43
	f	18	23	27	37	37	45
45–64	m	25	33	36	44	44	52
	f	25	32	35	44	45	54
65+	m	31	38	42	50	51	58
	f	31	37	40	50	53	61
Overall		20.9	26.0	28.9	36.8	37.1	43.5

Table 27.11. *Numbers (in thousands) of the total population of Wales, in age and sex categories, at successive censuses*

Age	Sex	1971	1961	1951	1931	1921	1911
3–4	m	44	41	48	42	48	56
	f	42	39	47	42	47	56
5–9	m	116	99	97	123	136	135
	f	109	94	94	120	135	134
10–14	m	106	112	91	122	137	121
	f	101	107	87	120	136	121
15–24	m	197	175	166	225	239	229
	f	190	168	171	213	238	214
25–44	m	321	344	375	367	376	368
	f	316	341	380	384	382	340
45–64	m	329	327	302	271	244	184
	f	353	352	331	268	229	174
65+	m	149	129	125	82	64	51
	f	230	189	156	93	74	62

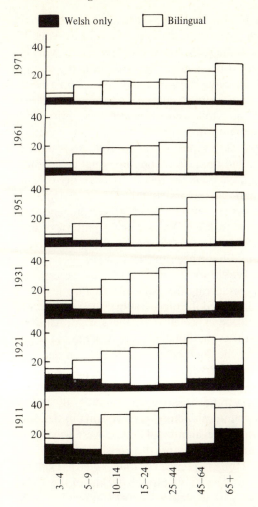

Figure 27.1 Welsh only and bilinguals by age group, 1911–1971

more. Bellin (1982) explains what happens if deviations from the best fitting trends of more than 5,000 are studied, taking male-female differences into account. Individual patterns emerge in nearly every census. (All the calculations with contingency tables in this chapter were performed using the package known as GLIM on the ICL 1904S computer, or on the Nord 100 computer, at Reading University.)

The evidence derived from departures from simplifying trends is that up until 1921, the overall composition of the population was all important for the fate of the language. Lewis (1971, 1973) explains how powerful the effects of such factors can be, just on their own, on language contact. Table 27.11 contains male-female ratios which reflect large scale in-migration to Wales till 1921. In 1911, there were far fewer male Welsh speakers in the young working age group than would be expected from a straightforward linear trend in the bottom graph in figure 27.1. Such economically active new people had a profound influence socially, so 'aggregate structural factors' in the terminology of Williams (1980) took their toll. Ten years later, a cohort study described in the 1921 Census report on the language found that some previously bilingual children had shifted to reporting themselves as speakers of only English in adulthood. There had been effects on individual behaviour.

The 1931 Census showed a big increase in the relative importance of what Williams calls 'behavioural-evaluational factors'. In table 27.11, male/female ratios in the groups aged 25–44 in 1931 reflect a much greater likelihood of male out-migration than of women to leave Wales. Such a pattern of migration should have produced fewer male Welsh speakers than age trends would predict. The situation should have been the same as in 1911 for the opposite reasons (loss of male Welsh speakers lowering the percentages instead of extra non-Welsh-speakers having the same effect). But in 1931 it was the women aged 25–44 who produced the biggest shortfall in numbers of Welsh speakers below what would be expected from the age gradient (see Bellin, 1982 for details). Behavioural-evaluational factors must have taken on a much greater importance during the great economic depression and produced a female-led shift away from Welsh which persisted through the Second World War and afterwards. However, the male/female differences in the fluctuations around the best fitting trends disappeared by 1971. By 1971 it could be claimed that aggregate-structural factors were working in the same way as before, but by then behavioural-evaluational factors were working in conflicting directions instead of uniformly against the Welsh language.

All the survey evidence quoted in this chapter can be interpreted as evidence against a consistent and uniform process leading to the decline of the Welsh language. It has been shown also how to detect lack of uniformity in the picture obtainable from the ten-year census returns. The figures from the 1981 Census were therefore awaited with great tension. Could the dispersion of speakers and the dissolution of communities be offset to any extent by mass media communication and benefits of bilingual education? Could improvement in the status of the language affect language choices with the next generation, as well as producing appreciable numbers of second-language speakers? Had imprisonment and protests been in vain? The level of public awareness and the evidence from surveys with intermediate categories of linguistic ability meant that the census figures for bilinguals would have to be taken seriously.

The first information from the 1981 Census concerned the population changes (see map 27.4) and indicated very negative influences from aggregate-structural factors. Nevertheless, Bellin (1982) gave 17 per cent as the most optimistic prediction for the overall percentage of Welsh speakers, and 14.5 per cent as an extrapolation from previous censuses. In the event, the overall percentage turned out to be 19 per cent, which must be a vindication of the endeavours made to save the language in the 1960s and 1970s.

The prediction that can be uncovered in the 'death' metaphor is that of a uniform continuous process. Both the ten-year census and survey evidence can be used to show that there was something distinctive about 1971 and even optimistic about 1981. The sting in the 'death' metaphor is the suggestion of inevitability. If Welsh speakers maintain their commitment, and the monolingual majority gain enthusiasm for measures taken to draw that sting, then Wales may become a stomping ground for students of language stability instead of students of language shift.

APPENDIX: Government reports and other documents quoted

WHITE PAPER
Our changing democracy: devolution to Wales and Scotland. Cmnd 6348, 1975.

CENSUS REPORTS
Census 1971: Report on the Welsh language in Wales. Office of Population Censuses and Surveys, 1973.
Census 1981: preliminary report; England and Wales. Office of Population Censuses and Surveys, 1982.

Figures were also taken from reports of previous censuses (1911–61).

OTHER REPORTS
Primary education in Wales. Department of Education and Science: Central Advisory Council for Education (Wales), 1967.
Welsh in the primary schools of Gwynedd, Powys and Dyfed/Y Gymraeg yn yr ysgolion cynradd Gwynedd, Powys a Dyfed. Welsh Education Office/Swyddfa Addysg Cymru. Survey no. 5/Arolwg Rhif 5, 1977.
A Future for the Welsh language/Dyfodol i'r iaith Gymraeg. Council for the Welsh Language/Cyngor yr Iaith Gymraeg, 1978.
Migration into, out of and within Wales in the 1966–71 period/Mudo i Gymru, o Gymru ac oddimewn i Gymru yn ystod y cyfnod 1966–1971. Welsh Office Occasional Paper no. 4/Papur achlysurol rhif 4 y Swyddfa Gymreig, 1979.

CONSULTATIVE DOCUMENTS
Welsh in the school curriculum: proposal for consultation by the Secretary of State for Wales/Y Gymraeg yng nghwrs addysg yr ysgolion: cynigion ymgynghorol gan Ysgrifennydd Gwladol Cymru. 1980.
Welsh in the schools/Y Gymraeg yn yr ysgolion. 1981.

REFERENCES

Note: References to official publications (HMSO, Office of Population, Censuses and Surveys, Welsh Office and the Department of Education and Science) are given in the Appendix.

Ambrose, J. E. 1980. Micro-scale language mapping: an experiment in Wales and Britanny. *Discussion papers in geolinguistics* 2: 1–52.

Aull, C. H. 1978. Ethnic nationalism in Wales: an analysis of the factors governing the politicization of ethnic identity. Ph.D. dissertation, Duke University, Durham, North Carolina, USA.

Bellin, W. 1982. The application of loglinear models to figures from the Welsh language question in the Census. Paper given at the Sheffield Sociolinguistic Conference.

——— 1984. Welsh phonology in acquisition. In Ball, M. and Jones, G. (eds.) *Readings in Welsh phonology.* Cardiff: University of Wales Press.

Betts, C. 1976. *Culture in crisis: the future of the Welsh language.* Upton, Merseyside: The Ffynnon Press.

Boissevain, J. 1974. *Friends of friends: networks, manipulators and coalitions.* Oxford: Blackwell.

Bowen, E. G. and Carter, H. 1974. Preliminary observations on the distribution of the Welsh language at the 1971 census. *Geographical Journal* 140: 432–40.

——— 1975. The distribution of the Welsh language in 1971: an analysis. *Geography* 60: 1–15.

Bracken, I. 1980. Socioeconomic profiles for rural areas: a study in mid-Wales. *Cambria: a Welsh Geographical Review* 7: 29–44.

British Broadcasting Corporation and Independent Broadcasting Authority. 1981. *Listening and viewing among Welsh speaking people in Wales.* Broadcasting Research Department report LR/81/1.

Carter, H. and Griffiths, H. M. (eds.) 1981. *National atlas of Wales.* Cardiff: University of Wales Press.

Carter, H. and Williams, S. W. 1978. *Aggregate studies of language and cultural change in contemporary Wales.* London: Routledge and Kegan Paul.

Centre for Information on Language Teaching. 1976. *Bilingualism and British Education: the dimensions of diversity.* CILT Reports and Papers 14. London: Centre for Information on Language Teaching.

Coupland, R. 1954. *Welsh and Scottish nationalism: a study.* London: Collins.

Davies, C. 1973. Cymdeithas yr Iaith Gymraeg. In Stephens, M. (1973).

Emmett, I. 1978. Blaenau boys in the mid-1960's. In Williams, G. (1978).

Evans, G. 1975. *Land of my fathers: two thousand years of Welsh history.* Swansea: John Penry.

Fienberg, S. E. 1977. *The analysis of cross-classified categorical data.* Cambridge, Mass.: MIT Press.

Gal, S. 1979. *Language shift: social determinants of linguistic change in bilingual Austria.* New York: Academic Press.

Giles, H. and Powesland, P. F. 1975. *Speech style and social evaluation.* London and New York: Academic Press.

Giles, H., Robinson, W. P. and Smith, P. M. (eds.) 1980. *Language: social psychological perspectives.* Oxford: Pergamon Press.

Harrison, G. H. 1980. Social motives in the transmission of a minority language: a Welsh study. In Giles, H. *et al.* (1980).

Harrison, G. H., Bellin, W. and Piette, A. B. 1981. *Bilingual mothers in Wales and the language of their children.* Cardiff: University of Wales Press.

Jones, D. G. 1973. The Welsh language movement. In Stephens, M. (1973).

Jones, G. 1978. *Dyddiadur dyn dŵad.* Caernarfon: Cyhoeddiadau Mei.

Jones, R.B. 1972. *Anatomy of Wales*. Peterston Super Ely, Glamorgan: Gwerin publications.

Jones, W.R. 1966. *Bilingualism in Welsh education*. Cardiff: University of Wales Press.

Khleif, B.B. 1980. *Language, ethnicity and education in Wales*. The Hague: Mouton.

Le Calvez, A. 1970. *Un cas de bilinguisme, le pays de Galles. Histoire, littérature, enseignement*. Lannion: Skol.

Lewis, E.G. 1971. Migration and language in the USSR. *International Migration Review* 5: 147–79.

——— 1973. Language contact in the USSR and Wales. *Planet* 20: 53–64.

Morgan, K.O. 1981. *Rebirth of a nation: Wales 1880–1980*. London/Cardiff: Oxford University Press/University of Wales Press.

Pryce, W.T.R. 1978a. Welsh and English in Wales: a spatial analysis based on the linguistic affiliation of parochial communities. *Bulletin of the Board of Celtic Studies* 28: 1–36.

——— 1978b. Wales as a culture region: patterns of change 1750–1971. *Transactions of the Honourable Society of the Cymmrodorion* 103: 229–61.

Rees, C. 1973. The Welsh language in politics. In Stephens, M. (1973).

Roberts, C. and Williams, G. 1980. Attitudes and ideological bases of support for Welsh as a minority language. In Giles, H. *et al.* (1980).

Schools Council Committee for Wales. 1978. *Bilingual education in Wales 5–11: Report by Eurwen Price with an independent evaluation by C.J. Dodson*. London: Evans/Methuen Educational.

Sharp, D., Thomas, B., Price, E., Francis, G. and Davies, I. 1973. *Attitudes to Welsh and English in the schools of Wales*. London and Cardiff: Macmillan/University of Wales Press.

Singer, B.R. 1979. *Distribution-free methods for nonparametric problems: a classified and selected bibliography*. Leicester: British Psychological Society.

Stephens, M. (ed.) 1973. *The Welsh language today*. Llandysul, Dyfed: Gomer Press.

Stephens, M. 1976. *Linguistic minorities in Western Europe* Llandysul, Dyfed: Gomer Press.

Williams, C.H. 1977. Non-violence and the development of the Welsh language society *Welsh History Review* 8: 426–55.

——— 1980. Language contact and language change in Wales, 1901–1971: a study in historical geolinguistics. *Welsh History Review* 10: 207–38.

Williams, G. 1978. *Social and cultural change in contemporary Wales*. London: Routledge and Kegan Paul.

Williams, S.W. 1979. Language erosion: a spatial perspective. *Cambria: a Welsh Geographical Review* 6: 54–69.

——— 1981. The urban hierarchy, diffusion and the Welsh language: a preliminary analysis 1901–1971. *Cambria: a Welsh Geographical Review* 8: 35–50.

28

Irish and English in Ireland

JOHN EDWARDS

Constitution of the Irish Free State, Article 4:
The national language of the Irish Free State is the Irish language,
but the English language shall be equally recognised as an official
language ...
Constitution of Ireland, Article 8:
1. The Irish language as the national language is the first official
   language.
2. The English language is recognised as a second official language.
3. Provision may, however, be made by law for the exclusive use of
   either of the said languages for any one or more official purposes,
   either throughout the state or in any part thereof.

Introduction

Up until the Norman invasions of Ireland in the twelfth century, the Irish
language was secure. Indeed, Adams (1970) notes that it had been so for five
hundred years, having displaced earlier varieties and established itself as a
language of literary use. With the advent of French and English speakers,
however, the process of change was set in motion. This change was not a rapid
one. Only in the towns within the Pale did French and English become
established and the Pale itself tended to shrink. In fact there was considerable
Gaelicizing of the new arrivals and their descendants (*Hibernis ipsis
Hiberniores*, as the saying has it). In 1366, the passage of the Statutes of
Kilkenny – intended to support the English language – attests to this trend.
The Statutes (written, incidentally, in Norman French) were not effective.

Thus, in 1600, English existed only within a diminished Pale along the
eastern coast and in one or two rural enclaves. Overall, the early period of
Irish contact with English (and French) is characterized by expansion of the
former at the expense of the latter.

When Plantagenet gave way to Tudor, the fortunes of Irish really began to
change, however. Henry VIII, for example, issued many proclamations in
which Irish was, directly or indirectly, discouraged. More importantly, the
plantation schemes – the intention of which was the replacement of Irish with

480

English settlers – which began in the mid-sixteenth century and which reached their zenith under Cromwell a century later brought about movements of Irish speakers to the south and west. The conquest of Ireland, however, was not completed until the end of Elizabeth I's reign. Hugh O'Neill and his Spanish allies were decisively beaten by Lord Mountjoy in 1601 at Kinsale; this was followed in 1607 by the 'flight of the Earls' (i.e. the exile of a number of Irish chiefs). After, and because of, this came the acts of plantation in Ulster which have had such longstanding consequences (see e.g. Beckett, 1981). All of this amounted to the passing of the Gaelic order and, although Irish was still the majority language at the end of the Tudor period, many see the first decade of the seventeenth century as decisive for Ireland and Irish.

Elizabeth had earlier encouraged the use of Irish for proselytizing purposes (a theme to be revived in the nineteenth century), providing type and press for an Irish Bible (although one was not produced until the end of her reign). She was also behind the founding of Trinity College, Dublin (1591) with the same end in mind. So, in matters large as well as more restricted, there is some reason to emphasize the first years of the seventeenth century.

English began to make steady advances, although these were to be counted more in terms of status than in numbers. Between 1600 and 1800, it grew to become the language of regular use for about half the population – the more powerful half. Irish speakers were more and more the poor, the disadvantaged, and their language received no official recognition. In the first half of the nineteenth century, other problems beset Irish. Wall thus notes that 'every school child in Ireland will tell you that Daniel O'Connell, the Catholic clergy and the National schools together killed the Irish language' (1969: 81). While an oversimplistic statement of the case, there is no doubt that each strand here was important. O'Connell, the Great Emancipator, was an Irish speaker; yet, in his own famous phrase, he was 'sufficiently utilitarian not to regret its [Irish] gradual abandonment'. The Catholic clergy had turned to English, especially since the British had founded Maynooth College in 1795, and since the Irish language continued to be used by Protestant proselytizing societies (e.g. the Irish Society, established in 1818). The general view here seemed to be that it was better to save souls than to save Irish and, as priests were often managers of primary schools, they often worked actively against the Irish language in the educational context (O'Donnell, 1903). The educational context itself, the National School system established in 1831, was British-run of course, and excluded Irish; it was called the 'murder machine' by Patrick Pearse (1976).

Also within the first half of the nineteenth century came the famine. Its depredations and the emigration which it prompted were felt most severely in rural Irish-speaking areas. Thus, we might agree with Adams who states that 'it is clear that English quite suddenly gained an advantage about the middle of the last century' (1970: 163). In fact, the 1851 Census indicated only 23 per cent of the population as being Irish-speaking. Although the figure may not be very precise, we can understand why Macnamara (1971) has noted that, by this time, the number of MONOLINGUAL Irish speakers was very small.

All of these factors in the decline of Irish are subject to much interpretation. De Fréine (1977, 1978) and others have, for example, seen them as reflections of other, deeper matters and not as causes in themselves (the famine excepted, of course). There is no doubt, however, that the first half of the nineteenth century was disastrous for the Irish language.

After the middle of the nineteenth century, the more relevant matters have to do with attempts to maintain, encourage and revive Irish. These attempts were generally made by upper-middle-class individuals and organizations, in many of whom Irish fluency was an acquired talent rather than a maternal one. In 1876, the Society for the Preservation of the Irish Language was founded, followed by the Gaelic Union in 1880 and, in 1893, the Gaelic League (*Conradh na Gaeilge*). This last – the largest and most important of the language organizations – was prompted in large part by Douglas Hyde's famous address to the Irish National Literary Society in November 1892 ('The necessity for de-anglicising Ireland'). The Gaelic League's objective was essentially to maintain Irish but it is generally, and not unfairly, seen as wishing to do more: to revive Irish as the ordinary language of the mass of the population (though Hyde himself did not think this a very likely possibility; see Hyde, 1886). The beginnings and spread of the Gaelic League make a fascinating story in themselves; suffice it to say here that it was a significant movement, in terms of its supporters, its propagandizing and, indeed, its success, for it gained a place for the Irish language in schools and at the university.

The Gaelic League declined in importance (though it still exists today) with the establishment of the Irish Free State in December 1921. Many of the political leaders were members of the League and, as the larger national movement grew, the language aspect waned. And, as Macnamara (1971) points out, the Gaelic League felt that the restoration of the language could now be reasonably transferred to governmental responsibility. Daniel Corkery, in his *Fortunes of the Irish language*, noted that 'for the first time since 1169, the Irish language has a state behind it. To say this is equivalent to saying that everything has changed for it' (1968: 128).

The modern scene

As the two quotations at the beginning of the chapter show, Irish was enshrined as the national and first official language from the inception of the Irish Free State. However, by this time, the number of Irish speakers was very small. In this respect, the efforts of the Gaelic League had been in vain; by 1922, the mass of the Irish people had long since switched to English, as the Census figures in table 28.1 indicate. So far as monoglot Irish speakers go, it

Table 28.1. *Census figures for Irish speakers*

Date	Irish speakers	(% of total population)
1901	619,710	(19.2)
1911	553,717	(17.6)
1926	543,511	(18.3)

may be assumed that these were very few indeed; in 1901, about 21,000 were recorded, representing only about 0.5 per cent of the population (about 4,400 in each of Munster and Ulster, about 12,000 in Connaught, and 7(!) in Leinster; see Akenson, 1970).

Despite these figures Irish obviously had a special hold upon the founders of the new state. It was closely tied to Irish nationalism and, as Akenson (1975) suggests, possessed a value quite beyond purely educational, intellectual and, indeed, pragmatic concerns. De Valera himself stated his opinion that 'Ireland with its language and without freedom is preferable to Ireland with freedom and without its language' (Akenson, 1975: 36). In this sentiment, De Valera and others like him were essentially carrying on in the highly romanticized tradition so carefully accented by the Gaelic League. At the same time, it was also good political sense to endorse (or appear to endorse) Irish, because doing so established a clear, non-British line. Under these circumstances, the government passed the burden of Irish restoration to the schools. Although Akenson and others refuse to accept the simplistic notion, mentioned above, that the National School system in Ireland was a prime factor in the decline of Irish, the idea presented an immediate and much-discussed possibility – the British schools had killed Irish; let the Irish schools revive it. Even if the first half of this statement were true, the second does not necessarily follow. Nevertheless, from the first, the Irish language was seen largely to be within the domain of the school.

Irish and education

From the beginning, Irish was to be a compulsory subject. In addition, infants' classes were to be conducted entirely through the medium of Irish. This arose from a recommendation of the Irish National Teachers' Organization (INTO) conference of 1921 largely, it would seem, on the advice of the Reverend T. Corcoran, then Professor of Education at University College, Dublin. This man has a very interesting place in the Irish language–education situation of the 1920s and 1930s, and is worth a brief look here. Clearly pro-Irish and anti-English, Corcoran was the *éminence grise* of the INTO conference, and published several articles which today have the flavour of an odd combination of nationalism and naiveté. In 1923, for example, he outlined a scheme for the revival of Irish which was totally unsupported by any evidence (1923a). He also (1923b) felt that virtually all girls who had been educated in Irish would be 'natural teachers'. His views on English were that it served to transmit English thought, which itself reflected 'narrow insularity, repellent materialism and chronic indifference to what is of real worth in life' (1923c: 272). In 1925 Corcoran made the astonishing statement that 'the popular schools can give and can restore our native language. They can do it even without positive aid from the home' (1925: 387). Later (1934), Corcoran made it clear that he thought the main task of the school was restoration of Irish. Later still he noted that the policy of restoration had been 'ratified and reinforced by the emphatic, if quiet, mind of the whole mass of the Irish people' (1939: 285). The two words between the commas must have been distasteful to Corcoran, but even he can hardly have failed to notice the lack of general activity in support of the Irish language. Corcoran was not, of course, alone in his naive and poorly-considered views, but his position at the university gave them considerable weight. They were naturally seized upon by revivalists and may be taken as generally representative of a large section of that group. This group was not without its critics, however; even at the height of language nationalism, there were those who saw difficulties. Sean O'Faolain, for example, regularly thundered against the language fanatics in the pages of *The Bell* (see, e.g., 1943).

The finding of suitable teachers of Irish was something of a problem from the beginning, and necessitated the establishment of preparatory colleges, a system which lasted until the 1960s. Generally, as O'Connell (1968) points out, teachers were (and continue to be) uneasy with aspects of Irish at school. In particular, they objected to the use of the language as a teaching medium in cases in which this might not be 'profitably done'. This is NOT to say that the INTO desired the removal of obligatory Irish from the roster of school subjects. Nevertheless, it is probably fair to say that teachers resented the implicit decision to revive Irish through schools alone. Certainly, the INTO reports of 1942 and 1947 tend to bear this out; the 1942 document in particular, a survey into the use of Irish as a medium of instruction for English-speaking children, emphasized the need for teachers to have greater curricular flexibility (see also Binchy, 1945 on this point). More recently, individual teachers have commented on the matter. Comber, for example, noted that 'the teacher loses heart flogging a dead horse while the experts debate whether another whip might not revive him' (1960: 27). Harrison continued on the same theme when he stated that 'Irish, except as an arcane minority rite, is on its way out. Don't blame the teachers for its demise' (1976: 35).

Macnamara, in a useful summary of the Irish restoration movement generally, deals with the place of Irish in education as follows:

... in the middle 1930s, it was forbidden to teach English or to use English in the infant classes of the state-financed national (primary) schools. Irish as a subject was compulsory in all classes, and English as a subject was compulsory in the second class ... and all higher classes. Further, the rule was that Irish was to be used as the medium of instruction in all classes and subjects where the teacher was competent to do so and where the children were competent to learn in this manner. (1971: 71)

Since this was written, things have not changed greatly, although the all-Irish infants' class has been abolished, and increasing recognition has been given to the idea that the use of Irish as a medium of instruction for other subjects is not always productive. In secondary education, Irish is a compulsory subject and, until quite recently (1973), a pass in Irish was necessary to obtain the Leaving Certificate. At universities, Irish courses are naturally on offer.

However, there is no doubt that the bulk of the restoration effort (and therefore most of the interest, for present purposes) has occurred at the primary school level. This has created enduring difficulties, since the system has not been self-supporting. The teacher-training colleges no longer instruct their students mainly through Irish; consequently, those who are to be the next generation of teachers of Irish are not themselves especially competent. All of this has led to what a recent newspaper report (Murphy, 1981) has termed 'the crisis in Irish'. Standards of Irish are allegedly low, both in terms of teaching quality and student competence. Students who have taken Irish for a dozen years at school cannot speak the language. Part of the difficulty here may be that the secondary school requirements still centre largely upon written work; at the primary level, emphasis has recently been put upon conversational proficiency. There is thus a confusing mismatch. Murphy's report cites teachers who point to poor oral language proficiency as well as those who condemn students' poor Irish grammatical skills. In all of this, one can see the traditional complaints made of second-language teaching and learning. It must be remembered, however, that there is a special piquancy here – Irish is indeed a second language to most Irish children but it is a rather special second language, at least in the eyes of many. This makes the failure of the schools a bitter one, even though a thin wash of Irish competence HAS been applied to almost everyone who has gone through the system. The failure may indeed be bitter, but it is hardly surprising; as we shall see below, there is very little to be found in other spheres of current Irish life which could be seen as supporting the schools' effort. So perhaps their failure is not so great as might first be thought; perhaps, in fact, they should be commended for what they HAVE managed to do.

Finally, it can be noted that the government in 1980 produced a White Paper on educational development which deals, among other things, with the Irish language. The aim of Irish restoration is affirmed here although it is now recognized that schools alone cannot achieve this. Methods and teacher competence in spoken Irish are singled out for attention, and emphasis is given to regular objective evaluation of Irish standards at school. Also stressed (and not before time) is continuity between first and second levels of education. Remarks are also made about the need for *Gaeltacht* support (see below) and for broadcast media time to be given to Irish. Generally, the emphasis is now to be upon spoken Irish, how teachers can be assisted to develop and maintain competence in this area, and continuous evaluation of Irish standards. All of these proposals are to be welcomed.

As in other parts of this chapter, I have had to be brief here. Irish and education is a most interesting aspect of the whole restoration issue (see O'Connell, 1968; Akenson, 1975; and Edwards, 1983 for a listing of many articles on the topic).

The *Gaeltacht*

The *Gaeltacht* – Irish-speaking district – must be given special attention here. As we have seen, all Ireland was once a *Gaeltacht*; over time, the areas in which Irish predominated shrunk. As well, because of the plantation policies, these districts were also those most poverty-stricken. Today the *Gaeltacht* is almost entirely to be found on the western seaboard (in Donegal, Mayo, Galway, Kerry and Cork). The total *Gaeltacht* population is now about 70,000. This number cannot, however, be equated with the number of regular Irish speakers there (which Ó Danachair (1969) estimates to be on the order of 50,000 – i.e. under 2 per cent of the total Irish population).

Despite the small numbers, however, the *Gaeltacht* Irish speakers have always occupied a central position in discussions on the language, constituting as they do the remaining concentrations of Irish. Indeed, in 1891, a 'Congested Districts Board' was established to enquire into life in poor areas in the west. The areas looked at included almost every part of the *Gaeltacht*. Relief of congestion, however, entailed population decline, and the establishment of industry led to English-speaking incursions. In short, the *Gaeltacht* has always been a problem for the language movement, inasmuch as the lifestyle there has created an association between the Irish language and 'penury, drudgery and backwardness' (Ó Danachair, 1969: 120).

The paradox is this: the *Gaeltacht* is vital to the language, since it provides the only sizeable groups of Irish speakers. At the same time, it is constantly being encroached upon by modern influences of all kinds (which usually means English-language influences). If nothing is done, the *Gaeltacht* will continue to shrink; if things ARE done there is the very real danger of creating an enclave which is seen, by those inside as well as by those without, as essentially artificial – an area not allowed to follow larger social and economic currents. In such a situation, can a language survive in anything like its usual unselfconscious state? Ó Sé (1966) noted that, since the *Gaeltacht* is not urbanized, emigration continues; yet if it were urbanized, why then would it not go the way of the rest of the country and become anglicized as well?

The *Gaeltacht* has been at the heart of agonized discussion since the Gaelic League focused attention on it in the 1890s (see e.g., Bergin, 1911; Gaelic

League, 1937; Byrne, 1938; Lyons, 1971). It is undoubtedly the centre of a rich oral culture. Yet the *Gaeltacht* continues to diminish; the 'material advantages that the *Gaeltacht* people have seen in Irish have not outweighed those that they could see in English' (Macnamara, 1971: 85). In 1972, *Comhairle na Gaeilge* (a body set up by the government to advise on Irish-language matters) formally recommended that all *Gaeltacht* development be under a central agency. This body, *Údarás na Gaeltachta*, was established in 1979 and began official functions in 1980; it is to oversee all aspects of *Gaeltacht* life, with a special view to linguistic and cultural matters. So far, it has had to wrestle with inherited problems and it remains to be seen what can be done.

The most recent assessment of *Gaeltacht* life is that of Fennell (1980). He feels that the attempt to save the *Gaeltacht* has failed – all that now remains is a 'crumbling archipelago'. Much of the failure Fennell ascribes to the language movement, who saw in the *Gaeltacht* a sort of 'never-never land', and to the inadequacy of various governmental measures. Fennell also notes, however, that the people themselves seem not to be as devoted to the language as many might have wished. Echoing Macnamara, Fennell states that 'the majority of parents *throughout the entire Gaeltacht* have decided to rear their children in English'. This seems reminiscent of the countrywide process a century and more ago with regard to Irish parents and the National School system.

Irish in government and official life

At the state level, support of Irish continues. Naturally, most state documents are printed in both English and Irish but, in addition, the government has made specific moves to help in the restoration effort. In 1958, for example, the Commission on the Restoration of the Irish Language was established to advise on steps to hasten the revival. In their report (1963), the Commissioners noted the national goodwill towards Irish, and how this could 'spark off' national advance. Many recommendations were made, applying to all areas of Irish life. In 1965, the government responded with a White Paper setting out its policy *vis-à-vis* these recommendations. This report is prefaced by the observation that the 'national aim is to restore the Irish language as a general medium of communication' (p. 4), and calls for the widespread passive support for Irish to be translated into something more active. Progress reports were issued in 1966 and 1969 detailing grants for Irish books, for the *Gaeltacht* and for language organizations. The Linguistics Institute of Ireland was established and a 'Buy Irish' campaign begun. Yet, for all of this, there seems little transformation apparent in the lives of ordinary Irish people. It would be easy to say that commissions and White Papers provide an immediate and facile way of giving lip service to a cause – easy to say and true, at least in part. Yet, the government is caught in a difficult position. It cannot realistically go all out for Irish and advocate widescale switching to that language. Neither, perhaps, can it renounce the language movement altogether (although some would say this to be the more honest course, in the light of history and the contemporary scene).

The government established, in 1975, *Bord na Gaeilge* which is charged with promoting Irish generally. Progress here has been slow, and many have been critical of the board; it has suffered, too, from a certain amount of internal disruption. It has attempted to put Irish before the people via media advertisements and the like. With the end of its first statutory term, in 1980, the board had not succeeded, according to Ó Gadhra (1981), in creating a great deal of public awareness of its role. Other, non-governmental bodies continue to promote Irish. The Gaelic League is still extant, *Gael Linn* promotes Irish in the business world, and there are several Irish teachers' organizations. Publications in Irish are fairly healthy, both at the magazine and book level. Yet, the big push put on by the Gaelic League from the 1890s to about 1915 has not been repeated, and there seems little likelihood that it will.

In ordinary Irish life, there are places for the Irish language. Almost all of them, however, are either ceremonial, trivial or exist only in tandem with English. Bus scrolls, street signs, bits and pieces of advertisements, labels on the bottom of souvenirs which say 'Made in Japan' in Irish, the beginnings and endings of official letters (e.g. the salutation *A chara* – then the text of the letter in English – then, at the end, *Mise, le meas*), and so on. In addition, until very recently (1974) entrance to the Civil Service required a knowledge of Irish; this was, however, almost entirely nominal. Indeed, a recent report notes that even in sections designated officially as Irish-speaking the majority of people 'rarely if ever *spoke* Irish ... during work hours' (Committee on Irish Language Attitudes Research, 1975: 196). Nominal Irish-language qualifications are also required (or have been required) for the police, the army and for the practice of law.

With regard to broadcasting, there are state requirements for Irish on television and radio. Macnamara (1971) reports that during a monitored week in 1969 8 per cent of television time and 4 per cent of radio time were given to Irish. In 1974 Conor Cruise O'Brien, then the Minister for Posts and Telegraphs, mentioned a proposed reform for broadcasting policy on Irish, to take the form of an amendment to Section 17 of the Broadcasting Act which refers to national cultural development. Dr O'Brien wanted this concept re-examined with a view to a more realistic appraisal of the position of Irish and English. Naturally, this caused outrage among language supporters, who felt it to be the thin end of the wedge to eventually displace Irish altogether. O'Brien did not, however, propose to omit Irish completely. More recently, the creation of the second national television channel (RTE-2) has aroused a good deal of discussion as to whether or not it should give more time to the Irish language.

Research

Despite the view of Corkery (noted on page 482) the revival of Irish as a
regularly spoken language has not succeeded. It is true that, in the 1971
Census, 789,429 people (three years-of-age and over) reported themselves as
Irish speakers. This is 28.3 per cent of the total and is the highest figure for
almost a hundred years. Indeed, the reported Irish speakers in 1861 were 24.5
per cent of the total population. However, that quarter of the populace were
Irish speakers in a sense not applicable to the present quarter. That is, there
has been a steady decline in speakers of Irish as a first language and, with
school Irish compulsory since 1922, a great increase in a more cursory
knowledge of Irish. Today, outside the *Gaeltacht*, perhaps 4 per cent of the
Irish people use the language with any regularity.

With all the rhetoric surrounding Irish, comparatively little has ever been
done to investigate matters of attitude, ability and usage. It may well be that
the results of such research would prove to be unpalatable. Indeed, when
Macnamara (1966) published his survey of bilingualism and primary education, there was a furore. His major point, that the amount of time in the
school day devoted to Irish caused lower standards in English for Irish
children generally, and for *Gaeltacht* children in particular, has proved a
provoking one for students of bilingualism in general. In Ireland the effect was
considerable. It was only two years previously, for example, that Brennan had
said:

if research were to show an undoubted drop in standards of English it would be
regrettable; but it would have to be tolerated for the greater good: the production of
integrated *Irish* personalities. (1964: 271)

The quotation clearly demonstrates the emotive power of the Irish-language
issue. Indeed, this is not surprising. What is of particular interest in the Irish
case, with the reliance upon education, is the way in which many have
perceived the children to be pawns in some political game. 'Digits in the Irish
revival statistics', Akenson called them (1975: 60); and O'Doherty stated that
'children's minds must not be made the battleground of a political wrangle'
(1958: 268).

I have already mentioned the Irish teachers' survey which called for more
curricular flexibility with regard to Irish (INTO, 1942; see also INTO, 1947).
This report prompted silence from the Minister of Education at first, followed
by anger, criticisms from other members of the government and from the
Gaelic League (O'Connell, 1968). In 1974, Streib reported on what he termed
'patterned evasion' – a process by which conflicts between language ideals and
actual language behaviour are reduced. It would seem as if patterned evasion,
in one form or another, has been characteristic of the Irish language scene for
a long time. In 1971, Macnamara reported some findings of an Irish
Marketing Survey's attitude poll. Although 83 per cent felt that Irish could

not be restored as the vernacular, there still existed considerable goodwill towards Irish and towards efforts in its behalf, especially at school (see also Ernest Dichter Institute, 1968). This general goodwill would still seem to exist (Committee on Irish Language Attitudes Research, 1975); yet Ó Catháin (1973) reported hostility towards Irish as well. This apparent paradox can be resolved if one takes into account the difference between volition and coercion in language matters. Many people, for example, were upset over the compulsory Irish for Civil Service appointments, and over the need to pass Irish to pass the overall secondary school Leaving Certificate, both of which requirements have now gone.

Attitudes towards Irish are also clearer if one bears in mind communicative and non-communicative aspects of language. In societies in which the ancestral language is also the vernacular these two facets are not separated – but they are separable, as the Irish case shows. The report mentioned in the previous paragraph (Committee on Irish Language Attitudes Research, 1975; see also Edwards, 1977a) made clear that most people value the language as a 'symbol of national or ethnic identity, or as a symbol of cultural distinctiveness'. Here, a national sample of about 2,500 people, as well as a special *Gaeltacht* sample of about 500, supplied information on Irish attitudes, ability and use. Apart from support for the language as an ethnic symbol, there was also found pessimism about the future of the language, support for governmental moves in its behalf, and a general lack of interest in restoration–promotion groups. With regard to ability, results show, as expected, a decrease in conversational ability (which native speakers possess) and an increase in basic reading and writing skills (which have been emphasized in school Irish). This, interestingly enough, shows the importance of school instruction in a language in situations in which larger social support is lacking. For language usage, the findings mirror subjective evaluations – Irish is little used. Even where it would be most expected (e.g. in Civil Service units designated as Irish-speaking, among teachers, and even in the *Gaeltacht*), usage is disappointingly infrequent.

Overall then research, such as it is, tends to show that Irish restoration is not likely. By the time the state was established, the mass of the population had been English-speaking for some generations and vague, abstract or cultural/traditional appeals for widespread change have not succeeded. And, unless one is a fanatical revivalist, this is not to be wondered at. As in other matters, people are linguistically pragmatic. A more cynical view was expressed by Ussher when he noted that 'the Irish of course like their Irish, but they like it *dead*' (1949: 107). At the same time, of course, one should not conclude that the Irish people have completely turned their backs on the language, or that the restoration movement has been a total failure. Indeed, of all the Celtic revival efforts, that for Irish has been in some ways the most successful. Nevertheless, it has been severely criticized. The only movement to proceed from a national base, it has been a 'terrible failure' in the eyes of some (e.g. Ellis and Mac A'Ghobhainn, 1971). Yet, as Macnamara aptly notes:

It seems unlikely, indeed, that the native government could ever have secured a substantial material advantage for Irish at any level of society without methods so dictatorial that Irish democracy would have been destroyed. And in the final analysis, neither Irish politicians nor the Irish people wanted that. (1971: 86)

What the Irish have done is not to lose their national identity through language, but rather to enshrine it in English; that is, they have taken English and made it peculiarly their own. There has, of course, been much debate over the language–identity issue in Ireland. Many have held the view that Irish is essential to identity (see, e.g., O'Hickey, 1898; Cahill, 1935; Brennan, 1964, 1969). However, other more reasoned views have co-existed with these. Ryan (1905) made the point three-quarters of a century ago, and Brown noted that language is not an 'essential constituent of a distinctive nationality' (1912: p. 503; see also Dillon, 1958; and Kavanagh, 1948, on the 'humbug' revival).

Others have emphasized points which now have a curious ring to them. For example, the view that Catholicism was enshrined in the Irish language has proved a popular theme (see, e.g., O'Reilly, 1898; Cashel, 1917; Malone, 1935); keeping Irish was a way of keeping out crass English materialism and irreligious thought. Others, including Hyde himself (1886) felt that the vocal organs of Irish people were especially suited to the Irish language (see also Fullerton, 1912).

English in Ireland

I can be brief here, for two reasons: (1) chapters 7 and 8 in this volume deal effectively with Irish English; (2) for my purposes, having delineated the role of Irish *vis-à-vis* English, the other side of the coin should be more or less apparent. Nevertheless, I do want to deal with the position of regional varieties and of nonstandard English in Ireland.

Over the years there have of course developed a number of regional varieties of English in Ireland; in addition there exists a supra-regional variety in some ways akin to British RP (see chapter 8). Henry (1977) provides some useful examples, first of all, of the differences between Anglo-Irish (essentially rural, and composed of Irish and English minglings) and Hiberno-English (from the usage of British settlers, and approximating a standard). These examples are taken from current Galway speech:

(1) Anglo-Irish: 'There no word o' a lie in it'
     (relates to Irish: 'Níl aon fhocal bréige ann')
     Hiberno-English equivalent: 'That (this) is quite true'

(2) Anglo-Irish: 'There's misfortune shook down on 'im'
     (relates to Irish: 'Tá 'n mí-ádh craití anuas air')
     Hiberno-English equivalent: 'He's very unlucky'

Accent varieties occur within both Anglo-Irish and Hiberno-English. Standard Hiberno-English is the Irish equivalent to Standard English English, while the so-called 'Ascendancy' accent, being one pronunciation of the standard, is to be compared to RP.

Delahunty (1977) has noted that only a small number of distinct Irish accents are generally recognized, although some people are able to make many fine-grained discriminations. Thus, the Irish scene in this regard is analogous to others elsewhere, resembling the British most of all perhaps. There are varieties of Dublin accent and, in the country at large, Delahunty suggests Cork, northern Irish (including Donegal), Kerry and Midlands accents as being the major varieties. He also adverts to the 'no-accent' accent, which he states is the standard Irish pronunciation of English, or Hiberno-English (which is, in fact, a standard Irish English rather than a standard pronunciation – see previous paragraph).

Anecdotally, there is much evidence that stereotypes attach to Irish regional accents, as they do to those elsewhere, but little work has been done here. In one study, Edwards (1977b) employed the matched guise technique to investigate the reactions of Irish secondary school students to five regional accents. The students were boys and girls from several social strata in Dublin; the accents – those of Galway, Cavan, Cork, Dublin and Donegal – were all produced by a professional actor reading an emotionally-neutral passage as an educated middle-class speaker. All of the guises were evaluated along 9 rating scales. Underlying these were three broad personality dimensions: 'competence' (traits such as intelligence and industriousness), 'social-attractiveness' (friendliness, sense of humour) and 'personal integrity' (trustworthiness, generosity). The results showed that the Donegal guise was seen as most competent and the Dublin guise least so. This appears to validate the popular stereotypic view of northerners in general – one of ambition and a business-like demeanour – which may well have longstanding historical precedent. The Dublin guise was seen as higher in attractiveness but lower in integrity than the others, and the Cavan, Cork and Galway guises were generally rated between those of Dublin and Donegal. Since the judges here were from Dublin themselves, it seems as if the results corroborate those of Giles and his colleagues (e.g. Giles, 1971; Giles and Powesland, 1975) in which local speakers are not evaluated highly in terms of competence but are rated more positively along the attractiveness dimension than are other varieties (in Giles' studies, mainly RP; in the present study, the Donegal guise seems to occupy this role; see also Edwards, 1979a).

Another Irish study in this vein is that of Milroy and McClenaghan (1977). Fifteen Belfast undergraduates listened to four stimulus speakers possessing Scottish, southern Irish, RP and Ulster accents. Overall, the RP speaker was evaluated most favourably, especially so on competence dimensions; on integrity and attractiveness, however, the RP speaker was seen somewhat less positively than the Scot and the Ulsterman. Evaluations of the southern Irish speaker were generally favourable in terms of competence, but were the lowest on the other two broad scales. Milroy and McClenaghan related their findings to the Ulster–Republic interaction in general and, more particularly, to the fact that 13 of their 15 raters were Protestant. It is interesting that the high competence ratings accorded to northerners (Donegal speakers) in the Edwards (1977b) study noted above were not found here, where northern Irish judges were evaluating northerners (Ulstermen) but where, of course, an RP speaker was included among the stimuli.

The findings generally that regional varieties of English may be downgraded relative to what are perceived as more standard ones takes on special significance when one considers varieties spoken by the poor, especially the urban poor. Trudgill (1975) has suggested that urban speech patterns in Britain (e.g. those of Birmingham and Liverpool) are generally seen as more unpleasant than rural varieties (e.g. Devon). Wilkinson (1965) proposed a three-part accent hierarchy – at the top is RP, next are various regional accents, and at the bottom of the scale are the urban varieties. This leads directly to a consideration of the speech of the socioeconomically disadvantaged. Studies reveal generally that this is downgraded, especially in the educational context (see Edwards, 1979a). Two Irish studies may be cited here. In the first (Edwards, 1977c), twenty disadvantaged and twenty non-disadvantaged boys in fifth class (11- to 12-year-olds) provided speech samples via a story-retelling task. Adult middle-class judges consistently downgraded the former group along the dimensions of intelligence, fluency, vocabulary, pronunciation and intonation, and communicative ability. A further and more detailed study (Edwards, 1979b) found that, on each of 17 semantic-differential scales, disadvantaged 10-year-old Dublin boys and girls were evaluated less favourably than their non-disadvantaged counterparts, on the basis of short recorded speech samples. Overall, the evidence suggests that the patterns of disadvantaged, nonstandard speech and the reactions which these prompt are remarkably similar in the Irish context to findings from other parts of the world.

Conclusions

To the casual observer, the sociolinguistic scene in Ireland is one in which English predominates and in which there exists a very limited role for Irish. Within the English-speaking dominance, there exists the regional variation and the differing prestige which this leads to, although research on this matter in Ireland is still in its infancy. In this sense, a sociolinguistic study of Ireland could easily be seen as a mere extension of a larger study of varieties of English.

To do so, however, would be to miss out on the more latent influences of Irish. I have attempted in this chapter to show the role that Irish has (and had) in various aspects of Irish life; in so doing, I hope that I have given a sense of the overall sociolinguistic situation which must take into account both languages. In this concluding section I want to summarize along two main lines: (1) the reasons for the decline of Irish, and why investigation of this has been so sparse; (2) the future of Irish in Ireland.

In general, the decline of Irish has been often put down to English occupation. This is, of course, the overriding reason; if English had not arrived in Ireland, it could hardly have displaced Irish. But to say this is to be simplistic. Why did Irish first successfully counter English, and then lose out to it? Why didn't things follow the course of, say, Norman French and English in England?

The facts relate, above all, to the increasing prestige of English and its speakers which, from about 1800, proved a powerful attraction. The view that the National School system, the Catholic clergy and Daniel O'Connell were the killers of Irish is, as I noted in the introduction, an oversimplification. Yet all of these do relate to the declining prestige of Irish, increasingly associated with rural backwardness, poverty and an unsophisticated peasantry, and the power of a formidable language with two great nations behind it. Thus, de Fréine states, with regard to the Irish decline:

The worst excesses were not imposed from outside. The whole paraphernalia of tally sticks, wooden gags, humiliation and mockery – often enforced by encouraging children to spy on their brothers and sisters, or on the children of neighbouring townlands – were not the product of any law or official regulation, but of a social self-generated movement of collective behaviour among the people themselves. Most of the reasons adduced for the suppression of the Irish language are not so much reasons as consequences of the decision to give up the language. (1977: 83–4)

This he feels is of special importance with regard to the role and function of the National School system. De Fréine expands his thesis on the decline of Irish in his book, *The great silence* (1978). The title does not refer to the loss of Irish itself, but rather to the fact that historians have virtually ignored the decline in their treatments of eighteenth- and nineteenth-century Irish social history. De Fréine dilates at some length on the reasons for this ignorance, which he essentially ascribes to national psychological inhibitions. Whatever can be made of de Fréine's psychologizing (and it *is* an interesting approach to the massive Irish language shift of the last century), one fact does seem to emerge, and to be corroborated in other writings. This is that the mass of the Irish people were more or less active contributors to the spread of English for pragmatic reasons brought into being by longstanding historical forces. Binchy (1945), for example, notes that the 'persecution' theory does not fully explain the dramatic Irish decline; Brooks states that, although the English are far from blameless, 'it is impossible to stamp out a language which the people are determined to keep alive' (1907: 22). Irish, he feels, committed suicide rather than having been murdered (see also Ó Conaire, 1973, citing the views of Flann O'Brien, the well-known Irish writer, on this matter). In any event, to use phrases like '700 years of English oppression' or 'the stifling of the will of a nation' is to fall prey to the 'black and white' theory of history.

If one accepts that the Irish people themselves accepted English and increasingly rejected Irish, then it is easier to understand why so few investigations have been made into the sociolinguistics of Irish and English. For this would be formally to recognize an unpalatable fact that language revivalists and, indeed, the State itself to a greater or lesser degree have been unwilling to accept – at least publicly (see Breatnach, 1956). It explains why those critical of any aspect of Irish revival or Irish teaching have very often been unwilling to make public their feelings; and why, when they HAVE done so, they have aroused such hostility. In short, the Irish sociolinguistic scene has been, more than most, a powerful exemplar of the highly-charged emotive topic of language and nationalism. A very recent example here is given by Murphy (1981) in her discussion of teachers' views of Irish at school. One teacher, critical of teaching Irish to disadvantaged pupils 'did not want his name used, as was the case with many teachers criticizing the situation in relation to Irish. It is still a very sensitive area.' In the atmosphere which has prevailed, and which prevails still, it is often difficult to induce people to express their true feelings towards Irish and when they do so the results are often interpreted very widely indeed. Thus, when the Committee on Irish Language Attitudes Research produced its report (1975), both the Gaelic League (ardently pro-Irish) and the Language Freedom Movement (a modern organization, supporting a *laissez-faire* approach to Irish) welcomed it as vindicating their positions. Given all this, it seems reasonable to say that, in gross terms at least, the overwhelmingly English-speaking tenor of modern Irish life is the best and most accurate indicator of real attitudes and desires *vis-à-vis* Irish.

What of the future? It is inconceivable that Irish will ever be restored as the vernacular of Ireland. It will continue to live, of course, in certain highly-circumscribed areas, and the school policy will continue to ensure a widespread, if thin, competence among the general population. Recently, especially in the Dublin area, there has been a steady if small demand for Irish-medium education and preschool Irish. However, in terms of the country as a whole, this should not be overemphasized. Indeed, if compulsory Irish at school were ever to be abolished, the situation could in a relatively short time come to resemble that of Cornish – a language now no longer the maternal tongue of anyone, but which is nevertheless sustained through various formal and informal means amongst those who desire it.

For the Irish language, the future (as the past) will be more determined by larger social trends than by any selfconscious, if well-meaning, revival efforts on the part of relatively few people within relatively limited boundaries. As Fennell (1980) notes, attempts to stop the erosion of shrinking minority languages have not succeeded generally, and certainly not in the Irish case. Irish proves the point that language – in its growth, its spread and its decline – is virtually an organic entity closely allied to real-life exigencies. Those ignorant of this, or those who choose to ignore it, will continue to be disappointed.

REFERENCES

Adams, G. B. 1970. Language and man in Ireland. *Ulster Folklife* 15/16: 140–71.
Akenson, D. H. 1970. *The Irish education experiment*. London: Routledge and Kegan Paul.
——— 1975. *A mirror to Kathleen's face*. Montreal: McGill-Queen's University Press.
Beckett, J. C. 1981. *A short history of Ireland*. London: Hutchinson.
Bergin, O. 1911. *Irish spelling*. Dublin: Browne and Nolan.
Binchy, D. A. 1945. Review of J. L. Campbell's *Gaelic and Scottish education and life*. *The Bell* 10: 362–6.
Breatnach, R. A. 1956. Revival or survival? An examination of the Irish language policy of the state. *Studies* 45: 129–45.
Brennan, M. 1964. The restoration of Irish. *Studies* 53: 263–77.
——— 1969. Language, personality and the nation. In B. Ó Cuív (ed.) *A view of the Irish language*. Dublin: Government Stationery Office.
Brooks, S. 1907. *The new Ireland*. Dublin: Maunsell.
Brown, S. J. 1912. What is a nation? *Studies* 1: 496–510.
Byrne, E. 1938. Where the Irish language still lives. *Ireland-American Review* 1: 50–5.
Cahill, E. 1935. The Irish national tradition. *Irish Ecclesiastical Record* 46: 2–10.
Cashel, A. 1917. Language and thought. *Irish Monthly* 45: 397–403.
Comber, T. 1960. The revival? *Múinteoir Náisiúnta* 5, 7: 23, 24, 27.
Commission on the Restoration of the Irish Language. 1963. *Summary, in English, of final report*. Dublin: Government Stationery Office.
Committee on Irish Language Attitudes Research. 1975. *Report*. Dublin: Government Stationery Office.
Corcoran, T. 1923a. How the Irish language can be revived. *Irish Monthly* 51: 26–30.
——— 1923b. The native speaker as teacher. *Irish Monthly* 51: 187–90.
——— 1923c. How English may be taught without anglicising. *Irish Monthly* 51: 269–73.
——— 1925. The Irish language in the Irish schools. *Studies* 14: 377–88.
——— 1934. The home within the school. *Irish Monthly* 62: 35–9.
——— 1939. Education in Éire. *Yearbook of Education*. pp. 282–94.
Corkery, D. 1968. *The fortunes of the Irish language*. Cork: Mercier Press.
De Fréine, S. 1977. The dominance of the English language in the nineteenth century. In D. Ó Muirithe (ed.), *The English language in Ireland*. Cork: Mercier Press.
——— 1978. *The great silence*. Cork: Mercier Press.
Delahunty, G. P. 1977. Dialect and local accent. In D. Ó Muirithe (ed.) *The English language in Ireland*. Cork: Mercier Press.
Dillon, M. 1958. Comment. *University Review* 2, 2: 22–7.
Edwards, J. R. 1977a. Review of *Report of the Committee on Irish Language Attitudes Research*. *Language Problems and Language Planning* 1: 54–9.
——— 1977b. Students' reactions to Irish regional accents. *Language and Speech* 20: 280–6.
——— 1977c. The speech of disadvantaged Dublin children. *Language Problems and Language Planning* 1: 65–72.
——— 1979a. *Language and disadvantage*. London: Edward Arnold.
——— 1979b. Judgements and confidence in reactions to disadvantaged speech. In H. Giles and R. St.Clair (eds.) 1979. *Language and social psychology*. Oxford: Blackwell.

—— 1983. *The Irish language: an annotated bibliography of sociolinguistic publications, 1772–1982.* New York: Garland.

Ellis, P. B. and Mac A'Ghobhainn, S. 1971. *The problem of language revival.* Inverness: Club Leabhar.

Ernest Dichter International Institute for Motivational Research. 1968. *A motivational study for the greater use of the Irish language.* Croton-on-Hudson, NY: Ernest Dichter Institute.

Fennell, D. 1980. The last days of the Gaeltacht/Why the Gaeltacht wasn't saved. *Irish Times* 3 and 4 June.

Fullerton, R. 1912. The place of Irish in Ireland's education. *Irish Educational Review* 5: 456–66.

Gaelic League. 1937. *You may revive the Gaelic language.* Dublin: Gaelic League.

Giles, H. 1971. Patterns of evaluation to R.P., South Welsh and Somerset accented speech. *British Journal of Social and Clinical Psychology* 10: 280–1.

Giles, H. and Powesland, P. 1975. *Speech style and social evaluation.* London: Academic Press.

Harrison, M. 1976. The revival of Irish. *Secondary Teacher* 6, 1: 34–5.

Henry, P. L. 1977. Anglo-Irish and its Irish background. In D. Ó Muirithe (ed.) *The English language in Ireland.* Cork: Mercier Press.

Hyde, D. 1886. A plea for the Irish language. *Dublin University Review*, 2: 666–76.

—— 1894. The necessity for de-anglicising Ireland. In C. G. Duffy, G. Sigerson and D. Hyde (eds) *The revival of Irish literature.* London: T. Fisher Unwin.

Ireland, 1965. *The restoration of the Irish language.* Dublin: Government Stationery Office.

—— 1966. *White paper on the restoration of the Irish language: Progress report for the period ended 31 March, 1966.* Dublin: Government Stationery Office.

—— 1969. *White paper on the restoration of the Irish language: Progress report for the period ended 31 March, 1968.* Dublin: Government Stationery Office.

—— 1980. *White paper on educational development.* Dublin: Government Stationery Office.

Irish National Teachers' Organization. 1942. *Report of committee of inquiry into the use of Irish as a teaching medium to children whose home language is English.* Dublin: INTO.

—— 1947. *A plan for education.* Dublin: INTO.

Kavanagh, P. 1948. The bones of the dead. *The Bell* 15, 4: 62–4.

Lyons, F. S. L. 1971. *Ireland since the famine.* London: Weidenfeld and Nicolson.

Macnamara, J. 1966. *Bilingualism and primary education.* Edinburgh: Edinburgh University Press.

—— 1971. Successes and failures in the movement for the restoration of Irish. In J. Rubin and B. Jernudd (eds.) *Can language be planned?* Honolulu: East-West Center Press.

Malone, C. 1935. English literature in Ireland: a comment on school courses. *Catholic Bulletin* 25: 199–204.

Milroy, L. and McClenaghan, P. 1977. Stereotyped reactions to four educated accents in Ulster. *Belfast Working Papers in Language and Linguistics* 2, 4.

Murphy, C. 1981. The crisis in Irish. *Irish Times* 25 May.

Ó Catháin, S. 1973. The future of the Irish language. *Studies* 62: 303–22.

Ó Conaire, B. 1973. Flann O'Brien, 'An Béal Bocht' and other Irish matters. *Irish University Review* 3: 121–40.

O'Connell, T. J. 1968. *History of the Irish National Teachers' Organization, 1868–1968.* Dublin: INTO.

Ó Danachair, C. 1969. The Gaeltacht. In B. Ó Cuív (ed.) *A view of the Irish language.* Dublin: Government Stationery Office.

O'Doherty, E. F. 1958. Bilingual school policy. *Studies* 47: 259–68.

O'Donnell, F. H. 1903. *The ruin of education in Ireland.* London: David Nutt.

O'Faolain, S. 1943. Gaelic – the truth. *The Bell* 5: 335–40.

Ó Gadhra, N. 1981. Language report: Developments in 1980. *Éire-Ireland*, 16, 1: 109–18.

O'Hickey, M. P. 1898. *The true national idea.* Dublin: Gaelic League.

O'Reilly, J. M. 1898. What religion has lost by the decay of the Irish language. *New Ireland Review* 8: 362–74.

Ó Sé, L. 1966. The Irish language revival: Achilles heel. *Éire-Ireland* 1, 1: 26–49.

Pearse, P. H. 1976. *The murder machine and other essays.* Cork: Mercier Press. (Original, 1912).

Ryan, F. 1905. On language and political ideals. *Dana,* 1: 273–89.

Streib, G. F. 1974. The restoration of the Irish language: behavioral and symbolic aspects. *Ethnicity* 1: 73–89.

Trudgill, P. 1975. *Accent, dialect and the school.* London: Edward Arnold.

Ussher, A. 1949. *The face and mind of Ireland.* London: Gollancz.

Wall, M. 1969. The decline of the Irish language. In B. Ó Cuív (ed.) *A view of the Irish language.* Dublin: Government Stationery Office.

Wilkinson, A. 1965. Spoken English. *Educational Review* 17 (supplement).

29

Scottish Gaelic and English in the Highlands

KENNETH MACKINNON

Gaelic: who speaks it and where

The number of speakers of Scottish Gaelic at the present time is about 80,000. The 1961 Census enumerated 80,978 Gaelic speakers in Scotland (of whom 974 were monoglot). Surprisingly the number of speakers rose at the 1971 Census to 88,415 (of whom 477 were monoglot) – an increase of 9.2 per cent. (General Register Office, 1975). In comparison, Welsh (for which census questions on reading and writing ability were also asked for the first time in 1971) registered a 15 per cent decennial decline (see chapter 27). Enhanced awareness of Gaelic within Scotland, together with increased opportunities to learn Gaelic at school, in adult education, and through radio and television might have perpetuated this upward trend. The 1961–71 increase was, however, a feature of the Lowland area. In its traditional homeland of the Highlands and Hebrides, the number of speakers of Gaelic continued to decline both absolutely and proportionately (MacKinnon, 1978). Between 1961 and 1971 this decline was around 12 per cent, in contrast to the increase of around 62 per cent in Lowland counties and cities. By this time Gaelic monolingualism had become vestigial: a feature of the oldest generation of women and, transitionally, of pre-school-aged children only. (For the general background to Gaelic in Scotland see, among others, Campbell, 1950; Chapman, 1978; Aitken and McArthur, 1979; Ennew, 1980; Durkacz, 1983.)

Preliminary returns for the 1981 Census were published in April 1982 (General Register Office, 1982). These indicated a return to a similar position as in 1961 with a total of 79,307 Gaelic speakers. For the first time, however, separate specification of all those able to speak, read or write Gaelic produced a total of 82,620. For the first time also there were actual increases in numbers of Gaelic speakers in some Highland and Island areas. The Western Isles, the present-day heartland of Gaelic, registered an overall maintenance of its Gaelic speakers and a small increase in its total Gaelic population. Similar numerical increases were also registered in Ross and Cromarty and Inverness Districts and in the Orkney and Shetland Island Areas. These areas had developed oil-related and other growth industries attracting employment from Gaelic communities. Some suburban Lowland districts also evidenced

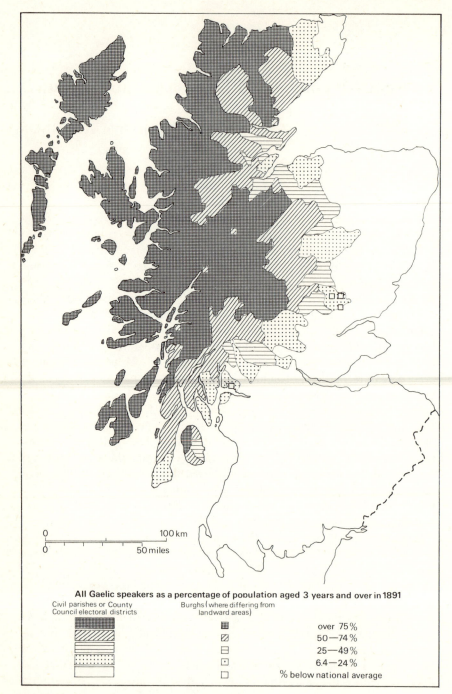

All Gaelic speakers as a percentage of population aged 3 years and over in 1891

Civil parishes or County
Council electoral districts

Burghs (where differing from
landward areas)

		over 75 %
		50 — 74 %
		25 — 49 %
		6.4 — 24 %
		% below national average

Map 29.1. Incidence of Gaelic speakers in 1891

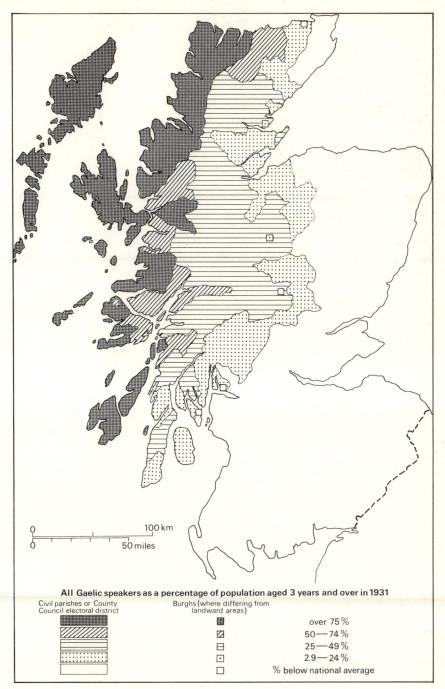

All Gaelic speakers as a percentage of population aged 3 years and over in 1931

Civil parishes or County Council electoral district	Burghs (where differing from landward areas)	
		over 75 %
		50 — 74 %
		25 — 49 %
		2.9 — 24 %
		% below national average

Map 29.2. Incidence of Gaelic speakers in 1931

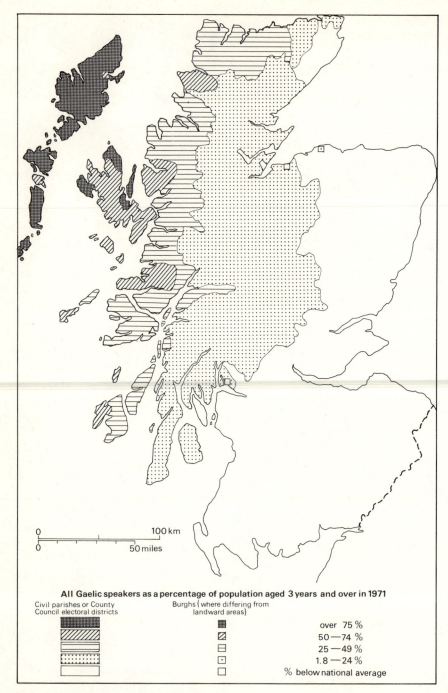

All Gaelic speakers as a percentage of population aged 3 years and over in 1971

Civil parishes or County Council electoral districts

Burghs (where differing from landward areas)

over 75 %
50—74 %
25—49 %
1.8—24 %
% below national average

Map 29.3. Incidence of Gaelic speakers in 1971

some increases in numbers of Gaelic speakers. Further analysis is not possible until the publication of fuller details.

Today native Gaelic-speaking communities are to be found only in the Hebrides and north-west coastal fringes of the Highlands. The Outer Hebrides were over 90 per cent Gaelic-speaking at the time of the 1971 Census, with the exceptions of Benbecula and Stornoway (areas of adventitious incomer settlement). The only other areas over 75 per cent Gaelic-speaking were the northern extremities of Skye, Portree East and Raasay. The only other areas of 50 per cent incidence and over were the remainder of Skye, the Small Isles, Tiree, Colonsay and western Islay in the Inner Hebrides, and the mainland areas of Stoer (Sutherland), Applecross (Wester Ross), Moidart (Inverness), and Ardnamurchan (Argyll). These, then, were the only areas in which a majority of the population aged three years and over spoke Gaelic. The picture though was not one of universal decline of Gaelic over age. A number of areas were more strongly Gaelic in the age groups of youth (5–24 years) than in older age categories: most of northern and western Lewis, Harris, North Uist, South Uist, Barra and the Duirinish West, Kilmuir and Sleat divisions of Skye.

The remainder of the northern and western coastal fringes of the Highland mainland, from Farr in Sutherlandshire to North Lorne in Argyll, together with the remaining Argyllshire islands comprised a zone of between 25–50 per cent incidence of Gaelic. Within this area over half the middle-aged population (45–64 years) was Gaelic speaking and over three-quarters of the elderly (65 years and over).

The area enclosed by the traditional 'Highland Line' of Scottish history still retained almost everywhere an incidence of Gaelic speakers higher than the national average (1.8%). At the time of the 1891 Census this area was almost entirely 75 per cent or more Gaelic-speaking. Decline to 50 per cent or under was a feature of the eastern and southern fringe areas only at that time. A short ride out from any of the larger Scottish cities at the end of the nineteenth century would have brought the traveller into a Gaelic-speaking countryside. Today of course these cities have attracted population from the remoter, declining rural areas and so contain sizeable minority Gaelic-speaking populations. Taken by themselves these dispersed Gaelic speakers would form a 'Gaelic Archipelago' numerically more consequential than the Hebrides themselves – but of course these Lowland Gaelic populations do not constitute true communities. Relatively few of these people are second- or third-generation Gaelic speakers removed from the *Gàidhealtachd* (the Gaelic-speaking area).

The distribution of Scotland's 79,307 Gaelic speakers at the 1981 Census, in terms of the post-1975 local government areas, resulted in well over one-quarter (23,447 or 29.6%) of Scotland's Gaelic speakers residing under the authority of Comhairle nan Eilean in the Western Isles Island Area. Just over one-fifth (16,632 or 21%) of the total lived within the Highland Region, and almost one-third (24,805 or 31.3%) within Strathclyde. The most urbanized of Scotland's new regional authorities thus contained the largest number of Gaelic speakers. Overall, almost two-thirds (50,754 or 64%) of all Gaelic speakers lived in local authority areas which were less than 50 per cent Gaelic-speaking.

The core Gaelic areas however lie within the 'crofting counties' and the survival of the language has been bound up with the distinctive way of life and social institutions of Gaelic Scotland. When the Gaelic social structure of the 'clan system' broke down after the Jacobite Rebellion, the introduction of commercial exploitation of land and resources and the 'Highland clearances', Gaelic society underwent a transformation into the 'crofting community' based upon subsistence agriculture and mutual assistance (MacKinnon, 1974; Hunter, 1976). The system became recognized in law and a government department, the Crofting Commission, was created to supervise and maintain it. The typical traditional Gaelic community is thus based upon an economy of small-scale farming, augmented by fishing, weaving and employment in tertiary occupations. Social structure is not based so much upon divisions of economic class as in urban industrial society. Professional, managerial and technical posts are typically filled by non-Gaelic-speaking incomers, with the exception of teachers and clergy. Local resources generally do not enable all the local children to find work at home. In the past, even secondary education required many to board away from home. In places, some still do. Further and higher education have generally necessitated young people to leave the Highland area altogether. Few have returned to the *Gàidhealtachd*. The 'rooted Gael' may therefore typically be a crofter, fisherman or weaver, a semi- or unskilled manual worker or employee in routine service occupations (see Prattis, 1980 for a study of Lewis). The 'exiled Gael' may, in contrast, be a professional, higher managerial or skilled craftsman. The police, merchant navy, health and educational services have attracted many Gaelic speakers from their home areas and many Gaelic 'exiles' have risen to conspicuous positions in such fields. Traditional attitudes have resulted in younger women being differentially extruded from some of the home Gaelic areas, especially those women in the 15–44 age-range (MacKinnon, 1978: 75–8). Many of these take up work elsewhere in teaching, nursing and catering.

Scottish Gaeldom: its demographic structure

The population structure of the Gaelic-speaking communities is thus substantially distorted in terms of age and sex composition. Migration renders the age pyramid top-heavy in terms of older age groups and produces a 'waistline' or gap in the young to middle-aged cohorts, which are asymmetrically biased with males and depleted of females of child-bearing age.

This is apparent from figure 29.1 and this distribution of population in terms of age and sex clearly indicates that the ability of the Gaelic

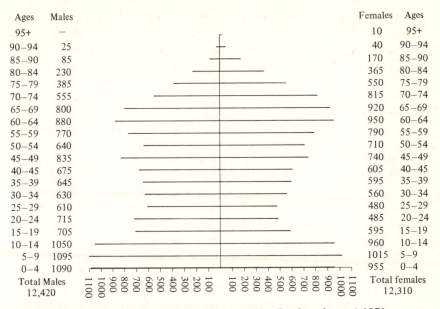

Ages	Males		Females	Ages
95+	–		10	95+
90–94	25		40	90–94
85–90	85		170	85–90
80–84	230		365	80–84
75–79	385		550	75–79
70–74	555		815	70–74
65–69	800		920	65–69
60–64	880		950	60–64
55–59	770		790	55–59
50–54	640		710	50–54
45–49	835		740	45–49
40–45	675		605	40–45
35–39	645		595	35–39
30–34	630		560	30–34
25–29	610		480	25–29
20–24	715		485	20–24
15–19	705		595	15–19
10–14	1050		960	10–14
5–9	1095		1015	5–9
0–4	1090		955	0–4
Total Males	12,420		Total females	12,310

Figure 29.1. Age and sex composition: Western Isles (landward areas) 1971

Source: 1971 Census County reports (aggregation of District Council tables for Lewis D.C., Harris D.C., North Uist D.C., South Uist D.C., and Barra D.C.)

community to renew itself by natural increase is inhibited. There are, of course, other factors which together promote language shift from Gaelic to English: clearances of population in the past and the continued migration today in many areas, economic developments promoting new social uses of English, changeover of population as new activities encourage out-migration of natives and immigration of newcomers, changes in social morale as a community loses confidence in using its ethnic language, and most recently, the widespread use of English in education, the communications media and public life. The cultural retreat model of the *Gàidhealtachd* is the resultant of all such forces but it must be remembered that the 'frontier zone' of culture clash lies not so much along a linguistic boundary or 'Highland Line' as within the mind of every Gaelic speaker (Weinreich, 1953; MacKinnon, 1977: 16). In actuality the line of bilingualism runs through every home and meeting place in Gaelic Scotland.

Gaelic literacy

With the loss of a Gaelic-speaking nobility and gentry in early modern times, the suppression of the bardic schools and orders of Gaelic literati in the early seventeenth century (Thomson, 1968, 1983) and the loss of the older literary language and its associated vocabulary of a 'higher culture' (Jackson, 1951), Gaelic became the repository of a 'little tradition' of vernacular poetry and song. It ceased as a literary language, but in the early nineteenth century the Gaelic Schools' Societies promoted popular education and Gaelic literacy. Gaelic publishing and journalism enjoyed some success during the nineteenth century as a result. However public education, introduced after the 1872 Education Act, neglected Gaelic and until recent decades there was little attempt made through the schools to promote Gaelic literacy. Since the mid 1950s the Inverness-shire and Ross and Cromarty education authorities introduced a bilingual approach as a bridge to English at the initial primary stages in Gaelic-speaking areas, coupled with some attention to Gaelic in successive stages of schooling. Improvements in Gaelic literacy amongst younger people in these areas may be contrasted with the poorer literacy levels in the Gaelic areas of Sutherland, Perthshire and Argyll, as revealed in the 1971 Census report. Gaelic literacy rates amongst 10–19 year-olds in these counties were 0 per cent, 34 per cent and 43 per cent respectively, as compared with 72 per cent in Inverness-shire and 75 per cent in Ross and Cromarty (General Register Office, 1975: 10–18; MacKinnon, 1978: 48–50). Levels of Gaelic literacy comparable with English literacy levels appear to occur only where three factors are present: high incidence of Gaelic speakers, supportive educational policies and adherence to a presbyterian form of protestantism. In 1971 Gaelic literacy levels above 75 per cent in the 15-year-old-and-over age groups occurred only in such protestant areas, which were over 75 per cent Gaelic-speaking and administered by the Inverness-shire and Ross and Cromarty county councils. In the catholic areas of South Uist and Barra Gaelic literacy levels amongst older school-aged children and among young adults were demonstrably lower than those in the core Gaelic protestant areas of the Western Isles: 69 per cent as compared with 85 per cent in the 10–14 age-range, and 68 per cent as compared with 80 per cent in the 15–24 age-range.

The 1971 Census also revealed, on closer analysis, differential Gaelic literacy levels by age and sex. In general, Gaelic literacy increases through the older school ages with a slight diminution amongst young adults, an increase amongst the middle-aged and a further decrease amongst the elderly. This pattern remained true throughout all areas of Scotland except for the very strongly Gaelic protestant areas, within which Gaelic literacy is increased amongst the elderly. The effects of a religious culture emphasizing the reading of scripture and singing of psalms as features of home and congregational worship are apparent.

Almost all areas evidenced larger numbers of females than males claiming ability to speak Gaelic (as indeed there were more females than males within the population generally). However, more Gaelic-speaking women than men claimed the ability to read and write Gaelic: 62 per cent of Gaelic-speaking women in the *Gàidhealtachd*, compared with 57 per cent of the men, claimed reading ability. For ability to write, these proportions were 36 per cent and 32 per cent respectively. In the areas below national average incidence of Gaelic speakers in the population the proportions were lower, but of similar patterning: for Gaelic reading ability 39 per cent and 35 per cent respectively, and for writing 28 per cent and 25 per cent (MacKinnon, 1978: 41–3). Gaelic-speaking women may be regarded as being more likely to be literate in their mother tongue than men. It would be interesting to know whether in other respects women evidenced greater language skills or more supportive attitudes towards the language and culture than did men.

Attitudes towards Gaelic

In order to assess whether women do, in fact, support the language better than men, a national sample would be required, and to date no national survey of Gaelic has been attempted on the lines of the Irish Languages Attitudes Survey, Canadian Non-Official Languages Survey (O'Bryan *et al.*, 1975), surveys of Welsh in Wales or ethnic languages in England. However, the author has undertaken more limited surveys in Harris, Barra and Skye as well as a national opinion poll in Scotland as a whole relating to attitudes towards Gaelic (MacKinnon 1977, 1982; MacKinnon and MacDonald, 1980). The difficulty in interpreting results from these studies lies in the fact that migration from the more strongly Gaelic areas means that many of the more socially mobile people do not remain within the community and are not available to be contacted in the study, and the differential extrusion of the sexes renders comparisons especially difficult to make. In the study of Harris undertaken in 1972–4 (MacKinnon, 1977) it was found that language loyalty increased with age and was stronger amongst men than women. The least language loyal of all age and sex categories was in fact that of younger women aged between 18 and 39. A study of the younger Harris women boarding away at schools and technical colleges indicated very strongly supportive attitudes towards Gaelic language and culture. Since few of these women returned permanently to their home communities, a distortion of the community language loyalty profile is a clear result (MacKinnon, 1977: 75, 96–134). This factor has crucial implications for both the demographic viability of the home community and for the transmission of ethnic language and culture. There is a lack of young women of child-bearing age in the Gaelic communities, and those that are left are the least supportive of all groups towards the language and culture.

Attitude surveys carried out in southern Skye, North Uist and Barra in 1981 produced a very similar patterning of loyalty towards Gaelic in terms of age and sex categories (MacKinnon, 1982). Again the younger women of child-bearing age evidenced the least favourable attitudes towards the use of Gaelic in local and public life.

Occupational class has proved a difficult form of social categorization with which to compare abilities to speak, read and write Gaelic or to compare attitudes towards language use. As we have seen, the whole occupational spectrum and ability range may not be present within the local community, neither is economic occupation a particularly meaningful social categorization within these communities. Some relationship between occupation and language loyalty was found in the earlier Harris study (MacKinnon, 1977). The highest loyalty scores were evidenced amongst the 'agricultural' group, i.e. the crofting core of the local community. Also rating highly were Gaelic-speaking public employees. Unemployed and manual groups were less loyal, with the professional and technical groups ranking marginally lower and the commercial group lowest of all (MacKinnon, 1977: 161).

Social surveys undertaken in South Harris and Barra in 1976–8 enabled a more detailed study to be effected of the relationship of loyalties towards the Gaelic language and its associated culture with salient sociological characteristics of its speakers. Indices of language and cultural loyalties were analysed by sex, age, educational level, occupational type, religious adherence and voting record. No significant differences of levels of loyalty resulted between the sexes overall, but there were definite associations with age: older groups evidencing higher loyalty levels. In terms of educational level, the highest loyalty scores were associated with respondents whose education did not proceed beyond the junior secondary level. (The study was unable of course to assess the loyalties of local people who had left these communities for senior secondary, further or higher education and who had not returned.) Of the religious groupings, Church of Scotland adherents registered the lowest loyalty scores, whilst Roman Catholic, Free Church and Free Presbyterian adherents evidenced similar and higher levels of support for the language and culture. On the whole there were no salient differences resulting from political affiliations, except that in South Harris the higher cultural loyalties were associated with Labour rather than Scottish Nationalist Party support. Outside the *Gàidhealtachd* SNP voters tended to be the most supportive towards Gaelic (MacKinnon, 1982) but in the Western Isles and Skye it must be remembered that traditional loyalties towards Gaelic tend to be associated with the political parties which have been traditionally supported by the local community core: Labour and Liberal.

An opinion poll and attitude survey undertaken nationally in Scotland in 1981 evidenced a wide measure of support for Gaelic amongst a predominantly non-Gaelic-speaking population (MacKinnon, 1982). A clear majority, of 54% (or 67% if 'don't knows' are eliminated) favoured official recognition of Gaelic. Almost as many, 46% (or 55%) supported expenditure of more public money in support of Gaelic; 49 per cent (64%) supported the promotion of Gaelic throughout Scotland as a whole; 47 per cent (71%) supported the provision of more programmes for Gaelic learners on the media. Eliminating the 20 per cent of 'don't knows', the sample was almost equally divided on whether there should be more or less radio and television time in Gaelic. A bilingual policy for public signs, notices and advertisements was supported by 42 per cent (68%), and over two-thirds of the respondents, 70 per cent (82%), agreed that Gaelic should be available in schools throughout Scotland.

Gaelic usage patterns

The diglossic character of the present-day Gaelic communities apportions domains or speech situations within which Gaelic or English may predominate, or within which there may be a nearly equal use of either. In the 1972–4 Harris survey, respondents were asked whether they used Gaelic always, both languages or English always in some 55 typical speech situations. It was possible to assess how far across the spectrum of local social life each language extended. The concepts of 'dominance configuration' and 'balance of bilingualism' were felt to be unsatisfactory in describing this situation, within which bilingual speakers felt the legitimacy of both their languages in different aspects of social life. These respondents used a language of local social or community solidarity in the speech situations of personal, familial and communal domains whereas a language of wider communication or bureaucratic power was used in certain transactional, commercial and administrative domains. The term 'demesne extension' was proposed for this concept which utilized language as an index to illustrate the extent of social networks which were locally, as opposed to externally, controlled. At the stronger end of the local or Gaelic 'demesne' 96 per cent of respondents claimed to use Gaelic always when speaking to older relations and parents. Almost as strongly Gaelic were exchanges between other family members, religious situations and crofting business (92–68%). Still very high were exchanges with other adults and children within the community and at work (66–54% of respondents claiming use of Gaelic always). Exactly half of the respondents claimed to use Gaelic always when discussing a child with a teacher – and this situation might serve as the boundary between the two 'demesnes'. Just within the predominatingly English 'demesne' came dreaming (49%) and more substantially English were exchanges in local clubs, societies and council business, swearing, counting, dealings with inspectors, telephone operators, banks, police, doctors and letter writing.

Intergenerational language shift from Gaelic to English has occurred in most – but not all – of these speech situations. As between the oldest age groups (70 years-and-over) and the youngest (18–29 years) there were smaller declines in usage of Gaelic always for familial purposes (with spouse and other family members) from 94 per cent of respondents to 68 per cent, and for communal purposes (work, township matters, quarrels, church affairs) from 84 per cent to 55 per cent of respondents. Larger shifts occurred for intrapersonal matters (dreaming, praying, swearing, counting) from 70 per cent to 43 per cent, for transactional matters (at garages, shops, post office and on public transport) from 75 per cent to 43 per cent and in official business (local government, dealings with teachers, district clerk and crofting assessor) from 79 per cent to 43 per cent. Gaelic usage thus stood up best in the familial and communal domains and was weakest in intrapersonal, transactional and official domains. There were still strong social pressures to maintain Gaelic in communal affairs in Harris at that time, but church and work were two fields within which there was a pronounced shift towards English amongst younger respondents. However, the rules enjoining use of Gaelic or English in particular fields or domains are weaker amongst the young – and there were shifts in favour of Gaelic usage amongst younger respondents in dealings with the bank, telephone operators, police, inspectors, local councillors, at public entertainments and with a workman at the door.

The surveys of South Harris and Barra in 1976–8 (MacKinnon and MacDonald, 1980) asked respondents to report on levels of Gaelic usage in their own families of origin in comparison with their own circumstances at the time of the survey. In Barra, 86 per cent, and in South Harris 79 per cent of the respondents reported on Gaelic always being used in their family of origin for conversations with spouse, at meals, between parents and children, with friends and visitors, when angry or excited, for family prayers and church, and between children. Considerably lower incidence of use of Gaelic was reported for public entertainments (81% in Barra, 57% in Harris) and helping children with homework (47% and 16% respectively) in respondents' families of origin. Present-day Gaelic usage levels in the respondents' own families at the time of survey were rather lower for conversations with spouse and at meals (some 70–76% of respondents), somewhat lower still between parents and children, with friends and visitors and when angry or excited (68–58% of respondents), much lower for family prayers or at church and between children (61–36%), at public entertainments (53% in Barra, 23% in Harris), and least of all for helping children with homework (16% and 8% in the two communities). In terms of language shift, Gaelic usage levels were lower among younger age groups, especially in Harris; however, although language shift has proceeded further in Harris it seems to have stabilized more in the present generation than in Barra. Barra evidenced a virtually consistent higher rate of Gaelic usage than Harris in all these instances. Intergenerational maintenance of Gaelic usage was significantly associated with downward social mobility.

Cultural transmission

A study similar to that described above was also undertaken of the transmission of popular entertainment skills and cultural practices (performance as musician, singer, dancer, storyteller, attendance at *céilidhs*, concerts, listening to Gaelic programmes and recordings, reading Gaelic books and periodicals, and writing any Gaelic at all). There was a lower incidence of these skills on Harris than in Barra, doubtless as the result of contrasted religious cultures: calvinist and catholic. Fifteen per cent of Harris respondents reported involvement in popular entertainment skills, as compared with 27 per cent of the

Barra respondents. Differences were salient in terms of family of origin (58%
of the Harris respondents reporting these skills in their family of origin
compared with 86% in Barra). An intergenerational reproduction rate of
these skills comprised 28 per cent of respondents' families of origin passing
on these skills to the respondent in Harris, compared with 58 per cent in
Barra. Such skills were always transmitted through the family. There were
no cases of respondents developing these skills independently of their presence
in the family of origin.

Intergenerational change in the other cultural practices were also in contrast between the two communities. Only 31 per cent of the Harris respondents whose families went to *céilidhs* and concerts did so themselves, as
compared with 45 per cent in Barra. For those listening to Gaelic programmes
and recordings there was an intergenerational increase to 145 per cent in
Barra and 121 per cent in Harris. The practice of reading Gaelic books and
periodicals decayed to 79 per cent in Barra but only to 84 per cent in Harris,
whilst those writing any Gaelic decayed by 25 per cent in Barra but in contrast
by 41 per cent in Harris.

The survey also asked respondents to state how important they felt various
cultural institutions or innovations to be for encouraging Gaelic in their areas.
The two institutions regarded as 'very important' for the future of Gaelic by
the greatest number of respondents were the broadcasting media (by 77% of
Barra respondents and 68% of Harris respondents) and the schools (by 70%
and 62% respectively). Of moderate importance were regarded the establishment of summer schools for Gaelic learners (51%, 63%) and Gaelic cultural
centres (45%, 50%). Respondents attached least importance to the presence of
Gaelic on public signs and notices (only 27% of respondents in Barra and 25%
in Harris regarded this as very important for the future of the language).

Gaelic in official and public life: old stock – new shoots

When the Gaelic poet George Campbell Hay wrote these lines in the 1940s few
might have shared his optimism for the language:

Thalla, Eudòchais, is beachdaich.
  A' chraobh a leag iad an uiridh –
seall! – cha n-fhaic thu 'stoc am bliadhna
  aig lionmhorachd nam fiùran uime ...
          (Deòrsa mac Iain Dheòrsa: 'Stoc is Failleanan')

(Come, Despondency, gaze on this sign and ponder.
  The tree they felled in the Spring of the year that is gone –
look! seek for the stump – this Spring you cannot find it
      for the young shoots around it, so close have they grown ...
          George Campbell Hay: 'Old Stump and Young Shoots')

Nevertheless it has been the poet's vision which has prevailed. As concern for

Gaelic faded out of public consciousness in the aftermath of war, there was little to hold out the prospect of a Gaelic renaissance, yet four decades later prospects for the language have awakened and it is an issue which has come into the forefront of affairs, in the Highlands at least – an issue with political as well as cultural dimensions (see for example, Thompson, 1972).

The principal Gaelic language loyalty organization An Comunn Gàidhealach came into being in 1891 in the wake of numbers of Highland district and clan societies in the Scottish cities, in order to give a more specifically Gaelic focus in public affairs. Earlier, there had been Gaelic societies, which still continue, in London (from 1777) and Inverness (from 1871). Apart from some activity in publishing, education and as a pressure group of a somewhat mild and apolitical character, its principal efforts were until recently concerned with promoting the annual National *Mòd* – a cultural festival copied from the model of the Welsh *Eisteddfod*. Since the appointment of its first professional director in the mid-1960s it has become more effective as a pressure group and has been active within the Gaelic areas themselves in many ways. It had become very clear by this time that the cultivation of Gaelic in universities, its admission as a specific subject in schools, the cultural activities of voluntary bodies and a token presence (about $1\frac{3}{4}$ hours per week) on BBC radio were insufficient to ensure a continued place for the language in public life. Gaelic was scarcely recognized in public administration and by the early 1950s Gaelic publishing had reached its lowest ebb ever.

However, in 1952 a new all-Gaelic periodical *Gairm* commenced and a new publishing venture followed from it. During the 1950s and 1960s the Committee on Bilingualism of the Scottish Council for Research in Education developed concern for Gaelic (SCRE, 1961) and stimulated research and publishing initiatives. A committee for school texts got underway during the 1960s, and in the 1970s a state-funded Gaelic Books Council and a commercial Gaelic book club. In education, improved examination schemes for natives and learners were developed. Commercial Gaelic recordings developed considerably at this time from initiatives by smaller companies and the larger groups. An Comunn brought out a Gaelic course on LP records around 1967 and this was followed a few years later by a commercial audio course.

The 1970s witnessed an increased pace in Gaelic cultural revival. There was a modest increase in broadcasting time and, with the introduction of VHF, some expansion of the Gaelic services occurred, but the transfer to that channel meant that many Gaelic areas were deprived of Gaelic radio altogether. BBC television introduced a weekly current affairs feature in Gaelic from time to time, but it was not until the opening of the Lewis transmitter that a more truly regular Gaelic series started: *Cuir Car*, a Gaelic children's programme on Saturday mornings on ITV, followed by a regular weekly news programme *Seachd Làithean* – also on ITV. The BBC did however empanel an official Gaelic Advisory Committee which reported on the future of Gaelic broadcasting (MacDonald, 1979) and created local 'opt-out' stations in

Inverness (Radio Highland/Radio air a' Ghàidhealtachd) and Stornoway (Radio nan Eilean) in 1976 and 1979, respectively. Although both stations carry much of their station output in Gaelic they only broadcast for an hour or two a day as an alternative to BBC Radio Scotland. Nevertheless, even this modest type of local radio has stimulated Gaelic affairs, brought back able young Gaels to the *Gàidhealtachd* – and even has a 'first' or two to its credit. The world's first intercontinental live entertainment programme by satellite was a Gaelic Hogmanay *céilidh* linking the Hebrides and Cape Breton Island Nova Scotia at the turn of the decade, and a regular two-way Gaelic international programme was established with Radio na Gaeltachta in Donegal. It is tempting to think that these advances in Gaelic public service broadcasting followed quickly upon a series of public demonstrations organized by the newly-formed Gaelic students' organization COGA (Comhairle Oileanaich Gàidhealach Alba) in 1974–75 – the first ever on behalf of Gaelic. Their success both in outflanking the Gaelic 'Establishment' and in forcing its pace, as well as in getting results from a public body, deserves commemoration in Gaelic history. In 1979 the BBC provided an ambitious and well produced Gaelic learners' series on television, *Can Seo*, together with series on radio for school and adult learners. ITV also ran a number of series *About Gaelic* which were valuable in terms of public information.

The reform of Scottish local government which took effect in 1975 divided the *Gàidhealtachd* between a most-purpose Island Area Authority of the Western Isles, which took a Gaelic title as its official name: Comhairle nan Eilean (the name of the old parliament of the Lordship of the Isles), and two-tier regional authorites dividing the Highland mainland between them: Highland and Strathclyde regional councils. In the Western Isles the new authority undertook a public consultation through its 'Rae Report' on a policy of bilingualism in administration and public affairs, and in fact introduced a moderate and permissive bilingual policy in its early years of operation. As an education authority it quickly moved to establish a bilingual education project jointly funded with the Scottish Education Department, and in 1978 the project widened to include all island primary schools. Unfortunately, the move to extend the scheme into the secondary schools in 1980–1 was vitiated by council indecision and vacillation and by a change of heart in the SED. The project developed spin-offs in the commissioning of a new Gaelic books series for children, *Cliath*, using contemporary spoken Gaelic, a Gaelic publishing venture, Acair, a community video and film unit Cinema Sgìre in 1976, a travelling repertory group Fir Chlis in 1978 and a community education project assisted by the Van Leer Foundation earlier in that year, with units in Lewis, Harris and South Uist, Proisect Muinntir nan Eilean. Local government expenditure cuts resulted in the curtailment of Cinema Sgìre and Fir Chlis early in 1981. Meanwhile a new Gaelic newspaper commenced in 1977, *Crùisgean*. This was the first since *MacTalla* ceased publication in 1904 in Sydney, Nova Scotia.

A Gaelic college, run on semi-independent lines with assistance from the Scottish Education Department, charitable trusts and Stirling University, had developed on Skye during the 1970s – chiefly as a centre for summer school courses, special events and conferences. It undertook a feasibility study between 1978 and 1980 into the possibility of developing Gaelic-medium higher education courses. In 1980–1 it was assisted by the Highlands and Islands Development Board with a grant for course development and running expenses, and in 1983 began full-time courses.

Also on Skye, demands for bilingual education schemes in the schools similar to those in the Western Isles led to the Director of Education for Highland Region circularizing parents in 1978, and to the appointment of peripatetic staff for Gaelic in Skye and south-west Ross. Similar demands were subsequently met in Ardnamurchan, Badenoch, Inverness, Easter and Wester Ross, Sutherland and Mull (the latter area of course now under Strathclyde). In Perthshire, Tayside Education Authority has provided Gaelic instruction in 13 of its primary, and in two of its secondary, schools. There are a number of articles and books which have dealt with Gaelic and education; among them are Smith (1948), Campbell (1950), Nisbet (1963), MacLeod (1966), MacLeod (1974) and Mulholland (1981).

In the run-up to the general election of 1979 the political parties awoke to the sensitivity of Gaelic as an election issue. The SNP announced its policy at New Year (having previously 'leaked' a Gaelic version to the periodical *Gairm*). Labour announced the creation of a working party on Gaelic and the Conservatives promised greater support through Mr Whitelaw during an official visit to An Comunn headquarters. The Liberals issued a statement shortly before the commencement of the election campaign. An Comunn had in fact been involved in a parliamentary lobby since 1978 and had attracted about 50 MPs interested in furthering the Gaelic cause. A Gaelic 'parliamentary group' was officially constituted at Westminster. Gaelic had become an issue. After the 1979 elections representations were made through MPs at Westminster and through MEPs in Europe. In 1981 Donald Stewart (MP for the Western Isles and parliamentary SNP leader) had the chance to present a private members' bill and chose to introduce a Gaelic (Miscellaneous Provisions) Bill to give official recognition to the language, to define Gaelic-speaking areas within which the 1918 'Gaelic clause' (obliging education authorities to provide for the teaching of Gaelic in Gaelic-speaking areas) must operate, to secure a comparable place for Gaelic in broadcasting as had been secured for Welsh, and to provide for the right to use Gaelic in court proceedings. The Bill was talked out after a five-hour filibuster on Friday, 13 February 1981, and subsequent attempts to introduce similar provisions in the Education and Broadcasting Bills in the ensuing weeks were unsuccessful. These setbacks for Gaelic did, however, have the effect of provoking a civil disobedience campaign on similar lines to the Welsh road-signs campaign through a new activist organization, Ceartas (Justice), which led to arrests and confiscations by the police in August 1981. Another militant group, Strì (Struggle), threatened a television licence campaign on similar lines to that in Wales. Subsequently, Gaelic was given recognition in the Nationality Act (of 1982) together with English and Welsh, as one of the languages in which an applicant for British citizenship must be fluent.

The effervescence of the Gaelic scene at this time, coinciding with setbacks for the Gaelic theatre, cinema and video units in the Western Isles, may raise questions for the future. There has been no official enquiry into Gaelic problems as has been enjoyed in Wales through the Hughes-Parry, Gittens, Bowen and Welsh language Commissions. However the Highlands and Islands Development Board constituted a Gaelic 'think-tank', or advisory committee, in 1981 charged with producing an authoritative report on what needs to be done to secure the prospects for the language. The freelance broadcaster and researcher Martin MacDonald was commissioned to produce the report which was published in 1983. In 1981–2 Strì assisted in the formation of a national Gaelic playgroup organization.

At no time in recent centuries has there been such a welling up of good writing of prose, verse and drama in Gaelic than over the last decade or two. Neither has there been such an awakening of possibilities for an enhanced place for the language in public life, education, popular entertainment and the media. There has begun to be an appreciation that administrative and language planning policies may even secure the continuance of the language in Scottish and Highland life. Such efforts might even succeed!

Ar caint s ar cultur, car sealain
  ged rachadh an leagadh buileach
cuiridh am freumhan s an seann stoc dhiubh
  failleanan snodhach is duilleach.
          (Deòrsa mac Iain Dheòrsa: 'Stoc is Failleanan')

(Our speech and culture – Despondency, consider –
  though they be brought low for a time and forgotten by men,
the old stock still has its roots, and the roots will bring us
  shoots and sap, branches and leaves again.
          George Campbell Hay: 'Old Stump and Young Shoots')

REFERENCES

Aitken, A.J. and McArthur, T. 1979. *Languages of Scotland.* Edinburgh: Chambers.
Campbell, J.L. 1950. *Gaelic in Scottish education and life.* Edinburgh: Wand A.K. Johnston.
Census Scotland 1981. 1982. *Information Bulletin on Scottish Gaelic.* Ref CEN81 SB1. Edinburgh: Census Office.
Chapman, M. 1978. *The Gaelic vision in Scottish culture.* London: Croom Helm.
Comhairle nan Eilean 1977. *Consultative document on bilingualism* ('Rae Report'). Stornoway.

—— 1977. Proisect Foghlum Da-Chananach – *Report*. Stornoway.

Committee on Irish Language Attitudes Research 1975. *Report*. Dublin: Oifig Dhiolta Foilseachán Rialtais.

Durkacz, V. E. 1983. *The decline of the Celtic languages*. Edinburgh: John Donald.

Ennew, J. 1980. *The Western Isles today*. Cambridge: CUP.

General Register Office 1975. *Census 1971 Scotland Gaelic report*. Edinburgh: HMSO.

Hunter, J. 1976. *The making of the crofting community*. Edinburgh: John Donald.

Jackson, K. H. 1951. Common Gaelic. *Proceedings of the British Academy* XXXVII.

MacDonald, M. 1979. *Consultative draft of survey on Gaelic and broadcasting*. Inverness: An Comunn Gàidhealach.

—— 1983. *Cor na Gàidhlig – language, community and development in the Gaelic situation*. Inverness: Highlands and Islands Development Board.

MacKinnon, K. 1974. *The lion's tongue*. Inverness: Club Leabhar.

—— 1977. *Language, education and social processes in a Gaelic community*. London: Routledge and Kegan Paul.

—— 1978. *Gaelic in Scotland 1971: some sociological and demographic considerations of the census report for Gaelic*. Hatfield: The Hatfield Polytechnic.

—— 1982. *Scottish opinion on Gaelic: a report on a national attitude survey for An Comunn Gàidhealach undertaken in 1981*. Hatfield: The Hatfield Polytechnic.

MacKinnon, K. and MacDonald, M. 1980. *Ethnic communities: the transmission of language and culture in Harris and Barra, Report to the SSRC*. London: Social Science Research Council.

MacLeod, F. 1974. Gaelic: out of date model slows drive to bilingualism. In *Education in the North*. Aberdeen: the College of Education.

MacLeod, M. 1966. Gaelic in Highland education. *Transactions of the Gaelic Society of Inverness*. XLIII.

Mulholland, G. 1981. *The struggle for a language – Gaelic in education*. Edinburgh: Rank and File.

Nisbet, J. 1963. Bilingualism and the school. *Scottish Gaelic Studies* X, part I. Aberdeen: University of Aberdeen.

O'Bryan, K. G., Reitz, J. G. and Kuplowska, O. 1975. *Non-official languages – a study in Canadian multiculturalism*. Ottawa: Minister Responsible for Multiculturalism.

Prattis, J. I. 1980. *Industrialisation and minority language loyalty: the example of Lewis*. Ottawa: Carleton University.

Scottish Council for Research in Education 1961. *Gaelic speaking children in Highland Schools*. London: University of London Press.

Smith, C. A. 1948. *Mental testing of Hebridean children in Gaelic and English*. London: University of London Press.

Thompson, F. G. 1972. Gaelic in politics. *Transactions of the Gaelic Society Inverness* XLVII.

Thomson, D. S. 1968. Gaelic learned orders and literati in medieval Scotland. *Scottish Studies* 12, part I, 57–78.

—— (ed.) 1976. *Gàidhlig an an Albainn/Gaelic in Scotland*. Glasgow: Gairm.

—— 1983. *Companion to Gaelic studies*. Oxford: Blackwell.

Weinreich, U. 1953. *Languages in contact*. The Hague: Mouton.

30

Scots and English in Scotland

A.J. AITKEN

Introduction

Nearly all Scots of the present day command some variety of English and most Scots have it as their native language. In this chapter we are concerned only with the varieties of English and Lowland Scots native to those parts of Scotland which lie east and south of the 'Highland Line', the Scottish Lowlands. For a brief discussion of the Highland Line and a map showing the limits of the Lowland area, see chapter 6. For the other indigenous languages of modern Scotland – Scots Gaelic, still spoken, mostly in the Hebrides, by 1.5 per cent of the country's total population of 5.2 million, and for the 'post-Gaelic' or 'Hebridean' and 'Highland' English which accompanies or has succeeded it in the Hebridean and Highland areas in which it still is or formerly was spoken, see chapters 29 and 9, respectively.

Northern English in earlier Scotland: the origins of 'Scots'

The first speakers of an Anglo-Saxon language, the ancestor of Lowland Scots, arrived in what is now southern Scotland early in the seventh century, as a northern offshoot of the Anglian peoples then comprising the kingdom of Bernicia or northern Northumbria. The areas which these first English speakers in Scotland occupied, as defined by place names containing 'early' Anglo-Saxon place-name elements, consisted of a wide swathe of what is now south-eastern and southern Scotland, then and later known as Lothian, along with less extensive settlements along Solway and, perhaps rather later, in Kyle in mid-Ayrshire.

Before the twelfth century the English-speaking part of Scotland was limited to these south-eastern and southern areas (except, perhaps, for the royal court of King Malcolm III and his queen, Margaret, a princess of the ancient royal house of Wessex, whom he married about 1070). There is also evidence, from chronicle record and place names (see Nicolaisen, 1976: 121 f) that by the tenth and eleventh centuries the Gaelic language was in use throughout the whole of Scotland, not excluding English-speaking Lothian, though no doubt the longer established northern English continued to be the

dominant language there. In origin Gaelic was the native language of the
Scots of Alba or Scotland, the kingdom centred north of the Forth and Clyde,
whose kings in the tenth and eleventh centuries also gained dominion of the
more southerly parts of an expanded Scottish kingdom. Brythonic or British
(i.e. Welsh) in the south, Pictish in the east and Scandinavian in the west and
north also contributed importantly to the place nomenclature of Scotland.

Until the late eleventh century the trend was toward the linguistic dominance of Scotland by Gaelic. The reversal of this trend followed the accession
of the 'Normanized' kings of Scotland, particularly King David I (1124–53)
and his immediate successors. Thereafter place names and other indications
show a spread of the English-speaking area beyond the confines of Lothian,
first to other parts of southern Scotland, then in the late twelfth and thirteenth
centuries to eastern Scotland north of the Forth. This expansion of English
speaking in Scotland accompanies, and is evidently closely associated with,
the acquisition of lands in Scotland by Anglo-Norman and Flemish land-
owners, with the establishment in the areas concerned of new monastic houses
with monks from England and France, and with the foundation of new royal
and baronial 'burghs' peopled with immigrant burgesses from England and
elsewhere, whose *lingua franca* was northern English (see especially the discussions and maps of mottes, religious houses and burghs in McNeill and
Nicholson, 1975). So began the long retreat of Gaelic before varieties of
English, a retreat which, despite strenuous efforts on the part of some Gaels to
arrest it, seems still to be continuing today.

By the fourteenth century the dominant spoken tongue of all ranks of
Scotsmen east and south of the Highland Line was the northern dialect of
English known to its users first as 'Inglis' (or 'English') but later (from 1494)
also as 'Scots'), and to modern philologists as 'Older Scots'. By the eighteenth
century the same tongue had superseded the old Norse or Norn speech
formerly spoken under the Norse earls in Caithness, Orkney and Shetland (see
chapter 22). By the second half of the fifteenth century Older Scots had become
the principal literary and record language of the Scottish nation, having successfully competed in this function with Latin. Hence in the later fifteenth and
the sixteenth centuries there were two national languages in use in Britain,
metropolitan Tudor English in the kingdom of England, and metropolitan
Older Scots in the kingdom of Scotland. Linguistically these two were close
relatives, representing respectively southern and northern dialects of 'English',
the tongue descended (with many transmutations) from that of the Anglo-
Saxon invaders of fifth-century Britain. But they were, of course, far from identical. Metropolitan Tudor English was the sixteenth century ancestor of modern
Standard English, supplying the 'English' component of table 30.1, below.
Older Scots (an exhaustive record of which is supplied by the *Dictionary of the
Older Scottish Tongue*) is the ancestor of the modern Lowland Scots dialects,
and supplies the 'Scots' (i.e. the non-standard) component of table 30.1.

In the seventeenth and eighteenth centuries considerable numbers of land-hungry Scots, chiefly from the western and south-western shires from Clyde southwards, settled in large enclaves in northern Ireland, in the Plantation of Ulster. As a result the speech of their present-day descendants shares many of the features of Scots described in chapter 6 and indeed must be reckoned as dialects of Scots (see further chapter 7).

The current situation: options and varieties

Had Older Scots retained its former autonomy from English, we might have had in Britain today a language situation resembling that of modern Scandinavia, with Scots occupying a position like that of, say, Swedish, and (Standard) English that of Danish; or (perhaps a closer parallel) Scots might be occupying the position of Catalan, (Standard) English that of Castilian Spanish. But Scots did not retain its autonomy. The attractions of the great literature of late medieval and early modern southern English, the fact that the Scottish Reformed Church, before and after the Reformation of 1560, depended upon Tudor English versions of the Bible and the Psalter, and other political and social influences predictable from the history of the times (the Union of the Crowns of the two nations came in 1603), led to the adoption by Scottish writers, from about the middle of the sixteenth century, of a 'mixed dialect' in which both Older Scots and Tudor English equivalent forms (e.g. both *guid* and *good*, both *hale* and *whole*, both *kirk* and *church*, both *ken* and *know*) co-existed as options. Through the late sixteenth and the seventeenth centuries the non-Scottish options gained in popularity over their Scottish equivalents. And this 'mixed' form of literary Scots began in the seventeenth century to be followed by a 'mixed dialect' of a similar sort on the lips of the Scottish aristocracy, by now in frequent communication, and at times inter-marriage, with their English compeers. (For a much fuller account of these events and of the later history of Scots and English in Scotland, see Aitken 1979a.) So there arose the modern Scots linguistic situation, modelled in table 30.1. This model offers a macrocosmic sample of the total body of vocabulary and morphology in principle available to all native Scottish speakers, and a microcosmic view of the options accessible to each individual speaker. It will be seen that it contains a large 'common core' of invariants (column 3) and variants or options of selectional phonology and of vocabulary and grammar in the outer columns. Further examples of the various categories are to be found in chapter 6.

Being only two-dimensional, the model has inevitable limitations, such as its failure to incorporate a regional dimension (on which also see chapter 6 *passim*). It also ignores the important fact that the different items which make up the totality of choices vary individually and collectively in their social and stylistic markedness between groups of speakers and for each individual speaker of the 5 million or so speakers concerned. For many middle-class speakers column 4 and 5 items are stylistically unmarked, whereas most items of columns 1 and 2 are stylistically marked as 'Scotticisms' (see chapter 6, page 107) and some in other ways (e.g. also as 'vulgarisms' chapter 6, page 108). Some working-class speakers have, however, rather different, and to

Table 30.1. *A model of modern Scottish speech*

'Scots'		'English'		
1	2	3	4	5
bairn	hame	name	home	child
brae	hale	hole	whole	slope
kirk	mare	before	more	church
ken	puir	soup	poor	know
darg	muin	room	moon	job of work
cuit	yuis (n.)	miss	use (n.)	ankle
kenspeckle	yaize (v.)	raise	use (v.)	conspicuous
birl	cauld		cold	spin
girn	auld	young	old	whine
mind	coo	row /rʌu/	cow	remember
sort	hoose	Loudon	house	mend
	loose	winter	louse	
	louse /lʌus/	feckless	loose	
ay /əi/	pay /pəi/	bite /bəit/	pay	always
gey /gəi/	way /wəi/	tide /təid/	way	very
kye /ka·e/		tie /ta·e/		cows
een	deed /did/	feed	dead	eyes
shuin	dee /di:/	see	die	shoes
deave /di:v/	scart	leave	scratch	deafen, vex
gaed	twaw, twae	agree	two	went
ben the hoose	no /no:/	he	not	in or into the inner part of the house
	-na, -nae	his	-n't	
		they		
		some		
	/ʌ/ (= I)	I		
	/o/ (= of)	of /ʌv/		

'Obligatory covert
    Scotticisms'
Most of word-order
Morphology
Syntax
Phonology (system
    and rules of
    realization)

some extent converse, stylistic values. The localized and non-standard items, the Scotticisms, have for long been regarded as appropriate to 'lower-class' speech or highly informal middle-class speech styles, and occur chiefly there (and in certain literary settings such as 'broad Scots' lyric, comic and satiric verse and Scots drama, both the realist and the farcical).

Though the matter remains uninvestigated, it is possible to suggest tentative groupings of speakers in terms of their habitual responses to the sets of choices offered by the model.

At one extreme there are those numerous speakers who operate fairly exclusively from columns 3 to 5, except that they employ both 'obligatory covert' and sporadic 'stylistic overt' Scotticisms (see chapter 6) and they do this in one of the Scottish accents. Hereafter we shall term this variety, as realized with one of the Scottish accents described below on page 524, Scottish Standard English and when, most usually, it is realized with one of the accents favoured by middle-class or 'educated' speakers it will be termed Educated Scottish Standard English. Of all Scottish speakers, users of Educated Scottish Standard English display the smallest stylistic range between their informal and formal styles. Scottish Standard English is commonly heard also from lower middle- and working-class speakers in public speaking and when addressing middle-class interlocutors. This is our group 1 variety.

A second group of middle-class speakers (our group 2), perhaps with the men outnumbering the women, along with many or most of the lower middle-class and some of those whom some sociologists have dubbed 'respectable working-class', operate much less exclusively, though still preponderantly, from columns 3 to 5. Such speakers make moderately frequent, though inconsistent, recourse to column 2, though more often for function words including 'weak forms', such as [ʌ] for *I*, *-na* or *nae* for *-n't*, *no* for *not*, *-in* rather than *-ing* (pres.part.), than for content words. Speakers of this group have recourse to column 1 much less frequently than to column 2, except in 'stylistic overt Scotticism' function.

A more frequent recourse to column 2 content-words (*hame* for *home*, *hoose* for *house*) and some column 1 items, with quite regular and consistent preference for some items from both of these, but inconsistency for many other items, is characteristic of informal working-class speech. Such speakers may be thought of as straddling the table but with a bias towards the Scottish (columns 1 and 2) side of it. These we shall call group 3.

A small number of working-class speakers, chiefly elderly, from some rural districts, are rather more consistently Scottish than this. They may be thought of as based firmly on columns 1 to 3. Some of these may be mono-dialectal: they fail to adjust their styles towards columns 4 and 5 when addressing non-local interlocutors or in more formal settings as most other Scottish speakers do. These speakers supply our group 4.

Speakers of groups 1 and 2, more unequivocally speakers of group 1, are held to speak what they and other Scots call 'English', though, as we have seen, they pronounce this in a Scottish manner. Speakers of groups 3 and 4, especially the latter, are described by their compatriots, and often by themselves, as speakers of 'Scots', of 'broad Scots', even of 'good Scots' or, sometimes, simply as 'broad' speakers.

There is another variety of Scots. This is the imaginary 'Ideal Scots' which stands as an ideal of perfect performance in 'Scots' for the 'best' speakers and writers. A performer in this variety would select columns 1 and 2 items with total consistency, never permitting his discourse to be diluted with column 4 and 5 options. It need hardly be added that, a few literary *tours de force* (*Johnny Gibb of Gushetneuk*?, *Eppie Elrick*?) apart, this variety exists only in the imagination of its advocates, who are however, more often than not, themselves Educated Scottish Standard English speakers: no one actually speaks, and few even write, with this consistency to the Scottish options, not even group 4 speakers.

Speakers of all four groups vary widely in the size and make-up of their repertories of column 1 and column 2 items: the 'educated' Scot, more or less well versed in Scottish vernacular literature, will command a different list of Scots words and forms from that at the disposal of the rural peasant, and the lists of both of these are likely to be more extensive than, and different from, that of the urban working-class housewife (see further, chapter 6, pages 107–8). It will be seen that groups 2 and 3 allow of wide variation between individual speakers in preferences for particular single items, and there is little doubt that such variation does exist: probably no two speakers of these groups agree exactly in their behaviour in this respect. With some speakers there may also be a tendency to polarization of choices: with such speakers either *You hae a guid hame* or *You have a good home* are more likely than, say, *You hae a good hame* or *You have a guid home*, and *Yaize* (= Use) *your ain* is more likely than *Yaize your own*. Yet there are certainly other speakers who appear (in their less formal styles) to display little consistency of this sort. In truth, no studies of the vagaries of practice in this respect have yet been made, though in one investigation the inconsistent behaviour of some Edinburgh schoolchildren in operating variants of this sort has been noted (Romaine, 1975).

Some speakers of groups 2–4 display a tendency to 'drift' in the direction of the more prestigious, fully English, variety, by more frequently (though not necessarily invariably) preferring an 'English' (columns 4 or 5) item when addressing 'English-speaking' interlocutors. As well as this common 'upwards convergence' phenomenon (towards the more socially prestigious variety, group 1 Educated Scottish Standard English), the situation also offers opportunities for observing 'downwards convergence' (say, of group 2 speakers in a mainly group 3-speaking environment) and, no doubt occasionally, of 'divergence' (of group 3 or 4 speakers reacting hostilely to what they take to be linguistic pretentiousness, say of group 1 speakers). 'Style-drifters' may also be observed to drift away from preferring English (columns 4 and 5) options, as they become familiarized to a strange interlocutor or a formal setting.

Style-drifting is not, however, the only possibility. Many group 3 and 4 speakers are capable of 'dialect-switching' from their habitual vernacular into school English (i.e. a style based almost entirely on columns 3 to 5), with or without a de-localizing adjustment of accent, in addressing non-vernacular-speaking strangers or when away from home. The ability to switch cleanly from one 'dialect' to the other in this way seems to be most common with speakers from the most conservatively-spoken regions (perhaps the only regions in which group 4-type speech occurs at all commonly) but some working-class group 3 speakers from all regions possess it also.

Every small Scottish community – a hamlet, a school staff-room, a hospital ward – is likely to contain speakers from several of the groups of Scottish speakers described above, as well as speakers of Hebridean or Highland and of non-Scottish, most commonly England-derived, varieties of English. Customarily, all intercommunicate freely and without difficulty. Where inter-locutors are familiar and at ease with one another, but of course only if this is so, convergence may be slight or non-existent.

Something like this situation has probably operated from the time when southern English influence became a noticeable feature of Scottish speech in the seventeenth century. Clear indications that a situation of the sort existed become numerous in the second half of the eighteenth century, when we hear often of 'hybrid' Scots-English: 'Neither gueed fish nor flesh nor yet sa't herrin' (1768); or of local Scots speech that is 'improving and approaching nearer the English' (*First Statistical Account of Scotland,* 1791–; many of the accounts of the local speech in this collection imply a 'hybrid' situation of this sort); and similar remarks appear constantly thereafter. Some of these ac-counts are cited in Aitken (1979a, and 1981).

One slightly surprising result of the few sociolinguistic investigations of Scots speech which have as yet been completed (Romaine (1975), Macaulay (1977), Reid (1978) which are chiefly of phonological items whose range of realizations includes pronunciation 'vulgarisms' (see chapter 6, page 107)) is the surprisingly early age (below six) by which children have learned to dialect-switch or style-drift according to the sociolinguistic rules of their community, perfecting this skill in the next few years (Romaine, 1975, 1979; Reid, 1978). The ability to recognize the different stylistic options and to perform in this way is, it seems, an important part of the language competence of Scots.

Accents of English in Scotland

The accents with which the several varieties of Scots speech described in the previous section are realized range from fully local and vernacular accents, many of the features of which are mentioned in chapter 6, to 'hybrid' varieties approximating Anglo-English accents such as RP. To date the fullest overall account of these accents appears in Abercrombie (1979) and in Aitken (1979a).

All Educated Scottish Standard English accents, as employed regularly by most group 1 and some group 2 speakers (as these are characterized on pages 521) share a large number of systemic and realizational features with local vernacular Scottish accents, as employed by group 3 and group 4 speakers. The shared systemic items can be seen in table 6.1 on pages 95–8, and some of the shared realizations are mentioned in chapter 6, pages 100 and 102, as well as the Scottish Vowel-length Rule described on pages 94–9; others are mentioned in Aitken, 1979a: 99f). Some Educated Scottish Standard English speakers have characteristic local realizations of some vowels, and all Educated Scottish Standard English speakers have local realizations of some consonants shared with working-class speakers of their own localities. Many Educated Scottish Standard English speakers adopt the vernacular local treatment of unstressed syllables ('educated' north-eastern speakers, for example, commonly operate Buchan vowel-harmony, without, as a rule, being aware of this); and most share some local supra-segmental habits: in all such ways Educated Scottish Standard English speakers possess more or less localized accents. Just as the range of Scotticisms employed by users of these accents is not homogeneous throughout Scotland (see chapter 6, page 108), so the Educated Scottish Standard English accents themselves display regional variation.

In other ways, however, the Educated Scottish Standard English accents as a whole are differentiated from local vernacular speech and approximate a single national norm: in the differences of vowel system and vowel selection from vernacular Scots displayed in tables 6.1 and 6.2 and, at the realizational level, in giving some vowels, (notably vowel 15 /ɪ/, and vowel 6 /u/, and vowels 12a /ɔ/ and 18a /ɔ/ or /ɒ/) realizations approximating those of RP rather than the realizations current in the vernacular of their locality (for example most vernacular Scottish accents employ much opener and more centralized realizations of vowel 15 /ɪ/ than are acceptable as Educated Scottish Standard English). Vowel 16a appears to be predominantly an Educated Scottish Standard English, not a vernacular Scottish, phenomenon. And the 'vulgarisms' of pronunciation described on page 108 of chapter 6 are eschewed by Educated Scottish Standard English speakers.

The several sets of features just summarized are criterial for the group of Scottish accents we are calling Educated Scottish Standard English – those accents which Scots find acceptable as 'educated' accents or appropriate for 'educated' (really, middle-class) speakers, which indeed are almost invariably used by such speakers, and which most usually accompany the group 1 set of lexical choices identified on page 521. Speakers operating the group 1 or group 2 varieties, but failing to preserve the distinctions from local vernacular speech specified in the previous paragraph, qualify as Scottish Standard English, but not Educated Scottish Standard English, speakers. Many such speakers do, of course, exist, especially among the 'lower middle classes' and the 'respectable working class', many as habitual Scottish Standard English speakers, some as speakers of this variety only on formal occasions, with strangers or away from their own locality.

The types of Educated Scottish Standard English accent we have just described are the most conservative, most fully Scottish and most socially widespread of this group of accents, each local version sharing some, but not all, features with its own local vernacular. Another sort of accent of this group, which typically displays fewer localized features (replacing these with standardized national features) and which, in system and realizations, is more closely assimilated to RP and other Anglo-English accents, is the type which might be called 'hybrid'. This range of accents is further identified on page 526, below.

Alongside the more or less native and Scottish forms of Scots speech which we have been considering, there is widely current in Scotland a prestigious and influential variety which cannot in the same way be considered as in any sense native to Scotland: namely, Standard English pronounced with an RP accent. Both as dialect and as accent this variety of English derives from England; however, RP-accented English (often, it is true, accompanied by a few stylistic overt Scotticisms) is, without exception, the speech of all members of the hereditary landed gentry of Scotland, the lairds and clan chiefs and of the Scottish member of the royal family, the Queen Mother, since these persons have from the eighteenth century and earlier been accustomed to educate their children in expensive English private schools (the so-called 'Public Schools') or the few similar establishments in Scotland, and have, since the seventeenth century, mixed (and intermarried) with the same social caste in England. Similar kinds of English, also originating in England, are to be heard from the large and growing number of English immigrants (5% in the 1971 Census) to be found everywhere throughout Scotland, many of these occupying senior managerial and technical posts and often active and of standing in local affairs.

Until recently this kind of English, differing from typically Scots varieties and accents, was manifestly the ultimate 'top-dog' variety in Scotland as well as in England. It remains the variety which is most in evidence on the grandest social occasions. It is the variety most often heard from airline employees (though not from the servants of the railway or the bus companies). Cinema and television advertisements are most often in RP accents (but not those for beer, which are commonly in Scots accents). Announcers and newsreaders for the BBC in Scotland are invariably RP-accented speakers or speakers with hybrid accents. Today, presenters and speakers on Scottish radio (both the BBC and local stations) more often than not have Scottish accents, but these are predominantly middle-class ones: working-class dialects and accents are largely confined to interviews, phone-ins and fictional dialogue. The Scottish presence is even less on television, but on similar lines. Of course Scottish listeners are even more exposed to media from furth of [furth = 'outside': Ed.] Scotland, where non-Scottish accents, especially RP, naturally predominate.

The prestige enjoyed by RP and similar English-accented varieties of English in Scotland, evidenced in all these and other ways (in Muriel Spark's *The Prime of Miss Jean Brodie* it is the ENGLISH school girl who is the model of elegant diction in the Scottish girls' school class), appears to provide the explanation for the emergence (at what date is at present unclear) of a range of Scottish accents which are in essence compromises or hybrids between the more conservatively Scottish of the Educated Scottish Standard English accents described on page 524, above and RP. These hybrid accents are characterized linguistically in Abercrombie (1979: 75–81) and in Aitken (1979a: 110–14).

Whereas (as we noted on page 525) the more conservatively Scottish of the Educated Scottish Standard English accents encompass a wide social range of users, from 'respectable working-class' through 'lower middle-class' to 'middle-class', these 'hybrid' accents are fairly exclusively middle-class in their provenance. Among the social group which includes advocates, solicitors, accountants, doctors, professors and some teachers they appear to predominate. As Abercrombie has pointed out (1979: 75), these accents are fully established, 'hereditary' and institutionalized, just as much as the more distinctively Scottish ones: they are not just casual imitations by single individuals of RP speakers.

In attractiveness, 'elegance', absence of 'uncouthness', it is probable that some of the 'hybrid' accents we have just considered would rate higher for many native speakers of English, and for most Scots, than the more conservative Educated Scottish Standard English varieties, though both could fairly be described as socially 'acceptable'. The same cannot be said of the more distinctively working-class accents; nor can it be said of the so-called 'Morningside' or 'Kelvinside' accent (so named from these middle-class districts in Edinburgh and Glasgow where this type of accent is held – probably erroneously – specially to flourish). This accent is widely believed to represent casual and inaccurate imitations by its speakers of their social betters – to result from pretentiousness, affectation or 'talking posh'. Its salient characteristics are a few features, mainly of realizations of vowels, which do indeed appear to have resulted, at least originally, from 'hypercorrect' imitation of RP: *naice* for *nice*, *faive* for *five*, *ectually* for *actually*, and others; the presence of only one or two of these features is enough to identify and stigmatize this stereotype. It has been known as a stereotype for at least the whole of the present century. Its speakers are typically middle-class and (perhaps especially) lower middle-class group 1 speakers, much more often women than men, it seems; I have observed it only in speakers from Central Scotland; but it is not apparently otherwise regionally restricted, and is certainly not confined to the districts which give it its most popular names – there are others – though it does indeed occur there.

The very few subjective reaction investigations of attitudes to the different types of Scots accents so far reported (Cheyne, 1971; Romaine, 1980) confirm that speakers with RP-like accents are regularly judged to be of higher wealth, status, ambition, leadership, good looks and self-confidence; to native Scots accents are left only the more homely and likeable personality traits, such as 'goodheartedness'.

What is special about Scots?

Part of the answer to this question is, obviously, the linguistic substance itself, much of it, as we saw in chapter 6, unique to Scotland.

Lowland Scotland is not, of course, alone in manifesting a bi-polar stylistic continuum, with styles ranging from a more prestigious SE, in Scottish and non-Scottish varieties and accents, to fully local non-standard varieties, in which the choice of Scottish elements (columns 1 and 2, and Scottish phonology and phonetics) is maximal. Similar ranges between local varieties of SE and 'the full local dialect' operate, for example, in English regions such as Yorkshire, and in 'post-creole continuum' situations such as that of Jamaica (see e.g. De Camp, 1971).

But it has been and can be claimed, first, that the 'linguistic distance' between the two extreme poles of the Scottish continuum is 'greater' than in any comparable case in the English-speaking world, and, second, that distinctively Scottish elements are in more frequent spoken (and, as we shall see, also written) use over a socially much more widely dispersed range than in any of these other cases. The term 'linguistic distance' is used as a way of expressing the fact that Scottish speech possesses more numerous contrasts of the column 2 versus column 4 sort, and that more of these are phonetically striking (of a considerable phonetic distance, like the phonetic distance between the vowels of *hame* [hem] and *home* [hom], or *yaize* [jeːz] and *use* [juːz]). The term also conveys that there are also more numerous lexical oppositions to SE (column 1 versus column 5) than in other British dialect regions: the most important witnesses to this are the contents of the *Scottish National Dictionary* (*SND*) (over 30,000 entries, few obsolete) and the *English Dialect Dictionary* (*EDD*). In addition, I am asserting that the Scots use more of these non-standardisms more often and over virtually the whole social range, than are similar non-standardisms used elsewhere in the English-speaking world, including creole-speaking areas.

The greater durability of Scotticisms in Scottish tradition and the greater willingness of the Scots to use them reflect what appears to be a greater 'dialect-loyalty' by Scottish speakers of all the Scottish regions than is evinced by their English cousins towards THEIR non-standard dialects. According to Glauser (1974: 276, 282–3), it is much more common to find that a 'dialect' form or word continues to be used on the Scots side of the Scottish-English Border than the converse of this, i.e. survival of a 'dialect' item on the English side when Scottish speakers know only the standard item.

This more persistent dialect-loyalty of the Scots is loyalty to more than a dialect. The non-standardisms (of columns 1 and 2) used by them and which they regard (erroneously in some cases; see chapter 6, page 105) as peculiar to Scotland, they label Scots, and some Scots at least regard them as part of the Scots 'language'. The Scots language has strong associations with Scotland's identity as a nation and it has, since the fifteenth century, shared the national name. Among those who have written or spoken of Scots as the national language of the Scottish nation have been Gavin Douglas in 1513, King James VI (of Scotland) and I (of England), various seventeenth-century Scots writers, Allan Ramsay the poet, Alexander Ross the eighteenth-century regional poet, Robert Burns, Walter Scott, Lord Cockburn the celebrated Edinburgh judge and raconteur, Robert Louis Stevenson, Lewis Grassic Gibbon, Hugh MacDiarmid and many Scots today, including, of course, the advocates of a 'restored' or 'promoted' Scots (on which see below). However, there has also been a (perhaps smaller) body of Scots, including J. A. H. Murray (1873: 91) who have regarded 'Scots' as a mere 'dialect' of English, or, in Murray's case, as merely part of the northern English dialect.

Further support to the notion of a Scottish 'language' comes from Scotland's uniquely copious and distinguished vernacular literature, albeit this has been until quite recently restricted to genre and lyric verse, prose dialogue and first-person (quasi-oral) narrative, and to settings and topics of purely Scottish provenance. Most of this literature is in the 'mainstream literary Scots' tradition, in something like a standard variety of literary Scots. This is based loosely on an idealized conservative form of spoken Central Scots – a Central Scots version of 'Ideal Scots'. This form of literary Scots employs an orthography that is variable within certain circumscribed limits. This orthography draws most of its symbolizations from literary SE but retains also a few of the conventions of Older Scots (e.g. *ui* optionally with *u-e* and *oo* to represent vowel 7 (see table 6.1) and *ch*, optionally with *gh*, the phoneme x). The mainstream literary tradition includes probably all of the internationally known names of Scottish literature – Burns, Scott, Hogg, Stevenson, MacDiarmid – and many others. But there have also established themselves several deviant traditions, drawing on the stereotypes and shibboleths of certain regions and conforming to the 'local standards' of these regions, or specialized in other ways. A distinctive literature in the Scots of north-eastern Scotland has existed since the eighteenth century (beginning with Robert Forbes, Andrew Shirrefs, John Skinner), a Shetlandic literature since the nineteenth (see Robertson and Graham, 1952). Since then the range of local and social varieties expressed in literature has continued to expand, most strikingly in recent decades (on which see McClure, 1979a).

In quantity, distinction and variety this literature far outshines the 'dialect literatures' of any other part of the English-speaking world. Scotland is unique among English-speaking nations and regions in possessing its own great literature in both 'standard' and 'dialect' versions of its own language, even though this is restricted to 'literary' functions and localized settings.

Furthermore, many Scots, such as Walter Scott and Hugh MacDiarmid, are very conscious that a form of Scots formerly was (in the sixteenth century) the full 'standard' or 'official language' of the then separate Scottish nation. Nevertheless, though Scots in this way possesses literary status and though some of those who (more or less) speak it are influenced by patriotic loyalty towards it, the sole official and transactional language of the country today, in ordinary general reference, remains SE, and SE in its various accents and varieties is manifestly the prestige speech.

Good and Bad Scots

In this chapter we have operated a binary model of the potential claimants for the allegiance of Lowland Scottish speakers – 'English' and 'Scots'. In this form the binary model implies an awareness that Scotland and Scots do have their own distinctive traditions. As Sandred (forthcoming) and others have pointed out, many working-class Scots appear, to some extent at least, to lack this awareness and hold a version of the binary model in which the opposed varieties are simply 'proper English' and 'slang'. As is often the case, the members of society most strongly conscious of traditions and culture are the 'educated' – who are perhaps rather better represented among the middle class; and this also accounts for the greater knowledge and use by this group of the stylistic overt Scotticisms described in chapter 6 (pages 107–8).

In the course of the last two centuries the binary model of Scots has been giving place to a trinary one, particularly among 'educated' and middle-class Scots, themselves normally Educated Scottish Standard English speakers. The components of this trinary model are (approvable) 'Scots-English' (i.e. Educated Scottish Standard English), (said to be approvable) 'genuine Scots' or 'Good Scots', and (not approvable) 'slovenly corruptions of Scots' or 'Bad Scots'. 'Good Scots' is commonly identified with archaic and rural varieties 'whether of the Borders or of Buchan', and is believed to approximate to 'Ideal Scots' (see page 522); 'Bad Scots' is the variety of Scots common among the working-classes of urbanized Central Scotland – 'Urban Demotic' – marked by free use of those 'vulgarisms' of accent and of usage identified in chapter 6, page 108.

Yet without the protection of an 'educated' accent or an approved literary setting, it is certain that even 'Good Scots' vocables are far from finding universal or unqualified approval. Tape-recorded specimens of conservative rural Scots speech (our group 4) have been known to amuse middle-class Scottish audiences almost as much as specimens of more unquestionably Urban Demotic varieties; and Sandred's findings in his investigation into attitudes to lexical Scotticisms seem to point in the same direction. It seems that approval of 'Good Scots' items and loyalty to the 'Scots language' is by many more readily accorded to 'Ideal Scots' and its abstracted components than to the coarse reality of actual performance, associated as this is with socially objectionable speakers. Some who profess approval of 'Good Scots' for historical and patriotic reasons, and who admire its use in literature, may yet discourage in children's speech the use on any occasion of identifiably vernacular Scots forms (i.e. those which are not covert – see chapter 6, pages 105–7) for social reasons (see Sandred, forthcoming). The whole issue of attitude and its relation to performance and to education is clearly highly various and complex but as yet far from fully understood and virtually unstudied.

Reviving Scots?

From 1776 to the present, almost every commentator on Scots has repeated the almost universally agreed belief that it is 'dying'. Some earlier suggestions for restoring or reviving it are mentioned in Aitken (1981), and a recent discussion of ways of doing so is McClure, Aitken and Low (1980). It was not however till the early 1970s that there arose several organizations devoted to 'the promotion of Scots as a language' or 'the furtherance of Scotland's languages', including the Association for Scottish Literary Studies, with a membership, in 1980, of over 700 and which has a very active Language Committee, and the Scots Language Society, originally called the Lallans Society, with several hundred members. One aim of these organizations is to promote awareness of the language and literature of Scotland, present and past, which was until recently almost totally and scandalously neglected in Scottish education (see Aitken, 1979b, 1981; McClure 1979b). Another aim of some people, for example McClure, has been the preservation and development of Scots as a distinct language, as an important part of the cultural heritage of the Scot. One proposal for so doing is reminiscent of the methods used for the (more or less) successful promotion of 'Nynorsk' in Norway: see especially McClure (1980) and Aitken's riposte in the same volume.

If what I have called 'New Scots' (Aitken, 1980), in imitation of the term 'Nynorsk', were somehow to be made available as a literary, official, private and transactional language in the manner proposed by McClure, it would require to have norms to preserve its own distinctiveness and for pedagogic reasons. It can hardly be doubted that these would be on the lines of existing mainstream literary Scots (rather than one of the divergent varieties of literary Scots). A foretaste of what this might be like can be seen in the Scots Language Society's journal *Lallans*. *Lallans* is almost entirely in literary Scots and with a few other, very much more occasional, pieces in other publications, it breaks new ground in that it uses Scots for the narrative as well as the dialogue of its short stories and for serious essays on a variety of topics (but mainly of particular Scottish concern). These *genres* have hitherto been virtually confined to SE rather than Scots. *Lallans* also contains notices and advertisements in Scots, such as the following:

Scots Literature Competition 1978

The Scots Language Society offers prizes for scrievin in the Scots tongue. There are three clesses: Age 18 and owre wi prizes o £20, £10 and £5; age 12–17 wi prizes o £10, £5 and £2.50; and under 12, prizes o £5, £3 and £2.

Entries maun be original and ne'er afore prentit. They may be (a) Poems up to 60 lines; (b) tales up to 3,000 words; (c) plays that tak nae mair nor 25 meenits to perform. Ilk entry maun be signed wi a byname, and the byname should be prentit on the outside o a sealed envelope, that has inside the entrant's real name and address, and, for them under 18, the date o birth.

(From *Lallans* 9, Mairtinmas 1977)

This is evidently a word-for-word rendering of an equivalent notice in SE. As a performance it looks as if it is derived from a competence in SE. The choice of the modal *may* is perhaps revealing of this, since this is unidiomatic in modern spoken Scots (and in Scottish Standard English), which has only *can* in this application (the advertisement appeared repeatedly without correction of this). It is doubtful if many Scots today would share the belief of the committed few that there is any real point in having this in 'Scots' at all, rather than in the simple SE which underlies it.

Even if the Scots ever do achieve political devolution or Independence, it does not seem at all likely that the small group of New Scots enthusiasts will convert the mass of uncommitted and uninterested Scots to anything like a full New Scots revival, with all the drastic changes in linguistic and literary habits (and the consequences for education and publication) that this would entail. On the contrary, we can probably look forward to a continuation of the present slow drift of Scottish speech habits in an anglicizing direction. Yet it might be that, if Independence did come, native Scottish habits of speech (and even writing?) might gain enhanced prestige, so that the drift might be decelerated or even arrested. Perhaps a new SE of Scotland might be stabilized, in which rather greater recourse to occasional Scottish elements in both speech and writing would become normal.

REFERENCES

Abercrombie, D. 1979. The accents of Standard English in Scotland. In A. J. Aitken and T. McArthur (eds.) *Languages of Scotland.* Edinburgh: W. and R. Chambers. pp. 68–84.

Aitken, A. J. 1979a. Scottish speech: a historical view with special reference to the Standard English of Scotland. In A. J. Aitken and T. McArthur (eds.) *Languages of Scotland.* Edinburgh W. and R. Chambers. pp. 85–118.

——— 1979b. Studies in Scots and Scottish Standard English today. In A. J. Aitken and T. McArthur (eds.) *Languages of Scotland.* Edinburgh: Chambers. pp. 137–58.

——— 1980. New Scots: the problems. In J. D. McClure, A. J. Aitken and J. T. Low (1980). pp. 45–63.

——— 1981. The good old Scots tongue: does Scots have an identity? In E. Haugen,

J.D. McClure and D. Thomson (eds.) *Minority languages today*. Edinburgh: Edinburgh University Press. pp. 72–90.

——— 1982. Bad Scots: some superstitions about Scots speech. *Scottish Language* 1: 30–44.

Cheyne, W.M. 1971. Stereotyped reactions to speakers with Scottish and English regional accents. *British Journal of Social and Clinical Psychology* 9: 77–9.

De Camp, D. 1971. Towards a generative analysis of a post-Creole speech continuum. In D. Hymes (ed.) *Pidginization and creolization of languages*. London: CUP. pp. 349–70.

DOST. 1931–. *A dictionary of the older Scottish tongue*. Edited by W.A. Craigie, A.J. Aitken, J.M. Templeton and J.A.C. Stevenson. Aberdeen: Aberdeen University Press.

EDD 1898–1905. *The English dialect dictionary*. Edited by J. Wright. London: OUP.

Glauser, B. 1974. *The Scottish-English linguistic border: lexical aspects*. The Cooper monographs. Bern: Francke.

Macaulay, R.K.S. 1977. *Language, social class and education: a Glasgow study*. Edinburgh: Edinburgh University Press.

McClure, J.D. 1979a. Scots: its range of uses. In A.J. Aitken and T. McArthur (eds.) *Languages of Scotland* Edinburgh: Chambers. pp. 26–48.

——— 1979b. The concept of Standard Scots. *Chapman* 23, 24: 90–6.

——— 1980. In J.D. McClure, A.J. Aitken and T. Low (1980) pp. 11–41.

McClure, J.D., Aitken, A.J. and Low, T. 1980. *The Scots language: planning for modern usage*. Edinburgh: the Ramsay Head Press.

McNeill, P. and Nicholson, R. (eds.) 1975. *An historical atlas of Scotland, c. 400–c. 1600*. Conference of Scottish Medievalists.

Murray, J.A.H. 1873. *The dialect of the southern counties of Scotland*. London: Philological Society.

Nicolaisen, W.F.H. 1976. *Scottish place-names*. London: Batsford.

Reid, E.C. 1976. Social and stylistic variation in the speech of some Edinburgh schoolchildren. M. Litt. thesis, University of Edinburgh.

——— 1978. Social and stylistic variation in the speech of children: some evidence from Edinburgh. In P. Trudgill (ed.) *Sociolinguistic patterns in British English*. London: Edward Arnold. pp. 158–171.

Robertson, T.A. and Graham, J.J. 1952. *Grammar and usage of the Shetland dialect*. Lerwick: The Shetland Times Ltd.

Romaine, S. 1975. Linguistic variability in the speech of some Edinburgh schoolchildren. M. Litt. thesis, University of Edinburgh.

——— 1979. The language of Edinburgh schoolchildren: the acquisition of sociolinguistic competence. *Scottish Literary Journal* Supplement 9: 55–61

——— 1980. Stylistic variation and evaluative reactions to speech: problems in the investigation of linguistic attitudes in Scotland. *Language and Speech* 23: 213–32.

Sandred, K.I. forthcoming. *Attitudes to optional lexical and grammatical usages in Edinburgh*. Stokholm: Almqvist and Wiksell.

SND 1931–76. *The Scottish national dictionary*. Edited by W. Grant and D.D. Murison. Scottish National Dictionary Association Ltd.

31

The sociolinguistic situation in Northern Ireland

ELLEN DOUGLAS-COWIE

Accent types in Northern Ireland

Accents of Northern Ireland English can be distinguished first of all at a regional level. Regional varieties include the major Ulster Scots and mid-Ulster accent types and a number of more minor types, for example those found in the area where Northern Ireland borders the Republic of Ireland (see, for example, Adams, 1964; and, for Belfast regional varieties, see Milroy, 1981; for a summary see this volume, chapter 7).

Cutting across regional types are a number of other accent varieties. Milroy (1981) is the first to attempt to set out in any systematic manner what these varieties are (see also earlier attempts by Adams, 1948), though their interactions and their functions in society have not yet been clearly described. This chapter attempts, briefly, such a description.

The accent types described by Milroy (1981) are: (i) local vernaculars; (ii) careful vernaculars; (iii) localized standard; (iv) RP-influenced speech.

Three factors, not previously indicated in the literature, may be involved in the decision to single out the above categories. Firstly, although many people may have more than one category in their linguistic repertoires, they probably gravitate over stretches of speech in any one social situation towards one of the varieties. The varieties are, in a sense, target points for the speakers.

Secondly, listeners in Northern Ireland may perceive their fellow country-men's speech in terms of its similarity to one of these varieties. Of particular interest here is speech which does not approximate particularly closely to any of the varieties, but shows (over a short stretch) features of different varieties. Such speech seems to be heard as inconsistent and fluctuating in style and may be felt to be false or unacceptable (see discussion on page 542 of listeners' reactions to RP-influenced speech).

A third point is that for both listeners and speakers these categories are probably social reference points.

The linguistic traits of accent types

Local vernaculars
These are forms of speech which differ from region to region and, within the
linguistic spectrum in Northern Ireland, are farthest away in phonological
systems from RP. Further information on some local vernaculars can be
found in Adams (1956), Gregg (1958, 1959), Douglas-Cowie (1979), Milroy
(1980) and Milroy (1981).

Careful vernaculars
Milroy (1981) describes these as modifications of speakers' vernacular speech
in three ways:

(a) The phonetic differences between two variants of a phoneme may not be
    as extreme as in the vernacular.
(b) Certain vernacular variants may be adopted rather than others.
(c) Much of the lexical distribution of phonemes may be different from that
    in the vernacular and much more in line with the localized standard
    variety.

Localized standard
This variety receives more attention here than any of the other varieties. This
is because very little information on it can be found in the existing literature.

Localized standard can be described at segmental and non-segmental
levels. The literature on it has concentrated only on the segmental level (Barry,
1980; Adams, 1981) but, as this section will indicate, non-segmental descriptions are probably very important in the discussion of social varieties of this
category.

At a segmental level localized standard is like careful vernacular in that
speakers still retain a localized accent, but many of the allophonic rules of the
vernacular are lost or modified. The distribution of phonemes over the
vocabulary is, with few exceptions, that of their nearest equivalents in RP: for
example, in the Ulster Scots local vernacular /ʉ/ may occur in *cow*, *town* etc.,
whereas in the localized standard /ɑʉ/ is used. At the realizational level,
however, localized standard is very different from RP: for example, /o/ in
home, *rose* etc. is often realized as a monophthong. There are also many
differences of system between localized standard and RP. For example, there
is one phoneme /ʉ/ for RP /uː/ and /ʊ/; one phoneme /a/ for RP /æ/ and
/ɑː/; and, very unlike RP, post-vocalic /r/ is represented in pronunciation,
e.g. *hour* /ɑʉər/ and *there* /ðɛər/. For further details on the phonology of
the localized standard see Barry (1980).

There is some debate in the scanty literature on the localized standard as to
what linguistic leeway is permissible within the category (Adams, 1981). This
debate seems fairly sterile, however, since the identification of the category by

listeners in the province probably involves a good deal of variation at a number of levels. Perhaps the term 'standard' here is inappropriate. This term tends to give the idea that it is a well-established and clearly defined category, linguistically and socially. In fact it is not. The term 'neutral' accent may be more appropriate.

The linguistic variation that may be involved in this category is probably both regional and social. Regional variation has been pointed to before by Gregg (1964), who talks of an Ulster Scots standard as opposed to a mid Ulster standard. Milroy's term 'localized' may also be taken to involve regional variation. This variation may involve some phonemic differences, for example an /aɪ/ ~ /aːe/ opposition in Ulster Scots, (cf. *die* /daɪ/ *dye* /daːe/) as opposed to the one phoneme /aɪ/ in mid Ulster, but mainly involves phonetic variation, for example the monophthongization of some vowels in Ulster Scots standard speech rather than diphthongization in mid Ulster (see chapter 7).

Variation in the localized standard related to social groups has not been discussed before. It is the writer's intuition as a native Ulster speaker that this level of variation manifests itself at non-segmental levels, for example voice quality or perhaps rhythm, and can be found when one compares the accents of certain schools in Northern Ireland or certain professions. Perhaps a good example of a social variant of the localized standard is the accent of Presbyterian ministers who seem to have certain suprasegmental features imposed on speech that, at the segmental level, might be called localized standard. One such feature seems to be a tendency to linger over the articulation of the initial syllables of some words.

There are some other varieties which probably fit the category. One of these is what might be called an old-fashioned or local-genteel accent. One of the features of this variety is its slow and deliberate rate of articulation, or even somewhat 'exaggerated' articulation. Another variety is what might be called the cultured variety. Some of the distinguishing features of this may be volume and pitch. The accent seems to be 'softer' (or perhaps it is a matter of having a less tense overall voice setting) and seems often to be higher pitched than some of the other varieties. (It is recognized that the descriptive terms used here are imprecise, but it is impossible to be more specific without proper voice settings analyses.)

It is clear from the above discussion that the category localized standard encompasses quite a lot of linguistic variation on different levels which, to the native listener, contains interesting social innuendoes not immediately obvious to the outsider.

RP-influenced speech

For reasons that will be apparent later this category, as defined by Milroy (1981), is perhaps better referred to as RP-like speech. This accent results from fairly consistent attempts by Ulster speakers to speak RP. It sounds quite like

RP, although there are usually certain Ulster features which intrude, such as the Ulster post-vocalic /r/. This type of speech has fairly restricted use, and is probably mostly used by some Northern Ireland television and radio news announcers. RP influence, however, can also be detected from time to time in the other speech categories already discussed. For example, the speech of careful vernacular or localized standard speakers may take off sporadically in the direction of RP.

RP influence may manifest itself at the segmental level. For example, common RP features used occasionally in place of Ulster features include the use of an RP diphthong [əʊ] for Ulster [o]; the use of a more RP-type [u] for Ulster [ʉ]; the indiscriminate use of either RP [æ] or [ɑː] for Ulster [a]; and the absence of post-vocalic /r/. It is probably true that RP influence also manifests itself in both RP-like speech and other varieties at non-segmental levels, for example voice quality. It is probable that speakers model their attempts at RP on a more global level than knowledge simply of isolated articulatory characteristics.

Individuals' repertoires

This chapter has so far described the linguistic resources of the community. How do users in the community draw on those resources to form individual repertoires? The discussion is based on the writer's intuitive knowledge as a native of Northern Ireland and on empirical evidence taken from Douglas-Cowie (1979).

Accent varieties occurring in individuals' repertoires

Most speakers probably have more than one variety involved in their repertoires. It is the writer's intuition, however, that some people who speak localized standard are simply not able to use other varieties: in particular they cannot use the more vernacular varieties, though they may sometimes show RP influence.

Probably many people have two adjacent varieties in their repertoires or one variety with and without RP influence. There are undoubtedly others, however, whose speech involves more than two categories. The combinations of varieties which seem to occur most frequently are: vernacular and careful vernacular; careful vernacular (possibly with some elements of vernacular), with and without RP influence; localized standard, with and without RP influence.

A number of points about these combinations and missing combinations can be made. Firstly, as already indicated, localized standard probably does not often combine with more vernacular speech in an individual's repertoire. Secondly, it is the writer's intuition that speakers of careful vernacular are more likely, when they want to be more formal, to superimpose RP influence on their speech than to use localized standard. Thirdly, RP-like speech is missing from the combinations above. This is because the writer has no intuitions on whether RP-like speakers have any other varieties in their repertoires or not. Her knowledge of them is from the media, but she suspects that RP-like speech is an acquired form rather than one with which some people in Northern Ireland grow up and that therefore probably some RP-like speakers, in other situations, may use, for example, localized standard. Others, however, may acquire RP-like speech and have social pressures to maintain it in all circumstances.

The use of accent varieties

Probably most people who have the vernacular and careful vernacular varieties in their repertoires will use both in differing proportions in different social situations. It is the writer's intuition that people switch from fairly consistent careful vernacular in one situation to careful vernacular with RP influence in another, more formal, setting (typically when such people are on the phone or talking to someone of higher educational status or to RP speakers).

People who have localized standard with and without RP influence seem to use consistent localized standard in one situation and add RP influence in another, particularly in the context of talking to an RP speaker or educated English person with a modified regional accent. There may, however, be some exceptions. For example, the writer knows speakers of localized standard who will show RP influence even in fairly informal circumstances among friends when they are referring to particular places in England or to things associated in their minds with social superiority.

Interaction of accent varieties in stretches of speech

There is evidence from Douglas-Cowie (1979) to show that elements of the different accent varieties can interact quite rapidly within short stretches of speech, as illustrated in the following example which shows RP elements interacting with elements at the more vernacular end of the linguistic spectrum:

She lives up at the top of that big hill
[ʃi lɪvz ʌp əʔ ðə tap ə ðɒn bɪg hæl]

↑ ←——————————→ ↑ ↔
RP   vernacular   RP vernacular

This rapid interaction often seems to be completely random, though some people focus on particular words, and will always produce them in, for example, localized standard, while other words containing the same linguistic form may often be produced in the vernacular. This is true of Douglas-Cowie's Subject D in Articlave who always says [ŋ] in *teaching*, but not necessarily in other words (Douglas-Cowie, 1979: 327).

On some occasions people do seem to shift from fairly consistent use of one variety over a particular stretch of speech to fairly consistent use of another variety over a stretch of speech. This shift often coincides with topic changes (see below).

Acquisition of linguistic repertoires

Research seems to have ignored what is surely an important question for sociolinguists, that is, how do individuals acquire their repertoires? This question is highlighted by data from Northern Ireland from Douglas-Cowie (1979). The data show that socially motivated speakers who are lacking in high level educational status seem unable to acquire the more prestigious variants of certain variables (some of those belonging to her 'covert' variables class), although they can use the more prestigious variants of many other variables. For example, they cannot acquire the more prestigious pronunciations [ı] or [ɪ] for the vowel in *bin*, *sin* etc., but continue to use the vernacular pronunciation [ä]. They do, however, abandon the vernacular [a] for the vowel in *wander*, *watch*, *one* etc. in favour of the more prestigious [ɒ]. Less socially motivated but better educated subjects, on the other hand, can, when the occasion demands, use the prestige variants of all variables. One would like to know more about the nature of limitations determining the linguistic repertoires that people acquire.

The social significance of accent varieties in Northern Ireland

As indicated, a description in terms of social classes fails to capture a great deal of structure which is basic to the sociolinguistic fabric of the province. Such descriptions are also generally lacking in explanatory power, a point which has been noted by Milroy (1980) and explored in more depth by Douglas-Cowie and Cowie (1980). The approach adopted here focuses instead on the fact that an individual is typically a member of a set of nested social and cultural constituencies, and may have various affiliations to these various constituencies.

Social and cultural constituencies in Northern Ireland

Immediate tight-knit sociogeographic communities

In Northern Ireland, both urban and rural societies tend to be characterized by tight-knit, 'internally focused' communities. Members of such a community tend to have strong loyalties to each other, know each other's business, and are often interrelated. Milroy (1980) describes three such communities in the urban context of Belfast, and suggests that some tight-knit communities may be associated with individual streets. Members of streets are reported to be territorially aggressive. Douglas-Cowie (1979) describes a tight-knit rural community, the village of Articlave.

Intermediate constituencies

In the urban setting, people clearly tend to be aware of belonging to a city (e.g. Belfast) and perhaps to areas of the city (e.g. west Belfast). Correspondingly, in the bulk of rural Northern Ireland, villages form clusters which are satellites to a larger town. Many people work or shop outside their immediate communities, and thus participate directly in these larger and more diffuse communities; and their influence (as well as the mass media) brings influences from outside into the immediate communities. Note that because of this, rural communities in Northern Ireland tend not to be isolated and self-contained – though there are exceptions, particularly in areas bordering the Republic of Ireland. For fuller evidence on these points, see Douglas-Cowie (1979) and Milroy (1980).

Less immediate cultural constituencies

People in Northern Ireland also belong to wider cultural groups. They are members of Northern Ireland, Ireland and Great Britain.

Attitudes to cultural constituencies

In both urban and rural Northern Ireland, it is probably the case that dual membership of tight-knit communities and intermediate communities leads to conflicts of allegiances: between internal allegiances to the tight-knit network and external allegiances. Some people, for example those eager for social advancement, might be more eager than others to mark their allegiance to external and perhaps socially superior communities; others might be socially aggressive about being members of a tight-knit community; yet others might be aware of the pull of different allegiances depending on situation and occasion.

Milroy (1980) and Douglas-Cowie (1979), in very different ways, have both shown that there are conflicts of allegiances in tight-knit communities, Milroy by measuring people's degrees of internal allegiances to networks in Belfast, and Douglas-Cowie, in rural Articlave, by measuring people's degrees of external allegiances to what they perceive as the socially superior values of the neighbouring town. This is done by measuring what is called 'social ambition'.

Many people in Northern Ireland, depending on their political and cultural backgrounds, have different attitudes to Northern Ireland, the Republic of Ireland, Ireland and Great Britain. For example, many have allegiances to Northern Ireland, but some see it as part of Great Britain, others as part of the political state of the Republic of Ireland (not the actual status of Northern Ireland). Others may want to see it as an independent entity. Yet others may have clashes of allegiances which manifest themselves differently in different situations. For example, it is possible for some people to feel pro-British in the presence of Republic of Ireland supporters, but often to feel anti-British in the presence of the British. There are probably other possible combinations of allegiances.

The linguistic consequences of people's attitudes to social and cultural constituencies

Tight-knit and intermediate communities

Both Milroy (1980) and Douglas-Cowie (1979) have shown that conflicts of allegiances manifest themselves linguistically.

Milroy (1980) studied three tight-knit communities in Belfast: the Clonard, the Hammer and Ballymacarrett. She shows that within these communities there is considerable linguistic variation from person to person, and attempts to explain the variation in terms of people's differing degrees of allegiance to the networks in which they live. A strong relationship was found between network allegiance and linguistic variation in Ballymacarrett, which suggests that the nested communities model may be useful. But her evidence does not rule out alternative explanations: it could be explained in more traditional terms, on the basis of differences associated with age and sex, as well as in terms of network allegiances (Milroy, 1980: 161, fig. 6.1).

Douglas-Cowie's (1979) study of Articlave investigated the relationship between linguistic variation and people's desire to identify with the social values and attitudes of external communities. The study showed that people who aspired to the social values of the outside world tended to gravitate towards RP-influenced speech, while those who had high socioeconomic status, but whose allegiances were firmly tied to the village community, tended to gravitate towards the local vernacular. Thus subject I, who is a prosperous farmer but clearly considered his place to be in the village (as he put it, 'Sure I'm only an oul' farmer, workin' wi' muck and beasts an' things'), speaks something like the local vernacular. On the other hand subject A who has much lower social status, but who works outside the community and has the less parochial values of the outside world, speaks something like careful vernacular with RP influence.

The Articlave study shows that the villagers can also switch linguistically, for example, from vernacular speech to something more like careful vernacular, depending on whether they are in their roles as members of a tight-knit community or in their roles as members of the 'outside' world. Thus villagers talking to each other used more vernacular forms than when talking to an RP-speaking outsider introduced to each of them: when speaking to him a lot of the subjects spoke RP-influenced speech.

The Articlave subjects also code-switch linguistically according to topic of conversation. Topics concerned with the daily events of the immediate community or with the values of that community tend to produce the speech varieties at the vernacular end of the spectrum, while topics associated with the 'outside' world or with the values of villagers who aspire to things outside of their tight-knit community, produce varieties at the other end of the linguistic spectrum.

Larger cultural constituencies

Two cultural-linguistic relationships in Northern Ireland are particularly noticeable. The attitude of 'blatantly Ulster and proud of it' is typical of some people in the province and manifests itself linguistically in a display of vernacular forms in the speech of people whose socioeconomic class would lead one to expect much more 'standard' linguistic behaviour. This is perhaps particularly true of some Ulster Protestants. It should be realized that people of educated or high social status in Northern Ireland who want to mark themselves as strongly 'Ulster' cannot do so in the same way as an educated Scot can mark himself linguistically as strongly Scottish. Probably their only way of marking strong Ulster allegiance is to turn to vernacular speech.

There are also those from all social classes who appear to be ashamed of sounding 'Ulster'. Perhaps their shame at their speech may be linked to a sense of being inferior or subservient to other cultures, in particular to England. (The early dominance of the English culture and English speech as the superior culture and language in Northern Ireland in the centuries following the Plantation is noted in Connolly, 1981.) Many people in Northern Ireland who show attitudes of shame at sounding Ulster tend to have RP-influenced speech and, on being questioned on why they use RP forms, come out with statements like 'The English have no bad vowels like us', or 'Ulster speech is inferior to English speech.' There is evidence that a number of people in Ulster attend elocution or speech and drama classes where RP-influenced speech appears to be taught (see Douglas-Cowie, 1979).

Listeners' evaluations of speech related to cultural allegiances

There has been comparatively little work done on Northern Ireland listeners' evaluations both of Northern Ireland accent types and of non-Ulster accent types. The research that has been conducted, however, suggests that researchers intuitively feel that people's evaluations of Ulster and non-Ulster accent types reflect their attitudes to the types of cultural constituencies considered in this chapter.

A brief synopsis of the three studies conducted in Northern Ireland on listeners' reactions indicates the anticipated interaction of cultural, political and linguistic attitudes. (In these studies religious divisions are taken as indicative of political and cultural divisions.) It should be noted that the researchers' intuitions are not always proved in their findings, nor always investigated with sufficient regard for linguistic precision. There is clearly need for further research on listeners' attitudes.

Ward (1980) studied the evaluative reactions of adolescents to four accents, the last three of which are very loosely defined, English (RP), Southern Irish, Northern Irish and Scottish, with the hypothesis that Catholics would have very favourable opinions of the Southern Irish speaker and would be least favourably disposed to the RP speaker, while Protestants would have more favourable impressions of the RP speaker and would have unfavourable opinions of the Southern Irish speaker. His hypothesis is not at all clearly borne out by his findings.

Milroy and McClenaghan (1977) also carried out a pilot study on reactions in Ulster to four accents – what they call educated Scots, RP, educated Ulster and educated Southern Irish. Their listeners consisted of 14 Protestants and only one Catholic, so no useful information on the relation between cultural divisions and linguistic attitudes can be gleaned.

Cairns and Duriez (1976) looked at the influence of a speaker's accent on recall by Catholic and Protestant children in Northern Ireland. Speakers were played three accents which were defined as middle-class Dublin, middle-class Belfast and RP. It was found that Catholic children listening to the RP accent scored less well than Protestant children listening to RP and that Protestants listening to Southern Irish did less well than Catholics listening to the Northern Ireland accent, thus suggesting a cultural and political basis for a complex speaker–hearer interaction in the Province.

No other empirical research has been carried out on listeners' attitudes, but some other general impressions can be gleaned from random observations. One point in particular can be made, which concerns attitudes to RP-influenced speech and the RP-like variety. Speakers with these accents probably want to be held in high social esteem, yet listeners in the community often express contempt of or anger at such speech, accusing it of being false and 'put on'. The speaker's desired image is different from his attained image.

The relation of social class, age and sex to linguistic behaviour in Northern Ireland

Social class

Published work on Belfast speech has focused on working-class communities alone. More recently however, Milroy and Milroy (1979–82) have undertaken linguistic investigation of other social classes with a view to looking for linguistic correlations with social class stratification for sensitive variables throughout the city. Milroy (1981: 84) states that there are broad class differences in speech and gives some examples.

Douglas-Cowie, working with only twelve subjects of differing social backgrounds in the rural community of Articlave, looked for relationships between linguistic behaviour and social class, but found that her subjects' linguistic behaviour very often showed a greater relationship to their social aspirations than to their social class in terms of the traditional markers of education, occupation and income. She suggests that her results may not be atypical of other rural communities. It is worth suggesting that class distinc-

Table 31.1. *Percentage deletion of intervocalic (th): conflated figures for three areas of Belfast*

	Men (40–55)	Women (40–55)	Men (18–25)	Women (18–25)
Interview style	57	32	80	30
Spontaneous style	69	53	89	47

Source: Milroy and Milroy (1977).

tions may be less marked in rural communities, where everyone is geographically lumped together, than in cities, where classes tend to be geographically segregated into particular regions of the city.

Age and sex

Age and sex are undoubtedly related to linguistic behaviour in Northern Ireland. The data used here are taken from work on Belfast speech, although some more information on the linguistic behaviour of different age groups in Northern Ireland should be available in the future from the Hiberno-English Dialect Survey (Adams, Barry and Tilling), which has been concerned with three age groups.

The Belfast data tend to indicate the same types of relationships between sex and linguistic behaviour as are indicated in other sociolinguistic research in Britain and the USA. Females in Belfast are more linguistically ambitious and standard than males. This can be demonstrated both from their linguistic behaviour and from their linguistic attitudes: for example, female groups tend to show more marked style shifting than men, usually avoid vernacular indicators in 'interview' style (Milroy, 1981), and also over-report their linguistic behaviour (O'Kane, 1977). Males tend to be conservative, females innovative. Hence linguistic change tends to be initiated by females.

These generalizations need refinement in the light of some interesting details from the Belfast data which involve the dimension of age interacting with sex. Two points in particular are mentioned here. Firstly, young males are particularly assertive in maintaining the urban vernacular, as demonstrated in the case of the variable (th) in the table 31.1. Milroy and Milroy (1977) consider it unlikely, however, that the high scores of the young men indicate a change in progress which will go to completion. It is rather a case of vernacular assertiveness or covert prestige, and occurs in the case of the young men for other variables also.

Secondly, there can be exceptions to the general findings on the relationship between sex and linguistic behaviour. In the Clonard community in Belfast Maclaren (1976) and Milroy and Milroy (1978) point to the case of the binary variable (ʌ) i.e. the use of vernacular [ʌ] in place of Ulster [ʉ] in a restricted lexical set (see chapter 13), where the older women show as nearly nonstandard behaviour as the young men. Milroy and Milroy (1978) and Maclaren (1976) interpret the high use of the nonstandard form [ʌ] as a case of covert prestige for the young men, and interpret the older women's high use of it as the residue of a former linguistic change that they were leading, perceiving [ʌ] as carrying the status of some higher-ranked community.

These findings on the relationship of sex and age to linguistic behaviour in Northern Ireland not only provide data on the sociolinguistic situation in Northern Ireland but further our general knowledge on more complex interplays of sex and age with linguistic behaviour than have hitherto been detailed in sociolinguistic studies.

REFERENCES

Adams, G. B. 1948. An introduction to the study of Ulster dialects. *Proceedings of the Royal Irish Academy* 52, cl: 1–25.

———— 1956. The phonology of the Antrim dialect (part 1). *Proceedings of the Royal Irish Academy* 57, c3: 69–152.

———— (ed.) 1964. Ulster dialects. In G. B. Adams (ed.) *Ulster dialects: an introductory symposium*. Holywood, Co. Down: Ulster Folk Museum.

———— 1981. Correspondence. *The Journal of the Northern Ireland Speech and Language Forum* 7: 70–7.

Adams, G. B., Barry, H. V. and Tilling, P. M. In progress. A Tape-recorded Survey of Hiberno-English Dialects.

Barry, M. V. 1980. Towards a description of a regional standard pronunciation of English in Ulster. *Journal of the Northern Ireland Speech and Language Forum* 6: 43–7.

Cairns, E. and Duriez, B. 1976. The influence of speaker's accent on recall by Catholic and Protestant schoolchildren in Northern Ireland. *British Journal of Social and Clinical Psychology* 15: 441–2.

Connolly, R. I. 1981. An analysis of some linguistic information obtained from eighteenth and nineteenth century Ulster poetry. Ph.D. thesis, The Queen's University of Belfast.

Douglas-Cowie, E. E. 1979. A sociolinguistic study of Articlave, Co. Londonderry. D.Phil. thesis, The New University of Ulster.

Douglas-Cowie, E. E. and Cowie, R. 1980. Sociolinguistics: what are the relevant variables? Unpublished paper presented at the Third British Sociolinguistic Symposium.

Gregg, R. J. 1958. Notes on the phonology of a County Antrim Scotch-Irish dialect, part 1. *Orbis* 7: 392–406.

———— 1959. Notes on the phonology of a County Antrim Scotch-Irish dialect, part 2. *Orbis* 8: 400–24.

———— 1964. Scotch-Irish urban speech in Ulster. In G. B. Adams (ed.) *Ulster dialects: an introductory symposium*. Cultra: Ulster Folk Museum.

Maclaran, R. 1976. The variable (ʌ), a relic form with social correlates. *Belfast Working Papers in Language and Linguistics* 1: 45–69.

Milroy, J. 1981. *Regional accents of English: Belfast*. Belfast: Blackstaff Press.

Milroy, J. and Milroy, L. 1977. *Language variety and speech community in Belfast.* Report to Social Science Research Council.

—— 1978. Belfast: change and variation in an urban vernacular. In P. Trudgill (ed.) *Sociolinguistic patterns in British English.* London: Edward Arnold.

—— 1979–82. *Sociolinguistic variation and linguistic change in Belfast.* Report to Social Science Research Council.

Milroy, L. 1980. *Language and social networks.* Oxford: Blackwell.

Milroy, L. and McClenaghan, P. 1977. Stereotyped reaction to four educated accents in Ulster. *Belfast Working Papers in Language and Linguistics* 2: 4.

O'Kane, D. 1977. Overt and covert prestige in Belfast vernacular speakers: the results of self-report tests. *Belfast Working Papers in Language and Linguistics* 2: 3.

Ward, M. F. 1980. Evaluative reactions of adolescents in Northern Ireland to four regional accents. Undergraduate dissertation submitted to the Department of Psychology, The Queen's University of Belfast.

32

Indigenous nonstandard English varieties and education

JENNY CHESHIRE

Nonstandard accents

The term 'nonstandard accent' is used here to refer to a regional pronunciation of 'General English', of the kind discussed in chapter 4: it refers, that is to say, to an accent that is NOT Received Pronunciation (RP). The vast majority of English speakers in the British Isles speak with the nonstandard regional accent typical of the area in which they grew up; it has been estimated, in fact, that only about 3 per cent of the English-speaking population use RP (Trudgill, 1979). The number of nonstandard phonological features that are used and the frequency with which they occur is closely correlated with social class, so that speakers from the higher end of the socioeconomic spectrum use fewer nonstandard features less frequently than speakers from the lower end of the scale. The use of nonstandard features is correlated with other social characteristics also, such as the age and sex of speakers, and the degree to which they are integrated into their local social network (for discussion see Chambers and Trudgill, 1980: ch. 5).

RP has traditionally been the prestigious accent in Britain, because of its associations with the aristocracy and with the professional and wealthy classes (see chapters 3 and 4). In recent years, however, changes in British society have resulted in professional and influential positions being held by speakers who have regional accents, and accents other than RP are now heard even from BBC newsreaders. Nevertheless, the more widespread occurrence of regional accents does not appear to have led to a decline in the prestige of RP (see chapter 3). Experiments using the 'matched guise' technique have shown that RP speakers are considered to be more competent (in terms of intelligence, industriousness and self-confidence) than speakers who have a nonstandard accent, and these opinions are held even by people who themselves have a nonstandard accent (see Giles, 1971; and this volume, chapter 28). Of particular relevance to the educational context is an experiment performed by Edwards (1978), in which both middle-class and working-class judges rated a child who used RP as better on a range of attributes relating to intellectual competence, and also as better behaved, more helpful, and as having greater academic potential than children with nonstandard accents.

But although speakers with nonstandard accents receive a negative evaluation in terms of intellectual ability, they are rated very highly on more personal attributes. They have been judged, for example, as more trustworthy and kind hearted than RP speakers (see Bourhis, Giles and Lambert, 1975) and as more likeable and sincere (see Elyan *et al.*, 1978).

Linguistic prejudices of this kind can be of crucial importance at school. It appears, for example, that teachers often unconsciously use language as a cue for assessment of the academic potential of their pupils (see Seligman, Tucker and Lambert, 1972), and it is well known that teachers' expectations have a significant effect on the school performance of their pupils (see, for example, Rosenthal and Jakobson, 1968; Pidgeon, 1970). It might be hoped that a positive evaluation in terms of personal attributes would to some extent offset any negative stereotyped reactions to accent; however, the situation is complicated by the relationship that holds between nonstandard accents and nonstandard dialects, as will be shown later in this chapter.

Nonstandard dialects

The term 'dialect' is used here to refer to vocabulary items and to features of morphology and syntax. Nonstandard English dialects differ from accents in that a standard dialect exists that has become institutionalized in society, so that it is used in the media, in teaching and by all speakers who consider themselves 'educated' (see Trudgill, 1975: 18) as well as in all forms of writing (the use of dialect in literature is a rare exception). Therefore, although nonstandard accents may nowadays be heard from BBC newsreaders, nonstandard dialects are not.

This implies, of course, that it is possible to speak Standard English with a nonstandard accent, and this is indeed the case. For speakers of a nonstandard dialect the use of nonstandard morphological and syntactic features is correlated with social characteristics in the same way as nonstandard phonological features are, so that it is again speakers from the lower end of the socioeconomic scale who use the higher proportion of nonstandard forms. Since SE is used by speakers from the higher social classes it is, like RP, considered prestigious. Furthermore, the fact that it is the variety of English used in writing has led to the view that this is 'correct' or 'proper' English and that the use of nonstandard grammatical forms is 'careless', 'incorrect' or 'bad' English.

This has very serious implications for the education of children who speak a nonstandard dialect. These children will almost certainly have a nonstandard accent also, which, as we have seen, may mean that they are branded as having lower intelligence and less academic potential than other children. If they are also considered to use slovenly, incorrect English then these negative evaluations will be very strongly reinforced.

Furthermore, since the use of nonstandard phonological and grammatical features is correlated with socioeconomic class, it is working-class children who will suffer most severely from value judgements about nonstandard English. Educationists have been worried for many years by the fact that working-class children under-achieve at school; and although it is now recognized that to a large extent this is because their language and cultural background are different from those of the school (and of middle-class children) rather than in some way inferior, the myth that working-class children under-achieve because they are culturally and linguistically deprived still persists in many schools. Rosen and Rosen, for example, write:

A generation of young teachers has gone into schools recently, convinced that working-class parents never talk to their children, that the children are never taken anywhere, never see anything or do anything, and that the language they do possess is lacking many essential features. (1973: 54).

Clearly views of this kind will further reinforce the impression that working-class pupils who speak a nonstandard variety of English have low intelligence and low academic potential.

Linguistic problems

Although attitudes towards nonstandard varieties of English are of clear importance in education, it is usually thought that there are few, if any, LINGUISTIC problems involved. Varieties of English share a very large common core (see Quirk et al., 1972: 13), and the formal differences between SE and nonstandard dialects are few in number and linguistically rather trivial (see, for example, Trudgill, 1979). Furthermore, the majority of nonstandard features alternate in occurrence with the SE equivalent forms, so that children who use nonstandard features already possess the corresponding SE features as part of their linguistic repertoire. They are also, of course, exposed to SE through the media and through contact with SE speakers. However, although ATTITUDES towards nonstandard varieties constitute the major language obstacle in education, recent research suggests that there may also be problems of a linguistic nature. What, then, are the problems faced by speakers of nonstandard English in reading, writing, and in speech and comprehension at school?

Problems in learning to read

Reading can be considered only briefly here, since there is a wide range of opinions on the psycholinguistic mechanisms that are involved, and on the ways in which reading should be taught. Recent research into some reading materials used in infant schools, however, confirms that it is the attitude of teachers towards nonstandard forms that is of key importance, rather than the forms themselves (Wight et al., 1978). Goodman and Buck (1973) point out that the only way in which speaking a nonstandard dialect may interfere with learning to read is if teachers insist on 'word for word' correct reading rather than on 'reading for meaning'. They argue that if a nonstandard form is used in place of an SE form, this is an indication that the meaning has been understood, and should be seen as a mark of progress in learning to read. If teachers correct nonstandard forms learners may be confused and their linguistic confidence may be undermined. As Rosen and Burgess (1980: 133) point out: 'The onus is here placed firmly on the teachers, not only to adopt a positive attitude to dialect, but also to make sufficient effort to learn about the features of dialect to avoid confusing children.'

Confusion may also arise where nonstandard accents are concerned. If the teacher and the child have different accents the teacher may unwittingly correct a word that has been understood correctly, but pronounced in accordance with the rules of the child's accent. Trudgill (1975: 49) gives a good example of the kind of mutual confusion that can arise. A boy read aloud the word *road* with his local Norwich pronunciation, which distinguishes between pairs of words like *road* and *rowed*, that are indistinguishable in RP and many other English accents. His reading was misinterpreted by the teacher as *rude*, and she therefore attempted to correct him by saying 'No, it's not *rude*, it's *road*'. This in turn was misunderstood by the boy as meaning that the word in question had been *rowed*. The problem was caused, quite simply, by ignorance on both sides of the difference between the local accent and the teacher's accent.

Recent research suggests that confusion caused by the correction of nonstandard forms may be of a very serious nature. Learning to read is a difficult, complex task for all children, partly because they begin the learning process before they have developed the ability to distinguish words as discrete elements within utterances. Twite (1981: 186) points out that below the age of 6 or 7 children find it difficult to disregard what they see as the whole meaning of an utterance, in order to focus on individual details within it. Thus young children whose usage of nonstandard morphosyntactic or phonological forms is corrected may be completely bewildered by the correction; they will have read what they saw as a complete item, and may not be able to perceive the nature of the teacher's objection.

There is the additional factor that since language functions as a symbol of personal identity, persistent corrections by the teacher may result in children who speak a nonstandard variety of English becoming totally alienated from the school. A striking example of this was observed in research carried out into the use of language by adolescents in the town of Reading, in Berkshire (Cheshire, 1982a). Two boys were considered by their teachers as 'hopelessly backward' at reading; furthermore, they refused to participate in reading activities when they were at school. It transpired, however, in meetings that took place outside school, that both boys were in fact fluent readers; one of them read a James Bond novel to his friends, with great skill and obvious enjoyment, in an adventure playground one day when they were playing truant from school.

Table 32.1. *Style shifting in written work*

Nonstandard feature	Group frequency index: playground speech	Group frequency index: written work
Boys:		
present tense suffix e.g. *I sings*	64.42	0.00
was e.g. *we was happy*	88.06	60.00
negative concord e.g. *I didn't do nothing*	93.33	40.00
what e.g. *a boy what I know*	80.00	0.00
Girls:		
present tense suffix	61.51	0.00
was	73.42	19.44
past tense *come* e.g. *we come here yesterday*	92.59	20.00

Source: Cheshire (1982b: 56).

Thus correction of nonstandard features may not only add to the state of 'cognitive confusion' in which all children start the task of learning to read (Twite, 1981) but those children who do learn to read may become so alienated from the school that they give teachers a false impression of their linguistic ability.

Writing

The problems discussed in the previous section also apply when children who speak a nonstandard variety of English are learning to write – the expectation is that they should use SE forms, and nonstandard forms may be mis-interpreted by teachers as grammatical mistakes.

Children who use nonstandard forms in speech naturally tend to use them in writing also. The following sentences, for example, were written at schools in the town of Reading by working-class children aged between 11 and 14:

(1) Last Christmas Eve Mum and Dad *was* out round the pub drinking
(2) The rescuers *couldn't* do *nothing* more
(3) I *wants* to be a farmer

In fact, however, these children used fewer nonstandard forms in their school written work than in their speech. This can be seen in table 32.1, which compares the frequency of occurrence of five nonstandard morphosyntactic forms in the speech of two groups of children (4 boys and 4 girls) in their school written work and in their conversational speech. The analysis of the spoken forms is based on group recordings made outside school, in adventure

Word	Past tense
hurry	hurried
horrify	horrified
throw	~~throwed~~ thron
take	take
bring	~~bringed~~ brong
laugh	laughed
tell	told
go	~~gond~~ gone
write	~~writed~~ wrote

Figure 32.1. Past tense verb-form exercise

playgrounds. As the table shows, these nonstandard forms occur less often in the children's written work than in their conversational speech, and some nonstandard forms do not occur at all in their written work. Clearly, then, these children were aware that they needed to adjust the forms they normally used, in order to produce a style appropriate for school written work, though this awareness may not necessarily have been at a conscious level.

Other forms that they used in writing, however, suggest that they were unsure of the precise adjustments that had to be made. The exercise reproduced in figure 32.1, for example, indicates that the child whose work it is was confused about the verb forms he was expected to produce. It also, incidentally, illustrates the way in which school English exercises can severely discriminate against pupils who speak a nonstandard variety of English. The children were given a verb and were asked to supply the correct past tense form. The crossings-out in the exercise illustrated provide a useful indication of the child's approach to the exercise. Clearly, his first impulse was to add the regular -*ed* suffix to the majority of the verbs. This is the most common way of forming past tense forms in SE, and it is often used in nonstandard English with verbs that have 'irregular' past tense forms in SE. (The verbs *wake* and *fight*, for example, occur with an -*ed* suffix in their past tense forms in the nonstandard English spoken in the town of Reading.) However, the child appears to have reconsidered this initial decision, perhaps because he remembers that at school he is expected to give some verbs irregular forms that he does not always use himself. He identifies correctly those verbs that have irregular past tense forms in English (*throw*, *take*, *bring*, *tell*, *go*, and *write*), but although the forms that he gives them are forms that he does not use himself, they are not always the appropriate SE forms.

Hypercorrect forms of this kind were used throughout the children's written work. Some appeared to result from differences between present tense verb forms in the nonstandard variety and in SE. Whereas in SE an -*s* suffix occurs only with 3rd person singular verb forms, in Reading English the suffix occurs throughout the paradigm, so that *I knows, you knows, we knows* and *they knows* occur, as well as *(s)he knows*. Table 32.1 showed that the children in the Reading study did not use the nonstandard suffix in their written work: they had realized, in other words, that use of the *-s* suffix was inappropriate in school writing. However, they also omitted the *-s* suffix in other places, where the rules of both SE and nonstandard, Reading English *do* require it: for example, with 3rd person singular forms of present tense verbs:

(4)   It *taste* all rich and creamy
(5)   A hedgehog *live* in a hole

and with plural nouns:

(6)   There are two *house* on the left
(7)   Walter also drunk a lot and backed *horse*

They also added the suffix in a number of constructions where neither SE nor nonstandard Reading English require it: for example, with singular nouns:

(8)   There is one *tractors* on the right
(9)   And a *stones* fell on his head, too

and elsewhere:

(10)   All I saw was boys and girls crying, running to find *theirs* mums and
       dads

All children tend to make mistakes of this kind when they are first learning to write (Wiles, 1981). However, the fact that children were still making these mistakes at secondary school suggests that they may be caused by linguistic confusion between SE and the nonstandard variety (see also chapter 33).

Differences between English accents can also cause problems in writing. There are several sets of homonyms in English that can give rise to spelling difficulties (for example, *there/their*; *meet/meat*; *to/too/two*). Speakers with nonstandard accents often have to learn different sets of homonyms: most Scottish speakers, for example, make no distinction in speech between *caught* and *cot* (Trudgill, 1975). As Trudgill points out, this is not a serious problem, since English spelling does not always bear a close relationship to pronunciation, and all children face problems of this kind, though the words involved will vary from region to region. Problems *can* arise, however, if teachers are not aware of the causes of children's spelling mistakes.

Word-initial *h*, for example, is not always pronounced in the variety of English spoken in the town of Reading, and this creates several pairs of homonyms that do not exist in SE, such as *as/has*; *ill/hill*; *is/his*. This presumably accounts for the spelling mistakes in the following examples (again from the Reading study), particularly since it is only *his* that is spelt wrongly in the first example, and not *he*, which is not a homonym:

(11)   He finds *is* food and he closes *is* mouth
(12)   Mary's grandad *as* a plain, dull, garden

It may also account for the mistakes made in the sentences below:

(13)   And other people stuck to the goose *has* well
(14)   When *his* he coming back?
(15)   Off Debra went, and ran *has* fast as she could

Some homonyms lead to forms being used in writing that are probably spelling mistakes, but that give the impression of being serious grammatical errors. The words *are* and *our*, for example, are pronounced in the same way in Reading English, which may well account for the following:

(16)   All *are* food, air, water, fuel and waste as to be take and put back in the land, sea and air around us

It is not yet known whether children who speak a nonstandard variety of English make more mistakes in their written work than children who speak the standard. Clearly, however, children who speak a nonstandard variety encounter a different set of problems from those who do not, and the extent to which this affects their educational progress will depend on whether the teacher recognizes the nature of the problem. If children do not understand the reason for their teacher's corrections, they are likely, as we have seen, to become linguistically confused. This may lead them to produce written forms that belong neither to the standard nor the nonstandard variety.

Speech and comprehension

All children encounter language problems when they start school. They may have difficulty understanding unfamiliar forms used by the teacher, and at later stages in their school career they have to learn to understand the language used in textbooks and on workcards, and to write about academic topics in the appropriate impersonal style (for discussion see Perera, 1981). Children who speak a nonstandard variety of English, however, have the additional task of learning to use SE forms in writing; they may also come to realize that they are more likely to win their teacher's approval if they use these forms in speech.

Research findings indicate that children learn to adjust their use of nonstandard features at a relatively early age. The children in the Reading study, for example, used most of the nonstandard morphosyntactic features less often in school than in the playground (Cheshire, 1982b). Reid (1978) reports that in Edinburgh, also, children as young as 10 were able to make appropriate stylistic adjustments to the frequency with which they used nonstandard phonological forms (though Macaulay (1977) did not find consistent stylistic adjustment in the speech of children younger than 15). As far as the children in Reading were concerned, this stylistic adjustment occurred without any apparent awareness of the existence of SE (except in so far as they distinguished 'talking posh' from talking 'normally').

Clearly, if fewer nonstandard forms are used at school, negative reactions from the teacher to the nonstandard variety will be minimized. Many writers have pointed out, however, that a child's use of a standard or nonstandard form depends on whether (s)he wishes to show respect for the formality of the school, or solidarity to the family and the peer group (see, for example, Mercer and Maybin, 1981). For example, those children in the Reading study who disliked school and their teacher made little change when they were at school to the frequency with which they used nonstandard present tense verb forms, and one boy who was a persistent truant asserted his independence and hostility to the school by using *more* nonstandard verb forms when he spoke to his teacher than when he spoke to his friends. On the other hand, those children who enjoyed a good relationship with their teacher used fewer nonstandard forms when talking to him than when talking in the playground (Cheshire, 1982a: ch. 9).

The variable nature of language, then, forces children who speak a nonstandard variety of English to choose whether to assert their allegiance linguistically to the peer group or to the school. This places a burden on them that is not shared by children who come to school speaking SE, and it must account, in part at least, for the fact that SE speakers adjust more readily to the school environment.

Furthermore, if children recognize, even unconsciously, that SE is more appropriate in school, then speakers of a nonstandard variety may be reticent and unforthcoming in oral work. This will further hamper their academic progress. It may also mean that when they leave school they continue to feel inadequate and inarticulate in formal situations, a feeling which will have a crucial effect on their performance in job interviews (Macaulay, 1977).

Prospects

The educational prospects of speakers of nonstandard English have improved during the course of this century. The Newbolt report (Board of Education, 1921) not only confuses SE with RP, but also equates 'Standard English' with 'correctness' and 'clearness', suggesting that important components of a language curriculum are:

... first, systematic training in the sounded speech of standard English, to secure pronunciation and clear articulation: second, systematic training in the use of standard English, to secure clearness and correctness both in oral expression and in writing.

The Bullock report (Department of Education and Science, 1975) avoids value judgements of this kind, and sees SE as appropriate in certain situations only:

The aim is not to alienate the child from a form of language with which he has grown up and which serves him effectively in the speech community of his neighbourhood. It is to enlarge his repertoire so that he can use language effectively in other speech situations and use standard forms when they are needed.

Current mainstream policy aims to teach children to become proficient in writing SE, recognizing that this is what many parents and children want (see, for example, Richmond, 1979) and that as things stand at present this is what is necessary if children are not to fail the examination system. It recognizes, however, that nonstandard forms may be more appropriate in informal writing, and that it is undesirable (and probably impossible) to teach children who normally speak a nonstandard variety to speak SE when they are at school (for discussion see Rosen and Burgess, 1980: 129–31, 134–6).

This policy has led to a number of developments in the school curriculum. For example, the *Language in Use* scheme, which was sponsored by the Schools Council, consists of a set of classroom activities aimed at increasing the awareness of secondary school pupils of the different varieties of English (such as scientific, instructional and persuasive English) that are appropriate in different situations. The ILEA English Centre, which provides a workshop approach towards the development of curriculum materials to aid the study of linguistic diversity, has produced a number of publications that contain ideas for teachers (for example, *The English Magazine* 1979a) or for pupils (for example, the *Languages* book, 1979b). And some schools are now using other material designed to promote dialect appreciation and the recognition of the social significance of varieties of English (see Edwards, 1979 for some examples).

The importance of using a coherent marking technique for correcting pupils' written work is gradually becoming recognized (see Cheshire, 1982b for discussion). Richmond (1979) suggests that teachers should separate dialect forms in children's written work from genuine mistakes – 'errors, confusions or miscues in grammaticality, meaning, punctuation and spelling' – and a recent Workshop on Literacy in Further Education Business and Communication Studies, sponsored by the Welsh Joint Education Committee, attempted to put this scheme into practice.

There have also been changes in the books used as reading primers in infant schools. The *Nipper* books, first published in 1968 (Berg *et al.*), contain some nonstandard dialect forms in conversation, and this 'true to life' approach persists in the settings of the stories, which are intentionally working-class. The aim was to alleviate the cultural conflict faced by working-class children at school, a conflict which was not helped by the leafy suburban settings of the previously popular *Janet and John* books (O'Donnell and Munro, 1949–).

Not all of these developments, however, have been successful. Many rely upon teachers having some formal knowledge of language structure; Crystal (1976), for example, points out that without this it is not possible to assess the progress of pupils using the *Language in Use* scheme. And clearly Richmond's marking scheme can only be of use if teachers are aware of the systematic differences between SE and the nonstandard variety of their pupils. Some teachers are reluctant to use the *Nipper* and *Little Nipper* reading books, because they feel that they are 'ungrammatical' and that they deal with 'a side of life from which we are trying to lead the children away' (Dixon, 1977: 88, quoted in Hoffman, 1981: 196). Furthermore, it is not always realized that discussions of linguistic diversity need to be handled with great care and sensitivity in order to avoid alienating nonstandard speakers. The material in the English Centre's (1979c) booklet on *Dialect and language variety*, for example, has been criticized for adopting an 'us and them' approach which does nothing to help those children who have to choose between in-group loyalty and educational participation (see Mercer and Maybin, 1981: 92).

Many teachers still subscribe to the uninformed prejudices towards non-standard English that were discussed at the beginning of this chapter. All the teachers who took part in the study carried out in the town of Reading, for example, interpreted the use of nonstandard forms in writing as 'slovenly, careless grammar'. It has long been recognized that teachers need special skills in order to help those pupils for whom English is a second language, and courses on teaching in the multicultural classroom exist in most teacher training institutions. In-service training sessions are also arranged. It is not often recognized, however, that children for whom English is a first language, but who speak a nonstandard variety of English, also need expert help. Their teachers need to be aware of the linguistic characteristics of social and regional accents and dialects, of the origins and social significance of SE and RP, and of the POSITIVE characteristics of nonstandard varieties – for example, of the special verbal skills that are used in working-class narratives, jokes and rhymes.

Finally, educational policy is often inconsistent and contradictory in its approach to language. The Assessment of Performance Unit (1978), for example, notes that the style of a writing task should be appropriate to subject matter, audience and intention, but goes on to state that *he done it* should be treated as a 'morphological error'. As Mercer and Maybin (1981: 90) point out, this is inconsistent with allowing the subject matter, audience or intention to determine the choice of the appropriate language style; it is, instead, using SE as an inflexible guide for correctness. This contradictory approach is particularly unfortunate since the Assessment of Performance Unit (if it remains in being) is likely to have a great deal of influence on practice in schools.

Further inconsistencies lie in the fact that any successful teaching in the classroom of linguistic diversity will be thwarted by the 'Advice to the Examiner' of most English GCE 'O' level and CSE boards (Mercer and Maybin, 1981: 90). As Rosen and Burgess (1980: 112) point out: 'The classic pattern of examinations, in English and other subjects, rests heavily on mastery of standard written English, and perhaps even a narrow view of that.'

It seems, then, that although there have been considerable advances in our knowledge of the linguistic characteristics of nonstandard English, this knowledge has not yet eradicated negative attitudes and ill-informed prejudices towards nonstandard varieties. In education, confusion, ignorance and prejudice concerning nonstandard English can have extremely serious consequences, and clearly there is an urgent need for a consistent policy on nonstandard English to be implemented in schools. Without this there can be little hope of improving to any significant extent the educational prospects of the majority of school children in the British Isles.

REFERENCES

Assessment of Performance Unit. 1978. *Criteria for assessing writing.* London: Department of Education and Science.

Berg, L. *et al.* 1968– *Nippers.* London: Macmillan.

Board of Education. 1921. *The teaching of English in England.* 'The Newbolt report'. London: HMSO.

Bourhis, R.Y., Giles, H. and Lambert, W.E. 1975. Social consequences of accommodating one's style of speech: a cross-national investigation. *International Journal of the Sociology of Language* 6: 55–72.

Chambers, J.K. and Trudgill, P. 1980. *Dialectology.* London: CUP.

Cheshire, J. 1982a. *Variation in an English dialect: a sociolinguistic study.* London: CUP.

——— 1982b. Dialect features and linguistic conflict in schools. *Educational Review* 34 (1); 53–67.

Crystal, D. 1976. *Child language, learning and linguistics.* London: Edward Arnold.

Department of Education and Science. 1975. *A language for life.* 'The Bullock Report'. London: HMSO.

Dixon, B. 1977. *Catching them young.* London: Pluto Press.

Edwards, V.K. 1978. Language attitudes and underperformance in West Indian children. *Educational Review* 30: 51–8.

——— 1979. *The West Indian language issue in British schools.* London: Routledge and Kegan Paul.

Elyan, O., Smith, P., Giles, M. and Bourhis, R. 1978. RP accented female speech: the voice of perceived androgyny? In P. Trudgill (ed.) *Sociolinguistic patterns in British English.* London: Edward Arnold.

Giles, H. 1971. Patterns of evaluation to RP, South Welsh and Somerset accented speech. *British Journal of Social and Clinical Psychology* 10: 280–1.

Goodman, K.S. and Buck, C. 1973. Dialect barriers to reading comprehension revisited. *The Reading Teacher* 27 (1): 6–12.

Hoffman, M. 1981. Children's reading and social values. In N. Mercer (ed.) *Language in school and community.* London: Edward Arnold.

ILEA English Centre. 1979a. *The English Magazine.* London: Ebury Teachers' Centre.

——— 1979b. *Languages.* London: Ebury Teachers' Centre.

——— 1979c. *Dialect and language variety.* London: Ebury Teachers' Centre.

Macaulay, R.K.S. 1977. *Language, social class and education.* Edinburgh: Edinburgh University Press.

Mercer, N. (ed.) 1981. *Language in school and community.* London: Edward Arnold.

Mercer, N. and Maybin, J. 1981. Community language and education. In N. Mercer (ed.) *Language in school and community.* London: Edward Arnold.

O'Donnell, M. and Munro, R. 1949. *Janet and John*. Welwyn, Herts.: Nisbet.

Perera, K. 1981. Some language problems in school learning. In N. Mercer (ed.) *Language in school and community*. London: Edward Arnold.

Pidgeon, D. A. 1970. *Expectation and pupil performance*. Slough: National Foundation for Educational Research.

Quirk, C. R., Greenbaum, S., Leech, G. and Svartvik, J. 1972. *A grammar of contemporary English*. London: Longman.

Reid, E. 1978. Social and stylistic variation in the speech of children: some evidence from Edinburgh. In P. Trudgill (ed.) *Sociolinguistic patterns in British English*. London: Edward Arnold.

Richmond, J. 1979. Dialect features in mainstream school writing. *New Approaches to Multiracial Education* 8: 10–15.

Rosen, C. and Rosen, H. 1973. *The language of primary school children*. Harmondsworth, Middx.: Penguin (for the Schools Council).

Rosen, H. and Burgess, T. 1980. *Languages and dialects of London school children*. London: Ward Lock Educational.

Rosenthal, R. and Jakobson, L. 1968. *Pygmalion in the classroom*. New York: Holt, Rinehart and Winston.

Seligman, C. R., Tucker, G. R., and Lambert, W. E. 1972. The effects of speech style and other attributes on teachers' attitudes towards pupils. *Language and Society* 1(1): 131–42.

Trudgill, P. 1975. *Accent, dialect and the school*. London: Edward Arnold.

——— (ed.) 1978. *Sociolinguistic patterns in British English*. London: Edward Arnold.

——— 1979. Standard and non-standard dialects of English in the United Kingdom: problems and policies. *International Journal of the Sociology of Language* 21: 9–24.

Twite, S. 1981. Language development in and out of school. In N. Mercer (ed.) *Language in school and community*. London: Edward Arnold.

Wight, J., Hunt, P., Sapara, S. and Sinclair, H. 1978. *Make-a-story* Teachers' notes. London: Holmes McDougall and ILEA.

Wiles, S. 1981. Language issues in the multi-cultural classroom. In N. Mercer (ed.) *Language in school and community*. London: Edward Arnold.

33

British Black English and education

V. K. EDWARDS

Introduction

The response of British schools to the arrival of large numbers of West Indian children in the 1950s and 1960s was slow and confused. The situation of the children from the Indian sub-continent (who started to arrive a short while after the first influx from the Caribbean) was relatively straightforward inasmuch as their most urgent need was to learn English, and specialist help was made available quite rapidly (see chapters 25 and 26). The needs of West Indian children, on the other hand, proved far more difficult to define. Since these children came from British colonies where English was the official language and the medium of education, it was considered that they could not be experiencing language difficulties. This stance was very much reinforced by West Indian parents who regarded England as the 'mother country' and were quite clear in their own minds that they spoke English. Yet the unwavering confidence on both sides that no special provision should be made for West Indian children diverted attention from a very complex linguistic situation (see chapter 14).

The slaves transported to the Caribbean in the seventeenth and eighteenth centuries came from a wide area of West Africa and spoke a variety of languages. There was a conscious policy of mixing Africans from different linguistic backgrounds and so the need urgently arose among the slaves themselves for some mutually intelligible form of communication. This need was in fact far more pressing than the need to communicate with the white planters, with whom most Africans would have had very little contact (Alleyne, 1971). In the early stages, a pidgin drawing heavily on English vocabulary but retaining many features of African phonology and syntax would have evolved. But as this pidgin became the native language of subsequent generations of slaves, it would have undergone a process of expansion which allowed it to fulfil all the communication needs of its speakers. The precise form of the resulting creole varied from one West Indian territory to the next, but the similar conditions created by slavery and the sugar industry and the considerable movement from one island to another (Lowenthal, 1972) laid the foundations for a common culture and language, and there remains a core of common features which can be found in any of the English-based Caribbean creoles.

Over the centuries the continuing influence of English as the language of government and education has given rise to an extremely complex linguistic situation. Some writers (see chapter 14) have chosen to describe this in terms of a continuum between Broad Creole and Standard English; others talk in terms of basilectal, mesolectal or acrolectal speech. West Indians show considerable variation in their speech, and language selection depends on a wide range of factors including social class, education and formality. But although Broad or basilectal Creole is not used consistently by any given speaker or speakers it does appear to have considerable psychological reality as an autonomous variety (Reisman, 1970; Sutcliffe, 1982).

On the one hand, Broad Creole is characterized by West Indians as the language of sincerity, the variety which they would use to express strong emotion (Reisman, 1970). On the other hand, it is heavily stigmatized. Children have been taught in school that it is 'bad talk' or 'monkey talk' and that they will never amount to anything if they do not learn to speak the standard. The resulting state of linguistic schizophrenia is clearly to be seen in the protestations of West Indian parents that they speak English. To admit otherwise would be tantamount to an acceptance of low social worth and limited intelligence.

The school response

Many British teachers seemed to have existed for a number of years in an uneasy state of cognitive dissonance. On the one hand, West Indian parents insisted that their children spoke English, and it was a matter of common knowledge that English was the official language in the British West Indies. On the other hand, teachers often had considerable difficulty in understanding these children and making themselves understood, and had very few ideas about what they should do. The lack of official guidance or any well thought out school policy resulted in teachers either ignoring the problem or trying to cope with it on the basis of rather unsatisfactory *ad hoc* arrangements. Townsend and Brittan's (1972) survey of *Organization in multiracial schools* is the most comprehensive account of opinion and practice current at that time and is particularly illuminating in this respect:

As the West Indians officially speak English no special allowance of staff is given.

Boys of West Indian origin: In each year we have a class for retarded pupils. Although not designed as such, all of these classes have about 90 per cent West Indians or pupils of West Indian origin. (Townsend and Brittan, 1972: 26)

This approach was often the result of an egalitarian philosophy which did not recognize that special needs require special provision. In the words of one headmaster:

Some allowance may be made for any immigrant with language difficulty, but the whole aim of the school is gradually to treat all children alike, be they immigrant or non-immigrant. (Townsend and Brittan, 1972: 37)

This is not to suggest, however, that the subject was not an extremely sensitive one which needed to be handled with great tact:

We once arranged special coaching for West Indians whose English was very poor, but they tended to resent this, not accepting that there was anything wrong with their English, so little progress was made, and the project abandoned. (Townsend and Brittan, 1972: 26)

The magnitude of the difficulties created by influxes of West Indian and Asian children both for the school and for individual teachers should not be underestimated. Many of these difficulties derived not from the overall numbers of immigrant children, but from their concentration in particular schools. Because of the nature of labour demand, immigrant populations are concentrated in conurbations and particularly within Greater London, the Midlands and West Yorkshire. There is a further concentration within these areas and Department of Education and Science statistics for 1973 show that, in the country as a whole, nearly a thousand schools had over a quarter immigrant pupils. The DES definition of immigrant, however, excluded children whose parents had lived in Britain for ten years or more, so that the actual concentration of ethnic minority children is greater than official statistics suggest. While not wishing to minimize the enormous strain on the British education system created by schools having a high proportion of children with problems of language and adjustment, it seems certain that the difficulties of West Indian children, in particular, were exacerbated by an inflexibility in the system. This is clearly illustrated by the whole area of assessment procedures. While intelligence tests were waived in the case of Asian and European immigrants, they were a normal part of the evaluation of West Indian children. This remained standard practice for a number of years despite strong evidence that intelligence tests have considerable cultural and linguistic bias (V. Edwards, 1979).

Adherence to practices and teaching strategies inappropriate for the situation inevitably contributed to widespread under-performance among West Indian children. The extent of their under-performance finally received official recognition with the publication of the DES statistics of education in 1970 (see table 33.1). The publication of these statistics and various other studies relating to the achievement of ethnic minority children (e.g. Blair, 1971; Townsend and Brittan, 1972; Select Committee, 1977; Little, 1975) made it clear that different ethnic groups were performing at different levels. There appeared to be a hierarchical situation in which non-immigrants did better than immigrants and all immigrants did better than West Indians. Even when ethnic minority children had received all their education in Britain, their performance was below that of the indigenous population. The figures which

Table 33.1. *Analysis of educational achievement according to ethnic group*

	West Indians	Indians	Pakistanis	Non-immigrants
in educationally sub-normal schools	2.33	0.32	0.44	0.68
in selective schools	4	9	9	25
doing non-exam courses	23	26	32	3
doing 'O' levels	6	6	6	42

Source: Provisional figures from the DES reported in Townsend (1971: 57).

produced the greatest protest, however, were those which revealed the over-representation of West Indian children in schools for the educationally sub-normal. On a national level there were proportionately four times as many West Indian children in ESN schools as indigenous children, and in Greater London these figures were higher still. It had been hoped that the phenomenon of low average attainment would disappear with the virtual ending of immigration from the Caribbean, but this has not proved to be the case. The analysis of levels of achievement for school leavers in 1978/79 for six local education authorities shows, for instance, that only 3 per cent of West Indian children obtained higher grades in CSE and 'O' level examinations, compared with 18 per cent of Asians and 16 per cent of other leavers. It would also seem that the majority of the middle band of achievers fall at the lower end of the range of achievement (Rampton, 1981).

Factors in educational under-performance

The main focus of this chapter is the role of language in the education of children of West Indian origin. Language cannot, however, be discussed in isolation from the other factors which have clearly contributed to the low achievement of West Indian children as a group. There can be little doubt, for instance, of the critical part which alienation and rejection of British society by many black children is playing in educational under-performance. The British black community and, in particular, young blacks feel very angry at the racial discrimination which they experience at all levels of employment, in housing and in public services (Smith, 1976, 1977; CRC, 1977). This anger is bound to affect the attitudes of younger children towards the value of education. When brothers and sisters are unemployed, find they have to attend many more interviews than white peers before finding jobs for which they are qualified (CRE, 1978), are paid less, and have to wait longer for promotion, the validity of examination success as a sure passport to social mobility is clearly open to question.

Much has been written about the institutional racism embodied in the educational process. Rampton (1981), for instance, describes 'unintentional' racism in teachers whose negative views of the academic potential of West Indian children, when combined with a tendency to show stereotyped or patronizing attitudes towards them, may prove to be self-fulfilling prophecies. Almost as important, schools tend to convey an all-white system in their visual environment, their books and their curriculum. Little and Willey (1981) report that depressingly little progress has been made since the last major survey (Townsend and Brittan, 1972) in initiatives aimed at giving all children an understanding of the cultural diversity of the wider society. Younger children often seek refuge in denying their blackness, painting their skin white in self-portraits, stating a preference for white dolls and characters and even saying that they look more like white characters than black ones (Milner, 1975). Older children, in contrast, often find it necessary to reject this white-centred society and retreat to the all black world of reggae, sound systems, Rastafarianism and shebeens, which promotes as something positive the very blackness which society as a whole rejects. An essential part of this process is the retention or indeed the intensification of features of West Indian speech. Hebdige (1976), for instance, comments on the ways in which West Indian youths have developed Creole as a symbol of group identity:

Language is used [by members of certain West Indian sub-cultures] as a particularly effective way of resisting assimilation and preventing infiltration by members of the dominant groups. As a screening device it has proved to be invaluable; and the 'Bongo talk' and patois of the Rude Boy deliberately emphasize its subversive rhythms so that it becomes an aggressive assertion of racial and class identities. As a living index of the extent of the black's alienation from the cultural norms and goals of those who occupy high positions in the social structure the Creole language is unique.

Crump's (1979) study of the language use of black children in a London comprehensive school relating the language varieties of black adolescents to their involvement in particular youth cultures, throws further light on the importance of language as an integral part of a person's identity. Children's comments together with observations of the classroom and playground suggest that it is only when pupils develop an orientation towards one or other of the major youth cultural groupings that differences in language use become apparent. Those pupils who by the third and fourth years of secondary school use Patois (see chapter 14) and take pride in 'talking black' are those who turn to the all-black world of reggae and sound systems.

The extremely complex interconnections between educational performance, discrimination and language have on occasions, however, been oversimplified or ignored. The inability or unwillingness of many West Indian children to speak SE, for instance, has sometimes been identified as the reason for educational under-achievement. As Richards (1980) observes:

The facts of failure and dialect interference have recently been placed together; the one has been used increasingly to explain the other. The teachers in language centres, for instance, have begun to argue that they should deal with West Indian children, as well as Indian or Pakistani, Vietnamese, Italian or Chinese children.

Yet this diverts attention from the crucial question of why many West Indian children born in Britain persist in fostering an independent linguistic and cultural identity.

Teacher attitudes towards West Indian language

Earliest reactions to West Indian speech were typical of those towards non-standard British varieties. Anecdotal accounts are plentiful though actual documentation is scarce. An interesting source, however, is the 1970 report of the Birmingham branch of ATEPO (Association of Teachers of English to Pupils from Overseas) on West Indian children. In this report West Indian language is described variously as 'babyish', 'careless' and 'slovenly', 'lacking proper grammar' and even 'very relaxed like the way they walk'. It was considered that they communicated 'by sign language' in 'a glut of speech' but 'a poverty of correct expression'.

Reactions such as these in the educational world need to be discussed in the context of the heated debate which took place in both Britain and America in the 1960s on the subject of whether nonstandard varieties were deficient or merely different. Many educationalists influenced by the work of Bernstein, or, in some cases, a misinterpretation of the work of Bernstein, felt that nonstandard speakers were restricted by their language, and linked alleged linguistic deficiencies with cognitive deficiencies (Hess and Shipman, 1965; Bereiter and Engelmann, 1966; Blank, 1970). This position has been strongly criticized by Labov (1969) and others who have demonstrated that non-standard varieties are just as regular, flexible and logical as the standard.

The Concept 7–9 project materials produced by the Schools Council project on 'Teaching English to West Indian children' (Wight, 1969, 1970; Wight and Norris, 1970) can be seen to some extent as a weak statement of the verbal deprivation hypothesis. Originally the materials were envisaged as a language course for West Indian children, but later the emphasis was changed and it was decided that many of the language skills that could be usefully developed with West Indian children would also be beneficial to a good number of native British children. The authors of the materials maintained that the language of West Indian children (and, presumably, working-class white children) was perfectly logical and regular and that attempts to teach SE should be reserved for children's writing and not their speech. However, they did feel that nonstandard speakers needed to develop a whole range of verbal strategies which would enable them to take part more successfully in the education process. Yet no reference is made to the children's language outside the classroom and V. Edwards (1979) and Sutcliffe (1978) point to the pos-sibility that the strategies the materials were designed to teach can be found in the language which children use in non-school settings. Certainly American research (e.g. Houston, 1973) has demonstrated that deficiencies which intervention programmes were seeking to remedy did not exist when children were studied in a wide range of settings. No attempt has been made to evaluate the Concept 7–9 materials in use, but the American findings suggest that it is unlikely that positive transfer will take place from the various activities in the pack to the classroom. A more plausible explanation for why children do not use particular verbal strategies in the classroom – and it is far from certain that they do not – would seem to be in terms of situational constraints rather than an inability to do so.

V. Edwards (1978) rejects the verbal deprivation hypothesis and seeks rather to explore the relationship between attitudes towards language and under-performance. She describes an experiment in which recordings of four children – a middle-class English boy, a working-class English boy, a recently arrived Jamaican girl and a British-born Barbadian girl – were heard by various panels of 'judges', including student teachers. Each child spoke for approximately thirty seconds on the subject of a visit to the dentist. Unbeknown to the judges, however, the Barbadian girl spoke twice, once in the working-class dialect which she habitually used at school and once in the Barbadian dialect which she used in certain peer-group and family situations. Using the semantic differential technique (Osgood *et al.*, 1971), a hierarchical situation emerged in which the middle-class boy was evaluated most favourably, followed by the working-class children (the English boy and the English guise of the Barbadian girl) and then the West Indian girls (the Jamaican girl and the Barbadian girl's West Indian guise). Significantly, the Barbadian girl was judged quite differently when she used different dialects. Her English guise was felt to be more valuable, more careful, more helpful and better behaved than her West Indian guise. Equally significant, student teacher judges were prepared to make predictions about achievement on the basis of short snatches of speech. As a group, they considered the middle-class boy likely to achieve 'A' levels, while the working-class children would do 'O' levels and the West Indian girls CSE. This, it can be argued, is a reflection of educational reality, but when taken in conjunction with the finding that 33 per cent of the student-teacher judges did not feel that the West Indian girls would be interesting members of the class, it seems reasonable to consider their predictions for levels of academic success as still further evidence of gross stereotyping behaviour. It is not possible to assert, of course, that these students would behave in the classroom in accordance with views expressed as part of an extremely artificial exercise performed in isolation, but the findings of the survey confirm the very widespread tendency to resort to stereotyping behaviour of this kind (see Seligman, Tucker and Lambert, 1972; Williams, 1973). They also point to a very real danger that teachers may convey their negative feelings to children and so translate the stereotypes into reality (Rosenthal and Jakobson, 1968; Bagley, 1975).

Educational strategy

Styles of teaching and approaches towards the language differences of West Indian children are many and varied, but it seems that throughout the 1960s and 1970s the most common approach can be conveniently described as what some writers (Trudgill, 1975; V. Edwards, 1979) have labelled 'dialect eradication'. Until relatively recently attempts to stamp out linguistic diversity have sometimes been crude and occasionally cruel. More recently, however, attempts at dialect eradication have been more benign and well-intentioned, though scarcely more successful. The feeling is that, since SE is the language of educational success and social mobility, the school's duty is to teach the standard, and dialect therefore has no place in the classroom. Very often this approach is extremely subtle. The sensitive teacher would not dream of telling a child that a particular form is 'bad' or 'wrong' and would be more likely to respond with interest, pointing out that this is the form the child uses in speech, but that in writing an alternative form is more appropriate.

Teachers who adopt this gentler technique usually believe that they are in fact pursuing a policy of bidialectalism, in which both standard and dialect are considered 'correct' and the differences between the two are discussed as an interesting fact in an attempt to teach the child how to convert his or her dialect forms into the standard when this is required (Trudgill, 1975: 68–9). However, any approach which effectively dismisses the use of dialect inside the classroom, except for purposes of comparison with the standard, is unlikely to have any more credibility with dialect speakers than blatant condemnation of nonstandard speech. It is not enough simply to say that nonstandard dialects are equal to the standard. Teachers must be able to show by their choice of materials and activities that there is a range of situations, such as drama, poetry and dialogue in story writing, where dialect is both considered appropriate and valued.

It is not difficult to understand why all such attempts to exclude dialect are doomed to failure. Language is inextricably bound up with identity and the only thing which can motivate children to change their speech is the desire to identify with another group of people. While standard speech is perceived by standard and nonstandard speakers alike as having greater prestige (Giles and Powesland, 1975; J. Edwards, 1979), it very often has unfavourable connotations for nonstandard speakers (Labov, 1966; Trudgill, 1974). SE, particularly when RP accented, is often perceived as affected and effeminate, and can be strongly resisted, especially by boys. Craig (1971), for instance, reports the case of West Indian boys imitating the standard in high pitched female voices. And J. Edwards (1979) cites the Cockney woman in the BBC series 'Word of Mouth' who remarked that if her grandson were to talk 'la-di-da', his mates would think he was a 'queer'. Certainly, the current socio-political situation and tension within the West Indian community makes it extremely unlikely that black children will be receptive to attempts to change speech patterns which are an integral part of their identity.

Nevertheless, there has been a move in some quarters towards providing special language classes for West Indian children. Richards (1980) explains the kind of thinking which has been taking place in certain educational circles:

Teachers of English in primary and secondary schools are now wondering if the failure of their black pupils is to do with their relative incompetence in English. Already some schools are devising language development programmes specifically for their black pupils.

Attempts to impose SE are likely to be resisted for reasons of linguistic identity. They are also doomed to failure for other more pragmatic reasons. Differences between West Indian varieties of English and SE affect structures which occur so frequently that teachers find it impossible to 'correct' every dialect form. Even if it were possible, constant correction would certainly demoralize the child. Many teachers therefore resort to selective correction, a practice which can be extremely confusing for the child. In this piece of written work by a 10-year-old West Indian, for instance, the only alteration was to the second line where the teacher changed *smell* to *smells*:

(1)   It look very good
      It smell creamy
      It's very smooth texture
      It's very brown
      It stand like a stone
      It smell like milk

It is difficult to imagine, however, what conclusions the child is supposed to draw when the teacher has chosen to add *-s* to *smell* but not to *stand*, nor indeed to *smell* when it reappears in the last line.

A frequent consequence of *ad hoc* teaching strategies such as these would seem to be over-generalization and hypercorrection (see also chapter 30). All the commonly occurring areas of difference between Creole and Standard English are subject to hypercorrection as is illustrated in the examples below taken from the writing of second generation West Indian children. Thus, not only do we find examples of the unmarked Creole plural, as in:

(2)   The headlight are *thing* you put on at night to look out for *thing* like *dog* or *cat*

but we also encounter hypercorrect forms like:

(3)   They picked up the sacks of *golds*
(4)   Some of her friends had a *fights*

By the same token, we find examples of both the invariable Creole verb form:

(5)   One Christmas day father Christmas *give* me a present
(6)   Minerva *know* all about spiders

and hypercorrect forms:

(7)   The butterflies *dies*
(8)   I *haved* met you before
(9)   Radiator is to *keeps* the car engine cool

It is unfortunate that several of the areas of difference between Creole and SE – noun plurals, genitives and 3rd person singular present tense verbs – are all expressed with the -*s* suffix in English and are unmarked in Creole. Such is the confusion experienced by some children that they fall into the 'if in doubt add an -*s*' syndrome, neatly illustrated by the following example:

(10)   The *slides makes* the sugar *canes turns* into the box

Spelling is also affected and alongside renditions of *tin* for *thin* and *den* for *then* (/θ/ and /ð/ do not occur in Creole) we also find instances when *th* has been substituted for *t* or *d*:

(11)   He got the tools from the *booth* (boot) of the car

Most combinations of consonants are not admissible in word-final position in Creole and so examples such as *pars* for *passed* or *fine* for *find* are not uncommon. Conversely, many West Indian children tend to add a consonant at the end of a word when it is not necessary:

(12)   Long long ago *went* (when) the Saxons live in England
(13)   *Guest* (guess) what?
(14)   I was going down the road and *thereupond* (thereupon) I saw a bear

There are equally strong arguments to be made against 'correcting' dialect features in children's oral reading. Reading researchers see the reading process as heavily dependent on various kinds of cue systems which help us to predict what lies ahead and confirm or modify these predictions as we proceed (Smith, 1971; Goodman, 1972). The dialect-influenced child who reads *I give it to my brother* for *I gave it to my brothers* is in fact demonstrating very healthy reading strategies, since he or she is drawing on knowledge of his language to predict what comes next and has clearly understood what the writer intended to convey. Following Goodman and Buck (1973), Wight (1976) and V. Edwards (1979, 1980) suggest that the teacher who corrects dialect features is encouraging the child to read for accuracy and not for meaning. It may well be that the most realistic explanation of reading failure in nonstandard speakers is rejection of their dialects by the school. Goodman and Buck sum the situation up thus:

In encouraging divergent speakers to use their language competence, both receptive and productive, and accepting their dialect based miscues, we minimize the effect of dialect differences. In rejecting their dialects we maximize the effect.

It would thus appear that many teachers have pursued a course of dialect eradication because they have been unable to conceive of any viable alternative. The exigencies of the examination system are such that SE is a prerequisite for success and examination qualifications are the only route to white-collar jobs and social mobility. Most teachers, therefore, cannot entertain the idea of not correcting dialect features. There is nonetheless a very strong case for doing just this. Richmond (1979) points out in an analysis of the writing of Pat, a second-generation West Indian girl born in London, that 'errors, miscues and confusions' (EMCs) which arise from the technical aspects of writing, such as spelling and punctuation, outnumber the dialect features by four to one. He argues that the teacher can far more profitably focus on these EMCs, leaving the dialect features alone until the last two years or so of school. By this time many dialect features will have been edited out spontaneously and children are likely to be far more motivated in terms of examination success. At this stage any differences which remain between the standard and the dialect can be explained clearly and systematically.

A school language policy (see Department of Education and Science, 1975) which ensures consistency in the treatment of dialect features is clearly a prerequisite for such an approach. Linguistic prescriptivism currently remains a high priority for many teachers – and parents, too – and it is therefore difficult to foresee how such a policy could be implemented on a wide scale in the near future. It must also be admitted that such an approach is unlikely to work with all children. Many pupils in their final years of school have become so alienated that they consider examination success futile and will be unaffected by even this more sympathetic handling of the issue. Nevertheless an approach which waits for the child to become firmly literate in his or her own language variety before attempting to point out the differences between that variety and the standard has much to recommend it. It bypasses the confusion and insecurity which so often result from present practices and, even though it will not work with all children, it is likely to make an impact on a far larger proportion than those being reached by current teaching techniques.

Other important developments include the increasing use of Creole in the classroom. This has met with a good deal of resistance in certain quarters. Some West Indian parents, for instance, have reacted with alarm to the suggestion that Creole should be used in school. This is partly because Creole was allowed to play no part in their own school experience and they are unaware of changes in attitude which have recently taken place in the Caribbean (Carrington and Borely, 1977). It also derives in part from a fear that the use of Creole represents yet another attempt to hold their children back. Teachers, too, are reluctant to experiment and one London headteacher is reported as saying that he would allow Creole in his school only 'over his dead body' (*Sunday Times*, 16 October 1977). In spite of such reactions, the Inner London Education Authority has been encouraging its teachers to use Creole in poetry and drama since 1977. The rationale for such a policy is that

Creole should be used to supplement – though not to replace – the use of SE. Rampton (1981) fully endorses such a policy, and also stresses the need for initial and in-service training for teachers on West Indian language. Little and Willey (1981) take a similar stance. Their survey of seventy local education authorities shows that no more than a handful have made serious attempts to evaluate the needs of West Indian pupils. They point to the importance of clarifying the extent to which, and the ways in which, these children have 'special' language needs, and of providing guidance and support to teachers.

It has been argued that because Creole functions for many children as a language of resistance its legitimization in the classroom will simply lead to modification and adaptation by children who do not wish to be absorbed into mainstream culture (Stone, 1981). Whilst conceding that this is a possible development, it should be remembered that a number of teachers such as McGuigan (1976), Griffin (1977), Hoyle (1978) and Richmond (1978) have shown that it can be used most effectively as a motivational tool in the acquisition and development of literacy.

The West Indian language issue has helped to highlight the whole question of dialect difference in British schools and there is a growing understanding that West Indian dialect speakers and nonstandard British dialect speakers have a great deal in common. A sociolinguistic assessment of present educational practice shows clearly why we are not producing children who use SE, even at the end of eleven years of full-time schooling, and suggests directions for improvement. The difficulties in implementing such improvements, however, are considerable and much work clearly remains to be done in educating teachers as to the nature of language and language difference.

REFERENCES

Alleyne, M. 1971. The cultural matrix of creolization. In D. Hymes (ed.) *Pidginization and creolization*. Cambridge: CUP. pp. 169–86.

Association of Teachers of English to Pupils from Overseas (ATEPO: Birmingham branch). 1970. *Work group on West Indian pupils report.*

Bagley, C. 1975. On the intellectual equality of races. In G. Verma and C. Bagley (eds.) *Race and education across cultures*. London: Heinemann.

Bereiter, C. and Engelmann, S. 1966. *Teaching disadvantaged children in the pre-school.* Englewood Cliffs, NJ: Prentice-Hall.

Blair, C. 1971. Immigrant education and social class. *Race Today* August.

Blank, M. 1970. Some philosophical influences underlying pre-school intervention for disadvantaged children. In F. Williams (ed.) *Language and poverty*. Chicago: Markham.

Carrington, D. and Borely, C. (eds.) 1977. *The language arts syllabus, 1975: comment and countercomment*. Trinidad: University of Saint Augustine.

Commission for Racial Equality (CRE) 1978. *Looking for work. Black and white school leavers in Lewisham*. London: HMSO.

Community Relations Commission (CRC) 1977. *Urban deprivation, racial inequality and social policy*. London: HMSO.

Craig, D. 1971. Education and Creole English in the West Indies. In D. Hymes (ed.) *Pidginization and creolization*. pp. 371–91.

Crump, S. 1979. The language of West Indian children and its relevance for schools. Unpublished M.A. dissertation, University of London, Institute of Education.

Department of Education and Science 1975. *A language for life*. 'The Bullock report'. London: HMSO.

——— 1970. *Statistics of education*. London: HMSO.

Edwards, J. 1979. *Language and disadvantage*. London: Edward Arnold.

Edwards, V. 1978. Language attitudes and underperformance in West Indian children. *Educational Review* 30: 5–12.

——— 1979. *The West Indian language issue in British schools*. London: Routledge and Kegan Paul.

——— 1980. Black British English: a bibliographical essay on the language of children of West Indian origin. *Sage Race Relations Abstracts* 5, parts 3/4: 1–25.

Giles, H. and Powesland, P. 1975. *Speech style and social evaluation*. London: Academic Press.

Goodman, K.S. 1972. Reading: a psycholinguistic guessing game. In N.C. Farnes (ed.) *Reading purpose, comprehension and the use of context*. Milton Keynes: Open University Press. pp. 78–84.

Goodman, K.S. and Buck, C. 1973. Dialect barriers to reading comprehension revisited. *The Reading Teacher* 27(1): 6–12.

Griffin, C. 1977. Dialect in practice. *Issues in Race and Education* March.

Hebdige, D. 1976. Reggae, Rastas and Rudies. In S. Hall and T. Jefferson (eds.) *Resistance through ritual: youth sub-cultures in post war Britain*. London: Hutchison. pp. 135–54.

Hess, R. and Shipman, V. 1965. Early experience and the socialization of cognitive modes in children. *Child Development* 36: 869–86.

Houston, S. 1973. A re-examination of some assumptions about the language of the disadvantaged child. In M.H. Moss *Deprivation and disadvantage?* Milton Keynes: Open University Press. pp. 67–70.

Hoyle, S. 1978. Street language in an urban primary school. *Issues in Race and Education* 12.

Labov, W. 1966. *Social stratification of English in New York City*. Washington DC: Center for Applied Linguistics.

——— 1969. The logic of non-standard English. *Georgetown Monographs on Language and Linguistics* 22: 1–131. Reprinted in P.P. Giglioli (ed.) 1972. *Language and social context*. Harmondsworth: Penguin.

Little, A. 1975. Educational achievement of ethnic minority children in London. In G. Verma and C. Bagley (eds.) *Race and education across cultures*. London: Heinemann.

Little, A. and Willey, R. 1981. *Multi-ethnic education: the way forward*. London: Schools Council Pamphlet 18.

Lowenthal, D. 1972. *West Indian societies*. London: OUP.

McGuigan, G. 1976. Talking and writing by black fifth formers. *Multiracial School*, Summer.

Milner, D. 1975. *Children and Race*. Harmondsworth, Middx.: Penguin.

Osgood, C.E., Suci, G.J. and Tannenbaum, P.H. 1971. *Measurement of meaning*. 8th edn. Chicago: University of Illinois Press.

Rampton, A. 1981. *West Indian children in our schools*. Interim report of the Committee of Inquiry into the Education of Children from Ethnic Minority Groups. London: HMSO.

Reisman, K. 1970. Cultural and linguistic ambiguity in a West Indian village. In J. Whitten and J. Szwed (eds.) *Afro-American anthropology: contemporary perspectives*. New York: Free Press.

Richards, K. 1980. The language debate continued. *Education Journal* 3(1).

Richmond, J. 1978. Jennifer and Brixton Blues. *New Approaches to Multiracial Education* 6(3).

——— 1979. Dialect features in mainstream school writing. *New Approaches to Multiracial Education* 8(1): 9–15.

Rosenthal, R. and Jakobson, L. 1968. *Pygmalion in the classroom: teacher expectation and pupils' intellectual development*. New York: Holt, Rinehart and Winston.

Select Committee on Race Relations and Immigration. 1977. *The West Indian community report*. London: HMSO.

Seligman, G., Tucker, G. R. and Lambert, W. 1972. The effect of speech style and other attributes on teachers' attitudes towards pupils. *Language in Society* 1: 131–42.

Smith, D. 1976. *The facts of racial disadvantage*. London: Political and Economic Planning.

——— 1977. *Racial disadvantage in Britain*. Harmondsworth, Middx.: Penguin.

Smith, F. 1971. *Understanding reading*. New York: Holt, Rinehart and Winston.

Stone, M. 1981. *The education of the black child in Britain*. Glasgow: Fontana.

Sutcliffe, D. 1978. The language of first and second generation West Indian children in Bedfordshire. M.Ed. thesis, University of Leicester.

——— 1982. *British Black English*. Oxford: Basil Blackwell.

Townsend, H. E. R. 1971. *Immigrants in England: the LEA response*. Windsor: National Foundation for Educational Research.

Townsend, H. E. R. and Brittan, E. M. 1972. *Organization in multiracial schools*. Windsor: National Foundation for Educational Research.

Trudgill, P. 1974. *The social differentiation of English in Norwich*. Cambridge: CUP.

——— 1975. *Accent, dialect and the school*. London: Edward Arnold.

Wight, J. 1969. Teaching English to West Indian children. *English for Immigrants* 2(2), and in ATEPO (1970) pp. 58–60.

——— 1970. Language deprivation and remedial teaching techniques. In ATEPO (1970).

——— 1976. How much interference? *Times Educational Supplement* 14 May.

Wight, J. and Norris, R. 1970. *Teaching English to West Indian children: the research stage of the project*. Schools Council Working Paper 29. London: Evans/Methuen Educational.

Williams, F. 1973. Some research notes on dialect attitudes and stereotypes. In R. Shuy and R. Fasold (eds.) *Language attitudes: current trends and prospects*. Washington DC: Georgetown University Press. pp. 113–28.

Glossary

ABLAUT Vowel variations in the same root word; e.g. *find: found, was: were.*

ACCENT The particular pronunciation of a variety of language, which may include features that locate the speaker regionally and/or socially.

ACROLECT The DIALECT of highest prestige in a speech community with several social dialects.

ADSTRATUM A term used to cover both SUBSTRATUM and its opposite, superstratum.

AFFIXATION The process of adding lexical or grammatical MORPHEMES to a stem; e.g. *re*employ*ing.*

AFFRICATE A consonant characterized by the gradual release of air after a complete closure; e.g. *ch* [ʧ] in *church, j* [ʤ] in *jam.*

ALLOPHONE A particular REALIZATION of a PHONEME; e.g. the two different allophones of /p/ in *pin* [pʰɪn] and *spin* [spɪn].

ALVEOLAR A manner of articulation in which the tip or blade of the tongue touches the alveolar ridge (the ridge behind the upper teeth); e.g. [t], [s], [l], [n].

ANALYTIC In language typology, a language which uses few or no inflections, but rather relies on separate grammatical elements in particular orders in a phrase or sentence to signal syntactic relationships; e.g. Chinese (see also PERIPHRASIS).

APPROXIMANT A consonant produced by constriction of the vocal tract without causing audible friction; e.g. [w], [j], [r], [l].

ASPECT A grammatical category indicating duration or type of activity denoted by the verb; e.g., progressive, habitual, perfective, inceptive.

ASPIRATION The audible rush of air which may accompany the production of a consonant; e.g., *pin* [pʰɪn].

ASSIBILATION The process of making a sound into a SIBILANT.

ASSIMILATION The influence of one sound on another so that the sounds become more like each other or identical in articulation; e.g., good boy > goobboy.

AUXILIARY (VERB) A verb which is subordinate to the main lexical verb, has different grammatical properties from a lexical verb, and helps to make distinctions in mood, ASPECT, voice, etc.

BACK-FORMATION A type of word-formation process whereby a shorter word is derived from a longer one by deleting a supposed affix; e.g., *to burgle* from *burglar.*

BACKING Articulating a sound farther back in the mouth.

BASILECT (most often with reference to CREOLE language situations) The variety furthest from the prestige variety (ACROLECT).

BIDIALECTALISM Proficiency in the use of two DIALECTS (either social or regional) of a language.

BILABIAL A consonant produced with both lips coming together; e.g. [p], [b], [m].

BORROWING The taking into one language or DIALECT of linguistic forms from another; borrowed words are also known as LOAN-WORDS.

BREAKING The process by which a MONOPHTHONG becomes a centralized DIPHTHONG.

BREATHY VOICE A type of VOICE QUALITY, produced by letting a great amount of air pass through slightly opened vocal cords.

BRYTHONIC One of the two branches of the Celtic language family, including Welsh, Cornish and Breton.

CALQUE A type of borrowing where the MORPHEMES of the borrowed word or phrase are each translated into equivalent morphemes in the new language; e.g. English *handbook* from Latin *manualis liber*, German *Schöngeist* from French *bel esprit*.

CARDINAL VOWEL SYSTEM The standard reference points for identifying vowels based on tongue position along two dimensions: *open* vs. *close* and *front* vs. *back*. A given point corresponds roughly to the position in the mouth of the highest point of the tongue in the production of that vowel. Parentheses indicate the presence of lip rounding.

	Front		Back
Close	i, (y)		(u), ɯ
Half-close	e, (ø)		(o), ɤ
Half-open	ɛ, (œ)		(ɔ), ʌ
Open	a		(ɑ), ɒ

CENTRING DIPHTHONG A DIPHTHONG which involves a GLIDE towards the centre of the mouth; e.g. in *here* [hɪə].

CLEFTING A grammatical process for focusing on an item, which involves moving it to the front of its clause and preceding it by *it is/was/* etc.; e.g. *John bought a bicycle* can be clefted as *It was John who bought a bicycle* (focusing on John) or as *It was a bicycle that John bought* (focusing on the bicycle).

CLITIC A form which is word-like but which is structurally dependent upon a neighbouring word, may attach to the neighbouring word, and which typically is not capable of bearing stress; e.g. *n't* (vs. *not*) as in *You shouldn't really do that* (vs. *You should really NOT do that*).

CODA In phonetics, a PHONE which can follow the syllabic nucleus; e.g. /t/ of /kæt/.

CODE-SWITCHING Changing from one language variety to another, depending on the participants, setting, image the speaker wishes to project, etc.

COGNATE A language or form which is historically derived from the same source as another; e.g. Latin *unus*, Welsh *un*, English *one*, Icelandic *einn*, Dutch *een*, Spanish *uno* are all cognates.

COMMUNITY LANGUAGE A language which is especially characteristic of a particular sub-group of society.

CONCORD Grammatical agreement (e.g. in number, gender, case) whereby a form of one word requires a corresponding form of another.

CONTINUANT A consonant produced by incomplete closure of the vocal tract; e.g. all vowels and FRICATIVES.

COPULA A (stative) verb whose main function is to link or equate the subject and complement of a sentence; e.g. *is* as in *He is a teacher*, *feel* as in *That feels good*, *look* as in *She looks intelligent*.

CORONAL A consonant produced with the blade of the tongue raised from its neutral position; e.g. ALVEOLAR, DENTAL, and palato-alveolar consonants.

CRASIS The fusion of the final vowel of a word with the initial vowel of a following word.

CREOLE A PIDGIN language which has become the MOTHER TONGUE of a speech community.

CREOLIZATION The process by which a PIDGIN becomes a CREOLE, typically involving expansion of structural (vocabulary, grammar) and stylistic range.

DEIXIS (DEICTIC) The use of an item which has no fixed meaning and whose reference is semantically dependent on the temporal or locational characteristics of the situation within which an utterance takes place; e.g. *here/there, now/then, I/you, this/that.*

DENTAL A consonant made with the tip of the tongue against the teeth; e.g. /θ/, /t̪/.

DETERMINER An item whose main role is to co-occur with nouns to express such semantic notions as definiteness and quantity; e.g. *a/the, some/any.*

DIACHRONIC From the point of view of historical development.

DIALECT A regional or social variety of a language which is distinguished from other varieties by particular features of grammar and vocabulary, and which may be associated with a distinctive ACCENT.

DIAPHONE A unit of phonological analysis used to represent the fact that two different ACCENTS may use different pronunciations of the same phoneme; e.g., the phoneme /æ/ is [æ] in the south of England and [a] in the north of England.

DIGLOSSIA A language situation in which two very different varieties of a language are used for complementary functions, a 'High' variety normally used for written and formal purposes, and a 'Low' variety for ordinary conversation.

DIGRAPH A graphic unit which combines two symbols to function as a single unit; e.g. æ and œ.

DIPHTHONG A vowel where there is a change in quality during the syllable; e.g. *time* [taim].

DO-SUPPORT The use of the semantically empty auxiliary verb *do* to carry a TENSE maker; e.g. in question formation, *Did he go?*

DUAL FORM A form marked for reference to exactly two things; e.g., English *both.* Many languages have dual pronouns, e.g., 'we two', 'you two', and dual verb forms.

ENCLITIC A CLITIC which attaches to, or depends on, a preceding word.

EPENTHETIC (EPENTHESIS) An extra sound inserted medially in a word; e.g., as in *film* [fɪləm].

FIRST CONSONANT SHIFT (GRIMM'S LAW) A 'law' formulated to account for the correspondence of Germanic stops to Proto-Indo-European stops, it states basically that PIE voiceless stops became Gmc voiceless aspirates, PIE voiced aspirates became Gmc voiced stops, and PIE voiced stops became Gmc voiceless stops. There are several exceptions to these rules.

FLECTION/FLEXION A term sometimes employed to include both inflection and root modification; e.g. *ring, rang.*

FRICATIVE A consonant sound produced by constricting the vocal tract enough to cause audible friction when air moves through; e.g. [f], [z], [h].

FRONT MUTATION (see *i*-UMLAUT).

FRONTING Articulating a sound further forward in the mouth.

GAELTACHT Areas of the Republic of Ireland which are (officially deemed to be) natively Irish-speaking. The equivalent term in Scotland for the Scottish Gaelic-speaking area is *Gàidhealtachd.*

GEMINATION The doubling of a sound within a morpheme.

GENERATIVE GRAMMAR A set of formal rules which projects a finite set of sentences upon the potentially infinite set of sentences of a language, assigning to each a set of structural descriptions.

GLIDE A transitional sound made as the vocal organs move towards (on-glide) or away from (off-glide) a particular articulation; e.g. in British English *tune* [tʲu:n].

GLOTTAL STOP A sound made by the complete closure of the glottis (the opening between the vocal cords); e.g. as in *oh-oh* or Cockney *better* [bɛʔə].

GOIDELIC One of the two branches of the Celtic language family, including Irish, Scots Gaelic and Manx.

GOVERNMENT A syntactic linkage whereby one word requires a specific morphological form of another; e.g. in the assignment of case, as in *to him* rather than *to he*.

GREAT VOWEL SHIFT, THE The change in the pronunciation of long vowels between Middle English and present-day English, whereby these vowels were all raised and diphthongized: /ī/ → /ai/, /ē/ and /ɛ̄/ → /i:/, /ā/ → /ei/ /ɔ̄/ → /ou/, /ō/ → /u:/, and /ū/ → /au/.

GRIMM'S LAW see FIRST CONSONANT SHIFT.

HOMOPHONY Refers to words having the same pronunciation but different meaning; e.g. *two/too/to*.

HOMORGANIC Sounds which are pronounced at the same place of articulation; e.g. [p], [b], [m].

ICONIC An item whose form closely resembles characteristics of its referent; e.g. onomatopoeic words.

IDIOM A sequence of words which functions as a single unit and for which the meaning of the whole is not deducible from the meaning of the parts; e.g., *kick the bucket* (meaning 'to die').

INFLECTION An AFFIX which signals a grammatical relationship; e.g. plurality, tense, case.

INTERLANGUAGE A form of language which arises when a speaker is attempting to learn a foreign language, combining the target language with features from the native language and maybe some features not present in either.

INTONATION The patterns of pitch levels of sentences or clauses which signal grammatical structure (e.g. questions vs. statements) and attitude (e.g. surprise, sarcasm).

ISOGLOSS A line on a map marking the boundary of the usage of a particular linguistic feature.

ISOLATIVE (ISOLATING) In language typology, an ANALYTIC language in which all words are separate, invariable, and equivalent to a root; e.g. Chinese.

i-UMLAUT An historical process by which back vowels became fronted when an /i/ or /j/ occurred in the following syllable; e.g. Pre-Gmc, **musiz* became English *mice*.

LABIAL A sound where the lips are actively involved in pronunciation; e.g. as in liprounding.

LANGUAGE SHIFT The change in regular use of MOTHER-TONGUE status from one language to another, as happens often in immigrant communities.

LENITION The weakening of the articulation of an intervocalic consonant.

LEVELLING A process by which dialects or accents lose their distinctive traits and become more like each other.

LEXIS, LEXICON The vocabulary of a language.

LINGUA FRANCA See chapter 24 for the original Lingua Franca. The term *lingua franca* is used to identify an auxiliary language used for communication between people who speak different MOTHER-TONGUE languages.

LIQUID Sounds of the type [l] and [r].

LOAN-WORD A word taken into one language or dialect from another; the form and meaning of the word are borrowed intact, but pronunciation may be altered to conform to the phonological system of the new language; e.g. English *garage* from French.

LOWERING Articulating a vowel with the highest point of the tongue lower down.

MATCHED GUISE TECHNIQUE A technique employing the SEMANTIC DIFFERENTIAL TECHNIQUE for investigating reactions to language varieties in which recordings are played to subjects, including at least two made by the same speaker in different guises, i.e. speaking in different ACCENTS, DIALECTS or languages.

MESOLECT A variety intermediate between ACROLECT and BASILECT.

MINIMAL PAIR Two words which differ in only one sound; e.g. *pit/pet, pit/bit*.

MODALITY Refers to contrasts in grammatical mood signalled by the verb through inflections (e.g. subjunctive mood) or auxiliaries.

MONOPHTHONG A vowel which has no discernible change in quality during a syllable; e.g. cot [kɒt].

MORA A unit of timing in segmental phonology; e.g. a CVV structure would have two moras.

MORPHEME A minimal distinctive unit of meaning used in word formation; e.g., *unthinking* consists of three morphemes: *un-*, *think*, *-ing*.

MORPHOLOGY The study of word structure or word-formation; the system of word structure or formation of a given language.

MORPHO-SYNTACTIC Referring to something that depends on both MORPHOLOGY and SYNTAX for its definition; e.g. many inflectional categories affect both morphological description and syntax (e.g. pluralization).

MOTHER TONGUE The language acquired naturally in one's childhood; the first language acquired or the language primarily used at home by a child.

MUTATION (in Celtic languages) A process whereby the initial consonant of a word changes phonetically as a way of marking different grammatical functions or in response to the preceding phonetic environment.

NASALIZATION The process by which normally or formerly non-nasal sounds are modified by the lowering of the soft palate, allowing an audible escape of air through the nose.

NATURAL CLASS In phonetics, a set of segments for which fewer phonetic features are needed to specify the set as a whole than to specify any particular member of the set; also, the set should undergo similar phonological processes together; e.g. in English, [p], [t], [k] form a natural class (voiceless plosives).

NEOLOGISM A newly coined word or linguistic form.

NEUTRALIZATION The loss of distinction between two PHONEMES in a particular linguistic environment; e.g. final devoicing of consonants in German.

PALATAL The manner of articulation of a consonant where the blade of the tongue is in contact with, or approaching, the hard palate (roof of the mouth).

PARTICLE An invariable item with grammatical function; e.g. English infinitival *to*, subordinate units in phrasal verbs.

PATOIS A non-standard local variety of a language.

PERIPHRASIS The use of separate words rather than inflections to express a grammatical relationship; e.g. *He made the room dark* vs. *He darkened the room.*

PHARYNGEAL The manner of articulation of a sound made in the pharynx (the part of the throat above the larynx).

PHONE A speech sound considered purely as a sound.

PHONEME A minimal distinctive unit of sound. The substitution of one phoneme for another in a word causes a change in meaning.

PHONETIC Referring to the articulatory, acoustic and/or auditory characteristics of speech sounds.

PHONOLOGY The study of the organization of speech sounds into sound systems of languages; the particular sound system of a given language.

PHONOTACTIC The particular sequential constraints of PHONEMES of a language; e.g. the consonant cluster /kt/ cannot occur initially in English.

PIDGIN A linguistically simplified, mixed and restricted language used in limited contact situations between people who have no common language. It is not a MOTHER TONGUE.

PIDGINIZATION The process of forming a PIDGIN language, by simplifying the grammar and vocabulary of the contact languages.

PRETONIC Occurring before the stressed syllable.

PROCLITIC A CLITIC which attaches to or depends on a following word.

PROTHETIC An extra sound inserted initially in a word.

PROTOTONIC Stressed on the first syllable.

REALIZATION The actual pronunciation of a PHONEME.

RECESSIVE FORM An old-fashioned word, structure or pronunciation that is receding in use (geographically or socially) in the face of a newer form.

REGISTER A variety of language used in specific social settings for specific purposes; e.g. formal, scientific and religious registers.

RETRACTED A manner of articulation in which the tongue is moved backward.

RETROFLEX The manner of articulation whereby the tip of the tongue is curled back behind the ALVEOLAR ridge.

ROOT The base form of a word which is left when all the AFFIXES are removed and which cannot be further analysed; e.g. the root of *unskilfully* is *skill.*

SANDHI The phonological modification of forms which have been juxtaposed, as at word boundaries.

SCHWA The neutral central vowel [ə], as found in English *the* and initially in *ago.*

SEGMENT Any discrete unit; e.g., in phonology, a vowel or consonant phoneme.

SELECTIONAL RESTRICTIONS Restrictions on permitted combinations of words in a given syntactic context; e.g. the verb *dream* requires an animate subject.

SEMANTIC DIFFERENTIAL TECHNIQUE A way of testing emotional or attitudinal reactions of speakers to lexical items in order to describe the affective dimensions of a language's organization of concepts.

SEMANTICS The study of meaning in natural languages.

SERIAL VERBS In some languages it is possible to string two or more main verbs together in a single clause; e.g. *he run go market* = 'he runs to market' or 'he runs and goes to market'.

SIBILANT A FRICATIVE with a high-frequency hissing characteristic, produced by grooving the blade of the tongue behind the ALVEOLAR ridge; e.g. [s], [š].

SONORANT A sound produced with a relatively free flow of air and where VOICING is possible; e.g. vowels, [r], [l], [n].

SPIRANT A sound with high noise intensity; FRICATIVES and AFFRICATES; e.g. [s], [č].

STEM The form of a word after all inflectional affixes are removed; a stem may be simple or compound (e.g. *man, manmade*), and may include derivational affixes (e.g. *manly*).

STOP A consonant produced by complete closure of the vocal tract at some point; e.g. [p], [t], [k].

STRESS The degree of force or loudness used in pronouncing a syllable.

STRONG Verb: using internal vowel change to form the preterite and participle forms (e.g. *drive/drove/driven, sing/sang/sung*), as opposed to a weak verb, which uses a dental suffix (*talk/talked*). Adjective: an adjective which does not occur after a demonstrative, possessive pronoun or article, and which usually differs in inflection from a weak adjective.

STYLE A variety of language dependent on the situation, described in terms of formality vs. informality.

STYLE SHIFT The changing from one STYLE to another, depending on the situation.

SUBORDINATOR A conjunction which introduces a dependent clause; e.g. *when, since*.

SUBSTRATUM A linguistic variety which has, through time, influenced a more dominant variety in the community; e.g. the substratum effect of Welsh on Welsh English such that even the English of Welsh people who speak no Welsh shows the influence of Welsh pronunciation.

SUPRASEGMENTAL In phonetics and phonology, a feature which extends over more than one SEGMENT; e.g. PITCH, STRESS.

SVARABHAKTI VOWEL (see EPENTHETIC).

SYNCOPE The loss of medial vowels, often due to strong accent on the preceding syllable.

SYNTAX, GRAMMAR The study of the arrangement of items in sentences, the constructions which make up the parts of sentences, and the structural relationships between sentences.

SYNTHETIC In language typology, a language typically having words which contain more than one MORPHEME; e.g. Latin.

TAG QUESTION A question structure at the end of a statement which consists usually (in English) of an AUXILIARY + pronoun; e.g. *You're coming, aren't you?*

TAPPING Producing a sound by a single brief contact with the tongue on the roof of the mouth; e.g. the pronunciation of *t* in American English *better*.

TAUTOSYLLABIC Occurring in the same syllable as.

TENSE A grammatical category referring to the way the grammar marks the time at which the action of the verb took place.

TOKEN An actual instance of a particular TYPE or linguistic category.

TONE The pitch level(s) of a syllable.

TYPE (see TOKEN).

UNIVERSAL A property common to all languages, either a formal condition on the construction of grammars, a primitive element in a grammar, or an implicational condition (if X occurs, then Y occurs).

UVULAR The manner of articulation of a consonant made by the back of the tongue against the uvula (the dangling bit of skin at the back of the throat).

VELAR The manner of articulation of a consonant, made by the tongue against the velum (soft palate).

VERNACULAR The ordinary spoken language of a community, as opposed to a dominant or standard language which is not the local variety.

VERNER'S LAW Formulated to account for an exception to GRIMM'S LAW, it states that Proto-Indo-European voiceless stops became Proto-Germanic voiceless fricatives, except that in voiced environments these voiceless fricatives (plus /s/) became voiced when not immediately preceded by the accent.

VOCOID A sound which is vowel-like in that it does not involve complete closure or narrowing of the vocal tract sufficient to produce audible friction, but which functions as a consonant (i.e. it is not the centre of a syllable); e.g. [w], [j].

VOICE QUALITY The permanent, personally identifying features of someone's speech, including both physiologically determined and learned features.

VOICE SETTING Culturally or individually learned aspects of VOICE QUALITY; e.g. pitch, tempo, loudness.

VOICING Refers to vibration of the vocal cords. Voiced sounds are produced with the vocal cords vibrating, and *voiceless* sounds are produced without them vibrating; thus, VOICING refers to sounds which are normally voiceless being pronounced with vibrating vocal cords, and DEVOICING refers to sounds which are normally voiced being pronounced with less or no vibration of the vocal cords.

VOWEL HARMONY A phonological pattern in some languages where all vowels in a word share certain features; e.g. all are rounded, or high or fronted.

WORD-CLASS A grouping of words into sets based on similarities in grammatical and semantic properties; a *closed* class has limited or fixed membership, e.g. the class of articles in English.

ZERO MORPH A morpheme which has no REALIZATION; e.g. the plural morpheme for *deer*.

Note. Many of these definitions are based on those found in David Crystal, 1980. *A first dictionary of linguistics and phonetics*. London: André Deutsch.

Index of topics

Page numbers in italics refer to tables and figures.

Index of places